DATE DUE

JE 23 '94			
DE 22 '95			

DEMCO 38-296

THE BEST PLAYS OF 1992–1993

THE OTIS GUERNSEY BURNS MANTLE THEATER YEARBOOK

THE BEST PLAYS OF
1992-1993

EDITED BY OTIS L. GUERNSEY JR.
AND JEFFREY SWEET

*Illustrated with photographs and
with drawings by* HIRSCHFELD

LIMELIGHT EDITIONS

EDITOR'S NOTE

THIS 74th volume in the Best Plays series of theater yearbooks first published after the 1919–20 season by Dodd, Mead adds another number to its record in 1993: its third publisher, Melvyn B. Zerman's Limelight Editions. Limelight now succeeds Applause Theater Books, which shepherded the Best Plays series through its first five post-Dodd, Mead volumes. The fifth and sixth editors of this series gratefully extend their appreciation to Applause for its past sponsorship, while welcoming Mel Zerman and Limelight to our project in the same capacity.

Another new member of the Best Plays team for 1992–93 is Jeffrey A. Finn, who has replaced the late Stanley Green as the organizer of our coverage in the cast-replacements section and has expanded it to include the casts of first-class touring companies of shows *not* spinoffs from recent New York productions. Otherwise, *The Best Plays of 1992–93* is the mixture of theater lore and review as before, with associate editor Jeffrey Sweet—not only one of the most perceptive of the 1990s theater critics (c.f. his book *The Dramatist's Toolkit* recently published by Heinemann) but by far the most diligent, covering just about every Broadway and off-Broadway production—reviewing the New York season and singling out its best work. Jonathan Dodd and the editor's wife continue to oversee the many publication chores, making sure that the vast amount of detailed information contained in our 1992–93 summaries is both accurate and comprehensive.

Camille Croce Dee is in charge of the ever-growing list of off-off-Broadway casts and credits, while Mel Gussow reviews the year's outstanding events in that energetic and creative venue. Likewise, Sheridan Sellers gathers the cast-and-credits information on new plays produced in cross-country theater, and T.H. McCulloh is the chairman of the American Theater Critics Association committee which annually selects three outstanding new playscripts to be honored by that group's citations, recorded in this Best Plays volume with excerpts from the chosen scripts. And Rue E. Canvin remains on duty with the necrology and list of theatrical publications, while William Schelble keeps our Tony Award records up to date.

The scores of men and women in the theater's press offices both in New York and across the country annually make these hundreds of pages of information possible with their support at every step of the way. And we benefit from the additional helping hands of Sally Dixon Wiener (two Best Play synopses), Thomas T. Foose (historical advisories), Michael Kuchwara (New York Drama Critics Circle voting), Dan Sullivan and Roger Downey (ATCA citations),

Henry Hewes (former Best Plays editor, following whose suggestion we've added a section to this volume listing Theater Hall of Fame members) and Ralph Newman of the Drama Book Shop.

As ever, the spirit of the theater season is gloriously captured in the incomparable drawings by Al Hirschfeld, honored in this the year of his 90th birthday by a special Tony Award and honoring us in this the 40th year of his work's reproduction season by season in the Best Plays volumes. So do the original sketches of scenery and costume designs illustrating this season's best, provided to us by their creators, John Arnone, Chris Parry, Paul Tazewell and David C. Woolard, for representation here. And the "look" of the season is sampled throughout these pages in the photographs of stage action by photographers in New York and across the country, including David Allen, Judy Andrews, Chris Bennion, Michal Daniel, Lisa Ebright, T. Charles Erickson, Suellen Fitzsimmons, Tim Fuller, Gerry Goodstein, Grossman/Goldsmith/Schier, John Haynes, Ken Howard, Sherman Howe Jr., Susan Johann, Brigitte Lacombe, Liz Lauren, Marcus/Bryan-Brown, Joan Marcus, Jack Mitchell, Miguel Pagliere, Robert Schnellbacher, Arlene Schulman, Martha Swope and her associates (William Gibson and Carol Rosegg), Richard Termine, Jay Thompson, Richard Trigg, Sheila Trow, Leslie Troxell, Michael Wakefield and Bengt Wanselius.

Before we send *The Best Plays of 1992–93* to press, let us express our profound thanks to our former publisher and to our new publisher for their faith in our project; to the members of the Best Plays information-gathering team and their ever-present helpers in the theater production staffs; to the graphic artists, and to the many, many others to whom not only the Best Plays series but the theater itself owes its very existence. Among these, above all, we thank the playwrights, composers, lyricists and librettists who keep hope and sometimes even exhilaration alive with their continuing supply of new material for stage presentation. In a very real sense, their worst is like their best, as essential as a heartbeat. In 1992–93 they've given us a living theater in which we can all take pride.

OTIS L. GUERNSEY Jr.
Editor

September 1, 1993

CONTENTS

Drawings by HIRSCHFELD

Herndon Lackey, Merle Louise, Chita Rivera, Brent Carver, Anthony
   Crivello and Kirsti Carnahan in *Kiss of the Spider Woman*   50-51
The late Roy Cohn; Marcia Gay Harden, David Marshall Grant, Kathleen
   Chalfant, Ellen McLaughlin, Stephen Spinella, Joe Mantello, Jeffrey
   Wright and Ron Leibman in *Angels in America*   52-53
Rodgers and Hammerstein surrounded by their greatest shows   54
Tommy Tune in *Tommy Tune Tonite!*   55
Paul Kandel, Cheryl Freeman, Buddy Smith, Michael Cerveris, Marcia
   Mitzman and Jonathan Dokuchitz in *The Who's Tommy*   56–57
Wrong Turn at Lungfish with Tony Danza, Kelli Williams, Jami Gertz,
   George C. Scott and Garry Marshall (co-author and director)   58-59
Jon Voight and Tyne Daly in *The Seagull*   60
Christine Lahti and Ron Rifkin in *Three Hotels*   61
Cameron Mackintosh manipulates the cast and creative team of
   Sondheim—Putting It Together   62-63
Carol Woods, Tammy Minoff, John Christopher Jones, Martin Short,
   Bernadette Peters in *The Goodbye Girl*   64-65

THE SEASON
ON AND OFF
BROADWAY

*Dramatic
Confrontations
1992–93*

PATIENT VS. DOCTOR: Ron Leibman as Roy Cohn with Kathleen Chalfant, *above,* in *Angels in America*

STUDENT VS. TEACHER: Rebecca Pidgeon and William H. Macy, *left,* in *Oleanna*

STRAIGHT VS. GAY: *Below,* Anthony Crivello *(right)* and Brent Carver in *Kiss of the Spider Woman*'s "I Draw the Line" scene

BROADWAY AND OFF BROADWAY
By Jeffrey Sweet

ONE of the leading characters is a gay man. In moments of stress, the stage is filled with his frequently hilarious fantasies.

I've just described the best Broadway play of the season, *Angels in America: Millennium Approaches*. Also the best Broadway musical, *Kiss of the Spider Woman*. Also one of the best off-Broadway plays, *Jeffrey*.

The New York *Times* ran a front-page story this year on a study which challenged the old Kinsey Report estimate that 10 percent of Americans are homosexual. According to the experts cited in the article, a more accurate figure is one percent. A study of the *dramatis personae* of this season would probably result in a figure higher than Kinsey's. In addition to the three Best Plays cited above, new theatrical works which presented major gay characters or dealt with gay themes included *The Destiny of Me, Flaubert's Latest, And Baby Makes Seven, Aven' U Boys, Someone Who'll Watch Over Me, The Sisters Rosensweig, The Years, Deep in a Dream of You, Spic-O-Rama, Memory Tricks, Later Life, The Night Larry Kramer Kissed Me* and *The Who's Tommy*. (*The Goodbye Girl* didn't. At least not in New York. In its pre-Broadway tryout in Chicago, the musical adaptation of the film of the same name contained a scene in which a straight actor is compelled to play Richard III as a homosexual, but this was revised for fear of giving offense.)

The reason for the prevalence of gay characters and themes is not hard to fathom. Writers often find inspiration in the issues which intrude on their lives, and nobody writing for the stage today can be oblivious to the devastation AIDS has wreaked among fellow artists. Though a number of these plays are by gay writers, some of the plays dealing with gay themes are, in fact, by heterosexuals trying to address their time. (Turnabout is fair play; after all, for years gay writers like Tennessee Williams and William Inge made their reputations writing about heterosexual characters.)

This is the theater doing some of what it is supposed to do—reflecting the society it serves. On Sunday, April 25, while many of these works were attracting matinee audiences in New York, what some estimated as a million gay men, women and supporters marched in Washington, D.C. to impress upon our nation's politicians their determination that homosexuals be treated as full and equal citizens.

The 1992–93 Season on Broadway

PLAYS (5)

Chinese Coffee
THE SISTERS ROSENSWEIG (transfer)
The Song of Jacob Zulu
Redwood Curtain
ANGELS IN AMERICA: MILLENNIUM APPROACHES

HOLDOVERS WHICH BECAME HITS IN 1992–93 (4)

Catskills on Broadway
Conversations With
My Father
Falsettos
Guys and Dolls

MUSICALS (7)

Anna Karenina
My Favorite Year
The Goodbye Girl
Ain't Broadway Grand
THE WHO'S TOMMY
Blood Brothers
KISS OF THE SPIDER WOMAN

REVUES (2)

3 From Brooklyn
The Sheik of Avenue B

FOREIGN LANGUAGE PRODUCTIONS (4)

Oba Oba 93
Gypsy Passion (return engagement)
Yabuhara Kengyo
Tango Pasión

FOREIGN PLAY IN ENGLISH (1)

Someone Who'll Watch Over Me

REVIVALS (12)

Roundabout 1992:
  The Price
  The Real Inspector Hound & The Fifteen Minute Hamlet
Salome
New York City Opera:
  110 in the Shade
  Regina
Roundabout 1993:
  The Show-Off
  Anna Christie
  Candida
Nat'l Actors Theater:
  The Seagull
  Saint Joan
  Three Men on a Horse
  Wilder, Wilder, Wilder

ONE-ACTOR PERFORMANCES (3)

Solitary Confinement
A Christmas Carol (return engagement)
Shakespeare for My Father

SPECIALTIES (3)

Radio City Music Hall:
  Christmas Spectacular
  Easter Show
Fool Moon

Categorized above are all the plays listed in the Plays Produced on Broadway section of this volume.
Plays listed in CAPITAL LETTERS have been designated Best Plays of 1992–93.
Plays listed in *italics* were still running June 1, 1993.
Plays listed in **bold face type** were classified as hits in *Variety's* annual estimate published June 21, 1993.

The fact that a society which 20 years ago seldom (if ever) saw a sympathetic gay character in a leading role on a Broadway stage now confers hit status on works such as *Kiss of the Spider Woman* and *Angels in America* says a good deal about the growing tolerance of the audience. It would be comforting to believe that the theater has helped advance the cause of tolerance by dramatizing the human face of the gay experience.

Given that so many of the plays dealt with AIDS, we saw a lot of scenes set in hospitals, clinics or nursing homes. Some non-AIDS works also had scenes set in medical facilities—*Wrong Turn at Lungfish,* the musical version of *Wings,* and *The Last Yankee.* The theater has long been called the Fabulous Invalid, but I cannot recall a time when more patients appeared as characters.

This season also hosted a large number of pieces for solo performers. At one point, both the Joseph Papp Public Theater and Manhattan Theater Club were running two solo performance pieces in repertory (Marga Gomez's *Memory Tricks* and David Cale's *Deep in a Dream of You* at the former, and Richard Greenberg's *Jenny Keeps Talking* and Charlayne Woodard's *Pretty Fire* at the latter). This impulse to address the audience directly rather than share scenes with other actors is partially owing to the relatively modest financial investment such pieces usually require. Whatever their points of origin, several of these were evenings to be treasured—Josh Kornbluth's *Red Diaper Baby,* Lynn Redgrave's *Shakespeare for My Father* and John Leguizamo's *Spic-O-Rama* in particular.

These solo pieces were the source of most of the views of ethnicity in America offered this season, Leguizamo and Gomez offering insight into Hispanic family life and Woodard relating stories about growing up as a black girl. Except for Jose Rivera's *Marisol* and Mustapha Matura's *Playboy of the West Indies* (a Caribbean adaptation of Synge's *Playboy of the Western World*), the only other works with significant black or Hispanic characters *(Someone Who'll Watch Over Me, The Song of Jacob Zulu, The Heliotrope Bouquet by Scott Joplin and Louis Chauvin, Kiss of the Spider Woman, Angels in America, The Goodbye Girl, The Destiny of Me,* and *Aven' U Boys)* were written by white writers. Aside from the Vietnamese-American girl in Lanford Wilson's *Redwood Curtain* and the Filipino ex-bantamweight fighter in *My Favorite Year,* Asian-Americans were little seen onstage this season, though there would have been more representation if David Henry Hwang's play, *Face Value,* hadn't closed in previews. I'm not suggesting white writers shouldn't write for non-white performers, but it is worth noting that a season so dominated by a sexual minority offered little room for works by ethnic minorities.

Also, it provided little room for plays by women who, according to the census, have the numerical edge over men in America. If one doesn't count the solo pieces (where several women were represented), women who saw their new works produced on or off Broadway still were in a minority—among them, Wendy Wasserstein (Best Play *The Sisters Rosensweig*), Catherine Butterfield (Best Play *Joined at the Head*), Tina Howe *(One Shoe Off),* Paula Vogel *(And*

Baby Makes Seven), Lynn Ahrens (the lyrics for *My Favorite Year*) and Cindy Lou Johnson *(The Years).*

Though two musicals are cited as Best Plays this year *(Kiss of the Spider Woman* and *Wings),* and a third *(Tommy)* is given a special citation, it was hardly a banner year for musical theater. *My Favorite Year* was an unsuccessful attempt by the non-profit Lincoln Center Theater company to mount a big Broadway show in the Fifties style. Another non-profit company, Circle in the Square, came to similar grief with its attempt at a Broadway musical, an adaptation of Tolstoy's *Anna Karenina. Anna Karenina, The Goodbye Girl, My Favorite Year, Kiss of the Spider Woman* and *Tommy* all were based on works familiar to many in the audience from other media. *(Karenina* and *Spider Woman,* of course, began as novels, *Tommy* began as a record album, and all five have been seen in movie versions.) Off Broadway, the Best Play *Wings* was based on Arthur Kopit's play of the same title. *Ain't Broadway Grand* technically was an original, but the plot bore a strong resemblance to the film of *The Band Wagon.* Other musical entertainments *(Sondheim—Putting It Together,* Carole King's *Tapestry* and *Hello Muddah, Hello Fadduh)* found new settings for old material. Willy Russell's *Blood Brothers,* the Craig Lucas-Gerald Busby collaboration *Orpheus in Love* and *Wild Men* were written directly for the stage.

As usual, most of what appeared under Broadway and off-Broadway lights began their lives elsewhere. On Broadway, productions originated in London *(Blood Brothers, Someone Who'll Watch Over Me),* Toronto *(Kiss of the Spider Woman),* the La Jolla Playhouse *(Tommy),* the Mark Taper Forum of Los Angeles *(Angels in America),* the Steppenwolf Theater of Chicago *(The Song of Jacob Zulu),* the Seattle Rep *(The Sisters Rosensweig),* the Pasadena Playhouse *(Solitary Confinement),* and the John Harms Theater Center in Englewood, New Jersey *(Anna Karenina).* Off Broadway, four productions were nurtured at the Goodman Theater of Chicago *(Wings, Deep in a Dream of You, Spic-O-Rama* and *On the Open Road).* Other off-Broadway works made their way here from such New York-based developmental stages as Naked Angels, Ensemble Studio Theater, the WPA, the Women's Project and Second Stage, as well as such regional and international venues as Long Wharf, Steppenwolf, Baltimore's CenterStage, the Back Bay Theater Company of Cambridge, the Marsh Theater of San Francisco, the Fountainhead Theater Company of Los Angeles, the Arena Stage of Washington, the Arizona Theater Company, and the City Arts Center in Dublin.

The season was dominated by such veteran writers as Lanford Wilson, David Mamet, Wendy Wasserstein, Terrence McNally, Arthur Miller, John Kander, Paul Rudnick, Fred Ebb, Neil Simon, Marvin Hamlisch, Keith Reddin, David Zippel, Jon Robin Baitz, Willy Russell, Larry Kramer, Neal Bell, Paula Vogel, Simon Gray, Eric Overmyer, Peter Parnell, Tina Howe, Rupert Holmes, A.R. Gurney and Steve Tesich, most of whom have won Best Play citations in the past. While not previously as well-known as many of the above, *Angels in*

Outstanding designs of the musical year were those for *Tommy*, with samples pictured here: *above,* John Arnone (scene designer, *left*) and Chris Parry (lighting) with a model of the set; *below,* David C. Woolard's costume sketches for three of the characters—Mrs. Walker *(left),* Sally Simpson and the title role, Tommy at the age of 18

America author Tony Kushner has been represented on New York stages before. The most impressive playwriting debut of the season was by the aforementioned Catherine Butterfield, who wrote and played one of the leading roles in *Joined at the Head*. (Incidentally, one of her earlier acting jobs was as understudy for the tour of Wendy Wasserstein's *The Heidi Chronicles*.)

Audiences in search of stars found them in a variety of venues. Julie Andrews and George C. Scott both chose to return to the New York stage in off-Broadway projects. Al Pacino played two roles in repertory at Circle in the Square's uptown stage. The Roundabout attracted such impressive names as Natasha Richardson, Mary Steenburgen, Liam Neeson, Rip Torn and Eli Wallach to perform in its series of revivals. Musicals prompted the returns of past Tony winners Chita Rivera and Bernadette Peters. And valuable contributions were made by several alumni of the Compass and Second City comedy troupes—Martin Short, Robert Klein, Andrea Martin, George Wendt, Anne Meara and Jerry Stiller.

Marshall W. Mason and Gloria Muzio were among the busiest directors of the year, Mason clocking in with four productions *(Redwood Curtain, The Destiny of Me, The Seagull* and *Solitary Confinement)* and Muzio with three *(Bubbe Meises Bubbe Stories* and the Roundabout productions of *The Real Inspector Hound* and *Candida)*. Such other established directorial names as George C. Wolfe, Harold Prince and Daniel Sullivan reaffirmed their positions by directing the hit productions of *Angels in America, Kiss of the Spider Woman* and *The Sisters Rosensweig*, respectively. Three playwrights, David Mamet *(Oleanna)*, Garry Marshall *(Wrong Turn at Lungfish,* co-written with Lowell Ganz) and Simon Gray *(The Holy Terror)*, directed their own work, though not always to good effect.

As recognized by this volume's special citation for stage imagery, *Tommy* was a state-of-the-art display of theatrical wizardry, integrating the scenery of John Arnone, the lighting of Chris Parry and the projections of Wendall K. Harrington into a breathtaking barrage of images which announced that the MTV sensibility had arrived on Broadway. The high points of production design for non-musicals included the work for *Angels in America* (sets by Robin Wagner, lights by Jules Fisher), *Richard III* (sets by Bob Crowley), *On the Open Road* (sets by Donald Eastman, lights by Kenneth Posner), and *One Shoe Off* (set by Heidi Landesman).

The worlds these theatrical magicians conjured were first glimmerings in the imaginations of the dramatists this annual is dedicated to honoring with citations for Best Plays. To quote Otis L. Guernsey Jr. in past volumes, "The choice is made without any regard whatever to the play's type—musical, comedy or drama—or origin on or off Broadway, or popularity at the box office or lack of same.

"We don't take the scripts of bygone eras into consideration for Best Play citation in this one, whatever their technical status as American or New York 'premieres' which didn't have a previous production of record. We draw the line between adaptations and revivals, the former eligible for Best Play selection but the latter not, on a case-by-case basis. If a script influences the character of a season, or by some function of consensus wins the Critics, Pulitzer or Tony Awards, we take into account its future historical as well as present esthetic importance. This is the only special consideration we give, and we don't always tilt in its direction, as the record shows." This season, we've expanded our citations to honor distinguished achievements in the field of writing for solo performance.

Our choices for the Best Plays of 1992–93 are listed below in the order in which they opened in New York (a plus sign + with the performance number signifies that the play was still running on June 1, 1993).

Best Monologues:
Red Diaper Baby
  (Off B'way, 59 perfs.)
Spic-O-Rama
  (Off B'way, 86 perfs.)

The Destiny of Me
  (Off B'way, 175 perfs.)

The Sisters Rosensweig
  (Off B'way, 149 perfs.)
  (B'way, 85 + perfs.)

Oleanna
  (Off B'way, 249 + perfs.)

Joined at the Head
  (Off B'way, 41 perfs.)

Jeffrey
  (Off B'way, 99 + perfs.)

Wings
  (Off B'way, 47 perfs.)

The Who's Tommy (special citation)
  (B'way, 46 + perfs.)

Kiss of the Spider Woman
  (B'way, 32 + perfs.)

Angels in America: Millennium Approaches
  (B'way, 32 + perfs.)

Later Life
  (Off B'way, 9 + perfs.)

SOMEONE WHO'LL WATCH OVER ME—Stephen Rea and Michael York (who replaced Alec McCowen) in Frank McGuinness's play

New Plays

Paul Rudnick's Best Play *Jeffrey* is a gay play employing the devices of traditional romantic comedy, even to the point of ending with its leading couple dancing against the background of the Manhattan skyline. Rudnick manages the not-inconsiderable trick of serving a whipped cream topping on a very bleak base—the AIDS epidemic in today's Greenwich Village. The title character, a self-confessed sexual obsessive, relieved when his tests show him to be HIV-negative, decides to avoid further risk by vowing celibacy. As luck would have it, temptation appears in the form of the man of his dreams. Unfortunately, the man of his dreams is HIV-positive. Against the constantly shifting backgrounds of bars, gyms, AIDS benefits and (inevitably) hospitals, Jeffrey confronts his dilemma, ultimately moving to the conclusion that the best response to encroaching death is to embrace life rather than avoid it. This is not a script marked by deep characterization—few of the characters have more substance than clever *New Yorker* cartoons—rather it is an engaging hybrid of play and topical revue with the title character acting as the lens through which various aspects of the gay scene are depicted in satiric but affectionate terms. Under the direction of Christopher Ashley, the ensemble dashed about with a precision and spirit one would associate with a Jerry Zaks production.

The three sisters of Wendy Wasserstein's *The Sisters Rosensweig* have a clear advantage over Chekhov's threesome, to whom they make occasional joking reference. Chekhov's yearned to leave their provincial lives for the sophisticated world represented by Moscow; Wasserstein's Sara, Gorgeous and Pfeni can pretty much go where they want (if only they had a clear idea of where that is). The three gather in Sara's London townhouse to celebrate her 54th birthday and to take stock of their mid-lives. Sara, the eldest, is an international banker, twice divorced, the mother of a young woman who will soon leave the nest. Gorgeous is a housewife whose chattiness has propelled her to local celebrity as the host of a radio show on which she gives advice. And Pfeni alternates between roaming the world as a journalist and keeping company with a British director whose relationship with her represents a detour from homosexuality. And, to a large extent, all three women are characterized by their response to their Jewish background.

Pfeni's reaction is to be the modern version of the Wandering Jew, embracing a profession which encourages rootlessness. Gorgeous's is to revel in her ethnicity to the point of excess. Sara sees herself as a citizen of the world, more or less discounting her Jewishness, though she did get satisfaction out of having helped rehabilitate the economy of an Eastern European country from which her ancestors had fled anti-Semitism.

That Gorgeous and Mervyn Kant, the purveyor of synthetic furs who takes a shine to Sara, get the largest share of the jokes indicates where Wasserstein's sympathies lie. Gorgeous and Mervyn may be "too" Jewish; but, especially as performed by Madeline Kahn and Robert Klein, they share an optimism and vitality which buoy the play. Much of the pleasure of the production came from Mervyn's courtship of Sara, the odd-coupleness of the characters reinforced by the different but complementary acting styles of Klein and Jane Alexander.

Though contemporary political topics are invoked, *The Sisters Rosensweig* is intended as the kind of comedy which flourished on Broadway some decades ago (e.g., *Cactus Flower* and *Forty Carats*), the kind in which no character can leave the stage without hesitating at the door and tossing out a nimble, defining quip. That the play works well cannot be disputed. We laugh when we're supposed to, and at well-paced intervals a little gem of an aphorism tickles the brain. But, following *The Heidi Chronicles,* I couldn't help feeling just a little let down. *Heidi* may have been structurally awkward, but it had an urgency and an edge that *Sisters Rosensweig,* for all its craft, lacks. It seems like a determinedly

The 1992–93 Season Off Broadway

PLAYS (25)

Playwrights Horizons 1992:
Flaubert's Latest
MTC 1992:
  The Innocents' Crusade
Distant Fires
Young Playwrights Festival
The Roads to Home
Circle Repertory
THE DESTINY OF ME
Three Hotels
And Baby Makes Seven
THE SISTERS ROSENSWEIG
OLEANNA
Dog Logic
MTC 1993:
JOINED AT THE HEAD
The Last Yankee
The Years
Playwrights Horizons 1993:
On the Bum, or The Next Train Through
The Heliotrope Bouquet by Scott Joplin and Louis Chauvin
LATER LIFE

Program for Murder
Papp Public Theater:
On the Open Road
Marisol
Wrong Turn at Lungfish
JEFFREY
Aven' U Boys
The Second Annual Heart o' Texas Eczema Telethon
One Shoe Off

MUSICALS (5)

Balancing Act
Orpheus in Love
Madison Avenue
WINGS
Wild Men

REVUES (6)

Cut the Ribbons
Hello Muddah, Hello Fadduh
Manhattan Moves
Forbidden Broadway 1993
Back to Bacharach and David
Sondheim—Putting It Together

FOREIGN LANGUAGE PRODUCTIONS (6)

Brooklyn Academy:
(Les Atrides)
Iphigenia in Aulis
Agamemnon
The Libation Bearers
The Eumenides
Peer Gynt
Madame de Sade

ONE-ACTOR PERFORMANCES (16)

RED DIAPER BABY
Ethel Merman's Broadway
The Night Larry Kramer Kissed Me
Ali
Papp Public Theater:
You Could Be Home Now
Texts for Nothing
Memory Tricks
Deep in a Dream of You
SPIC-O-RAMA
Bubbe Meises Bubbe Stories
American Place:
The Confessions of Stepin Fetchit
On the Way Home
Manhattan Theater Club:
Pretty Fire
Jenny Keeps Talking
Time on Fire
Lypsinka!

SPECIALTIES (2)

CBS Live
Mo' Madness

REVIVALS (6)

Richard III
Shakespeare Marathon:
As You Like It
The Comedy of Errors
Remembrance
Jacques Brel Is Alive and Well and Living in Paris
Woyzeck

FOREIGN PLAYS IN ENGLISH (5)

Mad Forest
(return engagement)
The Holy Terror
The Madame MacAdam Travelling Theater
The Best of Friends
Playboy of the West Indies

Categorized above are all the new productions listed in the Plays Produced Off Broadway section of this volume. Plays listed in CAPITAL LETTERS have been designated Best Plays of 1992–93. Plays listed in *italics* were still running June 1, 1993.

"nice" play from a writer who has more than proved her ability to accomplish more. Still, its presence provided Broadway with much-needed sparkle and intelligence.

There is nothing "nice" about *Oleanna,* David Mamet's tale of a college professor's disastrous series of encounters with a student. In the first scene, John, seeing the befuddlement of Carol in his class, offers to give the young woman private tutorials. In the second scene, Carol has evidently instituted procedures against John, claiming that John's seemingly generous offer was in actuality an incident of sexual harassment. She offers to drop the procedure if he modifies his course to her ideological tastes (and the tastes of the mysterious group of radical feminists who apparently support her). At the play's end, his career ruined by what we in the audience know to be unfounded charges, John snaps and assaults the student. Mamet seems to be saying that by relentlessly attacking John, Carol has turned him into what she accused him of being. (We become what we're called?)

Some discussed the play as if it were intended to be Mamet's even-handed view of the conflict between the sexes. But there is nothing even-handed about the characterization of the two. While somewhat patronizing and more than a little foolish, John is presented as a patently well-intentioned man whose attempts to extend himself to a student in trouble are misinterpreted and turned against him. Carol is clearly in the wrong. The only question is whether she misinterprets out of a willful and evil desire to destroy, or because she is genuinely so dense or warped not to have the ability correctly to interpret reality. In this way, she is reminiscent of Karen in Mamet's *Speed-the-Plow,* who could be played, with equal conviction, as an idealist, a nut case or a schemer. With the exception of his remarkable one-act, *Reunion,* Mamet's writing for women is akin to that of his friend Harold Pinter—both seem to view women as ultimately unfathomable. So, rather than write women with the same concreteness as they do their men, they assign actions to the female characters and leave it to the actresses to try to find a logic to support the frequently mysterious behavior. (Incidentally, at this writing, Pinter is scheduled to direct the London production of *Oleanna.*)

Under Mamet's direction, *Oleanna* was a galvanizing theatrical experience. With the Clarence Thomas-Anita Hill hearings fresh in mind, it could hardly fail to stimulate passionate discussion. I must, however, register some reservations about the script. The inarticulate woman of the first scene who asks for definitions of fairly common words bears little resemblance to the feminist warrior of the rest of the play, capable of extended articulate jeremiads. The transformation is merely presented, not accounted for, and I, for one, find it unpersuasive. Being unable to believe in the journey of the character, I find it difficult to believe in the action of the play, except on the more abstract level of a fable.

I am also troubled by the degree to which the stylization of Mamet's dialogue overwhelms the characters' individual voices. In his Best Plays, *American Buf-*

falo and *Glengarry Glen Ross,* the characters speak with specific and unique voices. In *Oleanna,* there are too many stretches when I stop hearing John and Carol and hear only Mamet speaking through them. Of course, playwrights do speak through their characters, but the most artful dramatic writing creates the illusion that the characters speak only for themselves. All in all, to my taste, *Oleanna* is a provocative if flawed work.

Frank Pugliese's *Aven' U Boys* is full of male abusiveness—three young thugs in a Queens neighborhood, bonded by mindless violent ritual and a sense of hopelessness, for two acts bully each other and the women unfortunate enough to be part of their lives. Individually, many of the scenes have a nasty vitality, but assembled into an evening, the yelling and punching and swearing gets numbing. The play's central idea—that hopelessness and lack of effect breed frustration, which in turn breeds violence—is not developed so much as reiterated. Under the direction of Frederick Zollo, the play received a strong production, aided by a talented young cast and Kert Lundell's ingenious set summoning up a world under elevated train tracks.

The relationship of Larry Kramer's Best Play *The Destiny of Me* to *The Normal Heart* is similar to that of *The Godfather, Part II* to *The Godfather,* containing action which both precedes and follows the earlier work. In *The Normal Heart,* one of the first dramas to deal with AIDS, Kramer introduced Ned Weeks, the frequently abrasive gay activist (an autobiographical character), and portrayed him simultaneously fighting political battles and coping with the illness of his lover. One of the most explosive moments in that work came when Weeks smashed a carton of milk on the floor. In *The Destiny of Me,* he smashes packets containing blood samples against the wall. Clearly, neither Kramer nor his alter ego has mellowed in the intervening years. *Destiny* deals with Weeks, himself now suffering from AIDS, undergoing experimental treatment. Between scenes in which he confronts the hospital personnel are scenes from his youth, charting the source of the anger and abrasiveness. The picture Kramer paints of his childhood—of a distant and homophobic father and a mother overflowing with charity for the rest of the world but offering little comfort at home—is a grim one, and Kramer does nothing to make it any less grim. Marshall W. Mason's production featured affecting work by Jonathan Hadary and John Cameron Mitchell as the older and younger Weeks.

On Broadway, Mason also directed Lanford Wilson's new play, *Redwood Curtain.* The central figure is Geri, a young woman born of a Vietnamese mother and a G.I. father. Brought to the States when she was a child and adopted and raised by a wealthy American family, she haunts the redwood forest where Lyman, a Vietnam vet she suspects might be her father, lives a hermetic life. The aspect of the story which deals with the mystery of Geri's paternity builds to a moving and resonant revelation, but Wilson muddies the script with other elements. For instance, he endows Geri with magical powers, but the powers are not well defined, and they have little bearing on the resolu-

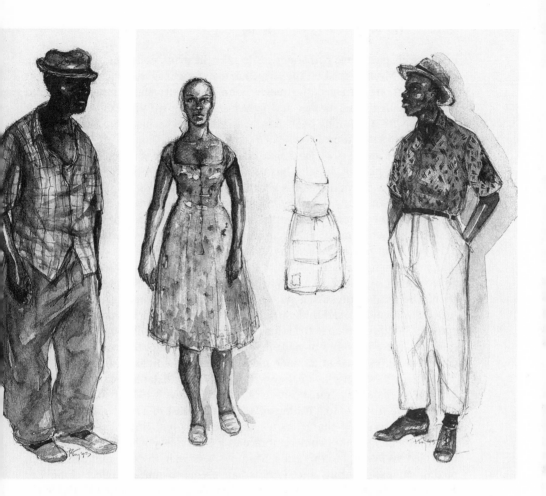

Examples of Paul Tazewell's costume designs for *Playboy of the West Indies*, outstanding in the straight-play year, are pictured here as created for the characters Mikey *(left)*, Peggy *(center)* and Stanley

tion of the story. He invokes environmental issues with a subplot concerning Geri's Aunt Geneva being forced to part with the land she owns, but rather than complementing the play's main concerns, it comes across as a digression. In addition, Wilson returns to the motif of the blocked artist he employed with characters of the novelist in *The Mound Builders* and the choreographer in *Burn This* by making Geri a famous concert pianist reluctant to play. As in *Burn This,* her return to her art is meant to represent coming to terms with the conflicts which have plagued her, but the moment strikes me as constructed rather than felt.

This is not to say that the production was without rewards. Jeff Daniels extended his range, putting aside the passivity which has been the hallmark of many of his past stage performances to play the gruff, confrontational Lyman; and Debra Monk tossed off the script's many witty lines with such panache that she won a Tony for her performance. John Lee Beatty and Dennis Parichy did wonders with the set design and lighting, winning a well-deserved round of applause with a stunning change in which the trees seemed to waltz aside and reveal Geneva's house.

Redwood Curtain is of particular concern because it is the first new play in years from a playwright who has probably composed more major plays than any American dramatist of his generation. In interviews prior to the show's opening, Wilson made rumbling noises about his reluctance to continue writing plays if this one weren't sufficiently welcomed. We have to hope that he will get past his discouragement. His compassionate and lyrical voice is needed.

In Tug Yourgrau's *The Song of Jacob Zulu,* the use of the black South African *a cappella* singing group Ladysmith Black Mambazo as a kind of Greek chorus gave an enticing frame to a play whose text was otherwise earnest but pedestrian. The most impressive aspect of the production of this fact-based story of the evolution of a black South African terrorist was the performance of Chicago actor K. Todd Freeman in the lead. Freeman carried with him an eerie combination of vulnerability and menace that ultimately, despite the explicitness of his climactic confessional aria, made him a hauntingly enigmatic figure.

The season's other play dealing with black life, Mustapha Matura's *Playboy of the West Indies,* is a transposition of John M. Synge's 1921 Irish play *Playboy of the Western World* to a fishing village on the coast of Trinidad in 1950. I am one of those grumpy characters who have always had trouble swallowing the idea that a community would embrace as a hero a boy who proclaims that he has killed his father; but this aside, Matura's version is an exuberant concoction, mixing calypso rhythms and Trinidadian patois to musical effect. John Lee Beatty contributed another of his first-rate designs, complemented by the colorful costuming of Paul Tazewell. Lorraine Toussaint was superb, managing the difficult transitions from being a figure of defiant strength to a woman intoxicated by passion to bitterness and regret. Victor Love was a touching combination of naivete and braggadocio as the title character, Michele Shay made a wonderfully lusty voodoo lady, and Kelly Taffe and Melissa Murray gave winning turns as two youngsters smitten by the newcomer.

The tale of a mildly retarded boy put into prison because nobody can figure out what else to do with him, *Seconds Out,* written by a group of Irish teenagers, has a vitality and a clear-sightedness many a more experienced playwright would do well to emulate. It was given a strong production at the Public Theater by the Irish Arts company under the direction of Jack Hofsiss.

Another play about imprisonment, *Someone Who'll Watch Over Me,* puts political hostages from Ireland, England and America into the same room and eavesdrops on the conversational strategies they employ to keep their wits about them. Along the way, writer Frank McGuinness scores some interesting points about the different ways the three use the English language, but, despite some graceful writing, the play struck me as being too neat and predictable; time after time I found myself anticipating the sense of whole passages. The best reason to see the production was to watch Stephen Rea (whose starring role in the hit film *The Crying Game* helped attract audiences to the play) as the rambunctious Irish journalist. I have long been an admirer of Alec McCowen, but his performance as a gay English teacher struck me as so reminiscent of some of his past performances in similarly prim and fussy parts as to be distracting.

Playwrights Horizons produced two plays this year about artists being summoned back from the dead, Peter Parnell's *Flaubert's Latest,* and Eric Overmyer's *The Heliotrope Bouquet by Scott Joplin and Louis Chauvin.* In the former, a contemporary writer summons the French author to help him cope with writer's block. In the latter, the celebrated ragtime composer is haunted by memories of a lesser known and unjustly ignored ragtime pianist. Parnell's script has gleeful flashes of literary humor, but Albert Innaurato's *Gus and Al* (a Best Play produced by Playwrights Horizons a few years back) told a similar story with greater resonance. Overmyer's script offers interesting historical insights into the exploitation of ragtime music, but the title characters fail to come alive or engage in genuinely illuminating dramatic action. I hope that Playwrights Horizons has exhausted its appetite for telling stories of artists kidnapped out of their eras and urge Parnell, Overmyer and the other talented writers whose work is produced there to explore other motifs. Yet a third play produced at Playwrights Horizons, Neal Bell's *On the Bum, or The Next Train Through,* deals with the place of the artist in American society, offering a number of vivid scenes of a young actress's struggle in the Depression, but it gets bogged down in an awkwardly-constructed plot meant to show the parallels between the travails of WPA-supported theater and the recent controversies at the National Endowment for the Arts.

Artists were characters again in Ira Lewis's *Chinese Coffee,* a one-act, two-handed play about two middle-aged, struggling Bohemians and the prospects for success one of them now has because of a novel he has written based on the other's life. Al Pacino and Charles Cioffi, as the novelist and his photographer friend, had a good deal of fun for the first half batting amiable invective back and forth, but the second half, supposedly a debate about the competing interests of friendship and ambition, never caught fire.

Keith Reddin's *The Innocents' Crusade* concerns a directionless young man who, while being driven around to interviews at various college admissions offices, attracts some other aimless characters to an ill-defined crusade. Reddin may be trying to make a point with the very lack of definition of the young man's crusade—that we are a society desperately searching for something to generate passion and purpose—but it's hard to respond to a character with so vague an agenda. Ultimately, despite the clever writing one expects from Reddin, the play founders from lack of specificity and a too-studied antic tone.

Daniel Gerroll played frazzled book editors twice this season, as the lead in Simon Gray's *The Holy Terror* and one of the ensemble of Tina Howe's *One Shoe Off.* The latest of Gray's portraits of British literati falling to pieces, *The Holy Terror* offers no reason for us to care about the disintegration of his protagonist, Mark Melon, and in production his two-hour aria of justifiable self-loathing (interrupted only by an intermission) proved wearing. Howe's play, an absurdist look at a floundering middle-aged couple and their attempt at a dinner party, also disappoints, though its production featured a marvelous set by Heidi Landesman depicting a house overcome by intrusive plant life.

Wrong Turn at Lungfish, by Garry Marshall and Lowell Ganz, brings to mind Israel Horovitz's *Park Your Car in Harvard Yard* of last season; both concern cranky professors on death's door awakening new dignity in working class women who have come to work for them. Being the handiwork of writers who have contributed some skilled film and TV comedy, *Lungfish* moves along snappily enough, but the piece ultimately collapses under its selfconscious literary references and the schematic nature of the plotting. George C. Scott imbued the character of the blind, hospitalized pedant with his own particular brand of hostile charm, making one hungry to see him again in a piece that would make fuller use of his great gifts. On the other hand, despite conscientious work, Jami Gertz, as the young woman who has volunteered to read to him, couldn't transcend the pattern of mispronunciations, malapropisms and cheerful trampiness which marked the character as a stereotype.

Arthur Miller's *The Last Yankee* is also set in a hospital, though of a psychiatric sort. This short work begins on a beguiling note with a nicely-observed dialogue between the philosophical Yankee craftsman of the title and a rigid materialist. With the introduction of their wives, both institutionalized at the facility, the play seems to lose its way. The characters talk earnestly among themselves, but what is at issue is elusive. The piece ends with the middle-aged wife of the materialist putting on top hat and tails and tapping to the banjo playing of the Yankee, and I couldn't begin to tell you what this signifies, though John Heard gave a performance of easy assurance in the title role.

Catherine Butterfield's Best Play *Joined at the Head,* which preceded *The Last Yankee* on the Manhattan Theater Club's invaluable second stage, also spends time in a hospital. Novelist Maggie Mulroney, returning to the Boston-area town to promote her new semi-autobiographical book, is invited to dinner by Jim, an old boy friend, to meet his wife, similarly named Maggy. The complicated feelings this encounter engenders are further complicated by the fact that Maggy is dying of cancer. The meat of the play is in the relationship that grows between the two women. There is little by way of story, but the evening offers the rare treat of the company of believable, articulate and sympathetic grown-ups calling on the best in themselves to cope with loss in a series of sensitively-written scenes. Butterfield not only gave Ellen Parker her best role in years as the acerbic Maggie, but, under the direction of Pamela Berlin, did credit to her own writing with a solid performance as Maggy. I thought hers the most auspicious playwriting debut of the season.

Another Manhattan Theater Club production, Cindy Lou Johnson's *The Years*, was less satisfying. Using an upper middle class family's gatherings as the occasions for various absurd disasters and coincidences, despite some witty passages, the overall effect was of facetiousness. Johnson's intention seems to have been to trigger the audience's sympathy for characters mistreated by the randomness of life, but the curious result was to trigger sympathy for them because of the mistreatment they were suffering at the hands of their creator.

In last season's *The Baltimore Waltz*, actress Cherry Jones depicted a woman who used fantasy to deal with her brother's death from AIDS. Jones returned to fantasize in another play by *Waltz*'s author, Paula Vogel, *And Baby Makes Seven*, this time with two fantasizing companions—the gay male roommate whom she urged to impregnate her and her lesbian lover. Reportedly a script whose composition pre-dates *Waltz*, *Baby*'s characters were so aggressively cute as to be off-putting.

The Joseph Papp Public Theater offered two plays in which leading characters picked their way across apocalyptic landscapes. Steve Tesich's script for *On the Open Road* alternates between exhilarating bursts of black comedy and sincere but trying passages of pseudo-poetry in his tale of how a good-hearted proletarian ruffian named Angel teams up with a cynical esthete named Al in an attempt to escape an unnamed wartorn country. Robert Falls directed forcefully, but the script couldn't help encouraging him to reprise imagery from his notable production in Chicago of *Mother Courage*.

Tesich's angel was followed into the Public's Martinson Hall by the black angel played by Danitra Vance in Jose Rivera's Obie-winning *Marisol*. Being preoccupied with her guerrilla battle against a senile white God, this angel takes a vacation from acting as the title character's guardian, leaving Marisol to the mercy of a New York City gone mad. Much of Rivera's nightmare imagery is arresting, but the play suffers from Marisol's passivity. She seems to be present chiefly to be battered and brutalized, her only object being to survive in a world which would drive any reasonable person to suicide.

Subscribers to the Public also got to see the season's most talked-about angel, the one who crashed through the ceiling of a man dying of AIDS in Tony Kushner's Pulitzer Prize-winning Best Play, *Angels in America: Millennium Approaches*. Subtitled *A Gay Fantasia on National Themes*, the play (actually the first of two parts) views the journey of four gay men through the Reagan years—a WASP drag queen named Prior Walter and his Jewish lover, Louis Ironson, who takes off when he can no longer cope with Walter's illness, a married Mormon lawyer named Joe Pitt who tries to use his religious beliefs to ward off his homosexual drive, and Pitt's mentor, Roy Cohn, the real-life, spectacularly corrupt, red-baiting attorney who made his name as Sen. Joseph McCarthy's hatchet man. Though the play is a large one, most of the scenes are

WRONG TURN AT LUNGFISH—George C. Scott, Jami Gertz and Tony
Danza in a scene from the play by Garry Marshall and Lowell Ganz

encounters between two or three characters wrangling over moral issues. To my
mind, the script marks a substantial advance over Kushner's last New York
presentation, *A Bright Room Called Day.* In *Angels,* he is no less concerned with
the effect of a corrupt body politic on the private ethical dilemmas than he was
in *Bright Room,* but in this script he has managed to illuminate his subject with
biting humor and characters who for the most part not only represent positions
but also have real depth and individuality. Running in excess of three hours, in
production the evening was almost relentlessly entertaining. Small wonder that
it was greeted with open arms by the critical community and the Pulitzer Prize
Committee.

This is not to say that there aren't some bumps along the way. The passages
Kushner wrote in which the distraught Mormon wife Harper Pitt is enticed by
the hallucinatory embodiment of her need to escape through drugs—a gaudily
dressed black travel agent wearing shades named Mr. Lies—are repetitive and
too calculatingly outrageous. Too many of the scenes for Harper seem to be
there to give the character equal time with the play's other leading characters.

If it falls short of perfection, this first part of *Angels in America* offers scene
after vivid scene of sharp satiric writing as well as wrenching confrontations

between most of its major characters. Under George C. Wolfe's direction (which, according to *Newsday* critic Linda Winer, built on the foundation of the Los Angeles production directed by Oskar Eustis), Stephen Spinella and Joe Mantello as the lovers and David Marshall Grant and Marcia Gay Harden as the Mormon couple gave brave and complex performances, Kathleen Chalfant did strong work in a variety of supporting characters (including some male ones), and Jeffrey Wright did a memorable turn as Belize, a black gay man with 20/20 moral vision. In the extravagant and malevolent role of Roy Cohn, Ron Leibman seized the opportunity to give a performance full of gigantic comic flourishes and gestures, making him one of the most exuberant and compelling monsters to hit the stage since Richard III.

In addition to starring in one Best Play, Joe Mantello directed another, Jon Robin Baitz's *Three Hotels,* an expansion of a television piece Baitz wrote for public television. Like Kushner, Baitz is concerned with the relationship between public and private morality. In the pursuit of profits and a higher place in the corporate ladder through the aggressive and deceptive sale of baby formula to third world mothers, a multinational food corporation executive, Kenneth Hoyle, has spread death and disease. (Switching babies to formula keeps the babies from receiving needed antibodies in their mothers' milk; and illness may result because the formula's powder frequently is mixed with unclean water.) Yet a moral sense is not dead within Hoyle, particularly given his awareness of the consequences of his work on his emotionally fragile wife, Barbara. The piece is written in the form of three monologues, the first and third featuring Hoyle, the second Barbara. The device is most effective in the contrast between the second section, in which Barbara proudly announces the success she's had speaking to the wives of corporate officers, and the third, in which Kenneth reveals what that "success" looked like to more objective eyes. As Kenneth describes the speech and its aftermath, the audience finds itself reevaluating Barbara's monologue, even as Kenneth is reevaluating the premises of his life. The writing is characterized by Baitz's usual elegance and, guided by Mantello, Ron Rifkin and Christine Lahti gave virtuoso performances. My only regret is that Baitz's construction didn't allow the pleasure of seeing what would happen if these two superb actors had a real scene together. But then, yes, that would have been a different play.

Truth to tell, some members of the audience raised on more traditional theatrical subject matter than what dominated this season must have blinked and wondered what happened to the world they used to take for granted. They have a kinship with Austin (played by Charles Kimbrough), the hero of A.R. Gurney's latest Best Play *Later Life.* A recently divorced man in his 50s who has spent the bulk of his life in a kind of protected cocoon in Boston, we first see him on a terrace overlooking Boston Harbor. At the request of a woman named Ruth (played by Maureen Anderman), the hostess of the party going on just inside has arranged an introduction. Actually, it is a reintroduction. Years ago, when Austin was in the service, Ruth met him in Italy and they almost began a relationship. Handed a second chance, the two now explore the possibility of taking up where they left off. During their conversational dance, the separate paths they took in the intervening years are revealed.

But the conversation is constantly interrupted by other of the party's guests. In one way or another, all of them represent aspects of Austin's changing Boston—a relentlessly charming couple from the new South, a computer obsessive, a humorless lesbian, an aged pair of Bostonians with different attitudes about relocating in Florida, etc. In a stroke of theatricality, all of these roles are written to be played by two actors. In Don Scardino's production, the two were Anthony Heald and Carole Shelley, both of whom played with enormous wit and specificity. Shelley scored a particular success, drawing as never before on her facility with accents and astonishing sense of comic timing—a brilliant comic performance.

Given all of the thrilling and flashy work going on around him, there is a tendency to underestimate the less showy work of Kimbrough. But his, too, was an extraordinary performance. The script establishes that the normally staid Austin is flirting with danger by drinking wine on top of the Prozac he takes for depression. As he fights for Ruth's affection, he also copes with the giddiness which threatens to throw him off balance. The final image of Austin, alone again, standing on the terrace, looking in through the doorway at a party he cannot bring himself to join—a party made up of people not dissimilar to the citizens of the diverse new society so many of this season's plays reflect—served as a bittersweet coda to the season.

Here's where we list the Best Plays choices for the outstanding straight play achievements of 1992–93 in New York, on and off Broadway. In the acting categories, clear distinction among "starring," "featured" or "supporting" players can't be made on the basis of official billing, which is as much a matter of contracts as of esthetics. Here in these volumes we divide acting into "primary" or "secondary" roles, a primary role being one which might some day cause a star to inspire a revival in order to appear in that character. All others, be they vivid as Mercutio, are classed as secondary. Furthermore, our list of individual standouts makes room for more than a single choice when appropriate. We believe that no useful purpose is served by forcing ourselves into an arbitrary selection of a single best when we come upon multiple examples of equal distinction.

PLAYS

BEST PLAY: *Angels in America: Millennium Approaches* by Tony Kushner

BEST REVIVAL: *Richard III* by William Shakespeare

BEST ACTOR IN A PRIMARY ROLE: K. Todd Freeman as Jacob Zulu in *The Song of Jacob Zulu;* Ian McKellen as Richard in *Richard III*

BEST ACTRESS IN A PRIMARY ROLE: Ellen Parker as Maggie Mulroney in *Joined at the Head;* Christine Lahti as Barbara Hoyle in *Three Hotels*

BEST ACTOR IN A SECONDARY ROLE: Robert Sean Leonard as Marchbanks in *Candida;* Joe Mantello as Louis Ironson in *Angels in America: Millennium Approaches*

BEST ACTRESS IN A SECONDARY ROLE: Ann Dowd as Miss Proserpine Garnett in *Candida;* Carole Shelley as Other Women in *Later Life*

BEST DIRECTOR: Pamela Berlin for *Joined at the Head;* Richard Eyre for *Richard III;* George C. Wolfe for *Angels in America: Millennium Approaches*

BEST SCENERY: Bob Crowley for *Richard III*

BEST COSTUMES: Jess Goldstein for *Later Life;* Paul Tazewell for *Playboy of the West Indies*

BEST LIGHTING: Jean Kalman for *Richard III;* Natasha Katz for *Joined at the Head;* Kenneth Posner for *On the Open Road*

SPECIAL CITATIONS: Josh Kornbluth for *Red Diaper Baby;* John Leguizamo in *Spic-O-Rama;* Lynn Redgrave in *Shakespeare for My Father*

FOOL MOON—Bill Irwin *(right)* and David Shiner in
one of the comedy numbers in the show which they created

Musicals and Special Entertainments

Once upon a time, the word "musical" summoned up an image of lightweight
material. Tragedy was for grand opera, musicals were supposed to be fun,
suitable for the whole family, upbeat.

Upbeat, though, is not a word one would apply to several of this season's
musical theater entries. *Kiss of the Spider Woman, Blood Brothers, Anna
Karenina* and *Wings* all featured leading characters who went to their deaths by
the final curtain.

Paradoxically, in *Spider Woman* the death is the occasion for a celebratory
number. As Molina, the gay window dresser, is about to be shot, the defense
mechanism that he's been invoking throughout the evening—evading the grim-
ness of reality through fantasies featuring Aurora, his favorite movie star—
kicks in again. Suddenly he imagines himself in a movie theater surrounded by
all of the supporting characters, sharing a musical number and a kiss with

Aurora. The shot rings out, but the show's creators would have us believe that his spirit has escaped.

Escape, which is what Broadway musicals have for so long represented, is in fact the subject matter of *Spider Woman*. For the bulk of the show, Molina shares a cell with a political prisoner named Valentin in a jail in an unnamed Latin American country where torture is an active part of the penal modus operandi. Throughout the evening, as the pain and degradation of prison life threaten to become overwhelming, Molina submerges himself in memories of Aurora's films. Valentin, who is new to the cell, initially is repelled by Molina's homosexuality as well as his escapist tactics. By the end of the evening, Valentin has had sex with Molina (admittedly for less than pure reasons) and learned to appreciate the value of escapism in attempting to cope with the nearly intolerable.

As an examination of repression in South American dictatorships, *Spider Woman* is pretty shallow. There are a few glancing references to Marxism and a song of political idealism which could be sung in the service of virtually any political philosophy. But then, I don't think the show is really about South America. Though AIDS is not mentioned in the show, it is easy to see the prison as a metaphor for the prison of a body whose dignity is being assaulted by the torture of that disease, and certainly the fantasies Molina summons up bring to mind the hallucinatory images many AIDS patients experience.

Much of *Spider Woman* is wonderful. A good deal of the score by John Kander and Fred Ebb ranks with their very best work, some of it written with a lyricism they have never previously achieved. In a season of notably disappointing Broadway books, Terrence McNally's graceful and literate adaptation is a particularly welcome and instructive contrast. Hal Prince's production displays his characteristically bravura touch, in collaboration with designers Jerome Sirlin and Howell Binkley, effecting nearly magical transformations from the cells of the prison to the exotic landscapes of Molina's imagination.

Yes, I have a quibble or two. The first act could profitably lose a good 15 minutes; Molina's narcotic-induced ballet in the clinic seems unnecessary, and a few expositional points are repeated to little effect. And some of the pastiche material written for Aurora seems less than fresh, given how frequently in the past Broadway and off-Broadway have satirized the conventions of overdone production numbers.

But this is the one Broadway musical of the season which is by and large successful in telling an involving story through a new score and book. What's more, it presented Brent Carver in an extremely impressive Broadway musical debut as Molina, simultaneously heroic and a little ridiculous. Anthony Crivello as Valentin was essentially used as Molina's straight man (in both senses of "straight"), establishing the reality which served as the platform from which his cellmate launched his flights of fantasy. Aurora is virtually a mythological character, and being something of show biz legend herself, it was a natural for

Chita Rivera who, in her 60s, set a daunting pace for the ensemble of dancers who supported her.

In a continuing vein of tragedy, *Anna Karenina,* of course, is the story of a Russian woman whose adulterous affair leads her to suicide. To attempt to condense Tolstoy's huge novel into an evening of musical theater is asking for trouble, and trouble is what Peter Kellogg (author of the book and lyrics) and Daniel Levine (composer) got. Although the enterprise floundered, I don't think it deserved the easy mockery with which it was greeted. Kellogg and Levine may well have made a mistake in their choice of material to adapt, but throughout the evening there were flashes of real talent. One song in particular, "There's More to Life Than Love," showed a flair in the Cole Porter vein. But who would suggest that Cole Porter and Tolstoy are a natural match? I hope that Kellogg and Levine will not be daunted by the fate of this effort and will return with a project better suited to their abilities. I hope, too, one day to see the gifted Ann Crumb cast in a musical that shows her to better advantage.

Tragedy again in *Blood Brothers,* a musical parable about a woman who gives up one of her twin sons at birth to a wealthy family, then is powerless to help as the two boys, unaware of being brothers, fall prey to the inequities of the British class system and ultimately destroy each other. Of course, this is meant to be a warning that such inequities threaten to cause a mutually destructive civil war on a national level. Unfortunately, Willy Russell, the author of both book and score, writes with an oppressively heavy hand, relentlessly pounding home through an ominous black-clad narrator the significance of every word and action. If only the whole show had been able to maintain the deftness of a beguiling ballad Russell introduces in the second act, "I'm Not Saying a Word." I must report that, in contrast to me, many of the audience were very deeply affected; I saw more than a few tear-stained faces at the end as the twins' mother led the chorus in "Tell Me It's Not True" over the bodies of her sons. As indifferent as I was to much of the material, it was a pleasure to make the acquaintance of Con O'Neill and Jan Graveson as the working class brother and his wife, both of whom played with great heart.

There were attempts at lighter fare. Neil Simon refashioned his charming screen play for *The Goodbye Girl* into a musical in collaboration with composer Marvin Hamlisch, lyricist David Zippel and director Michael Kidd. Estimable talents all, but the transfer to the new form fell flat. Part of the problem has to do with the inclusion of a chorus which seems to have no function other than to pump up the small story to a size that would justify occupying a Broadway stage. More seriously, though Bernadette Peters and Martin Short are both gifted performers, they didn't generate much believable chemistry as a dancer and an actor who begin as involuntary roommates and end up falling in love. This may have something to do with Peters's role being written as such a grump that one didn't care much what she found. Short was the show's one unmitigated asset, a marvelous clown who managed to be ingratiating and funny even without much support from the material, though Hamlisch and Zippel did come through for him with a sweet ballad about the appeal of fatherhood to Peters's daughter called "I Can Play This Part."

If Simon, Hamlisch and Zippel began with too little story for their show, book writer Joseph Dougherty, composer Stephen Flaherty and lyricist Lynn Ahrens apparently thought they began with too much when adapting the film *My Favorite Year*. The movie told the story of a movie star named Alan Swann (think Errol Flynn) and his relationship with a young writer named Benjy Stone (think a young Mel Brooks) into whose care he is entrusted during the rehearsals for and broadcast of an episode of the 1950s TV show for which Stone writes and on which Swann is supposed to appear as a guest, a show starring an outrageous and slightly mad comic genius named King Kaiser (think Sid Caesar). In his swashbuckling film roles, Swann has long been a hero to the movie-obsessed Benjy, but in real-life, Swann is an alcoholic has-been with a disillusioning streak of cowardice. The original film contained a subplot in which a gangsterish labor leader (Jimmy Hoffa?) threatened Kaiser for satirizing him; at the picture's climax, Swann sailed into action and rescued Kaiser from a bunch of goons in an on-air donnybrook, thus becoming a real-life hero. For some reason, Dougherty's book eliminates the gangster, so Swann has no persuasive opportunity to take a large and heroic action that redeems him in Benjy's eyes. Ah well, Flaherty and Ahrens proved with the Best Play *Once on This Island* that they are a team to be reckoned with; they'll be back with another, better show. Dougherty too has established his gifts with a series of fine scripts for the television series *Thirtysomething,* and I am hopeful he too will be returning to the stage. The best reason to remember *My Favorite Year* was Andrea Martin, who brought her Second City experience to bear getting the most out of every comic opportunity in the role of the wise-cracking Alice Miller, the only female member of the writing staff.

I doubt that the 1992–93 season will be remembered by David Lipman as *his* favorite year. He began it by playing a zhlub in *My Favorite Year,* an ode to TV in the Fifties, and ended it by playing another zhlub in *Ain't Broadway Grand,* an even less successful ode to Broadway in the late Forties. I'm not suggesting that Lipman bears any responsibility for the quality of the productions where he clocked time, but it must have been discouraging for him. At least *My Favorite Year* had several genuinely funny lines and some amiable songs. *Ain't Broadway Grand,* which purported to be a portrait of flamboyant producer Mike Todd, featured three able performers—Mike Burstyn as Todd, Debbie Shapiro Gravitte as Gypsy Rose Lee and Maureen McNamara as Joan Blondell—and gave them little of consequence to do. As I mentioned in the introduction, the plot bears an uncomfortable resemblance to the movie *The Band Wagon,* with a musical comedy veteran attempting high art by producing a pretentious show; and then, after out-of-town embarrassment, revamping the production as an old-fashioned audience-pleaser. The score, too, frequently sounds familiar. (The opening bars of "Tall Dames and Low Comedy," for instance, sounds like a carbon of *Damn Yankees'* "A Little Brains, a Little Talent.") David Mitchell's romanticized views of the world of Broadway during its glory days were graces that were insufficient to save this venture.

The only light musical to score this season took itself so un-seriously as to bear the subtitle, "a musical . . . sort of." *Wild Men* is not a musical so much as it is a sketch blown up to two hours—not too surprising, given that many in the production's cast and creative team were Second City alumni, among them star George Wendt and co-writer and director Rob Riley. The target of the show is the sort of retreat designed to help disaffected contemporary American males get in touch with their masculine essence by bonding with other men under the guidance of a Robert Bly wannabe. God knows, there's a lot of pretension on the fringes of the men's movement, and *Wild Men* has a good deal of fun mocking the jargon and attitudinizing, in the process generating the kind of stupid comedy that only smart people can create. In between the sketchy scenes

THE GOODBYE GIRL—Bernadette Peters *(right)* and Tammy Minoff as mother and daughter in the musical by Neil Simon, Marvin Hamlisch and David Zippel

are interludes by composer-lyricist Mark Nutter which continue the nonsense in combination with parodies of popular musical styles. The fun begins to wane a bit in the middle of the second act when some plot threatens to intrude, but still it offered an engagingly silly evening.

Productions derived from the catalogues of popular songwriters continued to pop up this season. *Back to Bacharach and David* was well received. *Tapestry,* a concert of songs by Carole King, fared less well. Part of the problem with theatrical presentation of popular songs is that pop lyrics tend to be short of the subtext which characterizes theater lyrics, and so the performers find it difficult to play much but sincerity. Sincerity may sustain the performance of a three-minute song, but a whole evening is another matter. (Pop lyric writers generally find the transition to theater writing difficult. The whole approach to writing for the stage—writing for characters in the middle of an ongoing dramatic situation—is significantly different from that of composing the brief explosion of words and music for a song designed to stand on its own.) Yes, re-encountering King's tuneful songs was agreeable, but past the hour mark the evening began to succumb to monotony.

Douglas Bernstein and Rob Krausz created characters and a plot (of sorts) to contain the work of Allan Sherman in *Hello Muddah, Hello Fadduh.* Sherman came to fame in the early Sixties by writing new words to old songs, the imagery for his lyrics being derived from middle-class suburban Jewish life. In his hands, "Frere Jacques" became a gossipy dialogue about the exploits of various relatives called "Sarah Jackman" and "Down By the Riverside" was transformed into "Don't Buy the Liverwurst." Bernstein and Krausz introduced a Jewish Everyman and followed him from birth to Miami Beach, illustrating his life with selections from the Sherman *oeuvre,* occasionally augmented with deft rewrites. The piece was most entertaining when Tovah Feldshuh cut loose in various amiable caricatures that would give Philip Roth nightmares.

A new plot of sorts was also concocted by composer-lyricist Stephen Sondheim and director Julia McKenzie to provide a context for the songs collected in *Sondheim—Putting It Together.* The scene is a Manhattan party. The well-heeled host and hostess are combative, the maid hired to help out for the evening is enticing, one party guest seems to be in a constant state of emotional turmoil, and another fellow, frequently found at the piano, tosses out wry comments and generally acts as if he knows things nobody else does. The first act consists of a series of flirtations and conflicts between these five. In the second, a bit battered, they perch and, prompted by a truth game, share bits of their souls.

Most of the characters register as self-centered and self-pitying, and the truth game of the second act is a shopworn device. These things might matter more if this were an attempt to construct a work that could stand on its own as a musical.

But the reason for the evening, of course, isn't the plot or the characters, it's to revisit the Sondheim treasure chest. If the characters are appalling, the cast assembled to play them were appealing, and all of them had several opportunities to shine. The production attracted a good deal of attention for being the occasion of Julie Andrews's first regular run on the New York stage since playing Guenevere in *Camelot* more than thirty years ago, and she gave the audience ample reason to regret all of those years of absence, particularly with a crystal-perfect interpretation of "Every Day a Little Death." Faced with the daunting challenge of playing her husband, Stephen Collins more than held his own, particularly in the duet, "Country House" (from the London version of *Follies*). Rachel York did a smashing version of *A Little Night Music*'s "The Miller's Son," Michael Rupert quivered with comic lust with "Bang!", and playwright Chris Durang, possessor of a surprisingly appealing singing voice, started the evening with a little-known song from *The Frogs* offering injunctions to the audience called "Invocation and Instructions." (Surely it was a coincidence that, with his beard and bemused manner, Durang brought a certain composer-lyricist to mind.) In addition to all of these treats, Sondheim aficionados had the fun of identifying all of the nimble new lyrics and variations their hero had whipped up for the occasion. For once, *Sondheim—Putting It Together* was a special event that lived up to anticipation.

Still more familiar music blasted through the St. James Theater with *The Who's Tommy*. For the uninitiated, The Who was one of the wave of British rock bands to win popularity in the 1960s, and the bulk of the material in this production was first heard by millions when it was released as a double album more than two decades ago. The tale introduces Tommy as a child who is traumatized into something like catatonia when he witnesses the death of his mother's lover at his father's hands. Various specialists, orthodox and un-, are consulted and unable to do anything for the boy, who spends much of his time racking up huge scores by feel on pinball machines or standing in front of a mirror. The spell binding him is somehow broken when his mother smashes the mirror. Thereafter, he goes on to become a celebrity, ultimately using his influence with his followers to try to promote family values. I think.

Frankly, having experienced *Tommy* in various forms—as an album, a movie and now a stage show—I have yet to see in it the profound meanings much of my generation has. Some of the songs are stirring, but I can't pretend that it speaks to me in the way it seems to speak to the seemingly limitless Tommyphiles.

That said, director Des McAnuff has put on a hell of a spectacle, the theatrical equivalent of a giant pop-up book. John Arnone's set designs, Chris Parry's lighting and Wendall K. Harrington's projections were in conjunction to serve up a ceaseless roil of images with a cinematic fluidity. Much of their work draws on techniques developed for rock concerts, and influences from Robert Wilson's brand of spectacle can also be seen. Though I am less than overwhelmed by the material all this technical legerdemain supports, the effects were startling and stirring enough to make the show a must-see for anyone interested in the possibilities of image-dominated musical theater, and, as such, it merits a special citation.

When it was first released as a recording, *Tommy* was billed as a rock opera. In a stylistic departure, Circle Rep attempted another kind of opera with *Orpheus in Love,* featuring words by Craig Lucas (author of Best Play *Prelude to a Kiss*) and music by Gerald Busby. The first act is made up of the title character's dreams. The absurdist dreamscape of the first act is supplanted in Act II by a more straightforward narrative, retelling the Orpheus legend in the context of a contemporary community college, too archly whimsical for my taste.

Though billed as a musical, *Wings,* an adaptation of Arthur Kopit's play of the same title, was virtually an opera. Emily, who in her youth relished the freedom of the air as a pioneering wing-walker, suddenly finds herself a prisoner in her body in the wake of a stroke. The bulk of the piece shows her working to make a recovery from the resulting aphasia, aided by a therapist whose techniques include music. Composer Jeffrey Lunden and librettist Arthur Perlman have created a work of rare delicacy and beauty, the structures of the songs reflecting the growing capabilities of their heroine, building to a duet about snow between her and her therapist which was the musical high point of the season. Michael Maggio directed this gem, winning from Linda Stephens as the lead the most memorable female performance in a musical. Special mention is also due to composer Lunden for the variety of colors and effects he achieved with his orchestration for five pieces.

Music figured in several of the season's special attractions. *3 From Brooklyn* was a revue designed to showcase talents bred in that borough. Best of a mixed bag was Adrianne Tolsch, a comic who managed some fresh insights out of the familiar field of Jewish family life. *Saltimbanco,* the latest edition of the French Canadian Cirque du Soleil, featured an eclectic group of acrobats, dancers, musicians and clowns performing a series of acts with a touch of poetry in a world that could have sprung from Fellini's dreams.

An alumnus of Cirque du Soleil, David Shiner, teamed with Bill Irwin to create an evening of non-verbal clowning called *Fool Moon.* Shiner's hostile and competitive personality, which led him to pick fights with members of the audience, was contrasted with Irwin's sweet-tempered innocence. Between their routines, a group called the Red Clay Ramblers sang a clutch of country-flavored songs which had nothing to do with what Shiner and Irwin did. Which, of course, was the point. The sight of the two sailing into the rafters on a crescent moon cut-out must have given a lift to all but the most jaded heart.

To end this chapter on the most positive note, here's where we list the *Best Plays* choices for the musical, revue and special attraction bests of 1992–93.

MUSICALS, REVUES AND SPECIAL ATTRACTIONS

BEST MUSICAL OR REVUE: *Wings*

BEST REVIVAL: *110 in the Shade*

BEST BOOK: Terrence McNally for *Kiss of the Spider Woman*

BEST MUSIC: John Kander for *Kiss of the Spider Woman;* Jeffrey Lunden for *Wings*

BEST LYRICS: Fred Ebb for *Kiss of the Spider Woman;* Arthur Perlman for *Wings*

BEST ACTOR IN A PRIMARY ROLE: Brent Carver as Molina in *Kiss of the Spider Woman*

BEST ACTRESS IN A PRIMARY ROLE: Linda Stephens as Emily in *Wings*

BEST ACTOR IN A SECONDARY ROLE: Michael Rupert in *Sondheim—Putting It Together*

BEST ACTRESS IN A SECONDARY ROLE: Julie Andrews in *Sondheim—Putting It Together;* Jan Graveson as Linda in *Blood Brothers;* Andrea Martin as Alice Miller in *My Favorite Year*

BEST DIRECTOR: Michael Maggio for *Wings;* Hal Prince for *Kiss of the Spider Woman*

BEST CHOREOGRAPHY: Susan Stroman for *110 in the Shade*

BEST SCENERY: John Arnone for *The Who's Tommy*

BEST LIGHTING: Chris Parry for *The Who's Tommy*

BEST COSTUMES: David C. Woolard for *The Who's Tommy*

SPECIAL CITATIONS: Wendall K. Harrington for projections for *The Who's Tommy;* David Shiner and Bill Irwin for *Fool Moon*

SHAKESPEARE FOR MY FATHER—Lynn Redgrave in
the solo show which she conceived, wrote and performed

Solo Performances

In a sense, to segregate the productions which featured solo performances
creates a false impression. Many of these works bear comparison only by virtue
of their number of characters.

Some of these pieces are actually plays. That is to say, they could be played
by other actors; though, of course, usually the authors had themselves in mind
when writing.

Take, for instance, John Leguizamo's *Spic-O-Rama.* In scene after scene,
author-actor Leguizamo introduces us to the various members (male, female,
straight and gay) of a Latin family on the day of the marriage of one of the sons.

The picture is not a cheerful one. The parents' marriage is over, and their kids are in various stages of crisis (though one has hopes for the hyperkinetic youngest son with the big teeth and the glasses). The first half hour or so of this work is richly funny, most outrageous in a passage dealing with the son who flees from his Latin identity by acting out a fantasy life as Laurence Olivier's illegitimate child. Though Leguizamo's comic skills never falter, in performance at a certain point the laughs began to stick in my throat. As funny as he is, what he is presenting is a group portrait of waste and destruction, seemingly beyond the reach of hope, rivalling Larry Kramer's *The Destiny of Me* in its depiction of familial misery.

Director Peter Askin is credited with having "developed" the show, which marks a giant step forward for Leguizamo as a writer. His potential was clearly evident in his previous solo effort *Mambo Mouth,* but that work was more impressive for its display of his performing skills than for his writing. In *Spic-O-Rama,* his writing has attained the same high level as his acting.

Though Leguizamo starred in *Spic-O-Rama,* the show is organized in such a way that another talented performer might be able to star in a production elsewhere. Because the script could be presented independently of its writer, I think it is fair to view this piece as a play.

Some of the season's other solo pieces, having been written to be performed by actors other than the writers, clearly also are plays. *Solitary Confinement* by Rupert Holmes, a heavily plotted suspense novelty, featured star Stacy Keach in a variety of roles, live and on tape. The twisty tale focusses on a megalomaniacal recluse and how he defends himself against the attempt by subordinates to murder him. (To be absolutely technical, the play does require two actors; at one point, the script called for Keach to battle a character who is his supposed double, though the resemblance remained untested because the other happened to be in armor with a visor over his head.) The gimmick is amusing for a while, but ultimately it runs far longer than its matter warrants, though Keach himself was never less than entertaining.

Richard Greenberg, who has been represented in this series by three Best Plays, wrote a trio of pieces about two sisters and a grandmother for actress Leslie Ayvazian called *Jenny Keeps Talking.* The first of the portraits, concerning the efforts of the title character to piece her life back together after being dumped as the firebrand columnist of a newspaper, is Greenberg in fine form, a bracing blend of social commentary and precisely-observed character. Jenny's sister, a would-be singer named Claudia, is the subject of the second section; the writing here is crafty but the relentlessly self-absorbed Claudia is a less compelling creation. The third section, a brief look at their grandmother, resolves the evening's plot too neatly for my taste. Though Greenberg didn't make the second and third characters as interesting as Jenny, Ayzavian did scrupulously specific work throughout the evening.

The chief pleasure of *Texts for Nothing,* a work adapted from Samuel Beckett's prose by director Joseph Chaikin in association with Steven Kent (who directed the original production, starring Chaikin, in 1981 under the title of *Texts*), was in being reminded that performer Bill Irwin has a speaking voice as supple and expressive as his body. As much as I admire Beckett and Irwin, however, more than an hour of eventless musings about nothing concrete, even graced by Beckett's rueful language, seemed too much.

Ann Magnuson was warmly received by many in her performance piece, *You Could Be Home Now.* I found her performing more engaging than the material she wrote, which circled with ironic intelligence about the concept of home without striking many sparks. Another performance artist, John Epperson, brought his character Lypsinka to the stage in a piece called *Lypsinka! A Day in the Life.* The conceit of the evening involves Epperson in drag doing an entire performance in precisely timed coordination with a pre-recorded sound track. As technically impressive as this is, the target at which Epperson aims—the absurdity of the images of women promoted by American popular culture—already seems to me to be riddled with holes from assaults by countless past satirists.

David Cale's *Deep in a Dream of You* offered the writer-performer in a series of image-laden monologues about various bizarre characters and their erotic obsessions. Some of these—particularly one about a man remembering sexual abuse as a child at the hands of a serviceman—were haunting; others crossed the border into self-indulgence and obscurity. Most were accompanied by Roy Nathanson's imaginative score, which was played by a chamber orchestra sitting upstage behind him.

The American Place Theater played host to Stephen Wade in *On the Way Home.* Wade is a fearsomely proficient banjo player, a prowess he demonstrated throughout this entertainment, which also included a selection of stories and other passages he's collected rummaging through arcane corners of Americana. His appeal as a performer appears to be curiously regional—in New York he attracted a modest audience; at the Arena Stage in Washington, D.C., his *Banjo Dancing* (which had flopped in New York), ran for years.

There were a few of the usual biographical solo shows. Both Matt Robinson's *The Confessions of Stepin Fetchit* (featuring Roscoe Orman as the black actor who attained stardom by creating a character that reinforced racial stereotypes) and *Ali* (actor-writer Geoffrey C. Ewing's enactment of the controversial heavyweight champion) were well-received, but neither ran long enough to be seen by a wide audience.

In a distinctly different category of the theatrical monologue, there were also several notable autobiographical efforts. Evan Handler told the gruelling and darkly funny story of his battle with leukemia and Sloan-Kettering Hospital in *Time on Fire.* Ellen Gould fashioned a slight but charming musical entertainment out of her relationship with her two Jewish grandmothers called *Bubbe Meises Bubbe Stories.* Mining much of the same imagery as Paul Rudnick's

Jeffrey (which opened later in the season), David Drake presented an evening of vignettes on young homosexual manhood in Greenwich Village in *The Night Larry Kramer Kissed Me,* an offering which became a cult hit. Charlayne Woodard told five stories of growing up black in *Pretty Fire,* establishing herself not only as a gifted writer but as an actress whose power has previously been barely tapped.

Three of the more compelling autobiographical pieces dealt with the performers' relationships with their parents. Marga Gomez, a San Francisco-based lesbian performance artist, viewed her Puerto Rican exotic dancer mother with a blend of love, irritation and bemusement in *Memory Tricks,* reaching comic peaks when she shifted from her own body language to the extravagant gestures of her parents' Latin show biz circle. In *Shakespeare for My Father,* actress-writer Lynn Redgrave dramatized the influence the two men in the title have had on her life. Her father, of course, was Michael Redgrave, one of the great stars of the English stage, whom she portrayed as kind but often moody and austere. During the course of her show, Redgrave told the story of undertaking her career in the shadow of her imposing parent (not to mention the rest of the talented Redgrave family), offering thematically-related passages from Shakespeare in counterpoint. (Not all of the text related to Shakespearean work, though. The performance's most hilarious passage concerned the actress's memories of Noel Coward trying to maintain composure while rehearsing Edith Evans and a young Maggie Smith in the National Theater's revival of *Hay Fever.*) This was a grand entertainment on a number of accounts—as theater history made vivid, as a moving personal story, and as the opportunity to make deeper acquaintance of this extraordinarily gifted actress. At the evening's end, my only regret was of never having had the opportunity to see her onstage in a classical role. (What I would give to see her Beatrice!)

Josh Kornbluth's *Red Diaper Baby* focussed on his relationship with his extravagant father, a gifted teacher of boundless energy who kept getting himself fired by trumpeting his Marxist beliefs at inappropriate moments and banging heads with his superiors. Kornbluth deftly sketched the gallery of querulous political characters surrounding his father and the would-be writers who gathered to share their treasures in a creative writing salon his divorced mother organized. With an eye for detail, irony and incident that would do credit to a novelist, Kornbluth recalled the effect his eccentric background had on his youth, chronicling the loss of both his political and sexual innocence and charting the relationship between them. *Red Diaper Baby* was simultaneously a valuable social document and a comic meditation on the way we weave the values inherited from our parents into the fabric of our own lives. Kornbluth may not be as skilled an actor as many of the others discussed in this section, but he has few peers as a storyteller.

ANNA CHRISTIE—Liam Neeson, Natasha Richardson and
Rip Torn in the Roundabout revival of Eugene O'Neill's play

Revivals

A critical colleague this season remarked to me about the improvement in the
general quality of the productions by the Roundabout Theater. Whereas the
Roundabout used to produce the occasional distinguished production among
seasons of less-inspired work, this year it staked a claim to being among the
most artistically successful companies in the city. Did I have a theory covering
the change?

I think much of it can be traced to the move from the acoustical nightmare
that housed it off Broadway on Union Square to the much more appealing
Criterion Center on Broadway. By producing on Broadway, Roundabout has
access to a whole new range of talent attracted by limited runs and the eligibility
for Tony Awards.

The Tony for best revival, in fact, went to a Roundabout production, *Anna
Christie.* Eugene O'Neill's tale of a former prostitute's dealings with her father
and her fiance (neither of whom know of her past) received a freshly-imagined
production under the direction of David Leveaux that did much to overcome

the creakiness and improbability of what is essentially a melodrama. Some parts of the script still seemed absurd—particularly the scene in which the half-drowned sailor Mat Burke goes from a stumbling, delusional state to ardent courtship of Anna in the space of about 15 minutes. And my heart went out to Rip Torn as the father, trying to find ways to negotiate past mutterings about "dat ole davil sea" without raising unintended laughs from the audience.

But for all of the clumsiness of the plotting and much of the language, the passions which fuel the play are still capable of eliciting fine work from a cast, and this production featured a cast born to the roles. Natasha Richardson was a vibrant and affecting Anna, constantly keeping alive the pulls between the poles of hope and cynicism. Liam Neeson was a commanding figure as Mat, physically strong yet emotionally vulnerable. Torn gave Anna's father Chris a nimbleness which went a long way toward redeeming the heavy-handed passages O'Neill wrote for the character, and Anne Meara offered an admirably unsentimental cameo as the philosophical gin-soaked barge tramp who has kept Chris company. I still don't think *Anna Christie* is anything like a great play, but this production did it up proud. Who could have anticipated that this would be one of the season's hottest tickets?

All of the skill of a cast of some of our finest actors—Pat Carroll, Boyd Gaines, Laura Esterman and Sophie Hayden—and director Brian Murray couldn't resurrect the charms George Kelly's *The Show-Off* allegedly once had. Under John Tillinger's direction, Hector Elizondo made a fine straight man for Eli Wallach's philosophical antique dealer for the first half of Arthur Miller's *The Price;* but their conscientious work couldn't overcome a second half which is as ponderous as the first act is engaging. This was a strong production of a flawed play.

Gloria Muzio, an artistic associate at the Roundabout, directed two successful offerings from the repertory of British comedy, a bill of Tom Stoppard's *The Real Inspector Hound* and *The Fifteen Minute Hamlet* and George Bernard Shaw's *Candida. Hound*'s forced mating of Pirandello and Agatha Christie is no longer as outrageous as when it first appeared; the passing years have made the outrageous almost quaint. But *Hamlet,* which presents an abbreviated version of Shakespeare's tragedy, and then an abbreviation of that abbreviation, is a silly gem, transforming shards of the theater's greatest language into punch lines. The wry Simon Jones was invaluable to both enterprises. I seem to be in the minority in my appreciation of Mary Steenburgen's Candida—I thought she made Shaw's heroine a beguiling repository of sense and wit. She was well partnered by Robert Foxworth as her minister husband and Robert Sean Leonard as the lovestruck Marchbanks. Shaw's articulateness sometimes reduces actors to being the mere instruments of his debates with himself; Foxworth and Leonard managed to imbue the two with individual souls. As the reverend's repressed assistant, Miss Prosperine Garnett, Ann Dowd gave a performance on which I can't imagine an improvement.

Around the corner from the Roundabout at the National Actors Theater, Shaw received another creditable revival this season. Michael Langham guided the N.A.T.'s most reliable asset, Maryann Plunkett, through a sturdy *Saint Joan,* illuminating this tale of the charismatic young woman who died because others saw her representing intellectual principles of which she, in her simplicity of purpose, had little ken. Plunkett received strong support from her husband Jay O. Sanders as Dunois and John Neville as Beauchamp. After all of the critical brickbats aimed at the N.A.T., it must have been a special satisfaction for founder Tony Randall to see this production receive a well-deserved Tony nomination for best revival.

The other N.A.T. productions were not on this level. Randall and Jack Klugman starred in John Cecil Holm and George Abbott's *Three Men on a Horse.* The script, alas, doesn't hold up very well; and, as was almost universally noted, Randall and Klugman were way too old for the parts they played. The audience, however, didn't let any of this get in the way of enjoying the reteaming of the co-stars of TV's *The Odd Couple* series. Certainly there was pleasure in watching two pros having a lark, and Jerry Stiller was on hand to give the evening some of the drive a farce should have.

Marshall W. Mason directed the N.A.T. attempt at *The Seagull.* I thought Tyne Daly approached Madame Arkadina with great intelligence, but she simply had the wrong instrument for the part. Laura Linney, on the other hand, is a marvelous actress who would seem to have the right instrument for Nina, but somehow didn't find her way in this production. Maryann Plunkett was a fine Masha; her scenes with Jon Voight, as Trigorin, were easily the most successful in this otherwise earnest but uninspired revival.

At the uptown Circle in the Square, Al Pacino played Herod in Oscar Wilde's *Salome.* He seemed to be having a good time camping it up, but it was hard to figure out in the audience why this awkward play merited reviving. Better use was made of the stage late in the season when a group featuring many alumni of the Circle in the Square's school presented *Wilder, Wilder, Wilder,* a bill of three short plays by Thornton Wilder. Only one of them, *The Happy Journey to Trenton and Camden,* depicting a family drive with a surface of trivial detail and an undercurrent of tragedy, seemed to overstay its welcome in performance. *The Long Christmas Dinner,* the chronicle of a family's tenancy of a house as seen through excerpts from holiday dinners over the years, and *Pullman Car Hiawatha,* in which an *Our Town*-style narrator places passengers in the berths of a railway car within ever-widening contexts, both seem remarkably fresh and provocative, especially given the fact that they were published in 1931. Not many experimental plays of more recent vintage possess anything like such endurance.

Composer Philip Glass was represented by two theatrical revivals this season. I thought his music for JoAnne Akalaitis's production of Buchner's *Woyzeck* as translated by Henry J. Schmidt to be one of the production's most conspicuous

RICHARD III—Ian McKellen in the Royal National Theater of Great Britain revival of Shakespeare's play at Brooklyn Academy of Music

assets. The production itself was what I've come to expect from Akalaitis as a director—a mixture of stage imagery alternately breathtaking and arbitrary. A footnote supplied by our historian Thomas T. Foose informs us that "The short-lived Georg Buchner (1813–1837) began to work on *Woyzeck* only in 1836. The play was unfinished at the time of his death, and it was not produced for the first time until 1913. Buchner's story first became widely known in the form of Alban Berg's 1925 opera version, which has the different title of *Wozzeck* . . . . . The set form has often been governed more by the opera libretto than by the original. The play has thus been a challenge for translators, and in

England and America there have been almost as many translations as productions."

Viewing the second Glass revival, *Einstein on the Beach,* for me was rather like what the astronauts of *2001* felt looking at the monolith; it was big, it was impressive, it sent out definite vibrations, and I can't pretend I could begin to make out what Glass and designer-director Robert Wilson intended.

The New York City Opera again produced revivals of pieces which had originated on the Broadway stage. Rosalind Elias's staging of *Regina,* Marc Blitzstein's adaptation of Lillian Hellman's *The Little Foxes,* seemed leaden, but there was the considerable consolation of the frequently glorious passages, particularly the third act's "Rain" quartet. Scott Ellis's production of *110 in the Shade,* Harvey Schmidt, Tom Jones and N. Richard Nash's adaptation of Nash's *The Rainmaker,* was a happier occasion. I've long believed this to be the most beguiling of the Schmidt and Jones scores, and with the benefit of an opera-scaled orchestra it had a special muscularity to support the Western setting. Best of all, it had Karen Ziemba. Miss Ziemba is a wonderful singer-dancer, a captivating clown and an actress of considerable power, and the leading role of Lizzy made full use of all of these gifts. Susan Stroman, who won a Tony last season for her work on *Crazy for You,* performed similar magic here, frequently integrating props and parts of the set into her spirited choreography. I could carp that an opera stage is not the ideal venue for a musical of such purposeful modesty, but better to have this delightful production in an inappropriate house than not to have it at all.

The New York Shakespeare Festival's *As You Like It* was an uneven affair. Elizabeth McGovern, who has had mixed success with Shakespeare in the past, here was a smart and spunky Rosalind. Curiously, Richard Libertini, who has the makings of a definitive Jaques, seemed to lack direction. I couldn't fathom why director Adrian Hall set the Forest of Arden on a farm; it made the references about foraging for food in the woods seem a little silly when chickens were handy. Despite the presence of such reliable comic actors as Marisa Tomei, Boyd Gaines, Elizabeth Franz and Larry Block, the Festival's *The Comedy of Errors* was low on merriment; but I can't pretend to have ever seen a production of this play that I've found genuinely funny. I'd much rather see *The Boys From Syracuse.*

Easily the most impressive production of Shakespeare was the Royal National Theater of Great Britain's touring *Richard III* featuring Ian McKellen in the title role. A few seasons back, I criticized Denzel Washington for playing Richard without any relish. In contrast to McKellen, Washington's performance was a model of enthusiasm. Yet, somehow McKellen made his choice work brilliantly. The setting for this production was a Britain featuring black-shirted fascists of the Thirties. McKellen's Richard, reportedly drawing some inspiration from the late Duke of Windsor, seemed to have all pleasure drained from his constitution, save a mordant appreciation of irony. The image of this monster passionlessly wreaking destruction on the world was all the more chilling because he seemed to destroy because of his nature rather than his appetite. One got little sense that he would find much genuine satisfaction in the prizes he sought. The production was further distinguished by the series of bold images created by director Richard Eyre in collaboration with set designer Bob Crowley and lighting designer Jean Kalman—most chillingly a public address on a towering platform by Richard reminiscent of a Nuremberg rally, and a breathtakingly balletic contrapuntal staging of Richard's nightmares and Richmond's dreams on the night before the climactic battle. All in all, an accomplishment of epic proportions.

Offstage

According to the League of American Theaters and Producers, the 1992–93 season was another record year for Broadway income. The League's figures state that Broadway ticket sales brought in $327.7 million dollars, an 11.9 percent increase over the $293 million which itself established a record last season. This increase occurred despite the fact that, according to the League, there were four fewer new Broadway productions—33 this season as opposed to last season's 37. Even more impressive was the reported $621 million in ticket sales for Broadway touring productions, bringing the total to something approaching the $1 billion mark. A New York *Times* article confirmed what these figures suggest—that increasingly Broadway serves as the place where properties establish identities which are then used to support their promotion in other markets, where the majority of the income is realized.

Much of the income, in and out of New York, could of course be attributed to the continuing strength of musical juggernauts such as *Cats, Les Misérables, The Phantom of the Opera, Miss Saigon, Crazy for You* and *Guys and Dolls,* as well as the holdovers *The Will Rogers Follies* and *Jelly's Last Jam.* This season, it appeared likely that *Tommy* would join the elect group of musical money-making machines.

One project that did not join the group was *Annie Warbucks,* the sequel to the hit musical *Annie.* Announced to open in the spring, the production had to be cancelled because the producers failed to raise the last million of its $5.5 million budget. At season's end, the creators of this often scheduled, often postponed show announced their intention to open a smaller version on a correspondingly smaller budget off Broadway.

Though $5.5 million is considerably less than the capitalization required to open some of the larger extravaganzas (*Miss Saigon* still holds the record with a figure approaching $10 million), it is still a hefty sum, though not an unusual one for a large-scale Broadway musical; $6 million was required for the technically sophisticated production of *Tommy.* It was still possible, however, to mount a show on Broadway for considerably less. *Fool Moon* came in for $600,000, and *Redwood Curtain,* with its dazzling set, came in at $925,000. The upper reaches of capitalization for non-musical Broadway production were $2.2 million for *Angels in America* and $2 million for the aborted production of *Face Value.* In the off-Broadway, non-profit world, money goes a good deal farther; $6 million was reportedly the budget for Manhattan Theater Club's entire season.

There were no productions this season under the Broadway Alliance contract, the agreement hammered out between producers and the various unions and guilds to facilitate the production of new plays on Broadway offered at lower ticket prices and financed with reduced capitalizations. Looking to the future,

REDWOOD CURTAIN—Jeff Daniels and Sung
Yun Cho in a scene from Lanford Wilson's play

though, the principals agreed to add seven more houses to the original roster of
three that would be eligible to host productions under this contract. Whether the
availability of these additional houses will attract more Broadway Alliance
productions remains to be seen. So far, the track record has not been encouraging; the three Broadway Alliance productions attempted in seasons past all
failed, though much of their failures must be attributed to the unenthusiastic
critical response that met two of them.

If discount production hasn't yet scored a success, discount sales, in the form
of cut-price tickets available through the TKTS booths, continued to account
for a substantial percentage of the theater's income. This year, the Theater
Development Fund, which administers the booths, expanded its operations to
include the option of the purchase of advance sale tickets at full price at two of
its locations—the booths at the World Trade Center and Brooklyn's Borough
Hall Park. It was decided that the volume of activity at the flagship booth on
Duffy Square, in the heart of the Broadway district, precluded adding this
service there. Ticketmaster, another major outlet for ticket sales, also announced a new service: whereas, previously, people purchasing tickets over the

phone could only get confirmations of general seating areas, Ticketmaster announced it would identify the specific locations of seats for shows in theaters owned by the Nederlander organization. (After criticizing this move, Tele-Charge, the Shubert-owned service, fell into line and announced it too would offer this information to the ticket-buying public.)

There were highly visible exits—some voluntary, some not—at theatrical institutions, including those of Arthur Rubin, vice president of the Nederlander organization, Paul S. Daniels, the executive director at Playwrights Horizons, Henry Guettel of TDF and David E. LeVine, the longtime executive director of the Dramatists Guild. There was also a headline-making split of an artistic collaboration—Gene Saks, who had guided many of Neil Simon's plays to acclaimed runs on Broadway, was replaced by Michael Kidd while Simon's *The Goodbye Girl* was trying out in Chicago. After Saks's angry reaction was quoted in the *Times,* Simon suggested that a future reteaming with the director was unlikely.

Speaking of the *Times,* Alex Witchel, who had excited much controversy during her stewardship of its widely read Friday theater column—both because of her aggressive muckraking writing style and because some thought her marriage to first-string critic Frank Rich resulted in too much power being vested in one couple—left that post to concentrate on writing features and interviews for the paper.

Perhaps the most publicly debated departure was at the Joseph Papp Public Theater (a/k/a, the New York Shakespeare Festival), and some claimed to see Rich's influence in it. Avant garde director JoAnne Akalaitis, whom Papp had named in October 1991 as his successor as the theater's producer, and whom Rich and Witchel had criticized frequently, was ousted in March by the company's board and replaced by George C. Wolfe, the writer-director perceived to be a Rich favorite. I don't pretend to have always admired productions Akalaitis has directed, but I admired much of what she did as head of the Public, particularly in view of the budget crunch that organization has experienced. The addition of a theater bookstore and a cafe in the lobby as well as the institution of a Friday night cabaret series (out of which some mainstage projects have emerged) deserve applause and appreciation for encouraging a greater sense of community among those in the theater. In booting her out, the chairman of the board's executive committee, Larry Condon, issued a statement thanking Akalaitis for her work "during this time of transition." As Jeremy Gerard wrote in *Variety,* Condon's statement "is Stalinism, pure and simple: Transition is not what Akalaitis had in mind when she agreed to take over the New York Shakespeare Festival." To regret the rude and abrupt treatment to which Akalaitis was subjected is not, however, to disparage Wolfe, who grew to artistic maturity under Papp's sponsorship at the Public. Being perceived as one of the theater's golden boys may well help Wolfe boost that company's sagging image.

Wolfe and Rich were linked in another controversy. Rich's review of the Los

Angeles production of *Angels in America* was critical of director Oskar Eustis's work. Shortly after the publication of this notice, Eustis (who was intimately involved in the genesis of the play) withdrew as director, and Wolfe was hired to replace him for the Broadway production. In order to accept the Broadway assignment, Wolfe withdrew from his commitment to direct Jose Rivera's *Marisol* at the Hartford Stage, which was scheduled to move to the Public after its Connecticut run. There was much muttering about this from Hartford. Ironically, by the time *Marisol* was produced at the Public, Wolfe had taken over at that theater and was the titular producer of the production from which he had resigned.

In labor news, Equity and the League of American Theaters and Producers agreed to a new four-year contract which will increase the minimum Broadway wage to $1,000 a week by 1996 and boost health care contributions. Provisions were also designed to make Equity touring companies more competitive with the flourishing non-Equity tours. Equity also successfully negotiated a three-year agreement with managements operating under League of Resident Theaters contracts. An election saw a change in the leadership of the American Federation of Musicians, the union representing the musicians who, among other things, play for Broadway musicals. There is no clear-cut indication what this bodes for the union's dealings with producers who hope to reduce musical expenses by using more synthesizers to substitute for instrumentalists.

The rejection of the Bush presidency by the American voters promised a change in the tone of government's relationship to the arts. Under Bush, there had been a distinct anti-homosexual tinge to the dealings of the National Endowment for the Arts, extending at one point to wording in legislation discouraging the funding of projects which could be accused of promoting a gay lifestyle. The Clinton administration, the first to embrace many goals of the gay community and to install openly gay figures in high government posts, is expected to promote a more tolerant attitude. Expectation is about all the arts community has to sustain itself at the moment; at press time Jane Alexander had been named the new head for the N.E.A.; and, given the charge to cut the federal deficit, it isn't likely that there will be much increase in federal funding. (This despite a survey by the National Cultural Alliance reporting that, to quote *Variety*, "an overwhelming percentage of Americans not only support public funding for the arts but also believe the arts are crucial in making their communities a better place to live.")

Incidentally, a federal court, reviewing the Bush-era decision by the N.E.A. to refuse grants to four artists on the basis of content, sided with the artists who brought suit against the agency, awarding them the withheld grants.

There was the usual muttering concerning the Tony Awards. When the nominations were announced, *The Goodbye Girl*'s book writer, composer and lyricist were not nominated, whereas the team behind a flop from earlier in the season, *Anna Karenina*, were. (Peter Kellogg nominated instead of Neil Simon?!) It doesn't take much imagination to guess the disgruntlement of members of the League who consider nominations for shows that have closed to be wasted. By those terms, there were a fair number of "wasted" nominations, not just for *Anna Karenina,* but *My Favorite Year, Redwood Curtain, The Song of Jacob Zulu* and various Roundabout and National Actors Theater limited-run productions. There was also grumbling (and I was one of the grumblers) at the idea of *Tommy*'s composer-lyricist Pete Townshend being deemed eligible for nomination as writer of the best score, given that the score didn't make its debut in a theatrical context and was, in fact, more than two decades old. (Under this logic, McCartney and Lennon should have been eligible for *Beatlemania.*) The award is diminished in value if the score is deemed eligible only by virtue of making a Broadway debut rather than by virtue of being genuinely new material written for the stage.

The Tony Awards themselves proved to be among the least suspenseful in recent memory. The biggest question seemed to be whether *Tommy* or *Kiss of the Spider Woman* would prevail as best musical (*Kiss* did.) The biggest surprise was that both Townshend and the team of Kander and Ebb won for best score in an unusual tie award. The best play award to *Angels in America* was a foregone conclusion, given that Kushner had already picked up virtually every other playwriting award for his audacious work, including the Pulitzer Prize. As for the Awards show itself, most comment was excited by the bullying tactic of using the orchestra to begin drowning out winners' acceptance speeches after 30 seconds. This resulted in some winners trying to shout over the music to acknowledge dead friends. The broadcast may indeed have actually ended very shortly after the end of its scheduled time period (it usually ends much later), but the spectacle was galling.

On March 24, a year-long festival was inaugurated to celebrate the 100th birthday of Broadway (this birthdate derived from the 100th anniversary of the opening of the American Theater, the first stage on 42d Street). Planned events include live performances, TV specials, concerts, exhibits and educational programs to highlight the contribution Broadway has made. There is indeed much in the past to celebrate; and, despite periodic lulls in activity, there continues to be much today to celebrate. But, as this season dramatized, the sense of what constitutes Broadway entertainment is constantly being redefined.

A GRAPHIC GLANCE

Herndon Lackey, Merle Louise, Chita Rivera, Brent Carver, Anthony Crivello and Kirsti Carnahan in *Kiss of the Spider Woman*

The late Roy Cohn *(upper left)* overlooking Marcia Gay Harden, David Marshall Grant, Kathleen Chalfant, Ellen McLaughlin, Stephen Spinella, Joe Mantello, Jeffrey Wright and Ron Leibman (as Roy Cohn, with phone) in *Angels in America: Millennium Approaches*

Richard Rodgers and Oscar Hammerstein II surrounded by their greatest shows *(clockwise from upper left)*: *The Sound of Music* (Mary Martin and children), *Carousel* (Jan Clayton and John Raitt), *The King and I* (Gertrude Lawrence and Yul Brynner), *South Pacific* (Mary Martin) and *Oklahoma!* (Alfred Drake and Celeste Holm). The album cover for *An Evening with Rodgers and Hammerstein*

Tommy Tune in
Tommy Tune Tonite!

Paul Kandel, Cheryl Freeman, Buddy Smith, Michael Cerveris, Marcia Mitzman and Jonathan Dokuchitz in *The Who's Tommy*

Wrong Turn at Lungfish with Tony Danza, Kelli Williams, Jami Gertz, George C. Scott and Garry Marshall (co-author and director)

Jon Voight and Tyne Daly in *The Seagull*

Christine Lahti and Ron Rifkin in *Three Hotels*

(Opposite page) Cameron Mackintosh manipulates the cast and creative team of *Sondheim—Putting It Together: (cast)* Julie Andrews, Stephen Collins, Christopher Durang, Michael Rupert and Rachel York *(creative team)* Lynne Meadow (artistic director of the Manhattan Theater Club), Stephen Sondheim (author), Julia McKenzie (director), Bob Avian (choreographer), Robin Wagner (scenery), Theoni V. Aldredge (costumes) and Tharon Musser (lighting)

Carol Woods, Tammy Minoff, John Christopher Jones, Martin Short, Bernadette Peters—and students "working out" in a dance class—in *The Goodbye Girl*

Freddie Roman, Dick Capri, Louise DuArt and Mal Z. Laurence in *Cat-skills on Broadway*

Frankie Hewitt, director of Ford's Theater, Washington, D.C.

Frances McDormand, Jane Alexander and Madeline Kahn in *The Sisters Rosenweig*

Josh Mostel, Colleen Dunn, Lainie Kazan, Evan Pappas, Tom Mardirosian, Andrea Martin, Tim Curry and Lannyl Stephens in *My Favorite Year*

Betty Comden and Adolph Green *(left to right): On the Town* rehearsal
October, 1944; celebrating the opening of *Wonderful Town,* February 25,
1953; *On the Town* opening, December 28, 1944; Betty Comden in *Isn't It
Romantic,* December 15, 1983; *A Party With Comden and Green,* February
10, 1977

Julie Hagerty, Jack Klugman, Tony Randall, Ellen Greene and Jerry Stiller in *Three Men on a Horse*

Melissa Errico, Gregg Edelman, John Cunningham, Ann Crumb and Scott Wentworth in *Anna Karenina*

Lynne Meadow, artistic director of the Manhattan Theater Club

Frank Rich, drama critic of the New York *Times*

Jake Weber, Kathryn Meisle, Elizabeth McGovern, Donald Moffat and Richard Libertini in *As You Like It*

Richard Rodgers and Oscar Hammerstein II

Julie Andrews in *Sondheim—Putting It Together*

Al Hirschfeld, self-portrait of the artist at work

THE TEN
BEST PLAYS

Here are the details of 1992–93's Best Plays—synopses, biographical sketches of authors and other material. By permission of the playwrights, their representatives, publishers, and others who own the exclusive rights to publish these scripts in full, most of our continuities include substantial quotations from crucial/pivotal scenes in order to provide a permanent reference to style and quality as well as theme, structure and story line.

In the case of such quotations, scenes and lines of dialogue, stage directions and descriptions appear *exactly* as in the stage version or published script unless (in a very few instances, for technical reasons) an abridgement is indicated by five dots (.....). The appearance of three dots (...) is the script's own punctuation to denote the timing of a spkoen line.

BEST MONOLOGUES

Excerpts From Two One-Performer Shows

RED DIAPER BABY

BY JOSH KORNBLUTH

and

SPIC-O-RAMA

BY JOHN LEGUIZAMO

Casts and credits appear on pages 332 and 340-341

THE EXPANDING presence and importance both on and off Broadway of the one-performer show, usually both acted and written by one person and sometimes providing a theatrical impact equal in power to the best of the multi-character offerings, is winning a place among our Best Play citations more and more often. Eric Bogosian's Drinking in America *(1986) and* Sex, Drugs, Rock & Roll *(1990) and Anna Deavere Smith's* Fires in the Mirror *(1992) are recent Best Play examples. This year, to illustrate each of the two genres in which the one-performer material generally falls (see Jeffrey Sweet's comments in The Season in New York section of this volume), we cite the two best 1992–93 monologues of their kinds as a Best Play. They are Josh Kornbluth's* Red Diaper Baby, *an example of the autobiographical genre, which opened off Broadway June 12 for a 59-performance run, and John Leguizamo's* Spic-O-Rama, *an example of the genre with fictional characters, presented off Broadway October 27 for 86 performances.*

Red Diaper Baby

JOSH KORNBLUTH was born in Roslyn, N.Y. to a teacher father and librarian mother on May 21, 1959. He received his early education in Manhattan at P.S. 128 and the Cathedral School of St. John the Divine through 8th grade, in the Bronx at the High School of Science and then to Princeton, graduating in 1980. He was working on the Boston Phoenix as a writer and editor in 1983 when his father died, an event that caused him to rethink his life plan and look for a profession that would allow him a more personal expression than journalism was providing him. He tried cartooning but found he couldn't draw. He had been deeply impressed by the solo performances of Spalding Gray, and after preparing a skit which he performed at a party, he decided that this kind of activity was so much fun he'd pursue it further. This he did in a Boston radio show called The Urban Happiness Radio Hour *and in standup gigs. Moving on to San Francisco, Kornbluth began performing in his own material in 1989 in* Josh Kornbluth's Daily World, Haiku Tunnel *and* The Moisture Seekers. *Finally he came up with* Red Diaper Baby *and brought it to New York April 1, 1992 for a five-week OOB run at Second Stage, moving in June to full off-Broadway status for his first Best Play citation and a Drama Desk nomination. Kornbluth now resides in San Francisco.*

The following excerpt from the script of Red Diaper Baby *was designated by the author to represent his work in these pages.*

My father, Paul Kornbluth, was a Communist. He believed there was going to be a violent Communist revolution in this country—and that I was going to lead it. Just so you can get a sense of the pressure.

And anything my father told me I'd believe, because my father was such a physically magnificent man: he was big, and he had this great big pot belly—not a wiggly-jiggly, Social Democratic pot belly; a firm, Communist pot belly. You bopped it, it would bop you back. It was strong.

And he had powerful legs, from running track at City College. And he had these beefy arms. And he was naked—virtually all the time; naked in the apartment. And all over his body he had these patches of talcum powder—you know, Johnson's Baby Powder—I guess, because he was a big man and he would chafe. Especially around his private parts.

And he had me on the weekends, and I would've loved to have slept in late on the weekends, but I couldn't because my father wouldn't let me. He would wake me up. And this is how he'd wake me up: he'd come *bursting* into my room and then he'd *stop* in the doorway; and when he stopped, the talcum powder would come *bouncing* off of his balls—it was like the entrance of a great magician. And then he'd come running up to my bed, and looming over me he'd sing:

Arise, ye prisoner of starvation
Arise, ye wretched of the earth.

I didn't know that was the "Internationale"; I didn't know that was the international Communist anthem. I thought it was my own personal wake-up song. Check it out: "Arise, ye prisoner of starvation"—it's time for breakfast. "Arise, ye wretched of the earth"—it's five o'clock in the morning and I'm being woken up!

And if I didn't show the proper signs of life right away, my father would lean down over me—and his long, graying hair would straggle down, his beard would flutter down into my nose—and he'd go, "Wake up, Little Fucker! Wake up, Little Fucker!" That was his nickname for me: Little Fucker. Nothing at all pejorative about it, as far as my father was concerned. For my dad, calling me "Little Fucker" was like calling me "Junior" . . . "Beloved Little One" . . . "Little Fucker."

I knew from an early age that one day I must grow up and become . . . a Big Fucker. And I assumed that that would be around the time that I would lead the Revolution. 'Cause my dad had told me over and over that all the great revolutionaries were also great fuckers.

But for now I was just lying there in my bed, my father looming over me with his—to me—enormous penis . . . swinging around, spewing smoke, powder, whatever . . . while I just had this little, six-year-old . . . training penis, if you will.

"Little Fucker." I didn't realize at the time that my father had his own language—not only his own English, but his own Yiddish. I used to think it was real Yiddish, but then my mom would go, "That's not Yiddish. What your father speaks is not Yiddish. *I* went to Yiddish school in Bensonhurst—and what your father speaks is not Yiddish."

I'd go, "You mean, 'ouska' is not—"

"No. There's an 'oyska,' but there's no 'ouska' . . ."

Well, in my *father's* Yiddish, there was a term "ouska." "Ouska" was a prefix, meaning "a lot of," "very"—as in, "I am ouska-cold, my son!"

I'd say, "Of course you're ouska-cold, Dad; you're ouska-naked. The window is ouska-open."

As it would be in the kitchen, where we'd go for breakfast. Dad and I would sit around the kitchen table having hard-boiled eggs (my father, not really a soft-boiled kind of guy). And never little eggs: when Dad went shopping for eggs, he always got ouska-jumbo-large-size eggs, so we would not want for eggs. And we would smear on our eggs, in my father's language, "salad dressing"—meaning mayonnaise. And we'd drink juice—apple juice and orange juice . . .

And Dad would regale me with his stories of organizing in the South with the Henry Wallace campaign. (That's *Henry* Wallace. *Henry*. Okay?) And he'd drill me over and over in the catechisms of our faith—of Communism. Like how society has been driven from one stage to the next, driven inexorably by the forces of dialectical materialism, until . . .

I sense I'm covering old ground. But just to review:

According to Marx and Engels—and my dad—the first human society was Primitive Communalism: everyone's just kind of dancing around, like at a Grateful Dead concert.

The next stage after Primitive Communalism was Slavery—which must have been a bummer of a transition.

Then from Slavery to Feudalism, and from Feudalism . . . Well, we've learned from history, it's very important after Feudalism to stop in Capitalism before moving on to Socialism. Very important to stop in Capitalism. 'Cause that's where you get your appliances.

So you stop in Capitalism, you get your stuff, and *then* you move on to Socialism, and finally to Communism—and you're back at the concert.

After breakfast, me and my dad would move from the kitchen into the living room—although when I say "kitchen" and "living room," I'm being euphemistic. There was one basic room—except for my bedroom: Dad always insisted that I have my own bedroom for my privacy—he'd just come bursting in at any moment. But aside from my bedroom, there was just one basic room. That's 'cause when my father moved into an apartment, the first thing he'd do is, he'd knock down all the walls. I don't mean that metaphorically; he'd knock down all the walls.

The first time he did this, we had to move—right away. 'Cause we lived on the first floor, and the building came . . . ouska-down.

So we moved into the next building—same landlord, who insisted on giving my dad a lecture on the crucial architectural concept of *the supporting wall.* That's the wall you must not knock down.

So my dad went knocking around with his hammer to find the one wall that wasn't hollow, left that wall up, knocked down all the other walls. And all along the external walls of our kitchen-cum-bathroom-cum-living-room-cum-dining-room area were posters of our heroes, our gods: W.E.B. Du Bois, Malcolm X, Dr. King, Ho Chi Minh, Bertolt Brecht, Emma Goldman . . . And then, at the end of all these posters: my height chart. See how the Little Fucker measures up.

And then we'd go outside for our walks. And when we went outside, my father—in his one true concession to society—he would put on clothing. This is back in Sixty-five, when I was about six years old. Dad wore this one-piece, bright orange jumpsuit—a parachute outfit—with a broad collar and a big zipper with a peace-symbol pull-thing that would seal in the freshness of the powder.

Josh Kornbluth in his *Red Diaper Baby*

And being Communists, we had songs associated with every activity. But me and Dad didn't just have generic walking songs; we had specific going-up-the-hill songs, specific going-down-the-hill songs.

We had learned our biggest going-up-the-hill song off an album by Paul Robeson, a great Jewish folksinger. It was a record my dad had borrowed from the public library, and then—as a revolutionary act—refused to return. (And my mom was a librarian . . .)

Going up the hill, me and my dad would sing:

Ey yuch nyem
Ey yuch nyem
O Volga, Volga
Ey yuch nyem.

Very hard to walk fast while singing "Ey Yuch Nyem."

A lot easier on our going-down-the-hill song, which we had learned off an album by Doc Watson—a great Jewish folksinger from the Appalachians (another record that my dad had liberated from the library).

Going down the hill, me and my dad would sing:

As I go down in the valley to pray
Stu—

—as we went down in the valley to pray on East Seventh Street, between C and D—

As I go down in the valley to pray
Studying about that good old way
And who shall wear the robe and crown
Good Lord show me the way.

My father couldn't hear me. He thought I wasn't singing. He didn't connect it with the fact that he was singing so ouska-loud he was drowning me out. So periodically he'd turn to me on the sidewalk and go, "Sing louder, my son—I can't hear you!"

YOUNG JOSH *(sings):*
Oh, fathers, let's go down
Let's go down, come on down.
Oh, fathers, let's go down
Down in the valley to pray.

DAD: Try singing even louder, my son—and perhaps with more . . . melodic invention.

YOUNG JOSH *(sings, inventively):*
Come on, fathers, let's go *down!*
Down in the valley to pra-a-a-ay . . . to pray-*yee!*

DAD: And a child shall lead them!

And then we'd hit the flatlands of Manhattan, as we continued north on our walks towards Herald Square. And along the flatlands we'd sing what, for us, were flat songs—rounds—which were easier for me, more *even* between the two singers. And along the flatlands we would stop at the *bodega* to pick up supplies, and we'd stop at the pharmacy to get Dad's pills—and we'd continue north along the flatlands, singing rounds like:

Come follow, follow, follow, follow, follow, follow me.
Whither shall I follow, follow, follow
Whither shall I follow, follow thee?
To the greenwood, to the greenwood
To the greenwood, greenwood tree!

A nice, cheerful walking song—though confusing lyrically, to an urban child. "Follow thee to the greenwood tree"—why? I'd much rather follow thee to, say, Chock Full O' Nuts.

Which was the kind of place we had to eat, me and Dad, 'cause we had to live ouska-cheaply. 'Cause my father . . .

Well, he was a schoolteacher—he was a very good schoolteacher. But my dad would get a job and be teaching his students with great passion, yet at the same time he would be developing this *anger* towards his bosses: the principal, the assistant principals, the school board. And this *anger* at his bosses would build and build, until finally Dad couldn't take it anymore. This would take about two weeks. And at the end of those two weeks, Dad would go storming into the principal's office and go, "Fuck you!"

Often the guy would never have seen my Dad before. And he'd go, "You're fired! . . . If you work for me, you're fired!"

And then Dad would get another job, and he'd be teaching his new students with great passion but developing this anger towards his new bosses. And at the end of two weeks he would storm into his new principal's office and go, "Fuck you!"

And the new principal would go, "You're fired!"

So Dad would find another job—perhaps a little further away from New York, as he lost his license to teach in this gradually growing radius. And at the end of two weeks at his new job:

"Fuck you!"

"You're fired!"

And another job:

"Fuck you!"

"You're fired!"

"Fuck you!" "You're fired!" "Fuck you!" "You're fired!"

This went on for years and years; my father never saw the pattern. He never saw the cause-and-effect between "Fuck you!" and "You're fired!"

So we had to live ouska-cheaply. But that was fine with me: I *loved* eating at places like Chock Full. You could have a nice hot dog, maybe some coconut cake . . . then we'd continue north for further ouska-cheap adventures, like the Museum of Natural History—where at the time the admission was whatever you would care to donate. They've since changed that policy—I think, 'cause of my dad. ("Pay them a penny and not a penny more, Fucker!" "You're right, Dad! We're not gonna give in to those imperialistic paleontologists!")

And then we'd go running up to the dinosaur exhibit, where Dad would give me a tour. I don't think he was an expert in the field, but he did have his bright orange tour-guide outfit. "The *tyrannosaurus rex,* my son—one of the largest . . . reptilian fuckers ever to walk the earth!" And other kids would break away from their field trips and join us. The field was a lot more interesting the way my dad described it.

And then, after a weekend of this kind of ouska-fun, my dad—as the courts had mandated—had to return me to . . . my mom.

My mom, Bernice "Bunny" Selden: also Jewish, also a New Yorker, also a City College grad, also a Communist—but so different from my father in temperament. If my father was an out-there, *ouska* Communist, my mom . . . *inska.*

And she had her own inska wake-up song for me too—and like I thought Dad had written the "Internationale" for me, I thought my mom had written *her* wake-up song for me; I only found out years later that Irving Berlin wrote it.

My mom would be getting ready to go to work at the library across the river. She'd go into the bathroom in her nightgown and come back out with her hair in a bun. Then she'd go back into the bathroom and come out with another bun having been added from some mysterious source. And she'd stand in my open doorway—which was easy for her to do, 'cause for some reason she would not let me have a door. And she'd tiptoe up to my bed and she'd lean down and sing "Oh, How I Hate to Get Up in the Morning." A pretty nice wake-up song. Unless you know the second verse, which to me gets to a surreal level of violence that I find almost Sam Peckinpah-esque.

I thought she could snap at any moment. So I'd get out of bed; I didn't want my reveille amputated!

But I still didn't have that get-up-and-go that the "Internationale" gives a kid. So she'd guide me gently up from my bed and lead me into the living room and sit me down on the couch, and then—this goes back to when I was at least four or five—she had this little motherly trick she'd play to get me going in the morning: she'd serve me a tall cup of double-espresso—with whipped cream and a maraschino cherry on top, 'cause I'm a little kid!

And I'd sit there sipping my double-espresso on the couch, beneath the half-dozen or so ceramic disks that she bought in Mexico, where she went to divorce my dad—which, by the way, was when I was six months old.

They were married for nine years, then I was born—then, when I was six months old, they divorced. From time to time I'd wonder why.

But then I was reading this article in the *Village Voice* about this guy named Saul Newton, a psychoanalyst who ran this psychoanalytical cult called the Sullivanians. They had a co-op on the Upper West Side. I was reading about this Saul Newton guy, and how he told his patients that the family is evil—parents are intrinsically evil, and they can only wreak havoc on their children; you must break up the family.

Reading about this guy—Saul Newton, Saul Newton, Saul Newton—and suddenly it hit me: "Wait a second! My *Dad's* therapist was named Saul." So I called up my mom and said, "Mom, I'm reading about this Saul Newton guy," and she said, "Yeah, that was your father's therapist."

Evidently, Dad was an early patient of Saul's—sort of a test case. And after I was born, Saul convinced my dad that now that he had a family, and families were evil, his family must be broken up. So Dad left me and my mom up in Washington Heights and he got an apartment down on the Lower East Side.

And then, according to my mom, after a couple of weeks Dad started to miss us. He came running up the island to reconcile with us. But Mom saw him coming and escaped with me down to Mexico, where she got the divorce, bought big floppy hats, danced around in circles with strangers, and got the half-dozen-or-so ceramic disks; each one of those disks depicts a woman escaping from slavery.

So I'd sit there under the disks on the couch, sipping my double-espresso, as my mom went up to the old radio console and turned on WBAI—listener-sponsored, sometimes listener-taken-over WBAI. And the morning disc jockey at the time was Julius Lester—he of the ouska-deep voice. And supposedly, Julius's program was a classical-music show. But what Julius would do is, he'd play about five minutes of a Baroque oboe concerto . . . and then speak for hours, about his various ex-wives and their sexual peccadillos.

And I'd listen real carefully to Julius, and I'd sip my double-espresso, and I'd listen to Julius, and I'd sip my double-espresso . . . and then I'd go running off to school—jazzed!

I was so excited my first day of kindergarten. After spending the first five years of my life exclusively in the company of my parents and their friends, today—for the first time—I was going to get to mingle with the masses.

Boy, was I disappointed! That first day, I walked into my kindergarten classroom at P.S. 128—and I saw all these little kids running around screaming, pulling hair, bopping each other, crying. I thought, "How will I ever organize *these* people?"

Spic-O-Rama

JOHN LEGUIZAMO was born in Bogota, Columbia July 22, 1964 but moved to Jackson Heights, Queens at an early enough age to be educated in New York City schools. From about the age of 17 he participated in as many theater activities as he could, dropping out of N.Y.U. (where he appeared in the student film Five Out of Six*) in order to pursue a career of acting and writing. His first recorded appearance on the New York stage was as a performer in the Public Theater's* La Puta Vida Trilogy *in 1987. Three years later, on November 8, 1990, he appeared as actor and author in his own monodrama* Mambo Mouth *at American Place for*

114 performances, winning a performance Obie and the Outer Critics Circle Award for achievement and coming back for a 77-performance return engagement in independent off-Broadway production June 5, 1991. He presented his one-man performance of his Spic-O-Rama *as a work-in-progress in George C. Wolfe's* Festival of New Voices *at the Public Theater December 1, 1991 for 15 perform-ances and at Chicago's Goodman Theater January 16, 1992 before moving to the Briar Street Theater for a regular Chicago run. He opened* Spic-O-Rama *off Broadway on October 27 for an 86-performance run, winning this Best Play citation and the Dramatist Guild's Hull-Warriner Award, among other honors.*

In other dramatic media, Leguizamo has appeared in the Miami Vice *TV series and several films, costarring in* Super Mario Brothers *with Bob Hoskins and Dennis Hopper. He lives in Manhattan and is now writing his first screen play,* White Chocolate, *with Peter Askin.*

In this multi-character monologue, Miguel ("Miggy") Gigante is presenting a description of his brothers and his parents as a science project, profusely illustrated with videos. He introduces himself ("This is me of course. With my handsome preColombian features") then goes on to his brother Willie (a vet-eran of Desert Storm) and then to his brother Raffi, "brains not included."

MIGGY:

> I have to share my room with
> Him too. And he's weird,
> Cause he thinks he's white.
> Oh yeah, even whiter than you, Mister!
>
> One day, he locked himself in our
> Room for hours and hours.
> And when he finally came out,
> He was screaming
> "Look, look—a miracle, a miracle,
> The Most Sacred Lady of Flushing
> Has appeared before me
> Transforming me into a albino
> White person." And he has blonde
> Hair and blue eyes.
> Na-ah. Na-ah. Not even.
>
> Cause I searched our
> Room and found that miracle—
> Holy water by "Saint Clorox."
>
> And I don't dislike him
> I just hate him intensely.

Cause if he's not talkin' about himself,
He's talkin' to himself . . . . .

One day my mother was going
Through my father's pants and
She found a letter from Yolanda.
        Pulls pants out of middle drawer.
So she set all my
Father's his pants on fire . . .
And my father came home and
Caught her and called her,

"La negra india puta immunda del carajo."
The nastiest black indian ho of hell.
And my mother cursed right back,
"Tu eres un maricon, malparido y guevon."
Look it up.

And my father smacked my moms
So she ran and told my grandmother
And my grandmother said,
"Bueno, tu lo merece,"
Good, you deserve it.
In her nasty parrot voice.
And my mother gave her the evil
"Chupame la teta!" Suck my tit!

And my grandmother reslapped my moms.
And my mom jumped on her and
Started choking her . . .

And then my father came into the room
And grabbed my mom in a half Nelson
        Big arm movement.
And I jumped on him and started
Kickin' him and punchin' him
And kickin' him . . . . .

And I'm a miss him.
I'm a miss him . . .
Especially when he's drunk . . .

Spit basketball . . .
Oh, you played it before
Where everyone had to spit in a bucket
And the first person to get twenty-one won

And this big kid came along all
Uninvited and pushed Ivan so I had to
Play with him. And I beat him.
And I don't know what came
Over him. Cause all I said was,
"I murdelized you. I destroyed you.
Miggy's in the house." And the sore
Loser picked up the bucket and poured
It all over me and said,
"Get out of my country you stupid ugly spic."
Now I could have beat him up so bad,
Cause when you're angry, oh my God,
You can beat up people who are a
Million zillion trillion times your size.
But I didn't do nothing.
Cause I didn't want to act like it counted.

So I just stared at the kid and said,
"Yes, yes, yes, I am a spic.
I'm, I'm spic-tacular!
I'm, I'm spic-torious!
I'm indi-spic-able!"
And I stared at him and stared at him
Till he couldn't take it no more.

Later on that night, in our tent,
Me and Ivan figured out: that
Since we were spics, then our
Whole families must be
Spic-sapiens mondongo-morphs
And that when we have picnics together
It's a *spic-nic.*

And we made a promise to each other
That no matter where we went or
What we did our whole lives
Would be nothing less than a
Spic-O-Rama!!

RAFFI *(at mirror in bedroom; stares out at the audience):*
. . . . . Do you like my British accent?
Do you think it's real?
I'm not telling you.
Do you like my albino looks?

John Leguizamo as Raffi in his *Spic-O-Rama*

Do you think they're real?
I'm not telling you that either.

. . . . . You see, I am an understudy at the
Not-for-profit production of
The Canterbury Tales.

Yes, yes . . . Someone finally took ill
So I'm going on as the cuckolded
Innkeeper's manservant's best
Friend's friend's . . . friend . . . . .

You got it? It's a major opportunity
Any actor in his right mind would
Kill for it.
And acting jobs are like

Sex—all around, but I don't seem
To be getting any . . . . .

All right, I confess.
You were going to find out anyway . . .
Please look me in the face!
The rumors are true! I am the
Love child of Sir Laurence Olivier.
Here's the true untold story,
Laurence, Larry, met me mum, in
Puerto Rico while shooting
The Boys From Brazil.
Me mum was pressing his trousers . . . . .
When Larry sneaks up behind her,
In his undies, grabs her bum and whispers,
"Ooh, I like young girls. Their stories are
Shorter." Et voila, mon freres!! Je suis ici.
      Turns to mirror.
Excuse me, aren't you that love child?
Aren't you that famous bastard?
      To camera.
Guilty as charged . . . . .

Oh God, I don't want to be
With anyone whom I love
More than myself.
      Makes love to himself in mirror.
I'm not black. I'm not white.
What am I? I'm urine colored,
      Closes mirror doors.
I'm actually urine colored.
      Turns out to audience.
Well, I don't know why people
Insist on knowing themselves.
It's hard enough to know what to wear.

I don't care. I don't care.
I'm not going to do anything
I'm supposed to any more.
I'm going home.
      As he opens window, loud Spanish Harlem cacophony. Closes window.
It's so hard being Elizabethan
In Jackson Heights.
Exeunt dramatis personae.

The boys and their father (Felix) and mother (Gladys) are attending the wedding of the oldest son (Willie) and his bride Yvonne. Felix is preparing to give a toast.

FELIX:

> Now, I know the newlyweds would
> Be disappointed if I did not speak at
> Length about matrimonio.
> So listen up, amigos y socios.
> Yvonne, Willie, as I told you from
> The time you were yo high,
> And I can never tell you enough,
> Lies, distortions, half truths and
> Critical omissions are
> The glue to all relationships . . . . .
>
> So I'm going to teach you two
> How to keep that matrimonio fresh
> And alive when what you really
> Wanna do sometimes is put a bullet
> Through your head.
> Fantasize. Fantaasize.
> There is absolutely nothing wrong
> With taking the body of a woman
> You desire and superimposing it over
> The tired old thing at home.
> What else? What else?
> You're also gonna fight a lot
> Which is really a lucky thing,
> Cause sex is never as good as
> After a vicious fight.
> Right, Gladys?
> My little gladiatress.
> Nothing like rough sex.
> *(Barks.)* When I was younger I used to have . . .
> What do they call that now?
> Anybody!
> Performance anxiety.
> Now I just look forward to giving it
> My best shot and coming out of it alive.
>
> Many a night I have come home
> To Gladys and ask her for a little
> Cabeza, and she says, "I'm too tired,

I'm too tired," And I tell her,
"Baby, it'll be over before you
Know it. You won't feel a thing."

If I was a young puppy again, instead of
The old dog that I am, Yvonne, yum,
Yvonne, you look nice. There're so
Many things I could've done to your
Bosco candy coated thighs . . . . .

What can be said about me that I
Tried to be more and better. That I
Tried not to make the same
Stupid mistakes my father made.

At least I was there for youse.
I gave up a lot to provide for youse.
I never told you this but I had a shot
To travel with Carlos Santana.
That's right, Mr. Oye Como Va.
He came up to me personally and
Said that I was the best maracas
Player he'd ever heard.
Then Gladys got pregnant with Willie . . . . .
And it just destroyed my chance.
Cause I could of played with one of
The great Latin rock and rollers . . .
Grabbed God by the ears and kissed
Him right smack on the lips.

But I chose to stick it out and give
You what I could and what do I
Got, my memories, youse . . .
        Pause.
I have a confession to make.
Unbeknownst to Gladys here,
I had an affair once.

I'm sorry baby, I admit it.
But it kept me from running away
And it helped me to understand you.
        Pats gut.
Kept me young. It's not that we men
Want more sex than women,

It's that we want a different kind
Of sex more often. Right, fellas?

Well, don't all back me up at once.

Ever since you had the kids,
You only want it when
Jupiter aligns with Mars.
I ask myself where would I be
Without you by my side.
Pushing me, kicking me,
Nailing me to the wall.
Cause deep in my heart, I believe
That any woman can make love to
A handsome man, but it take a
Great woman to keep making
Love to an ugly pig like me . . . . .

Go, get out of here.
Go to him, Yvonne.
You have my blessing . . .
Enjoy your honeymoon . . . . .
But promise me, Yvonne,
My new daughter, that you'll
Always be there to fix it, mend it,
Make it better, and if it doesn't
Work out then . . . remember, you
Always have family—and tell my
Son that no matter how much he
Hates me, I'll always be here for him,
Cause we're stuck with each other.

○○○
○○○
○○○
○○○
○○○
○○○ # THE DESTINY OF ME

A Play in Three Acts

BY LARRY KRAMER

Cast and credits appear on page 337

LARRY KRAMER was born June 25, 1935 in Bridgeport, Conn., where his father was a lawyer. He was educated in Washington, D.C. public schools and Yale University, graduating in 1957. He was attracted by the theater from childhood and became a frequent customer of the National Theater's second balcony. His plays Sissie's Scrapbook *and* Four Friends *were done in OOB workshops in 1972 and 1973, respectively, but his first major production was* The Normal Heart *at New York Shakespeare Festival April 21, 1985, winning him immediate acclaim for sounding an alarm about AIDS and the George and Elisabeth Marton Award for its quality. It ran for 294 performances (the Public Theater group's longest off-Broadway run) and has gone on to more than 600 productions worldwide.*

Kramer's Just Say No, a Play About a Farce *was produced OOB by WPA Theater October 28, 1988 for 34 performances. A portion of his volume of essays* Reports From the Holocaust: The Making of an AIDS Activist *was adapted as a one-act on New York Shakespeare Festival's 14-performance program* Indecent Materials *in 1990. This season's* The Destiny of Me, *which opened off Broadway on October 20, is its author's first Best Play.*

Outside the theater, Kramer is probably best known for his participation in AIDS activism which, he remarks in a program note to his new play, has "fostered

Gay Men's Health Crisis and ACT UP—the 'problem' kids I often no longer recognize, often don't like, who give me a lot of lip and grief, but of which I'm fiercely proud and protective, and fight like an angry mother to defend when they're in trouble. Which is often." His authorship extends beyond the stage to the movies, where his screen play Women in Love *won him an Oscar nomination. He has also written a novel,* Faggots, *and has been working for the past ten years on what he characterizes as "a very long novel,"* The American People. *He lives and works in New York City and environs.*

Place: Just outside Washington, D.C.

ACT I

SYNOPSIS: The curtain rises on a white-walled hospital room fully equipped with appurtenances of sophisticated modern medicine—and also equipped to accommodate, with the automated addition of props and furnishings, all of the other locations to be represented in the memory of Ned Weeks. Ned, in his mid-50s, enters and unpacks the suitcase he's brought with him, as Hanniman, a black nurse, about 35, comes in pushing a cart loaded with medical materials. Hanniman explains to Ned that this is the Infectious Diseases floor, and he mustn't visit other floors or wander outside the hospital.

Dr. Anthony (Tony) Della Vida *("short, dynamic, handsome and very smooth . . . . . the consummate bureaucrat"),* about 40, enters and embraces Ned, whom Tony considers a friend in spite of the fact that Ned has attacked the doctor and his programs in the press, often and vigorously. Tony studies Ned's medical record and comments, "All your numbers are going down pretty consistently. You didn't listen to me when you should have." Ned quotes a New York *Times* article reporting a new treatment that is one of the promising results of the two billion dollars so far spent on Tony's programs, a treatment involving reconstituted genes which has suppressed the growth of the AIDS virus in mice.

TONY: How have you been feeling?
NED: Okay physically. Emotionally shitty. We've lost.
TONY: You are depressed. That's too bad. You've been very useful.
    He starts examining Ned.
Such attention as this illness has received has been because of you guys. All your anger has kept us on our toes.
HANNIMAN: Useful? They have yelled at, screamed at, shrieked at, hollered at, threatened, insulted, castigated, crucified every person on our staff and at every other agency, in every publication, on every network, on every street corner, from every soap box . . .

NED *(as Tony's examination becomes more intimate):* I've been infected for so long, and I still don't get sick. What's that all about? Everyone thinks I *am* sick. Everyone around me *is* sick. I keep waiting to get sick. I don't know why I'm *not* sick. All my friends are dead. I think I'm guilty I'm still alive.

TONY: Not everybody dies in any disease. You know that. Your numbers could even go back up on their own. Why is my hospital surrounded by your army of activists? Am I going to be burned at the stake if I can't restore your immune system?

NED: I'm not so active these days.

TONY: You?

NED *(softly):* They don't know I'm here.

HANNIMAN: Why don't I believe that?

NED: What have we achieved? I'm here begging.

> *Ned suddenly reaches out and touches Tony's face. Tony nervously looks at Hanniman, whose back happens to be turned.*

This new treatment—you can't even stick it into me legally. Can you? Why are you doing this for me?

TONY: Ned—I do think I'm on to something. You've really got to keep your mouth shut. You've got to promise me. And then you've got to keep that promise.

NED: The world can't be saved with our mouths shut.

TONY: Give me lessons later.

NED: Can you keep me alive three, four more years? I've got work to finish. Two years. Can you do that?

TONY: You know there aren't any promises. Two years, the way you look now, doesn't seem impossible.

NED: How about three? It's a very long novel. Why are you willing to give it to me?

HANNIMAN: Because if it works, you'll scream bloody murder if anyone stands in his way. Because if it doesn't work, you'll scream bloody murder for him to find something else. That's *his* reasoning. Now I would just as soon you weren't here. You're a sore loser.

Tony orders an injection and leaves, as Hanniman prepares to administer it with a very large needle. Hanniman reminds Ned that he once wrote that Mrs. Della Vida was a lesbian—and Hanniman, approaching Ned with the threatening needle, informs him that *she* is Mrs. Della Vida. This makes Ned think, "I want my Mommy," conjuring up the memory of himself as a 13-year-old boy, Alexander (a name Ned insisted on using as a teen-ager) Weeks. Alexander enters the hospital room wrapped in a towel, wet from a shower, and watches Hanniman give Ned, his grown-up self, the shots. Hanniman exits while Alexander, sensing that "Something awful's happening," asks Ned what's going on but departs before Ned answers him.

Alone, Ned remembers the battle to call public attention and action toward this disease, then the fear at realizing your days are numbered, and then "You talk yourself into believing the quack is a genius and his latest vat of voodoo is a major scientific breakthrough. And you check yourself in. So here I am. At the National Institute of Quacks." Twelve years of anger and screaming, Ned recalls, and now the fight seems lost. "When I started yelling there were 41 cases of a mysterious disease. Now they're talking about 150 million. And it's still mysterious. And the mystery isn't why they don't know anything, it's why they don't want to know anything."

Alexander (Ned at 13, aging to 24 in the course of the play) comes back with his own protest to Ned: "If you die I die!" He gave Ned a good start in life—"How did you fuck it up?" Alexander goes to his bedroom, decorated with full-page ads of Broadway shows, and remembers how he loved going to the theater and wished that he could be an actress making believe "so many wonderful things that never happen in real life." He hated living in the apartment complex Eden Heights, not far from this hospital, and once ran away to New York hoping to see a play every day.

They hear their father coming home, and Alexander rushes to get dressed, Ned helping him. Their father, Richard Weeks, about Ned's present age, enters. *"He is impeccably dressed . . . . . takes off his jacket and tie and cuff links and rolls up his shirtsleeves. He keeps on his vest with its gold chain that holds his Phi Beta Kappa and Yale Law Journal keys. "* Richard chides Alexander for reading comic books—"You'll never get into Yale." In an aside to Ned, Alexander explains that a man down the block gives him the comic books in exchange for sexual favors.

Hanniman enters (she, of course, doesn't see Alexander or others of Ned's memory figures), gives Ned some pills and reports that a crowd of "unusually dressed people" is gathering outside the hospital. Hanniman exits (as does Richard). Then Rena Weeks, Ned's mother, about 40, enters dressed in her Red Cross uniform, carrying groceries. Alexander asks his mother what a penis is (he had asked his father, who had refused to answer him), and Rena immediately replies in matter-of-fact, clinical detail. "Is that all?" Alexander asks, somewhat disappointed, as Richard returns. Rena answers Richard's complaints that she's late coming home, while Alexander sits and reads his father's newspaper, jiggling his leg up and down.

Richard continues to complain that Rena is so busy on her affairs that he never gets a hot meal; then he *"suddenly and furiously swats Alexander's leg with his part of the newspaper. "* He comments on his son's choosing to be called Alexander rather than Ned, and Alexander notes that his older brother Benjamin likes to be called by his full name, not Ben. Richard complains that his ailment he calls "Alexander's ulcer" is acting up. For one thing, Richard is annoyed because Alexander talks all the time, never shuts up. He complains again about his wife's many compassionate activities which take a lot of her time and attention from him.

Rena exits, as Alexander speaks to Ned.

ALEXANDER: I don't have to tell you there are a lot of comic books hidden in this house.

NED: So you like it?

ALEXANDER: It feels good. Except when it's over. When it feels bad.

RICHARD: I got a raise.

ALEXANDER: How could I be bar mitzvah when I don't believe in God?

RICHARD: Why do you say things like that?

ALEXANDER: What's wrong with saying what you believe?

RICHARD: You're just an obnoxious show-off!

ALEXANDER: And you're my father!

> Richard raises his hand to hit him. Alexander moves adeptly out of the way.

Do you believe in God?

RICHARD: Of course I believe in God!

ALEXANDER: I don't know why. He hasn't been very good to you.

NED (whistles, impressed): Did we learn to fight from them?

Hanniman comes in to check on Ned, who belabors her with his opinion of the pills he is supposed to take: "Rat shit is rat shit . . . . . if the virus within us itself does not kill us, this will." It's the standard treatment these days, Hanniman explains, "The standard of care against which we must test anything new . . . . . That's the only way we can find out if *anything* is better." She looks out the window at the growing mob of demonstraters, then forces Ned to take the pills and exits.

Rena returns wearing a different uniform, on her way to help out at the Stage Door Canteen. Richard won't accompany her; Alexander wishes he could go with his mother, he could sing all the Andrews Sisters song numbers. Richard wishes they were back living in Connecticut; Rena likes it here in Washington with all the activities. She's going to take a Pentagon course in prosthetic devices so that she can teach department store clerks not to be put off by the devices while dealing with their ex-servicemen customers.

When Rena goes back into the bedroom, Alexander starts singing and dancing, to Richard's extreme annoyance. Richard stops him with more force than he had intended to use. Alexander exclaims to Ned, "I am going to do with my life every single thing I want to do, I don't care what, and you better too!"

Rena comes in with a couple of the prosthetic devices, leaves them with Alexander and goes out for the evening. Richard starts laying the table for breakfast, while thinking about his job with the government documenting ocean traffic (of which there is very little now, in wartime). His security is guaranteed, but his job is monotonous.

RICHARD: . . . . . Each day is like the one before. Each week and month and year are the same. For this I went to Yale and Yale Law School. For this I get up every day at dawn while everyone's asleep. So I can go through life stamping papers. Yes. I got a raise . . . . .

ALEXANDER *(tries awkwardly and unsuccessfully to kiss him):* Poppa, would you like me to get up early and have breakfast with you?

RICHARD: That's okay. You finish your homework, boy?

ALEXANDER: Yes, Poppa.

RICHARD: That's good. You've got to get into Yale. Goodnight, boy.

ALEXANDER: Goodnight, Poppa. Poppa . . .

> *Alexander wants to kiss and be kissed. But Richard goes into his bedroom . . . . .*

Does the fighting stop some day?

NED: No.

ALEXANDER: Does any dream come true? *(No answer.)* Should I stop wishing?

NED *(pause):* A few dreams do.

ALEXANDER: You had me worried.

NED: Not many.

ALEXANDER: Are you afraid if you tell me the truth I'll slit my wrists?

NED *(pause):* I wish you could know now everything that happened so you could avoid the things that hurt.

ALEXANDER: Would I do anything differently?

NED: I don't know if we can.

ALEXANDER: Then don't tell me. I guess it wouldn't be much fun anyway if I knew everything in advance. It *will* become fun . . . ? Oh, Ned, I want a friend so bad . . . ly!

NED: I know.

Alexander has been reading Krafft-Ebbing on the subject of teen-aged homosexual sex and is confused about his identity. He decides to consult his older brother Benjamin, though Ned warns him against doing this: "You will be but you're not good friends yet." Benjamin enters, in Ned's memory a handsome figure dressed in a West Point uniform. Hanniman breaks Ned's thoughts by entering with several glasses of colored liquids which he must drink to aid in the complicated diagnosis. And she tells him that the picketers are now camped outside in sleeping bags.

After Hanniman exits, Alexander is bubbling over in an attempt to communicate with his brother. But Richard comes in in his bathrobe, and the subject switches to Benjamin's impending court-martial. Benjamin feels that he didn't get the support from his parents he should have at this time of trouble. Rena

John Cameron Mitchell as Alexander, Piper Laurie as Rena,
Peter Frechette as Benjamin and Jonathan Hadary as Ned in a
scene from *The Destiny of Me* by Larry Kramer

(entering) and Richard claim it was because they were distracted: Richard had
to go to the hospital for an operation and nearly died.

RICHARD: Why are you deliberately choosing to fight the system!

BENJAMIN: Where do you find choice? I'm accused of turning my head during
a dress parade, when the man next to me tripped, all of two inches. For this a
lieutenant colonel, a major, a captain, eight cadets, have spent two months
haggling over whether it was really four inches instead of two inches. But in
reality I lose a year of my life not because I turned my head at all but because
my drill inspector, Lieutenant Futrell, hates Jews.

RICHARD: That's right. They don't like Jew boys. Why do you want to make
so much trouble?

BENJAMIN: Why do you take their side?

RICHARD: It's your word against theirs.

BENJAMIN: He lied.

RICHARD: Yes, he called you a liar.

BENJAMIN: He called me a kike. At 4:30 in the morning, I was pulled out of
my bed and hauled naked out into the snow by a bunch of upper-classmen and
forced to stand up against a brick wall, which was covered with ice . . .

ALEXANDER: Poor Benjamin . . .

RENA: Such a good education going to waste.

BENJAMIN: Please stop saying things like that.

RICHARD: Can't you see how impossible it is to be the only one on your side?

BENJAMIN: Can't you see I don't mind being the only one on my side?

Alexander offers Benjamin the kind of unquestioning support his brother Benjamin wishes he were getting from his parents. Benjamin has no intention of remaining at West Point, but he is going to make them give him a hearing.

Richard and Rena digress from Benjamin's problem to a discussion of Richard's troubles with his brother Leon, also a lawyer. At one time Rena left Richard to force him to make a break with Leon, who she feels treated them shabbily. But Richard thinks highly of Leon's abilities and sent for him to help Benjamin in his case at West Point.

The brothers go into their own bedroom, and Benjamin informs Alexander that he plans to go to Yale—"The surest way I know to get rich." Alexander, Benjamin believes, would "be better off at some small liberal artsy place where they don't mind your being different." How is he different? Alexander begs Benjamin to tell him. But Benjamin has had enough for one day and prepares to go to sleep.

Hanniman comes in to take some tests and report on the demonstrations outside: "Speeches. Firecrackers. Bullhorns. Rockets. Red glares. Colored smoke . . . . . Lots of men dressed up like nurses . . . . . Over fifty arrests so far." She explains what Tony is doing for Ned: mixing healthy cells with Ned's infected ones in the hope that reinjected into his blood they will combat the disease. Hanniman finishes, "Why don't they know out there that you're in here? *(No answer.)* Would they think you'd crossed over to the enemy? *(No answer.)* They hate us that much?"

Ned tries to explain, "There's not one person out there who doesn't believe that intentional genocide is going on." He recalls that when his lover Felix died, Felix's wife Darlene (who hadn't seen her husband in fifteen years) made a homophobic scene at the funeral and has continued to contest Felix's will, which left everything to Ned. "I was in love for five minutes with someone who was dying. I guess that's all I get," Ned concludes.

Alexander runs into his mother's bedroom, asking her, "Mom! Mommy! What's wrong with me?" *"Rena wears only a half slip and can't hook her bra up in the back."* Alexander assists her, while telling her "I'm different! Even Benjamin says so," and Ned advises her, "Do not sit half-naked with your adolescent son." But his mother's state of undress doesn't bother Alexander; what catches his attention is the size of male genitals in the locker room, he unselfconsciously declares.

Rena tells him about a time when she almost had an audition for a radio program, finishing, "We're all different in many ways and alike in many ways and special in some sort of way." Alexander is further perplexed when his mother advises him to stick to his own kind and marry a Jewish girl. He says he never wants to get married, and his mother might have been happier married to Cary Grant, for example, whom he calls "gorgeous," a word which (Rena suggests) is too effusive for a man to use. Rena assures Alexander that she chose Richard over a great many suitors. "Please tell me what to do!" Alexander begs, and his mother replies, "About what?"

Hanniman enters to take blood samples, as Alexander goes to a trunk in the living room and pulls out clothing that looks like a woman's costume but is a leftover from the days when Rena's family fled from Russian persecution of the Jews. And Rena recalls having had a romance with a gentile who was her professor—but then she met Richard. She saw the professor one more time when he came to New York and took her to Delmonico's, but she declined his invitation to visit his hotel room afterwards.

While they talk, Alexander dresses in the Russian costume, puts in padding to simulate breasts, and Rena helps him with his makeup. Richard comes in, sees Alexander dressed as a girl and hits him again and again, calling him "Sissy!" Alexander doesn't fight back. *"Richard rips the skirt and underpants off Alexander,"* while Rena exclaims, "Stop tearing my dress! It's all that's left!" But Richard continues, demonstrating that Alexander has been using depilatory cream on his private parts because he's embarrassed to be growing pubic hair.

Richard turns from Alexander to the theater posters and starts ripping them down. Alexander tries to stop Richard from destroying his precious posters, but Richard persists.

RICHARD: This is what we do to sissies.

ALEXANDER: It's Halloween! Mr. Mills divided my Scout troop for my play, half into boys and half into girls. I didn't have any choice!

RICHARD: *Your* play?

ALEXANDER: I invited you. Tonight's my opening night.

RICHARD: Your what?

RENA: He wants to become a writer! Of plays!

ALEXANDER *(screaming with all his might):* I hate you!

RENA: Don't say that!

ALEXANDER: You taught me to always tell the truth!

NED: Go for it!

> *He feels dizzy. He hungrily swallows more pills.*

ALEXANDER *(to Ned, furious):* Get me out of this!

RENA: Apologize to your father immediately!

ALEXANDER *(to Rena and Richard):* I hate both of you!

RICHARD *(really swatting him):* Do what your mother says!

ALEXANDER *(grabbing the Russian shawl, stepping into women's shoes and standing up to both of them):* Go to hell! *(Running off as best he can, screaming.)* Trick or treat! Trick or treat!

Hanniman rushes into the room. She and her uniform are heavily bloodied.

HANNIMAN: Look what your people did to me!
Curtain.

ACT II

Ned (in a wheelchair), Tony and Hanniman (wheeling a cart with a bottle of blood, in a clean uniform) enter the hospital room, now equipped with elaborate machinery in the background. Ned carries posters with a picture of Tony and the caption "Tony, you are murdering us." The demonstrators have plastered them all over the hospital. Ned evokes a cheer from the group outside by showing one at his window. Hanniman tears it up, but Ned has another which he puts up over his bed. Tony wonders why they hate him so.

TONY: You drown my wife in fake blood. You chop the legs off my lab tables. You've got some crazy gay newspaper up in New York that claims I'm not even studying the right virus. They call me Public Enemy Number One. "The little man with the compensatory ego." Why aren't you guys proud of me? If I'm not in my lab, I'm testifying, lobbying, pressuring, I'm on TV ten times a week, I fly to conferences all over the world, I churn out papers for the journals, I supervise hundreds of scientists, I dole out research grants like I'm Santa Claus—what more do you want?
        Hanniman gives the blood to Tony. She handles it like it's liquid gold. He inserts the bottle into the machine.
NED: A cure.
TONY: I'm not a magician.
        He and Hanniman attach Ned to the machine.
NED: Now's not the time to tell me. There's no end in sight. That's why they hate you. You tell every reporter you have enough money. That's why they hate you. You tell Congress you have everything you need. That's why they hate you. You say more has been learned about this disease than any disease in the history of disease. That's why they hate you. You say the President cares. That's why they hate you.
TONY: He does care! He tells me all the time how much he cares!
NED: You asked me. I told you. You're the one in charge, and you're an apologist for your boss. That's why they . . .
TONY: If I weren't, do you think I'd get *anything!* You don't understand the realities of this town.

Tony pulls the lever which releases the prepared blood, explaining that he hopes the treatment will block the virus's proliferation. Ned is frightened. Tony reassures him but doesn't claim that there might not be a down side to the treatment.

Meanwhile, Rena, Richard and Alexander enter as though they were on vacation at their annual spot on the Connecticut seashore, Mrs. Pennington's boarding house. Alexander, only two weeks away from his entry into Yale, pulls Ned along with him into the scene because "We don't have much time left before I grow into you and you kick me out."

Rena is phoning old friends, announcing their arrival and making dates. Alexander reminds Ned that he felt more different and more frightened in some way each summer, and that it seems all the family's friends got richer and richer as the years passed. As Rena continues on the phone, she finds that everyone except themselves has made major upward gains—new houses, new cars—or taken expensive and glamorous trips, while Rena and family are back in the same old summer boarding house.

Meanwhile, Richard and Ned (as Alexander) are quarreling about the salt Alexander uses. Finishing her phone conversation, Rena demands that this argument cease at once, they're here for a good time. But Richard and Alexander are still squabbling when Ned, feeling a bit faint, returns to bed, leaving Alexander to continue challenging Richard: "Benjamin is driving from New Haven in the new second-hand Ford he bought with his own money. He has jobs and he has scholarships and he's paying his own way and he's free, he's a free man, ever since he beat West Point and they said he wasn't a liar. So what do you know what's right for him or me or anybody. He won! My brother, whom you said wouldn't win, won!"

Richard, defeated, exits. Rena clearly disapproves of Alexander's talking to his father that way, but Alexander is not sorry. "The point is, we're all healthy and together, and he loves you very much," declares Rena. It's Ned who answers her: "The point is, in my entire life I never believed for one single minute that my father ever loved me. The point is, I can't even figure out if I've ever been loved at all."

Alexander admits to his mother that he found the letters from her admiring professor hidden in a purse in her closet. Rena is reminded that the purse was crocheted by Alexander's great grandmother, Sybil, who lived until the age of 99 with Rena's father taking care of her. Sybil once threw her husband out of the house permanently after he'd slept with another woman, and Rena recalls other such family incidents, remembering that she had a miscarriage once while visiting the old lady.

Rena seeks relief from these unpleasant memories in Ned/Alexander's arms. Benjamin comes in, disapproving of their closeness. He and Alexander exit, as Ned, feeling unwell, returns to bed and presses his buzzer after his machine sends out its signals with a soft bell and yellow lights.

Richard comes in and tells Rena how devoted to her he is, in part to console her for spending yet another vacation here in the boarding house instead of going on a glamorous trip. He promises her that in four more years, when the boys are educated, they can start spending their money on themselves. Rena reminds him, "You know how much all this fighting upsets me. You just can't seem to stop. Why can't you stop? Why can't you leave the boy alone?"

Before Richard can answer, Benjamin and Alexander come back. Hanniman runs in, checks the measuring devices, then departs quickly as Rena asks Benjamin about Yale and is told that he's doing his thesis on twentieth century Negro poets.

Hanniman returns with Tony. Ned begins to convulse slightly.

TONY *(checking the dials, then Ned)*: Insulin reaction.

Hanniman hands him a huge syringe which he injects into Ned's groin or neck.

ALEXANDER *(to Ned)*: Benjamin doesn't want to go to law school. He wants to be a teacher or a writer. He wants to help people. What are they doing to you?

BENJAMIN: I'll be all right . . . . . Law is helping people, too.

ALEXANDER: That's not what you told me. Ned, what's wrong? Why aren't you answering?

RICHARD *(to Benjamin)*: Listen, mister smart ass big guy, don't make it sound like such a holy sacrifice! I got you this far. I got both of you this far. I got all of us this far.

RENA: Stop it, stop it, stop it!

ALEXANDER: *NED!*

RICHARD: You and your ungrateful prick of a brother.

ALEXANDER: Why do you bring us back to this stupid place every year anyway? Just so we can feel poor? Benjamin is going to marry a rich girl he doesn't even love!

RENA: You're getting married?

RICHARD: Hey, I always say it's just as easy to marry a rich one.

BENJAMIN: You promised me you'd keep your mouth shut. Let's go for a swim.

Throws Alexander his suit.

RENA: Don't go. It's getting dark.

BENJAMIN *(gets his own suit)*: Fast!

RENA: Wait until tomorrow. I'll go with you.

RICHARD *(grabbing Alexander as he starts out)*: Every time I look at you, every single time I see you, I wish to Christ your mother had that abortion!

RENA *(a wail)*: NOOOOOO!

RICHARD: She wouldn't have another one. And I've been paying for it ever since.

RENA: I beg you!

ALEXANDER: Ned, help me! Where are you?

Tony is holding on to Ned, telling him he's going to be O.K., as Benjamin helps Alexander, who is going to vomit. Richard continues complaining that he's spent his life at a job he hates in order to support his family, and his sons haven't even turned out to be anything he'd wanted. Richard lets his frustration lead him into attacking Alexander physically, pulling him down and hitting him like a punching bag, despite Benjamin's best efforts to restrain him.

> *Benjamin somehow separates his father from his brother. He carries Alexander off in his arms.*

BENJAMIN: It's too late. There's nothing we can do. I shouldn't have come.
> *Richard pulls himself off the floor. He doesn't know which way to go. Hanniman comes in with another transfusion bottle—green—of blood. She hands it to Tony, who inserts it in the machine. Richard, dazed, walks off.*

NED: It's too late. There's nothing we can do. I shouldn't have come.
HANNIMAN: Why, we're just starting.
TONY: You just had a little imbalance. It wasn't unexpected. It's a good sign. It means we're knocking out more of your infected cells than we expected. I think we just may be seeing some progress.

Tony departs and so does Hanniman after listening to Ned recite an anecdote of vicious homophobia in 18th century Holland. Benjamin (now Ben) and Alexander (now Ned) enter Alexander's Yale room. The older brother hears that the younger is flunking just about everything. Ben is wearing his Y for one of his many athletic achievements. He asks Alexander why he hasn't accepted the offer of a friend named Theo to accompany him on a trip to Europe. Ned, looking back on this moment, realizes that it was an important one in his life. If Alexander answers the question truthfully, Ben's reaction is uncertain.

ALEXANDER *(to Benjamin):* We were lovers.
BENJAMIN: We were what!
ALEXANDER: Me and Theo!
NED: And so the journey begins. Do you feel any better?
BENJAMIN: Did he ask you?
ALEXANDER *(to Benjamin):* Yes. *(To Ned.)* Yes.
BENJAMIN: He shouldn't have done that.
ALEXANDER: Oh, I wanted to do it.

Alexander explains to Ben, "We made love. Right here. I went to Theo and asked him: I'm flunking out of your German class, could I do something for extra credit?, and we went out and drank beer, and we came back here, and he asked me: would you like to make love?, and I walked to this door, and opened it, and said: I think you'd better go, and I closed the door and ran right back into his arms. And I passed."

Ben considers this kind of love an unhealthy trait which as "everybody knows" is the result of having a possessive mother and an absent father and can be corrected by modern psychiatry. What Alexander wants Ben to say to him, though, is something like, "I don't care if you've got purple spots, I love you." Ben supposes that Alexander refused Theo's invitation for a trip because he knew this was wrong and "sick," but Alexander insists that he refused because he didn't love Theo.

Ned predicts the future to Alexander: he's going around a circle of psychiatrists who will identify him as a homosexual—"That's what you are"—and try to tell him that it's because he's "sick, sick, sick," ignoring the demands of the heart. Alexander, undaunted, departs with Ben, as Hanniman enters to get still another blood sample. Ned wonders whether marrying a white husband solved any of her problems, which causes her to comment, "Boy, you are one piece of cake." Ned feels that he has failed his young followers, adding, "In a few more years, more Africans will be dying from this plague than are being born. If this stuff works, only rich white men will get it. I call that genocide. What do you call it? How do you go to sleep at night lying beside your husband knowing all that?" Hanniman walks out on him, and he calls after her, "What are you doing for *your* people out there?"

Meanwhile, Ben pounds on the door and pushes into Alexander's New York studio, carrying a bottle of champagne. Alexander has isolated himself from his series of doctors and from his office for a week, not answering the phone. Ben opens the champagne, while chiding Alexander for never visiting Ben's children and asking about the status of his psychiatric treatment. Alexander has been called a pervert and a violator of God's laws by the doctors, but what he really longs for is someone to love. He began a promising relationship with one man he thought "beautiful," a Harvard doctorate candidate named Peter, but then he was brainwashed by the psychiatrist into sending Peter away.

Alexander asks himself again and again why he listens to Ben. He is virtually forced to seek psychiatric advice because he fears Ben won't love him if he doesn't manage to change. "It's much too powerful a force to change!", Alexander exclaims, "It's got to be a part of me! Especially when it doesn't want to die. And fights tenaciously to stay alive, against all odds. And no matter what anyone does to try and kill it. Why are you so terrified of what I might become? Why don't you just leave me alone? We don't have to see each other. Are you afraid to let go of me, too? Why? Why am I—why are we both—such collaborators? And how can I love you when part of me thinks you're murdering me?"

And as for Ben (Alexander continues), why did he spend so little time at home? Because he never had a mother, Ben believes. Rena had so many projects on hand she never had time to love him. He can't forgive her for that; she is so self-centered (Ben continues) that she pulled her husband away from a lucrative career with his brother Leon to suit her convenience, and they turned down a good job in the Virgin Islands for the same reason—"She had to be the star." And in Ben's opinion she smothered Alexander, never giving him room to develop in his own way.

Alexander agrees to the point that during his psychoanalyzing sessions he can't remember any happy memories of childhood. Ben admits that he too is under psychoanalysis, and so is his wife Sara, who is much too hard on their son Timmy (who consequently feels at times that he is unloved, and has developed a stomach ulcer).

This has been very painful for Ben to verbalize and confide. He suddenly turns away. Alexander kneels on the mattress beside him and tries to put his arms around him.

John Cameron Mitchell *(seated)* as young Ned "Alexander" Weeks and Jonathan Hadary as Ned Weeks grown up in *The Destiny of Me*

BENJAMIN: I . . . I get frightened my mind is going to leave me. I'll be in court, I'll be trying a case, in a courtroom, before a judge, and I'll start getting clammy and freezing, and then I'm bathed in a terror that I'm about to lose my mind. *(Looks at his watch.)* I've got to get out of here. I'm late . . .

ALEXANDER: What happens when a kid is chosen for the wrong team? He's chosen, and he doesn't want to be on that team. Doesn't want to be the beloved of the parent. I wanted him but could only have her. You wanted her but could only have him. And he adored you so. You didn't like Richard either, did you?

BENJAMIN: I felt sorry for him.

ALEXANDER: It's as if we each took one parent for our very own. And each of them chose one of us. The whole procedure had nothing to do with love.

NED: "And the sins of the fathers shall visit unto the third and fourth generations."

BENJAMIN: No! I don't believe that! We can change it!

Impulsively, Ben advises his brother, "Go and call Peter back." So Alexander did call his Harvard friend and arrange a rendezvous at the Savoy Plaza, only to find that Peter was in love with someone else. Ben encourages Alexander, "The answers will present themselves . . . . . Keep fighting," and departs.

Ned confesses to the audience a moment of extreme despair when he was facing final exams he knew he couldn't pass and there was no escape.

NED: . . . . . Every social structure I'm supposed to be a part of—my family, my religion, my school, my friends, my neighborhood, my work, my city, my state, my country, my government, my newspaper, my television . . . tells me over and over what I feel and see and think and do is sick. The only safe place left is the dark. I want to go to sleep. It's Saturday. I want to sleep till Tuesday.
Swallowing Hanniman's pills with Ben's champagne.
This couple of pills will take me till tomorrow and these until Sunday and . . . Monday . . . now I can sleep till Tuesday. Might as well take a few more. Just in case. Pop's right, of course. I'm a failure. *(Looking at himself in the mirror.)* You even look like Richard. You'll look like him for the rest of your life. I am more my father's child than ever I wanted to be. I've fought so hard not to look like you. I've fought so hard not to inherit your failure. Poor newly-named Ned. Trying so hard to fight against failure. Now increasing at an awful rate.

ALEXANDER'S VOICE: Help! I'm drowning! Don't let me drown!

NED: I woke up in a hospital and Ben was there beside me.

TONY *(entering and disconnecting him):* I've run the tests. The new genes are adhering. We're half way there. We can go on with the final part. Say Thank You. Say Congratulations. You begged for a few more years. I may have bought you life. Lay off my wife, will you? Any fights you got with me, pick them with me. *(He leaves.)*

Ned looks out the window. Chanting is heard. He steps back quickly when he fears someone may have seen him.

NED: Okay, Ned—be happy. Be exuberant! You're half way there. *(Singing.)* "Hold my hand and we're half way there, Hold my hand and I'll take you there. Somehow. Someday. Somewhere . . ." That night when Benjamin and I left Mrs. Pennington's and went swimming, he carried me down to the shore. We swam and played and ducked under each other's arms and legs. We lay on the big raft, way out on the Sound, side by side, not saying a word, looking at the stars. I held his hand. He said, "Come dive with me." I dived in after he did, and I got caught under the raft, and I couldn't get out from under. I thrashed desperately this way and that, and I had no more breath. When I thought I would surely die, he rescued and saved me, Benjamin did.

Benjamin comes back in carrying a limp Alexander both of them wet from the ocean. He lays him on the ground, and we see the action Ned describes.

He got me to the shore, and he laid me out on the sand, and he pressed my stomach so the poison came out, and he kissed me on the lips so I might breathe again.

Curtain.

ACT III

Tony, dressed for a visit to the White House, is connecting a group of new bottles to still another machine called an Ex-Cell-Aerator closely watched by Ned, who comments that the activists outside have created a large enough disturbance to cause 370 arrests, but so far no press coverage. Ned taunts Tony, "Why is everyone down here afraid to call a plague a plague? Are you punishing us or yourself?"

Tony leaves without comment, and Ned takes off his bathrobe, picks up a suitcase and joins Rena, now 70, who is waiting in a hospital where Richard is gravely ill. Ned has come on from London and steers the conversation toward his mother's onetime romance which she gave up because "Your father came along and said, 'I'll always take care of you,' and he always has." Ned even inquires about her sex life with Richard.

RENA: Stop it!

NED: You used to tell me everything.

RENA: Well, here's something I'm not going to. Our lives weren't about sex. Is sex what controls your life?

NED: Kids are some sort of sum total of both their parents. We've got both of you in us. We pick up a lot of traits from whatever kind of emotional subtext is going on.

RENA: I'm supposed to understand that mouthful of jargon? You must still be going to a psychiatrist.

NED: I can go every day for $75 a week.

RENA: That used to be three months' rent. How in God's name do you find enough to talk about every day?

NED: I fall asleep a lot.

RENA: You pay someone to fall asleep? You kids, you and your psychiatrists think you know it all. Then why aren't we perfect after all these years?

NED: I don't fall in love. People don't fall in love with me.

RENA: That's too bad. Everyone should have someone.

NED: I want to love them. I want them to love me back.

RENA: Are we getting blamed for all of this?

NED: I've just finally got the courage to say what I want to say.

RENA: I don't recall your ever being delinquent in that department.

NED: Without caring what anyone thinks back.

RENA: Well, I always tried to instill courage in you. But you can't always just say what you think.

NED: That's a very mixed message.

RENA: Why? Why is it?

NED: Do you feel guilty for not being more courageous yourself?

RENA: Why do I have to feel guilty?

NED: You saw how much Pop hated me. You must have had some sense that if you'd only left him, I wouldn't have had to go through all that shit.

RENA: Don't use that language. I tried to make up for it by loving you more.

NED: It doesn't work that way.

RENA: It would appear it doesn't.

Ned has accepted the fact that he's homosexual, and he doesn't care whether Rena does or not. Rena thinks this makes her seem like a bad mother and wonders why under these circumstances Ben didn't turn out the same way. Ned replies, "Because it isn't caused by anything. You *or* Richard. I was born this way. You didn't do anything to make me this way," declaring further, "I like being gay. It's taken me a long time. I don't want to waste any more, tolerating your being ashamed of me, or anyone I care about being ashamed of me. If you can't accept that, you won't see your younger son again."

Rena doesn't see much of him as it is, she replies grudgingly, and sends Ned into his dying father's room. Richard wishes Ned had been a big success like Ben, who is supervising 200 lawyers and earning millions. Ned tries to explain that he is a success as the author of plays and movies. Richard complains that he has been in stomach pain all his life—"I never had a father either"—as part of the cost of hating his own father, who eventually deserted his family. Richard shifts position so that his back is turned to Ned, who summons up the courage to make one final declaration: "I'm sorry your life was a disappointment, Poppa. Poppa, you were cruel to me, Poppa."

After his father died (Ned recalls) he achieved greater and greater success, much to his gratification. As a writer, "I would address the problems of my new world. Every gay man I knew was fucking himself to death. I wrote about that. Every gay man I knew wanted a lover. I wrote about that. I said that having so much sex made finding love impossible. I made my new world very angry. As when I was a child, such defiance made me flourish. My writing and my notoriety prospered."

Ned gets back into bed and (as Tony and Hanniman enter and connect him to the machine) recalls that he stopped going to psychiatrists and finally found a lover, Felix, who became sick and died 19 months later. Thanks to Ben's investment sagacity, Ned is well enough off to indulge in such non-profitable pursuits as activism.

Tony and Hanniman assure Ned he has a 50-50 chance. They turn on the machine and exit.

In their old Eden Heights apartment, Ned and Ben are packing up the family possessions while Rena, now 80, finishes a phone conversation. She's moving to an "adult residence" and, like Ben, wants to throw everything away. It's Ned who values the mementos and the memories. Rena remembers that they moved here for a three-month temporary job and stayed here 50 years, after the job became permanent. She finds the batch of letters from her onetime admirer and decides, "I don't want to meet another man. One was enough. *(Ned looks at her.)* I always thought Richard was inadequate. *(Ben looks up at her too.)* I just never had the guts to really leave him. It's no great crime to choose security over passion. My grand passion was the two of you. *(To Ben.)* You have the wonderful wife and the wonderful marriage and have given me my wonderful grandchildren. *(To Ned.)* You have the artistic talent, which you inherited from me. Hurry up and write whatever it is you're going to write about me so I can get through all the pain it'll no doubt cause me."

As Rena exits to her bedroom, Ben informs Ned that his son is going to have an operation to fix a nerve problem in his stomach which he inherited from Richard—a genetic flaw, apparently, not psychosomatic. He sneaks off before Rena returns dressed in the Russian costume which Ned once wore, causing Richard to give him a beating (Rena denies that anything like this ever happened). She wants her sons to know she's aware that they treat her with disdain but puts up with it.

Hanniman makes a quick in-and-out visit to take Ned's pulse, and Rena expounds on the subject of her mother's very old age, an unhappy experience for all concerned. Rena's planning to review her life in an autobiography class offered by the home she's going to, and she confesses to Ned that she tried to get in touch with her onetime lover but found that he had died: "I guess we couldn't expect him to wait around for me forever, could we?" She tells Ned that she used to receive a lot of friends' comments like, "Your son's sick with that queer disease," or "I saw your son on TV saying homosexuals are the same as everyone else," but their attitude has changed with all the progress being made.

NED: There hasn't been any progress.

RENA: Of course there has. Goodbye, darling. It's a long trip back. And I'm having trouble with my tooth. Every time I say goodbye I'm never sure I'm going to see you again. Give me a kiss.

> *She comes to his bed and they kiss, Ned hugging her with his arms all tubed up.*

NED: I wouldn't be a writer if you guys hadn't done what you did.

RENA: Is that something else I'm meant to feel guilty for, or a thank you?

NED: I love being a writer.

RENA: At last.

> *Walks off, slowly, holding on to things. She is almost blind . . . . .*
> *Hanniman enters, with Tony, and takes another blood test.*

NED: What happened at the White House? What did he say?

TONY: They're cutting our budget.

NED: Your buddy. Is it too pushy of me to inquire as to my and/or your progress?

TONY: We have a 50-50 chance.

NED: That's your idea of progress?

TONY: You're not only pushy, you're . . . how do your people say it, a kvetch? Just imagine this is the cure and you're the first person in the world getting it.

Tony leaves, and Hanniman, drawing still more blood, informs Ned that he's her last patient; she's now going to turn her attention to having and raising a baby. Ned is tossing, feverish, and calls for Ben, who appears and comforts him.

> *A young man, Jack, wearing an ACT UP baseball cap, comes in.*

JACK: You fucking traitor! Why aren't you out there with us! Just when we need you most, you're not there.

NED: Who are you?

JACK: You don't remember me? I'm Jack.

NED: Jack, whatever we're doing isn't working.

JACK: Don't say that! You're the reason I got into this! How dare you walk out on us!

NED: I'm tired. It's somebody else's turn now.

JACK: Oh, bullshit! Bullshit! You're supposed to be the angriest gay man in the world.

NED: How are you doing?

JACK: You remember my lover, Chris? He took an overdose. I came home and he was still alive, and I didn't know what to do. What would you have done?

NED: I don't know. What did you do?

JACK: I called 911. He lived six more months in awful pain. And it was me who saved him for that. Come back and fight with us! *(No answer. Re: the machinery.)* I hope all this shit works. I read all the literature and . . . I wish to God they'd just admit they don't know what the fuck's going on and go back to the drawing board . . . . .

They plan to raid Tony's lab in the early morning hours, Jack informs Ned, and departs.

Ben is still there comforting Ned, who tells his older brother he wants to be buried, not cremated, so people can see his tombstone and remember him. He's picked out a spot in a cemetery and hopes Ben will choose to be buried by his side. And he wants Ben, as his lawyer, to arrange for something at Yale or in New York to be named after him as a permanent memorial.

Ben, weeping, tells Ned that he is proud, even a little bit jealous, of Ned's firm stand on behalf of his cause. "You're the only one I've ever totally trusted," Ben finishes. "There never was a moment I would have not put my fate in your hands."

Tony comes in with a long computer printout—the results of the treatment—complaining that the raid on his lab destroyed his records of ten years of work. Ned grabs the printout, peruses it, and sees that it's bad news.

NED: I'm worse? I'm worse!

TONY: Yes.

NED: What are you going to do?

TONY: There's nothing I can do.

NED: What do you mean there's nothing you can do? You gave me the fucking stuff! You must have considered such a possibility! You must have some emergency measures!

TONY: Oh, shut up! I am sick to death of you, your mouth, your offspring! You think changing Presidents will change anything? Will make any difference? The system will always be here. The system doesn't change. No matter who's President. It doesn't make any difference who's President! You're scared of dying? Let me tell you the facts of life: it isn't easy to die: you don't die until you have tubes in every single, possible, opening and orifice and vent and passage and outlet and hole and slit in your ungrateful body. Why, it can take years and years to die. You haven't suffered nearly enough. *(Leaves.)*

> *Ned slowly begins to disconnect himself, as best he can, from all the tubes to the machines. Blood starts to trickle and spurt from the freed tubes.*

NED: The miracle cure didn't work. Again. Ben, it gets harder and harder to want to stay alive. I can feel my fear of death overtaking any joy in still being alive.

The flowings of blood increase.

What will it be like? Will I be conscious? Will my breath suddenly be taken away? Cut off at the pass? Is there a split second when you accept the fact that it *is* about to happen—that, at last, it's been personalized—that the obit in the *Times* . . . is mine?

More blood.

Who will want me? An aging, lonely, diseased once-angry man . . . . . I wanted it so much. A love of my own.

He yanks the tubes violently out of the machine, causing blood to gush out. Then he picks up one of the bottles of blood and smashes it against a wall.

My straight friends . . .

Smashes another bottle.

. . . ask me over and over again: Why is it so hard for you to find love?

Another bottle.

Ah, that is the question, answered, . . .

Another bottle.

. . . I hope, . . .

Another bottle.

. . . for you . . .

Another bottle.

. . . tonight. Why do I never stop believing this fucking plague can be cured?

ALEXANDER *(appearing wet from the shower and in the bath towel we first saw him in)*: What's going to happen to me?

NED: You're going to go to eleven shrinks. You won't fall in love for forty years. And when a nice man finally comes along and tries to teach you to love him and love yourself, he dies from a plague.

ALEXANDER: I'm sorry I asked. Do I learn . . . *anything?*

NED: Does it make any sense, a life?   —

ALEXANDER: You made me go through all of this just for that?

NED: I wonder, Alexander, if the search is all.

ALEXANDER: All?

NED: When Felix was offered the morphine drip for the first time in the hospital, I asked him, "Do you want it now?" Felix somehow found the strength to answer back, "I want to stay a little longer."

Ned starts singing "This Nearly Was Mine," and as he continues, Alexander questions him about how the future is to be. In between verses of the song, Ned tells him they become rich. "I gave you great stuff to work with," Alexander declares and adds, "Excuse me for saying so, but I still think you're a mess." He joins Ned in the end of the song, after which Ned comments, "I want to stay a little longer." *Curtain.*

○○○
○○○
○○○
○○○
○○○
○○○ THE SISTERS ROSENSWEIG

A Play in Two Acts

BY WENDY WASSERSTEIN

Cast and credits appear on pages 300, 302, 338, 339

WENDY WASSERSTEIN was born in Brooklyn in 1950. Her father was a textile manufacturer, and her mother saw to it that her daughter developed an enthusiasm for the theater at an early age, combining classes at a dancing school in the Broadway area with visits to matinee performances. Wasserstein received her formal education at Calhoun School in Manhattan, Mount Holyoke College (B.A.), CCNY (M.A.) and Yale Drama School, graduating in 1976. Before that, in 1973, she was testing her mettle as a playwright with a staged reading of Any Woman Can't *at Playwrights Horizons. Her* Uncommon Women and Others *was first staged at Yale, followed by readings at Playwrights Horizons and the Eugene O'Neill Theater Center (1977), and finally—her first produced play—off Broadway by the Phoenix Theater November 17, 1977 for 22 performances. The Phoenix also presented Wasserstein's* Isn't It Romantic *in 1981 for 37 perform- ances; and on December 15, 1983 Playwrights Horizons produced a revised version of* Isn't It Romantic *which ran for 733 performances.*

A Wasserstein one-acter, The Man in a Case, *based on a Chekhov story, appeared off Broadway in 1986 on an Acting Company program; and then her first Broadway production,* The Heidi Chronicles, *also became her first Best Play and won her the Pulitzer Prize, the Drama Critics and Tony Awards for best play and the Elizabeth Hull-Kate Warriner Award to "the playwright whose work dealt with controversial subjects involving the fields of political, religious or social mores of the time," the latter being a major concern of this feminist-oriented script. It was written with a National Theater British American Arts Association grant and produced in a Seattle Repertory workshop in association with Playwrights Horizons, which then presented it off Broadway December 11, 1988 for 81 performances before moving it to Broadway March 9, 1989 for its 621-performance, multi-prizewinning run. Wasserstein's second Best Play is this season's* The Sisters Rosensweig, *which also played in Seattle Repertory workshop, this time in association with Lincoln Center Theater, which then opened it as an off-Broadway production October 22, 1992 at the Mitzi E. Newhouse Theater for 149 performances before moving it to Broadway at the Ethel Barrymore Theater March 18, 1993.*

Among Wasserstein works staged in New York and other venues are the skit Smart Women/Brilliant Choices *for the Manhattan Theater Club Revue* Urban Blight *(1988),* When Dinah Shore Ruled the Earth *(written with Christopher Durang, as was the screen play* The House of Husbands*),* Montpelier Pazazz, *the books of the musicals* Miami *and* Tender Offer *and additional material for the musical* Hard Sell. *She is also the author of the TV plays* Kiss, Kiss Darling; Drive, She Said, *and an adaptation of John Cheever's* The Sorrows of Gin *for PBS, as well as a book of essays entitled* Bachelor Girls.

Wasserstein is a contributing editor of New York Woman *and* Harper's Bazaar, *a recipient of NEA and Guggenheim grants and a member of the Dramatists Guild, serving on its Council and as one of the dramaturges for the Young Playwright's Festival of plays by teen-agers, presented annually in New York, where she now lives.*

The following synopsis of The Sisters Rosenweig *was prepared by Sally Dixon Wiener.*

Time: A weekend in late August, 1991

Place: A sitting room in Queen Anne's Gate, London

Scene 1: Late Friday morning

SYNOPSIS: *"The room is decorator 'done' with cozy, comfy, but expensive chintz couches, chairs and window treatments. There is a dining room upstage right and a staircase upstage left leading to the bedrooms."* Stage left there is an entrance to a downstairs apartment and also stage left is the front door of the house. As the play begins, Tess, Sara's daughter, an attractive 17, *"in blue jeans and T-shirt is listening to Sara's collegiate all-women's singing group, The Cliffe Clefs, doing an a cappella version of 'Shine on Harvest Moon'.* "Tess is speaking into her tape recorder, commenting on "the use of the vernacular—'I ain't had no lovin',"' when her Aunt Pfeni, 40, one of her mother's sisters, arrives carrying several shopping bags. She is youthful in appearance, wearing loose-fitting ethnic clothes, and has just come from Bombay. The occasion is Sara's birthday. Sara's and Pfeni's other sister, Gorgeous, is due to arrive soon from Newton, Massachusetts.

Tess explains to Pfeni she's listening to her mother's college singing group recordings because biographies of parents' younger days is her school's summer project. Tess would like to leave London and go to school in America, but her mother, who named her for Tess of the D'Urbervilles, is not in favor of that.

Sara, 54, the oldest of the Rosensweig sisters, enters and greets her youngest sister, almost immediately asking her if it isn't about time she won the Overseas Press Award. Tess backs up her aunt by announcing that her English teacher at Westminster assigned Pfeni's book *Life in the Afghan Village* for the next semester for the women's writing segment. Her teacher also called her aunt counter-revolutionary for writing travel columns now. It doesn't matter to Tess, however, because she plans to study hairdressing so she can make her way in the world. A "less luxury-oriented field" might be better in view of the economy, Sara thinks. Pfeni suggests welding.

When Sara goes off to the kitchen to take a phone call, Tess confesses her mother worries about her because she's like Pfeni, a compulsive traveler because she fears commitment. Pfeni is searching through her shopping bags for a gift she's brought Tess (Tess's grandmother Rita said "only crazy people travel with shopping bags," so Pfeni has made shopping bags her "personal signature ever since") and finds it, proudly presenting it to Tess. It is Shiva, the many-armed destroyer, to destroy evil and bring her "hope, rebirth, and a life-time guarantee" that Tess won't grow up like Pfeni. Tess asks if she can give it to her mother whom she suggests is "in desperate need of hope and rebirth."

Sara returns, pleased that Nick Pym is coming for dinner. Tess takes umbrage, pointing out that with homeless people sleeping under Charing Cross Station it doesn't seem right having "bourgeois dinner parties with capitalists like Nicholas Pym." Sara remarks how brilliantly Tess has grown up, she's perfect, and Pfeni should have a child because Sara's main joy in life is Tess. Tess isn't buying. She's been told by someone's father Sara has "the biggest balls at the Hong Kong/Shanghai Bank worldwide."

Tess would like to ask Tom Valiunus, her current young man, to dinner. It seems his father owns a radio supply store in Liverpool, and he hopes to go into the business. Sara doesn't understand what Tess has in common with someone who wants to sell radio parts, and doesn't think Tess needs to go to Latvia with him either. Tess corrects her—it's Lithuania, and she and Tom have a commitment to the Lithuanian resistance. Pfeni points out that Vilnius was at one time the Jerusalem of Lithuania, adding that there's the famous Old Cellar restaurant there, plus the Central Theater of Vilnius. "That way, Tessie, when they send the tanks in, you and Tom can take in a quick hamburger and a show," Sara remarks.

The sparring goes on until Tess points out that Tom comes from a normal family, something her mother's not managed to maintain, "despite being on the cover of *Fortune* twice," but if Sara wants her to, she'll tell Tom he isn't invited for dinner with "socially acceptable, racist, sexist, and more than likely anti-Semitic Nicholas Pym." Sara backs down, urges Tess to invite Tom to dinner, and kisses her on the cheek. Tess, who has invited Pfeni earlier to join them for tea, reminds her they'll be at Fortnum's at five o'clock as she goes off.

Sara tells Pfeni Tess wants to make her life the opposite of hers. Pfeni points out that's what they set out to do because of their mother. They were right, Sara insists. Pfeni thinks Tessie might be, too. Sara picks up the Shiva.

PFENI: This will destroy all evil and bring you hope and rebirth.

SARA: I'm too old.

PFENI: You're not too old.

SARA: You don't know. You're only forty.

PFENI: Forty is old.

SARA: Oh, Pfeni, I'm so glad you're here.

PFENI: Did you think I'd let Dr. Gorgeous show up for your birthday and not be here?

SARA: Your sister's not just showing up for my birthday. She's leading the Temple Beth El sisterhood on a tour of the crown jewels.

PFENI: But she managed to plan it in time for your birthday.

SARA: True. You're a good sister, Pfeni Rosensweig. Pfeni! God, what an awful name! Why do you keep it?

PFENI: Penny Rosensweig wasn't any better. Now, Sara Goode, on the other hand, is a great name.

SARA: Multiple divorce is a brilliant thing. You get so many names to choose from. But my second was definitely my best. And how nice that there is now a Mrs. Samantha Goode, Mrs. Melissa Goode, Mrs. Pamela Goode, and, as of last year, the twenty-four-year-old Mrs. Sushiro Goode. We could form the Wives of Kenneth Goode Club with branches in Chicago, New York, London, and Tokyo. Well, never mind. I'm looking forward to us growing old together. Like two old-maid spinsters in a Muriel Spark novel.

PFENI: Sara, that's beyond depressing.

SARA: No it isn't. It could be rather cozy. You could stop traveling, finally settle into the downstairs flat and grow more and more eccentric, and I could get meaner and crabbier.

PFENI: But I have Geoffrey.

SARA: Well, he can visit us. He's here all the time anyway.

PFENI: Geoffrey says we'll live together when his house is finished.

SARA: That man has no intention of ever living there when he can enjoy the hospitality of all his friends.

PFENI: Geoffrey adds a little texture to your life.

SARA: I don't need that much texture in my life. You'd be better off getting old with me. Is Geoffrey joining us for dinner tonight?

PFENI: I hope so.

SARA: Good. Maybe he'll solve both our problems and fall madly in love with Tom and lead him on the children's crusade to Vilnius.
    Pause.
Indulge me, Pfeni. I told you, I'm an old and bitter woman.

PFENI: You're not old and bitter. You're anticipating an era of hope and rebirth.

Pfeni makes a reference to Tessie's summer project. It's to prove that Sara's early years don't have any bearing on her life now, Sara explains. But hearing the music recently has got her wondering about an old lyric of which she's forgotten some of the words—"The Cannibal King with the big nose ring." Pfeni recalls it, and they are still singing, along with vigorous clapping, when Geoffrey arrives. *"Geoffrey, an attractive 40-year-old man in a handsome leather jacket and a Sunset in Penang T-shirt . . . . . carries an overnight bag and immediately begins applauding."* But the recitative must go faster, he insists, as he sings along with them and conducts. They pick up the pace and he again applauds. "Bravo the sisters Rosensweig!"

Scene 2: Later that afternoon, around 6:30.

"Pfeni enters from her apartment, which is downstairs. Geoffrey follows her." They seem to be continuing a conversation they've been having, and their bantering invariably includes references to show business and/or popular music. Geoffrey is always "on." Pfeni interrupts.

PFENI: Sara says we should stop seeing each other. She says she and I should grow old together.

GEOFFREY: Pfeni my luv, all you've talked about since you've arrived here is Sara. How guilty you feel that she was ill. How guilty you feel that she's alone. How much you love her. How much you can't bear to be around her. How much you want her praise. How little you care for her opinions.

PFENI: That's not true.

GEOFFREY: All I know is that whenever you're around that woman you tell me we have to stop seeing each other. My darling, we hardly ever do see each other. I'm always in rehearsal and you're in Timbuktu half the year. It's a bloody brilliant relationship.
    He kisses her on the forehead.

PFENI: Oh my God, my life is stuck. "I've forgotten the Italian for window."

GEOFFREY: Very good! *The Three Sisters.* Act III. Now, Pfeni darling, see how worthwhile it's been knowing me. If not for me, you'd still think that *Uncle Vanya* was a Neil Simon play about his pathetic uncle in the Bronx.

PFENI: And now instead I've had a three-year relationship with an internationally renowned director and bisexual.

GEOFFREY: You left out botanist. I read botany at Cambridge. And I also put that "f" betwixt your name. If not for me, you'd be plain and simple Penny Rosensweig.

PFENI: Thank you. I have your "f" to keep me warm.

GEOFFREY: For Christ's sake, Pfeni, if you want to find unconditional love, have a baby. Adopt a red and fuzzy brood of them. Better yet, have artificial insemination.

> *He lifts up a water glass.*

"Hello, darling, this is Daddy. Say good morning to your Daddy." "Morning, Daddy." Or you could become a lesbian. Most of the really interesting women I know are lesbians.

PFENI: Just tell me one thing? What do you still get out of this?

GEOFFREY: T-shirts from all over the world. Would I be sporting Sunset in Penang if not for you? I've been meaning to ask you, darling, where is Penang?

PFENI: Malaysia. Somerset Maugham lived there.

GEOFFREY: This is what's so wonderful about dating a nice American Jewish girl! You're all so well versed in British colonial history.

> *He embraces her.*

Pfeni, my luv, trust me. I am still very happy with you.

Pfeni is not convinced he wouldn't like to meet a nice man to come home to. Geoffrey claims he's already done that, but the man, Jordan, left Geoffrey for a chorus boy from *Cats.* Geoffrey and Pfeni then met at the ballet. Geoffrey does not now have his eye on anyone, he claims, and is committed, "signed exclusively," with Pfeni.

Geoffrey is expecting a delegation of the homeless who live under Charing Cross Station, but when the bell rings it's not the downstairs bell, so Pfeni agrees to answer it and send them to meet Geoffrey downstairs. At the door, when Pfeni opens it, is not the delegation, but Merv Kant, *"a 58-year-old American in a wrinkled linen suit . . . . . carrying a Turnbull & Asser bag."* No, he doesn't live under Charing Cross Station. He lives over it, at the Savoy Hotel, and wants to leave something for Geoffrey. When Geoffrey appears, Merv starts dancing in glee and singing at having found the purple shirts they'd been looking for, one for Geoffrey and one for himself, and they finish the dance together. Merv claims Geoffrey left him a message to meet him at seven, but Geoffrey plays up his concern for the homeless, telling Merv he believes he told the homeless to meet him at the Savoy where he thought he'd be seeing Merv. In the midst of this confusion he rushes off, asking Pfeni to give Merv a drink.

Merv is curious as to whose house he is in. Pfeni tells him it's her sister Sara's, and that her sister is the managing director of the Hong Kong/Shanghai Bank Europe. When Sara comes on, Merv remarks that she must be Pfeni's younger sister. Sara finds out that Merv was in Budapest last week and is going to Ireland on Sunday for brunch with the rabbi of Dublin. Pfeni goes off at last to join Tess and Tom, leaving Sara and Merv alone. Merv reports that Pfeni considers Sara brilliant, the first Jewish woman to run a Hong Kong bank. She is the first *woman* to run one, she tells him. When she calls him Mr. Kant, he says it used to be Kantlowitz. He notices she's looking at her watch and asks if she'd like him to leave. She's concerned about when her daughter is coming home.

MERV: Relax. I had three children who never came home and they're all fine now. My oldest, Kip, is a semiotics professor at Boston University. That means he screens *Hiroshima, Mon Amour* once a week. The other boy is a radiologist in North Carolina, Chapel Hill, and my baby, Eva, is a forest ranger in Israel. That means she works for the parks department in Haifa. And your daughter?

SARA: We're hoping she'll be up at Oxford next year.

MERV: She wants to stay here for school?

SARA: From what we've heard about the States now, I think it's wise.

MERV: Tell me what "we've heard."

SARA: It's conventional wisdom, really.

MERV: Really?

SARA: Well, obviously what you have is a society in transition. You've got an industrial economy that is rapidly being transformed into a transactional one. And that's exacerbated by a growing disenfranchised class, decaying inner cities, and a bankrupt educational system. Don't misunderstand me, Mr. Kantlowitz . . .

MERV: Kant, like the philosopher.

SARA: In many ways America is a brilliant country. But it's becoming as class-driven a society as this one.

MERV: So you're a hot-shot Jewish lady banker who's secretly a Marxist.

SARA: This is hardly the time to be a Marxist.

MERV: But your sister's right. You are a brilliant woman!

SARA: Excuse me, Mr. Kant, I really should check on my roast.

MERV: Are we having roast beef and Yorkshire pudding? Blimey, I've been hoping for a good old-fashioned, high-cholesterol English meal. I had a banger for breakfast this morning.

Sara extends her hand.

SARA: It was lovely to meet you, Mr. Kant.

MERV: Whenever I come over here, I treat myself to one blow-out meal at Simpson's on the Strand.

SARA: Only Americans eat there. It's a tourist trap.

MERV: That's why I was so delighted when Geoffrey invited me here for dinner tonight.

SARA: Geoffrey did what?

MERV: And I said to myself, "Merv, this way you can avoid that tourist trap Simpson's on the Strand and have a good old-fashioned Anglo-Saxon Jewish meal."

It seems Merv and Geoffrey have had a working relationship since Geoffrey's musical *The Scarlet Pimpernel* came to New York the preceding season. The anti-fur lobby was picketing the show and Merv, formerly a show biz and novelty furrier and now the world leader in synthetic animal protective covering, was called in to save the day.

Sara points out that it's her 54th birthday, and she's expecting her two other

Robert Klein as Merv and Jane Alexander as Sara
in Wendy Wasserstein's *The Sisters Rosensweig*

sisters shortly. The roast is part of a cassoulet which also includes, among other ingredients, pork sausage, and he might want to go to Simpson's after all.

Sara asks about Merv's wife. She was a Roslyn housewife who died three years ago. Her name was Helene. Merv asks about Sara's husband. Her second is on his fifth wife, she snaps. Her first she's lost track of, and she is doubtful there will be another. "You've closed shop," Merv remarks. Sara says she's busy and excuses herself.

Merv pokes about, helping himself to a drink, approving of her LP records. He's still talking to himself about a Broadway show tune when Gorgeous Teitelbaum comes on, *"a very attractive, slightly overdone woman of around 46 . . . . . She wears a mock Chanel suit with too many accessories."* Merv must be a friend of Geoffrey's, Gorgeous figures, because Geoffrey's friends all like musicals. Merv realizes she must be the third Rosensweig sister. And her sisters are "such funsy people," she assures Merv. Maybe he should marry Sara, she suggests, his having known her for only five minutes doesn't mean a thing. People call Gorgeous from the Massachusetts Turnpike to tell her they've met someone at a rest stop and fallen in love.

Gorgeous asks if Merv's been to Boston. His son lives there, so if Merv listens to the radio when he visits his son he'd know Dr. Gorgeous's call-in program. She sings her theme song and pretends she's having a phone conversation with Merv. She tells him she's a Newton housewife with four children and an attorney husband. Their lifestyle is comfortable but she needed "just a little sparkle to make it all perfect." The sister who did it all the right way, Merv comments. No, she's more than that, Gorgeous assures him, before revealing that she hopes her show is making the move from radio to cable.

"Talking has always come easily to me," she confides. It all began when the women in her Newton temple sisterhood (a group of whom are now on a London tour with Gorgeous) asked her to speak to them about how she maintained "a warm and traditional home" in these "frantic modern times." And who should be in the audience but Rabbi Pearlstein, host of "Newton at Sunrise," who asked her to be on his show.

Gorgeous had become a regular on the rabbi's show, and now Dr. Gorgeous is known through the area. Her husband must be proud, Merv ventures. "And so supportive," she agrees. About becoming a doctor: "You've heard of Dr. Pepper?" Of course he has. "So I'm Dr. Gorgeous." But she must say hello to her sister—"brilliant" but vulnerable, loving, tender as well. Sara's had a difficult year, "urgent female trouble," and was not able to come to their mother's funeral. That's why she and her other sister are here for her birthday.

When Sara comes on, she's surprised that Gorgeous's husband Henry has not come with her. He hasn't because his case load is too heavy, and he wanted to see their daughter Lily playing lacrosse. Merv mentions going back to the Savoy to freshen up, and Gorgeous suggests he go downstairs instead.

Gorgeous takes a gift from a shopping bag, wishes Sara a happy birthday and

announces she will stay with her ladies. *"She picks up her suitcase and her purse."*
Sara urges Gorgeous to at least stay to say hello to Pfeni. If Pfeni's still sleeping
with Geoffrey then she doesn't need to see her, Gorgeous replies; she thinks it's
time Pfeni began to think about someone "even remotely available" and stop
living as if she were on "an extended junior year abroad." Gorgeous announces
that she'll stay for dinner if Merv will. Sara gives in. She can put the sausage on
a separate plate. When Merv starts downstairs to change his shirt, Gorgeous
suggests the guest room upstairs is "cozier." Merv thanks her. "Tonight could
be funsy" he remarks as he goes up the stairs.

Gorgeous likes Merv, but Sara regards him as "a certain type." She's gotten
hard, Gorgeous tells her. Her rabbi claims Sara needs a man "to make her soft
again." There IS a man in Sara's life—Nick Pym's coming for dinner. A Nazi,
Gorgeous snaps, and a philanderer. He dates some other women, Sara admits.
Whatever, it's important after Sara's "procedure" to get back "on the saddle,"
Gorgeous advises. Sara's not the only woman who's been sick. According to
Newsweek it's around three in ten, Gorgeous points out. A larger sisterhood
than Hadassah, Sara remarks. "Female trouble" is Gorgeous's way of putting
it, but there are real words, Sara states: "Ovarian abcess. Hysterectomy."

GORGEOUS: Do you want to share your anger, your rage?

SARA: Actually, I prefer to get on with my life.

GORGEOUS: Rabbi Pearlstein says we should openly discuss our feelings.

SARA: I can't tell you what a comfort it is to live in a country where "our
feelings" are so openly repressed. End of conversation, Gorgeous!

GORGEOUS: Fine. Have it your way. Achhhh! My feet are killing me.
        She slips her shoes off and lies on the sofa.
I schlepped twenty ladies through Harrod's and up and down Sloane Street.
One of them, Mrs. Hershkovitz, her daughter was a counselor at Lily's summer
camp, everywhere she goes she has to have another piece of Wedgewood. She's
got Wedgewood clocks, Wedgewood bells, Wedgewood napkin holders, and
meanwhile her daughter was the biggest dope dealer at Camp Pinehurst.

SARA *(laughing):* I don't know how you do it. I couldn't put up with them.

GORGEOUS: Believe me, Sara, they wouldn't like you either.

SARA: Oh, God, I'm sure not.

GORGEOUS: I don't mind, really. The one thing that bothers me is my feet. I
told Henry if I get this cable job the first thing I'm going to do is stop wearing
cheap shoes. I'm marching myself right into Saks and treating myself to Bruno
Maglis, Ferragamos and Manulo Blanchikis.

SARA: Manulo who?

GORGEOUS: Manulo Blahnick. Whatever. It's all the brands the ladies in my
group tell me are the best. Do you know those bitches—achh, I shouldn't use
that language—what those ladies said to me this morning. "Gorgeous, you're
a celebrity now. Why don't you treat yourself to a real Chanel suit? You're such

a brilliant and attractive women, it kills us to see you with an imitation Louis Vuitton purse." Do you know how much one of those Chanel suits costs? Sarah, you're my brilliant big sister, when we were growing up, why didn't Daddy tell us about money?

SARA: Because girls weren't supposed to know about money.

GORGEOUS: But you became a banker.

SARA: That's because no one ever called me Gorgeous.

Sara begins to stroke Gorgeous's hair.

GORGEOUS: I'm so tired, Sara. So very tired. Up a little higher. Mmmmmmmmmm. That feels so good. Remember when mother stroked our hair.

SARA: I remember coming home with a ninety-nine and her shrieking at me, "Where's the other point?"

GORGEOUS: Mother really missed saying goodbye to you.

SARA: Mother and I had a female trouble conflict.

GORGEOUS: She wanted to see us all happy.

SARA: We are happy, Gorgeous. It's just not our mother's kind of happiness . . . . .

Sara's anxious about Tessie. It's getting late. The sun's going down, and suddenly Gorgeous rises and insists they must light the Sabbath candles. She takes two candlesticks from the mantel, finds something to put over her head and asks for matches. Sara suggests they wait for her birthday candles, but Gorgeous chides her. She is going through the Sabbath eve rite, when Tess enters with Tom, who loudly asks if there is a seance in session. It's an ancient tribal ritual, Sara explains. Pfeni comes in, interrupting as well. When Gorgeous ends the prayer, Sara asks if she's finished. Again Gorgeous tells her she's become hard, and she goes upstairs. Tess is upset at her mother's behavior. Sara tells Pfeni to blow the candles out. Pfeni doesn't want to, but Sara insists. When the room is *"suddenly dark,"* Sara announces, "Drinks here in the sitting room at half-past."

Scene 3: Around 8:30 P.M.

Everyone is gradually gathering for a drinks scene before the birthday dinner. The talk is brisk, brittle, sometimes erudite, and covers history, politics and anti-Semitism, past and present—a sort of Mad Hatter's tea party with everyone very much in character. Sara's special guest, Nicholas Pym, admires the chevre, which Tom won't try. And when Nick discusses the availability of gefilte sandwiches, Sara, to Tess's annoyance, tells Tom he'd like them: "They're a fish cake, very much like quenelles."

Gorgeous, entering in mock Chanel evening wear, raves about her beautiful niece. Her daughters are jealous of Tess, but Gorgeous remembers knowing girls who were like Tess at this age and then had hard times later on.

Geoffrey and Pfeni appear in evening clothes (actually, Pfeni's got on Sara's good evening gown) and have prepared a playlet in honor of Sara's birthday and the collapse of the Soviet Union. Geoffrey introduces Pfeni as Anastasia Rosensweig Romanov and doesn't forget her sister, either, "the eminent Petrograd physician, Dr. Gorgeous 'Noodles' Romanov."

Geoffrey admires Merv in his new shirt. Nick asks why so many Jewish American men, professional men, wear shirts like this. "It's a money-lending uniform," Merv explains. "They're so well designed you'd never know it costs a pound of flesh to get them." Sara calls for the play to begin, and they start singing from *The Scarlet Pimpernel,* eventually marching into the dining room.

Scene 4: After dinner, around 11:30

Everyone except Gorgeous (who is clearing the table) returns to the sitting room, continuing a dinner conversation about Danny Kaye and Laurence Olivier, shocking Sara a bit. Geoffrey and Pfeni exit, off to a late meeting. Gorgeous appears with the napkin holders she hasn't known what to do with. It was a "funsy evening" but she is exhausted and exchanges goodnights. Nick must leave, as well—he's meeting his niece early the next day. He hands Sara a large gift-wrapped box and wishes Tom and Tess well on their trip. "You know the shocking thing about all this business with the Soviets is one questions what in God's name the entire twentieth century was for," he proclaims as his farewell statement.

Tess and Tom also leave. They're coordinating a candlelight vigil the next day in Hyde Park, Tom explains, thanking Sara for the party.

Sara and Merv are alone, and she begins straightening up the living room, suggesting that it's late. But Merv isn't about to be sent off, he'd rather watch her clean. He imagines her mother was a good cook, but it seems she never cooked, or cleaned. Asked if her mother was Jewish, Sara is annoyed, declaring he has a narrow perspective for a "supposedly intelligent man." He's pleased she called him intelligent. He's like all the men she went to high school with, Sara recites: smart, good provider, reads the *Times,* started running at 50, thinks about affairs but doesn't have them, and now that she's dead, his wife is saintly. Sara's upset, and Merv's telling her, "Take it easy," annoys her even further. She wants him to leave and begins to cry, then calms down a bit, and they continue talking. He's nice, but not her type, she tells him. She's not his, either, Merv admits, but he'd like to know when it was that she'd figured out "she had all the answers." It was in high school, when she realized she knew what the teacher was going to ask before she asked it, knew what would become of each girl in her class, and knew somehow she was different. She wasn't "a nice Jewish girl," Merv comments, annoying Sara again. He didn't get 800's on his college boards, Merv admits, and Sara did, it seems.

SARA: It was no big deal.

MERV: Of course it was a big deal. I'll bet the valedictorian was nowhere as intelligent as you.

SARA: Sonia Kirschenblatt. Went to Bryn Mawr, married an astronomy professor, lives in Princeton, works for educational testing.

MERV: Fuzzy brown hair. Poodle skirts. Started going to Greenwich Village bookstores at sixteen.

SARA: You knew her?

MERV: Her parents had a cabana at the Brighton Beach Baths. I was a cabana boy. I shtupped her the year before she went to Bryn Mawr.

SARA: So Sonia Kirschenblatt went to Bryn Mawr not a virgin.

MERV: It was no big deal.

SARA: Are you kidding? Thirty years ago it was a very big deal.

MERV: Look, thank God she didn't get pregnant, or today I'd be an astronomy professor at Princeton. I like talking to you, Sadie. You're a very smart woman. You're a very nice woman, and I wish you'd stop pushing the ashtray back and forth and maybe your shoulders could come down from your ears.

He starts to rub her neck.

I didn't think they could get any higher. Pretty soon they'll be on the ceiling.

SARA: Merv, do you want to "shtup" me tonight in Queen Anne's Gate, like you did Sonia Kirschenblatt that hot and lusty summer night at the Brighton Beach Baths?

MERV: We did it at Columbia in my dorm room in John Jay Hall.

SARA: They didn't allow women in Columbia rooms then.

MERV: Sonia was a woman of ingenuity. She didn't get to be valedictorian by being a half-wit.

SARA: But she wasn't so smart, either. She just worked hard. Look, Merv, if you're thinking, "I know who this woman is sitting next to me. I grew up with her, with women like her, only sometime in her life she decided to run away. She moved to England, she dyed her hair, she named her daughter Tess and sent her to Westminster. She assimilated beyond her wildest dreams, and now she's lonely and wants to come home," you're being too obvious. Yes, I'm lonely, Merv, but I don't want to come home.

When Merv talks about connecting with another person, Sara asks how many support groups he joined when his wife died—then apologizes. But he did join two, plus signing up for an Outward Bound trip to find himself. He learned that he couldn't write poetry or solve the Middle East, but that he did want to be in love again. "To have someone take care of you," Sara remarks. Merv confesses his wife was not a saint. "She drank a little, she was depressed, a little, and she thought she could have been a contender if it wasn't for me." She put Merv through school, raised the children and at last was able to take art classes at the museum for a few years before she died. He questions whether that's fair, and assures Sara that having someone take care of him has already been done.

Merv kisses Sara. She says she could never love him, and she's "old enough and kind enough" not to let him love her, but for a night she could be Sonia Kirschenblatt, and he could be a Columbia sophomore. As they start to go upstairs, Merv asks her to sing for him, but Sara won't, she just can't, and Merv sings alone to the Sinatra record he's put on as they continue up the stairs. *Curtain.*

ACT II

Scene 1: Early Saturday morning

It's 6 A.M., as Pfeni enters and Geoffrey is already "on," clowning, a one-man show in turquoise underwear and a T-shirt, dancing and lipsynching to a record of The Four Tops singing "Sugar Pie Honey Bunch." When Pfeni finally turns off the music he intimates that Sara is with Merv. Geoffrey has got to find a special plate he'd loaned to Sara that belongs to Jordan, with whom he's going to the country this afternoon. Pfeni inquires about Jordan's *Cats* friend and whether or not he's going to the country as well. Geoffrey claims Jordan is his best friend and Pfeni ought not to make things more complicated. Whenever Pfeni leaves, Geoffrey confesses, he wonders why she's going, that she belongs here with him. If getting married is what she wants, they will, and if she wants children, they'll have "a troop of them."

Geoffrey wants to know what Pfeni's working on now, and she claims she has a book on "gender and class working in a crock-pot somewhere in Tajikistan. It's writing itself." She's talked about that for years. "It's time to move on," he warns her.

GEOFFREY: Pfeni, I am serious. I've changed address books three times this year because I couldn't bear to cross out any more names. I've lost too many friends. I've seen too many lights that never had their chance to glow burn out overnight. I've tried for years now to make sense of all this, and all I know is life is random and there is no case to be made for a just or loving god. So how then do we proceed? In directing terms, what is the objective? Of course, we must cherish those that we love. That's a given. But just as important, people like you and I have to work even harder to create the best art, the best theater, the best bloody book about gender and class in Tajikistan that we possibly can. And the rest, the children, the country kitchen, the domestic bliss, we leave to others who will have different regrets. Pfeni, you and I can't idle time.

PFENI: I love you, Geoffrey. I'm not going to travel any more. I want to stay with you.

Gorgeous enters in her flannel nightgown and admires Geoffrey's legs. She noticed them because her legs are great, too, she explains. Her tour ladies are very excited about Geoffrey's agreeing to breakfast with them this morning, something Geoffrey seems to have forgotten agreeing to. When he goes off, Pfeni expresses her belief that if Geoffrey isn't every mother's dream date for her daughter, she isn't every mother's dream daughter. It's Gorgeous's view that men have no interest in "eccentric women in their forties." Maybe eccentric women in their twenties, or in their thirties, "only if you're super thin and arty successful," however. At her age now, Pfeni is liable to not even be in the marketplace.

As for Geoffrey, Gorgeous claims you can't judge a book by its cover, but Pfeni's "at the wrong library altogether." Doesn't Pfeni want what every normal woman wants? Pfeni's never sure what Gorgeous means by normal. "You and I are people people . . . . . We need warmth and cuddles and kisses," Gorgeous explains, urging Pfeni not to waste time.

Tom and Tess come downstairs and report that Sara had been dancing with the furrier last evening and that he'd been singing Frank Sinatra. When Sara enters, Gorgeous doesn't take long in getting to the point: "How was your night?" she asks, winking at her. Everyone knows she slept with the furrier, Tess tells her. "We like him," Gorgeous adds. Sara assures her she's not going "off into the sunset" with someone she's had dinner with once, and wonders if Gorgeous has ever heard of privacy. She might be the happiest woman in Newton, but Gorgeous is not her mother, Sara states. "Our mother is dead."

Gorgeous feels attacked and has quite a tirade. Gorgeous will not let Sara go on hurting her feelings because she's threatened by Gorgeous's pride in her husband, family and accomplishments. It's all very well for Sara to talk with a British accent and for Pfeni to send postcards to her children from all over the world, but Gorgeous knows that they both wish they were her. She carries on, only to upstage her own exit by tripping.

They were all having a nice time, feeling happy for her, "and then you came down and spoiled it," Tess pouts to Sara. She wants her passport because they're leaving tomorrow. Sara would rather talk about it later, but Tess wants to talk about it with Tom at hand. They may as well leave, Tess tells Tom, because Sara's thinking it's not important to have passion in one's life doesn't mean they shouldn't. Tom, before departing, tries to reassure Sara by confessing his mother and his sisters do not get on always, and that his dad sings Sinatra, too.

Sara, when she and Pfeni are alone, admits the furrier "has some very special skills." Pfeni wonders about Gorgeous and Henry having "the most delicious sex" that she's always talking about. Sara wonders if Gorgeous is the smartest of them. If Sara were settled, maybe Tess would not be on the verge of turning into "a new age Emma Goldman." Pfeni knows Sara doesn't believe that. Sara admits it, but she does want Pfeni to talk to Tess. How can she, Pfeni wonders. She spent much of last night watching Kurdish refugees on the TV, but she doesn't write about that sort of thing any more.

PFENI: Sara, I had the most unsettling experience last week. Before Bombay I went back to Doubandi, my Afghan village. I wanted to visit the women I'd written about, but when I arrived I was told that half of them were dead and the rest refugees. And Sara, with every bit of dire information, I became more and more excited to listen.

SARA: I don't understand.

PFENI: Somewhere I need the hardship of the Afghan women and the Kurdish suffering to fill up my life for me. And if I'm that empty then I might as well continue to wander to the best hotels, restaurants and poori stands.

SARA: But how are you helping them if you don't tell their stories. Is it morally better to dispatch four-star Karachi hotel reviews?

PFENI: It's wrong for me to use these women.

SARA: Pfeni, real compassion is genuinely rarer than any correct agenda. I'm a pretty good banker, but it's not a passion. You, on the other hand, have a true calling, and the sad and surprisingly weak thing is, you're actively trying to avoid it. Tessie says I should have a talk show instead of Gorgeous. "Opinions With Sara Goode."

PFENI: There is no one I rely on in my life more than you. There is no one I am more grateful to than you.

Pfeni goes off after Merv comes on. It seems Sara has a morning tennis date, and she wants to know Merv's agenda. He doesn't have a tennis date.

MERV: I've never met anyone like you, Sara. You're warm and cold all at the same time. Your face is so familiar and so distant. Sometimes I look at you and see all my mother's photographs of her mother and her mother's entire family.

SARA: Well, it's a look.

MERV: My mother's family had a villa in a spa resort in Poland called Ciechocinek. And the pictures we had were of the family gathered by the seaside. The men waving at the camera or smiling, holding up a cantaloupe! They were sweet, these men, some even handsome, but they couldn't hold a candle to the women. The women in their too-large dresses with their arms folded all had your brilliant eyes—they sparkled even from those curled and faded photographs. Unfortunately, most of them and their families didn't survive. But Sara, when I look into your eyes, I see those women's strength and their intelligence. To me you are a beautiful and most remarkable woman. Why are you laughing? You're like a teenager. I say you're beautiful, and you start laughing?

SARA: You want to hear something cuckoo, Merv?

MERV: You cuckoo? You're too "not cuckoo" for your own good.

SARA: I've been to Ciechocinek. I was sent there by the Hong Kong/Shanghai Bank.

MERV: My mother always said it was the Palm Beach of Poland.

SARA: It's now a post-modern, pre-fab, post-cold-war resort of the grey cinder block variety.

MERV: Thank God there's somewhere for me to retire besides Coral Gables. Sadie . . .

    He begins laughing.

Why did the Hong Kong Shanghainese send you to Ciechocinek? Never in my life did I think I'd be asking a woman such a question!

SARA: Someone has to pay to privatize the state industries. Capitalism is expensive, Merv. They were asking for a loan, and I was being reasonably clear.

MERV: I'm sure you were brilliant.

SARA: I was all right. But while I reviewed their detailed proposals for renovating heating services and redistricting agricultural cooperatives, I couldn't help but see it all as a minor triumph for the women with those same sparkling eyes in my mother's faded photographs. Fifty years after the lucky few had escaped with false passports, Esther Malchah's granddaughter Sara was deciding how to put bread on the tables of those who had driven them all away.

Merv wants to get to know Sara better, but she believes he would be happier with someone like Gorgeous. They are both "lively." "Too lively" and "too Jewish" is what Sara means, Merv points out. Sara reminds him of his DeWitt Clinton classmates who pretend it was a prep school not far from Groton or St. Paul's. His world differs from hers, Sara insists. It doesn't, Merv counters. He changed his name from Kantlowitz, and his daughter went to St. Paul's. He calls Sara "an American Jewish woman living in London, working for a Chinese Hong Kong bank and taking weekends at a Polish resort with a daughter who's running off to Lithuania."

Sara wants Merv to give up on her, describing herself as cold and bitter, having turned her back on family, religion and country. He wonders if it bothers her that he reminds her of home, but Sara thinks the home he means, "the Bronx, Brooklyn, the America of 40 years ago," no longer exists. She didn't have someone like him in her life at 16 and isn't going to now. He deserves someone different, someone in a "tasteful, but cheery crêpe orange suit."

MERV *(extends his hand):* It was a pleasure to meet you, Sara.

SARA: You're a very nice man.

MERV: Do women like it when a man says, "I'm sorry. You're very nice"?

SARA: No. Especially not when the man has just spent the night.

MERV: You still have all the answers, Sara.

He exits. Sara goes to the record player and puts away the Sinatra album. She picks up the Cliffe Clef album and puts it on the record player, when the phone rings. She picks up the phone.

SARA: Oh, hello, Nick. Yes it was a lovely evening. Glynebourne Tuesday would be terrific. Oh, I'm so sorry. Your gift was absolutely brilliant. And Tessie thought it was brilliant as well. Thanks so much. See you Tuesday. Goodbye.

She turns on the record player and picks up a gift box that has remained wrapped on the window seat. As she sits to open the gift, we hear on the record, "Hi, I'm Sara Rosensweig of Brooklyn, New York and we're the Cliffe Clef of 1959." There are assorted cheers. "Tonight is our concert of Europe." There are assorted laughs. Sara laughs and shrugs her shoulders. "Well, we call it that as a tribute to Metternich, Talleyrand, and other well known Harvard men." There are more laughs. "Those of us who are graduating this year . . ." (there is a whooping cheer and Sara raises her arm in triumph) ". . . each have a chance tonight to lead with her favorite song, and this one, ever since freshman year, has been mine." The group begins to sing a cappella "MacNamara's Band." Sara listens. She continues to unwrap the gift when she hears herself singing solo on the record. Suddenly she begins to sing a different verse softly.

Oh my name is Moishe Pupick
And I come from Palestine,
I live on bread and honey
And on Manischewitz wine.
Oh my mother makes the best
Gefilte fish in all the land
    Her voice cracks.
And I'm the only Yiddish girl
In MacNamara's Band.
    Sara is crying as she lifts up a standard tea kettle from the gift box.
It's brilliant, Nick. Absolutely fucking brilliant.

Scene 2: Later that afternoon

It's about 4 P.M. when Tess brings in tea for Pfeni, who is on the window seat working with her lap-top computer. When Geoffrey enters, Tess goes up to pack for her trip.

Geoffrey describes his consciousness raising by the Temple Beth El sisterhood. Mrs. Hershkovitz questioned why as a director he's paid good money to do nothing, since he did not write *The Scarlet Pimpernel* or compose the music, and he doesn't act in it. It seems Jordan was at the breakfast as well (the "Royal Jordan" flatware he designs is very popular in the U.S.).

Pfeni urges Geoffrey to sit down, but he sings and dances instead. He's "beyond manic," Pfeni remarks, and asks why. Geoffrey admits that he drove around for a long time after addressing the Gorgeous ladies. He went past the Isle of Dogs and to Greenwich and sat on the bow of the Cutty Sark thinking about the two of them. He loves her and always will, "But the truth is, I miss men." He wants to be friends with Pfeni, "the Noel and Gertie of our day." He claims he's never cheated on Pfeni. The only place she's at home, or even close to it, is when she's with him, she confesses. Geoffrey recalls their meeting at the ballet and what a dark time it was for him, that period in his life. Jordan had left him and his friends were getting more and more ill.

PFENI: So you thought to yourself, why not try something completely different. Why not get as far away from the hurt and the fear as possible. And there I was seated beside you; pretty, eccentric, and more than just a little bit lonely . . . . .

GEOFFREY: Pfeni, don't.

PFENI: Why? Am I being self-indulgent? And maybe even just a little bitchy? Geoffrey, you're the one who said we should get married that very first night. You're the one who said what beautiful children we'd have just this morning.

GEOFFREY: But we would have beautiful children. Pfeni, my friends need me.

PFENI: I never stopped you from being there for them.

GEOFFREY: I was frightened.

PFENI: And now you're not?

    Pause.

GEOFFREY: You really don't understand what it is to have absolutely no idea who you are.

PFENI: What?

GEOFFREY: I thought about this on the bow of the pirate ship. For all your wandering, you're always basically the same—you have your sisters, your point of view, and even in some casual drop-in way your God. Pfeni, the only time I have a real sense of who I am and where I'm going is when I'm in a darkened theater and we're making it all up. Starting from scratch. But now I want a real life outside the theater, too. So maybe I will regret this choice. I know I'll miss you. But I'm an instinctive person, my luv, and speaking to those ladies, it all just clicked. Today this is who I am. I have no other choice. I miss men.

PFENI: It's all right, Geoffrey, I do too.

    A car horn is heard.

Jordan.

GEOFFREY: I don't have to go.

PFENI: He's waiting for you.

GEOFFREY: We're in no rush.

PFENI: Please, Geoffrey, just go.

GEOFFREY *(he kisses her head):* Sugar pie, honey bunch.

Enter Sara in a tennis outfit, as Geoffrey is leaving.

SARA: Jordan's outside, Geoffrey. He's looking rather well. He's driving a red Miata convertible. Things must be booming in the flatware design business. I suggested he move into cups and saucers, and we'll all get into business. Pfeni can be in charge of world-wide distribution, Geoffrey, you'll be director of special events, and Jordan can introduce his new line of sheets on Gorgeous's talk show. There, I've solved all of our futures!

GEOFFREY: The thing that no one can appreciate about you, Sara, is you're remarkably sweet.

The horn honks again.

I think I have a crush on all the sisters Rosensweig.

He exits.

Pfeni has barely told Sara about Geoffrey when Gorgeous enters, sopping wet, carrying an umbrella and a shopping bag, and wearing one shoe. She perfunctorily hands the Wedgewood gift from the shopping bag to Sara with a "Thank you very much. I had a lovely stay. I'll just go upstairs and pack my things and be gone in an hour." She is going to share Mrs. Hershkovitz's room for the night. If Pfeni leaves before she comes down, it was great to see her.

Sara asks, as Gorgeous starts up the stairs, what happened to her other shoe. Irately, Gorgeous takes a heel from her bag, a four-hundred-dollar, imported-from-Italy heel, it seems. Sara urges her to sit, but she'd rather stand. Rabbi Pearlstein's told her she should finish the tour and go home. It has not been "an enjoyable trip" for her—two days with the Newton temple sisterhood and two nights with her own sisters telling her "everything I do is wrong." So she decided to treat herself to some expensive shoes, trying them on in eight stores and convincing herself she was worth it. She then decided not to take a taxi back, but when she went into the tube stop her heel caught in the escalator. Sara thinks her cobbler might repair the shoe, but Gorgeous claims they're ruined for good and throws them in the coal bin.

Sara is going to call Gorgeous's husband. He'll buy her another pair. Gorgeous is forced to admit he couldn't, that he has not worked for two years. There's a recession, she points out. Henry's partnership in a law firm was dissolved, and now he's not even looking for a job, he's "Writing mysteries in the basement. He says he could have been Raymond Chandler or Dashiell Hammett if only he hadn't been brought up in Scarsdale."

Gorgeous urges Pfeni to stick with Geoffrey who is handsome and rich, only to find out that Geoffrey's gone off with Jordan for the weekend. "I am so stupid," Pfeni says, but Gorgeous thinks she ought not to take it personally and that Sara should tell her that none of Rita Rosensweig's daughters is stupid. Then Sara reveals she's chased Merv away. She's not sure why.

Pfeni decides tea time has ended. She selects a bottle from the wine rack, a "cab-sauv." The sisters toast their mother. "And her stunningly brilliant daugh-

Christine Estabrook, Jane Alexander and Madeline Kahn as the Sisters Rosensweig—Pfeni, Sara and Gorgeous—in Wendy Wasserstein's play

ters," Sara adds. Gorgeous recalls their mother always said Sara was a shtarker, "a person who takes charge." Pfeni opines that Sara was that sort of person to Merv, and she and Gorgeous chant "Call him. Call him. Call him."

Gorgeous waxes sentimental and wishes that on some birthday just the three of them could be sitting together, and that each of them could say, that at some point, "We had a moment of pure, unadulterated happiness!" Does Sara think that's possible? "Brief. But a moment or two," Sara believes. Then she begins teasing Gorgeous, remarking that her neck is dry. Pfeni agrees. And they both agree she needs a special rejuvenation treatment. "Rabbi Pearlstein says more collagen shots!" Pfeni insists.

Scene 3: Early Sunday morning

"*Tom and Tess come downstairs. They hug, and Tom leaves with his bag.*" Tess begins talking into the tape recorder as she listens to the Clefs singing: "What did the nightingale sing in Berkeley Square?" Gorgeous comes on in an aerobic outfit, and Tess wants to interview her, first asking her to state her name. Gorgeous does so, adding that she's a housewife, mother and radio personality. Tess wants to know about Sara's girlhood. She had no sense of style, Gorgeous recalls. "Her dolls were always half-naked, and mine were perfectly groomed." It seems Gorgeous gave Sara her prescription for dressing for success. "Accessories are the key to fashion," she confides, urging Tess to put together an ensemble from her closet today and wear it around and let her check it. Gorgeous's own daughters were taught this way and have thanked her for it.

Pfeni comes on with her shopping bags, ready to leave. She's going to Tajikistan and wonders if Tess is leaving for Vilnius. Tess is not. At the rally the night before, with everyone holding hands and singing folk songs and smiling, she began to feel more and more apart from it all. She asks Pfeni if Rosensweigs are people who always watch and never belong. Pfeni wonders how Tess got to be "so young and intelligent."

Pfeni kisses Gorgeous, who reminds Pfeni to use sunblock. But what if she needs her aunt? Tess asks Pfeni. Pfeni reassures her that the best life advice she's ever had is from her mother and the best moisturizer was from Gorgeous, and between the two of them they are able to cover "the entire temporal and spiritual world."

The doorbell rings—it's Merv with a large box. He's come because there was a message from Sara he'd left his shirt. The box is for Sara, Gorgeous assumes, but actually it's for her. It was on the steps outside. It's a Chanel suit, plus purse, earrings and shoes, a thank-you gift from Mrs. Hershkovitz and the sisterhood. Gorgeous is ecstatic, putting it on immediately over her aerobic outfit. She hasn't been so happy since the day she learned she made cheerleader and Sara hadn't, and she feels like Audrey Hepburn. Gorgeous plans to go to Claridge's to show Mrs. Hershkovitz and the ladies how she looks and then to the House of Chanel to return everything. Pfeni's shocked, but Gorgeous explains that somebody has to pay tuition this fall. She asks Tess to put her sneakers and purse in the box. Pfeni can drop her off. She'll jog home "just for funsy." And they'd better hurry, or she will lose her will power. She goes off.

Pfeni calls off to Sara to say she's leaving. Sara comes down to find Merv there. Pfeni leaves, and Tess goes off to get Merv's shirt. Merv's got a lunch date with the rabbi of Dublin, and the car's waiting, but Sara's trying to stall him. He wonders what's on her mind. Did he know there were 46 cabbage rose bouquets on this wallpaper? she asks him. It seems she spent yesterday afternoon from tea time until sundown on the sofa counting them and waiting for Merv to call her. And after her sisters went to bed she did not enjoy getting into hers with her mystery novel and licking the chocolate off her favorite wheatmeal biscuits. She called him because she couldn't seem to "come up with a good enough answer for what's wrong with you." She likes him. Merv wants to know why. "You're a man who says he wants a grown-up," is her answer. Merv doesn't consider licking wheat-meal biscuits in bed grown up. He might like to try it, she remarks. It isn't that she's thinking about their getting married, but she doesn't seem to want the relationship to be over.

SARA: Grown-ups can be difficult.

MERV: But difficult can be engaging. Even surprising. I meant to tell you I had dinner last night at that tourist trap Simpson's on the Strand and the bubble and squeak was rather good, actually.

SARA: Actually?

MERV: There are real possibilities in life, Sara, even for left-over meat and cabbage. And speaking of cabbage. The rabbi of Dublin!!

SARA: Go, go, go! Here, take this on your pilgrimage. It's the god Shiva.

MERV: The destroyer! I'm getting on a plane.

SARA: It'll ward off evil and bring you hope and rebirth.

MERV: You want me to worship pagan imagery?

SARA: I want to stir up your life a little, Mervyn Kantlowitz. Jesus Christ, why did your name have to be Mervyn?

She starts to hit him.

And you're a furrier!

MERV: Goodbye, Sara.

He kisses her.

Merv leaves and Tess comes on, wearing Gorgeous's mock Chanel complete with accessories. She thinks it's very "too-too," as Gorgeous would say. "I think maybe too 'too-too' for the Lithuanian resistance," Sara comments. But Tess has told Tom to go without her. "You have to have your own life," Tess announces, but she doesn't even know what it is. She's never really been Jewish. She's not actually American now, or English or European—who is she?

SARA: Tessie, honey, as a child I was told that when your grandmother Rita was a girl she was so smart, so competent, so beautiful and brave, that on the day the Cossacks came they were so impressed with her they ran away.

TESS: I don't understand.

SARA: Everyone always told me, "Sadie, that Tessie of yours is just like Rita." So if Rita could make the Cossacks run away, you are smart enough, and brave enough, and certainly beautiful enough to find your place in the world.

TESS: Thank you, Mommy.

SARA: There are possibilities in life, Tessie.

TESS: Mother!

SARA: Yes, honey.

TESS: If she was so beautiful why did they run away?

SARA: I never understood that either.

Tess's paper is due the next day, so she needs to ask Sara more questions. She has to start with her name. "My name is Sara Rosensweig. I am the daughter of Rita and Maury Rosensweig. I was born in Brooklyn, New York, August twenty-third, 1937." As to the first time she sang, Sara claims she made her debut at La Scala at 14, then changes it to the Hanukkah Festival at East Midwood Jewish Center. She played a candle. And she became a Cliffe Clef because Tess's great-grandfather thought she could be a singer. Tess wants her to sing now. Sara protests, but when Tess begins singing "Shine on, Harvest Moon," Sara joins in. *Curtain.*

OLEANNA

A Play in Two Acts

BY DAVID MAMET

Cast and credits appear on page 340

DAVID MAMET was born November 30, 1947 in Chicago. He graduated from Goddard College in Vermont with a B.A. in English literature in 1969, after observing creative theater at close quarters as a busboy at Chicago's theater group Second City and having studied it at a professional school in New York. From 1971 to 1973 he was artist-in-residence at Goddard. In 1974 he became a member of the Illinois Arts Council faculty, and in 1975 he helped found and served for a time as artistic director of St. Nicholas Theater Company in Chicago, which mounted some of the first productions of his scripts including Reunion, Squirrels, Duck Variations *and* Sexual Perversity in Chicago.

Mamet's first New York production was Duck Variations *off off Broadway at St. Clements in May 1975, followed by* Sexual Perversity *at the same group in September 1975. His* American Buffalo *moved from its world premiere at Chicago's Goodman Theater in October 1975 to St. Clements in January 1976. Mamet received the 1975–76 Obie Award as best playwright for these OOB productions, but his career on the wider New York stages began officially with the off-Broadway program of* Duck Variations *and* Sexual Perversity *at the Cherry*

Lane theater for 273 performances beginning June 16, 1976. Later that season, on February 16, 1977, his American Buffalo *was produced on Broadway, ran 135 performances, was named a Best Play of its season, won the Critics Award for best American play and established its author in the front rank of contemporary American playwrights with productions all over the world. It has been revived in New York June 3, 1981 for 262 performances off Broadway and October 27, 1983 for 102 performances on Broadway.*

Mamet's second Best Play, A Life in the Theater, *was presented off Broadway October 20, 1977 for 288 performances. His third,* Glengarry Glen Ross, *premiered January 27, 1984 at the Goodman Theater and opened on Broadway March 25, 1984, winning the Critics Award for best American play and the Pulitzer Prize (for its original staging in Chicago). Tony nominations that year included* Glengarry Glen Ross *for best play and* American Buffalo *for best revival, an unusual instance of an author with two different plays cited in two different categories in the same season.*

Mamet's fourth Best Play was Speed-the-Plow, *produced on Broadway May 3, 1988 just in time for a Tony nomination and minority representation in the Critics Award voting. It ran for 278 performances. This season's* Oleanna *is his fifth Best Play, presented under Mamet's direction in the Back Bay Theater production, which had premiered May 1, 1992 at the American Repertory Theater in Cambridge, Mass. before arriving off Broadway October 25, 1992.*

Off-Broadway productions of works by this prolific and versatile playwright have included The Water Engine *(1977, transferred to Broadway with the curtain-raiser* Mr. Happiness*);* The Woods *(1979), a program of one-acts comprising* The Sanctity of Marriage, Dark Pony *and* Reunion; Edmond *(1982);* Prairie du Chien *and* The Shawl *(1985);* Vint *(1986, from a translation by Avrahm Yarmolinsky);* Where Were You When It Went Down *(1988, a sketch for the Manhattan Theater Club revue* Urban Blight*); and the one-act* Bobby Gould in Hell *on the Lincoln Center program* Oh, Hell! *(1989). For the theater Mamet is also the author of* Lakeboat, The Revenge of the Space Pandas, The Spanish Prisoner, The Frog Prince *(staged OOB in 1985);* Two War Scenes: Cross Patch *and* Goldberg Street *(staged OOB in Ensemble Studio Theater's 1990 Marathon),* The Old Neighborhood *and translations/adaptations of Pierre Laville's* Red River *and Anton Chekhov's* The Cherry Orchard, Uncle Vanya *and* Three Sisters *(the latter presented OOB by Atlantic Theater Company last season).*

Mamet's screen plays have included The Postman Always Rings Twice, The Verdict, The Untouchables, House of Games *(writer-director),* Things Change *(co-author-director),* Homicide *(writer-director) and* Hoffa. *His work for the printed page includes* Warm and Cold *(a children's book);* Writing in Restaurants, Some Freaks *and* The Cabin *(essays);* On Directing Film; The Hero Pony *(poems); and* The Owl *(a children's book co-authored with his first wife, Lindsay Crouse).*

Mamet's long list of honors features many Joseph Jefferson Awards for distin-

guished Chicago offerings and grants from New York State Council on the Arts Plays for Young Audiences, Rockefeller (as playwright-in-residence) and CBS at Yale. He has taught acting and directing at NYU and the University of Chicago as well as at Yale Drama School. His activities often extend to Vermont, New York, Los Angeles and beyond, but home base for his wife (Rebecca Pidgeon, who played the female role in Oleanna*) and himself is Cambridge, Mass.*

Place: John's office

ACT I

SYNOPSIS: Carol, a student, age 20, is seated across from John's desk, where John, a professor in his 40s, is talking on the phone—a lengthy conversation with his wife about their proposed purchase of a house. He promises to join her shortly to help straighten out some problems that have arisen.

John hangs up the phone and apologizes for having kept Carol waiting. Carol gropingly inquires about a real estate term she's overheard, as though trying to postpone getting down to the matter about which she's come to see John, who also seems reluctant to get down to brass tacks.

JOHN: I know how . . . *believe* me. I know how . . . potentially *humiliating* these . . . I have no desire to . . . I have no desire other than to help you. But:
He picks up some papers on his desk.
I won't even say "but." I'll say that as I go back over the . . .

CAROL: I'm just, I'm just trying to . . .

JOHN: . . . no, it will not do.

CAROL: . . . what? What will . . . ?

JOHN: No. I see, I see what you, it . . . *(He gestures to the papers.)* but your work . . .

CAROL: I'm just: I just sit in class I . . .
She holds up her notebook.
I take notes . . .

JOHN *(simultaneously with "notes")*: Yes. I understand. What I am trying to *tell* you is that some, some basic . . .

CAROL: . . . I . . .

JOHN: . . . one moment: some basic missed-communi . . .

CAROL: I'm doing what I'm told. I bought your book, I read your . . .

JOHN: No, I'm sure you . . .

CAROL: No, no, no. I'm doing what I'm told. It's *difficult* for me. It's *difficult* . . .

JOHN: . . . but . . .

CAROL: I don't . . . lots of the *language* . . .

JOHN: . . . please . . .

CAROL: The *language,* the "things" that you say . . .

JOHN: I'm sorry. No. I don't think that's true.

Carol is very bright, John insists, and shouldn't be having trouble under-standing. Carol implies that her limited social background may be making it difficult for her to adjust to this new world of learning. John in his turn implies that perhaps his course is not right for her. He illustrates by reading from one of her papers the meaningless sentence, "I think that the ideas contained in this work express the author's feelings in a way that he intended, based on his results." "What can that mean?" John wonders, but instead of answering him, Carol pleads that she *must* pass John's course, it's absolutely imperative.

JOHN: Well.

CAROL: . . . don't you . . .

JOHN: Either the . . .

CAROL: . . . I . . .

JOHN: . . . either the, I . . . either the *criteria* for *judging* progress in the class are . . .

CAROL: No, no, no, no, I have to pass it.

JOHN: Now look: I'm a human being, I . . .

CAROL: I did what you told me. I did, I did everything that, I read your *book,* you told me to buy your book and read it. Everything you *say* I . . . *(She gestures to her notebook. The phone rings.)* I do . . . Ev . . .

JOHN: . . . look:

CAROL: . . . everything I'm told . . .

JOHN: Look, look. I'm not your *father.*

CAROL: What?

JOHN: I'm.

CAROL: Did I say you were my father?

JOHN: . . . no . . .

CAROL: Why did you say that . . . ?

JOHN: I . . .

CAROL: . . . why . . . ?

But John must interrupt this exchange to answer the phone. He cuts the caller short, promising to call back, and hangs up.

John tries to explain that they are both in a rigidly prescribed, institutional, student-teacher relationship and wants to know what Carol expects him to do other than he's now doing within that relationship. Carol begs him to *teach* her; to help her understand, for example, the contents of his book, incomprehensible

The spring and summer replacement cast—Mary McCann as Carol and Treat Williams as John—in the opening scene of David Mamet's *Oleanna*

to her. Like others, she came here to be helped, to learn something in order "To get on in the world," but she can't learn if she understands nothing of what they're trying to teach her. It makes her think she's stupid. John denies that she is, but Carol had noticed John's question "What can that mean?" after he read the excerpt from her paper, and she insists that this was the equivalent of calling her stupid (and of course John denies that he'd ever do such a thing).

Carol goes on: "Nobody *tells* me anything. And I *sit* there . . . in the *corner*. In the *back*. And everybody's talking about 'This' all the time. And 'concepts,' and 'precepts' and, and, and, WHAT IN THE WORLD ARE YOU *TALKING* ABOUT? . . . . . I DON'T KNOW WHAT IT MEANS AND I'M *FAILING* . . . . . I know I'm stupid. I know what I am. *(Pause.)* I know what I am, Professor. You don't have to tell me. *(Pause.)* It's pathetic. Isn't it?"

Carol rises to leave, but John asks her to sit down and listen to him, which she does. John confesses to her that he was raised to believe he was stupid, his inadequacies repeated again and again by his elders. That's the very point he's been trying to explain in class: you can make a child lose confidence in himself simply by repeating denigration. He blames himself for not having been able to make Carol understand—maybe because he's been distracted by concerns over the purchase of the house. He likens himself to an airplane pilot whose attention is distracted for a moment and who then becomes so distressed by his awareness of this distraction that he loses control entirely and crashes the plane.

JOHN: . . . . . This is what I learned. It is Not Magic. Yes. Yes. *You.* You are going to be frightened. When faced with WHAT MAY OR MAY NOT BE BUT THAT WHICH YOU ARE GOING TO PERCEIVE AS a test. You will become frightened. And you will say: I am incapable of . . . and everything *in* you will think these two things. "I must. But I can't." And you will think: *(Pause.)* Why was I born to be the laughing stock of a world in which everyone is better than I? In which I am entitled to nothing. Where I can not learn.
　　　　Pause.
CAROL: Is that . . . *(Pause.)* Is that what I have . . . ?
JOHN: Well. I don't know if I'd put it that way. Listen: I'm talking to you as I'd talk to my son. Because that's what I'd like him to have that I never had. I'm talking to you the way I wish that someone had talked to me. I don't know how to do it other than to be *personal,* . . . with you, but . . .
CAROL: Why would you want to be personal with me?
JOHN: Well, you see? That's what I'm saying. We can only interpret the behavior of others through the screen we . . .

But the ringing phone interrupts. John assures the caller (his wife) that everything's going to be all right and that he'll join her as soon as he finishes this conference with a student.

John is buying a new house in line with his expected promotion, and Carol feels that he should attend to it instead of prolonging this meeting. John has stayed because "I like you," and he likes her because "Perhaps we're similar." Like her, he has "problems," and when she asks him what they are, he temporarily abandons the constraints of the student-teacher relationship, the "Artificial Stricture," to answer and tell her what his problems are. He came late to teaching because he was suspicious of the entire education process. "I *knew* I was going to fail. Because I was a *fuck* up," he confides in Carol. He finally learned to think well of himself and suggests to Carol that the tests encountered in the classroom and indeed in life are largely nonsense, not a test of real worth but of the mechanics of repeating memorized information.

CAROL: . . . no . . .
JOHN: Yes. They're *garbage.* They're a *joke.* Look at me. Look at me. The Tenure Committee. The Tenure Committee. Come to judge me. The Bad Tenure Committee. The "Test." Do you see? They put me to the test. Why, they had people voting on me I wouldn't employ to wax my car. And yet, I go before the

Great Tenure Committee, and I have an urge, to *vomit,* to, to, to, puke my *badness* on the table, to show them: "I'm no good. Why would you pick *me?*"

CAROL: They granted you tenure.

JOHN: Oh, no, they announced it, but they haven't *signed* it. Do you see? "At any moment . . ."

CAROL: . . . mm . . .

JOHN: "They might not *sign*" . . . "I might not" . . . "the *house* might not go through . . ." Eh? Eh? They'll find out "my dark secret."

     Pause.

CAROL: . . . what is it . . . ?

JOHN: There *isn't* one. But *they:* will find an index of my badness.

CAROL: Index?

JOHN: A ". . . pointer." A "Pointer." You see? Do you see? I *understand* you. I. Know. That. Feeling. Am I entitled to my job, and my nice *home* and my *wife,* and my *family,* and so on. This is what I'm *saying:* That theory of education which, that *theory* . . . . .

But Carol cannot follow John's reasoning. She wants to know what he's going to do about her grade, and John sympathizes with her preoccupation. The telephone rings, but John ignores it. He rummages in his desk, finds her test paper, tears it up and promises her an A if she will keep on meeting with him so that they can start over, from the beginning: "I'm going to say it was not you, it was I who was not paying attention . . . . . What's important is that I awake your interest, if I can, and that I answer your questions."

Carol doesn't believe that John can ignore the college rules and structure to the extent of starting the whole course over with her. He insists he can—"We won't tell anybody"—and assures her he'll do this for her because he likes her.

Carol checks her notes (though John wishes she'd talk from memory to see if his ideas have had any impact on her) and finds that John's classroom subjects have included hazing ("ritualized annoyance" such as a teacher's harrassment of his pupils, "a sick game"), justice and fair trials (but a trial is superfluous unless one stands accused) and universal entitlement to higher education ("A confusion between equity and *utility* . . . . . we confound the *usefulness* of higher education with our, granted, right to equal access to the same. We, in effect, create a *prejudice* toward it").

In her hesitant manner, Carol indicates that she can't agree with his calling the right of everyone to a college education a form of prejudice.

CAROL *(checks her notes):* How can you say in a class. Say in a college class, that college education is prejudice?

JOHN: I said that our predilection for it . . .

CAROL: Predilection . . .

JOHN: . . . you know what that means.

CAROL: Does it mean "liking"?

JOHN: Yes.

CAROL: But how can you say that? That college . . .

JOHN: . . . that's my *job*. Don't you know?

CAROL: What is?

JOHN: To provoke you.

CAROL: No.

JOHN: Oh. Yes, though.

CAROL: To provoke me?

JOHN: That's right.

CAROL: To make me mad?

JOHN: That's right. To force you . . .

CAROL: . . . to make me mad is your job?

JOHN: To force you to . . . listen: *(Pause.)* Ah. *(Pause.)* When I was young somebody told me, are you ready, the rich copulate less often than the poor. But when they do, they take more of their clothes off. Years. Years, mind you, I would compare experiences of my own to this dictum, saying, aha, this fits the norm, or ah, this is a variation from it.

The fact is, though (John continues), it's meaningless, and he can't understand why the saying has stuck so firmly in his memory all these years. In the same way, Carol has accepted the premise that "higher education is an unassailable good," though the fact is that the middle class has come to consider it a right, without asking themselves, "What is it good for?"

John pauses to make a note, not on the subject of education but re his purchase of the new house, close to a private school where he intends to send his child, muttering that mandatory support of the public schools is "The White Man's Burden."

Carol is taking notes on John's conversation, which she wants to remember, though she disagrees completely with his put-down of equal access to education, suggesting that he is telling his students they are wasting their time when he defines education as "prolongued and systematic hazing." John suggests that they look into the demographics, the charts of business success of college-educated men and women during the last century, but Carol declares she cannot get anything from charts and so-called "concepts."

CAROL: . . . . . I DON'T UNDERSTAND. DO YOU SEE??? I DON'T *UNDERSTAND* . . .

JOHN: What?

CAROL: *Any* of it. *Any* of it. I'm *smiling* in class, I'm *smiling,* the whole time. What are you *talking* about? What is everyone *talking* about? I don't *understand.* I don't know what it *means.* I don't know what it means to *be* here

. . . you tell me I'm intelligent, and then you tell me I should not be *here,* what do you *want* with me? What does it *mean?* Who should I *listen* to . . . I . . .
> *John goes over and embraces her.*

No.

JOHN: Sshhhh.

CAROL: No, I don't under . . .

JOHN: Sshhhh.

CAROL: I don't know what you're *saying* . . .

JOHN: Sshhhh. It's all right.

CAROL: . . . I have no . . .

JOHN: Sshhhh. Sshhhh. Let it go a moment. *(Pause.)* Sshhhh . . . let it go. *(Pause.)* Just let it go . . . . .

Carol is on the point of explaining her feelings ("I always . . . all my life . . . I have never told anyone this"), when the phone interrupts. John is told that there's some kind of technical problem with the purchase of the house and his presence is required immediately. When he angrily asserts that he won't take no for an answer, even if he must take the matter to court, the caller reassures him that there's really nothing wrong—they're just pretending a crisis in order to get him to come to the new house for a surprise party to celebrate the forthcoming tenure announcement. Carol and John agree that John must go, even though John considers a surprise party "a form of aggression." *Curtain.*

ACT II

Scene 1

John and Carol are seated across from each other at the same desk in the same office, but time has passed and brought with it one immediately obvious change: Carol is no longer clothed in the shapeless, ill-matched, nondescript raiment of the previous scene but is now "with it," in mannish attire bespeaking the sartorial correctness of her student world.

John is in the midst of a long explanation, almost a lecture, to Carol about his love and style of teaching and the present status of his career: on the threshold of tenure, which is very important to him, as it offers him and his family a much improved lifestyle. So he was shocked, and hurt as well, when he learned that Carol had filed a complaint against him with the Tenure Committee—a complaint which (he concedes) Carol had a right to make if she felt that way about it, but which the Committee is bound to dismiss. In the meantime, though, the delay may cause him to lose the house. John has asked her to meet with him here, not to force, bribe or convince her to retract, but simply to explain what she thinks he's done to her.

CAROL: Whatever you have done to me—to the extent that you've done it to *me,* do you know, rather than to me as a *student,* and, so to the student body, is contained in my report. To the Tenure Committee.

JOHN: Well, all right. *(Pause.)* Let's see. *(Reads.)* I find that I am sexist. I am *elitist.* I'm not sure I know what that means, other than it's a derogatory word meaning "bad." That I . . . That I insist on wasting time, in non-prescribed, self-aggrandizing and theatrical *diversions* from the prescribed *text . . .* that these have taken both sexist and pornographic forms . . . here we find listed . . . *(Pause.)* Here we find listed . . . instances ". . . closeted with a student" . . . "Told a rambling, sexually explicit story, in which the frequency and attitudes of fornication of the poor and rich are, it would seem, the central point . . . moved to *embrace* said student and . . . all part of a pattern . . ." *(Pause. Reading.)* That I used the phrase "The White Man's Burden" . . . that I told you how I'd asked you to my room because I quote "like you." *(Pause. He reads.)* "He said he 'liked' me. That he 'liked being with me.' He'd let me write my examination paper over, if I could come back oftener to see him in his office." *(Pause. To Carol.)* It's *ludicrous.* Don't you know that? It's not *necessary.* It's going to *humiliate* you, and it's going to cost me my *house,* and . . .

CAROL: It's "ludicrous" . . .?

JOHN *(picks up the report and reads again):* "He told me he had problems with his wife and that he wanted to take off the artifical stricture of Teacher and Student. He put his arm around me . . ."

CAROL: Do you deny it? Can you deny it . . . ? Do you see? *(Pause.)* Don't you see? You don't see, do you?

JOHN: I don't see.

These things happened, Carol insists, whatever interpretation of them John might prefer. John reads again from the report—"He told me that if I would stay alone with him in his office, he would change my grade to an A—and insists he was only trying to help." Carol replies, "Do you see? DO YOU SEE? You can't *do* that any more. You. Do. Not. Have. The. Power. Did you misuse it? *Someone* did. Are you part of that group? *Yes. Yes.* You Are. You've *done* these things. And to say, to say, 'Oh. Let me help you with your problem . . .' "

John understands that he has hurt Carol, somehow, but argues that he has rights too, and his whole career and lifestyle are at the mercy of the Tenure Committee, "Good men and true." Carol points out that this flippancy is sexually demeaning, as there is a woman on that committee. Carol has come to this meeting as a favor, at John's request, "On my behalf and on behalf of my group," to repeat her protest against his "manipulative" and even "porno-graphic" lording-it-over a female student in a private interview. Carol accuses John of enjoying the power he acquired while rising through the upward steps of his profession, and at the same time neglecting "the aspirations of your students, of *hard-working students,* who come here, who *slave* to come here—you have no idea what it cost me to come to this school—you *mock* us. You call education 'hazing,' and from your so-protected, so-elitist seat you hold our confusion as a *joke,* and our hopes and efforts with it. Then you sit there and say, 'What have I done?' And ask me to *understand* that *you* have aspirations too. But I tell you. I tell you. That you are vile. And that you are exploitative. And if you possess one ounce of that inner honesty you describe in your book, you can look in yourself and see those things that I see."

John explains carefully that neither of them is an extremist; they are both human and therefore imperfect, and in some ways in conflict. John's job in class (he continues) is to communicate what he thinks to his students, who have come to class to learn about education: "I don't know that I can teach you about education. But I know that I can tell you what I think about education, and then you decide. And you don't have to fight with me. *I'm* not the subject. *(Pause.)* And where I'm *wrong* . . . perhaps it's not your job to 'fix' me. I don't want to fix *you.*"

When John asks her what it is she feels and is driving at, Carol begins with "My group . . ." but before she can go on, the ringing phone interrupts. John assures the caller that the house deal will go through despite the problem that has arisen. After he hangs up he tries to return to a review of Carol's complaint to the Tenure Committee, but Carol refuses to go into it any deeper here—they'll have plenty of chance to express their views at the Committee hearing.

JOHN: Yes, but I'm saying: we can talk about it *now,* as easily as . . .

CAROL: No. I think that we should . . . stick to the process . . .

JOHN: . . . wait a . . .

CAROL: . . . the "conventional" process. As you said. *(She gets up.)* And you're right. I'm sorry if I was, um, if I was "discourteous" to you. You're right.

JOHN: Wait, wait a . . .

CAROL: I really should go.

JOHN: Now look, granted. I have an interest. In the status quo. All right? Everyone does. But what I'm saying is that the *Committee. .*

CAROL: Professor, you're right. Just don't impinge on me. We'll take our differences, and . . .

JOHN: You're going to make a . . . look, look, look, you're going to . . .

CAROL: I shouldn't have come here. They told me . . .

JOHN: One moment. No. No. There are *norms,* here, and there's no reason. Look: I'm trying to *save* you . . .

CAROL: No one *asked* you to . . . you're trying to save *me?* Do me the courtesy to . . .

JOHN: I *am* doing you the courtesy. I'm talking *straight* to you. We can settle this *now.* And I want you to sit *down* and . . .

CAROL: You must excuse me . . .

JOHN: Sit down, it seems we each have a . . . Wait one moment. Wait one moment . . . just do me the courtesy to . . .

He restrains her from leaving.

CAROL: LET ME GO.

JOHN: I have no desire to *hold* you, I just want to *talk* to you . . .

CAROL: LET ME GO. LET ME GO. WOULD SOMEBODY *HELP* ME? WOULD SOMEBODY *HELP* ME? PLEASE . . .

Blackout.

Scene 2

Again, John and Carol are seated across the desk in his office. John appears subdued, Carol more confident, as John explains why he's asked her to come here (though the Court Officers advised Carol not to come, and she was "shocked" that John asked to meet with her). John wants her to hear him out, admits that he probably owes her an apology, on the basis of her "accusations" to the Tenure Committee. Arrogantly, Carol reminds him that these are no longer "accusations," "They have been proved, they are facts." The Committee

The original cast—Rebecca Pidgeon as Carol and William H. Macy as John—in the final scene of *Oleanna*

has reviewed them and ruled against John on the basis of his behaviour in class and here in his office.

Haltingly, after being interrupted by a phone call, John tries to make Carol reflect on the serious consequences to him of her actions: "They're going to discharge me." Her reply is, "And full well they should." He has no one to blame but himself for these consequences, and if he's asked her here to try to charm her into taking back her testimony, he's making a mistake: "Why should I . . . ? What I say is right. You tell me, you are going to tell me that you have a wife and child. You are going to say that you have a career and that you've worked for twenty years for this. Do you know what you've *worked* for? *Power.* For *power.* Do you understand? You sit there, and you tell me *stories.* About your *house,* about all the private *schools,* and about *privilege,* and how you are entitled. To *buy,* to *Spend,* to *mock,* to *summon.* All your stories. All your silly weak *guilt,* it's all about *privilege;* and you won't know it. Don't you see? You worked twenty years for the right to *insult* me. And you feel entitled to be *paid* for it. Your Home. Your Wife . . . Your sweet 'deposit' on your house . . ."

John reacts: "Don't you have feelings?"—feelings which would make her hesitate wantonly to damage someone else's life. But Carol's responsibility to her fellow-sufferers, her "group," takes precedence over all else in opposing what she sees as John's push toward unlimited power to patronize his students even to the point of sexist remarks like "Have a good day, dear" or "Now: don't *you* look fetching." As Carol sees it, "What is that but rape?" And the tone of John's book (she continues, producing it) proves that he believes in nothing at all, not even in freedom of thought. He believes only in his own freedom to pursue his elitist objectives.

Carol suggests that John thinks of her as "a frightened, repressed, confused, I don't know, abandoned, young thing of some doubtful sexuality, who wants, power and revenge." She isn't interested in revenge, though. She hasn't come here for that, she's come to tell him he has been terribly wrong.

CAROL: . . . . . Do you hate me now?
　　　Pause.
JOHN: Yes.
CAROL: Why do you hate me? Because you think me wrong? No. Because I have, you think, *power* over you. Listen to me, Professor. *(Pause.)* It is the power that you hate. So DEEPLY that, that *any atmosphere of free discussion is impossible.* It's not "unlikely." It's *impossible.* Isn't it?
JOHN: Yes.
CAROL: *Isn't* it . . ."
JOHN: Yes. I suppose.
CAROL: Now. The thing which you find so cruel is the selfsame process of selection I, and my group, go through *every day of our lives.* In admittance to school. In our tests, in our class rankings . . . Is it unfair? I can't tell you. But,

if it is fair. Or even if it is "unfortunate but necessary" for us, then, by God, so must it be for you. *(Pause.)* You write of your "responsibility to the young." Treat us with respect, and that will *show* you your responsibility. You write that education is just hazing. *(Pause.)* But we worked to get to this school. *(Pause.)* And some of us. *(Pause.)* Overcame prejudices. Economic, sexual, you cannot begin to imagine. And endure humiliations I *pray* that you and those you love never will encounter. *(Pause.)* To gain admittance here. To pursue that same dream of security *you* pursue. We, who, who are, at any moment, in danger of being deprived of it. By . . .

JOHN: . . . by . . . ?

CAROL: By the administration. By the teachers. By *you.* By, say, one low grade, that keeps us out of graduate school; by one, say, one capricious or inventive answer on our parts which, perhaps, you don't find amusing. Now you *know,* do you see? What it is to be subject to that power.

Carol goes on, reviewing John's offenses, interpreting some of them as sexual misconduct whether or not John views them as such—"It's not for you to say." But then Carol insinuates that her group might consider saving John's job for him by withdrawing the complaint as a gesture of friendship—but they would want him to teach from certain books they have chosen (Carol hands him the list of titles) in the belief that the teacher has no God-given right to be the only one to delineate the course of study.

Even before he notices that his book is not on the group's list, John sees Carol's offer as a threat to academic freedom. Accepting it is "out of the question," his name is on the door of his classroom and on the title page of his book, and he has a responsibility to guard the integrity of his teaching, if only to pass along a reputation of which his son can some day be proud.

John informs Carol that he hasn't been home for a couple of days, he's been isolated in a hotel room thinking things out and has decided: "You're *dangerous,* you're wrong and it's my job . . . to say no to you." Meanwhile the phone has started ringing, and Carol, having commented "You haven't been home in two days," advises John to answer it. It's John's lawyer, who informs John of a new development in John's case. Carol has assumed John already knew about it and tells him, after he hangs up the phone, "You tried to rape me. I was leaving this office, you 'pressed' yourself into me." Her group is considering the possibility of filing criminal charges against John.

JOHN: . . . no . . .

CAROL: . . . under the statute. I am told. It was battery.

JOHN: . . . no . . .

CAROL: Yes. And attempted rape. That's right.
    Pause.

JOHN: I think that you should go.

CAROL: Of course. I thought you knew.

JOHN: I have to talk to my lawyer.

CAROL: Yes. Perhaps you should.

The phone rings again. John picks it up.

JOHN *(into phone):* Hello? I . . . Hello . . . ? I . . . Yes, he just called. No . . . I. I can't talk to you now, Baby. *(To Carol.)* Get out.

CAROL: . . . your wife . . . ?

JOHN: . . . who it is is no concern of yours. Get out. *(To phone.)* No, no, it's going to be all right. I. I can't talk now, Baby. *(To Carol.)* Get out of here.

CAROL: I'm going.

JOHN: Good.

CAROL *(exiting):* . . and don't call your wife "Baby."

JOHN: What?

CAROL: Don't call your wife "Baby." You heard what I said.

Carol starts to leave the room. John grabs her and begins to beat her.

JOHN: . . . You vicious little bitch. You think you can come in here with your Political Correctness and destroy my *life?*

He knocks her to the floor.

You should be . . . *Rape* you . . . ? I wouldn't touch you with a ten-foot pole.

He picks up a chair, raises it above his head and advances on her.

You little *cunt* . . .

She cowers on the floor below him. Pause. He looks down at her. He lowers the chair. He moves to his desk and arranges the papers on it. Pause. He looks over at her.

Well . . .

Pause. She looks at him.

CAROL: Yes. That's right. (*She looks away from him and lowers her head. To herself.*) Yes. That's right.

Curtain.

JOINED AT THE HEAD

A Play in Two Acts

BY CATHERINE BUTTERFIELD

Cast and credits appear on pages 329, 330

CATHERINE BUTTERFIELD was born in New York City but grew up in the 1960s in Minnesota and Massachusetts, where her father was a general manager of CBS affiliates and her mother, a graduate of Yale Drama School, wrote for CBS radio. Creating and acting in stage material was one of her enthusiasms from childhood on through school, high school and college at S.M.U. in Dallas, and afterwards in an acting career temporarily slowed by illness in 1983. Her first New York appearance of record was as both author and performer in her solo piece Bobo's Birthday *in the American Humorists series at American Place April 23, 1990. Her first full-fledged New York production,* Joined at the Head, *was produced by Manhattan Theater Club this season on November 15 for 41 performances and a Best Play citation for its author, who also played the major role of Maggy Burroughs in it.*

Butterfield's playscripts produced in cross-country theater have included Under My Skin, Life in the Trees *(winning her the Davie Award at the GeVa Theater in Rochester, N.Y.) and* Showing at Delphi. *Her acting credits include the national tour of* The Heidi Chronicles *and cross-country appearances in her own* Bobo's Birthday. *Butterfield recently received a Fund for American Plays Roger L. Stevens Award for outstanding promise as a playwright. She is married to Larry Corsa, a talent agent, and they live in California.*

Place: In and around Boston

ACT I

SYNOPSIS: Maggie Mulroney, a writer in her late thirties, is visiting Boston for a signing of her latest book.

Lights up on Maggie.

MAGGIE *(to the audience):* I was walking down Newbury Street in Boston on a very brisk, very clear day, late afternoon. Low on the horizon, the white winter sun shone directly in my face. It dazzled me, this light. I could see shadow forms of people coming toward me, but I couldn't make out faces, and I couldn't make out buildings, and I felt like I was almost blind, although my eyes were wide open. How to describe it—I felt like a camera with its lens open too far . . . . . Being blinded by this light, my sense of hearing was unusually keen. And without meaning to, I found myself eavesdropping on a number of conversations.

A line of people walks by Maggie in couples chatting of their special concerns—college boys, waiters, an engaged pair, even a man grumbling to himself, "Don't let it be what I think it is." Maggie absorbs these bits and pieces of conversation.

MAGGIE *(to the audience):* . . . . . I became so aware of how much life is going on all the time, how many stories, how many people were out there with their absolute reality that had nothing to do with my absolute reality. To them, I'm the backdrop. To me, they're mine. How often do we think of ourselves as backdrops for other peoples' lives? Not too often, I guess. We prefer to think of ourselves as terribly significant . . . . . We all live with that illusion, don't we? And we all parade the streets daily, back and forth . . . . . convinced that really, deep down in the truest part of life, we are nobody's backdrop.

Maggie moves to an area of the stage with bed and telephone (her hotel room). When the phone rings and she answers it, the lights come up on the caller: Jim Burroughs, *"A man of 38. He is slightly overweight, slightly graying. If he took care of himself he would be a good looking man, but he hasn't been."* Jim, who lives near Boston, is a high school classmate whom Maggie hasn't seen in 20 years.

MAGGIE: I can't believe it. What are you—I mean, how are you doing?
JIM: I'm fine. Just fine. Yourself?

MAGGIE: I'm fine too. *(A pause. They laugh.)* I'm sorry. I'm overwhelmed. I don't know what to say.

JIM: Me neither. Twenty years is a lot to catch up on. Would you like to get together and try this in person?

MAGGIE: I'd love to. *(To the audience.)* Now, psychologically, is the moment in a conversation where you establish the boundaries of what is going to happen between a man and a woman. Naturally, both of us knew this instinctively.

JIM: We can have dinner. Maybe you can come over to the house. I'd love you to meet my wife.

MAGGIE *(looks knowingly at the audience):* That sounds wonderful. You have kids, too?

JIM: No. No kids. We wanted to, but . . . oh look, we can talk about everything over dinner. How about tomorrow night? Eight o'clock? I'll pick you up.

MAGGIE: Great. See you then. *(She hangs up. To the audience.)* It was as easy as that. Twenty years of total silence, of not knowing, and rarely thinking about someone who was once a big reason you got up in the morning. And now, all at once, all of that is behind you. Now, you're suddenly going to have a civilized dinner with him and his wife. Ain't life strange?

Two chairs represent the car in which Jim has arrived to pick up Maggie the next day. Maggie didn't recognize Jim at first: "I searched his face, trying to find the boy I'd known, but I couldn't find him." They exchange conventional compliments on the ride to Jim's house, and Jim deliberately takes them past the "little detour" they once used as a lovers lane.

Jim had started out to become a musician but has been sidetracked into a career as a teacher of English: "I am great at it." Maggie notices tears in Jim's eyes when he comments that it's not exactly what he would have wanted to do. In her turn, Maggie tells Jim that her writing career has taken precedence in her life over all other concerns: "I get so annoyed with these people who think that if you're not married your life is a total failure. Sometimes I think I could win the Nobel Prize, and some people would still think I was a failure because I wasn't married."

Jim has been writing music on the side (this information helps Maggie to perceive the boy she knew in high school) but has played it for no one except his wife—whose name is "Maggy" with a "y." "The two big loves of my life, with the same name," Jim offers, adding that they are alike in a lot of other ways too. In school, Maggy went out for cheerleading as a form of spite, just for laughs, but was elected captain of the squad.

JIM: I never knew her in school. I just figured she was one of them.

MAGGIE: One of "them." Oh, yeah. How did you meet her? All those years later.

JIM: Fourth of July parade. We started making rude comments about the floats together and realized we had causticity in common. It's a wonderful bond, being caustic together. Don't you find?

MAGGIE: I guess. *(To the audience.)* My imagination was running wild. I was ready for some kind of cross between Christie Brinkley and Dorothy Parker.

JIM: Well, here we are.

MAGGIE: Wow. What a wonderful old houce.

They stand and walk toward the door of the house.

JIM: Uh, by the way. There's one other thing you should know about Maggy.

Maggy appears at the door. Her head is wrapped in a brightly flowered scarf.

She has cancer.

Maggy greets Maggie warmly, and they enter the house. They open a bottle of wine, and in the general course of the conversation some of the ordinary comments (about ghosts, about the fact that Maggie's father died of cancer) acquire unwanted overtones of irony in Maggy's circumstances. Maggie explains that she's in Boston to promote her book, which both Jim and Maggy have read and enjoyed for its humor. Maggy remembers Maggie from school, but not vice versa, and Jim goes to get their yearbook to jog their memories.

MAGGY: I think you probably made more of an impression on me than I made on you. You were pretty memorable in high school.

MAGGIE: Really? I always thought of myself as kind of disenfranchised and out of it.

MAGGY: No way. You were our resident angry young woman. I was completely in awe of you.

MAGGIE: You were?

MAGGY: Sure. Do you remember a thing called Moratorium Day?

MAGGIE: Yeah. The protest day. "Let's get our Dick out of Cambodia."

MAGGY: I'll never forget the day you charged into the auditorium where we were practicing cheers and shouted, "Cut school tomorrow and come into Boston for Moratorium Day. Everyone who objects to this obscene war is doing it, even people like you."

MAGGIE *(laughing):* I did?

MAGGY: Yes. I was completely intimidated.

MAGGIE: I was such a big mouth back then. I'm surprised somebody didn't pop me one.

MAGGY: Oh, no. I thought you were great. I just wish I'd had the nerve to drop everything and go.

MAGGIE: You didn't?

MAGGY: No. My mom was an alcoholic, the kids needed me at home. I wish I could have, though. I'll bet it was great.

MAGGIE: Yeah, I seem to remember it being kind of inspiring.

MAGGY: Oh, well. Next life.

Jim comes back with the yearbook evoking memories of senior prom night when Jim abandoned his date, Maggie, for a sexier creature named Gina Lazlo and left Maggie to hitchhike home. This seems to have been typical of their turbulent relationship in those days—the next day Maggie came around and threw a rock through one of the windows of Jim's house. Maggy persuades them to apologize to each other for this 20-year-old behavior, making Maggie feel as though Maggy were permitting her to share Jim.

Maggy asks Maggie if she's married. To Jim's surprise, Maggie takes the question in stride, commenting that she either scares all men off or hasn't found the right one yet. They find a picture of Maggy as cheerleader, and Maggie

Kevin O'Rourke and Catherine Butterfield as Jim and
Maggy Burroughs in Butterfield's *Joined at the Head*

instantly remembers her, telling the audience, "She had always struck me as the quiet type, maybe even a little prissy. I was surprised to hear she'd been a cheerleader. She was the kind of girl who never had a stain on her sweater or a pimple on her face, these things would never dare happen to her. I contrasted this with the chaotic mess of a person I was in high school and understood why we'd never had much to do with each other. But tonight, this woman before me was a totally different story. So warm and outgoing, so no-bullshit and real. I looked at her, and the same thought kept ringing in my head—this woman has cancer?"

The three decide to go out to an Italian restaurant for dinner where, seated at a table, they come close to making themselves conspicuous with over-reactions of laughter to anecdotes of the past—until Maggy comments that she's going to the hospital for chemotherapy at 9 o'clock the next morning. It's an unpleasant experience but a necessary one, as Maggy puts it: "I'd rather be on the beach at Maui, but that wasn't one of the options. They need to get in there and do this thing, so they do it." Usually it pays off in making Maggy feel better—for a while.

To the tune of Led Zeppelin's "Stairway to Heaven," Jim takes Maggy onto the dance floor. Maggie, watching, tells the audience the two make her feel like one of them, a third Musketeer; but then she notes the special magnetism between them. When they return to the table and are studying the dessert menu, Maggie observes a look that passes between Jim and Maggy, "so emotionally charged it almost knocked me off my chair. It spoke of a deep love, the kind that can only spring from pain." No wonder Maggy shows no sign of jealousy at Maggie's close presence—the relationship between Jim and Maggy is beyond such a trivial emotion as jealousy.

At this point, Maggy interrupts.

Maggy closes her menu and addresses the audience for the first time.
MAGGY: . . . . . I'm sorry, but I just can't sit here any longer and let this go on. This woman is romanticizing. Now, I can understand why she's doing it. I mean, she's a writer, I've read her stuff, and I can tell her heart's in the right place. But this is my life here, and she's turning it into some kind of Gothic novel. *(To Maggie.)* Please. Forgive me. I don't mean to ruin your little whatever-this-thing-is, but there's a certain amount of bullshit going on, and I'd like to take the opportunity to set the record straight. You don't mind, do you?
MAGGIE *(horrified):* What are you doing?
MAGGY: I just thought I'd correct a few misconceptions. Okay with you?
MAGGIE: No. I'm sorry, but it is not okay with me . . . . . I'll admit I've allowed myself a little artistic license. But all writers do that. Now, maybe I haven't gotten all the facts completely straight, but since this is fiction—
MAGGY: This is not fiction. This is my life you're serving up before everyone, and I think I have the right to put in my two cents worth.

MAGGIE: Well, could you maybe do it after I've told the whole story?

MAGGY: No. Sorry. I thought I could at first, but that last monologue of yours was so over the top, I just had to say something. Listen, I don't mean to rain on your parade. But I should think in the interests of accuracy, you'd like to hear what I have to say.

MAGGIE *(wounded):* Fine. Go Ahead.

MAGGY: I've hurt your feelings, right?

MAGGIE: No, no. Say what you have to say. *(Pause.)* But I'd just like to add that this story is meant to be a tribute to you. I have worked very hard to present your story in a light that will be an inspiration for others, and perhaps even immortalize you.

MAGGY: Immortalize me? Boy, are you barking up the wrong tree. I'm just one other person who got cancer. No more or less mortal than anybody else.

Under the circumstances of Maggie's fictionalizing Maggy's situation, Maggy addresses the audience to set the record straight: Yes, Maggy liked Maggie when they were at school (and still does) and might have been a lot happier if she had joined Maggie's angry, activist group; but the idea of Maggie's being a third Musketeer, so to speak, with Jim and Maggy is a wild fantasy. Maggie protests that this was just "an allusion," the lonely writer's life she leads permits her few close friends, and the evening at the restaurant with Jim and Maggy meant a great deal to her. But Maggie soon realizes that this isn't the story she's been trying to put together and tell: "I do not intend to get into my life, this is your life we're examining here." Maggy observes, "But I think you might want to look into that no-friends thing some time in the future."

Before getting back to their lives as seen in Maggie's "story," Maggy has one more comment to make, about the look that Maggie noticed passing between husband and wife.

MAGGY: . . . . . To us, it was one of a thousand looks we'd given each other since this whole thing began. And listen, it's not fair to paint Jim as the wimpy one and me as some kind of saint. You saw the guy, he was Mr. Positive the whole time. That might be easy when you're out to dinner and your wife's being charming. But you didn't get to see the days when I was a whiney baby, or totally bitchy, and he was *still* great. Now, that's an accomplishment. It's important you get that in, Mag. I want Jim to get his due.

MAGGIE: Okay.

MAGGY: And one more thing—

MAGGIE: Oh, come on, this isn't fair—

MAGGY: One more thing. I *was* jealous of you.

MAGGIE: . . . You were?

MAGGY: Yes. But not for the reason you think. I was jealous of you because you were healthy, because you had your whole life ahead of you. I started wishing Jim had married you, so he wouldn't have to go through this shit with me.

MAGGIE: No.

MAGGY: Yes! Of course, yes. Do you have any idea of the guilt that a sick person carries around, knowing that they're ruining the lives of everyone they love? The whole experience is one big fucking drag, but the guilt thing is definitely one of the highlights. *(Pause.)* Okay. I'm done. Carry on.

But Maggie can't easily pick up where she left off, ordering dessert—she feels that Maggy has taken "the heroic aspect" out of the story by telling more about herself than anyone needs to know. Finally, Maggie relaxes and resumes her narrative. They finish dinner, and Jim drops Maggy off before driving Maggie home.

In the "car," Maggie tells Jim how much she likes Maggy. Jim informs Maggie that Maggy is a nurse who works with groups of children and will probably be able to get back to it after this round of chemotherapy. Jim speeds up the car until they're going dangerously fast, but all at once he slows down, pulls over, stops the car and *"puts his head on the steering wheel and begins to weep."* Maggie puts her arms around Jim, but after a moment he regains control of himself, restarts the car and continues driving Maggie home, dropping her off with the comment, "You look great, Mag, you really do."

Maggy enters as the lights go down on Jim, and the two women have another of their objective discussions, about the car incident. "He never cried like that with me. Never. I guess he needed an outlet," Maggy comments and suggests that they might have kissed (Maggie denies that this would have been appropriate). Maggy wonders if it is wise for Jim and her to hide their feelings, protectively, to keep from upsetting the other person. Maggie thinks it is. Maggy isn't so sure, she indicates, as she exits.

Strolling down Newbury Street, Maggie considers buying a crystal as a present for Maggy (a salesman assures her that stones have been recognized for centuries as having mysterious curative powers). Under sales pressure, Maggie buys a piece of sugalite and takes it to the hospital, asking the nurse at the desk to deliver it to Maggy.

NURSE: . . . . . Don't you want to see her?

MAGGIE: Oh, I'm sure she can't have visitors.

NURSE: Yes, she can. She's down in X-ray, but she'll be back soon. Why don't you wait?

MAGGIE: Oh, I really don't want to bother her.

NURSE: You won't be bothering her. I'm sure she'd love to see you.

A man in pajamas walks down the hall pulling his I.V. along behind him. Maggie starts to panic.

MAGGIE: Gosh, I'd love to, I really would. But I'm on such a tight schedule.

NURSE: Would you like me to call down there and see when she—

MAGGIE: No! *(Attempting calmness.)* No, thanks a lot, but I really just wanted to drop this off. I'll be back soon, though. Real soon. Tell her that, okay?

NURSE *(she's seen this before)*: Right. Real soon.

MAGGIE *(to the audience)*: I know. I know. What a wuss. But have you ever been to a cancer ward? Please reserve judgment until you have.

Maggie proceeds to her book-signing, noting that the men readers seem to be more objective about her work than the women, who respond to her characters more personally.

In Maggie's bedroom, the phone rings. It's Jim telling Maggie that the suga-lite crystal was a perfect gift—Jim had given Maggy one years before, but she lost it. Maggy returned from X-ray just after Maggie left and was sorry to have missed her (which of course gives Maggie a twinge of guilt). Maggie offers to fix Jim some dinner, but he is headed for a good night's sleep. Impulsively, Mag-gie—who had planned to leave town the next day—suggests she might stay over to do some "research." Jim wishes her good luck and hangs up.

Alone in her hotel room, Maggie decides that in fact she isn't looking forward to getting back to her "lonely little apartment" in New York, and she decides to stay over in Boston for a week or so—but not in this institutional-seeming hotel room. She moves to a Bed and Breakfast whose motherly owner, Nora Delaney, takes Maggie Mulroney under her wing (Nora knows some Mulroneys from County Kerry, but Maggie, whose father is dead and mother lives out of touch across the country, doesn't know much about her family background). Nora gives Maggie her best room, once her daughter's. Nora exits, leaving Maggie reflecting that she seems to be hiring a family to go with the room she's renting.

MAGGIE: . . . . . There was something kind of comforting about this woman suggesting that I might actually belong to a tribe somewhere.

She bounces on the bed a minute, testing the mattress.

I considered for a moment calling someone to let them know I was staying. Then I realized there was no one I needed to call, except maybe my editor. I have to admit, I got a little depressed there for a minute. *(Thinking of Maggy's "no friends" comment.)* Not that I don't have any friends, don't get me wrong. I just couldn't think of who they were at that particular moment.

She stretches out on the bed.

So. Here I was in a Bed and Breakfast, for no apparent reason. And there was Maggy, Jim's Maggy, lying in a bed across town, with poison dripping into her veins. I lay on the bed for a very long time, trying to figure out the correlation.

Blackout. Curtain.

ACT II

Maggie leaves messages on Jim's and Maggy's home phone wishing them well, offering to help in any way, but telling herself she would be intruding if she visited Maggy personally in the hospital, even though Jim's recorded message on his answering machine pleads for visitors.

Maggie subjects herself to a pretentious PBS interviewer, Raymond, quizzing her on the subject of her new book, *Joined at the Head,* now topping the *Times* best-seller list. "A searing indictment of the father-daughter relationship," Raymond comments, and Maggie objects: "It's not a searing indictment of anything. It's funny." Raymond notes that Maggie's male characters tend to be "caddish, shallow, selfish, even perverted individuals." Maggie denies this, saying of a character in her new book that she'd go out with him.

MAGGIE: He's smart, funny and successful. What more do you need in a man?

RAYMOND *(pause):* You're not married, are you?

MAGGIE *(slow burn):* No, as a matter of fact I'm not.

RAYMOND: Anyone special in your life?

MAGGIE: I find it interesting that this question is asked of me so frequently. Tell me, if Saul Bellow were on the show tonight, would you ask him about that "special someone" in his life? I'm just curious.

RAYMOND: Touche. *(To the audience.)* We've been talking to Margaret Mulroney, feminist author of *Joined at the Head.* Tomorrow we'll be talking to Jeane Kirkpatrick.

MAGGIE: I hear she's dating someone really cute these days. Ask her to tell you about him.

RAYMOND *(dourly):* Ha-ha-ha. *(To audience.)* This has been *The Best of Boston. (Blackout.)*

Asleep in her room, Maggie is awakened by the phone, finds it's her mother, who's called to wish her happy birthday. She realizes this is only a dream when her father also comes on the phone and insists that he's arranged for her to come out to the Coast and read her book page by page, in defiance of a local critic. When Maggie protests to her father, "You're dead," the phone connection is broken along with the dream.

Nora, still up playing Scrabble with her husband Howard, has heard Maggie call out and comes in to see that she's all right. When Nora departs, Maggie checks her watch and dials the phone. The lights come up on Maggy in her hospital room, picking up the ringing phone.

MAGGY: . . . . . How are you?

MAGGIE: Fine, fine. I'm having the weirdest dreams.

MAGGY: You and me both. I'm even hallucinating from time to time. Jim finds it very unnerving.

MAGGIE: What are you hallucinating?

MAGGY: Oh, people, places. I thought you were here for awhile.

MAGGIE: Really? You know, I was going to come today, I really was, but I seem to be going through this thing, I don't even know how to describe it to you . . .

Maggie lowers the phone and closes her eyes.

I think about you all the time, Mag. Everything I do, I think of what you'd say and how you'd react. And it's really silly, because my God, we've only known each other a couple of days. But something about coming back, something about seeing you and seeing Jim, it's upset my balance.

A nurse walks in to check on Maggy, sees the phone and picks it up.

Suddenly I feel kind of lost and disconnected, and I don't even know why. I mean, did you have similar feelings when you met me? Am I just making this up?

NURSE: Hello?

MAGGIE: . . . Hello?

NURSE: Who is this?

MAGGIE: Who is *this?*

NURSE: This is the nurse.

MAGGIE: Where's Maggy?

NURSE: Mrs. Burroughs is asleep. I'm afraid you've been talking to yourself.

MAGGIE *(pause):* Yes, I'm afraid I have.

The lights black out and come up on a doctor's office. Maggie's trying to find out why she has headaches, can't sleep and seems to be imagining things, but the doctor is no help—Maggie's in good physical health.

In an out-of-reality interlude, Maggy comes into Maggie's room and urges her to keep on with the story, which seems to be tapering off in Maggie's imagination. Maggie wanted to create a tribute to Maggy, but other thoughts keep getting in the way. Okay, Maggy continues, if that won't work, then she should go ahead and tell her own story, which Maggy summarizes as, "When last we left our heroine, she was sitting on a bed wondering what the connection was between me, with poison dripping into my veins, and herself. She had just decided to stay on in Boston in order to be near Jim and me. She then proceeded to avoid us for the next three days."

Maggie protests that she didn't avoid them, but Maggy points out that her entire contact consisted of one late-night phone call and a lot of messages on the machine, calls which Jim didn't bother to return.

Maggy's return from the hospital with a painful mouth and throat is acted out, with Jim bringing her a milkshake which she can barely swallow. The phone rings—it's Maggie calling to see how things are going (she had expected to leave a message on the machine). "She seems so sad," Maggy comments, but Jim thinks she's having a busy good time.

Maggy explains to the audience that because of her difficulty in swallowing she became dehydrated and had to go back to the hospital, where "Maggie still did not visit me . . . . . although she sent many strange and exotic gifts." Maggy remembers that Jim invited Maggie over to their house for dinner one night, and Maggie argues that this wouldn't be part of Maggy's story, "It had nothing to do with you." Maggy imagines what must have occurred that evening: Jim is playing love songs to Maggie on his guitar, remembering how beautiful she was and still is.

JIM: . . . . . It's such a relief to be with someone who's healthy. God, I hate myself for saying that. But poor Maggy, I feel like I have to be so careful of her all the time. She's so fragile, it's like being with a wounded bird. I broke one of her ribs once making love, just snapped it in two. And we were both trying to be so careful, it was like making love to a teacup. But I broke her rib anyway. I heard it break.

MAGGIE: Oh Jim, how horrible.

JIM: Maggie, sometimes I wonder how much more of this I can take. And then I hate myself, because she's the one who's going through the pain. What the fuck right do I have to cave in?

MAGGIE (taking his hand): You're not caving in, Jim. It's hard. No one comes out a hero at a time like this. It's hard.

JIM: Come here. (She moves toward him. He kisses her. She responds.) Please forgive me. (He kisses her again.) Please, please forgive me.

> They are in each other's arms, obviously on their way to other things. Maggie breaks away.

MAGGIE: No, no, no, no, no. You've got it all wrong. God! How could you even think such a thing?

That wasn't the way the evening went at all, Maggie protests to Maggy and is reluctant to describe how it really went. Maggy insists, so Maggie remembers that she had a lot of wine at dinner, and then Jim played a song he wrote for Maggy. Jim had hoped to become a composer "Instead of a loser high school teacher," but then Maggy came along—and Jim wouldn't change anything, except of course for her getting cancer.

Acting out her description of what really happened that evening, Maggie hints that she's here to listen if Jim wants to talk, mentioning Jim's moment of weakness the other day in the car. Jim brushes it off and goes into another song, an old one he wrote for Maggie, who comments, "I couldn't believe it. It was as though he had never cried in my arms. We had never shared that moment of intimacy. Just because he said so, none of that existed."

Maggie doesn't want to hear any more of this song and interrupts Jim, much

Ellen Parker as Maggie Mulroney and Kevin
O'Rourke as Jim in *Joined at the Head*

to his aggravation. Childishly, they bring up old high school aggravations until they both realize what they are doing and become embarrassed, apologetic.

MAGGIE: You were shutting me out again. Just the way you used to do in school. It drives me crazy.

JIM: I wasn't shutting you out.

MAGGIE: Yes, you were. I want to be able to help, Jim, but you won't let me. How can you act like nothing happened in the car the other day? I can see you're in a lot of pain. I just want to be able to be there for you.

JIM: Why?

MAGGIE: Why? Because I think you need it.

JIM: Are you sure it's not because you need it? Listen, this is tough stuff, and I don't want to be too hard on you, but at the moment the last thing I need is to cry myself out in somebody's arms. Okay, that moment in the car happened. But I can't let it happen again. It weakens me too much. You can't let yourself get weak for a second with this thing, Mag, not a second. That's the reason I haven't been returning your calls. I just can't let myself do that any more.

Maggie is becoming weepy, and Jim puts his arms around her to comfort her. The subject of the recent broadcast comes up, and Maggie realizes that Jim doesn't really like her book. He finally admits he thinks the book "dishonest," with fictional distortions of reality-based characters like her father and himself in order to get laughs. "This is just a little more honesty than I can take in one evening," Maggie declares. Jim apologizes, as Maggie departs, coolly, until she gets into her car, starts to drive and dissolves in tears.

Maggy joins Maggie in the car, and their out-of-reality interlude continues. Maggie proceeds to try to explain her behavior.

MAGGIE: I couldn't go see you, Maggy. I was too scared. Every time I looked at you, I saw me. I saw the road I hadn't taken. I felt guilty for having somehow escaped what you were going through. And now, knowing you, and even loving you, I was afraid of something else.

MAGGY: What's that?

MAGGIE: The responsibility of being friends with you. It seemed like a very heavy burden, under the circumstances. I wasn't sure I could do it right. I'm not used to being a good friend, Maggy. And I knew that with you, that's what I would have to be. No halfway measures.

MAGGY: I understand. Hey, life's hard. People do what they have to do. It's a question of self preservation . . . . .

Maggy exits, and Maggie lies down on the bed in her room. She confesses to the audience, "I'm totally lost now. I give up. This is beyond my power. This story is just going to have to tell itself."

The phone rings. It's Jim with the information that Maggy has developed an infection. Maggie arrives at the hospital carrying a bedraggled plant for Maggy. She encounters Jim, who lets her know that Maggy is recovering nicely and would like to see her. Maggie departs for Maggy's room, and after she's gone *"Jim's face goes from hopeful and encouraging to a mask of grief."* He unburdens himself to the audience with his feelings about how much he loves Maggy and desires her even in this condition, and wishes they could have children; about his anger at this devastating twist of fate; about his dreams of the better life he could have; about "how desperately and deeply I love her. My partner. My life partner. The one I'm joined to forever. My love. My wife."

Jim exits, and the action changes to Maggy's hospital room, where Maggie enters.

MAGGIE: Maggy?

MAGGY: Hey! Come on in. Don't be shy. You look like you think I'm going to drop dead before your eyes.

MAGGIE: Actually, I think you look pretty good. I mean, you don't look ready for the Olympics, but you look better than I imagined.

MAGGY: Kind of makes me wonder what you imagined. *(Looking at the gift.)* What is that?

MAGGIE: I don't know. I found it in the gift shop.

MAGGY: I hope you weren't planning on giving it to me.

MAGGIE: No, no. I've been really needing something like this for my apartment. *(They laugh.)* I keep buying you the most ridiculous things. I don't know why.

Maggy particularly values the crystal, and Maggie agrees, "Yeah, the crystal's different." They had both been a little scared in anticipation of meeting again after all the years, Maggie because she feared their faces "would hurt from fake smiling," Maggy because she felt a little guilty at having won Jim away from Maggie when all their contemporaries considered Jim and Maggie inseparable. Maggy remembers that she happened to be standing next to Jim at a Fourth of July parade and asked herself what Maggie might say to him under these circumstance. Maggy came up with a sarcastically witty remark about the sexpot Gina Lazlo on one of the floats.

MAGGY: . . . . . He looked at me like I'd just arrived on the planet, one of those what-have-we-here looks, you know?

MAGGIE: Yeah.

MAGGY: And I felt like a million dollars. Suddenly, with my new persona, I felt like I could do or say anything. I could get angry, I could stand up for myself, I didn't let people push me around. It was so liberating. But after awhile I started to worry. I said to myself, "This isn't really you. Who is it?" And of course I knew the answer right away. It was you. *(Pause.)* I've always felt guilty about that. Like some kind of impostor waiting to be exposed. If I hadn't pretended to be you, Maggie, Jim would never have fallen in love with me. I know that.

MAGGIE: Oh, Maggy, that's not—

MAGGY: No, it is. I know. Look at that wimpy little girl I was in high school. So angry, so filled with rage about her mother, her lost childhood, but so conditioned to be a "good girl" that she just sat on it all and let it fester inside. You don't know how much I wanted to go to that demonstration in Boston. Nothing would have been better for me than to be out there with you yelling, "This is wrong! This is wrong! This is—"

Her face contorts.

Maggy is taken suddenly with a spell of vomiting but soon recovers and continues, "I kept telling myself it didn't matter that I had purloined your personality, and pretty soon I started to believe it." But the old guilt feeling returned when Jim announced that Maggie had returned to Boston for a visit.

Both were surprised by their warmth of feeling for each other. "I couldn't forget that you were the woman Jim first fell in love with. I couldn't help wondering how much of me was me and how much was you," Maggy confesses. Maggie reveals to her that Jim and she had a stormy relationship, not at all like the loving one Jim and Maggy have enjoyed over the years. Maggy is glad to hear it, but it kind of ruins her plan to make a last request of Maggie to look after Jim after she's gone. Maggie will be glad to look after Jim, she tells Maggy—but at long distance.

Maggy always admired Maggie's apparent fearlessness. Maggie remembers that as a little girl she was intensely in love with and connected to every aspect of life. But one day her gerbil died, and her parents tried to console her by explaining that death was an inevitable part of life for every living thing. "Boing! My radar went up," Maggie continues. *"Everybody?* Yes, everybody. The two of them as well? Yes, but not for a very long time. Me? I was going to die? Well, yes, but not until I was a very, very old lady. *(Pause.)* After that, my place in the world felt very different. I felt myself drawing away from feelings of delight, of connectedness. The world got a little blurry to me. My eyesight was fine, but the world had gotten blurry. It was as though I didn't want to be so intimately connected to a world that was going to so callously cast me out from it. It was a protective device. In realizing that I was going to die, I was filled with a terrible paralysing fear. And so, to shield myself from the fear of losing a world so beautiful to me, I blurred its edges. To make the loss less profound, I diminished its beauty. I still do it. I avoid life sometimes. I try not to, I know it's wasteful and wrong, but I truly think there are times when I avoid living my own life." Maggy responds, "Live it, Maggie . . . . . It won't count for anything if you don't live it."

Maggie and Maggy resolve to attend their next school reunion together. On the way out, Maggie accepts Jim's invitation to dinner that night, but not for an excursion the next day—Maggie has decided that "It's time to go home and take stock." She'll be looking forward to the reunion, and she leaves, after hugging Jim and telling him, "To me, you're a great man."

Maggie then tells the audience that she can't go on with this story, but Maggy joins her and accuses her of copping out at the last minute: "I think you've told a better story here than you even meant to tell, but to just send everybody home now, robbing them of the final satisfaction of knowing how everything turns out—that's just cruel." But the cruel part of it, to Maggie, is that Maggy died (and Maggy takes particular pleasure in describing this event with as many euphemisms as she can bring to mind—"gave up the ghost," "bought the farm," "kicked the bucket," "shook hands with Elvis").

But Maggie tells the story of Maggy's death to the audience more decorously: "I guess chemo took her just a little too close to the edge this time." Maggie attended the funeral, observing that "Jim was a mess. It was as though everything just broke loose inside him, now that he didn't have to be strong for someone else." After that, Maggie would phone him from time to time and went to their reunion with him—"but it wasn't much fun."

Maggy's death also influenced Maggie to make major changes in her life. She moved out of New York, accepted a previously disdained teaching job in Iowa and "wrote a furious novel about women in the Nineties which left everyone bewildered. They kept looking for the jokes."

On the walk back from the hospital on the day Maggy died, Maggie couldn't help hearing all the stories of the people around her, though she wanted to concentrate on her own. *"The same afternoon light appears from the first act,"* as Maggie hears one passer-by telling his companion, "Your problem is that you fragmentize"; another pair speaking of falling in love over a weekend; others calculating the mathematical odds against the repetition of some event or other.

The people move more slowly. Maggie approaches the light.

MAGGIE: I couldn't help listening to their conversations. Everyone with his own story. Each person deeply involved in his own activity. And it was the events of the day, I guess. Suddenly it all seemed to be too much. I'm afraid I started to feel very, very sorry for myself. Because I couldn't help noticing that while everyone else seemed to be in the company of another person or persons, I seemed to be the only person on the whole street who was walking entirely alone.

Maggie starts to walk. Maggy appears and begins to walk beside her. Together, they walk directly into the light. Blackout. Curtain.

○○○
○○○
○○○
○○○
○○○
○○○ JEFFREY

A Play in Two Acts

BY PAUL RUDNICK

Cast and credits appear on page 348

PAUL RUDNICK is a New Jerseyan, born there in 1957 and educated there through high school. His father was a physicist and an editor and his mother was a public relations director. He was experimenting with writing as early as age 7 and was deeply interested in theater by the time he went to Yale, where as an undergraduate he took and/or audited as many courses in the graduate Drama School as he could. He graduated B.A. in 1977, and his first play produced professionally in New York was Poor Little Lambs, *about the consequences of a woman joining Yale's all-male Whiffenpoof singing group, opening off Broadway March 14, 1982, playing for 73 performances and winning an Outer Critics Circle Award.*

A Rudnick play reached Broadway two seasons ago: I Hate Hamlet, *opening April 4, 1991 and playing for 80 performances. It has been produced in Australia, New Zealand, Japan, Austria, Brazil, and elsewhere in the U.S. This season's* Jeffrey, *its author's first Best Play, appeared as an OOB production by the WPA Theater and then moved up to full off-Broadway status March 6, winning an Obie, an Outer Critics Circle Award and the John Gassner Award for an outstanding new American play. Rudnick is also the author of the plays* Raving *and* Cosmetic Surgery, *the novels* Social Disease *and* I'll Take It, *and numerous articles for various periodicals. He is a member of the Dramatists Guild and lives in Manhattan.*

The following excerpts from the script of Jeffrey *were designated by the author to represent his play in these pages.*

Time: The Present

Place: New York

ACT I

The play is introduced with a series of slides, *"accompanied by a lush, moody Gershwin score,"* depicting scenes of Manhattan. After a shot of the windows of a brownstone we meet Jeffrey, *"in his 30s, attractive and well put-together. He is an innocent; he is outgoing and optimistic, cheerful despite all odds."* He is seen in a series of sexual encounters with men, becoming absurdly defensive, with heroic safe-sex measures. Finally Jeffrey gets out of bed and gets dressed.

JEFFREY *(to the audience):* Okay. Confession time. You know those articles, the ones all those right wingers use? The ones that talk about gay men who've had over five thousand sexual partners? Well, compared to me, they're shut-ins. Wallflowers. But I'm not promiscuous. That is such an ugly word. I'm cheap. I *love* sex. I don't know how else to say it. I always have, I always thought that sex was the reason to grow up. I couldn't wait! I didn't! I mean—sex! It's just one of the truly great ideas. I mean, the fact that our bodies have this built-in capacity for joy—it just makes me love God. Yes!

But I want to be politically correct about this. I know it's wrong to say that all gay men are obsessed with sex. Because that's not true. All *human beings* are obsessed with sex. All gay men are obsessed with opera. And it's not the same thing. Because you can have good sex.

Except—what's going on? I mean, you saw. Things are just—not what they should be. Sex is too sacred to be treated this way. Sex wasn't meant to be safe, or negotiated, or fatal. But you know what really did it? This guy. I'm in bed with him, and he starts crying. And he says, "I'm sorry, it's just—this used to be so much fun."

So. Enough. Facts of life. No more sex. Not for me. Done!

And you know what? It's going to be fine. Because I am a naturally cheerful person. And I will find a substitute for sex. Sex lite. Sex helper. I Can't Believe It's Not Sex. I will find a great new way to live, and a way to be happy. So—no more sex. The sexual revolution is over! England won. No sex! No sex. I'm ready! I'm willing! Let's go!

*   *   *

> *Sterling enters, wearing something outrageous, perhaps Chinese-in-spired lounging pajamas.*

STERLING: So—he was really cute, this bartender?

> *We are now in Sterling's elegant, if somewhat overdone Upper East Side apartment. Sterling holds a cigarette and a cocktail.*

JEFFREY: He was fantastic. But I just got so—I don't know! I went nuts!

STERLING: Jeffrey—you are beginning to have a problem.

> *Darius, Sterling's boy friend, enters wearing an overcoat. Darius is a true innocent, a handsome, completely sweet dancer in his 20s.*

DARIUS: Hi, guys.

STERLING: Hello, sweetheart.

DARIUS: What a day. I am exhausted.

> *Darius takes off his coat. He is wearing his costume from* Cats, *which consists of a heavily painted bodysuit, accentuated with yarn and fur, elaborate leg-warmers, knitted gauntlets and a tail. He has already removed his makeup.*

JEFFREY: Darius—aren't you supposed to leave your costume at the theater?

DARIUS: We were filming a commercial, the new one, and it went late. I got stuck. So you're not having sex any more.

STERLING: What he needs is to fall in love and have a relationship. And then this sex thing will fall into place.

DARIUS: Exactly. Look at us. Look at how happy we are. Don't we make you want to fall in love?

STERLING: You know, sometimes I think we should be on a brochure for Middle America. So that everyone can say, oh look, a wholesome gay couple.

JEFFREY: Excuse me? You're not wholesome. You're a decorator—excuse me, an interior designer, there, I said it without giggling. And you—you're a dancer. You two are like Martha Stewart and Ann Miller. Which believe me, I prefer. I hate that gay role models are supposed to be just like straight people. As if straight people were even like that.

STERLING: That's true. I was watching these two guys on *Nightline,* on Gay Pride Day. And one of them said, "I'm Bob Wheeler and I'm a surgeon. And my lover is an attorney. And we'd like to show America that all gays aren't limp-wristed, screaming queens. There are gay truck drivers and gay cops and gay lumberjacks." And I just thought, ooh—get her.

DARIUS: Who's Martha Stewart?

STERLING: She writes picture books about gracious living. Martha says that nothing else matters, if you can do a nice dried floral arrangement. I worship her.

DARIUS: And who's Ann Miller?

STERLING: Leave this house.

> *Jeffrey and Sterling freeze. Darius addresses the audience.*

DARIUS: Some people think I'm dumb, just because I'm a chorus boy with an eighth grade education. Well—I live in a penthouse, and I don't pay rent. I go to screenings, and I take cabs. Dumb, huh? And yes, I'm in *Cats.* Now and forever. And I love it! I do! I figure I'm too young for *A Chorus Line* and too happy for *Les Mis.* I never got that show—*Les Mis.* It's about this French guy, right, who steals a loaf of bread, and then he suffers for the rest of his life. For toast. Get over it!

> *Back to the scene.*

JEFFREY: That's why I came over. To be convinced about this love and relationship bit. Because I do believe that you two are truly in love. You have that special . . . smugness. You're like an advertisement for connubial bliss.

DARIUS: What's connubial?

STERLING: It's when one of us can afford a cleaning woman.

> *The doorbell rings. Steve enters carrying a bouquet of flowers.*

Steven! Hi!

DARIUS: What a surprise!

JEFFREY: Oh my God . . .

Tom Hewitt (Steve), Edward Hibbert (Sterling, *standing*), John Michael Higgins (Jeffrey) and Bryan Batt (Darius) in Paul Rudnick's *Jeffrey*

STERLING: Jeffrey, this is Steven. I met him at the showhouse opening, and we talked.

DARIUS: We love him.

STEVE: Hi there.

JEFFREY: How are you?

STERLING: I think they're perfect for each other.

DARIUS: Me too.

STERLING: Steve's a bartender, so they'll have something in common. They can fall in love and cater together, it'll be like *Roots.*

JEFFREY *(to Steve, with great accelerating passion):* Steve—since the first second I saw you, at the gym, I have thought of nothing and no one else. I have fantasized about you—naked, about you kissing me and talking to me and walking down the street with me, and letting you do things to me that I have only permitted with five thousand other men. I think you could change my life and change the world, and I would love more than anything to do exactly the same for you, and I think it's completely and totally possible that we could be the happiest people alive except—I'm not having sex any more, so—sorry!

STERLING: Wait—you two already know each other.

STEVE: We do.

DARIUS: Oh my God. Oh my God. *(To Sterling.)* It's like I told you. I'm psychic—I can predict boy friends!

JEFFREY: We're not boy friends!

STEVE: Jeffrey, calm down. Stop hyperventilating.

JEFFREY: I can't!

STEVE: Take a deep breath.

> *As orchestrated by Sterling, all four men take a deep breath.*

STEVE: Better?

JEFFREY: Sort of.

STEVE: Okay. Now, I want to see you. We can take this as slow as you like. First step. How about—tomorrow night?

JEFFREY: I'm working! Till ten!

STEVE: Afterwards. We'll have dinner.

STERLING *(to Jeffrey):* You must.

DARIUS: You can't ignore the karma. It's too dangerous.

STERLING: You have to get over this bizarre sex thing.

DARIUS: You'll have fun! You'll have appetizers!

STERLING: We're your friends.

DARIUS: We love you.

STERLING: You must obey us.

STEVE: You have no choice, Jeffrey. Dinner?

STERLING *(to Jeffrey):* Dinner?

DARIUS *(to Jeffrey):* Dinner?

JEFFREY: Well . . .

DARIUS: Oh, come on. You're gay. You're single.

STERLING: It isn't pretty.

JEFFREY: Yes.

> *Everyone cheers.*

STERLING *(hugging Jeffrey):* I'm so proud of you! You're dating again!

STEVE: How about the Paris Commune? On Bleecker? I know the maitre d'.

JEFFREY: Yes!

STEVE: And Jeffrey?

JEFFREY: Yes?

STEVE: I just . . . okay, just so there are no surprises.

JEFFREY: Uh-huh.

STEVE: I'm HIV-positive.

JEFFREY *(after a beat):* Um, okay, right.

STEVE: Does that make a difference?

JEFFREY: No. No. Of course not.

Debra Moorhouse enters as Jeffrey steps forward and the lights come down on the others. Debra is *"an attractive, vibrant, magnetic woman . . . . . the evangelist as pop star."* Debra addresses the audience as part of her flock.

DEBRA: I'm not here as a priest, or a guru, or as any sort of religious leader. I'm just someone who—likes to talk. And people come to me, and they say, Debra, I'm in love with an alcoholic, what should I do? And I tell them, don't look to me for answers, look to yourself. And then turn it all over to some higher power, whether that power is simply the collective strength of all the love in the world, or some dude named—Jesus Christ. *(She offers a nod and a salute to heaven.)* Find that source of unconditional love, find that all-encompassing, ultimate love, surrender to that unending, infinite love that will let you say, hey—*(Her voice shifts from cajoling to a harsh bellow.)* FUCK YOU! Get out of my house until you stop drinking! *(She smiles radiantly.)*

> *   *   *

JEFFREY *(in his waiter's uniform . . . . . to the audience):* I'm working. A memorial. Another one. At a townhouse. It's for a curator, at the Met. The speakers are great. His straight brother. His doctor. His gorgeous Italian boy friend. *(Jeffrey smiles at the boy friend, across the room.)* Oh my God. I am so disgusting. Do you know what I'm doing? I'm cruising a memorial.

> *Sterling enters, in a stylish black suit, with a cocktail.*

STERLING: Oh please—everybody is. That boy friend. Carlo. I'm telling you, while Jessye Norman was singing that hymn, everyone was watching *that* him. It's not that we're not sad, it's just . . . there are all these guys here.

JEFFREY: And we've been through so many of them—memorials. Each one more moving and creative than the last.

STERLING: The Gay Men's Chorus, doing Charles Ives.

JEFFREY: Vanessa Redgrave, reading Auden.

STERLING: Siegfried and Roy.

JEFFREY *(looking across the room):* Who is that? Talking to Darius?

STERLING: It's Todd Malcolm.

JEFFREY: What?

STERLING: You know, from the gym.

JEFFREY: Oh my God.

STERLING: Jeffrey . . .

JEFFREY: He must weigh eighty pounds.

STERLING: He just got out of the hospital.

JEFFREY: He's blind, isn't he?

STERLING: It's a side effect, they think that ninety percent of the vision will return.

JEFFREY: Oh my God.

STERLING: Don't stare.

JEFFREY: Don't stare? When I first came to this city, he was . . . a god. I'd never seen anything like that. I used to watch him, dancing with his lover. People would gasp. *(He begins taking off his service jacket.)* I'm sorry.

STERLING: What are you doing?

JEFFREY: I can't work here. I can't go to one more of these. I can't see one more twenty-eight-year-old man with a cane.

STERLING: Don't be ridiculous.

JEFFREY: What are we doing? Cruising? Giggling? Pretending it's all some sort of hoot? I can't keep passing hors d'oeuvres in a graveyard! I went out with Todd! I just saw him in the hospital, and I don't even recognize him!

STERLING: Stop it!

Darius enters, in a dark suit, with a cocktail.

DARIUS: Hi, guys. Did you see Todd?

STERLING: Of course.

DARIUS: He looks better.

JEFFREY: Darius, Todd is dying! *(Darius faces him; Jeffrey realizes his mistake.)* He's . . . doing okay, I guess.

DARIUS: At least he's out of St. Vincent's. I mean, three months. Remember that collage he made on the wall? With all those Armani ads, and anything with Ann-Margret? *(He realizes something is wrong.)* What's going on here?

STERLING: Jeffrey is just having some sort of anxiety moment.

DARIUS: About Todd, right? It's okay. Do you know what we were talking about? This memorial. The cannoli are frozen. The drinks are watered. And I hated that singer. At my memorial, I want Liza.

STERLING: You are not having a memorial.

DARIUS: I mean like, in a million years.

STERLING: You are not going to get sick. I thought I'd made that clear.

DARIUS: But I was sick. I had pneumonia, and it went away. But I want—the Winter Garden. I do! And I want all the other cats to come out . . . and sing "Darius" to the tune of "Memory." *(Sings, to the tune of "Memory," while making paw-like gestures.)*

Darius, we all thought you were fabulous . . .

STERLING: Fine. And the service will run for years.

JEFFREY: Sterling!

STERLING: What?

JEFFREY: I mean . . . aren't we all being just a bit much? About all this?

DARIUS: What do you mean?

JEFFREY: I mean . . . it's a memorial.

DARIUS: So?

JEFFREY: We're making remarks. We're dishing it.

STERLING: Really, darling. Picture mine. And Jeffrey, do remember—open coffin. They can say it to my face.

JEFFREY *(viciously)*: Good idea.

DARIUS: Well, I like it. I mean cute guys, and Liza . . . . . it's not a cure for AIDS, Jeffrey. But it's the opposite of AIDS . . . Right?

STERLING: Shh, bow your heads. We're supposed to be praying.

They all bow their heads.

JEFFREY *(to Sterling)*: What are you praying for?

STERLING: What do you think? No more disease, no more prejudice.

DARIUS: And?

STERLING *(glancing around)*: No more chintz.

As the lights fade on the memorial, a nurse's voice is heard as on a hospital public address system. *"Lights up on a row of fiberglass waiting room chairs. There is an exit sign, a sign reading 'St. Vincent's' and a metal cart holding an array of medical paraphernalia."* Waiting for an appointment, Jeffrey sits and is soon joined and engaged in conversation by Steve. Finally Jeffrey hears the nurse call his name.

JEFFREY: Do you want to go first?

STEVE: What?

JEFFREY: I don't mind.

STEVE: Jeffrey, I am not here to see the doctor. Surprise!

JEFFREY: You're not?

STEVE: No, I'm on my way to the tenth floor, to see the AIDS babies.

JEFFREY: Why?

STEVE: As a volunteer. The last time I was up there, there were eight. They were all abandoned, or their parents had died. And no one would touch them, the nurses were all scared, or busy. The first baby I saw was just lying there, staring, not even crying. But when I held her, she finally smiled and gurgled and acted like a baby. We're all AIDS babies, Jeffrey. And I don't want to die without being held.

*   *   *

In St. Patrick's Cathedral Jeffrey kneels in prayer. He is joined by a priest, Father Dan, *"very working class, a tough, two-fisted guy,"* who reaches out and makes a pass at Jeffrey. They withdraw to another part of the Cathedral. Father Dan continues to pursue Jeffrey, but Jeffrey only wants to talk about God.

JEFFREY: . . . . . There's no God! It's all just random, luck of the draw, bad luck of the draw.

FATHER DAN: Darling, my darling—have you ever been to a picnic? And someone blows up a balloon, and everyone starts tossing it around? And the balloon drifts and it catches the light, and it's always just about to touch the ground, but someone always gets there just in time, to tap it back up. That balloon—that's God. The very best in all of us. The kindness. The heavy petting. The eleven o'clock numbers.

JEFFREY: But what about the bad stuff? When the balloon does hit the ground, when it bursts?

FATHER DAN: Who cares? Evil bores me. It's one-note. It doesn't sing. Of course life sucks, it always will—so why not make the most of it? How dare you not lunge for any shred of happiness?

JEFFREY: With Steve, who's sick? Who I'm afraid to touch?

FATHER DAN: So maybe you need a rubber or a surgical mask or a roll of Saran Wrap! But how dare you give up sex, when there are children in Europe who can't get a date! There is only one real blasphemy—the refusal of joy! Of a corsage and a kiss!

*   *   *

Jeffrey and Sterling meet in the waiting room at St. Vincent's, and Jeffrey learns that Darius has just died.

> *Mother Theresa appears. She gestures at Sterling; he freezes. She gestures again, and Darius enters, in a dazzling, all-white version of his* Cats *costume.*

DARIUS: Jeffrey—guess what?

JEFFREY: Sterling!

DARIUS *(sitting on one of the fiberglass chairs):* You know that tunnel of light you're supposed to see, right before you die? It really happens! The first person I saw was my Aunt Berniece. She had emphysema. She hugged me and she said . . . *(As Aunt Berniece, taking a drag on a cigarette and speaking in a gravelly voice.)* . . . "Darling, can you get me a pair for the matinee?"

JEFFREY *(staggered):* What are you? Some sort of grief-induced hallucination? Are you a symptom? Why did you come back?

DARIUS: To see you. I figured you got here too late, after I was already in the coma. Did you bring me anything?

JEFFREY: Um . . . flowers!

DARIUS *(looking around):* Where?

JEFFREY: I was in a hurry!

DARIUS: Jeffrey, I'm dead. You're not.

JEFFREY: I know that.

DARIUS: You do? Prove it.

JEFFREY: What do you mean?

DARIUS: Go dancing. Go to a show. Make trouble. Make out. Hate AIDS, Jeffrey. Not life.

JEFFREY: How?

DARIUS: Just think of AIDS as . . . the guest that won't leave. The one we all hate. But you have to remember.

JEFFREY: What?

DARIUS: Hey—it's still our party.

*   *   *

Steve joins Jeffrey on the observation deck of the Empire State Building, with the Manhattan skyline lit by a full moon. Jeffrey has a balloon that Mother Theresa has given him.

JEFFREY: Steve, if I asked you to, could we have sex? Safe sex? Some kind of sex? Tonight?

STEVE: On top of the Empire State Building?

JEFFREY: Wherever. I needed . . . a moon. You haven't answered my question.

STEVE: Wait a minute! What is this? You think it's so easy? You leave a message, snap your fingers? Jeffrey, I'm still HIV-positive.

JEFFREY: So?

STEVE: So—it doesn't go away! It only gets worse!

JEFFREY: I know.

STEVE: Don't do this. Don't pretend. I will not be your good deed!

JEFFREY: Oh, you're not. I'm too selfish. I don't want a red ribbon. I want you.

STEVE: Say we have sex. Say we like it. And say tomorrow morning you decide to take off, for Wisconsin!

JEFFREY: I won't!

STEVE: How do I know that?

JEFFREY: Because I'm a gay man. And I live in New York. And I'm not an innocent bystander. Not any more.

Steve is now somewhat convinced. He studies Jeffrey for a moment.

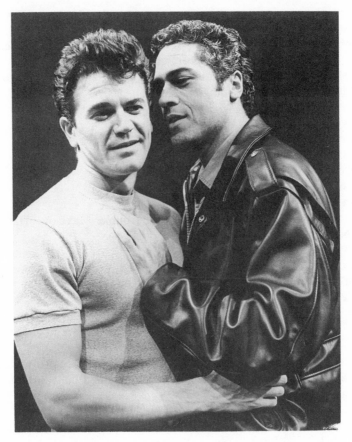

John Michael Higgins and Tom Hewitt in *Jeffrey*

STEVE: So . . . how bad do you want it?

JEFFREY: Find out.

STEVE: I like this. This is nice. You want it. Suddenly it's my decision. I get to be Jeffrey.

JEFFREY: Fuck you.

STEVE: Maybe.

JEFFREY: *Maybe?*

STEVE: You know, I think you should woo me. Maybe dinner. Maybe dancing.

JEFFREY: Yes!

STEVE: And then . . .

JEFFREY: Unbelievably hot sex!

STEVE: Not yet.

JEFFREY *(very frustrated):* What do you want?

STEVE: Jewelry.

JEFFREY: Yes!

STEVE: No, wait. What did my horoscope say this morning? "You will meet an incredibly fucked-up guy. Happiness is impossible. Go for it."

JEFFREY: Yes! *(After a beat.)* Yes?

STEVE *(after a moment):* Yes.

JEFFREY: But Steve—first you have to promise me something.

STEVE *(exasperated): What?*

JEFFREY: Promise me . . . you won't get sick.

STEVE: Done.

JEFFREY: And you won't die.

STEVE: Never.

JEFFREY *(staring at Steve, very emotional):* Liar.

> *Jeffrey and Steve move toward each other. Steve pulls back.*

STEVE: Jesus. We shouldn't do this. We are really asking for it. Give me one good reason. Give me one reason why we even have a prayer.

JEFFREY: You want one good reason?

STEVE: I do.

JEFFREY *(after a beat):* I dare you.

> *They stare at each other. Jeffrey tosses the balloon to Steve; the balloon almost hits the ground, but Steve leans forward and catches it. He holds the balloon for a moment and then tosses it back to Jeffrey. They move upstage, and toward each other, tapping the balloon back and forth. The balloon is caught in the light of the moon and glows translucently. Finally, Jeffrey catches the balloon. He and Steve embrace, and kiss, as the lights dim. Curtain.*

WINGS

A Full-Length Musical in One Act

BOOK AND LYRICS BY ARTHUR PERLMAN

MUSIC BY JEFFREY LUNDEN

BASED ON A PLAY BY ARTHUR KOPIT

Cast and credits appear on pages 332, 335

ARTHUR PERLMAN (book, lyrics) was born July 3, 1958 in Silver Spring, Md., the son of the assistant editor of an AFL-CIO labor journal. It was inevitable that he and his collaborator, Jeffrey Lunden, should meet at an early age, Lunden's father also being concerned with organized labor as a member of the U.S. Department of Labor. Meet at a pre-kindergarten age Perlman and Lunden did, and they collaborated on a show in 9th grade. They separated at the college level, Perlman getting his B.A. from Brown University in 1980, then they rejoined in the N.Y.U. musical theater program, getting their M.F.A.s in 1983.

The Perlman-Lunden musical collaboration has included Once on a Summer's Day *(1985) off off Broadway at Ensemble Studio Theater, two children's musicals (*Footprints on the Moon *and* From Sea to Shining Sea*) for Theaterworks/U.S.A. and material for the American Theater Festival revue* Let Freedom Sing! *at Kennedy Center. Their* Wings, *based on Arthur Kopit's play, produced March 9, 1993 for 47 performances at the Joseph Papp Public Theater after a premiere* *at the Goodman Theater, Chicago, in October 1992, is their first full-fledged New York production and their first Best Play.*

In addition to his work with Lunden, Perlman is the author of industrial shows. He lives in Manhattan with his wife and two sons.

JEFFREY LUNDEN (music) was born a few months after Arthur Perlman, on October 14, 1958 in Philadelphia, and shared school classes with his collaborator through high school but branched off to college at Oberlin, receiving his B.A. in 1980 and then rejoining Perlman in New York at N.Y.U. His solo activities have established him as a prominent producer of musical documentaries for National Public Radio, including presentations of the works of Burton Lane, Stephen Sondheim and a centenary tribute to Cole Porter which was hosted by Kitty Carlisle Hart and won Lunden a 1992 Public Radio Award.

Lunden and Perlman have received numerous ASCAP Awards, and both are members of the Dramatists Guild. At present they are preparing an adaptation of The Little Prince *for Theaterworks/USA. And Lunden, who lives in Brooklyn, was working solo this season on an NPR special celebrating the 50th anniversary of the Richard Rodgers-Oscar Hammerstein II collaboration and the opening of their* Oklahoma! *on Broadway on March 31, 1943.*

ARTHUR KOPIT (original play) was born on May 10, 1937 in New York City. He was educated at Lawrence, L.I. High School and Harvard (B.A. cum laude, 1959) where he began to write plays. Eight of them were produced from 1957 to 1960 by various groups: The Questioning of Nick, Gemini, On the Runway of Life You Never Know What's Coming Off Next, Across the River and Into the Jungle, Sing to Me Through Open Windows, Aubade, To Dwell in a Place of Strangers *and* Oh Dad, Poor Dad, Mamma's Hung You in the Closet and I'm Feelin' So Sad. *The latter was first staged by Cambridge, Mass. undergraduates in January 1960, then had a short run in its professional premiere in England during the summer of 1961, prior to its production off Broadway at the Phoenix Theater under the direction of Jerome Robbins on Feb. 26, 1962 for 454 performances. It was named a Best Play of its season (at which time its author was billing himself with a middle initial, Arthur L. Kopit) and won the Vernon Rice and Outer Circle Awards.* Oh, Dad *was revived on Broadway Aug. 27, 1963 for 47 performances.*

A double bill of Kopit one-acters, The Day the Whores Came Out to Play Tennis *and* Sing to Me Through Open Windows *appeared off Broadway March 15, 1965 for 24 performances. His second Best Play,* Indians, *was given its world premiere by the Royal Shakespeare Company in London in July 1968, its American premiere at the Arena Stage in Washington, D.C. in May 1969 and its New York premiere on Broadway Jan. 3, 1970 for 96 performances. Kopit's third Best Play,* Wings, *had its world premiere in March 1978 at the Yale School of Drama, where its author was Adjunct Professor of Playwriting. With Constance Cum-*

mings creating the central role, this full-evening one-acter moved to a limited off-Broadway engagement of 15 performances June 21, 1978 at the Public Theater. On Dec. 5 it reopened in Boston and headed for Washington and Broadway, where it played 113 performances starting Jan. 28, 1979. Now it is cited for the second time as a Best Play, in its 1993 reincarnation as a musical, and Kopit is preparing a movie version of the play for a Hallmark TV special.

A fourth Best Play citation went to Kopit for the authorship of the book for the musical Nine, *which opened on Broadway May 9, 1982, winning the Tony Award for the season's best musical and running for 739 performances. His adaptation of* Ghosts *came to Broadway for 40 performances the following summer on August 30; his* End of the World With Symposium to Follow *garnered two votes for best American play in the 1984 Critics Circle voting after playing Broadway for 33 performances starting May 6; and his* Road to Nirvana *came to Circle Rep off Broadway (after premiering at Actors Theater of Louisville as* Bone-the-Fish *in the spring of 1989) on March 7, 1991 for 30 performances. Kopit adapted* The Phantom of the Opera *with Maury Yeston as the musical* Phantom *in 1983, but it wasn't produced until after Andrew Lloyd Webber's famous 1988 version. It premiered in 1991 at Houston's Theater Under the Stars and has become a major multiple-production cross-country hit, with 40 more productions now planned.*

Kopit's other works for the theater have included What's Happened to the Thorne's House *(1972),* Conquest of Everest *and* Fame, the Hero *(OOB in 1973),* Louisiana Territory *(1975),* Secrets of the Rich *(1977 at the O'Neill Conference) and* Good Help Is Hard to Find *(OOB in 1981). He has received Guggenheim, Rockefeller, National Endowment, CBS and other grants, as well as an award in literature from the American Academy of Arts and Letters. He is the Secretary of the Dramatists Guild, the playwrights' organization, and lives in Connecticut with his wife Leslie Garis, who is also a writer, and their three children.*

Time: Over a period of two years

SYNOPSIS: Emily Stilson, age somewhere in her 70s, is sitting reading a book while on her phonograph a well-worn 78 rpm is playing a song whose lyrics extol the courage of adventurers, especially the "daredevils of the air."

> *Suddenly the sound begins to sound very echo-y and slow. Emily looks up. But the song quickly resumes its normal sound, and Emily goes back to her book. The lights begin to dim, as a spot comes up on Emily, who increasingly seems alone in the darkness.*

RECORD:
    Off they go in search of some new adventure
    Up among the clouds they are all alone . . .

Again, the song begins distorting. Emily looks up again, puzzled. Is something wrong with her record player?
They enjoy a life that is filled with wonder
Brave—you bet, on wings they can get to places as yet unknown
Abruptly, the sound stops. Silence. The book slips from Emily's hands. She stares out in terror. Blackout.

In the darkness is heard a cacophony of instrumental sounds, plus distorted impressions of a trip to the hospital in an ambulance, hospital noises; plus sounds and images of the outdoors, airplanes, blue sky. Light comes up on Emily seated downstage, surrounded by darkness, with the vague shapes and voices of a Doctor and Nurse who are questioning her. She shows no sign of hearing or noticing them, and they disappear.

EMILY *(sings):*
What if it happened but maybe it better soon no
But it globbridged and rubbidged me now till it's dofting
And nothing there
. . . Try again
We hear hospital sounds, vague and distorted. Lights reveal shadowy objects that appear and disappear.
Yes now I what of my son's name is can't but the face is too
Fleetish and floddered I hapst of the porship off into I lost it
Now
Sharp sound of a window opening. Sound of a bird chirping.
Now it's I heard of I can't think the word but I sound it so
Many off in out I know it it's . . . it's . . . it's . . .
Sound of bird.
. . . Bird
How long have I been here and wrapped in the dark?
How long have my arms no longer been mine?
Scurrying music as we see brief images of the Doctor, Nurses and Technicians moving behind her, pushing a bed. Curtains being pulled; lights change.

Emily, alone, tries to think out what has happened to her. She cannot speak, and her thoughts, often garbled, are expressed in song, or at least as words set to music. Visions of old propellor-driven airplanes cross her mind and then give way to on-and-off flashes of her hospital environment—a bed, a window, a door, etc. Doctors and Nurses gather round to question her, but she can't answer. She begins to understand the questions and is frustrated because she can't make the others understand that she hears them. Finally they manage to get a nod out of her in answer to one of their questions.

"Things could be worse/Though I can't imagine/How," Emily is singing to herself when Amy, an accordionist, begins playing "Let Me Call You Sweetheart," which we hear as Emily hears it, "knarled sound . . . . . threatening." But for the first time the hospital staff begins to deal with Emily directly. Like the music, the voices sound threatening to Emily. But *"her inner and outer worlds are beginning to come together."*

DOCTOR *(sings)*:
    Mrs. Stilson
    Makey your naming powers
EMILY: What?
NURSE: *(sings)*:
    Mrs. Stilson
    Canju spoke me?
EMILY: Can I what?
DOCTOR: *(sings)*:
    Can do peeper
    Insome to afterme do
NURSE *(sings)*:
    Ahwill

DOCTOR *(sings)*:   EMILY *(over)*: What . . . what's
    Howme feeder holeup?   going on? I don't . . . you don't . . .
NURSE *(sings)*:   this is . . . grotesque!
    Nodee youheed pause
DOCTOR *(sings)*:
    Pollycadjis
NURSE *(sings)*:
    Sewylada?

DOCTOR: *(sings)*:   NURSE *(sings)*:
    Mrs.   Mrs. Stilson
    Stilson
    Opee-eyes yourup
                                                 Blink
    Doteenot earwhat
                                                 Notty that
    Tak tor time-y Mrs.
    Stil-son   Pollycadjis
    Stil-son   Sewylada?
    Son-stil-son   Peppernotdo
    . . . Hmmmn
        The Doctor nods to the Nurse, and they exit. Music. Light change.
        Time passing.

EMILY *(sings)*:

How it came to pass that I was captured
How it came to pass that I came here
In this small and square and empty room. Where
Strangers come then quickly disappear
What means square?
—I'll come back to that . . . . .

As Emily tries to puzzle out what's happened to her, Amy comes in with her accordion, strokes Emily reassuringly and plays "Let Me Call You Sweetheart" again. This time Emily perceives the tune and moves her hand to its rhythm. It overstimulates her into excessive movement, however, and Amy calls for the Nurse.

Lights change as time passes, with Emily deciding that she's been in a plane crash and has been captured by unknown persons for unknown reasons. A Nurse comes in with a food cart and tries to interest the patient in a tray of food, singing "Yum yummy yum yummy yum" and smacking her lips, as one might with a child. But in the course of trying to feed Emily, the Nurse expresses a moment of compassion in song: "Is there someone behind those eyes/Those eyes that seem to see so much/Is there someone warm and wise/In there waiting; out of touch/How I wonder/Can you understand me?"

After the Nurse leaves, Emily resumes contemplating her situation in song: her plane has crashed, she's been captured and imprisoned in a farmhouse—probably in Rumania because the country's name sounds something like "insane"—and people keep on questioning her because she knows something they want to know. This line of reasoning eventually becomes too much for her, and again she breaks off with "I'll come back to . . . that."

Emily is taken to a session with the Doctor, who gets her to speak, with great effort, by questioning her about simple matters. He puts a number of objects before her and asks her to identify the one she'd use to clean her teeth. Emily picks up a comb.

DOCTOR *(hands her the toothbrush)*: Do you know what this object is called?
EMILY *(with great difficulty)*: Tooooovv . . . bbbrum?
DOCTOR: Very good. Now put it down. *(She puts it down.)* Now pretend you have it in your hand. Show me what you'd do with it. *(She does nothing.)* What does one do with an object such as that? *(No response.)* Mrs. Stilson, what is the name of the object you are looking at?
EMILY *(sings)*:

Well it's I think
Wombly and not
There's a toring to it

Works the clumbness of it
And the numbness of it
DOCTOR: Pick it up.
> *She does.*

EMILY *(as soon as she picks it up):* Toovbram . . . tooove-britch . . . bratch . . . brush . . . bridge. Two-bridge.
DOCTOR: Show me what you do with it.
> *Pause. She does nothing. Then she puts it to her lips, and holds it there*
> *motionless.*

Very good. Thank you.

When the Doctor leaves, Emily remembers that her children visited her the day before. She sings, "At least, that is, they said they were my children/Never saw them before in my life."

When the Doctor returns, he tries to make Emily understand why she's here, explaining carefully that she's had an accident to her brain, they don't know

William Brown (Mr. Brambilla), Ross Lehman (Billy), Hollis Resnik (Amy), Ora Jones (Nurse) and Linda Stephens (Emily Stilson) in the Arthur Perlman-Jeffrey Lunden musical version of Arthur Kopit's *Wings*

what caused it, and it's too soon to give a prognosis. But Emily pays little attention, not trusting him and believing he's playing tricks on her.

The Doctor comes in and out with his questions, and when the Yum Yummy Nurse appears and starts to go into her ingratiating routine, Emily throws a fit, screaming intelligibly, "Out! Get out! Take this shit away, I don't want it! Someone get me out of here," until she receives an injection that puts her to sleep.

The lights fade to black with the sound of wind and then come up on Amy wheeling Emily for a stroll outdoors. The sense of hospital confinement is gone, and Emily can now chat with Amy in words that are intelligible, but her thoughts are still confused. "I can't make it do it like it used to," Emily explains, and Amy reassures her that it's only because of the stroke she's suffered. Amy wonders whether Emily can remember her life before the accident. She can, at night, sometimes, as in a dream.

AMY: Your son is bringing a picture of you when you were younger. We thought you might like that. You used to fly, didn't you?

EMILY *(sings):*

Wings
I used to walk on
Wings . . .

> *Lights fade on Amy. Emily is alone again. Sound of wind and propellor turning, images of clouds and sky.*

I'm the
Middle Stilson in the show
Take a breath and out I go
Hold the wire feel the hum
Keep my balance, nerves are numb

Out on the wing

Out where the
Wind is howling, blowing through my hair
Underfoot is only air
Overhead the endless blue
Mist of white streams past as I soar through

> *The music soars as she feels herself walking on the wing.*

. . . Feel it bank and soar and spin
Then after time I climb back in
—The show is over, climb back in . . .

Wings
I used to walk on
Wings

> *Music continues as the lights return to normal. Amy enters.*

AMY: Hello, Emily.

EMILY: Oh, Amy! . . . Didn't hear what you was . . . coming . . . oh!

AMY: What is it?

EMILY *(sings):*

Something wet and

Don't know word but

Something wet from

Both my eyes

AMY: Can you name them? Do you know what they are?

EMILY *(sings):*

. . . Tears?

AMY: That's right, very good. And do you know what that means?

EMILY *(sings):*

It means that

I am . . . sad

> *Lights fade to black.*

The music continues, but it changes, and the setting is a rehabilitation center, in every way brighter than the hospital, with sounds of laughter and people in conversation. In song Emily remarks to herself about the maze of corridors and stairways—the place generally excites her—and wonders what's behind the closed doors. She meets a man, Billy, who offers her candy he says he's made. She refuses politely. And Amy comes to see her.

AMY: Do you like this new place better?

EMILY: Oh well oh well yes, much all . . . nice flowers here, people seem . . . more like me. Thank you.

> *Amy kisses her then disappears as Emily describes, singing:*

Amy kisses me

She puts her what—her thing

Her arm! Around my shoulder

Amy turns away

I know she knows I might

—Might *not* get too much better

No need—I want to tell her it's okay

She kisses me again, then walks away . . . . .

The scene changes to a therapy session directed by Amy with Emily, Billy and two other patients (Mr. Brambilla and Mrs. Timmins). The group is trying to sing "Let Me Call You Sweetheart," but in the middle of this Emily switches to the song "The New Daredevils of the Air." Emily apologizes, but Amy assures her she liked it. So did Billy, who comments, "Hey let me tell ya, it was really with the *(Bangs on drum.)* boom-de-boom-de-boom. Better 'an that other ya know, with the Sweetheart Let Me Call It: boom . . . boom . . . boom. Let me tell ya girlie, your song's got it better."

Gently, Amy attempts to prod the patients into exercising their memories, recalling little things like one another's names and what they were just watching on TV. Billy suddenly decides that he gave Amy his recipe for cheesecake and ought to have been paid for it. In song, Billy demands, "So let me have it, come on fork it over kiddo/Let's not be chief." Amy picks up on Billy's mistake immediately and urges him to pronounce the word "cheap," which he can't seem to do, even when he comes to it in the lyrics of his song.

BILLY *(sings):*
>   Okay I'm ready on my tongue I got it—simple
>   Now I'm gonna take the leap
>   It's nothin' hey now any kid could do it easy
>   —Let's not be chief
>   Charf . . .
>   Chafe . . . . .
>
>   I been a cook for nearly all my life
>   And hey I got it in me really deep.
>   A recipe like what I'm talkin' here ya know that's
>   Somethin' that you gotta keep
>   So I know you made it and you got it
>   And I know I had it but I guess I lost it
>   But I know it's somewheres and I gotta find it
>   So let me have it come on fork it over kiddo
>   Let's not be cheap
>
>   . . . Cheap
>   Cheap!
>   Cheap-cheap-cheap-cheeeeeeeeap!! . . . . .

Following Billy's triumph, the lights go to black, leaving only Emily visible as she continues trying to think out her situation in song.

EMILY *(sings):*
>   There are times
>   It goes in and out so fast
>   All the sounds I know they mean
>   Want to hold but they fly past
>   Like the clouds . . . . .
>
>   And there are times . . .
>   I think the end—I mean of death

I don't worry anymore
Know it's near and I'm not scared
But I don't open up the door . . . . .

Billy comes in with a tray of brownies. Emily takes one, remarking, "it looks deli ishes minds me since ovenish I-never-made-much-at-it-but . . ." Billy urges Emily to slow down. Doing so, she manages an intelligible "It . . . looks . . . delicious." She takes this opportunity to ask Billy, "Does it ever all of it come back?", but Billy doesn't know. He exits to fetch her some cookies.

The lights come up on Amy telling Emily she managed to get the record of "The New Daredevils of the Air" from Emily's son. Amy hands it to Emily, who puts it on the record player, and we hear the same song Emily was listening to when she suffered the stroke, extolling the new explorers who are no longer earthbound like Columbus and Peary but are "soaring through the sky." Sound of wind, propellors and cheering crowds are heard as Emily loses herself in the song. As it plays, she announces, "Ladies and gentlemen, my family and I will perform for you today feats of aeronautical skill such as have never been witnessed before! In the same spirit of adventure that propelled Lucky Lindy all the way across the Atlantic, I shall step out onto the wing of this airplane with only the vast blue sky beneath my feet! So prepare yourself for the thrill of a lifetime as you watch—the Flying Stilsons, Daredevils of the Air . . ."

Emily sings along with the record until it comes to an end and the sound effects fade, leaving only the sound of the needle on the revolving disc, as the lights go to black.

The lights come up on Amy and Emily going for a stroll outdoors, in winter. They stop by a snowy bench. Amy asks Emily to name the white stuff that's falling from the sky.

>   *Long silence.*
> EMILY: Where do you get names from?
> AMY: I? From in here, same as you.
> EMILY: Do you know how you do it?
> AMY: No . . .
> EMILY: Then how am I supposed . . . to learn?
> AMY *(softly):* I don't really know.
>> *Emily points at Amy and laughs—she's got her on that one. At first, Amy doesn't understand. Then she does. And then both of them are laughing.*
> EMILY: Look. You see?
>> *She scoops some snow off the bench; sings.*
> I reach out and I pick it up
> And suddenly I know

It's cold and crisp I'm feeling it
And suddenly—it's snow

It's peculiar I remember
If I hold it in my hand
When I hold it I remember
All at once I understand . . . . .

Emily remembers snowballs and eating snow with maple syrup, but when she drops her handful she forgets what snow is called. Amy gives Emily some more snow, and the names come back to her. Emily embraces Amy in gratitude for her help, then tells her of a strange thing that happened to her last night— perhaps a dream, Amy suggests.

EMILY: Yes, one of those, but I'm not . . . sure that it was . . . This . . . person . . . came into my room. I couldn't tell if it was a man or woman or . . . young or old. I was in my bed and it came. Didn't seem to have to walk just . . . came over to my . . . bed and . . . smiled at where I was. *(Pause.)* And then it said *(In a whisper.)* "Emily . . . we're glad you changed your mind." *(Pause.)* And then it turned and left.

Linda Stephens as Emily Stilson and Hollis Resnik as Amy in *Wings*

AMY: Was it a doctor? *(Emily shakes her head.)* One of the staff? *(Emily shakes her head.)* How do you know?

EMILY: I just know. *(Pause.)* Then . . . I left my body.

AMY: What?

EMILY *(with great excitement):* I was on the . . . what's the name over me . . .

AMY: Ceiling?

EMILY: Yes! I was floating like a . . .

AMY: Cloud? *(Emily shakes her head.)* Bird?

EMILY: Yes, up there at the *(She searches for the word; finds it.)* ceiling, and I looked down, and I was still there in my bed! Wasn't even scared, which you'd think I would be . . . And I thought, wow! this is the life, isn't it?

> *Music changes, sound of wind. The lights change and Amy recedes into the darkness. Emily sings:*

I am in a plane
—a Curtiss Jenny
How the sky is black
No stars—only snow
On my way to Omaha
I am lost my fuel is running low . . . . .

And her radio isn't working (the song continues) as she tries to guide the plane through the darkness. She sees a light below, through the gloom, and descends toward it, feeling greatly relieved—but it's just a street light, there's nowhere to land.

EMILY *(sings):*
. . . . . I need to use my
Wings
Into the darkness
Must go back into the night
Know that I somehow
Must let go of the light
My fuel is low, it's nearly gone
I am scared to—
I don't want to—
But I must go on . . .
> *The music soars.*
. . . Upside down, alone, and stranded
Think I'm dead, but single handed
Somehow I did it, made it—landed . . .
> *Amy is seen in the distance.*

AMY: Emily! Emily, are you all right?

> *Sudden, sharp, terrifying flapping sound. Emily gasps.*

EMILY *(sings):*

> I'm not in a plane
> But still I'm spinning
> How the sky is black
> No stars up above
> Falling through the emptiness
> Suddenly I feel the tremble of—
>
> Wings
> And now I fly on
> Wings
> I'm going on now
> Would you please touch her for me
> I'm going out now
> Where I land—well, we'll see
> Out on the wings
> I shut my eyes, I feel the wind
> And I am soaring on
> Wings
>
> > *The faint sound of wind as the lights close on her and fade to black.*
> > *Curtain.*

○○○
○○○
○○○
○○○
○○○
○○○
○○○ KISS OF THE SPIDER WOMAN

A Musical in Two Acts

BOOK BY TERRENCE McNALLY

MUSIC BY JOHN KANDER

LYRICS BY FRED EBB

BASED ON THE NOVEL BY MANUEL PUIG

Cast and credits appear on pages 313-315

TERRENCE McNALLY (book) was born in St. Petersburg, Fla., November 3, 1939 and grew up in Corpus Christi, Texas. He received his B.A. in English at Columbia where in his senior year he wrote the varsity show. After graduation he was awarded the Harry Evans Travelling Fellowship in creative writing. He made his professional stage debut with The Lady of the Camellias, *an adaptation of the Dumas story produced on Broadway in 1963. His first original full-length play,* And Things That Go Bump in the Night, *was produced on Broadway in 1965 following a production at the Tyrone Guthrie Theater in Minneapolis.*

McNally's short play Tour *was produced off Broadway in 1968 as part of the* Collision Course *program. In the next season, 1968–69, his one-acters were produced all over town:* Cuba Si! *off Broadway in the ANTA Matinee series;* Noon *on the Broadway program* Morning, Noon and Night; Sweet Eros *and* Witness *off Broadway that fall, and in early winter* Next *with Elaine May's* Adaptation *on an off-Broadway bill that was named a Best Play of its season.*

McNally's second Best Play, Where Has Tommy Flowers Gone?, *had its world premiere at the Yale Repertory Theater before opening on Broadway in 1971. His third,* Bad Habits, *was produced OOB in 1973 by New York Theater Strategy, directed then and in its off-Broadway and Broadway phases in the 1973–74 season by Robert Drivas. His fourth,* The Ritz, *played the Yale Repertory Theater as* The Tubs *before opening on Broadway January 20, 1975 for a run of 400 perform- ances. His fifth,* It's Only a Play, *was produced in a pre-Broadway tryout under the title* Broadway, *Broadway in 1978 and OOB under the new title by Manhattan Punch Line in 1982. It finally arrived in the full bloom of an off-Broadway production—and Best Play designation—January 12, 1986, for 17 performances at Manhattan Theater Club. This organization has produced most of his recent work including his sixth Best Play,* Lips Together, Teeth Apart, *which came onto the scene on June 25, 1991 and remained for 406 performances.*

Other notable McNally presentations in one of the most active and successful playwriting careers in his generation have included Whiskey *(1973, OOB); the book for the John Kander-Fred Ebb musical* The Rink *(1984, Broadway);* The Lisbon Traviata *(1985, OOB; 1989, off Broadway at MTC);* Frankie and Johnny in the Clair de Lune *(1987, off Broadway by MTC for 533 perform- ances); sketch material for MTC's musical revue* Urban Blight, *1988; in 1989,* Prelude and Liebestod *and* Hope *OOB and* Up in Saratoga *in regional theater at the Old Globe in San Diego; and in 1990, a revival at MTC of his* Bad Habits *and the book of the musical* Kiss of the Spider Woman *produced at SUNY Purchase, N.Y., in the short-lived New Musicals Program and continuing in production on an international scale until its arrival on Broadway this season to win McNally's seventh Best Play citation and the Tony Award for best book.*

McNally adapted his own The Ritz *and* Frankie and Johnny *for the movies and is the author of a number of TV plays, including the 1991 Emmy Award-winning* Andre's Mother. *He has been the recipient of Obies, Hull-Warriner Awards (for* Bad Habits *and* The Lisbon Traviata*); fellowships from CBS, Rockefeller and two from the Guggenheim Foundation; and a citation from the American Academy of Arts and Letters. He lives in Manhattan and has served as vice president of the Dramatists Guild, the organization of playwrights, composers, lyricists and libret- tists, since 1981.*

JOHN KANDER (music) was born in Kansas City, Mo., March 18, 1927. He received his B.A. at Oberlin in 1951 and his M.A. at Columbia in 1953. His early theatrical experience included conducting stock productions and doing the ar- rangements for Gypsy *and* Irma La Douce. *His first full Broadway score was* A Family Affair *(1962, with book and lyrics by James and William Goldman), and later that year he provided the incidental music for the Broadway comedy* Never Too Late.

Kander's collaboration with lyricist-librettist Fred Ebb—the most prolific and effective in the modern theater—began with the songs "My Coloring Book" and "I Don't Care Much" (a Barbra Streisand hit). It moved to Broadway with Kander *as composer and* Ebb *as lyricist with* Flora, the Red Menace *(1965),* Cabaret *(1966, a Best Play and the Tony and Critics Award-winner),* The Happy Time *(1968),* Zorba *(1968),* 70, Girls, 70 *(1971, with Ebb also providing the book),* Chicago *(1975, a Best Play Tony-nominated for both score and book, which again Ebb provided, with Bob Fosse),* The Act *(1977, with a Tony-nominated score),* Woman of the Year *(1981, a Tony-nominated score),* The Rink *(1984, again a Tony-nominated score) and now the tenth Kander-Ebb Broadway musical and third Best Play:* Kiss of the Spider Woman, *which took a circuitous route of a 1990 tryout production in Purchase, N.Y. and Toronto and award-winning 1992 London productions to arrive on Broadway May 3, 1993, just in time to win the Critics best-musical Award and Tony Awards for book, score and show.*

Off Broadway, the Kander-Ebb collaboration was recently celebrated in a 408-performance 1991 revue And the World Goes 'Round. *Kander is a member of the Songwriters Hall of Fame, the National Institute of Music Theater and the council of the Dramatists Guild. He lives in Manhattan.*

FRED EBB (lyrics) is a New Yorker born April 8, 1932 and educated at New York University and Columbia. He wrote both book and lyrics for the Phoenix Theater production of Morning Sun *(1963) and contributed to revues (*From A to Z, *1960 and* Put It in Writing, *1963) and* TV *(That Was the Week That Was). His collaboration with John Kander has progressed through the ten Broadway shows listed above in the composer's biographical sketch, and for two of those shows—*70, Girls, 70 *and* Chicago—*he also provided the book, the second named bringing him a Best Play citation and a best-book Tony nomination.*

The Kander-Ebb pairing began with songs, flourished on the Broadway stage and spread far and wide. Their off-Broadway cabaret revue 2 by 5 *(1976) has been followed by contributions to the revues* Joe Masiell Not at the Palace *(1977),* Diamonds *(1984) and* Hay Fever *(1986),* The Madwoman of Central Park West *(1979) and the Music Hall spectacular* Encore *(1982), while* Cabaret *and* Zorba *have enjoyed successful Broadway revivals. Their film credits include their own* Cabaret *plus* Norman Rockwell: A Short Subject; Lucky Lady; New York, New York; Funny Lady; Kramer vs. Kramer; A Matter of Times; Places in the Heart; French Postcards *and* Stepping Out. *They have created TV material for Liza Minnelli, Goldie Hawn, Frank Sinatra and Mikhail Baryshnikov and cabaret material for numerous other performers, and Ebb wrote a 1976 Broadway revue for Shirley MacLaine with Cy Coleman. Ebb and Kander were elected to New York's Theater Hall of Fame in 1991. Ebb is a member of the Dramatists Guild and like his collaborator lives in Manhattan and shares, for his lyrics, the 1993 best-score Tony Award voted to* Kiss of the Spider Woman.

MANUEL PUIG was an Argentinian born in Villegas in 1932 and died in Cuer-
navaca, Mexico in 1990. He studied philosophy at the University of Buenos Aires
and film direction at the Cinecitta in Rome, then worked as an assistant director
before beginning to write in 1962. His novels have included Betrayed by Rita
Hayworth *(1968),* Heartbreak Tango *(1969),* The Buenos Aires Affair *(1974)*
as well as Kiss of the Spider Woman *(1976). Puig's stage adaptation of the latter*
was an international success and was made into a 1985 film in which William Hurt
won an Oscar for his portrayal of Molina. Another Puig play, Mystery of the
Rose Bouquet, *opened in London in 1987 and was presented at the Mark Taper*
Forum in Los Angeles with Anne Bancroft and Jane Alexander.

Time: Sometime in the recent past

Place: A prison in Latin America

ACT I

SYNOPSIS: The Spider Woman is a voice singing in the darkness as the lights
come up—in a prologue—revealing a prison expressed in oppressive, changing
patterns of bars which sometimes blend with the lines of a projected spider's
web. The inmates include Molina, revealed in a spotlight sitting on his cot. *"A*
man—Valentin—is dragged onstage by two guards—Marcos and Esteban."

Scene 1

Guards freeze as the Warden, seen on a catwalk, declares, "Prisoner 16115.
Name—Valentin Arrequi Paz. Age 27. Arrested July 7th at Las Ventas Metro
stop. Apprehended in act of passing travel documents to political fugitives.
Suspect is key link to terrorist groups. Prisoner has been brought to La Hermosa
State Prison where he is now being held under executive power of the Federal
government and awaiting judgment." The Warden is sure that Valentin will
confess under torture (a scream is heard offstage). Then Valentin is dragged to
Molina's cell and thrown in with him. Before exiting, the Warden again declares, "Prisoner 57884. Name—Luis Albert Molina. Age 37. Sexual offender.
Arrested for corrupting a minor. Male. Serving third year of eight-year sentence."

The cell into which Valentin has been thrown has acquired a number of
decorative touches during its occupancy by Molina: a movie poster, a colorful
curtain, etc. Molina, whose appearance and mannerisms openly declare him a
homosexual, is a window dresser. Revolted by the brutal fashion in which he has

suddenly acquired a roommate, Molina calls upon his imagination to free him from this hostile environment.

MOLINA *(music under):* Aurora, help me! What scene? There were so many. What movie? Aurora, I need you. Come to me, like you always have. *(Sings.)*
> Her name is Aurora
> And she is so beautiful
> No man who has met her can ever forget her
> They're madly in love
> Forever in love.
I see her so clearly. I know her so well
> *Upstage we see Aurora looking in a mirror. Molina sings.*
> She steps to her glass now
> All almonds and roses
> She's powdered and pampered
> The sight of her dark eyes
> Igniting the screen . . .
> Scorching the screen.
> *Lights out on cell. We are totally in the movie.*

The singing continues, as Servants come on to tend Aurora and notice that she is aglow with happiness. Aurora tells them why.

AURORA *(sings):*
> Last night I went to see the gypsy
> And oh, the things she had to say
> She told me I would meet a stranger
> A lean, handsome hero
> Who'd sweep in and sweep me away
>
> I sat there trembling at her table
> And smelled the incense in the air
> "Someday, you'll hear a cry," she told me
> "A sharp, piercing sound
> And when you look around
> The love of your life
> Will be there!"

Indeed, there occurs a "sharp, piercing" sound which brings the song of Aurora and the Servants to an abrupt end. It is a scream from Valentin (dark-complexioned and masculine, in contrast to Molina), who is beginning to regain consciousness. Molina tries to comfort Valentin, advising him to take deep breaths, promising to tell him about Aurora and her movies, assuring Valentin that he can trust him. But the scene ends ominously, with a light on the Warden commenting, "I do, Molina. I trust you completely."

Scene 2

Prisoners in their cells sing of the delights to be found in life "Over the Wall," wondering if they'll ever be free to enjoy them again. The Spider Woman appears on the catwalk.

SPIDER WOMAN *(sings):*
 And the moon grows dimmer
 At the tide's low ebb
 And your breath comes faster
 And you're aching to move
 But you're caught in the web . . .
  Blackout.

Scene 3

In their cell, Valentin sits reading while Molina unrolls a movie poster of Aurora in *Forbidden Love*. Valentin is annoyed because instead of minding his own business in silence, Molina insists on singing (about Valentin being ungrateful for the care Molina has taken of him) and talking (about his being a window dresser in a large store). Molina is good at it, too (he confesses), because he insists on perfection.

MOLINA *(sings):*
 Once, I asked for a Balenciaga scarf
 To stuff in a mannequin's purse
 They told me, "No one on earth will see"
 I answered, "No one on earth but me"
 And I stood my ground as no other dresser does
 And darling guess what?
 Balenciaga it was!

 Dressing them up
 I was the creme de la creme
 As I adjusted each hem
 I kept on dazz-a-ling them
 At my particular store
 Which was the best in the town
 You'd never catch them wearing a frown
 Or catch them dressing me down
 For my finesse at
 Dressing them up . . . . .

Molina goes on describing his technique until Valentin can endure it no longer and begs him to shut up. Then Valentin draws an imaginary line across the cell, demanding that each keep to his own territory. The toilet happens to be on Valentin's side, Molina complains, so Valentin makes this an exception— otherwise, he draws the line.

VALENTIN *(sings):*
    . . . . . So don't ever try to be
    Don't ever dream you'll be
    Don't dare to think that you'll
    Ever be some fairy
    Friend of mine
    Cause no no no no no
    That's where I draw the line.
MOLINA: Fine!
VALENTIN *(sings):*
    I draw the line
MOLINA: Fine!
VALENTIN *(sings):*
    I draw the line
MOLINA: Fine!

Molina mocks Valentin for reading Karl Marx. He even creates a disturbance which draws the Guards and further annoys Valentin. The Guards threaten Molina with blackjacks and scare him into saying, "I'm a faggot piece of shit, and any time you want me, I'm here," before they exit.

> *Molina is on his knees, embarrassed and ashamed. Valentin raises himself on an elbow and looks at Molina.*
VALENTIN: Why do you let them humiliate you like that?
MOLINA: I don't let them. I'm a coward. *(Pause.)* Besides, darling, there are privileges in degradation. It got me my ravishing drapes and my pin-ups.
VALENTIN *(dismissing him):* Make yourself trivial.
MOLINA: We're both trivial. The only difference between us is that I know it and you don't.
VALENTIN: You go to hell.
MOLINA: We're already there.
VALENTIN: I will go mad alone in this cell with this person!

Molina advises Valentin to think about his girl to keep from going mad. Valentin's thoughts are of a girl named Marta and Molina's are of his mother. These thoughts are embodied by the appearance of the two women joining the men in a song which declares that these women are getting along very well without their absent men—which, they all assert at the end, is a lie.

Scene 4

The Prisoners are dreaming of life on the outside and singing their thoughts in another set of lyrics to "Over the Wall."

MOLINA *(sings):*
      So I sit on my cot and my memory whirls
As I think of the boys dressing up like girls
Wearing too much mascara and phony pearls
Over the wall . . . . .

PRISONERS *(sing):*
      Where are the children who bear my name?
Making a circle to play a game?
Do they say to the neighbors I'm not to blame?
Or spit at the thought of me
Over the wall . . . . .

VALENTIN *(sings):*
      So I wait in my cell feeling half alive
Sharing food with a rat, maybe four or five
While the rats with the power will all survive
Over the wall . . . . .

Meanwhile, the Warden amuses himself watching one of the Prisoners trying to escape. Just as the escaping Prisoner reaches almost to the top of the fence, a machine gun opens up, killing him, as the Prisoners continue to chant, "Over the Wall."

Scene 5

In the cell, Valentin shows signs of having taken a beating recently, while Molina is talking about himself, explaining that he is a "cineaste" addicted to movies because his mother was an usherette who took Molina with her to the movie house when she had to work nights. Molina sat in the front row where all the players on the screen seemed huge, and he first saw his Aurora and memorized "every line, every song, every costume, every kiss" of her every movie. Occasionally, in the background, is heard a scream, while Molina goes on explaining that there was one Aurora role he didn't like—a Spider Woman whose kiss was death. The Spider Woman scared him, and though his mother explained this was only a make-believe movie role, Molina is convinced that the Spider Woman is frighteningly real.

Brent Carver *(standing)* as Molina and Anthony Crivello as Valentin in the prizewinning musical *Kiss of the Spider Woman* by Terrence McNally, John Kander and Fred Ebb, directed by Harold Prince

Molina asks Valentin about someone named Marta whom Valentin mentioned while talking in his sleep, saying what he'd like to do to her.

VALENTIN: . . . . . What do you care? I thought you liked boys.

MOLINA: I do, but I'm always willing to expand my horizons.
       Staring at him provocatively. After a pause.
Don't worry, darling. You're not my type. I'm looking for someone to settle down with, not storm the barricades.

VALENTIN: When you're not molesting minors in some men's room.

MOLINA: Look, I didn't know he was a minor! When he smiled at me, I thought he was smiling at someone else. Men like me don't get smiled at a lot. But he kept smiling. So I smiled back. I followed him right into a trap. And it wasn't a men's room. It was a coffee bar.
       We hear another scream.
They're bringing a prisoner and they're going to make us look at him to frighten us. I'll look but I won't see. Deaf, dumb and blind. Take my advice, Mr. Revolutionary. *(Sings.)*

When you feel you've gone to hell in a handbasket
And the world in which you dwell's no paradise
> *The side curtain opens to reveal Aurora as she continues the song while*
> *Molina mouths the words.*

AURORA *(sings):*

I've some counsel I can give
You need but ask it
I'm so very glad to share this good advice

You've got to learn how not to be
Where you are
The more you face reality, the more you scar
So close your eyes and you can be a movie star
Why must you stay where you are?

You've got to learn how not to see
What you've seen
The slice of hell you call your life is harsh and mean
So why not lie beside me on a movie screen
Why must you see what you've seen? . . . . .

As Aurora continues her song, Prisoners join her and share her fantasy in a dance. Aurora and the dancers freeze, as Esteban and Marcos *"drag on a Prisoner with a cloth sack over his head."* They pull off the sack and challenge Valentin to look. As he does, he flinches—he obviously recognizes the victim but pretends he doesn't know him. Esteban and Marcos drag the Prisoner off, under orders from the Warden to step up the torture.

After they've gone, Valentin won't admit even to Molina that he knows the victim. "I *told* you not to look," Molina comments, while Valentin is trembling at the thought of what they're doing to the poor fellow.

Scene 6

An Observer from Amnesty International has come to look things over and questions the Warden about a political prisoner named Valentin Arrequi Paz. "Never heard of him," the Warden says.

Meanwhile, Valentin, Molina and other Prisoners are suffering an ordeal of being packed into a cell, so many of them so tightly, that they can hardly breathe. Valentin escapes into thoughts of Marta, as the others sing "Over the Wall."

Scene 7

The Warden questions Molina about his cellmate, asking Molina to supply the name of Valentin's girl friend so that through her they may penetrate the band of revolutionaries. Molina denies knowing anything, and the Warden suggests that they have various treatments that might refresh Molina's memory. The Guards are seen in the process of torturing a Prisoner by placing a metal bucket over his head and striking it with their batons; and at the same time, the Spider Woman appears above the action in a huge spider web. Molina still protests that he knows nothing, and the Warden mentions another kind of torture (which is seen about to begin), beating the soles of a Prisoner's feet.

> *Lights down.*

SPIDER WOMAN *(sings):*

Come—I'm the solution

Come—everlasting rest

Come—place your head on my welcoming breast

> *Lights up on the Prisoner and Guards.*

ESTEBAN: He's dead.

> *Music up as the Prisoner gets up from the chair and slowly starts climbing the web to reach the Spider Woman. Lights up on Molina and Warden.*

WARDEN: Ah, Molina, my friend! I'm afraid I have bad news for you. Your mother, she's very sick.

MOLINA: When? What happened? How do you know?

WARDEN: Find out for yourself, Molina. Life awaits you outside these walls. Life and your mother. His girlfriend's name is your key to freedom. No? Bring in the next one!

> *Esteban and Marcos exit. Lights up on Spider Woman. As she sings, the dead Prisoner . . . . . reaches her at the center of her web.*

SPIDER WOMAN *(sings):*

Come—I am the answer

Come—I can stop the pain

Come—I am the rainbow that follows the rain

Hear my song

Let me hold you

Here where you belong

Come! Come!

> *Esteban and Marcos return, open cell door—revealing Valentin. The Spider Woman kisses the dead Prisoner, who drops from the bars. Blackout.*

Scene 8

One Prisoner is singing a hymn, another moons the Guards, another paces up and down as though wearing a hole through which to escape, as Marcos and Esteban drag a battered Valentin back to Molina's cell. Molina wets a cloth to attend to the unconscious Valentin's wounds and summons Aurora to help him through this crisis, asking Aurora how Valentin can endure such suffering. "Love," is Aurora's answer, singing that love can do miracles. Soon she is joined by Marta.

AURORA *(sings):*
   I do miracles
MARTA *(sings):*
   As I cradle you close and caress each bruise
   What I've come here to give, you must not refuse
BOTH *(sing):*
   There is love in my touch that is yours to use
   And if you choose
   Just breathe my name
   And there I'll be
   Doing miracles
   I do miracles
   There are miracles in me
       Blackout.

Scene 9

Molina prepares to serve food on tin plates with napkins his mother brought him on her last visit. From his catwalk, the Warden advises Molina to be sure Valentin gets the larger portion, but Valentin isn't hungry and switches the plates, taking the smaller serving.

While they eat—Molina daintily (to Valentin's disgust), Valentin heartily—they query each other about their love lives. Molina admits to having his eye on a waiter named Gabriel, but they have never made any physical contact—Gabriel has a wife and child. Gabriel appears, singing the words of a sympathetic letter he might have written to Molina, a friend in prison, thanking Molina for gifts which Molina has sent to Gabriel's family, finishing, "And finally, I'm sorry for any pain I may have caused you/I know what you wanted of me but I'm just not that way/What a strange thing to be sorry for/But that's the way it is, isn't it?"

Molina is beginning to feel ill. Gabriel helps him to his cot and exits, leaving Valentin dreaming of his first woman.

VALENTIN *(not to Molina, but in reverie, sings):*
   My first woman
   I remember my first woman
   Back of a building
   Me and my friends
   A couple of pesos

There on the gravel
Down on her knees
What did she look like?
Probably plain
Who can remember
But to me she was the keeper of all mystery.

Gabriel returns to join Valentin in a duet. As Gabriel exits again, Molina is suffering severely from stomach cramps. Frightened, he begs Valentin to get him to the infirmary. Valentin calls for the Guards to take Molina away.

Scene 10

In the infirmary, Orderlies inject Molina with morphine that sets him to dreaming that the Orderlies are dancing and then, as they exit, that his mother appears. Molina asserts that she is still beautiful, and she reassures her son that he is not fatally ill. When Molina remarks "I've brought you such shame," she denies this in song.

MOTHER *(brushes Molina's hair from his forehead as if he were a little boy, sings):*
You could never shame me
There, I've told you so
Many things confuse me
But this I know

Let the neighbors gossip
At the mention of your name
You have never brought me shame

I know some mamas have roughnecks
Who never bring them joy
Thank God, you're not that kind of boy

I know that you're different
I don't really care
I would never change a hair . . . . .

Finally the Orderlies escort Mother out. As the lights dim, the spider web appears and the scene changes to Molina's cell, where the Spider Woman is revealed sitting on Molina's cot. "I've always been afraid of you," Molina confesses in song, and the Spider Woman, likewise in song, declares, "Someday you'll recognize me/As your friend."

SPIDER WOMAN *(sings)*:
> Someday you will understand
> I am your friend
> Someday you will kiss me

MOLINA *(sings)*:
> Never. Never. Go away. Go away

SPIDER WOMAN *(sings)*:
> Someday you'll give in
> Of course you will. All men do.
> Yes, all men kiss me and you will too
> You'll part my lips and rest yours there.
> You'll run your fingers through my hair
> Your cries of pleasure
> Will heat the cool, night air
> When you kiss me
> And you will kiss me
> But not now! Not yet! Not now!

As the Spider Woman exits and the scene returns to the infirmary, the Orderlies enter and help Molina back onto the gurney, then inject him with more morphine.

Scene 11

Molina, recovered, is led back to his cell by Esteban and Marcos, who also bring Valentin a plate of food—they've given him none for three days. Valentin, eating greedily after they exit, admits he missed Molina but warns him not to get any funny ideas about that. Valentin has been dreaming of Marta, hoping she's remaining faithful to him. Molina imagines her making bombs, but Valentin corrects him—their group doesn't have anything to do with making bombs; and besides, Marta isn't part of the movement.

MOLINA: What new twist is this?

VALENTIN: I have a confession to make. The fact is, she's upper class, drives a little red Mercedes, 180 SL, and plays golf.

MOLINA: She sounds divine. Does she have a brother?

VALENTIN: She's everything Golizar says we're supposed to hate, and I'm crazy about her.

MOLINA: Golizar? Alberto Golizar? That Golizar?

VALENTIN: Don't tell me you've heard of him.

MOLINA: I don't just read movie magazines. He's a great man.

VALENTIN: He changed my life. I didn't know there was another way until him.

I was seventeen years old when I heard him speak. There were thousands of people. He made us feel like one. He opened our eyes, our minds, our hearts, Molina. It's funny how your life can change forever in an instant.

MOLINA: No, it's not, Valentin.

VALENTIN: The man next to me was hiding a gun. There were plain-clothes police everywhere awaiting orders to open fire. It was a massacre. I never went back to my village. I slept in the streets. I stole. I got arrested. And then I joined the movement.

MOLINA: Please don't tell me any more.

VALENTIN: I started out just being Senor Golizar's personal bodyguard.

MOLINA: I don't want to know.

VALENTIN: Now, I'm in charge of getting fugitives . . .

But Valentin suddenly cries out with the pain of a cramp—his food was obviously poisoned, and this time it was consumed by the person for whom it was intended. Valentin suffers a spasm of the bowels, and Molina helps to clean him up. Valentin remarks on Molina's kindness but then cries out "Marta!" as he faints. "She's a Woman," Molina reflects in song directed at the unconscious Valentin.

MOLINA *(sings):*
     . . . . . Lilac waters
    Bathe her skin
    At the opera, ushers gasp
    When she sweeps in
    Gifts of chocolate
    Roses too
    Hand delivered notes
    Confessing "I love you"
    Milky lotions
    Scented creams
    She's the climax of your Technicolor dreams

    How lucky can you be?
    So lucky, you'll agree
    And I wish that she were me
    That
    Woman!

WARDEN: Hello, Molina, did you think I'd forgotten you?

MOLINA: No, I don't have anything for you yet. He's very suspicious. I just need time. I lost nearly a week when I was in the infirmary. He took the wrong plate. I nearly died. How is she?

WARDEN: Who?

MOLINA: My mother! You said if I cooperated with you I would be released for good behavior.

WARDEN: Did I? I don't remember.

MOLINA: We made a deal.

WARDEN: Then keep your end of it.

MOLINA: I'm not the person for this. I'm not political. I don't know about these things. I don't care about them.

WARDEN: That's exactly why I'm counting on you.

MOLINA: He told me he's willing to die for his cause.

WARDEN: And you're willing to betray him for yours.

MOLINA: I don't have a cause. I have a mother who needs me.

WARDEN: The sooner he talks, the sooner you'll be free to walk out of here and be with her.

Valentin regains consciousness and Molina, mopping his brow, becomes alarmed when the Spider Woman opens the cell curtains and appears. In great pain, Valentin begs to be taken to the infirmary, but Molina urges him to hold out—if he goes to the infirmary they'll dope him with morphine, and he's bound to talk. Valentin believes he's dying, but Molina refuses to accept this and distracts Valentin by summoning up an Aurora movie, *Bird of Paradise* (as the sound of birds is heard). Aurora's lover has escaped, and Aurora, a prisoner, will not betray him. "She is only a woman who loves!" says Molina, "Let them kill her even."

Dancers enter with Aurora in a birdcage, for a night club scene in the movie. She steps out of the cage for the song "Gimme Love."

Scene 12

AURORA *(sings)*:
    If there's a war on, don't bring me the news
    Ask me to bullfights and I must refuse
    But if you want to get my attention
    Let's make love.

MEN *(sing)*:
    Gimme love, gimme kisses, gimme love
    Gimme love, gimme kisses, gimme love

AURORA *(sings)*:
    If there's an earthquake I will not attend

MEN *(sing)*:
    Gimme kisses, gimme love.

AURORA *(sings)*:
    If there's a plague don't invite me my friend

MEN *(sing)*:
    Gimme kisses, gimme love, love love

AURORA *(sings)*:
But if you want to keep me looking in your direction,
Let's make love . . . . .

The night club movie scene with its song and dance continues until Marcos raps the bars of the cell with his nightstick and Molina returns to reality, making Valentin get up and pretend to be feeling O.K. so they won't take him to the infirmary. When the Guards leave, Valentin collapses into Molina's arms and the movie continues—but Molina opens his curtain and sees that the Spider Woman is gone.

MOLINA: She's gone. You're safe. Thank God, you're safe. Come with me. *(Sings.)*
Her name is Aurora
And she is so beautiful
No man who has met her can ever forget her
They're madly in love
Forever in love
Molina carries him into his movie. Bird calls swell up again suddenly.
Blackout. Curtain.

ACT II

Scene 1

The Spider Woman is heard singing about her kiss, but in the cell all is serene. Valentin is enjoying some chicken Molina's mother has sent them. And Valentin is now an addict of Molina's Aurora movie plots and requests the one where "To save her lover, Aurora agrees to marry a man she doesn't love on the eve of the Russian Revolution."

Obligingly, Molina sets the stage: Aurora, playing a cabaret singer (Tatyana) on the eve of her wedding to Count Ostrovsky, goes into her farewell number for an audience which includes the Tsar himself. She sings of the "Good Times" which are to replace all the bad times they're having, and the audience goes wild (the Count throws a diamond necklace at her feet). In her dressing room, Tatyana confesses to her faithful attendant, Lisette, that she does not love the Count, who has promised to save her lover but (she learns from a note of warning that has just arrived) has deceived her and intends to have the young man shot.

The Count knocks on her dressing-room door, but Tatyana escapes by the back way, goes to her lover to warn him but is shot and dies in his arms singing "There's going to be good times/Nothing but good times/Viva la guerra, viva

Chita Rivera as Aurora, with dancers in the "Gimme
Love" night club number of *Kiss of the Spider Woman*

la revolucion, viva . . ." The movie is at an end, and the prisoners return to
reality.

VALENTIN: You know there's one thing profoundly wrong with your movies,
don't you?

MOLINA: What is that, doctor?

VALENTIN: They're not real.

MOLINA: Thank you. Of course they're not real. They're better than real. I
need my movies to remind me that there can be beauty and grace and bravery
and loyalty and kindness and love and yes, dumb jokes and singing and dancing
and Technicolor and happy endings and love. I already said that.

VALENTIN: Why don't you try to find them in your own life?

MOLINA: I have tried. I failed. I am not a stupid man, Valentin.

VALENTIN: I guess I have a movie, too.

MOLINA: I hope you do, my friend.

VALENTIN: Only there's no part in mine for your Aurora. No singing, no dancing, no pretty costumes. Just the truth. *(Sings.)*

> It was made out of mud
> And pieces of tin
> And boxes nailed together
> Cardboard boxes
> My castle
> My home . . . . .

> And our mother poured soup
> Into little cracked bowls
> And she spoke of something better
> Beef steak, maybe, someday
> My home

> And that lady had eyes
> That were empty and cold
> At the ripe old age of thirty
> Death came
> Welcome
> To my home

> And still that Sunday
> On our knees
> How we thanked the Lord
> For his bountiful blessings . . . . .

Valentin and his sister (the song continues) came to the city and joined the movement to make the world a better place, "If not tomorrow/Then the day after that/Or the day after that." The chorus of men joins Valentin in this song until it is interrupted by Esteban and Marcos dragging in a battered Prisoner and showing him off to Valentin, who pretends not to recognize him. Molina blurts out, "You goddamn murdering bastards," nearly getting himself in trouble, so that when the Guards drag their man off Molina protests to Valentin, "You're a bad influence. Will you stop trying to make a man out of me?" And Valentin confides to Molina that the prisoner was one of his contacts.

Scene 2

Molina is fantasizing going shopping for various items requested by his mother, but in reality he is requesting them from the Warden. Molina is in the Warden's office with Esteban and Marcos, being interrogated. Molina asks for more time to get the information about Valentin's contacts, but the Warden warns him that he may not have much time, his mother is very sick. The Warden sends Esteban for the items Molina wants and offers to let Molina speak to his mother on the phone, leaving him in privacy to do so. Molina addresses his mother in song, assuring her he'll be coming home soon to take care of her: "Soon we'll be going to movies/I'll buy you beautiful things/Wait till you see what tomorrow brings."

When the Warden returns and cuts off the phone conversation, he returns to the subject of Valentin. "Tell him you're getting out in the morning—for good behavior. Ask him if there's anything you can do for him on the outside. *(Pause.)* There's the door to freedom and your mother. You have the key to open it." Molina agrees to get the names from Valentin for the Warden.

Scene 3

In the cell, Molina and Valentin have been enjoying a good meal with wine smuggled in by Molina's mother. Molina informs Valentin that he's leaving the next morning, and Valentin admits he'll miss Molina and his movies. Molina moves toward Valentin but remembers about the line dividing their territories.

VALENTIN *(strangely serious):* Let's forget about the line.

MOLINA: I hate feelings sometimes. Life is difficult enough.

VALENTIN: Our feelings are the only things that keep us from giving in to those bastards. You're leaving . . . my feelings for you aren't.

MOLINA: Thank you.

VALENTIN: Listen, Molina. When you get outside, there are a few phone calls you could make for me . . . I really need . . .

MOLINA *(holding his hands over his ears):* Please! I don't want to hear.

VALENTIN: There's nothing to it. You won't be in any danger.

MOLINA *(louder than before):* Please!

VALENTIN: Molina, it would mean so much to me! Only a few . . .

MOLINA: Please! Please!

> *We hear the Spider Woman's music. She appears. She paces provocatively above the two men as the music begins.*

SPIDER WOMAN *(sings):*

Soon, I feel it
Soon, somehow.
I will have him
Any minute now

MOLINA *(sings):*

I'd do anything for him.
He must know.
I'd do anything for him.
I want him so.
I've no interest in his cause.

Let that be.
Please, God, let him turn around
And look at me.
VALENTIN *(sings):*
He'd do anything for me
I can tell.
He'd do anything for me
I know him well
If we touch before he goes
He'll make that call
He'd do anything for me
Anything at all.

Molina, Valentin and the Spider Woman sing together, after which Valentin approaches Molina sitting on his cot. *"His hand slides under Molina's shirt."* In response, Molina touches Valentin's face.

MOLINA: How I've longed to do that. I've always longed to do that.
VALENTIN: Now you can. But you don't have to talk.
MOLINA: I want to tell you so many things.
VALENTIN: Jesus, I never knew anybody who liked to talk so much.
        Valentin blows out the candle, closes the curtains and removes his shirt.
        Embarrassed, Molina looks away.
Molina.
MOLINA: Valentin, if you like, you can do whatever you want with me . . . because I want you to.
        Valentin puts his hand out to Molina, who is still shy, and draws
        Molina to him.
The nicest thing about being happy is that you never think you'll be unhappy again.
VALENTIN: This time, maybe you won't be.
        Valentin draws Molina towards him on the bed. Lights down slowly.

Scene 4

The Spider Woman enters as the music for her song "Kiss of the Spider Woman" is heard. No one can escape her kiss, sooner or later it comes to everyone, even to lovers.

SPIDER WOMAN *(sings):*
. . . . . Sooner or later
You bathe in success
And your minions salute

They say nothing but "Yes"
But your power is empty, it fades like the mist
Once you've been kissed

And the moon grows dimmer
At the tide's low ebb
And your breath comes faster
And you're aching to move but you're caught in the web
Of the Spider Woman
In her velvet cape
You can run
You can scream
You can hide
But you cannot escape!
    Blackout.

Scene 5

In the cell, Molina is preparing to be released. He is leaving Valentin his Aurora poster and a red scarf to remember him by. Valentin again asks Molina to convey a message to someone, but Molina refuses.

VALENTIN: I wouldn't ask you to do anything dangerous.

MOLINA: I'd go to pieces. I'm not brave like you.

VALENTIN: Yes, you are. I've seen you.

MOLINA: I don't want to get involved. I'm not like you. Don't try to change me. Leave me alone, Valentin, or I will betray you.

VALENTIN: I understand.

MOLINA: No, you don't. You couldn't. I'm sorry I can't be the man you want me to be. Stay well. Maybe I'll write. I'll never forget you.

VALENTIN: Molina, I want you to promise me something. I want you to promise me you'll never let anyone humiliate you ever again.

He takes Molina's face in his hands and kisses him on the mouth.

MOLINA: Give me your message.

VALENTIN: You'll deliver it?

Molina quickly nods. Valentin pulls him close, whispers in his ear. We cannot hear his words.

Esteban and Marcos appear, to escort Molina away, leaving Valentin hoping Molina will prove to be man enough to deliver his message.

Scene 6

The Prisoners sing "Over the Wall" enviously as Molina passes their cells on his way to the Warden's office. He scribbles some names on a piece of paper, as promised, and hands it to the Warden. After Molina exits, the Warden tells the Guards he knows perfectly well that the names on the paper are phony—"The one I want he's taking with him" in his mind. Esteban and Marcos are ordered to follow Molina and never let him out of their sight. The Warden knows Molina will make his move because he's now in love. "I know him/I know him like the back/Of my hand," sings the Warden, "In the store where the alley ends/He'll be back with his fairy friends/Putting pins into ladies clothes."

Molina arrives back home, where his mother hopes that everything will be as it used to be. But Molina then goes to the store and tells his assistant, Aurelio, that he isn't going to do this kind of work any more. He looks up his waiter friend, Gabriel, but Gabriel doesn't want any part of this relationship that he doesn't understand.

Back at his mother's apartment, Molina gets ready to go across the street to make a phone call. Mother is frightened that something might happen to him if he goes outside, but Molina assures her it's perfectly safe, so she concedes, "Do what you must."

> *The scene fades. We hear the sound of a phone ringing. Lights up on Marta, who comes to answer it. She picks up the phone and we hear Molina's voice on the other end.*

MARTA: Hello?

MOLINA: Marta?

MARTA: Yes?

MOLINA: I have a message from The Eagle. Christ has risen.

MARTA: I don't know what you're talking about. Who is this?

MOLINA: A friend. I can't talk. I'm being followed. They're right across the street. He's alive. He's well. He loves you.

MARTA: I don't want to get involved.

MOLINA: Neither did I.

MARTA: Who is this? Who are you?

> *Sound of the phone hanging up.*

Hello? Hello?

Lights up on the Prisoners singing another chorus of "Over the Wall." *Blackout.*

Scene 7

In the Interrogation Room, Esteban, Marcos and the Warden are preparing to torture Valentin. The Warden tries to persuade Valentin to talk, but Valentin spits at him. As the Warden grinds out his cigarette on Valentin's chest, the guards exit and re-enter with a *"horribly bloodied"* Molina, whom they throw at Valentin's feet. Molina has not talked, and the Warden threatens to kill him if he doesn't. Valentin cries out in remorse.

VALENTIN: I betrayed you. Talk, give them what they want!
MOLINA: Darling, it all went right out of my dizzy head!
WARDEN: Last chance, Valentin.
VALENTIN: All right, I'll talk.
MOLINA: Then you *will* have betrayed me.
     The Warden takes out a pistol and puts it against Molina's temple.
I'm scared, Valentin. Look at me. Don't take your eyes off me!
WARDEN: I want names, or he dies.
MOLINA *(to Valentin):* Write my mother if they'll let you.
WARDEN *(to Molina):* I'll give you three. One.
VALENTIN: Why are you doing this?
MOLINA: I want to. And Gabriel. Write him.
WARDEN: Two.
VALENTIN: Not for me. It isn't worth it.
MOLINA: Wouldn't it be funny if that were true?
WARDEN: Three. Who were you calling? Talk, you fucking faggot, or I'll blow your fucking head off.
     Music.
MOLINA: I love you . . .
     Music. The Warden pulls the trigger. Pistol shot. Molina's body slumps lifelessly. Valentin cries out convulsively.
VALENTIN: Molina! Molina!
     Warden, Esteban and Marcos drag Valentin offstage. Music begins as Molina slowly rises. Suddenly, we see Molina's mother carrying a flashlight. Behind her are three or four rows of a movie theater. Valentin takes a seat in the theater. The Prisoners help Molina dress into white tie and tails. The Mother, with her flashlight, leads the Spider Woman to a seat. In the theater we come to recognize our entire company: Gabriel, Aurelio, Prisoners, the Warden, etc. At the sight of Molina fully dressed in front of the audience, Valentin begins to applaud. The rest of the theater audience joins him. Molina is receiving an ovation which he obviously savors. He turns and sings.

Molina's song, "Only in the Movies," is a summary of his lifestyle: only in the movies are there happy endings, so Molina sought refuge there from life's realities, "And though I knew the difference/I kept on pretending/I was in the movies." Meeting Valentin, though, changed his life: "I find I walk in Technicolor now!"

The Warden's harsh ultimatim and the pistol shot are suddenly repeated and

Molina "dies" once more. This time Valentin has Molina in his arms and laughs when Molina ends another verse of his song with "Viva la guerra/Viva la revolucion/Viva whatever it is."

The Spider Woman joins Molina, and they tango with the company circling around them. Valentin sings out "His name was Molina," and the company repeats these words like the chorus of a song. *"Molina and the Spider Woman kiss. The Company cheers. Blackout. Curtain."*

ANGELS IN AMERICA: MILLENNIUM APPROACHES

A Play in Three Acts

BY TONY KUSHNER

Cast and credits appear on page 315

TONY KUSHNER was born in New York City July 16, 1958, but his mother and father, both professional musicians, soon moved the family to Lake Charles, La., where the playwright-to-be grew up. His first memories of the theater were of his mother acting in amateur productions. When he came to New York for college at Columbia, he went to the theater almost every night. He received his B.A. in 1978 and went on to N.Y.U. for its graduate program in directing, getting his M.F.A. in 1984. At that time directing was "doable," Kushner felt, but "I never imagined I could write a play that was worth anything. It was unattainable." Such didn't turn out to be the case. The Eureka Theater Company in San Francisco produced his first play, A Bright Room Called Day, *in 1985 (it arrived at the Public Theater in New York January 7, 1991 for 14 performances). And Kushner's adaptation of Corneille's* L'Illusion Comique *provided him with his New York debut OOB at the New York Theater Workshop October 27, 1988 and has since been produced in regional theater venues including Hartford, Conn. and Berkeley, Calif.*

233

Angels in America *was commissioned through a special projects grant from the NEA. Its first version was a 250-page, six-act script workshopped at the Mark Taper Forum (it is now a two-parter,* Millennium Approaches *and* Perestroika, *the latter to be produced on Broadway next season). The two parts premiered at Eureka in 1991, winning the Fund for New American Plays/Kennedy Center, Joseph Kesselring and Bay Area Theater Critics Awards.* Millennium Approaches *then moved on to London's National Theater, winning the Evening Standard Award as the season's best new play. In November 1992, both parts of* Angels in America *(subtitled* A Gay Fantasia on National Themes) *were produced at the Mark Taper Forum and won the 1993 Pulitzer Prize as well as Los Angeles Drama Critics Award. The New York Drama Critics followed suit, voting the* Millennium Approaches *segment of* Angels in America *the best new play of this season after it opened on Broadway May 4. The best-play Tony Award soon followed, and it appears as a Best Play in this volume. Kushner, who lives in Brooklyn, has been additionally honored by a 1990 Whiting Foundation Writers Award.*

To convey insofar as possible the full flavor and texture of Kushner's extraordinary script, we represent it in these pages not in synopsis but with five of its 26 scenes—Act I, Scenes 8 and 9, Act II, Scenes 8 and 9 and Act III, Scene 5—presented in their entirety.

Place: New York City, Salt Lake City and Elsewhere

ACT I: Bad News, October–November 1985

Scene 8

Joe and Harper Pitt are a deeply troubled married couple. Prior Walter and Louis Ironson are homosexual lovers. It is night, and in a split scene Joe and Harper are in their home, and Prior and Louis are in bed.

HARPER: Where were you?
JOE: Out.
HARPER: Where?
JOE: Just out. Thinking.
HARPER: It's late.
JOE: I had a lot to think about.
HARPER: I burned dinner.
JOE: Sorry.
HARPER: Not my dinner. My dinner was fine. Your dinner. I put it back in the

oven and turned everything up as high as it could go and I watched till it burned black. It's still hot. Very hot. Want it?

JOE: You didn't have to do that.

HARPER: I know. It just seemed like the kind of thing a mentally deranged sex-starved pill-popping houswife would do.

JOE: Uh huh.

HARPER: So I did it. Who knows anymore what I have to do?

JOE: How many pills?

HARPER: A bunch. Don't change the subject.

JOE: I won't talk to you when you . . .

HARPER: No. No. Don't do that! I'm . . . I'm fine, pills are not the problem, not our problem, I WANT TO KNOW WHERE YOU'VE BEEN! I WANT TO KNOW WHAT'S GOING ON!

JOE: Going on with what? The job?

HARPER: Not the job.

JOE: I said I need more time.

HARPER: Not the job!

JOE: Mr. Cohn, I talked to him on the phone, he said I had to hurry . . .

HARPER: Not the . . .

JOE: But I can't get you to talk sensibly about anything so . . .

HARPER: SHUT UP!

JOE: Then what?

HARPER: Stick to the subject.

JOE: I don't know what that is. You have something you want to ask me? Ask me. Go.

HARPER: I . . . can't. I'm scared of you.

JOE: I'm tired, I'm going to bed.

HARPER: Tell me without making me ask. Please.

JOE: This is crazy, I'm not . . .

HARPER: When you come through the door at night your face is never exactly the way I remembered it. I get surprised by something . . . mean and hard about the way you look. Even the weight of you in the bed at night, the way you breathe in your sleep seems unfamiliar. You terrify me.

JOE *(cold):* I know who you are.

HARPER: Yes. I'm the enemy. That's easy. That doesn't change. You think you're the only one who hates sex; I do; I hate it with you; I do. I dream that you batter away at me till all my joints come apart, like wax, and I fall into pieces. It's like a punishment. It was wrong of me to marry you. I knew you . . . *(She stops herself.)* It's a sin, and it's killing us both.

JOE: I can always tell when you've taken pills because it makes you red-faced and sweaty and frankly that's very often why I don't want to . . .

HARPER: Because . . .

JOE: Well, you aren't pretty. Not like this.

HARPER: I have something to ask you.

JOE: Then ASK! ASK! What in hell are you . . .

HARPER: Are you a homo?

Pause.

Are you? If you try to walk out right now I'll put your dinner back in the oven and turn it up so high the whole building will fill with smoke and everyone in it will asphyxiate. So help me God I will. Now answer the question.

JOE: What if I . . .

Small pause.

HARPER: Then tell me, please. And we'll see.

JOE: No, I'm not. I don't see what difference it makes.

LOUIS: Jews don't have any clear textual guide to the afterlife; even that it exists. I don't think much about it. I see it as a perpetual rainy Thursday afternoon in March. Dead leaves.

PRIOR: Eeeugh. Very Greco-Roman.

LOUIS: Well, for us it's not the verdict that counts, it's the act of judgment. That's why I could never be a lawyer. In court all that matters is the verdict.

PRIOR: You could never be a lawyer because you are oversexed. You're too distracted.

LOUIS: Not distracted, *ab*stracted. I'm trying to make a point:

PRIOR: Namely:

LOUIS: It's the judge in his or her chambers, weighing, books open, pondering the evidence, ranging freely over categories: good, evil, innocent, guilty; the judge in the chamber of circumspection, not the judge on the bench with the gavel. The shaping of the law, not its execution.

PRIOR: The point, dear, the point . . .

LOUIS: That it should be the questions and shape of a life, its total complexity gathered, arranged and considered, which matters in the end, not some stamp of salvation or damnation which disperses all the complexity in some unsatisfying little decision—the balancing of the scales . . .

PRIOR: I like this, very Zen; it's . . . reassuringly incomprehensible and useless. We who are about to die thank you.

LOUIS: You are not about to die.

PRIOR: It's not going well, really . . . two new lesions. My leg hurts. There's protein in my urine, the doctor says, but who knows what the fuck that portends. Anyway it shouldn't be there, the protein. My butt is chapped from diarrhea and yesterday I shat blood.

LOUIS: I really hate this. You don't tell me . . .

PRIOR: You get too upset, I wind up comforting you. It's easier . . .

LOUIS: Oh thanks.

PRIOR: If it's bad I'll tell you.

LOUIS: Shitting blood sounds bad to me.

PRIOR: And I'm telling you.

LOUIS: And I'm handling it.

PRIOR: Tell me some more about justice.

LOUIS: I *am* handling it.

PRIOR: Well, Louis, you win Trooper of the Month.

    Louis starts to cry.

I take it back. You aren't Trooper of the Month. This isn't working . . . Tell me some more about justice.

LOUIS: You are not about to die.

PRIOR: Justice . . .

LOUIS: . . . is an immensity, a confusing vastness. Justice is God. Prior?

PRIOR: Hmmm?

LOUIS: You love me.

PRIOR: Yes.

LOUIS: What if I walked out on this? Would you hate me forever?

PRIOR *(kisses Louis on the forehead):* Yes.

JOE: I think we ought to pray. Ask God for help. Ask Him together . . .

HARPER: God won't talk to me. I have to make up people to talk to me.

JOE: You have to keep asking.

HARPER: I forgot the question. Oh yeah. God, is my husband a . . .

JOE *(scary):* Stop it. Stop it. I'm warning you. Does it make any difference? That I might be one thing deep within, no matter how wrong or ugly that thing is, so long as I have fought, with everything I have, to kill it. What do you want from me? What do you want from me, Harper? More than that? For God's sake, there's nothing left, I'm a shell. There's nothing left to kill. As long as my behavior is what I know it has to be. Decent. Correct. That alone in the eyes of God.

HARPER: No, no, not that, that's Utah talk, Mormon talk, I hate it, Joe, tell me, say it . . .

JOE: All I will say is that I am a very good man who has worked very hard to become good and you want to destroy that. You want to destroy me, but I am not going to let you do that.

    Pause.

HARPER: I'm going to have a baby.

JOE: Liar.

HARPER: You liar. A baby born addicted to pills. A baby who does not dream but who hallucinates, who stares up at us with big mirror eyes and who does not know who we are.

    Pause.

JOE: Are you really . . .

HARPER: No. Yes. No. Yes. Get away from me. Now we both have a secret.

PRIOR: One of my ancestors was a ship's captain who made money bringing whale oil to Europe and returning with immigrants—Irish mostly, packed in tight, so many dollars per head. The last ship he captained foundered off the coast of Nova Scotia in a winter tempest and sank to the bottom. He went down with the ship—la Grande Geste—but his crew took seventy women and kids in the ship's only longboat, this big, open rowboat, and when the weather got too rough, and they thought the boat was overcrowded, the crew started lifting people up and hurling them into the sea. Until they got the ballast right. They walked up and down the longboat, eyes to the waterline, and when the boat rode low in the water they'd grab the nearest passenger and throw them into the sea. The boat was leaky, see; seventy people; they arrived in Halifax with nine people on board.

LOUIS: Jesus.

PRIOR: I think about the story a lot now. People in a boat, waiting, terrified, while implacable, unsmiling men, irresistibly strong, seize . . . maybe the person next to you, maybe you, and with no warning at all, with time only for a quick intake of air you are pitched into freezing, turbulent water and salt and darkness to drown. I like your cosmology, baby. While time is running out I find myself drawn to anything that's suspended, that lacks an ending—but it seems to me that it lets you off scot-free.

LOUIS: What do you mean?

PRIOR: No judgment, no guilt or responsibility.

LOUIS: For me.

PRIOR: For anyone. It was an editorial "you."

LOUIS: Please get better. Please. Please don't get any sicker.

Scene 9

An author's note in the published script reads, "Roy M. Cohn, the character, is based on the late Roy M. Cohn (1927–1986), who was all too real . . . . . But this Roy is a work of dramatic fiction; his words are my invention, and liberties have been taken."

The third week in November 1985, the character Roy M. Cohn is visiting his doctor, Henry, in Henry's office.

HENRY: Nobody knows what causes it. And nobody knows how to cure it. The best theory is that we blame a retrovirus, the Human Immunodeficiency Virus. Its presence is made known to us by the useless antibodies which appear in reaction to its entrance into the bloodstream through a cut, or an orifice. The antibodies are powerless to protect the body against it. Why, we don't know. The body's immune system ceases to function. Sometimes the body even attacks itself. At any rate, it's left open to a whole horror house of infections from microbes which it usually defends against. Like Kaposi's sarcomas. These le-

Ron Leibman as Roy Cohn in *Angels in America*

sions. Or your throat problem. Or the glands. We think it may also be able to slip past the blood-brain barrier into the brain. Which is of course very bad news. And it's fatal in we don't know what percent of people with suppressed immune responses.

     Pause.

ROY: This is very interesting, Mr. Wizard, but why the fuck are you telling me this?

     Pause.

HENRY: Well, I have just removed one of three lesions which biopsy results will probably tell us is a Kaposi's sarcoma lesion. And you have a pronounced swelling of glands in your neck, groin and armpits—lymphadenopathy is another sign. And you have oral candidiasis and maybe a little more fungus under the fingernails of two digits on your right hand. So that's why . . .

ROY: This disease . . .

HENRY: Syndrome.

ROY: Whatever. It afflicts mostly homosexuals and drug addicts.

HENRY: Mostly. Hemophiliacs are also at risk.

ROY: Homosexuals and drug addicts. So why are you implying that I . . .

     Pause.

What are you implying, Henry?

HENRY: I don't . . .

ROY: I'm not a drug addict.

HENRY: Oh come on, Roy.

ROY: What, what, come on Roy what? Do you think I'm a junkie, Henry, do you see tracks?

HENRY: This is absurd.

ROY: Say it.

HENRY: Say what?

ROY: Say, "Roy Cohn, you are a . . ."

HENRY: Roy.

ROY: "You are a . . ." Go on. Not "Roy Cohn you are a drug fiend." "Roy Marcus Cohn, you are a . . ." Go on, Henry, it starts with an "H."

HENRY: Oh, I'm not going to . . .

ROY: *With an "H,"* Henry, and it isn't "Hemophiliac." Come on . . .

HENRY: What are you doing, Roy?

ROY: No, say it. I mean it. Say: "Roy Cohn, you are a homosexual."
> *Pause.*

And I will proceed, systematically, to destroy your reputation and your practice and your career in New York State, Henry. Which you know I can do.
> *Pause.*

HENRY: Roy, you have been seeing me since 1958. Apart from the facelifts, I have treated you for everything from syphilis . . .

ROY: From a whore in Dallas.

HENRY: From syphilis to venereal warts. In your rectum. Which you may have gotten from a whore in Dallas, but it wasn't a female whore.
> *Pause.*

ROY: So say it.

HENRY: Roy Cohn, you are . . . You have had sex with men many, many times, Roy, and one of them, or any number of them, has made you very sick. You have AIDS.

ROY: AIDS. Your problem, Henry, is that you are hung up on words, on labels, that you believe they mean what they seem to mean. AIDS. Homosexual. Gay. Lesbian. You think these are names that tell you who someone sleeps with, but they don't tell you that.

HENRY: No?

ROY: No. Like all labels they tell you one thing and one thing only: where does an individual so identified fit in the food chain, in the pecking order? Not ideology, or sexual taste, but something much simpler: clout. Not who I fuck or who fucks me, but who will pick up the phone when I call, who owes me favors. This is what a label refers to. Now to someone who does not understand this, homosexual is what I am because I have sex with men. But really this is wrong. Homosexuals are not men who sleep with other men. Homosexuals are men who in fifteen years of trying cannot get a pissant antidiscrimination bill through City Council. Homosexuals are men who know nobody and who nobody knows. Who have zero clout. Does this sound like me, Henry?

HENRY: No.

ROY: No. I have clout. A lot. I can pick up this phone, punch fifteen numbers, and you know who will be on the other end in under five minutes, Henry?

HENRY: The President.

ROY: Even better, Henry. His wife.

HENRY: I'm impressed.

ROY: I don't want you to be impressed. I want you to understand. This is not sophistry. And this is not hypocrisy. This is reality. I have sex with men. But unlike nearly every other man of whom this is true, I bring the guy I'm screwing to the White House and President Reagan smiles at us and shakes his hand. Because *what* I am is defined entirely by *who* I am. Roy Cohn is not a homosexual. Roy Cohn is a heterosexual man, Henry, who fucks around with guys.

HENRY: O.K., Roy.

ROY: And what is my diagnosis, Henry?

HENRY: You have AIDS, Roy.

ROY: No, Henry, No. AIDS is what homosexuals have. I have liver cancer.
    Pause.

HENRY: Well, whatever the fuck you have, Roy, it's very serious, and I haven't got a damn thing for you. The NIH in Bethesda has a new drug called AZT with a two-year waiting list that not even I can get you onto. So get on the phone, Roy, and dial the fifteen numbers, and tell the First Lady you need in on an experimental treatment for liver cancer, because you can call it any damn thing you want, Roy, but what it boils down to is very bad news.
    Curtain. End of Act I.

ACT II: In Vitro, December 1985–January 1986

Scene 8

Late at night, at a pay phone, Joe is calling his mother Hannah at her home in Salt Lake City.

JOE: Mom?

HANNAH: Joe?

JOE: Hi.

HANNAH: You're calling from the street. It's . . . it must be four in the morning. What's happened?

JOE: Nothing, nothing, I . . .

HANNAH: It's Harper. Is Harper . . . Joe? Joe?

JOE: Yeah, hi. No, Harper's fine. Well, no, she's . . . not fine. How are you, Mom?

HANNAH: What's happened?

JOE: I just wanted to talk to you. I, uh, wanted to try something out on you.

HANNAH: Joe, you haven't . . . have you been drinking, Joe?

JOE: Yes ma'am. I'm drunk.

HANNAH: That isn't like you.

JOE: No. I mean, who's to say?

HANNAH: Why are you out on the street at four a.m.? In that crazy city. It's dangerous.

JOE: Actually, Mom, I'm not on the street. I'm near the boathouse in the park.

HANNAH: What park?

JOE: Central Park.

HANNAH: CENTRAL PARK! Oh my Lord. What on earth are you doing in Central Park at this time of night? Are you . . . Joe, I think you ought to go home right now. Call me from home. *(Little pause.)* Joe?

JOE: I come here to watch, Mom. Sometimes. Just to watch.

HANNAH: Watch what? What's there to watch at four in the . . .

JOE: Mom, did Dad love me?

HANNAH: What?

JOE: Did he?

HANNAH: You ought to go home and call from there.

JOE: Answer.

HANNAH: Oh now really. This is maudlin. I don't like this conversation.

JOE: Yeah, well, it gets worse from here on.

> *Pause.*

HANNAH: Joe?

JOE: Mom. Momma. I'm a homosexual, Momma. Boy, did that come out awkward. *(Pause.)* Hello? Hello? I'm a homosexual. *(Pause.)* Please, Momma. Say something.

HANNAH: You're old enough to understand that your father didn't love you without being ridiculous about it.

JOE: What?

HANNAH: You're ridiculous. You're being ridiculous.

JOE: I'm . . . What?

HANNAH: You really ought to go home now to your wife. I need to go to bed. This phone call . . . We will just forget this phone call.

JOE: Mom.

HANNAH: No more talk. Tonight. This . . . *(Suddenly very angry.)* Drinking is a sin! A sin! I raised you better than that.

> *She hangs up.*

Scene 9

> *The following morning, early. Split scene: Harper and Joe at home; Louis and Prior in Prior's hospital room. Joe and Louis have just entered. This should be fast and obviously furious; overlapping is fine; the proceedings may be a little confusing but not the final results.*

HARPER: Oh God. Home. The moment of truth has arrived.

JOE: Harper.

LOUIS: I'm going to move out.

PRIOR: The fuck you are.

JOE: Harper. Please listen. I still love you very much. You're still my best buddy. I'm not going to leave you.

HARPER: No. I don't like the sound of this. I'm leaving.

LOUIS: I'm leaving. I already have.

JOE: Please listen. Stay. This is really hard. We have to talk.

HARPER: We are talking. Aren't we. Now please shut up. OK?

PRIOR: Bastard. Sneaking off while I'm flat out here, that's low. If I could get up now I'd beat the holy shit out of you.

JOE: Did you take pills? How many?

HARPER: No pills. Bad for the . . . *(Pats stomach.)*

JOE: You aren't pregnant. I called your gynecologist.

HARPER: I'm seeing a new gynecologist.

PRIOR: You have no right to do this.

LOUIS: Oh, that's ridiculous.

PRIOR: No right. It's criminal.

JOE: Forget about that. Just listen. You want the truth. This is the truth. I knew this when I married you. I've known this I guess for as long as I've known anything, but . . . I don't know, I thought maybe that with enough effort and will I could change myself . . . but I can't . . .

PRIOR: Criminal.

LOUIS: There oughta be a law.

PRIOR: There is a law. You'll see.

JOE: I'm losing ground here, I go walking, you want to know where I walk, I . . . go to the park, or up and down Fifty-third Street, or places where . . . And I keep swearing I won't go walking again, but I just can't.

LOUIS: I need some privacy.

PRIOR: That's new.

LOUIS: Everything's new, Prior.

JOE: I try to tighten my heart into a knot, a snarl, I try to learn to live dead, just numb, but then I see someone I want, and it's like a nail, like a hot spike right through my chest, and I know I'm losing.

PRIOR: Apartment too small for three? Louis and Prior comfy but not Louis and Prior and Prior's disease?

LOUIS: Something like that. I won't be judged by you. This isn't a crime, just—the inevitable consequence of people who run out of—whose limitations . . .

PRIOR: Bang bang bang. The court will come to order.

LOUIS: I mean let's talk practicalities, schedules; I'll come over if you want, spend nights with you when I can, I can . . .

PRIOR: Has the jury reached a verdict?

LOUIS: I'm doing the best I can.

PRIOR: Pathetic. Who cares?

JOE: My whole life has conspired to bring me to this place, and I can't despise my whole life. I think I believed when I met you I could save you, you at least if not myself, but . . . I don't have any sexual feelings for you, Harper. And I don't think I ever did.

> *Little pause.*

HARPER: I think you should go.

JOE: Where?

HARPER: Washington. Doesn't matter.

JOE: What are you talking about?

HARPER: Without me. Without me, Joe. Isn't that what you want to hear?

> *Little pause.*

JOE: Yes.

LOUIS: You can love someone and fail them. You can love someone and not be able to . . .

PRIOR: You *can,* theoretically, yes. A person can, maybe an editorial "you" can love, Louis, but not *you,* specifically you, I don't know, I think you are excluded from that general category.

HARPER: You were going to save me, but the whole time you were spinning a lie. I just don't understand that.

PRIOR: A person could theoretically love and maybe many do but we both know now you can't.

LOUIS: I do.

PRIOR: You can't even say it.

LOUIS: I love you, Prior.

PRIOR: I repeat. Who cares?

HARPER: This is so scary, I want this to stop, to go back . . .

PRIOR: We have reached a verdict, your honor. This man's heart is deficient. He loves, but his love is worth nothing.

JOE: Harper . . .

HARPER: Mr. Lies, I want to get away from here. Far away. Right now. Before he starts talking again. Please, please . . .

JOE: As long as I've known you, Harper, you've been afraid of . . . of men hiding under the bed, men hiding under the sofa, men with knives.

PRIOR *(shattered; almost pleading, trying to reach him):* I'm dying! You stupid fuck! Do you know what that is! Love! Do you know what love means? We lived together four and a half years, you animal, you idiot.

LOUIS: I have to find some way to save myself.

JOE: Who are these men? I never understood it. Now I know.

HARPER: What?

JOE: It's me.

Stephen Spinella as Prior Walter, David Marshall Grant as Joe Pitt, Marcia Gay Harden as Harper Pitt and Joe Mantello as Louis Ironson in a scene from Tony Kushner's prizewinning play *Angels in America*

HARPER: Is it?

PRIOR: GET OUT OF MY ROOM!

JOE: I'm the man with the knives.

HARPER: You are?

PRIOR: If I could get up now I'd kill you. I would. Go away. Go away or I'll scream.

HARPER: Oh God . . .

JOE: I'm sorry . . .

HARPER: It is you.

LOUIS: Please don't scream.

PRIOR: Go.

HARPER: I recognize you now.

LOUIS: Please . . .

JOE: Oh. Wait, I . . . Oh! (*He covers his mouth with his hand, gags, and removes his hand, red with blood.*) I'm bleeding.

     Prior screams.

HARPER: Mr. Lies.

MR. LIES *(appearing, dressed in Antarctic explorer's apparel):* Right here.

HARPER: I want to go away. I can't see him any more.

MR. LIES: Where?

HARPER: Anywhere. Far away.

MR. LIES: Absolutamento.

>*Harper and Mr. Lies vanish. Joe looks up, sees that she's gone.*

PRIOR *(closing his eyes):* When I open my eyes you'll be gone.

>*Louis leaves.*

JOE: Harper?

PRIOR *(opening his eyes):* Huh. It worked.

JOE *(calling):* Harper?

PRIOR: I hurt all over. I wish I was dead.

ACT III: Not-Yet-Conscious, Forward Dawning, January 1986

Scene 5

Joe Pitt is meeting Roy Cohn in the study of Roy's New York brownstone. Roy is dressed in an *"elegant"* bathrobe and *"has made a considerable effort to look well"* but hasn't managed very successfully. Joe is apologizing to Roy for turning down the job Roy has offered him.

JOE: My wife is missing. My mother's coming from Salt Lake to . . . to help look, I guess. I'm supposed to be at the airport now, picking her up but. . . . I just spent two days in a hospital, Roy, with a bleeding ulcer, I was spitting up blood.

ROY: Blood, huh? Look, I'm very busy here, and . . .

JOE: It's just a job.

ROY: A job? A *job? Washington!* Dumb Utah Mormon hick shit!

JOE: Roy . . .

ROY: *WASHINGTON!* When Washington called me I was younger than you, you think I said, "Aw fuck no I can't go I got two fingers up my asshole and a little moral nosebleed to boot!" When Washington calls you, my pretty young punk friend, you go or you can go fuck yourself sideways 'cause the train has pulled out of the station, and you are *out,* nowhere, out in the cold. Fuck you, Mary Jane, get outta here.

JOE: Just let me . . .

ROY: Explain? Ephemera. You broke my heart. Explain that. Explain that.

JOE: I love you, Roy. There's so much that I want, to be . . . what you see in me, I want to be a participant in the world, in your world, Roy, I want to be capable of that, I've tried, really I have but . . . I can't do this. Not because I don't believe in you, but because I believe in you so much, in what you stand for, at heart, the order, the decency. I would give anything to protect you, but . . . There are laws I can't break. It's too ingrained. It's not me. There's enough damage I've already done. Maybe you were right, maybe I'm dead.

ROY: You're not dead, boy, you're a sissy. You love me; that's moving, I'm moved. It's nice to be loved. I warned you about her, didn't I, Joe? But you don't listen to me, why, because you say Roy is smart and Roy's a friend but Roy . . . well, he isn't nice, and you wanna be nice. Right? A nice, nice man! *(Little pause.)* You know what my greatest accomplishment was, Joe, in my life, what I am able to look back on and be proudest of? And I have helped make Presidents and unmake them and mayors and more goddamn judges than anyone in NYC ever—AND several million dollars, tax free—and what do you think means the most to me? You ever hear of Ethel Rosenberg, Huh, Joe, huh?

JOE: Well, yeah, I guess I . . . Yes.

ROY: Yes. Yes. You have heard of Ethel Rosenberg. Yes. Maybe you even read about her in the history books. If it wasn't for me, Joe, Ethel Rosenberg would be alive today, writing some personal-advice column for *Ms.* magazine. She isn't. Because during the trial, Joe, I was on the phone every day, talking with the judge . . .

JOE: Roy . . .

ROY: Every day, doing what I do best, talking on the telephone, making sure that timid Yid nebbish on the bench did his duty to America, to history. That sweet unprepossessing woman, two kids, boo-hoo-hoo, reminded us all of our little Jewish mamas—she came this close to getting life; I pleaded till I wept to put her in the chair. Me. I did that. I would have fucking pulled the switch if they'd have let me. Why? Because I fucking hate traitors. Because I fucking hate communists. Was it legal? Fuck legal. Am I a nice man? Fuck nice. They say terrible things about me in the *Nation.* Fuck the *Nation.* You want to be Nice, or you want to be Effective? Make the law, or subject to it. Choose. Your wife chose. A week from today, she'll be back. SHE knows how to get what SHE wants. Maybe I ought to send *her* to Washington.

JOE: I don't believe you.

ROY: Gospel.

JOE: You can't possibly mean what you're saying. Roy, you were the Assistant United States Attorney on the Rosenberg case, ex-parte communication with the judge during the trial would be . . . censurable, at least, probably conspiracy and . . . in a case that resulted in execution, it's . . .

ROY: What? Murder?

JOE: You're not well is all.

ROY: What do you mean, not well? Who's not well?

Pause.

JOE: You said . . .

ROY: No. I didn't. I said what?

JOE: Roy, you have cancer.

ROY: No I don't.

> *Pause.*

JOE: You told me you were dying.

ROY: What the fuck are you talking about, Joe? I never said that. I'm in perfect health. There's not a goddamn thing wrong with me. *(He smiles.)* Shake?

> *Joe hesitates. He holds out his hand to Roy. Roy pulls Joe into a close, strong clinch.*

(More to himself than to Joe.) It's O.K. that you hurt me because I love you, baby Joe. That's why I'm so rough on you.

> *Roy releases Joe. Joe backs away a step or two.*

Prodigal son. The world will wipe its dirty hands all over you.

JOE: It already has, Roy.

ROY: Now go.

> *Roy shoves Joe, hard. Joe turns to leave. Roy stops him, turns him around.*

(Smoothing Joe's lapels, tenderly.) I'll always be here, waiting for you . . .

> *Then again, with sudden violence, he pulls Joe close, violently.*

What did you want from me, what was all this, what do you want, treacherous ungrateful little . . .

> *Joe, very close to belting Roy, grabs him by the front of his robe and propels him across the length of the room. He holds Roy at arm's length, the other arm ready to hit.*

(Laughing softly, almost pleading to be hit.) Transgress a little, Joseph.

> *Joe releases Roy.*

There are so many laws; find one you can break.

> *Joe hesitates, then leaves, backing out. When Joe has gone, Roy doubles over in great pain, which he's been hiding throughout the scene with Joe.*

Ah, Christ . . . Andy! Andy! Get in here! Andy!

> *The door opens, but it isn't Andy. A small Jewish woman dressed modestly in a Fifties hat and coat stands in the doorway. The room darkens.*

Who the fuck are you? The new nurse?

> *The figure in the doorway says nothing. She stares at Roy. A pause. Roy looks at her carefully, gets up, crosses to her. He crosses back to the chair, sits heavily.*

Aw, fuck. Ethel.

ETHEL ROSENBERG *(her manner is friendly, her voice is ice-cold):* You don't look good, Roy.

ROY: Well, Ethel. I don't feel good.

ETHEL ROSENBERG: But you lost a lot of weight. That suits you. You were heavy back then. Zaftig, mit hips.

ROY: I haven't been that heavy since 1960. We were all heavier back then, before the body thing started. Now I look like a skeleton. They stare.

ETHEL ROSENBERG: The shit's really hit the fan, huh, Roy?

> *Little pause. Roy nods.*

Well the fun's just started.

ROY: What is this, Ethel, Halloween? You trying to scare me? *(Ethel says nothing.)* Well, you're wasting your time! I'm scarier than you any day of the week! So beat it, Ethel! BOOO! BETTER DEAD THAN RED! Somebody trying to shake me up? HAH HAH! From the throne of God in heaven to the belly of hell, you can all fuck yourselves and then go jump in the lake because I'M NOT AFRAID OF YOU OR DEATH OR HELL OR ANYTHING!

ETHEL ROSENBERG: Be seeing you soon, Roy. Julius send his regards.

ROY: Yeah, well send this to Julius!

> *He flips the bird in her direction, stands and moves towards her. Halfway across the room he slumps to the floor, breathing laboriously, in pain.*

ETHEL ROSENBERG: You're a very sick man, Roy.

ROY: Oh God . . . ANDY!

ETHEL ROSENBERG: Hmmm. He doesn't hear you, I guess. We should call the ambulance. *(She goes to the phone.)* Hah! Buttons! Such things they got now. What do I dial, Roy?

> *Pause.*

ROY *(looks at her, then):* Nine-one-one.

ETHEL ROSENBERG *(dials the phone):* It sings! *(Imitating dial tones.)* La la la . . . Huh. Yes, you should please send an ambulance to the home of Mister Roy Cohn, the famous lawyer. What's the address, Roy?

ROY *(a beat, then):* Two-four-four East Eighty-seventh.

ETHEL ROSENBERG: Two-four-four East Eighty-seventh Street. No apartment number, he's got the whole building. My name? *(A beat.)* Ethel Greenglass Rosenberg. *(Small smile.)* Me? No, I'm not related to Mr. Cohn. An old friend.

> *She hangs up.*

They said a minute.

ROY: I have all the time in the world.

ETHEL ROSENBERG: You're immortal.

ROY: I'm immortal, Ethel. *(He forces himself to stand.)* I have *forced* my way into history. I ain't never gonna die.

ETHEL ROSENBERG *(a little laugh, then):* History is about to crack wide open. Millennium approaches.

As of the end of the play, Harper is on a symbolic trip to the Antarctic with Mr. Lies, Joe and Louis have found each other and Prior, at death's door, is visited by an Angel who crashes into his room through the ceiling and announces, "Greetings, Prophet; The Great Work begins: The Messenger has arrived." *Blackout. Curtain. End of Part One.*

○○○
○○○
○○○
○○○
○○○
○○○ LATER LIFE

A Full-Length Play in One Act

BY A.R. GURNEY

Cast and credits appear on pages 342, 343

A.R. GURNEY (who recently dropped "Jr." from his byline) was born Nov. 1, 1930 in Buffalo, N.Y., the son of a realtor. He was educated at St. Paul's School and Williams College, where he received his B.A. in 1952. After a stint in the Navy, he entered Yale Drama School in 1956 and emerged with an M.F.A. after studying playwriting in seminars conducted by Lemist Esler, Robert Penn Warren and John Gassner. His first production, the musical Love in Buffalo, *took place at Yale in 1958.*

"Pete" Gurney's first New York production of record was the short-lived The David Show *off Broadway in 1968, repeated in an off-Broadway program with his* The Golden Fleece *the following season. His* Scenes From American Life *premiered in Buffalo in 1970, then was produced by Repertory Theater of Lincoln Center for 30 performances in 1971, winning its author Drama Desk and Variety poll citations as a most promising playwright and achieving many subsequent productions at home and abroad.*

Gurney next made the off-Broadway scene with Who Killed Richard Cory? *for 31 performances at Circle Repertory in 1976, the same year that his* Children *premiered in Richmond, Va. and his* The Rape of Bunny Stunte *was done OOB. The next year,* Children *appeared at Manhattan Theater Club,* The Love Course *was produced OOB and* The Middle Ages *had its premiere at the Mark Taper Forum in Los Angeles. Gurney's* The Problem *and* The Wayside Motor Inn *were done OOB in the 1977–78 season. In 1981–82* The Middle Ages *came to New York OOB and Circle Rep workshopped* What I Did Last Summer.

In that same season, Gurney's first Best Play, The Dining Room, *began a 583-performance run at Playwrights Horizons on February 24. His second Best Play,* The Perfect Party, *opened a 238-performance run April 2, 1986, also at Playwrights Horizons. His third Best Play,* The Cocktail Hour, *reached independent off-Broadway production October 20, 1988. While it was chalking up 351 performances at the Promenade Theater, another Gurney script that had been staged at the Long Wharf Theater in New Haven in November 1988,* Love Letters, *was being put on in staged readings March 6–April 10 on Monday evenings at the Promenade, when* The Cocktail Hour *had the night off.* Love Letters *reopened August 22, 1989 as a full off-Broadway offering for 64 performances after which, on October 31, it moved to Broadway, its author's fourth Best Play. His fifth is* Later Life *which opened May 23 as the finale of Playwrights Horizons' 1992–93 season, then being moved on to an independent off-Broadway theater for a later life of its own.*

New York has also seen Gurney's What I Did Last Summer *for 31 performances in full production at Circle Rep and* The Middle Ages *for 110 off-Broadway performances, both in 1983;* The Golden Age, *suggested by Henry James's* The Aspern Papers, *on Broadway April 12, 1984 for 29 performances;* Sweet Sue *on Broadway January 8, 1987 for 164 performances; and* Another Antigone *January 11, 1988 for 30 performances and* The Old Boy *May 5, 1991 for 33 performances, both at Playwrights Horizons. The most recent Gurney works are* The Snow Ball *(based on his novel and produced in regional theater) and* The Fourth Wall.

Gurney is also the author of the TV adaptation from John Cheever's O Youth and Beauty! *and of two other novels* The Gospel According to Joe *and* Entertaining Strangers. *He has been the recipient of Rockefeller and National Endowment Awards, an Old Dominion Fellowship, an honorary degree from Williams, a New England Theater Conference citation for outstanding creative achievement and in 1987 an Award of Merit from the American Academy and Institute of Arts and Letters. He has taught literature at M.I.T. for 25 years. He is married, with four children, and lives in New York City, where he serves on the artistic board of Playwrights Horizons.*

The following synopsis of Later Life *was prepared by Sally Dixon Wiener.*

Time: A September evening

Place: The terrace of a high-rise apartment building, overlooking Boston Harbor

ACT I

SYNOPSIS: The terrace is conservatively planted, and in the dark green foliage there are, of course, the ubiquitous fall chrysanthemums in a muted shade. The outdoor furniture, of obviously excellent quality, is equally conservative. Two cushioned chairs with a small table between them are downstage, and a matching chaise longue is upstage. Another table, with a large hurricane lamp on it, is parallel to the upstage railing beyond which is the starry evening sky—its limitless view seemingly unable to be held in check by the strictures imposed on the terrace itself. There is an archway in the red brick wall at stage left that provides access to the unseen offstage apartment. Offstage right and also unseen is the view of Boston Harbor. (There are two main characters, Austin and Ruth, but all other characters, it should be noted, are played by one additional actress and actor.)

The stage is empty, but sounds indicate a party is going on inside. Sally, the hostess, appears, a perky, middle-aged blonde in a white blouse and long red skirt. She is carrying a gin and tonic and calls offstage to Austin to join her on the terrace. "I'm setting the stage here," she tells herself firmly, "That's all I can do." She calls to Austin again, and he rather reluctantly appears. *"He is a distinguished, good-looking, middle-aged man, who wears a gray suit, a blue shirt, and a conservative tie. He carries a glass."* Sally wants him to wait there so he can talk to someone. No, not her, Sally explains patiently, someone else. Austin demurs, but Sally insists he wait while she goes to get her.

While Austin's waiting, Jim, *"rather scruffily dressed,"* comes out, remarking that he supposes this is a place where people can smoke. He spots an ashtray on a table and wonders if there is anybody who still designs ashtrays. Austin, playing along with him, suggests there may be, in Europe. Jim goes on about cigarettes, the packaging, the taxes, and with Clinton the taxes will be more. "Yes well Clinton . . ." Austin comments. Jim taps out a cigarette, enjoying the process, and offers Austin one. It seems Austin has never really smoked.

JIM: Never even tried it?

AUSTIN: Oh well, I suppose behind the barn . . .   —

JIM *(taking a cigarette for himself)*: That's too bad. You've missed something in life. Smoking is one of the great pleasures of the phenomenal world. It's the closest we come to heaven on earth—particularly now it's forbidden fruit. *(He takes out a lighter.)* It adds depth and dimension to whatever we say or do. Oh, I know: it corrupts children, it exploits the Third World, it is gross, addictive and unnecessary. It is an image of capitalism in its last, most self-destructive stages. But . . . *(Puts cigarette in his mouth and lights the lighter.)* It is also a gesture of freedom in an absurd universe. *(Snaps lighter shut.)* And I'm giving it up.

AUSTIN: Are you serious?

JIM: I am. I have made the decision. That's why I'm behaving like such an asshole.

AUSTIN: Oh I wouldn't say that.

JIM: No, really. I've given it up before, of course, but tonight is the big night. Nothing becomes it like the leaving thereof. I bought this fresh pack and came out here because this time I'm trying to confront temptation. I am shaking hands with the Devil. I am deliberately immersing myself in the dangerous element.

AUSTIN: Do you teach around here?

JIM: That's not important. What I do—or rather, what I did, was smoke. I was an existential smoker. I smoked, therefore I was.

Jim finally admits he taught philosophy, at Brandeis, until he was forced to take early retirement. They claimed he "slept with too many students," he says.

"Sally comes back out, with Ruth in tow. Ruth is a lovely women, who wears a simple, slightly artsy dress." Sally sends Jim off because she wants Austin and Ruth to be left alone. She introduces them, saying to Austin that Ruth's from out of town. Austin welcomes her to Boston. The truth is, he doesn't remember Ruth; Ruth remembers him, however. Sally tells Ruth to get him to remember, and she also announces that Austin is divorced and tells Austin that Ruth is (separated, not divorced, Ruth corrects her). Sally leaves them, hoping they'll make the most of it.

Austin and Ruth begin a long round of cat and mouse, as Austin tries to recall when and where he is supposed to have met Ruth. Her last name wouldn't be a help, she assures him. He knew her only as Ruth. And she was not married at that time. He wonders if they could have met in school or in college. Ruth doesn't think that would have happened, because "Not everybody in the world went to Groton and Harvard." Austin feels foolish not to recall an attractive woman who came into his life. She offers to give him a hint, but he wants to remember on his own. He's proud of his memory, insisting he can remember an incident that occurred when he was two and a half. Ruth doubts it. Austin is sure. Ruth wants to know about it.

AUSTIN: I can remember being wakened in my crib by a strange sound. A kind of soft, rustling sound. And . . . *(He stops.)* Never mind.

RUTH: Go on. You can't stop now.

AUSTIN: It was my nurse—we had this young nurse. I specifically remember seeing her through the bars of my crib. Standing by the window. In the moonlight. Naked. Stroking her body. And I lay there watching her.

RUTH: Through the bars of your crib.

AUSTIN: Through the bars of my crib.

Pause.

RUTH: Austin.

AUSTIN: What?

RUTH: I am that nurse.

AUSTIN: No.

RUTH: No. Just kidding. *(Both laugh.)* No, we met after college.

AUSTIN: After college, but before I was married.

RUTH: And before I was.

AUSTIN: You are presenting a rather narrow window of opportunity, madam.

RUTH: I know it.

AUSTIN: I got married soon after college.

RUTH: As did I, sir. As did I.

AUSTIN: So we are talking about a moment in our lives when we were both . . . what? Relatively free and clear.

RUTH: That's what we were. Relatively. Free and clear.

AUSTIN: Those moments are rare.

Ruth is agreeing with Austin, when the party sounds are heard again. *"Marion comes out, gray-haired and maternal."* She oohs and aahs over the view and calls to her husband to come out. *"Roy comes out hesitatingly. He is grim and cold,"* dodders a bit and is obviously hard of hearing as well. Marion chats with Austin and dithers on about the view. She learns that Austin has lived his whole life in Boston and complains that Roy wants them to leave it to move south. Roy doesn't like the cold, has arthritis in his knees and hips.

ROY: I was once a runner.

MARION: He's never gotten over it.

ROY: I ran the marathon six times.

MARION: I had to line up the whole family on Commonwealth Avenue every Patriot's Day and cheer him on towards the Prudential Center.

RUTH: What's Patriot's Day?

AUSTIN: Ah. It's our own special holiday. It commemorates Paul Revere's ride to Lexington and Concord. "On the Eighteenth of April, in Seventy-Five . . ."

MARION *(taking over)*: ". . . Hardly a man is now alive/Who remembers that famous day and year . . ."

AUSTIN: Good for you. *(To RUTH.)* These days we celebrate it by running a marathon.

RUTH: Sounds very Boston.

AUSTIN: What do you mean?

RUTH: Everyone running madly towards an insurance building.

AUSTIN *(laughing)*: Ah well, I look at it in another way. We celebrate a Greek marathon because we're the Athens of America.

MARION: Exactly! *(To ROY.)* Listen to this man, Roy. He knows. He's chosen to live here all his life. *(To AUSTIN.)* I wish you'd tell my husband why.

AUSTIN: Chosen to live here? Oh, I don't think I ever *chose*. I was born here, I've lived here, I've been here, and now I don't think I could be anywhere else.

MARION *(to RUTH)*: That's because it's the most civilized city in America.

RUTH *(to AUSTIN)*: Do you agree?

AUSTIN *(bowing to MARION)*: I'd never disagree with such a passionate advocate.

Charles Kimbrough as Austin in *Later Life*

MARION: Thank you, sir.

ROY *(to* RUTH*):* I did the marathon of Seventy-Eight under four hours.

MARION: She doesn't *care,* Roy.

ROY: I came in six hundred and seventy-nine out of over fifteen thousand registered contenders.

MARION: Roy . . .

Roy has found a retirement place in Florida that has a golf course, but Marion thinks it "looks like a concentration camp" with its gates and guards. They'll leave friends, children and grandchildren. The purse opens, and the photographs of the grandchildren appear. Roy tells Marion people are not interested; furthermore, he wants to go inside and warm up. Marion wants to enjoy her grandchildren, but Roy is adamant. "You can enjoy them after I'm dead."

When Marion, exclaiming once more about the view, has followed Roy off, Austin informs Ruth that Boston Harbor could be turned into a theme park:

"One of the great natural harbors of the New World!" Austin still doesn't remember meeting Ruth. Was he working? he wonders. He was actually playing, Ruth retorts. It seems he was a good-looking young naval officer "steaming around the Mediterranean." She hums "The Isle of Capri," and gradually Austin recalls having liberty, going to Capri, the Blue Grotto, the funicular, and at a restaurant at the top of a hill having beers, and at the next table there were some American girls. "Summer Special for the sisters of Sigma Nu from the University of Southern Illinois," Ruth recites. "I struck up a conversation with a girl named . . . Ruth!" Austin triumphs. It seems they got along together right from the start and ended up on a terrace overlooking the Bay of Naples. "Which is one of the great natural harbors of the *Old* World," Austin interjects. Vesuvius was smoking in the distance, Ruth recalls. Austin begs to differ. He thinks Vesuvius had given up smoking. "There must have been pressure from the people of Pompeii," Ruth surmises.

They are both laughing as Duane comes out, a nerd whose native tongue seems to be computerese. He is looking for his wife, who might be a little over-emotional, he mentions, peering over the railing. He believes she's upset because she doesn't want him to upgrade (to a new IBM compatible with an Intel 486 processor), even though he's offered to upgrade her, too. It seems she's still using DOS 2.0., and Duane tells her she is "backspacing herself into the dark ages." He goes off cheerily.

Austin wants to know if he kissed Ruth on Capri. Almost at once, it seems. And he talked, and she listened, Ruth tells him. About himself. "I don't think I've ever heard anyone else say the things you said." That's why she remembered him, she explains.

Again they are interrupted. This time it's Nancy. *"She is carrying a plate of food. She wears austere clothes."* There is a mannered way about her that verges on the edge of ill-mannered. She announces that there's food inside. And they shouldn't think she's antisocial as she goes to sit on the chaise, but she is expecting someone to join her.

Nancy wants Ruth and Austin to go on talking. (They look "terribly intense" to her.) Nancy doesn't know what's become of her companion. They'd been talking and then gotten into line for food, and here Nancy is, but where is she? It's a mob scene, and Ruth thinks maybe Nancy's friend got lost in the shuffle. "If we went in, we might get lost in the shuffle, too," Austin comments to Ruth. Ruth agrees. Nancy's busy discussing the vegetable casserole, giving it a C minus. The bread is acceptable, but "no one serves butter in Boston any more."

Austin tries to continue their earlier discussion with Ruth, but she tells him to wait. "I'm always waiting," Austin replies. "I know," Ruth comments. It seems it's one of the things he told her on Capri. Nancy wonders if Austin and Ruth are married. Assured they're not, she asks if they're lovers. Again they say no. She assumes then that they are planning an assignation. Austin doesn't think so; he thinks they are just talking, just old friends talking. Nancy gives them the once-over again, remarking before she departs that life has taught her something: "Even if the main course is somewhat disappointing, there's always dessert." Austin feels it might have been rude of them not to include Nancy in their conversation. Ruth doesn't think so.

AUSTIN: . . . . . I believe in civility.

RUTH: Being from Boston . . .

AUSTIN: Well, I do. The more the world falls apart, the more I believe in it. Some guy elbows ahead of me in a line, I like to bow and say, "Go ahead, sir, if it's that important to you." Treat people with civility, and maybe they'll learn to behave that way.

RUTH: It's been my experience that they'll feel guilty and behave worse.

AUSTIN: Well *I* feel guilty now. Because I wasn't polite.

RUTH: I feel fine.

AUSTIN: You do?

RUTH: Yes, I do. Because we were doing something very rare in this world that is falling apart. We were making a connection. That's something that happens only once in a while, and less and less as we get older, so we shouldn't let anything get in its way.

AUSTIN: O.K., Ruth. I'll buy that. O.K.

Duane comes out to report he's found his wife: "Everything's batched and patched." They sat down to talk things out, and he suddenly remembered that today's her birthday. Quickly, he arranged by computer to have a dozen long-stem roses waiting for her when they get home, which may or may not smooth things over.

Duane exits, and Ruth wants to know if what Austin foretold on Capri ever happened. He claims not to know what she's talking about, so she tells him: "You said that you were sure something terrible was going to happen to you in the course of your life." He was waiting for it to happen and had already spent most of his life waiting. Austin seems embarrassed and tries to make light of it. He must have been "bombed out of his mind" in Capri and trying to "snow the pants off" Ruth. He succeeded, Ruth admits. She'd invited him up to her room, but he'd said no. He'd told her he liked her too much to drag her into his problem. He'd kissed her goodnight and returned to his ship.

What had she done?, Austin wonders, after he'd left. It seems she'd gone out on the town with some friend of his with an Irish name. Austin realizes it must have been Denny Doyle, a Bostonian who later ran for the state legislature. Ruth bets he won and Austin claims he surely did. He was fun, Ruth adds.

AUSTIN: I don't think he ever told me he took you out.

RUTH: I'm glad he didn't.

AUSTIN: He must have thought you were my girl.

RUTH: For a moment there, I thought I was.

AUSTIN *(bowing to her):* I apologize, Madam. For turning such a lovely lady down. And leaving her to the lascivious advances of Denny Doyle.

RUTH: Well, you had your reasons.

AUSTIN: Apparently I did.

RUTH: I'll never forget it, though. What you told me. I've met lots of men with lots of lines before and since—but no one ever told me anything like that.

AUSTIN: Some line. What a dumb thing to tell anyone.

RUTH: Oh no. It worked, in the long run.

AUSTIN: It worked?

RUTH: It's made me think about you ever since.

AUSTIN: Really? More than Denny Doyle?

RUTH: Much more. Particularly when . . .

AUSTIN: When what?

RUTH: When terrible things happened to me.

> *Pause.*

Austin asks Ruth if she would like a drink *now.* She wouldn't, but he would. He suggests they go in together, but she prefers to stay outside. It would be rude of him to leave her, he believes. Ruth says "nuts" to that, and he starts in.

RUTH: Austin . . .

> *He stops.*

How do I know you're not retreating back to your ship?

AUSTIN: Because I'm older now.

RUTH: Which means?

AUSTIN: Which means I learn from my mistakes.

RUTH: That's good to hear.

> *He starts in again, then stops.*

AUSTIN: Will you be here when I get back?

RUTH: Sure. Unless Denny Doyle shows up again.

AUSTIN: He just might. He's now head of the Port Authority, and wild as a Kennedy.

RUTH: Then you better hurry.

AUSTIN: I will. And I'll get us both drinks.

Ted and Esther McAlister join Ruth on the terrace. *"They wear bright suburban colors and have Southern accents."* They moved to Boston six months ago and are hell-bent on making it a memorable experience. It's not stuffy at all, they've found, the New Boston.

TED: We're making a point of meeting everyone at this party.

ESTHER: And everyone has a story.

TED: If you can just find out what it is. For example, we met this man, a perfectly ordinary looking man, who turns out to be a real Indian . . .

RUTH: Native American, honey . . .

TED: That's right. A Tuscarora, actually.

RUTH: He teaches history at Tufts.

TED: Think of that. A Tuscarora chief. Teaching history at Tufts. And there he was, drinking a dry martini.

ESTHER: Ted said, "Careful of the old fire-water."

TED: And he laughed.

ESTHER: He did. He laughed.

TED: Oh yes. And we met a couple who travels to Asia Minor every year.

ESTHER: To do archaeology.

TED: So I said, "Maybe we should all talk Turkey."

ESTHER: They didn't laugh.

TED: He did. She didn't.

ESTHER: She comes from Cambridge.

TED: And we met several Jewish people.

ESTHER: They're all so *frank.*

TED: That's because they've suffered throughout history. You'd be frank, too, if you'd suffered throughout history.

ESTHER: Oh, and there's an African-American woman in there. Who writes poetry.

TED: And we met this Hispanic gentleman . . .

ESTHER: Latino, honey. He prefers Latino. And he wants to . . . Shall I say this, Ted?

TED: Sure, say it, we're among friends.

ESTHER: He says he wants to become a woman.

TED: Said he was seriously thinking about it.

ESTHER: Can you imagine? Of course, they say Boston doctors are the finest in the world.

TED: He may have been pulling our leg.

ESTHER: I know. But still . . . I mean, ouch.

TED: And we met a woman from Cambodia, and a man from Peru . . .

ESTHER: He looked like an Aztec prince.

TED: Well, half-Aztec, anyway.

   Both laugh.

ESTHER: Anyway, he had a story. Everyone has a story.

They want to know Ruth's story. She's not sure they want to hear three volumes, but they pull up their chairs instantly. No, she's not a Bostonian. She's just visiting her friend Judith. Ruth reveals she's from the Midwest, has lived here and there and is now contemplating whether to move to Boston. Under their questioning Ruth admits to having been married four times, twice to the same man. Her first marriage ended after seven days when her husband was killed by a land mine in Korea. And, yes, she did have a child, by a second husband; and she reluctantly tells them her daughter died at 11 of leukemia.

ESTHER: You and your husband pulled together . . .

RUTH: Yes, we did. We pulled together. But when she was gone, we had nothing left to . . . pull. So we pulled apart.
      Pause.
Life goes on.

TED: It does, Ruth. It definitely does.

RUTH: So I married a Man of the West.

ESTHER: Number three?

RUTH: And four.

TED: He's a cowboy?

RUTH: He thinks he is . . . He'd like to be . . . He drives a Ford Bronco.

TED: At least he buys an American vehicle.

RUTH: Oh yes. He's very—American.

ESTHER: Do you like the West, Ruth?

RUTH: The answer to that is yes and no.
      Pause.
I'm a little at sea about that. *(Looks out.)* Maybe I'll find my moorings in Boston Harbor.

ESTHER: We're all wanderers, aren't we?

TED: Ships that pass in the night.

RUTH: Some are. *(Glances off where Austin has gone.)* Some aren't.
      Pause.
Lord knows I am.

When Austin returns with drinks and food, Ted and Esther announce they have reservations to go dancing and ask them to come. Ruth glances at Austin, who refuses the invitation but thanks them politely. Esther hopes to hear Austin's story another time. He has a special one, Ruth tells them. They leave.

RUTH: So it never happened.

AUSTIN: What?

RUTH: The terrible thing.

AUSTIN: Oh that.

RUTH: It never happened?

AUSTIN: Oh no. God no. No.

RUTH: You never made some terrible mistake?

AUSTIN: Not that I know of. No.

RUTH: You were never hit by some awful doom? Things always worked out?

Maureen Anderman (*left,* as Ruth) with Carole Shelley and Anthony Heald, players of multiple roles in A.R. Gurney's *Later Life*

AUSTIN: Absolutely. I mean, I think so. I mean, sure. After the Navy, I came back. Went to the Business School. Got a good job with the Bank of Boston. Married. Married the boss's daughter, actually. Two kids. Both educated. Both launched. Both doing well. Can't complain at all.

RUTH: Sally said you were divorced.

AUSTIN: Oh well, that . . .

 Pause.

That doesn't . . . she wasn't . . . we weren't . . .

 Pause.

She fell in love . . . *claimed* she had fallen in love . . . With this . . . this *creep.* I mean, the guy's half her age! . . . She got her face lifted. Dyed her hair. Does aerobics on demand . . . I mean, it's pathetic.

RUTH: So that's not the terrible thing?

AUSTIN: Her leaving? Christ no. That was a good thing. That was the best thing to happen in a long, long time.

RUTH: And nothing else even remotely terrible happened in your life?

AUSTIN: I don't think so.
Looking for some wood to knock on.
At least not yet.
RUTH: You still think something might?
Pause.
Austin? Hello? *(He looks at her.)* Do you?
Pause.
AUSTIN: I think it all the time.
RUTH: Really?
AUSTIN: All. The. Time.
Pause.
I've been very lucky, you know. Too lucky. From the beginning. It's not fair. Something's bound to . . .
Pause.
Want to know something?
RUTH: What?
AUSTIN: I'm on Prozac right now.
RUTH: You are?
AUSTIN: It's a drug. It calms you down.
RUTH: Oh, I know Prozac. I know what it does. And doesn't do.
AUSTIN: I don't tell people I'm on it. But I am.
RUTH: Does it help?
AUSTIN: Yes . . . no . . . a little.
RUTH: You shouldn't drink with it.
AUSTIN: I don't. Normally. That was a Perrier I was drinking before.
RUTH: But not now?
AUSTIN: This is a white wine spritzer. Tonight I'm becoming very reckless.
RUTH: Be careful. You might make some terrible mistake.
AUSTIN: Sometimes I wish I would. At least the shoe would drop.

Sally comes out briefly to turn on the terrace light, bringing Ruth's sweater at Judith's request. She gives them notice someone's going to be playing the piano, and that there will be singing, and goes back in.

Ruth confesses to liking Boston, except for the "shouldn't do this, have to do that" Puritanical attitude she senses. She sounds like his psychiatrist, Austin remarks. It seems his children gave him a couple of sessions as a present after his divorce, and he didn't want to hurt their feelings. And now, Ruth surmises, he's stayed on so as to not hurt the psychiatrist's feelings. When he dies, she assumes he'll say "Excuse me."

In any event, Austin feels that psychiatry isn't working for him. And even if it did, it seems a little late. He should not ever say that, Ruth warns him. He describes his psychiatrist as a woman who knows nothing about the world he is from, about all the surrogates, all the pressure, like a fly caught in a web. One move and the spider might . . . How would the psychiatrist know? he muses. "She grew up in a cozy little nuclear family in some kitchen in the Bronx." Ruth points out nuclear families could be explosive. Austin would choose an explosion over "death by spider."

The psychiatrist believes he has "a Puritan sense of damnation," and that he's been brought up to consider himself a member of the Elect. Austin finds it difficult to feel Elect, particularly since Bush's defeat. Now the psychiatrist tells him he is fighting against being one of the Damned and is so polite because he's hoping to propitiate God before the boom is lowered on him.

AUSTIN: . . . . . I feel good now. You've got me talking about these things. I've never done that before.

RUTH: Except with your shrink.

AUSTIN: It's different with you.

RUTH: You never talked about it with your wife?

AUSTIN: Oh God, no. Not with her. Never.

RUTH: Maybe that's why she left.

AUSTIN: Maybe: And maybe that's why you've stayed.

RUTH: Maybe.

AUSTIN: See? I've been snowing you again, just as I did on the Isle of Capri.

RUTH: Oh, is that what you've been doing?

AUSTIN: Has it worked?

RUTH: Oh yes. It's worked all over again.

AUSTIN: I'm glad.

He leans over and kisses her.

Walt comes out, "a little drunk. He wears a navy blazer with a crest on it and gray flannels." He sees them kissing, apologizes and goes inside. "That was my friend Walt," Austin tells Ruth. Walt returns, assuring Ruth he is Austin's best friend, ever since Groton (he was Austin's best man). Austin wants Walt to leave, but Walt simply goes on about Austin's family, his credentials as a banker, father and an "ultimately forgiving" husband. He assumes Austin's luring Ruth into his bed. She thinks not, but Austin concurs with Walt. Therefore Ruth should know she's going to bed with a squash player who'd be nationally ranked if he would play outside of Boston, Walt informs her, and "good at squash means good in bed." Austin walks away, impatient with Walt, who wants to describe Austin's squash game. Ruth wants him to.

WALT: The ayes have it. So. Now the secret to squash—we're talking about squash racquets here—is that you're obliged to be both brutally aggressive and ultimately courteous at the same time. At this, my friend Austin is a master. He will hit a cannon ball of a shot right down the rail, and then bow elegantly out of your way so you can hit it back.

RUTH: And what if you don't?

WALT: Then he'll ask if you'd like to play the point over.

AUSTIN: God, Walt.

RUTH: He sounds very special.

WALT: He is, Ruth.

Austin is embarrassed by Walt's fulsome praise, and Walt embarrasses him further by demonstrating how much he likes his old school chum by kissing him playfully on the cheek. Judith enters self-consciously, dressed in black with masses of wild, dark curly hair. There's a telephone call for Ruth, and Judith offers to say that Ruth isn't here, or even that Ruth doesn't want to speak to the caller, but Ruth feels she can speak to him, at least. Austin wonders if she'll be back. She will, she insists, and goes off after introducing Judith.

Judith is berating herself for bringing the message, explaining that it's Ruth's husband that's calling—"a deeply flawed person. . . . He hit her. That's for openers."

JUDITH: We met in this women's group two summers ago at the Aspen Music Festival. My husband and I played Mozart in the morning, and I signed up for Assertiveness Training in the afternoon. There was Ruth, dealing with her divorce. I thought we were all making great strides, but in the end she went back to her husband.

AUSTIN: So the group didn't help.

JUDITH: It helped me. I decided to leave mine.

AUSTIN: Oh dear.

JUDITH: I decided he was a weak man.

WALT: Weak—uh—physically?

JUDITH: Weak musically. Weak on Mozart, weak on Mahler, weak even on "Moon River."

AUSTIN: And this group had a say in that?

WALT: These women's groups work, man. *(To Judith)* My wife Ginny went to one. It improved her net game enormously.

JUDITH *(to Walt):* There you are. They open new horizons. I learned there's more to life than the string section. I'm now seriously involved with a French horn.

Austin interrupts. He wants to know more about Ruth. Ruth went back to Las Vegas where her husband prefers to live. He's a disaster, according to Judith. He even threw her television set out of the window. He's run through all Ruth's money. He's a gambler and manages a car rental business to support the habit. Judith's never met him, but she's seen his picture: "He looks like the Marlboro Man." Walt tells Austin it's time for him to make his move.

Austin's feeling pushed, but when Judith goes off to try to get Ruth off the telephone, Austin admits to Walt that he is strongly attracted to Ruth. Walt insists Austin needs somebody. Austin reminds him he has someone. But Walt doesn't mean Austin's "little friend up in Nashua" who's there when he needs her.

WALT: Give this one a chance.

AUSTIN: I'm not sure what you mean.

WALT: I mean, Ginny and I have tried to fix you up several times. But you gave those ladies short shift, or shrift, or whatever the fuck the expression is.

AUSTIN: Of course I'll give her a chance. I like to think I give everyone a chance. Why wouldn't I give her a chance?

WALT: Because you're acting like a jerk, that's why.

AUSTIN: What is it with you people in this town? Who do you think I am? Some new boy back at boarding school, being set up for the spring dance? I am a divorced man, Walt! I am the father of two grown children! I'll be a *grand*father any day! At our age, we don't just . . . *date* people, Walt. We don't just idly fool around. Every move is a big move. Every decision is a major decision. You ask a woman out, you take her to dinner, that's a statement, Walt. That says something important. Because there's no second chance this time, Walt. This is our last time at bat!

WALT: All the more reason not to be alone.

AUSTIN: And did you ever think, Walt, did you and Ginny ever think that maybe I *like* being alone? Ever think of that? Maybe I've discovered the pleasures of listening to opera while I'm shaving. And *walking* to work through the Common—rather than riding the damn train. And having a late lunch with a good book at the Union Oyster House! And reading it in bed at night! Maybe I like all that! Maybe I like feeling free to fart!

Ruth has returned with coffee and dessert, and Walt has gone off. Austin confesses Judith told him who was telephoning her. It seems Ruth's husband is at the Skyway Lounge at the airport and wants her to meet him there. She told him she was enjoying this party, and he'd said he could give her a better one there. Austin wonders if he could. "He can be . . . fun," Ruth admits. He's gotten two first class tickets on the red-eye for tonight and wants to have a bottle of champagne for them to drink while waiting for the plane. She likes champagne and is a sucker for first class, too, though she knows it will all be charged to her credit card. He has problems, Ruth admits, but don't we all, she muses. He is one of hers. "He's not good for me," she states frankly, but he loves her.

Austin is dubious about this, but Ruth isn't. "He's never traded me in for some young bimbo." He hasn't ever taken her for granted, and when she left him, he called everywhere to find out where she'd gone. He flew here, and called her, offering her champagne and begging her to come back. Austin can't believe he loves her if he hits her. "Once, maybe," Ruth insists, and it was by mistake. He can get carried away, she explains. That isn't love in Austin's book.

The singing has begun, and Austin suggests they go in and join the group, but Ruth indicates she's thinking of leaving. Austin proposes they go to the Ritz Bar and he'll buy her champagne, better than the Marlboro Man's, and pay for it as well. She tries to interrupt him, but he continues, desperately but unimpassionedly suggesting that afterward they walk from the Ritz to his apartment on Beacon Street. He has a guest room, with its own bath. He would like her to come with him, but she doesn't have to. If things were to work out, they might "make things more permanent." If not, she could leave whenever she wished. "We're back where we were, but this time we're getting a second chance," he points out, awaiting her decision.

"Austin from Boston. You're such a good man," Ruth tells him, giving him a kiss on the cheek and starting out. He wants to know where she's going. She doesn't want to tell him. "Why him and not me?" Austin wonders. How can she love him? If Austin doesn't know why, Ruth can't explain it. No, it isn't that she finds Austin unattractive, so it must be his problem, Austin reasons. Ruth agrees. He doesn't believe she takes his problem seriously, but she does, more so than he does, she informs him.

AUSTIN: You think something terrible is going to happen to me?
RUTH: I think it already has.
AUSTIN: When?
RUTH: I don't know.
AUSTIN: Where?
RUTH: I don't know that either.
AUSTIN: But you think I'm damned into outer darkness?
RUTH: I do. I really do.
AUSTIN: But you won't tell me why.
RUTH: I can't.
AUSTIN: Why not?
RUTH: It's too painful, Austin.
AUSTIN: Do you think I'll ever find out?
RUTH: Oh, I hope not.
AUSTIN: Why?
RUTH: Because you'll go through absolute hell.
AUSTIN: You mean I'll weep and wail and gnash my teeth?
RUTH: I don't think so, Austin. No. I think you'll clear your throat, and square your shoulders, and straighten your tie—and you'll stand there quietly and take it. That's the hellish part.

She gives him a tender look and says she must dash and, as Sally comes on, calls goodbye to her. Over the sounds of the singing offstage, Sally remarks on the abruptness of Ruth's departure; even so, Austin should call her at Judith's first thing tomorrow. Apprised of the fact that Ruth's flying back to Las Vegas with her husband, Sally is surprised. Austin doesn't understand how Ruth can do that. Sally suggests that perhaps Ruth thinks her husband will change.

AUSTIN: People don't change, Sally.

SALLY: Maybe they do in Las Vegas.

AUSTIN: Not at our age. We are who we are, only more so.

SALLY: No, Austin. I cannot agree with that. If that were true, I'd still be rattling around Ben's house on Brattle Street, having tea with his colleagues, talking about his books. But I sold the house, soon after he died. And I gave his books to the Widener. And I moved down here to the harbor, so I could live a different life with different people who talk about different things.

AUSTIN: Different they are, Sally. I'll say that.

SALLY: And they keep me *alive!* . . . Oh Austin, give it a try. Why not go after her!

AUSTIN: Sally . . .

SALLY: I mean it! She can't have gone that far!

    She finds the sweater.

Look! She even left her sweater!

    Holds it out.

You see? You're in luck! She's even given you a good excuse! Take it to her! Right now! Please!

AUSTIN: Sally, I'm not going to scamper off to some airport bar to deliver some sweater . . . She can come back any time she wants.

SALLY: Maybe she wants to be swept off her feet!

AUSTIN: I'm a little old to be sweeping people off their feet, Sally. Just a little too old for that.

SALLY: Austin, you're hopeless . . . . .

Sally begins cleaning up and urges Austin to join the others in the singing. And dancing may follow, she adds, as Jim comes out and lights a cigarette, apologizing. He'd gotten through most of the evening, but now the group is singing "Oh My Darling Clementine," and it got him down. It reminded him of a cat he'd had, and of his friend Dalton. They'd sing to their cat Clementine in the car on the way to Provincetown, with Jim taking the melody and Dalton taking the harmony. Jim puts out his cigarette and begins to cry.

SALLY: Now, Jimmy. Now, now.

JIM: Shit. I'm going to pieces here. I'm totally falling apart.

    To Austin.

Why are you staring? I'm just a sentimental old fag who smokes.

SALLY: Let's go in, Jimmy. It's cold out here.

JIM *(blowing his nose; wiping his eyes):* You're right. I'm embarrassing you, Sal, in front of your guest.

SALLY: Austin understands, don't you Austin?

> *Hands him Ruth's sweater.*

AUSTIN: Oh yes.

SALLY: Everyone in the world loves *some*thing. Am I right, Austin?

AUSTIN: Oh yes . . . yes . . .

JIM: Still, it's terrible to let go that way . . .

> *He goes off.*

SALLY *(blowing out the candle):* Think how much more terrible it would be if you couldn't!

> *Starting out.*

Coming, Austin?

AUSTIN: In a minute.

> *Sally goes off. The singing comes up inside. Austin stands alone, partly in the shadows. He takes a deep breath, clears his throat, squares his shoulders, straightens his tie and looks off toward the party. He clutches Ruth's sweater as the lights dim on him. Curtain.*

Special Citation for Stage Imagery

○○○
○○○
○○○
○○○
○○○
○○○ **THE WHO'S TOMMY**

A Musical in Two Acts

BOOK BY **PETE TOWNSHEND** AND **DES McANUFF**

MUSIC AND LYRICS BY **PETE TOWNSHEND**

ADDITIONAL MUSIC AND LYRICS BY **JOHN ENTWISTLE** AND **KEITH MOON**

Cast and credits appear on pages 308-310

PETE TOWNSHEND (music, lyrics, co-author of book) was a member of the rock group The Who at the time of its first recording in 1964—he joined it in 1963 and remained with it until 1982. He wrote and recorded the popular double-album rock opera Tommy *with The Who in 1969 and watched it ring its many changes to a concert version at the Metropolitan Opera House in New York in 1970, to a movie in 1975 (for which Townshend's score received an Academy Award), to this stage version which premiered at the La Jolla, Calif. Playhouse in summer 1992 under Des McAnuff's direction, and moved to Broadway April 22 for this special Best Play citation and Townshend's Tony Award for best score.*

Among the hundreds of songs and collections Townshend has written and re-corded are the rock operas (recorded with The Who) My Generation, Who's Next *and* Quadrophenia *and (recorded solo from 1980–1989)* Empty Glass, Chinese Eyes, White City *(with long-form video) and* Iron Man *(songs for a musical based on Ted Hughes's story). Then there are his publications,* The Story of Tommy *(with Richard Barnes) and* Horse's Neck. *His many honors include*
270

the Ivor Novello Award by his songwriting peers in 1981 and the British Phono-
graph Industry Award, both for outstanding service to the British music industry;
the 1991 International Rock Award for lifetime achievement; two Grammy nomi-
nations and induction into the Rock 'n' Roll Hall of Fame in 1990. Townshend is
now an editor at Faber and Faber, which he joined in 1983, and lives in Twicken-
ham, England, with his wife and three children.

DES McANUFF (co-author of book) was born June 19, 1952 in Princeton, Ill.
His father, a Canadian and former RAF Spitfire pilot and a doctor of veterinary
medicine living and working in the U.S., died after an auto accident a few months
before Des was born. His mother moved to Toronto with her infant son (and
another son, three-year-old Trevor), so that McAnuff grew up in the Toronto area
(in Buttonwillow, Guelph and Scarborough). He graduated from Woburn Colle-
giate Institute at 17, then moved on to the theater department of Ryerson Poly-
technical Institute, working as composer, playwright and director. Having learned
to play the guitar at age 12, he was also a performer who became an opening act
for Arlo Guthrie, Joni Mitchell and others and played in rock bands in the Toronto
area until he landed a role in the road company of Hair.

Convinced after his close association with this hit musical that he too could write
one, he came up with a science fiction rock musical, Urbania *(1971, produced at*
the Poor Alex Theater in Toronto). After five years of playwriting, composing and
directing, he moved to New York, connecting with the Chelsea Theater Center and
the Public Theater and cofounding Dodger Productions. His long list of authorship
credits includes, as composer, The Collected Works of Billy the Kid *(1975),* On
the Job *(1976, CBC TV),* Holeville *(1979, Dodger); and, as playwright,* Leave
It to Beaver Is Dead *(1979, SoHo Arts Award),* The Death of Von Richtofen
as Witnessed From Earth *(1982),* Alles Anfing/How It All Began *(1981,*
Dodger), Silent Edward *(1973, Toronto Young People's Theater),* A Lime in the
Morning *(1974, Toronto Center for the Arts),* The Pits *(1975, Toronto Free*
Theater), The Kids *and* Pigs Might Fly *(1976, CBC TV) and of course his first*
Best Play and Tony-nominated book, Tommy, *among whose many metamor-*
phoses was its world premiere as a stage musical at the La Jolla, Calif. Playhouse
under McAnuff's direction. Commenting on this production in Theater Week,
McAnuff told the interviewer, "We created a book and restructured the songs
. . . . . taking it from a song cycle into a fully realized production . . . . . We didn't
want to clutter up Tommy *with a lot of dialogue. We wanted to be respectful of*
the original. So we tell the story visually."

As a director, McAnuff has won Tony Awards for Tommy *and* Big River
(1985); a Rockefeller Grant for The Death of Von Richtofen *at the Public*
Theater, where he was artist-in-residence in 1982; and—since 1983—146 awards
and distinctions for the La Jolla Playhouse and its works under his artistic direc-
torship. Among plays he has directed elsewhere from time to time are The Crazy
Locomotive *(1977, Obie Award), the Best Plays* Gimme Shelter *(1979) and* A

Walk in the Woods *(1988)*, Henry IV, Part 1 *for Joseph Papp in Central Park (1981) and* Macbeth *at the Stratford, Canada, Festival (1983).*

McAnuff is a former faculty member of Juilliard and a present adjunct professor of theater at the University of California in San Diego. He is married to the actress Susan Berman, and they have one daughter.

Tommy *is specially cited as a Best Play of 1992–93 for the achievement which renders it uniquely a living theater work in this version: the visual stage imagery designed in the book by Pete Townshend and Des McAnuff to tell* Tommy's *story with live actors in dialogueless action, realized by McAnuff's direction and complemented by the Townshend score whose lyrics are familiar to rock music fans all over the world. To illustrate this specifically theatrical McAnuff-Townshend achievement, we represent it in these pages with Marcus/Bryan-Brown photos of some of the show's scenes as produced on Broadway April 22 by Pace Theatrical Group and Dodger Productions with Kardana Productions, as directed by Des McAnuff, with choreography by Wayne Cilento, scenery by John Arnone, costumes by David C. Woolard, lighting by Chris Parry and projections by Wendall K. Harrington.*

We offer our special thanks to the producers and their press representatives, Adrian Bryan-Brown, Chris Boneau and Susanne Tighe, for making available these excellent photos of the show.

ACT I

1. Capt. Walker, a British parachutist, is presumed dead after a mission *(above)*. When he turns up alive years later at his home *(below)*, Capt. Walker (Jonathan Dokuchitz, *right*) finds his wife (Marcia Mitzman) with a lover (Lee Morgan). Tommy Walker (Carly Jane Steinborn, *in background*), a 4-year-old who has never seen his father, is turned by his mother with his back to the fight that occurs. But Tommy is facing a mirrored wardrobe and watches the reflection of his mother being being pushed aside and a strange soldier shooting his mother's friend dead. The Walkers panic, begging Tommy never to tell what has happened here. No chance of that—poor Tommy has been stricken deaf, dumb and blind by the traumatic event.

2. Locked in a shell from which no medical help can free him, Tommy endures impassively. Reaching age 10, Tommy (Buddy Smith, *above* and *below*) has no reaction to his Cousin Kevin (Anthony Barrile, *above*) or a Christmas gift. Left alone with his besotted Uncle Ernie (Paul Kandel, *below*) as a baby sitter, Tommy can display no reaction even to molestation.

Later, Kevin takes Tommy out to a youth club where toughs treat Tommy roughly until Kevin puts a penny in the pinball machine and Tommy's hands on the controls. To everyone's amazement and awe, Tommy racks up a huge score. He becomes a sensation, a hero.

3. Reacting to Tommy's pinball wizardry, youths (Donnie Kehr, Anthony Barrile and Christian Hoff, *above*) dance, and a gypsy prostitute (Cheryl Freeman, *left*) suggests that a night of pleasure will cure whatever ails the boy.

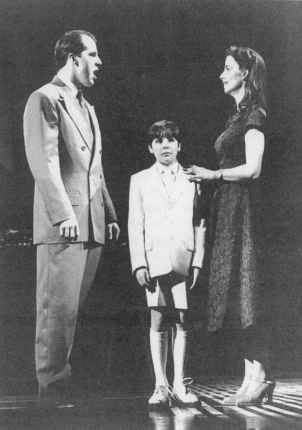

4. Hearing of their son's pinball prowess, the Walkers begin to hope again that Tommy might be starting to get better *(right)*. They renew their efforts, including a visit to a psychiatrist.

5. Despite Tommy's suddenly-discovered skill at pinball, neither the doctors' probing nor the gypsy's erotic dance arouse the boy from the depths of his deaf, dumb and blind isolation.

Teddy boys complain in song that they've been playing pinball all their lives but have never seen anyone who can handle the machine as well as Tommy does. Kevin observes in song that it must be a sense of smell and the lack of distraction from other senses that give Tommy his phenomenal edge.

Tommy rides in triumph into an arcade on a pinball machine (the lighted rectangle, *above*). As the display board shows, Tommy—now 18 years old—is racking up a super-score to bursts of light and sound. Kevin leads the throng in a salute to the pinball wizard. *Curtain. End of Act I.*

ACT II

6. Tommy, now a celebrity, is taken to a specialist for high-tech examination. Tests indicate that Tommy's eyes and ears are functioning, but all reaction seems to be mysteriously blocked. The doctor places Tommy before a mirror *(right)*. Doctor and parents, conferring, don't notice that 18-year-old Tommy (Michael Cerveris) sees 10-year-old Tommy and 4-year-old Tommy in the doctor's mirror.

Later, alone after leaving the laboratory, Tommy raises his hand and stares at it. His block is at last beginning to dissolve.

7. The Walkers, unaware that Tommy is getting better, are losing patience with their son as he stares *(left)* into the same mirrored wardrobe surface in which, as a terrified 4-year-old, he saw the shooting. Mrs. Walker, angrily, picks up a chair to smash the mirror. Lights black out, and in darkness there is the sound of breaking glass, a gunshot, the parents' command never to tell and, finally, Tommy's scream. Lights come up on the smashed mirror and Tommy and parents realizing that at last the spell has been broken.

8. Newspaper headlines tell of the pinball wizard's miraculous cure. In his newly-aware state, Tommy is distinctly cool toward his parents and even more so toward Uncle Ernie. But he invites the crowd to follow him, as a pinball machine rises from the floor. Tommy mounts it like a bronc rider, then plays it *(above)* until it emits sparks and smoke and finally explodes, with the crowd watching *(below)*, applauding and wondering in what manner they can accept Tommy's invitation to follow him.

9. At one of Tommy's appearances, an ardent fan, Sally Simpson (Sherie Scott, *above*)—convinced that she and Tommy are made for each other—is manhandled by guards after trying to join Tommy onstage. Tommy cradles Sally in his lap and resolves to return to his home, taking Sally with him, and inviting everyone within earshot to accompany him for an insight into his private life. Fans and press follow him home *(below),* where Tommy tells them it isn't they who should imitate him, it's he who must try to be more like them, now that he can see, hear and talk as they do.

Tommy angers his listeners by urging them to be themselves, with their own visions. Fans, press and guards desert him, leaving him with his family and Sally. Tommy embraces each member of his family—even Uncle Ernie—as a gesture of forgiveness. *Curtain.*

PLAYS PRODUCED
IN NEW YORK

PLAYS PRODUCED ON BROADWAY

Figures in parentheses following a play's title give number of performances. These figures do not include previews or extra non-profit performances. In the case of a transfer, the off-Broadway run is noted but not added to the figure in parentheses.

Plays marked with an asterisk (*) were still in a projected run June 1, 1993. Their number of performances is figured through May 31, 1993.

In a listing of a show's numbers—dances, sketches, musical scenes, etc.—the titles of songs are identified wherever possible by their appearance in quotation marks (").

HOLDOVERS FROM PREVIOUS SEASONS

Plays which were running on June 1, 1992 are listed below. More detailed information about them appears in previous *Best Plays* volumes of appropriate years. Important cast changes since opening night are recorded in the Cast Replacements section of this volume.

*Cats (4,447). Musical based on *Old Possum's Book of Practical Cats* by T.S. Eliot; music by Andrew Lloyd Webber; additional lyrics by Trevor Nunn and Richard Stilgoe. Opened October 7, 1982.

*Les Misérables (2,532). Musical based on the novel by Victor Hugo; book by Alain Boublil and Claude-Michel Schönberg; music by Claude-Michel Schönberg; lyrics by Herbert Kretzmer; original French text by Alain Boublil and Jean-Marc Natel; additional material by James Fenton. Opened March 12, 1987.

*The Phantom of the Opera (2,232). Musical adapted from the novel by Gaston Leroux; book by Richard Stilgoe and Andrew Lloyd Webber; music by Andrew Lloyd Webber; lyrics by Charles Hart; additional lyrics by Richard Stilgoe. Opened January 26, 1988.

Lost in Yonkers (780). By Neil Simon. Opened February 21, 1991. (Closed January 3, 1993)

*Miss Saigon (888). Musical with book by Alain Boublil and Claude-Michel Schönberg; music by Claude-Michel Schönberg; lyrics by Richard Maltby Jr. and Alain Boublil; additional material by Richard Maltby Jr. Opened April 11, 1991.

The Secret Garden (706). Musical based on the novel by Frances Hodgson Burnett; book and lyrics by Marsha Norman; music by Lucy Simon. Opened April 25, 1991. (Closed January 3, 1993)

*The Will Rogers Follies (870). Musical with book by Peter Stone; music by Cy Coleman; lyrics by Betty Comden and Adolph Green. Opened May 1, 1991.

Dancing at Lughnasa (421). By Brian Friel. Opened October 24, 1991. (Closed October 25, 1992)

Catskills on Broadway (452). Revue conceived by Freddie Roman. Opened December 5, 1991. (Closed January 3, 1993)

The Most Happy Fella (244). Revival of the musical based on Sidney Howard's play *They Knew What They Wanted;* book, music and lyrics by Frank Loesser. Opened February 13, 1992. (Closed August 30, 1992)

*Crazy for You (535). Musical with book by Ken Ludwig; co-conceived by Ken Ludwig and Mike Ockrent, inspired by material (in the musical *Girl Crazy*) by Guy Bolton and John McGowan; music by George Gershwin; lyrics by Ira Gershwin. Opened February 19, 1992.

Death and the Maiden (159). By Ariel Dorfman. Opened March 17, 1992. (Closed August 2, 1992)

Jake's Women (245). By Neil Simon. Opened March 24, 1992. (Closed October 25, 1992)

Conversations With My Father (402). By Herb Gardner. Opened March 29, 1992. (Closed March 14, 1993)

Five Guys Named Moe (445). Musical with book by Clarke Peters; music by various authors including Louis Jordan. Opened April 8, 1992. (Closed May 2, 1993)

A Streetcar Named Desire (137). Revival of the play by Tennessee Williams. Opened April 12, 1992. (Closed August 9, 1992)

Two Trains Running (160). By August Wilson. Opened April 13, 1992. (Closed August 30, 1992)

*Guys and Dolls (472). Revival of the musical based on a story and characters by Damon Runyon; book by Jo Swerling and Abe Burrows; music and lyrics by Frank Loesser. Opened April 14, 1992.

Man of La Mancha (108). Revival of the musical suggested by the life and works of Miguel de Cervantes y Saavedra; book by Dale Wasserman; music by Mitch Leigh; lyrics by Joe Darion. Opened April 24, 1992. (Closed July 26, 1992)

*Jelly's Last Jam (456). Musical with book by George C. Wolfe; music by Jelly Roll Morton; lyrics by Susan Birkenhead; musical adaptation and additional music by Luther Henderson. Opened April 26, 1992.

*Falsettos (456). Revival of the musicals *March of the Falsettos* and *Falsettoland;* book by William Finn and James Lapine; music and lyrics by William Finn. Opened April 29, 1992.

PLAYS PRODUCED JUNE 1, 1992–MAY 31, 1993

Roundabout Theater Company. 1991–92 season concluded with a schedule of two revival programs. **The Price** (47). By Arthur Miller. Opened June 10, 1992. (Closed July 19, 1992). **The Real Inspector Hound** and **The Fifteen Minute Hamlet** (61). By Tom Stoppard. Opened August 13, 1992. (Closed October 4, 1992). Produced by Roundabout Theater Company, Todd Haimes producing director, at Criterion Center Stage Right.

THE PRICE

Victor Franz	Hector Elizondo	Gregory Solomon	Eli Wallach
Esther Franz	Debra Mooney	Walter Franz	Joe Spano

Directed by John Tillinger; scenery, John Lee Beatty; costumes, Jane Greenwood; lighting, Dennis Parichy; sound, Douglas J. Cuomo; production stage manager, Matthew T. Mundinger; press, Joshua Ellis, Susanne Tighe.

The last major New York revival of *The Price* took place off Broadway 4/19/79 for 34 performances, then transferred to Broadway 6/19/79 for 144 performances.

THE REAL INSPECTOR HOUND
and
THE FIFTEEN MINUTE HAMLET

PERFORMER	"THE REAL INSPECTOR HOUND"	"THE FIFTEEN MINUTE HAMLET"
Patricia Conolly	Mrs. Drudge	Gertrude
Anthony Fusco	Simon	
David Healy	Birdboot	Marcellus/Bernardo; Ghost; Gravedigger; Osric; Fortinbras
Simon Jones	Moon	Hamlet
Rod McLachlan	Inspector Hound	Francisco; Horatio; Laertes
Gene Silvers	The Body	
J. Smith-Cameron	Felicity	Ophelia
Jane Summerhays	Cynthia	
Jeff Weiss	Magnus; Radio Announcer's Voice	Shakespeare; Claudius; Polonius

Understudies: Brennan Brown, Charles Gorder, Rod McLachlan, Shan Willis.

Directed by Gloria Muzio; scenery, John Lee Beatty; costumes, Jess Goldstein; lighting, Pat Collins; sound, Douglas J. Cuomo; fight director, Steve Rankin; production stage manager, Kathy J. Faul; stage manager, Matthew T. Mundinger; press, Boneau/Bryan-Brown, Adrian Bryan-Brown, Susanne Tighe.

The Real Inspector Hound was presented in two parts; *The Fifteen Minute Hamlet* was set at Elsinore Castle and was presented without intermission. *The Real Inspector Hound* was first produced as a one-acter on a double bill with the author's *After Magritte* off Broadway 4/23/72 for 465 performances. *The Fifteen Minute Hamlet* was first produced as *Dogg's Hamlet* on a bill with the author's *Cahoot's Macbeth* on Broadway 10/3/79 for 31 performances.

Circle in the Square Theater. 1991–92 season concluded with a schedule of three programs. Repertory of two plays: **Chinese Coffee** (25) by Ira Lewis, opened June 24, 1992 (Closed July 15, 1992); and **Salome** (34), revival of the play by Oscar Wilde, opened June 28, 1992 (Closed July 23, 1992). **Anna Karenina** (46). Musical adapted from the novel by Leo Tolstoy; book and lyrics by Peter Kellogg; music by Daniel Levine. Opened August 26, 1992. (Closed October 11, 1992) Produced by Circle in the Square Theater, Theodore Mann artistic director, Robert A. Buckley managing director, Paul Libin consulting director, at Circle in the Square Theater.

CHINESE COFFEE

Jacob Manheim	Charles Cioffi
Henry Levine	Al Pacino

THE FIFTEEN MINUTE HAMLET—J. Smith-Cameron, David Healy, Patricia Conolly, Rod McLachlan, Jeff Weiss and Simon Jones in the Roundabout Theater Company revival of Tom Stoppard's play

Directed by Arvin Brown; scenery and costumes, Zack Brown; lighting, Arden Fingerhut; production stage manager Wm. Hare; press, Maria Somma.

An artist insists on using material from his and others' life in his work. The play was presented without intermission.

SALOME

Soldier	Kevin Carrigan	Slave	Keith Randolph Smith
Manasseh	Mark Wilson	Herod Antipas	Al Pacino
Capt. of the Guard	Esai Morales	Herodias	Suzanne Bertish
Page of Herodias	Mark Kevin Lewis	Tigellinus	John Joseph Freeman
Soldier #1	John Robinson	Jew #1	Frank Raiter
Soldier #2	Neil Maffin	Jew #2	Kermit Brown
Cappodocian	Rene Rivera	Jew #3	John Straub
Naaman	Dennis P. Huggins	Jew #4	Tom Brennan
Jokanaan	Arnold Vosloo	Nazarene #1	Charles Cragon
Salome	Sheryl Lee	Nazarene #2	Alan Nebelthau

Roman .... Emilio Del Pozo   Attendants to
Slave .... William Edwin Wilson   Salome ..... Tanya M. Gibson, Molly Price

Understudies: Mr. Pacino—Emilio Del Pozo; Mr. Vosloo—Neil Maffin; Misses Lee, Bertish—Molly Price.

Directed by Robert Allan Ackerman; music, Richard Peaslee, Hamza El Din; choreography, Lar Lubovitch; scenery and costumes, Zack Brown; lighting, Arden Fingerhut; sound, Fox and Perla; production stage manager, Wm. Hare; stage managers, Jack Gianino, Joe Lorden.

Place: A great terrace in the palace of Herod, set above the banqueting hall. The play was presented without intermission.

The last major New York revival of Oscar Wilde's poetic drama took place on Broadway by the Ethiopian Art Theater 5/7/23.

ANNA KARENINA

Count Alexis Vronsky..... Scott Wentworth
Anna Karenina.............. Ann Crumb
Constantine Levin .... Gregg Edelman
Train Conductor; Fyodor; Basso;
  Levin's Foreman.......... David Pursley
Prince Stephen Oblonsky ..... Jerry Lanning
Princess Kitty Scherbatsky ... Melissa Errico
Dunyasha; Woman at Party ... Naz Edwards
Korsunsky; Man at Party;
Peasant.................. Gabriel Barre

Man at the Ball; Guard at the Station;
  Vasily.................... Larry Hansen
Man at the Ball; Finance
  Minister; Prince Yashvin .... Ray Wills
Masha; Gina.............. Amelia Prentice
Seryozha Karenin ...... Eric Houston Saari
Annushka................. Darcy Pulliam
Nicolai Karenin .... John Cunningham
Princess Elizabeth
  Tversky .... Jo Ann Cunningham

Swings: Jonathan Cerullo, Audrey Lavine. Extras: Jeremy Black, Billy Hipkins.

Orchestra: Nicholas Archer conductor, piano; David Geist assistant conductor, piano; Walter Kane, Edward Zuhlke woodwinds; Lorraine Cohen-Moses trumpet; Beverly Laridsen cello; David Carey percussion.

Understudies: Miss Crumb—Melissa Errico; Miss Errico—Amelia Prentice; Mr. Wentworth—Ray Wills; Mr. Cunningham—Larry Hansen; Mr. Edelman—Gabriel Barre; Mr. Lanning—David Pursley.

Directed by Theodore Mann; musical sequences staged by Patricia Birch; musical direction and dance music arrangements, Nicholas Archer; scenery, James Morgan; costumes, Carrie Robbins; lighting, Mary Jo Dondlinger; sound, Fox and Perla; orchestrations, Peter Matz; associate choreographer, Jonathan Cerullo; music coordinator, Seymour Red Press; production stage manager, Wm. Hare; stage manager, Jack Gianino.

Time: 1870s. Place: Act I, Russia; Act II, Russia and Italy.

Anna Karenina's obsessive love for Vronsky leads her to her doom, as in the Tolstoy novel.

ACT I

Prologue: St. Petersburg train station
  "On a Train" .... Anna, Vronsky, Levin, Chorus
Scene 1: Moscow train station, next morning
  "There's More to Life Than Love" .... Oblonsky, Anna
Scene 2: Kitty Scherbatsky's house, later the same day
  "How Awful"... Kitty
  "Would You?".. Levin
  "In a Room" .... Levin, Kitty, Anna, Vronsky
Scene 3: A ball, a few days later
  Waltz and "Mazurka"..................... Anna, Kitty, Vronsky, Oblonsky, Chorus
Scene 4: A small station between Moscow and St. Petersburg, the next night
Scene 5: Anna's house in St. Petersburg
  "Nothing Has Changed".. Anna
Scene 6: Prince Tversky's home, that night
  "Lowlands" .... Basso

Scene 7: Croquet lawn, several weeks later
"Rumors"... Chorus
Scene 8: Kitty's house
"How Many Men?"... Kitty
Scene 9: A small dance in St. Petersburg
"We Were Dancing"... Vronsky
Scene 10: On the way home
"I'm Lost" .... Anna
Scene 11: Anna's house
"Karenin's List" .... Karenin
Scene 12: Vronsky's apartment
"Waiting for You" .... Anna, Vronsky

ACT II

Scene 1: Anna's house, three months later
"This Can't Go On" .... Anna, Vronsky, Karenin
Scene 2: Levin's estate and Italy
"Peasants' Idyll" .... Chorus
"That Will Serve Her Right" .... Levin
Scene 3: A villa in Rome
"Everything's Fine"... Anna, Vronsky
Scene 4: Kitty's house
"Would You?" (Reprise)... Levin, Kitty
Scene 5: A hotel in Moscow
"Everything's Fine" (Reprise)... Anna
Scene 6: Karenin's house
"Only at Night"... Karenin
Scene 7: St. Petersburg train station
Finale .... Anna, Chorus

New York City Opera. 1992–93 repertory included two revivals of modern Broadway musicals. **110 in the Shade** (12). Musical based on the play *The Rainmaker* by N. Richard Nash; book by N. Richard Nash; music by Harvey Schmidt; lyrics by Tom Jones. Opened July 18, 1992. (Closed November 15, 1992) **Regina** (4). Musical based on the play *The Little Foxes* by Lillian Hellman; text and music by Marc Blitzstein. Opened October 9, 1992. (Closed October 24, 1992) Produced by New York City Opera, Christopher Keene general director, Donald Hassard managing director of artistic administration, at the New York State Theater.

110 IN THE SHADE

Tommy.............. Robert Mann Kayser	Noah Curry .... Walter Charles
Dance Couple........ Jennifer Paulson Lee,	H.C. Curry............ Henderson Forsythe
John Scott	Lizzie Curry .... Karen Ziemba
File .... Richard Muenz	Snookie Updegraff.......... Crista Moore
Jimmy Curry .... David Aaron Baker	Bill Starbuck............ Brian Sutherland

Directed by Scott Ellis; conductor, Paul Gemignani; choreographer, Susan Stroman; scenery, Michael Anania; costumes, Lindsay W. Davis; lighting, Jeff Davis; sound, Abe Jacob; chorus master, Joseph Colaneri; orchestrations, Hershy Kay; additional orchestrations, William D. Brohn; additional dance music arrangements, Peter Howard; press, Susan Woelzl.

Time: A summer day in a time of drought. Place: A Western state during a 24-hour period. Act I, Scene I: A fence and a windmill. Scene 2: The depot. Scene 3: A street in Three Point, File's office. Scene 4: The park. Scene 5: Outside the Curry house. Scene 6: An open space.

Act II, Scene 1: The park. Scene 2: Starbuck's truck. Scene 3: A picnic area. Scene 4: An open space. Scene 5: A fence and a windmill.

110 in the Shade was first produced on Broadway by David Merrick 10/24/63 for 330 performances. This is its first major New York revival of record.

ACT I

"Gonna Be Another Hot Day" .... File, Townspeople
"Lizzie's Comin' Home" .... Jimmy, Noah, H.C.
"Love, Don't Turn Away" .... Lizzie
"Overhead" .... Townspeople
"Poker Polka" .... Jimmy, Noah, H.C., File
"Why Can't They Leave Me Alone" .... File
"Come on Along" .... Townspeople
"Rain Song" .... Starbuck, Townspeople
"You're Not Foolin' Me" .... Lizzie, Starbuck
"Cinderella" .... Children
"Raunchy" .... Lizzie
"A Man and a Woman" .... File, Lizzie
"Old Maid" .... Lizzie

ACT II

"Come on Along" .... Townspeople
"Everything Beautiful Happens at Night" .... Townspeople
"Shooting Star" .... Starbuck
"Melisande" .... Starbuck
"Simple Little Things" .... Lizzie
"Little Red Hat" .... Jimmy, Snookie
"Is It Really Me?" .... Lizzie, Starbuck
"Wonderful Music" .... Starbuck, File, Lizzie
Finale: "Rain Song" .... Company

REGINA

Addie	Denise Woods	Leo Hubbard	John Daniecki
Cal	Michael Lofton	Regina Giddens	Leigh Munro
Alexandra Giddens	Elizabeth Futral	William Marshall	Paul Austin Kelly
Birdie Hubbard	Sheryl Woods	Benjamin Hubbard	Andrew Wentzel
Oscar Hubbard	Ron Baker	Horace Giddens	LeRoy Lehr

Directed by Rosalind Elias; conductor, Laurie Anne Hunter; scenery, James Leonard Joy; costumes, Joseph A. Citarella; lighting, Jeff Davis; chorus master, Joseph Colaneri; assistant stage director, Beth Greenberg; musical preparation, Laurie Anne Hunter; supertitles, Roberta Vincent Edles.

Time: Spring 1900. Place: The Giddens House in Bowden, Ala. Prologue: Morning. Act I: Evening the same day. Act II, Scene 1: One week later, early evening. Scene 2: Later that night. Act III: The following day.

Regina was first produced on Broadway 10/31/49 for 56 performances. Its only previous New York revivals of record have been in concert and opera venues, principally New York City Opera productions in 1953 and 1958.

Oba Oba '93 (45). 9th edition of the Brazilian musical revue. Produced by Franco Fontana at the Marquis Theater. Opened October 1, 1992. (Closed November 11, 1992)

Monica Acioli	Rodman Clayson
Edgar Aguiar	Nelaci Costa
Mercia Alexandre	Marquinho da Geralda
Messias Bastos	Iris da Rocha
Emerson Bernardes	Patricia Dantas
Ana Careca	Marcia Labios de Mel

Mauricio de Souza	Edval Boa Morte
Ray do Pendeiro	Jorge Boa Morte
Marcio do Repenique	Claudio Nascimento
Ana Paula Dos Reis	Rita de Cassia Nobre
Eliana Estevao	Carlos Oliveira
(Special Guest)	Julio Peluchi
Chico Filho	Rose Perola
Formiguinha	Arlindo Pipiu
Gamo	Toco Preto
Eliane Garcia	Giovani Ramos
Wellington Guzmao	Casemiro Raposo
Ilson Helvecio	Ratinho
Carlos Leca	Luciano Ribeiro
Claudia Lisboa	Sergio Rocha
Mac	Jorge Rum
R. Malaguti	Claudio Sampaio
Cobrinha Mansa	Jones Santana
Angela Mara	Claudio Santos
Nilton Maravilha	Jaime Santos
Valeria Matos	Carlos Silva
Wilson Mauro	Roberto Silva
Sete Mola	Ailto Souza
Sonia Regina Moraes	Paulo W. Takase
Cristiane Moreira	Lu Viana
Patricia Moreira	

Musical direction, Wilson Mauro; choreography, Roberto Abrahao; press, Peter Cromarty, David Lotz, David Bar Katz.

Act I, Scene I: Origins of Brazil (black culture from slavery to redemption). Scene 2: Homage to "Chorinho" (includes "Tico Tico No Fuba" and "Urubu Malandro" by Zequinha de Abreu). Scene 3A: Samba de Roda (talent competition among women in Sao Salvador). Scene 3B: "Lambada" (a merengue-like dance from Belem). Scene 3C: Samba Reggae (U.S. premiere of new dance form which originated in Sao Salvador). Scene 4: Homage to the Northeast (songs and dances of lament from deprived area). Scene 5: Brazil Cappella ("Aquarela de Brazil" by Ary Barroso). Scene 6: Homage to the Bossa Nova and the Seventies (includes "Desafinado" and "Girl From Ipanema" by Antonio Carlos Jobim). Scene 7: Tribute to Carmen Miranda, the "Brazilian Bomshell."

Act II, Scene 1: Macumba (a local form of worship). Scene 2: Afro-Brazilian Songs and Dances—Berimbau Medley; Part A, Capoeira of Angola (songs and dance imported from Africa); Part B, Maculele (Bahian dance, originated among African slaves); Part C, Acrobatic Capoeira. Scene 3: Partido Alto (carnival songs). Scene 4: Rhythm Beaters (samba rhythms expressed with percussive instruments). Scene 5: Show of Samba Dancers (performance by mulatto women). Scene 6: Grand Carnival (includes traditional parade of Rio de Janeiro's School of Samba).

A previous *Oba Oba* revue of popular music, folk songs and rhythms of Brazil was produced on Broadway 3/29/88 for 46 performances.

Roundabout Theater Company. Schedule of five revivals. **The Show-Off** (45). By George Kelly. Opened November 5, 1992. (Closed December 13, 1992) **Anna Christie** (54). By Eugene O'Neill. Opened January 14, 1993. (Closed February 28, 1993) **Candida** (45). By George Bernard Shaw. Opened March 25, 1993. (Closed May 2, 1993) And *She Loves Me,* musical based on the play by Miklos Laszlo, book by Joe Masteroff, music by Jerry Bock, lyrics by Sheldon Harnick, scheduled to open 6/10/93, and *Black Comedy* by Peter Shaffer, scheduled to open 8/8/93. Produced by Roundabout Theater Company, Todd Haimes artistic director, Gene Feist founding director, at Criterion Center Stage Right.

THE SHOW-OFF

Clara Fisher	Laura Esterman	Joe Fisher	Tim DeKay
Mrs. Fisher	Pat Carroll	Aubrey Piper	Boyd Gaines
Amy Fisher	Sophie Hayden	Mr. Gill	Kevin McClarnon
Frank Hyland	Edmund C. Davys	Mr. Rogers	J.R. Horne
Mr. Fisher	Richard Woods		

Standby: Miss Esterman—Patricia Kennell Carroll. Understudies: Messrs. DeKay, McClarnon, Horne—Trent Bright; Mr. Gaines—Edmund C. Davys; Mr. Woods—J.R. Horne.

Directed by Brian Murray; scenery, Ben Edwards; costumes, David Charles; lighting, Peter Kaczorowski; sound, Douglas J. Cuomo; production stage manager, Kathy J. Faul; stage manager, Matthew T. Mundinger; press, Boneau/Bryan-Brown, Susanne Tighe.

Time: 1922. Place: The Fishers' home, North Philadelphia. Act I, Scene 1: A Wednesday in May. Scene 2: Later that night. Act II: A Monday, six months later. Act III: A Monday, one week later.

The last major New York revival of *The Show-Off* was by the Roundabout Theater Company (now in its 27th season and second on Broadway) off Broadway 4/25/78 for 43 performances.

ANNA CHRISTIE

"Johnny-the-Priest" . . .	Christopher Wynkoop	Marthy Owen	Anne Meara
Larry	Barton Tinapp	Anna Christopherson . . .	Natasha Richardson
Chris Christopherson	Rip Torn	Mat Burke	Liam Neeson

Understudies: Mr. Neeson—Barton Tinapp; Mr. Torn—Christopher Wynkoop; Messrs. Wynkoop, Tinapp—Jeffrey Shore; Misses Richardson, Meara—Angelica Torn.

Directed by David Leveaux; scenery, John Lee Beatty; costumes, Martin Pakledinaz; lighting, Marc B. Weiss; composer and sound designer, Douglas J. Cuomo; fight director, Steve Rankin; production stage manager, Kathy J. Faul.

Act I: "Johnny-the-Priest's" saloon near the waterfront, New York City. Act II: The barge Simeon Winthrop at anchor in the harbor of Provincetown, Mass., ten days later. Act III: Cabin of the barge at dock in Boston, a week later. Act IV: The same, two days later. The play was presented in two parts with the intermission following Act II.

The last major New York revival of *Anna Christie* took place on Broadway 4/14/77 for 124 performances.

CANDIDA

Miss Proserpine Garnett	Ann Dowd	Mr. Burgess	William Duff-Griffin
Rev. James Mayor Morell . .	Robert Foxworth	Candida	Mary Steenburgen
Rev. Alexander Mill	Simon Brooking	Eugene Marchbanks . .	Robert Sean Leonard

Understudies: Misses Steenburgen, Dowd—Vivian Nesbitt; Mr. Leonard—Simon Brooking.

Directed by Gloria Muzio; scenery, David Jenkins; costumes, Jess Goldstein; lighting, Peter Kaczorowski; sound, Douglas J. Cuomo; production stage manager, Jay Adler.

Act I: St. Dominic's parsonage, London. Act II: Later that day. Act III: Past 10 that evening. The play was presented in three parts.

The last major New York revival of *Candida* was by Circle in the Square on Broadway 10/15/81 for 92 performances.

Solitary Confinement (25). By Rupert Holmes. Produced by Gladys Nederlander, James M. & Charlene Nederlander and Roger L. Stevens in association with Normand Kurtz at the Nederlander Theater. Opened November 8, 1992. (Closed November 29, 1992)

Richard Jannings . . . . Stacy Keach

Production supervised by Marshall W. Mason; based on original direction by Kenneth Frankel; scenery and art direction, William Barclay; costumes, Cathleen Detoro; lighting, Donald Holder;

SOLITARY CONFINEMENT—Stacy Keach in
a scene from Rupert Holmes's one-actor play

sound, Jack Allaway; fight direction, David Leong; production stage manager, Joe Cappelli; stage manager, Artie Gaffin; press, Jeffrey Richards Associates, David LeShay.

Place: The south tower study of the residence of Richard Jannings atop the Jannings Industries building in Albuquerque, N.M. The play was presented in two parts.

Reclusive billionaire communicates with the outside world only by videotapes of his employees (Fillip, Conroy, Girard, Eldridge, Fleischer and Miss Davis, all played on the tape also by Stacy Keach in various disguises) until his privacy is finally invaded. Previously produced at the Pasadena, Calif. Playhouse.

Radio City Music Hall. Schedule of two programs. **Radio City Christmas Spectacular** (179). 60th anniversary edition of the spectacle originally conceived and produced by Robert F. Jani. Opened November 13, 1992. (Closed January 6, 1993) **Easter Show** (28). Spectacle including *The Glory of Easter* pageant originally produced by Leon Leonidoff. Opened April 2, 1993. (Closed April 17, 1993) Produced by Radio City Music Hall Productions, J. Deet Jonker executive producer, David J. Nash producer, at Radio City Music Hall.

RADIO CITY CHRISTMAS SPECTACULAR

Scrooge; Santa;	Mrs. Cratchit .... Leigh-Anne Wencker
Narrator............ Charles Edward Hall	Belinda Cratchit.......... Suzanne Phillips
Bob Crachit .... Arte Phillips	Sarah Cratchit .... Fabiana Furgal,
Scrooge's Nephew .... Michael Berglund	Maria Skorobogatov
Marley's Ghost................ Scott Spahr	Peter Cratchit.... Robert Fidalgo, Joey Rigol
Ghost of Christmas Past..... Christiane Farr	Tiny Tim...... Christopher Boyce, Joey Cee
Ghost of Christmas Present ... Rod McCune	Poultry Man................ Todd Hunter

Skaters: Laurie Welch & Randy Coyne, Elena Tomelden & Jim Williams.

Elves: Tinker—Elena Gilden; Thinker—Phil Fondacaro; Tannenbaum—Michael J. Gilden; Bartholomew—Scott Seidman; Thumbs—Leslie Stump. Understudies—Pamela Danberg, Marty Klebba.

New Yorkers: Carol Bentley, Michael Berglund, John Clonts, John Dietrich, Lisa Embs, Angelo Fraboni, Kristen Howe, Nanci Jennings, Keith Locke, Joanne Manning, Erich McCall, Sharon Moore, Michael O'Donnell, Wendy Piper, Mary Jayne Waddell, Jim Weaver, Leigh-Anne Wencker, David Wood.

Dancers: Joe Bowerman, Christiane Farr, Scott Fowler, Bill Hastings, Todd Hunter, Terry Lacy, Bonnie Lynn, Rod McCune, Marty McDonough, Joan Mirabella, Arte Phillips, Suzanne Phillips, Kirk Ryder, Scott Spahr, Laura Streets.

Rockettes: Pauline Achillas, Dottie Belle, Kiki Bennett, Susan Boron, Julie Branam, Janice Cavargna, Eileen Collins, Lillian Colon, Linda Deacon, Susanne Doris, Rebecca Downing, Prudence Gray, Leslie Guy, Susan Heart, Vicki Hickerson, Ginny Hounsell, Connie House, Stephanie James, Jennifer Jiles, Jennifer Jones, Joan Peer Kelleher, Dee Dee Knapp-Brody, Debby Kole, Judy Little, Sonya Livingston, Setsuko Maruhashi, Anne Mason, Mary Frances McCatty, Patrice McConachie, Mary McNamara, Lori Mello, Laraine Memola, Elizabeth Mills, Marque Munday, Rosemary Noviello, Carol Paracat, Kerri Pearsall, Gerri Presky, Laureen Repp, Mary Six Rupert, Jereme Sheehan, Trina Simon, Terry Spano, Pam Stacey, Lynn Sullivan, Darlene Wendy, Beth Nolan Woods, Eileen Woods. (Rockettes appear in various roles throughout the show)

Orchestra: Don Pippin conductor; Bryan Louiselle associate conductor; Elliot Rosoff concert master; Andrea Andros, Gilbert Bauer, Carmine DeLeo, Joseph Kowalewski, Julius J. Kunstler, Nannette Levi, Samuel Marder, Holly Ovenden violin; Barbara H. Vaccaro, Richard Spencer viola; Frank Levy, Sarah Carter cello; Dean Crandall bass; Kenneth Emery flute; Gerard J. Niewood, Richard Oatts, John Cippola, Joshua Siegel, Kenneth Arzberger reeds; George Bartlett, Nancy Freimanis, French horn; Richard Raffio, Zachary Shnek, Hollis Burridge trumpet; John D. Schnupp, Thomas B. Olcott, Mark Johansen trombone; Andrew Rogers tuba; Thomas J. Oldakowski drums; Mario DeCiutiis, Maya Gunji percussion; Anthony Cesarano guitar; Susanna Nason, Henry Aronson piano; Jeanne Maier harp; George Wesner, Robert Maidhof organ.

Director, Scott Salmon; musical director, Don Pippin; restaging of original staging and choreography, Violet Holmes, Linda Lemac; choreography for "Carol of the Bells," "We Need a Little Christmas," "Santa's Toy Fantasy" and "A Christmas Carol," Scott Salmon; choreography for "Christmas in New York," Marianne Selbert; scenery, Charles Lisanby; original costume designs, Frank Spencer; costumes for "Carol of the Bells," "We Need a Little Christmas" and "Santa's Toy Fantasy," Pete Menefee; additional costume designs, Jose Lengson; lighting, Ken Billington; senior producer, Rockettes, Bruce Michael; dance music arrangements, Marvin Laird, Mark Hummel; associate producers, Giles Colahan, Robin C. Mathiesen; production stage manager, Howard Kolins; stage managers, Mimi Apfel, Andrew Feigin, Doug Fogel, Lynn M. Finkel, Janet Friedman, Zoya Kachadurian; press, Kevin M. Brockman.

Special credits: Writing—*Charles Dickens' A Christmas Carol* (play) by Charles Lisanby. Original music—"Sing a Little Song of Christmas" music by Don Pippin, lyrics by Carolyn Leigh; "What Do You Want for Christmas" music by Larry Grossman, lyrics by Hal Hackady; "Christmas in New York" by Billy Butt. Original orchestrations—Elman Anderson, Michael Gibson, Don Harper, Arthur Harris, Phillip J. Lang, Don Pippin. Santa film score arrangement—Bryan Louiselle. "Silent Night" arrangement—Percy Faith.

The 60th anniversary edition of the Music Hall's Christmas Show, starring the Rockettes, presented without an intermission.

SCENES AND MUSICAL NUMBERS: Herald Trumpeters. Scene 1: "We Need a Little Christmas"—Rockettes, Company. Overture—Radio City Music Hall Orchestra. Scene 2: *The Nutcracker; A Teddy Bear's Dream.* Scene 3: "The Parade of the Wooden Soldiers"—Rockettes. Scene 4: *Charles Dickens' A Christmas Carol.* Scene 5: "Christmas in New York"—New Yorkers, Rockettes, Orchestra. Scene 6: Ice Skating in the Plaza. Scene 7: Santa's Toy Fantasy. Scene 8: "Carol of the Bells"—Rockettes, Company. Scene 9: *The Living Nativity* with *One Solitary Life* ("Silent Night," "O Little Town of Bethlehem," "The First Noel," "We Three Kings," "O Come All Ye Faithful," "Hark, the Herald Angels Sing")—Company. Jubilant—Organ, Company.

EASTER SHOW

Rabbit. . . . . Joel Blum
Tortoise . . . . James Darrah

Dancers: Kim Culp, Kevin Gaudin, Chris Ghelfi, Bill Hastings, Jennifer Paulson Lee, David E. Liddell, Joanne Manning, Jeanine Meyers, Arte Phillips, Suzanne Phillips, Tom Porras, Ralph Ramirez, Sheri Ramirez, David Scala, Lynn Sterling, Susan Trainor.

Singers: Carol Bentley, Michael Berglund, James Darrah, John Dietrich, Sara Beth Lane, Keith Locke, Michelle Mallardi, Patrice McConachie, Clarence M. Sheridan, David A. Wood.

Singer/Dancer Swings: Laura Streets, Mark C. Reis.

Antigravity: Harrison Beal (rehearsal captain), Robin Fiederlein, Frederico Ferreira, Tony Flores, Chris Harrison (director/choreographer), Wendy Hilliard, Michele Maly, Jeanne-Marie Markwardt, Dominick Minicucci, Tabb Nance, Andrew Pacho (assistant director), Kara Redeka, Hector Salatzar, Jolaine Thoden.

Rockettes: Pauline Achillas, Dottie Belle, Kiki Bennett, Susan Boron, Julie Branam, Stephanie Chase, Eileen Collins, Lillian Colon, Susanne Doris, Joyce Dwyer (dance captain), Prudence Gray, Susan Heart, Vicki Hickerson, Ginny Hounsell, Connie House, Stephanie James, Jennifer Jones, Joan Peer Kelleher, Pam Kelleher, Dee Dee Knapp-Brody, Debby Kole, Judy Little, Sonya Livingston, Setsuko Maruhashi, Mary McNamara, Lori Mello, Laraine Memola, Lynn Newton, Carol Paracat, Gerri Presky, Laureen Repp, Linda Riley, Mary Six Rupert, Jereme Sheehan, Terry Spano, Pam Stacey, Darlene Wendy, Beth Nolan Woods, Eileen Woods.

Radio City Music Hall Orchestra: Don Pippin conductor; Bryan Louiselle assistant conductor; Louann Montesi concert master; Andrea Andres, Carmine DeLeo, Joseph Kowalewski, Julius J. Kunstler, Nannette Levi, Samuel Marder, Holly Ovenden violin; Barbara H. Vaccaro, Richard Spencer viola; Frank Levy, Sarah Carter cello; Dean Crandall bass; Kenneth Emery flute; Gerard J. Niewood, Richard Oatts, John Cippola, Joshua Siegel, Kenneth Arzberger reeds; George Bartlett, Nancy Freimanis, French horn; Richard Raffio, Zachary Shnek, Hollis Burridge trumpet; John D. Schnupp, Thomas B. Olcott, Mark Johansen trombone; Andrew Rogers tuba; Thomas Oldakowski drums; Mario DeCiutiis, Maya Gunji percussion; Anthony Cesarano guitar; Jeanne Maier harp; Susanna Nason piano; Robert Wendel keyboard; George Wesner organ.

Production conceived by Patricia M. Morinelli and William Michael Maher; directed and choreographed by Scott Salmon; musical direction and vocal arrangements, Don Pippin; scenery and costumes, Erté; additional scenery, Eduardo Sicanco; costumes, Eduardo Sicanco, Jose Lengson; lighting, Ken Billington, Jason Kantrowitz; orchestrations, Michael Gibson, Dick Lieb, Glenn Osser, Jim Tyler; dance music arrangements, Gordon Lowry Harrell, Mark Hummel, Marvin Laird, Ethyl Will; director of Rockettes, Violet Holmes; assistant musical director, Bryan Louiselle; special musical material, Larry Grossman; special material, Hal Hackady; additional material, Stuart Ross; *The Glory of Easter* lighting, Billy B. Walker; additional costumes, Pete Menefee; *The Glory of Easter* restaging, Linda Lemac; assistant director, Linda Haberman; assistant choreographers, Linda Haberman, Dennis Callahan; *The Glory of Easter* vocal solo recording, Marilyn Horne; associate producers, Giles Colahan, Robin C. Mathiesen; production stage manager, Howard Kolins; stage managers, Mimi Apfel, Doug Fogel, Janet Friedman, Peter Muste.

Original music credits: "Put a Little Spring in Your Step" (music and lyrics by Jeffrey Ernstoff), "Think About That," "I Know" and "How About Me" (music by Larry Grossman, lyrics by Hal Hackady).

Special music credits: "Put on Your Sunday Clothes" (music and lyrics by Jerry Herman), "Friends" (music by Larry Grossman, lyrics by Hal Hackady), "La Cage aux Folles" (music and lyrics by Jerry Herman), excerpt from "Hoe Down" section of "Rodeo" (by Aaron Copeland), "Optical Race" (composed and performed by Tangerine Dream).

SCENES: Prologue, *The Glory of Easter* (return engagement of the pageant performed annually from 1933 to 1979). Overture (Radio City Music Hall Orchestra). Scene 1: Pure Imagination. Scene 2: "Put a Little Spring in Your Step" (Rabbit, Singers, Dancers, Rockettes in "Happy Feet"). Scene 3: Yesteryear (1890s Easter Parade). Scene 4: Bunny Revelry (with Antigravity). Scene 5: The Chase (Tortoise vs. Hare, with the Rockettes). Scene 6: With Gershwin (Singers, Dancers, Radio City Music Hall Orchestra, with George and Ira Gershwin numbers). Scene 7: Optical Race (with Antigravity). Scene 8: "Dancing in the Dark" (laser show, Rockettes). Scene 9: Hats (Dancers). Scene 10: Rainbow Follies (Finale).

Note: In addition to its theater programs, concerts at Radio City Music Hall during the 1992–93 season included *The Music of Andrew Lloyd Webber* for 14 performances 9/22/92–10/4/92, produced by Broadway in Concert and Pace Theatrical Group, directed by Arlene Phillips, musical supervision by Michael Reed and musical direction by Paul Bogaev, with Luann Aronson, Laurie Beechman, Michael Crawford, Tom Donoghue, Willy Falk, Mark Hardy, Juliet Lambert, Jimmy Lockett, Donna Lee Marshall, Gary Mauer, Cathy Porter, Tami Tappan, Ty Taylor, Elizabeth Ward, Gay Willis.

Gypsy Passion (54). Return engagement of the Flamenco musical by Tomas Rodriguez-Pantoja; traditional music and lyrics. Produced by Roy A. Somlyo and Andalucia Productions for the Government of Andalucia, Spain, at the Plymouth Theater. Opened November 17, 1992. (Closed January 2, 1993)

CAST: First Generation—Manuel Morao, Lorenzo Galvez, Manuel Moneo, Juana la del Pipa; Second Generation—Antonio el Pipa, Sara Baras, Concha Vargas, Juan Antonio Ogalla, Pepe de la Joaquina, Luis Moneo, Antonio Moreno, Carmen de la Jeroma; Third Generation—Manuela Nunez, Mercedes Ruiz, Patricia Valdez, Estefania Aranda.

Directed by Tomas Rodriguez-Pantoja; artistic and musical direction, Manuel Morao; choreography, Gitanos de Jerez; scenery, David Sumner; costumes, Mercedes Muniz; lighting, Tom Sturge; sound, Otts Munderloh; special arrangements, Manuel Morao; production supervisor, Carlos Gorbea; press, Max Eisen, Madelon Rosen.

The life, music and dances of Spanish gypsies in their village and visits to Seville. Previously produced on Broadway at Town Hall 4/22/92 for 15 performances.

ACT I

Scene 1: The Patriarch
"Tona" .... Manuel Morao (singer)
Scene 2: The forest outside Seville
"Villancico" .... Company
"Solea" .... Juana la del Pipa (singer); Concha Vargas (dancer);
Morao, Luis Moneo, Antonio Moreno (guitarists)
"Cantina" .... Pepe de la Joaquina (singer); Antonio el Pipa (dancer);
Morao, Luis Moneo, Moreno (guitarists)
"Tangos" .... la del Pipa (singer, dancer)
"Tanguillos" .... la del Pipa (singer, dancer); Manuela Nunez,
Mercedes Ruiz, Patricia Valdez, Estefania Aranda (dancers);
Morao, Luis Moneo, Moreno (guitarists)
"Seguirillas" .... Manuel Moneo (singer); Sara Baras (dancer);
Morao, Luis Moneo, Moreno (guitarists)
Scene 3: In Seville, the next day
"Zapateado" .... Company
"Taranto" .... Lorenzo Galvez (singer); Juan Antonio Ogalla,
Carmen de la Jeroma (dancers); Morao (guitarist)
Scene 4: Seville, the market place
"Bulerias" .... de la Joaquina, la del Pipa (singers); Nunez, Ruiz,
Valdez, Aranda (dancers); Luis Moneo, Moreno (guitarists)

ACT II: The Gypsy Village

Scene 1. Romance
"Alegrias" .... de la Joaquina (singer); el Pipa, Baras, Ogalla, de la Jeroma (dancers);
Morao, Luis Moneo, Moreno (guitarists)
Scene 2: The wedding
"Alborea" .... Company
"El Polo de Tobalo" .... de la Joaquina (singer); el Pipa, Baras
(dancers); Morao, Luis Moneo, Moreno (guitarists)
Scene 3: At work
"Martinetes" .... Galvez, Manuel Moneo, de la Joaquina (singers); el Pipa, Baras (dancers)
Scene 4: Finale
"Bulerias" .... Company

3 From Brooklyn (9). Musical revue conceived by Sal Richards; original music and lyrics by Sandi Merle and Steve Michaels. Produced by Michael Frazier, Larry Spellman and Don Ravella at the Helen Hayes Theater. Opened November 19, 1992. (Closed December 27, 1992)

CAST: Sal Richards, Raymond Serra (as Cosmo the Cabbie), Roslyn Kind, Bobby Alto & Buddy Mantia, Adrianne Tolsch and the BQE Dancers (Guy Richards, John Michaels and Damon Rusignola).

Orchestra: Steve Michaels pianist; Dave Gross synthesizer; Ray Kilday bass; Bobby Shankin drums.

Directed by Sal Richards; musical direction, Steve Michaels; scenery, Charles E. McCarry; lighting, Phil Monat; sound, Raymond D. Schilke; production stage manager, Laura Kravets; stage manager, Bern Gautier; press, Judy Jacksina.

Time: The present. Place: A street in Brooklyn. The play was presented without intermission.

Homage to Brooklyn as seen through the eyes of a cab driver.

The Sheik of Avenue B (54). Musical revue conceived and written by Isaiah Sheffer; music and lyrics by various authors (see listing below). Produced by Mazel Musicals, Lawrence Topall and Alan & Kathi Glist at Town Hall. Opened November 22, 1992. (Closed December 27, 1992)

Don Gonfalon	Paul Harman	Sally Small	Michele Ragusa
Becky Barrett	Judy Premus	Pinky Pickles	Mark Nadler
Kevin Bailey	Jack Plotnick	Fanny Farina	Virginia Sandifur
Gretta Genug (Diana		Willy Wills	Larry Raiken
Darling)	Amanda Green		

Standbys: Steve Sterner, April Chestner.

Direction and musical staging, Dan Siretta; musical direction and arrangements, Lanny Meyers; scenery, Bruce Goodrich; costumes, Deirdre Burke; lighting, Robert Bessoir; production stage manager, Don Christy; press, Max Eisen, Madelon Rosen.

Time: The fall of 1932. Place: Two broadcasts of the Blue Radio Network hit show *Town Hall Tonight.* Act I: The first broadcast. Act II: Preparation and audience warm-up, the second broadcast.

With the cast playing radio performers, a collection of Jewish memories and little-known songs by well-known authors from the turn of the century to the 1930s, subtitled The Ragtime and Jazz Era Comedy Revue.

ACT I

"Doin' the Neighborhood Rag" .... Ensemble
    (1909, based on "The Yiddish Rag" by Harry Von Tilzer; additional lyrics by Isaiah Sheffer and
    Lanny Meyers)
"Ish-Ga-Bibble (I Should Worry)" .... Willie Wills, Ensemble
    (1913, by Sam M. Lewis and Leo W. Meyer; additional lyrics by Isaiah Sheffer and Lanny
    Meyers)
"Matinee Girl" .... Becky Barrett with Pinky Pickles and Don Gonfalon
    (1911, recorded by Rhoda Bernard)
"That's an Egg Cream!" .... Fanny Farina with Becky, Willie, Don, Pinky and Sally Small
    (by Isaiah Sheffer and Lanny Meyers)
"Nathan, Nathan, What Are You Waitin' For?" .... Gretta Genug with Don, Fanny,
                                              Pinky, Kevin Bailey and Sally
    (1915, recorded by Rhoda Bernard)
"Serenade Me Sadie With a Ragtime Tune" .... Kevin, Fanny
    (1912, by Joe Young and Bert Grant)
"Rosie Rosenblatt, Stop the Turkey Trot" .... Don; dance—Sally, Kevin
    (1911, recorded by Rhoda Bernard)

"My Yiddisha Colleen" .... Kevin
    (1911, by Edward Madden and Leo Edwards)
"Beckie, Stay in Your Own Back Yard"............ Don, Becky, Pinky, Fanny, Gretta, Sally
    (1910, by Norman & Young; additional lyrics by Lanny Meyers)
"Jake the Ball Player"... Willie
    (1913, by Irving Berlin)
"Nize Baby" .... Fanny, Pinky, Sally, Ensemble
    (1926, by Mac Rutchild and Lennie Whitcup)
"Rosenthal Ain't Rosenthal No More" .... Sally
    (1926, by Robert A. Simon)
"Sam, You Made the Pants Too Long" ...... Gretta with Pinky and Kevin; Willie with Becky,
                                                              Sally and Fanny
    (1932, by S. Lewis and Lew Young)

ACT II

"Yiddisha Charleston" .... Sally, Kevin, Ensemble
    (1927, by Fred Fischer and Billy Rose)
"Doin' the Neighborhood Rag" (Reprise) .... Ensemble
"Ish-Ga-Bibble" (Reprise) .... Willie, Ensemble
"Yiddisha Nightingale" .... Don
    (1911, by Irving Berlin)
"Abie and Me and the Baby" .... Becky, Ensemble
    (1915, by Harry Von Tilzer and Lew Brown with Fanny Brice)
"Cohen Owes Me $97"............... Fanny, Pinky with Don, Kevin, Diana Darling, Sally
    (1915, by Irving Berlin)
"Change Your Immigrant Ways" .... Diana
    (1909, based on "Roll Your Yiddisha Eyes"; lyrics by Isaiah Sheffer)
"Yiddisha Luck and Irisha Love (Kelly and Rosenbaum, That's Mazel-Toff)" ... Fanny, Becky
    (1911, by Alfred Bryan and Fred Fischer)
"A Rabbi's Daughter" .... Willie, Don, Diana, Ensemble Quartet
    (1899, by Charles K. Harris)
"Since Henry Ford Apologized to Me" .... Pinky
    (1922, by Billy Rose)
"Whose Izzy Is He?"....................... Becky, Diana, Fanny, Sally (female quartet)
    (1924, by Lew Brown, Bud Green and Murray Sturm; additional lyrics by Lanny Meyers)
"East Side Moon"... Fanny
    (1913, music by Sam M. Lewis and Leo Meyer; lyrics by Isaiah Sheffer)
"The Sheik of Avenue B".. Willie, Company
    (1922, by Bert Kalmar and Harry Ruby)

*Someone Who'll Watch Over Me (216). By Frank McGuinness. Produced by Noel
Pearson and The Shubert Organization in association with Joseph Harris at the Booth
Theater. Opened November 23, 1992.

Edward .... Stephen Rea   Michael.................... Alec McCowen
Adam .... James McDaniel

    Understudies: Mr. Rea—Tom Tammi; Mr. McDaniel—Chuck Cooper; Mr. McCowen—Denis
Holmes.
    Directed by Robin Lefevre; scenery and costumes, Robin Don; lighting, Natasha Katz; sound,
T. Richard Fitzgerald; production supervisor, Jeremiah J. Harris; production stage manager, Sally
Jacobs; press, Shirley Herz.
    Place: A basement somewhere in the Middle East. The play was presented in two parts.
    Three hostages—an American, an Englishman and an Irishmen—find that humor and mutual
support helps them to survive their ordeal. A foreign (Irish) play previously presented at the
Hampstead Theater, London and at the Vaudeville Theater, London in this production.

Chuck Cooper replaced James McDaniel 3/30/93. Michael York replaced Alec McCowen 4/6/93. David Dukes replaced Stephen Rea 6/1/93.

National Actors Theater. Schedule of three revivals. **The Seagull** (49). By Anton Chekhov; translated by David French. Opened November 29, 1992. (Closed January 10, 1993) **Saint Joan** (64). By George Bernard Shaw; produced in association with Duncan C. Weldon. Opened January 31, 1993 matinee. (Closed March 14, 1993) **Three Men on a Horse** (40). Revival of the play by John Cecil Holm and George Abbott. Opened April 13, 1993. (Closed May 16, 1993) Produced by National Actors Theater, Tony Randall founder and artistic director, Michael Langham artistic director, at the Lyceum Theater.

THE SEAGULL

Medvedenko.................. Zane Lasky	Dr. Dorn................... Tony Roberts
Masha................. Maryann Plunkett	Shamarev .... Russel Lunday
Sorin .... John Franklyn-Robbins	Madame Arkadina.............. Tyne Daly
Konstantin .... Ethan Hawke	Trigorin...................... Jon Voight
Yakov................... Danny Burstein	The Cook .... John Beal
Nina .... Laura Linney	Servants ...... Kam Metcalf, Kevin Shinick,
Polina .... Joan MacIntosh	David Watson

Standby: Miss Daly—Delphi Harrington. Understudies: Messrs. Lasky, Burstein, Beal—William Leone; Miss Plunkett—Elizabeth Marvel; Miss Linney—Daisy White; Messrs. Franklyn-Robbins, Lunday—Rand Mitchell; Mr. Hawke—Bill Camp; Miss MacIntosh—Delphi Harrington; Mr. Voight—Tom Stechschulte.

Directed by Marshall W. Mason; scenery, Marjorie Bradley Kellogg; costumes, Laura Crow; lighting, Richard Nelson; sound, Stewart Werner & Chuck London; original music, Peter Kater; production supervisor, Bonnie Panson; technical advisor, Christopher C. Smith; production stage manager, James Harker; stage managers, John M. Atherlay, Glen Gardali; press, John Springer, Gary Springer.

Act I: Dusk, by the lake, on a midsummer evening. Act II: Noon, a week later, on the croquet lawn. Act III: Midday, the following week, in the dining room. Act IV: Two years later, a stormy summer evening. The play was presented in three parts with intermissions following Acts I and III.

The last major New York revival of *The Seagull* was by New York Shakespeare Festival 11/11/80 for 40 performances in the Jean-Claude Van Itallie adaptation.

SAINT JOAN

Robert de Baudricourt;	Dauphin (later Charles
English Soldier .... Edmund C. Davys	VII)................. Michael Stuhlbarg
Steward; Delegate From	Duchesse de la
Rome.................... Ivar Brogger	Tremouille .... Elizabeth Marvel
Joan.............. Maryann Plunkett	Dunois .... Jay O. Sanders
Bertrand de Poulengey ..... Rod McLachlan	Dunois' Page .... Danny Burstein
Archbishop of Rheims;	Earl of Warwick.............. John Neville
Executioner .... John Franklyn-Robbins	Chaplain de Stogumber..... Remak Ramsay
La Tremouille; D'Estivet......... Tom Lacy	Bishop of Beauvais .... Louis Turenne
Court Page; De Courcelles .. Peter McRobbie	Warwick's Page .... David Adkins
Gilles de Rais (Bluebeard)....... Bill Camp	Inquisitor .... Nicholas Kepros
Captain la Hire ... Helmar Augustus Cooper	Brother Martin Ladvenu.... Lorne Kennedy

Knights, English Soldiers: David Adkins, Charles Geyer, Richard Holmes. Soldiers, Knights, Scribes: Emily Baer, Ted Brunson, Roslyn Cohn, Kam Metcalf, Kevin Shinick, David Watson.

Understudies: Miss Plunkett—Elizabeth Marvel; Mr. Camp—Danny Burstein; Mr. McRobbie—Lorne Kennedy, Rod McLachlan; Messrs. Neville, Stuhlbarg—Bill Camp; Messrs. Turenne, Franklyn-Robbins—Alan Mixon; Messrs. Kepros, Ramsay—Leo Leyden; Messrs. Brogger, Adkins,

NATIONAL ACTORS THEA-
TER—Highlights of the company's
season included revivals of *Three Men
on a Horse (above)* with Zane Lasky
(Frankie), Jack Klugman (Patsy),
Jerry Stiller (Charlie), Joey Faye
(Harry) and Tony Randall (Erwin);
and *Saint Joan (left)* with *(in fore-
ground)* Jay O. Sanders (Dunois) and
Maryann Plunkett (Joan)

Cooper—David Rainey; Messrs. McLachlan, Sanders—Richard Holmes; Messrs. Burstein, Kennedy—David Adkins.

Directed by Michael Langham; scenery, Marjorie Bradley Kellogg; costumes, Ann Hould-Ward; lighting, Richard Nelson; sound, T. Richard Fitzgerald; original music, Stanley Silverman; executive producer, Manny Kladitis; production stage manager, Perry Cline; stage manager, Marjorie Horne.

Part I, Scene 1: The castle of Vaucouleurs, occupied territory, 1429. Scene 2: The Dauphin's court at Chinon, unoccupied territory, March 8, 1429. Scene 3: Bank of the River Loire near Orleans, April 29, 1429. Scene 4: Earl of Warwick's tent in the English camp, Scene 5: Rheims Cathedral, July 17, 1429. Part 2, Scene 6: The Great Hall, Rouen, May 30, 1431. Epilogue: June 1456.

The last major New York production of record of *Saint Joan* was by Circle in the Square on Broadway 11/29/77 for 96 performances.

THREE MEN ON A HORSE

Audrey Trowbridge	Julie Hagerty	Mabel	Ellen Greene
Tailor	John Beal	Moses	Helmar Augustus Cooper
Erwin Trowbridge	Tony Randall	Gloria	Leslie Anderson
Clarence Dobbins	Ralph Williams	Mr. Carver	John Franklyn-Robbins
Delivery Boy	Danny Burstein	Al	Michael Stuhlbarg
Harry	Joey Faye	Hotel Maid	Heather Harlan
Charlie	Jerry Stiller	Sylvia (Chanteuse)	Nora Mae Lyng
Frankie	Zane Lasky	Gus (Piano Player)	David Geist
Patsy	Jack Klugman		

Understudies: Messrs. Klugman, Stiller, Faye—Andrew Bloch; Messrs. Beal, Stuhlbarg—Danny Burstein; Messrs. Randall, Williams, Franklyn-Robbins—Edmund C. Davys; Misses Hagerty, Greene—Margery Murray; Messrs. Lasky, Burstein—Michael Stuhlbarg.

Directed by John Tillinger; scenery, Marjorie Bradley Kellogg; costumes, Ann Hould-Ward; lighting, Richard Nelson; sound, T. Richard Fitzgerald; music direction, John Kander; fight choreographer, Jerry Mitchell; executive producer, Manny Kladitis; stage manager, Bob Borod.

Act I, Scene 1: The living room of the Trowbridge house, Ozone Heights, N.J., 1935. Scene 2: A barroom in the basement of the Lavillere Hotel, New York City. Scene 3: Ozone Heights. Scene 4: Patsy's room in the Lavillere Hotel. Act II, Scene 1: Patsy's room. Scene 2: Ozone Heights. Scene 3: Patsy's room.

The last major New York revival of *Three Men on a Horse* took place on Broadway 10/16/69 for 100 performances.

*Lincoln Center Theater. Schedule of two programs. **My Favorite Year** (37). Musical based on the motion picture *My Favorite Year;* book by Joseph Dougherty; music by Stephen Flaherty; lyrics by Lynn Ahrens. Opened December 10, 1992. (Closed January 10, 1993) ***The Sisters Rosensweig** (85). Transfer from off Broadway of the play by Wendy Wasserstein. Opened March 18, 1993. Produced by Lincoln Center Theater, Andre Bishop and Bernard Gersten directors, *My Favorite Year* at the Vivian Beaumont Theater, *The Sisters Rosensweig* at the Ethel Barrymore Theater.

MY FAVORITE YEAR

Benjy Stone	Evan Pappas	Leo Silver	Paul Stolarsky
King Kaiser	Tom Mardirosian	Alan Swann	Tim Curry
Sy Benson	Josh Mostel	Rookie Carroca	Thomas Ikeda
K.C. Downing	Lannyl Stephens	Tess	Katie Finneran
Alice Miller	Andrea Martin	Uncle Morty	David Lipman
Herb Lee	Ethan Phillips	Aunt Sadie	Mary Stout
Belle Steinberg Carroca	Lainie Kazan		

Ensemble: Leslie Bell, Maria Calabrese, Kevin Chamberlin, Colleen Dunn, Katie Finneran, James Gerth, Michael Gruber, David Lipman, Roxie Lucas, Nora Mae Ling, Michael McGrath, Alan Muraoka, Jay Poindexter, Russell Ricard, Mary Stout, Thomas Titone, Bruce Wynant, Christina Youngman.

Orchestra: Ted Sperling conductor; Jan Rosenberg associate conductor; Alva Hunt, Ken Hitchcock, Rick Heckman, Gene Scholtens woodwinds; Lawrence Lunetta, Phil Granger, Darryl Shaw trumpet; Sonny Russo, Jack Schatz trombone; Kaitilin Mahony, French horn; Belinda Whitney-Barratt, Janine Kam-Lal, Susan Lorentsen violin; Ruth Siegler viola; Matthias Naegele cello; John Babich bass; Joseph Thalken, Jan Rosenberg keyboards; John Redsecker drums; Larry Spivack percussion.

Standby: Mr. Curry—Michael O'Gorman. Understudies: Mr. Pappas—Michael McGrath, Thomas Titone; Mr. Mardirosian—Bruce Wynant, Michael McGrath; Mr. Mostel—Kevin Chamberlin, Bruce Wynant; Miss Stephens—Katie Finneran; Miss Martin—Roxie Lucas, Mary Stout; Mr. Phillips—Thomas Titone, Kevin Chamberlin; Miss Kazan—Nora Mae Ling, Mary Stout; Mr. Stolarsky—James Gerth, Bruce Wynant; Mr. Curry—James Gerth; Mr. Ikeda—Alan Muraoka; Swings—Robert Ashford, Aimee Turner.

Directed by Ron Lagomarsino; musical staging, Thommie Walsh; musical direction, Ted Sperling; scenery, Thomas Lynch; costumes, Patricia Zipprodt; lighting, Jules Fisher; sound, Scott Lehrer; orchestrations, Michael Starobin; dance music arrangements, Wally Harper; fight director, B.H. Barry; presented in association with AT&T:OnStage; production stage manager, Robin Rumpf; stage manager, Dale Kaufman; press, Merle Debuskey, Susan Chicoine.

Time: 1954. Place: New York City.

Nostalgia for the days of live TV and the Hit Parade mixed with intensive father-daughter and male-female relationships.

ACT I

Scene 1: The broadcast studio
"Twenty Million People" .... Benjy, Company
Scene 2: The writers' office, morning
"Larger Than Life" .... Benjy
Scene 3: The writers' office, later that day
"The Musketeer Sketch" .... Benjy, Sy, King, Alice, K.C., Leo, Herb
Scene 4: Swann's Waldorf suite
"Waldorf Suite" .... Benjy
"Rookie in the Ring" .... Belle
Scene 5: Streets of New York
"Manhattan" .... Swann, Benjy, Ensemble
    (orchestrations by Danny Troob)
Scene 6: The broadcast studio
"Naked in the Bethesda Fountain" .... Sy, Alice, Leo, Herb, K.C.
"The Gospel According to King" .... King, Swann, Company
"The Musketeer Sketch Rehearsal" .... Benjy, Swann, Ensemble
Scene 7: The ladies' room
"Funny/The Duck Joke" .... K.C., Alice
Scene 8: The broadcast studio
"The Musketeer Sketch Rehearsal" (Part II) .... King, Swann, Ensemble
Scene 9: Belle's apartment
"Welcome to Brooklyn" .... Morty, Rookie, Belle, Sadie, Benjy, Swann, Neighbors
"If the World Were Like the Movies" .... Swann

ACT II

Entr'acte .... Orchestra
Scene 1: Central Park
"Exits" .... Swann
Scene 2: The Plaza Hotel
Scene 3: Swann's Waldorf suite
"Shut Up and Dance" .... K.C., Benjy

Scene 4: The Broadhurst Studio
"Professional and Showbizness Comedy" . . . . Alice, King, Ensemble
Scene 5: Swann's dressing room
"The Lights Come Up" . . . . Swann, Benjy
Scene 6: The Broadhurst Studio
"Maxford House" . . . . Maxford House Girls
"The Musketeer Sketch Finale" . . . . Company
"My Favorite Year" . . . . Benjy, Company

THE SISTERS ROSENSWEIG

Tess Goode. . . . . Julie Dretzin	Marvyn Kant . . . . Robert Klein
Pfeni Rosensweig . . . . Christine Estabrook	Gorgeous Teitelbaum . . . . . . Madeline Kahn
Sara Goode . . . . Jane Alexander	Tom Valiunus. . . . . Patrick Fitzgerald
Geoffrey Duncan . . . . John Vickery	Nicholas Pym . . . . John Cunningham

Standbys: Miss Dretzin—Chiara Peacock; Misses Alexander, Estabrook—Robin Moseley; Misses Kahn, Alexander—Lucy Martin; Messrs. Vickery, Cunningham—Stephen Stout; Messrs. Klein, Cunningham—Stan Lachow; Mr. Fitzgerald—Jonathan Friedman.

Directed by Daniel Sullivan; scenery, John Lee Beatty; costumes, Jane Greenwood; lighting, Pat Collins; sound, Guy Sherman/Aural Fixation; production stage manager, Roy Harris; stage manager, Elise-Ann Konstantin.

Time: A weekend in August, 1991. Place: A sitting room in Queen Anne's Gate, London. The play was presented in two parts.

The character and relationship of three Brooklyn-born sisters celebrating the eldest's birthday. Previously produced off Broadway 10/22/92 for 149 performances by Lincoln Center Theater; see its entry in the Plays Produced Off Broadway section of this volume.

A Best Play; see page 126.

A Christmas Carol (22). Return engagement of the one-man performance by Patrick Stewart; adapted by Patrick Stewart from Charles Dickens. Produced by Timothy Childs at the Broadhurst Theater. Opened December 17, 1992. (Closed January 3, 1993)

Lighting, Fred Allen; executive producer, Kate Elliott; production stage manager, Kate Elliott; press, Boneau/Bryan-Brown, Bob Fennell. The play was presented in two parts and was previously produced on Broadway 1/12/19 for 14 performances. A foreign play first produced in 1988 and in a pre-Broadway tour of the United States.

*Fool Moon (109). Comic performance program created by Bill Irwin and David Shiner. Produced by James B. Freydberg, Kenneth Feld, Jeffrey Ash and Dori Berinstein at the Richard Rodgers Theater. Opened February 25, 1993.

With David Shiner, Bill Irwin.

The Red Clay Ramblers: Clay Buckner fiddle, harmonica; Chris Frank piano, tuba, accordion, ukulele; Jack Herrick trumpet, bass, banjolin, tin whistle, concertina; Tommy Thompson banjos; Ron Ladd drums.

Scenery, Douglas Stein; costumes, Bill Kellard; lighting, Nancy Schertler; sound, Tom Morse; flying by Foy; producing associate, Nancy Harrington; production stage manager, James Harker; press, Boneau/Bryan-Brown, Adrian Bryan-Brown, Chris Boneau, Jackie Green.

Two solo artists in episodes of clowning, much of it physical, with music. The show was presented in two parts.

*The Goodbye Girl (101). Musical with book by Neil Simon; music by Marvin Hamlisch; lyrics by David Zippel. Produced by Office Two-One Inc., Gladys Nederlander, Stewart F. Lane, James M. Nederlander, Richard Kagan and Emanuel Azenberg at the Marquis Theater. Opened March 4, 1993.

Lucy .... Tammy Minoff
Paula.................. Bernadette Peters
Billy......................... Scott Wise
Donna.................. Susann Fletcher
Jenna.................. Cynthia Onrubia
Cynthia.................... Erin Torpey
Melanie.................... Lisa Molina
Mrs. Crosby .... Carol Woods
Elliot..................... Martin Short

Mark; Ricky
  Simpson .... John Christopher Jones
Stage Manager .... Darlesia Cearcy
1st Man at Theater .... Larry Sousa
Woman at Theater........ Mary Ann Lamb
2d Man at Theater; TV Stage Manager;
  Ricky Simpson Announcer..... Rick Crom
Mark's Mother........... Ruth Gottschall

Cast of *Richard III:* Barry Bernal, Darlesia Cearcy, Jamie Beth Chandler, Dennis Daniels, Denise Faye, Nancy Hess, Joe Locarro, Rick Manning, Cynthia Onrubia, Linda Talcott, Scott Wise.

Audience at *Richard III:* Rick Crom, Ruth Gottschall, Sean Grant, Mary Ann Lamb, Larry Sousa.

Orchestra: Jack Everly conductor; Fran Forchetti assistant conductor; Al Regni, Bob Keller, Ed Zuhlke, John Winder reeds; Bob Millikan, Danny Cahn, Darryl Shaw trumpet; Keith O'Guinn trombone; George Flynn bass trombone; John Clark, French horn; Michael Keller drums; Jim Saporito percussion; Lee Musiker, Myles Chase keyboards; Ron Oakland concertmaster, violin; Janet Hill, Claudia Hafer Tondi, Deborah Wong violin; Alvin McCall, Mark Shuman, Ellen Westerman cello; Bill Sloat bass; Lise Nadeau harp.

Swings: Ned Hannah, Michele Pigliavento. Standbys: Miss Peters—Betsy Joslyn; Mr. Short— Michael McGrath. Understudies: Miss Peters—Nancy Hess; Messrs. Short, Jones—Rick Crom; Miss Minoff—Erin Torpey, Lisa Molina; Miss Woods—Darlesia Cearcy; Miss Fletcher—Ruth Gottschall; Misses Molina, Torpey—Ibijoke Akinola.

Directed by Michael Kidd; musical staging, Graciela Daniele; musical direction, Jack Everly; scenery and costumes, Santo Loquasto; lighting, Tharon Musser; sound, Tom Clark; assistant choreographer, Willie Rosario; production supervisor, Peter Lawrence; orchestrations, Billy Byers, Torrie Zito; dance music arrangements, Mark Hummel; associate producer, Kaede Seville; stage manager, Thomas A. Bartlett; press, Bill Evans and Associates, Jim Randolph, Erin Dunn, Sandy Manley.

Adapted from the 1977 film of the same title by Neil Simon, the mother of a ten-year-old girl finds herself sharing an apartment with an aspiring actor.

ACT I

Scene 1: Paula's apartment
  "This Is as Good as It Gets" .... Paula, Lucy
  "No More" .... Paula
Scene 2: A dance studio
  "A Beat Behind" .... Paula, Billy, Ensemble
Scene 3: In front of Paula's building
  "This Is as Good as It Gets" (Reprise)...................... Lucy, Melanie, Cynthia
Scene 4: Paula's apartment
  "My Rules"/"Elliot Garfield Grant"................................. Elliot, Paula
  "Good News, Bad News"................................... Elliot, Paula, Lucy
Scene 5: Paula's apartment
  "Good News, Bad News" (Reprise)................................ Mrs. Crosby
Scene 6: An off-off-Broadway theater
Scene 7: Central Park
  "Footsteps" .... Paula, Lucy
Scene 8: Paula's apartment
  "How Can I Win?" .... Paula
Scene 9: An off-off-Broadway theater
  "Richard Interred" .... Elliot, Paula, Lucy, Mark, Mrs. Crosby, Donna, Ensemble

ACT II

Scene 1: Paula's apartment
  "How Can I Win?" (Reprise).. Paula

Scene 2: Paula's Apartment
"Good News, Bad News" (Reprise)... Elliot
Scene 3: The Ricky Simpson Show
"Too Good To Be Bad".................................... Paula, Donna, Jenna
Scene 4: Paula's apartment
"2 Good 2 B Bad" .... Mrs. Crosby
Scene 5: Paula's apartment
"Who Would've Thought?" .... Paula, Elliot, Lucy, Melanie, Cynthia
Scene 6: The rooftop of Paula's building
"Paula (An Improvised Love Song)".................................. Elliot, Paula
Scene 7: Paula's apartment
Scene 8: A schoolyard
"Who Would've Thought?" (Reprise) .... Lucy, Melanie, Cynthia
Scene 9: The lake in Central Park
"I Can Play This Part".. Elliot
Scene 10: A TV studio
"Jump for Joy" .... Paula, Ensemble
Scene 11: Paula's apartment
"What a Guy"... Paula
Scene 12: In front of Paula's building
Finale .... Paula, Elliot, Lucy

Yabuhara Kengyo (The Great Doctor Yabuhara) (3). Play in the Japanese language by Hisashi Inoue. Produced by Chijinkai Theater Company in association with One Reel and Micocci Productions at the City Center. Opened March 4, 1993. (Closed March 6, 1993)

Blind Narrator............ Kikuo Kaneuchi	Kotonoichi; Zenbei .... Shinpei Suzuki
Suginoichi (Yabuhara	Oichi...................... Akiko Iwase
Kengyo)............... Yasuyoshi Hara	Kekke; Matsudaira
Shichibei; Hanawa Hokiichi;	Sadanobu.............. Kazuhiko Kura
Lover of Oshiho .... Takasha Fujiki	Widow................ Kyoko Yamaguchi
Oshiho.............. Kyoko Mitsubayashi	Daughter of the Widow .... Mie Koga
Kumanoichi;	Guitarist .... Naoya Mizumura
Sakuma-Kengyo .... Takehiko Ono	

Directed by Koichi Kimura; scenery, Setsu Asakura; music, Seiichiro Uno; choreography, Shunju Hanawaka; lighting, Yukio Furukawa; sound effects, Joji Fukagawa; music advisor, Sadako Miyamoto; titles, Sayuri Suzuki; stage manager, Tsukasa Mikami; press, the Zeisler Group, Suzanne Ford.

Black comedy of an evil blind musician, set in the Edo era (1603–1867). A foreign play previously produced in Japan, Hong Kong, Seattle, London and the Edinburgh Theater Festival.

The Song of Jacob Zulu (53). By Tug Yourgrau; original music by Ladysmith Black Mambazo; original lyrics by Tug Yourgrau and Ladysmith Black Mambazo. Produced by Steppenwolf Theater Company, Randall Arney, Stephen Eich, Albert Poland, Susan Liederman and Bette Cerf Hill in association with Maurice Rosenfield in the Steppenwolf Theater Company production at the Plymouth Theater. Opened March 24, 1993. (Closed May 9, 1993)

Marty Frankel .... Gerry Becker	Martin Zulu; Zebulun;
Mrs. Zulu; Mrs. Ngobese; Ma Bythelezi;	Guerrilla................. Leelai Demoz
Guerrilla................... Pat Bowie	Jacob Zulu .... K. Todd Freeman
Judge Neville .... Robert Breuler	Mrs. Sabelo; Beauty Dlamini;
John Dawkins; Dr. Shaw ... David Connelly	Guerrilla................ Erika L. Heard

THE SONG OF JACOB ZULU—The *a cappella* singing group
Ladysmith Black Mambazo in the play by Tug Yourgrau

Mr. Vilakazi; Fumani;
  Guerrilla............... Danny Johnson
Student; Policeman; Mbongeni;
  Michael Dube;
  Guerrilla......... Gary DeWitt Marshall
Rev. Zulu; Mr. X; Itshe ...... Zakes Mokae
Magistrate; Mr. Van Heerden;
  Mr. Jeppe............... Daniel Oreskes

Student; Aunt Miriam; Ruth Dube;
  Guerrilla................ Tania Richard
Interpreter; Policeman; Jacob's
  Superior.................. Seth Sibanda
Anthony Dent; Lt. Malan...... Alan Wilder
Michael Jeppe; Lt.
  Kramer.......... Nicholas Cross Wodtke
Uncle Mdishwa; Teacher; Policeman;
  Percy; Commissar .... Cedric Young

With Ladysmith Black Mambazo: Joseph Shabalala, Jubulani Dubazana, Abednego Mazibuko, Albert Mazibuko, Geophrey Mdletshe, Russel Mthembu, Inos Phungula, Jockey Shabalala, Ben Shabalala.

Understudies: David Connelly, Leelai Demoz, Erika L. Heard, Gary DeWitt Marshall, Daniel Oreskes, Seth Sibanda, Tania Richard, Nicholas Cross Wodtke, Cedric Young.

Directed by Eric Simonson; scenery, Kevin Rigdon; costumes, Erin Quigley; lighting, Robert Christen; sound, Rob Milburn; production stage manager, Malcolm Ewen; stage managers, Alden Vasquez, Femi Sarah Heggie; press, David Rothenberg Associates, Hugh Hayes, Manuel Igrejas, Terence Womble.

Play with music based on the true story of a young black man caught between his love of family and devotion to the cause of freedom, with additional music adapted from hymns and traditional South African songs. The play was presented in two parts. Previously produced in this production in Chicago and at the Festival of Perth, Australia.

Redwood Curtain (40). By Lanford Wilson. Produced by Robert Cole, Benjamin Mordecai, Deborah D. Mathews, James M. Nederlander, James D. Stern, William P. Suter and the Circle Repertory Company, Tanya Berezin artistic director, in the Circle Repertory Company Production at the Brooks Atkinson Theater. Opened March 30, 1993. (Closed May 2, 1993)

Lyman...................... Jeff Daniels	Geneva .... Debra Monk
Geri..................... Sung Yun Cho	

Understudy: Miss Monk—Pamela Dunlap.

Directed by Marshall W. Mason; scenery, John Lee Beatty; costumes, Laura Crow; lighting, Dennis Parichy; sound, Chuck London/Stewart Werner; original music, Peter Kater; fight director, Nels Hennum; associate producers, Susan Sampliner, Nick Scandalios; production stage manager, Fred Reinglas; stage manager, Denise Yaney; press, Bill Evans & Associates, Erin Dunn.

Time: Not long ago. Scene 1: A redwood forest neart Arcata, Calif., in the northwestern part of the state. Scene 2: Briefly, a car. The music room of Geneva's home in Arcata. Scene 3: A coffee shop. The forest. The music room. The play was presented without an intermission.

A teenage girl searches for her father among Viet Nam veterans living in the redwood forest. Commissioned by Circle Repertory Company but previously produced in regional theater at Seattle Repertory Theater, the Philadelphia Drama Guild and the Old Globe Theater, San Diego.

Ain't Broadway Grand (25). Musical with book by Thomas Meehan and Lee Adams; music by Mitch Leigh; lyrics by Lee Adams. Produced by Arthur Rubin in the Mitch Leigh production at the Lunt-Fontanne Theater. Opened April 18, 1993. (Closed May 9, 1993)

Bobby Clark.................. Gerry Vichi	*Of the People,* Part I
Gypsy Rose Lee.... Debbie Shapiro Gravitte	President & His Cabinet: Timothy Albrecht,
Mike Todd .... Mike Burstyn	Bill Corcoran, Scott Elliott, Scott Fowler, Je-
Harriet Popkin................ Alix Korey	rold Goldstein, Joe Istre, Rod McCune, Bill
Lou; Lindy's Waiter .... Bill Nabel	Nabel, Luis Perez, Mimi Cichanowicz Quillin,
Murray Pearl .... Mitchell Greenberg	Patrick Wetzel
Reuben Pelish.............. David Lipman	Riverside Drive Streetwalker.. Beverly Britton
Joan Blondell .... Maureen McNamara	Lili....................... Ginger Prince
Marvin Fischbein........... Gabriel Barre	Sheryl .... Jennifer Frankel
Waldo Klein................... Bill Kux	Linda........... Mimi Cichanowicz Quillin
Wally Farfle .... Scott Elliott	
Dexter Leslie .... Richard B. Shull	*Of the People,* Part II
Jaeger .... Merwin Goldsmith	President & His Cabinet: Leslie Bell, Beverly
Lindy's Waiter .... Bill Corcoran	Britton, Caitlin Carter, Colleen Dunn, Jennifer
Thelma .... Caitlin Carter	Frankel, Lauren Golar-Kosarin, Elizabeth
Floyd.................... Patrick Wetzel	Mills, Ginger Prince, Mimi Cichanowicz Quil-
Rocco .... Luis Perez	lin, Carol Denise Smith
Frankie.................... Scott Fowler	
Herbie; Lindy's Waiter ..... Jerold Goldstein	

Ensemble: Timothy Albrecht, Leslie Bell, Beverly Britton, Caitlin Carter, Bill Corcoran, Colleen Dunn, Scott Elliott, Scott Fowler, Jennifer Frankel, Jerold Goldstein, Lauren Goler-Kosarin, Joe Istre, Rod McCune, Elizabeth Mills, Bill Nabel, Luis Perez, Ginger Prince, Mimi Cichanowicz Quillin, Carol Denise Smith, Patrick Wetzel.

Standby: Mr. Burstyn—P.J. Benjamin. Understudies: Miss Gravitte—Mimi Cichanowicz Quillin; Miss McNamara—Beverly Britton; Messrs. Vichi, Lipman—Jerold Goldstein; Messrs. Barre,

Kux—Scott Elliott; Messrs. Greenberg, Goldsmith—Bill Nabel; Miss Korey—Ginger Prince; Mr. Shull—Merwin Goldsmith. Swings: Kelly Barclay, James Horvath, Lynn Sullivan.

Orchestra: Nicholas Archer conductor; Michael Dansicker associate conductor, keyboard; Lawrence Feldman, Bill Meade, Roger Rosenberg, Lauren Goldstein reeds; David Stahl, Don Downs trumpet; David Bargeron trombone; Alan Raph bass trombone; Paul Riggio, Chris Constanzi, French horn; Barry Finclair concert master; Robert Zubrycki, Carlos Villa, Rebekah Johnson, Valerie Levy, Susan Gellert violin; Anne Callahan, Curtis Woodside cello; Raymond Kilday bass; Ronald Zito drums; Ian Finkle percussion; Wayne Abravanel, Mark Lipman keyboards.

Directed by Scott Harris; choreography, Randy Skinner; musical direction, Nicholas Archer; scenery, David Mitchell; costumes, Suzy Benzinger; lighting, Ken Billington; sound, Otts Munderloh; musical supervision and vocal arrangements, Neil Warner; orchestrations, Chris Bankey; dance arrangements, Scot Woolley; production stage manager, Frank Marino; stage manager, John Actman; press, the Fred Nathan Company, William Schelble.

Time: Summer and early fall, 1948.

A year in the life of Broadway impresario Mike Todd as he produces a musical fictionally entitled *Of the People.*

Peter Gregus replaced Luis Perez 4/30/93.

ACT I

Scene 1: The stage of the Alvin Theater
"Girls Ahoy!" .... Bobby Clark, Gypsy Rose Lee, Ensemble
Scene 2: Backstage at the Alvin Theater
"Ain't Broadway Grand" .... Mike Todd, Harriet Popkin, Murray Pearl,
Reuben Pelish, Ensemble
"Class" .... Mike Todd, Chorus Girls
Scene 3: Backstage at a production meeting
"The Theater, The Theatre" .... Marvin Fischbein, Waldo Klein
"Ain't Broadway Grand" (Reprise) .... Mike Todd, Harriet Popkin, Murray Pearl,
Dexter Leslie, Marvin Fischbein, Waldo Klein, Wally Farfle, Ensemble
Scene 4: Lindy's Restaurant
"Lindy's" .... Jaeger, Waiters, Company
"It's Time to Go" .... Gypsy Rose Lee, Ensemble
Scene 5: The Bar at "21"
"Waiting in the Wings" .... Joan Blondell
"You're My Star" .... Mike Todd, Ensemble
Scene 6: Todd's office
Scene 7: *Of the People* show curtain
Scene 8: The Oval Office
"A Big Job" .... President, Ensemble
Scene 9: The stage of the Colonial Theater, Boston
"Ain't Broadway Grand" (Reprise) .... Company

ACT II

Scene 1: The street in front of Lindy's
"Ain't Broadway Grand" (Reprise) .... Jaeger, Waiters
Scene 2: Todd's suite, Ritz Carlton Hotel, Boston
"They'll Never Take Us Alive" .... Mike Todd, Harriet Popkin, Murray Pearl
Scene 3: Riverside Drive near Grant's Tomb
"On the Street" .... Mike Todd
"The Man I Married" .... Joan Blondell, Female Ensemble
Scene 4: A costume shop
"The Theater, The Theatre" (Reprise). .... Harriet Popkin, Murray Pearl
"Maybe, Maybe Not" .... Gypsy Rose Lee
Scene 5: Rehearsal backstage at the Alvin Theater
"Tall Dames and Low Comedy" .... Bobby Clark, Ensemble
Scene 6: Beverly Hills Hotel, Beverly Hills, California
"He's My Guy" .... Joan Blondell

Scene 7: Behind the curtain at the Alvin Theater
Scene 8: The Oval Office
  "A Big Job" (Reprise)... President, Ensemble
Scene 9: Backstage at the Alvin Theater
  "You're My Star" (Reprise).. Mike Todd
  "Ain't Broadway Grand" (Reprise)....................................... Company

Wilder, Wilder, Wilder (31). Revival program of three one-act plays by Thornton Wilder: *The Long Christmas Dinner, The Happy Journey to Trenton and Camden* and *Pullman Car Hiawatha*. Produced by Circle in the Square Theater, Theodore Mann artistic director, George Elmer managing director, Paul Libin consulting producer, in the Willow Cabin Theater Company production, Edward Berkeley artistic director, Adam Oliensis, Maria Radman producing directors, at Circle in the Square Theater. Opened April 21, 1993. (Closed May 16, 1993)

The Long Christmas Dinner

Lucia 1	Linda Powell
Roderick 1	Ken Forman
Mother Bayard; Lucia 2	Sabrina Boudot
Cousin Brandon.............	Jonathan Sea
Nurse	Rebecca Killy
Charles	Adam Oliensis
Genevieve	Angela Nevard
Leonora	Fiona Davis
Cousin Ermengarde......	Cynthia Besteman
Roderick 2	Stephen Mora
Sam.....................	David Goldman

The Happy Journey to Trenton and Camden

Stage Manager............	Michael Rispoli
Ma Kirby	Maria Radman
Arthur....................	Craig Zakarian
Caroline	Dede Pochos
Elmer	Laurence Gleason
Beulah..................	Tasha Lawrence

Pullman Car Hiawatha

Stage Manager...........	Michael Rispoli
Lower # 1	Dede Pochos

Lower # 3	Peter Killy
Lower #5.................	Maria Radman
Lower #7.................	Adam Oliensis
Lower #9.................	Jonathan Sea
Porter	Patrick Huey
Harriett...................	Angela Nevard
Philip.....................	Craig Zakarian
Insane Woman............	Tasha Lawrence
Nurse	Linda Powell
Attendant	Stephen Mora
Grover's Comers, Ohio;	
Mercury...............	David Goldman
The Field; Mars........	Laurence Gleason
Parkersburg, Ohio;	
Venus.................	Cynthia Besteman
Tramp..................	Ken Forman
German Workman..........	Bjarne Hecht
Watchman	John Billeci
The Weather..............	Charmaine Lord
10 O'Clock	Sabrina Boudot
11 O'Clock	Rebecca Killy
12 O'Clock	Fiona Davis
Archangel Gabriel	Timothy McNamara

Directed by Edward Berkeley; scenery, Miguel Lopez-Castillo; costumes, Dede Pochos, Fiona Davis; lighting, Steven Rust; stage manager, Wm. Hare; press, The Bruce Cohen Group, Bruce Cohen, Patty Onagan.

The most recent New York productions of record of these Wilder one-acts were: *Pullman Car Hiawatha* off Broadway at Circle in the Square for 33 performances 12/3/62; and *The Long Christmas Dinner* and *The Happy Journey to Trenton and Camden* on an off-Broadway program with Wilder's *Queens of France* for 72 performances 9/6/66. The present production was transferred from off off Broadway after a presentation at the Harold Clurman Theater in December 1992.

*The Who's Tommy (46). Musical with book by Pete Townshend and Des McAnuff; music and lyrics by Pete Townshend; additional music and lyrics by John Entwistle and Keith Moon. Produced by Pace Theatrical Group and Dodger Productions with Kardana Productions, Inc. at the St. James Theater. Opened April 22, 1993.

Mrs. Walker............	Marcia Mitzman	Uncle Ernie.................	Paul Kandel
Capt. Walker	Jonathan Dokuchitz	Minister; Mr. Simpson	Bill Buell

Minister's Wife.................. Jody Gelb
Nurse .... Lisa Leguillou
Officer #1; Hawker...... Michael McElroy
Officer #2 .... Timothy Warmen
Allied Soldier #1; 1st
   Pinball Lad .... Donnie Kehr
Allied Soldier #2......... Michael Arnold
Lover; Harmonica Player ...... Lee Morgan
(Tommy, Age 4)..... Carly Jane Steinborn,
                     Crysta Macalush
Tommy................ Michael Cerveris

Judge; Kevin's Father; News Vendor;
   D.J........................ Tom Flynn
Tommy, Age 10.............. Buddy Smith
Cousin Kevin .... Anthony Barrile
Kevin's Mother .... Maria Calabrese
Gypsy .... Cheryl Freeman
2d Pinball Lad .... Christian Hoff
Specialist.................... Norm Lewis
Specialist's Assistant .... Alice Ripley
Sally Simpson................. Sherie Scott
Mrs. Simpson............... Pam Klinger

(Parentheses indicate role in which the performers alternated)

Local Lads; Security Guards: Michael Arnold, Paul Dobie, Christian Hoff, Donnie Kehr, Michael McElroy, Timothy Warmen. Local Lasses: Maria Calabrese, Tracy Nicole Chapman, Pam Klinger, Lisa Leguillou, Alice Ripley, Sherie Scott.

Ensemble: Michael Arnold, Bill Buell, Maria Calabrese, Tracy Nicole Chapman, Paul Dobie, Tom Flynn, Jody Gelb, Christian Hoff, Donnie Kehr, Pam Klinger, Lisa Leguillou, Norm Lewis, Michael McElroy, Lee Morgan, Alice Ripley, Sherie Scott, Timothy Warmen.

Orchestra: Joseph Church conductor; Jeanine Levenson associate conductor, keyboard; Kevin Kuhn, John Putnam guitar; Luther Rix drums; David Kuhn bass; Ted Baker, Henry Aronson keyboards; Charles Descarfino, John Meyers percussion; Kaitilin Mahony, Alexandra Cook, French horn; Dale Stuckenbruck, Cecelia Hobbs Gardner violin; Crystal Garner viola; Maria Kitsopoulos cello.

Understudies: Mr. Cerveris—Romain Frugé, Donnie Kehr; Master Smith—Ari Vernon; Miss Mitzman—Alice Ripley, Jody Gelb; Mr. Dokuchitz—Paul Dobie, Timothy Warmen, Todd Hunter; Mr. Kandel—Bill Buell, Tom Flynn; Miss Freeman—Tracey Langran, Tracy Nicole Chapman; Mr. Barrile—Romain Frugé, Donnie Kehr. Swings—Victoria Lecta Cave, Romain Frugé, Todd Hunter, Tracey Langran.

Directed by Des McAnuff; choreography, Wayne Cilento; musical supervision and direction, Joseph Church; scenery, John Arnone; costumes, David C. Woolard; lighting, Chris Parry; projections, Wendall K. Harrington; sound, Steve Canyon Kennedy; video, Batwin & Robin Productions, Inc.; orchestrations, Steve Margoshes; musical coordinator, John Miller; special effects, Gregory Meeh; flying, Foy; fight direction, Steve Rankin; technical supervision, Gene O'Donovan; executive producers, David, Strong, Warner, Inc., Scott Zeiger/Gary Gunas; associate producer, John F. Kennedy Center for the Performing Arts; production stage manager, Frank Hartenstein; stage manager, Karen Armstrong; press, Boneau/Bryan-Brown, Adrian Bryan-Brown, Susanne Tighe.

Tommy, age 4, is rendered deaf, dumb and blind by a traumatic experience but grows up to become a pinball wizard, in the rock-opera context recorded in the double album *Tommy* in 1969 by the musical group known as The Who (which performed it in concert at the Metropolitan Opera House in 1970) and the 1975 movie adaptation. This stage version was previously produced last summer at the La Jolla, Calif. Playhouse.

A Best Play (special citation); see page 270.

ACT I

Overture: 1941 .... Company
Scene 1: 22 Heathfield Gardens, London, England/POW Camp, Germany, 1941
   "Captain Walker" .... Officers
Scene 2: Hospital/POW Camp, 1945
   "It's a Boy" .... Nurses, Mrs. Walker
   "We've Won"....................................... Capt. Walker, Allied Soldiers
Scene 3: 22 Heathfield Gardens
   "Twenty-One" .... Mrs. Walker, Lover, Capt. Walker
   "Amazing Journey"... Tommy
Scene 4: English courtroom
Scene 5: Hospital
   "Sparks"... Instrumental
   "Amazing Journey" (Reprise)... Tommy

Scene 6: Church/The home of the relatives, 1950
   "Christmas" . . . . Capt. and Mrs. Walker, Minister, Minister's Wife, Ensemble
   "See Me, Feel Me" . . . . Tommy
Scene 7: 22 Heathfield Gardens
   "Do You Think It's Alright" . . . . Capt. and Mrs. Walker
   "Fiddle About" . . . . Uncle Ernie, Ensemble
   "See Me, Feel Me" (Reprise) . . . . Tommy
Scene 8: 22 Heathfield Gardens/A youth club
   "Cousin Kevin" . . . . Cousin Kevin, Ensemble
   "Sensation" . . . . Tommy, Ensemble
Scene 9: Psychiatric clinic
   "Sparks" (Reprise). . . . . Instrumental
Scene 10: 22 Heathfield Gardens
   "Eyesight to the Blind" . . . . Hawker, Harmonica Player, Ensemble
Scene 11: The Isle of Dogs
   "Acid Queen" . . . . Gypsy
Scene 12: Amusement arcade
   "Pinball Wizard" . . . . Local Lads, Cousin Kevin, Ensemble

ACT II

Underture (Entr'acte): 1960 . . . . Orchestra
Scene 1: The Sunlight Laundry
   "There's a Doctor" . . . . Capt. and Mrs. Walker
Scene 2: Research laboratory
   "Go to the Mirror" . . . . Specialist, Specialist's Assistant, Capt. and Mrs. Walker
   "Listening to You" . . . . Tommy, Tommy Age 10, Tommy Age 4
Scene 3: The street/22 Heathfield Gardens
   "Tommy Can You Hear Me" . . . . Local Lads
Scene 4: 22 Heathfield Gardens
   "I Believe My Own Eyes" . . . . Capt. and Mrs. Walker
   "Smash the Mirror" . . . . Mrs. Walker
   "I'm Free" . . . . Tommy
Scene 5: The streets of London, 1961–1963
   "Miracle Cure" . . . . Newspaper Vendor, Local Lads
   "Sensation" (Reprise) . . . . Tommy, Ensemble
   "I'm Free"/"Pinball Wizard" (Reprise) . . . . Tommy, Company
Scene 6: Holiday Camp
   "Tommy's Holiday Camp" . . . . Uncle Ernie
Scene 7: The Simpsons
   "Sally Simpson" . . . . Cousin Kevin, Security Guards, Sally Simpson, Mr. and Mrs. Simpson
Scenes 8, 9, 10: Heathfield Gardens
   "Welcome" . . . . Tommy, Ensemble
   "We're Not Going to Take It" . . . . Tommy, Ensemble
   "See Me, Feel Me"/"Listening to You" (Reprise)/Finale . . . . Tommy, Company

*Blood Brothers (42). Musical with book, music and lyrics by Willy Russell. Produced by Bill Kenwright at the Music Box Theater. Opened April 25, 1993.

Mrs. Johnstone.	Stephanie Lawrence	Sammy	James Clow
Narrator	Warwick Evans	Linda.	Jan Graveson
Mrs. Lyons	Barbara Walsh	Perkins	Sam Samuelson
Mr. Lyons.	Ivar Brogger	Donna Marie; Miss Jones . .	Regina O'Malley
Mickey	Con O'Neill	Policeman; Teacher	Robin Haynes
Eddie.	Mark Michael Hutchinson	Brenda	Anne Torsiglieri

Other Parts: Ivar Brogger, Kerry Butler, James Clow, Robin Haynes, Philip Lehl, Regina O'Malley, Sam Samuelson, John Schiappa, Anne Torsiglieri, Douglas Weston.

BLOOD BROTHERS—Con O'Neill as Mickey *(center foreground)* Warwick Evans as the Narrator *(right foreground, wearing necktie)* and ensemble in the "Take a Letter, Miss Jones" number of the Willy Russell musical

Orchestra: Mark Berman assistant conductor, keyboards; Robert Kirshoff acoustic and electric guitar; Bob Renino acoustic and electric bass; Ray Grappone drums; Barry Centanni percussion; Mike Migliore, Billy Kerr reeds; Neil Balm trumpet, flugelhorn.

Understudies: Misses Lawrence, Walsh—Regina O'Malley; Mr. O'Neill—Philip Lehl; Messrs. Clow, Evans—John Schiappa; Mr. Hutchinson—Sam Samuelson; Miss Graveson—Anne Torsiglieri; Mr. Evans—Robin Haynes; Miss O'Malley—Kerry Butler.

Directed by Bill Kenwright and Bob Tomson; scenery and costumes, Andy Walmsley; lighting, Joe Atkins; sound, Paul Astbury; production musical direction, Rod Edwards; musical direction, Rick Fox; arrangements, Del Newman; technical supervisor, Gene O'Donovan; associate producer, Jon Miller; production stage manager, Mary Porter Hall; stage manager, John Lucas; press, Philip Rinaldi, Kathy Haberthur.

Place: Liverpool.

Twins separated at birth grow up in different classes under contrasting circumstances, one rich and the other poor, but destined for a tragic confrontation. A foreign play previously produced in London.

ACT I

"Easy Terms" (Reprise) .... Mrs. Johnstone
"Kids Game".................................... Sammy, Linda, Mickey, Ensemble
"Shoes Upon the Table" (Reprise) .... Narrator
"Shoes Upon the Table" (Reprise) .... Narrator
"Bright New Day" (Prelude) .... Mrs. Johnstone
"Long Sunday Afternoon"/"My Friend".............................. Mickey, Eddie
"Bright New Day" .... Mrs. Johnstone, Company

ACT II

"Marilyn Monroe" (Reprise) .... Mrs. Johnstone
"Shoes Upon the Table" (Reprise) .... Narrator
"That Guy".. Mickey, Eddie
"Shoes Upon the Table" (Reprise) .... Narrator
"I'm Not Saying a Word" .... Eddie
"Take a Letter, Miss Jones"........................ Mr. Lyons, Miss Jones, Ensemble
"Marilyn Monroe" (Reprise) .... Mrs. Johnstone
"Light Romance" .... Mrs. Johnstone, Narrator
"Madman".. Narrator
"Tell Me It's Not True" .... Mrs. Johnstone, Company

*Shakespeare for My Father (40). One-woman performance by Lynn Redgrave; conceived and written by Lynn Redgrave. Produced by John Clark at the Helen Hayes Theater. Opened April 26, 1993.

Directed by John Clark; lighting, Thomas R. Skelton; sound, Duncan Edwards; associate lighting designer, Beverly Emmons; production stage manager, C.A. Clark; press, Springer Associates, John Springer, Gary Springer.

Redgrave memories expressed in portrayals by Lynn of her father Michael Redgrave and others in and surrounding this family of performers, with examples of the many Shakespearean roles they filled in the course of the generations. The play was presented in two parts.

Characters From Life: Nanny, Dad, Mum, Vanessa, Corin, Roy (Grandfather), Daisy (Grandmother), Richard Burton, Laurence Olivier, Alfred Lunt, Lynn Fontanne, Maggie Smith, Noel Coward, Dame Edith Evans, Tony Richardson, Gillian (Child Actress) Miss Borchard (Teacher).

Shakespearean Scenes, Act I: "When That I Was a Little Tiny Boy" (song) from *Twelfth Night;* O Honey Nurse! What News? (Juliet, Nurse) from *Romeo and Juliet;* What Shall Cordelia Do? (Cordelia) from *King Lear;* Those Lines That I Before Have Writ Do Lie (Shakespeare) Sonnet CXV; Stay, Illusion! (Horatio) from *Hamlet;* What Must the King Do Now . . . ? and For God's Sake Let Us Sit Upon the Ground (Richard) from *Richard II;* To Be or Not To Be (Hamlet) from *Hamlet;* "O Mistress Mine" (song) from *Twelfth Night;* Give Me My Veil (Viola, Olivia, Malvolio) Willow Cabin Scene from *Twelfth Night;* Were You Not E'en Now (Viola, Malvolio) Ring Scene from *Twelfth Night.*

Shakespearean Scenes, Act II: The Quality of Mercy (Portia) from *The Merchant of Venice;* Oh My Dear Father (Cordelia, Lear) from *King Lear;* Noblest of Men, Woo't Die? and I Dreamt There Was an Emperor Antony (Cleopatra) from *Antony and Cleopatra;* "Come Away Death" (Feste) song from *Twelfth Night;* These Our Actors (Prospero) from *The Tempest;* "When That I Was a Little Tiny Boy" (Reprise) from *Twelfth Night;* If We Shadows Have Offended (Puck) from *A Midsummer Night's Dream.*

Tango Pasión (5). Dance musical conceived by Mel Howard. Produced by Mel Howard, Donald K. Donald and Irving Schwartz at the Longacre Theater. Opened April 28, 1993. (Closed May 2, 1993)

Ricardo.................	Alberto del Solar	Juan Larossa	Gustavo Russo
Pedro Montero..............	Jorge Torres	Senorita Virginia	Veronica Gardella
Lila Quintana................	Pilar Alvarez	Carmela	Alejandra Mantinan
Lucas....................	Osvaldo Ciliento	Julio Camargo	Marcelo Bernadaz

Dr. Bertolini.................	Luis Castro	Rosendo Frias	Fernando Jiminez
Senora Rosalinda		Angela...................	Judit Aberastain
Bertolini...............	Claudia Mendoza	Rodolfo..................	Daniel Bouchet
Carlos Bronco	Armando Orzuza	Flora Rosa	Yeni Patino
Senora Dora Bronco	Daniela Arcuri	Zully	Viviana Laguzzi
Grisel	Graciela Garcia	Lieutenant................	Juan Corvalan
Romero Brandan...........	Jorge Romano	Ludmilla Orlinskaya	Gunilla Wingquist

Dancing Couples: Armando & Daniela, Fernando & Judit, Gustavo & Alejandra, Jorge & Pilar, Juan & Viviana, Luis & Claudia, Marcelo & Veronica, Osvaldo & Graciela. Other Dancers: Jorge Romano, Gunilla Wingquist.

Singers: Daniel Bouchet, Alberto del Solar, Yeni Patino.

Sexteto Mayor: Jose Libertella, Luis Stazo bandoneon; Mario Abramovich, Eduardo Walczak violin; Oscar Palermo piano; Osvaldo Aulicino bass. And Thomas Giannini bandoneon; Juan Zunini keyboards, synthesizer; Jorge Orlando percussion.

Choreography, Hector Zaraspe; orchestrations, arrangements, musical direction and original music, Jose Libertella, Luis Stazo; scenery (based on paintings by Ricardo Carpani) and costumes by John Falabella; lighting, Richard Pilbrow, Dawn Chiang; sound, Jan Nebozenko; executive producer, Norman Rothstein; production stage manager, Joe Lorden; press, Boneau/Bryan-Brown, Ellen Levene.

The Argentine cast portrays Buenos Aires tango enthusiasts, inspired by Carpani decor, expressing themselves in the dance, in a Buenos Aires barroom setting. A foreign play previously produced in Buenos Aires.

Prologue: The present. Act I: The late 1940s. Act II: The present.

SCENES AND MUSICAL NUMBERS, ACT I: Mi Buenos Aires Querido; Payadora—Company; "Cafetin de Buenos Aires"—Alberto del Solar; El Internado—Armando & Daniela; El Moleston—Jorge Romano; Taquito Militar—Romano & Graciela Garcia; "Nostalgias"—Daniel Bouchet; Chique—Luis & Claudia; "Uno"—Yeni Patino; La Cumparsita; "Recitado"—del Solar; "Canto"—Bouchet; Danza—Juan & Viviana; Copete—Fernando & Judit; Milonga del 900— Gustavo Russo, Fernando Jiminez, Marcelo Bernadaz, Osvaldo Ciliento, Juan Corvalan; La Tablada—Osvaldo & Graciela; Ojos Negros—Gunilla Wingquist, Ciliento, del Solar; Hotel Victoria— Patino, Corvalan, Ciliento, Romano, Armando Orzuza, Gustavo Russo; El Firulete—Orzuza, Daniela Arcuri, Russo, Alejandra Mantinan, Luis Castro, Claudia Mendoza, Wingquist, Corvalan; Ojos Negros—Castro, Wingquist, Corvalan; Orgullo Criollo—Gustavo & Alejandra; Preludio a Francini—Luis & Claudia; "El Dia Que Me Quieras"—Bouchet, Patino; Milonga de Mis Amores— Fernando & Judit; Responso—Romano, Mendoza; Re Fa Si—Company; Canaro in Paris—Sexteto Mayor, Company.

ACT II: Rapsodia de Arrabal—del Solar, Jorge & Pilar; Bailonga—Company; Melancolico— Orzuza, Arcuri, Ciliento, Garcia; "A Media Luz"—Patino, Bouchet, Castro, Wingquist, Mantinan, Judit Aberastain, Mendoza, Veronica Gardella; Seleccion de Milongas—Corvalan, Russo, Jiminez, Romano; "Asi Se Baila el Tango"—del Solar, Arcuri, Orzuza, Bernadaz, Gardella; Quejas de Bandoneon—Jorge & Pilar; Celos—Sexteto Mayor; "Balada Para un Loco"—Castro, Pilar Alvarez, Wingquist, del Solar; Melancolico Buenos Aires—Marcelo & Veronica; Libert Tango— Garcia, Viviana Laguzzi, Mantinan, Aberastain, Ciliento, Corvalan, Russo, Jiminez; Verano Porteno—Corvalan, Romano; Fuga y Misterio—Bernadaz, Castro, Russo, Laguzzi; Adios Nonino—Sexteto Mayor; Provocacion: Paris Otonal, "Balada Para Mi Vida"—Romano, Alvarez, Company, del Solar, Patino, Bouchet; Onda 9—Company.

*Kiss of the Spider Woman (32). Musical based on the novel by Manuel Puig; book by Terrence McNally; music by John Kander; lyrics by Fred Ebb. Produced by Livent (U.S.) Inc. (Garth H. Drabinsky and Myron I. Gottlieb) at the Broadhurst Theater. Opened May 3, 1993.

Molina	Brent Carver	Esteban.................	Philip Hernandez
Warden................	Herndon Lackey	Marcos	Michael McCormick
Valentin	Anthony Crivello	Spider Woman; Aurora........	Chita Rivera

Molina's Mother . . . . Merle Louise

Marta . . . . Kirsti Carnahan

Escaping Prisoner . . . . Colton Green

Religious Fanatic;

   Prisoner . . . . John Norman Thomas

Amnesty International Observer;

   Prisoner Emilio . . . . Joshua Finkel

Prisoner Fuentes . . . . Gary Schwartz

Gabriel; Prisoner . . . . Jerry Christakos

Window Dresser at Montoya's;

   Prisoner . . . . Aurelio Padron

Aurora's Men; Prisoners: Keith McDaniel, Robert Montano, Dan O'Grady, Raymond Rodriguez.

Orchestra: Jeffrey Huard conductor; Greg Dlugos assistant conductor, keyboard II; Susan Follari concert mistress, viola I; Jeffrey Kievit 1st trumpet; Larry Lunetta 2d trumpet; Porter Poindexter trombone; Kate Dennis, Susan Panny, French horn; Al Hunt reed I; Mort Silver reed II; Richard Heckman reed III; Ken Berger reed IV; John Babich bass; John Redsecker drums; Mark Sherman percussion; Jeff Saver keyboard I; Ann Barak viola II; Matine Roach viola III; Katherine Sinsabaugh viola IV; Caryl Paisner cello.

Standbys: Misses Rivera, Carnahan—Dorothy Stanley; Miss Louise—Lorraine Foreman. Understudies: Mr. Carver—Joshua Finkel; Mr. Crivello—Philip Hernandez, Gary Schwartz; Mr. Hernandez—Gary Schwartz; Mr. McCormick—John Norman Thomas; Mr. Lackey—Michael McCormick; Mr. Christakos—Dan O'Grady; Mr. Finkel—Gary Schwartz. Swing—Gregory Mitchell; Partial Swing—Colton Green.

Directed by Harold Prince; choreography, Vincent Paterson; additional choreography, Rob Marshall; musical supervision, Jeffrey Huard; scenery and projections, Jerome Sirlin; costumes, Florence Klotz; lighting, Howell Binkley; sound, Martin Levan; orchestrations, Michael Gibson; dance music, David Krane; assistant to Mr. Prince, Ruth Mitchell; casting, Johnson-Liff & Zerman; production stage manager, Beverly Randolph; stage manager, Clayton Phillips; press, Mary Bryant (U.S.), Norman Zagier (Canada).

Time: Sometime in the recent past. Place: Latin America.

Marxist rebel and gay window decorator, thrown together as prisoners, develop a friendship as the latter diverts the former with movie plots. Previously produced in tryout 5/1/9 at SUNY Purchase, N.Y. and in Toronto and London, where it won the 1992 *Evening Standard* Award for best musical.

A Best Play; see page 208.

ACT I

Prologue . . . . Spider Woman, Prisoners

Scene 1

   "Her Name Is Aurora" . . . . Molina, Aurora, Aurora's Men, Prisoners

Scene 2

   "Over the Wall" . . . . Prisoners

Scene 3

   "Bluebloods" . . . . Molina

   "Dressing Them Up"/"I Draw the Line" . . . . Molina, Valentin

   "Dear One" . . . . Molina's Mother, Marta, Valentin, Molina

Scene 4

   "Over the Wall II" . . . . Prisoners, Molina, Valentin

Scene 5

   "Where You Are" . . . . Aurora, Aurora's Men, Prisoners

Scene 6

   "Over the Wall III—Marta" . . . . Valentin, Prisoners

Scene 7

   "Come" . . . . Spider Woman

Scene 8

   "I Do Miracles" . . . . Aurora, Marta

Scene 9

   "Gabriel's Letter"/"My First Woman" . . . . Gabriel, Valentin

Scene 10

   "Morphine Tango" . . . . Orderlies

"You Could Never Shame Me" .... Molina's Mother
"A Visit" .... Spider Woman, Molina
Scene 11
"She's a Woman" .... Molina
Scene 12
"Gimme Love" .... Aurora, Molina, Aurora's Men

ACT II

Scene 1
"Russian Movie"/"Good Times" .... Aurora, Molina, Valentin
"The Day After That" .... Valentin, Families of the Disappeared
Scene 2
"Mama, It's Me" .... Molina
Scene 3
"Anything for Him" .... Spider Woman, Molina, Valentin
Scene 4
"Kiss of the Spider Woman" .... Spider Woman
Scene 5: Molina, Valentin, Esteban, Marcos
Scene 6
"Over the Wall IV—Lucky Molina" .... Warden, Prisoners
Scene 7
"Only in the Movies" .... Molina, People in His Life

*Angels in America: Millennium Approaches (32). By Tony Kushner. Produced by Jujamcyn Theaters and Mark Taper Forum/Gordon Davidson with Margo Lion, Susan Quint
Gallin, Jon B. Platt, the Baruch-Frankel-Viertel Group and Frederick Zollo in association with Herb Alpert at the Walter Kerr Theater. Opened May 4, 1993.

Rabbi Chemelwitz; Henry; Hannah Pitt;
Ethel Rosenberg .... Kathleen Chalfant
Roy Cohn; Prior 2 .... Ron Leibman
Joe Pitt; Prior 1;
Eskimo .... David Marshall Grant
Harper Pitt; Martin
Heller .... Marcia Gay Harden

Mr. Lies; Belize .... Jeffrey Wright
Louis Ironson................ Joe Mantello
Prior Walter; Man in
the Park................ Stephen Spinella
Emily; Ella Chapter; Woman in the
South Bronx; Angel .... Ellen McLaughlin

Understudies: Messrs. Spinella, Grant, Mantello—Jay Goede; Messrs. Leibman, Mantello—
Matthew Sussman; Misses Harden, McLaughlin—Beth McDonald; Mr. Wright—Darnell Williams.

Directed by George C. Wolfe; scenery, Robin Wagner; costumes, Toni-Leslie James; lighting,
Jules Fisher; sound, Scott Lehrer; original music, Anthony Davis; executive producers, Benjamin
Mordecai, Robert Cole; produced in association with New York Shakespeare Festival; associate
producers, Dennis Grimaldi, Marilyn Hall, Ron Kastner, Hal Luftig/126 Second Avenue Corp.,
Suki Sandler; production stage manager, Perry Cline; stage managers, Mary K. Klinger, Michael
J. Passaro; press, Boneau/Bryan-Brown, Chris Boneau, Bob Fennell.

Place: New York City, Salt Lake City and elsewhere. Act I: Bad News October–November 1985.
Act II: In Vitro December 1985–January 1986. Act III: Not-Yet-Conscious, Forward Dawning
January 1986.

Subtitled A Gay Fantasia on National Themes, *Millennium Approaches* (Part I of *Angels in
America*, the second part being *Perestroika*, expected on Broadway next season) basically follows
three story lines: the demise of a violently power-hungry Roy Cohn from AIDS, the tragic separation by AIDS of a homosexual couple and the severe sexual-emotional problems of a man and wife.
Parts I and II of *Angels in America* were previously produced at the Eureka Theater, San Francisco
(1991) and at the Mark Taper Forum in Los Angeles in November 1992, winning the Pulitzer Prize.
Part I (*Millennium Approaches*) was also previously produced at the National Theater in London
(1991–92), winning the *Evening Standard* Award as the season's best new play.

A Best Play; see page 233.

PLAY WHICH CLOSED
PRIOR TO BROADWAY OPENING

A production which was organized by New York producers for Broadway presentation but which closed in 1992–93 during its production and tryout period is listed below.

Face Value. By David Henry Hwang. Produced in previews by Stuart Ostrow, Scott Rudin and Jujamcyn Theaters at the Cort Theater. Opened March 9, 1993. (Closed in previews March 14, 1993)

Randall Lee	B.D. Wong	Marci Williams	Gina Torres
Linda Ann Wing	Mia Korf	Jessica Ryan	Jane Krakowski
Bernard Sugarman	Mark Linn-Baker	Glenn Ebens	Jeff Weiss
Andrew Simpson	Michael Countryman	Pastor	Gus Rogerson

Directed by Jerry Zaks; scenery, Loy Arcenas; costumes, William Ivey Long; lighting, Paul Gallo; sound, Tony Meola; music and lyrics, David Henry Hwang; musical staging, Christopher Chadman; dance music, Mark Hummel; orchestrations, Michael Starobin; stage manager, Joe Cappelli; press, Springer Associates, Gary Springer.

Comedy of racial identity in the casting of a new Broadway musical, *The Real Manchu,* self-described as "a fairy-tale farce." The play was presented in two parts.

PLAYS PRODUCED OFF BROADWAY

Some distinctions between off-Broadway and Broadway productions at one end of the scale and off-off-Broadway productions at the other are blurred in the New York Theater of the 1990s. For the purposes of the *Best Plays* listing, the term "off Broadway" is used to distinguish a professional from a showcase (off-off-Broadway) production and signifies a show which opened for general audiences in a mid-Manhattan theater seating 499 or fewer and 1) employed an Equity cast, 2) planned a regular schedule of 8 performances a week in an open-ended run (7 a week for one-person shows) and 3) offered itself to public comment by critics at designated opening performances.

Occasional exceptions of inclusion (never of exclusion) are made to take in visiting troupes, borderline cases and nonqualifying productions which readers might expect to find in this list because they appear under an off-Broadway heading in other major sources of record.

Figures in parentheses following a play's title give number of performances. These figures do not include previews or extra non-profit performances.

Plays marked with an asterisk (*) were still in a projected run on June 1, 1993. Their number of performances is figured from opening night through May 31, 1993.

Certain programs of off-Broadway companies are exceptions to our rule of counting the number of performances from the date of the press coverage. When the official opening takes place late in the run of a play's regularly-priced public or subscription performances (after previews) we count the first performance of record, not the press date, as opening night—and in each such case in the listing we note the variance and give the press date.

In a listing of a show's numbers—dances, sketches, musical scenes, etc.—the titles of songs are identified wherever possible by their appearance in quotation marks (").

HOLDOVERS FROM PREVIOUS SEASONS

Plays which were running on June 1, 1992 are listed below. More detailed information about them appears in previous *Best Plays* volumes of appropriate date. Important cast changes since opening night are recorded in the Cast Replacements section of this volume.

*The Fantasticks (13,702; longest continuous run of record in the American theater). Musical suggested by the play *Les Romanesques* by Edmond Rostand; book and lyrics by Tom Jones; music by Harvey Schmidt. Opened May 30, 1960.

*Nunsense (3,097). Musical with book, music and lyrics by Dan Goggin. Opened December 12, 1985.

*Perfect Crime (2,501). By Warren Manzi. Opened October 16, 1987.

*Tony 'n' Tina's Wedding (1,705). By Artificial Intelligence. Opened February 6, 1988. (Editor's note: This show fits some but not all conditions of our off-Broadway category, in which it hasn't previously been listed. We list it now for informational purposes, recognizing the unique place it has made for itself on the New York theater scene.)

*Forever Plaid (1,352). Musical by Stuart Ross. Opened May 20, 1990.

Song of Singapore (459). Musical with book by Allan Katz, Erik Frandsen, Michael Garin, Robert Hipkens and Paula Lockheart; music and lyrics by Erik Frandsen, Michael Garin, Robert Hipkens and Paula Lockheart. Opened May 23, 1991. (Closed June 30, 1992)

Lips Together, Teeth Apart (406). By Terrence McNally. Opened June 25, 1991. (Closed June 27, 1992)

*Beau Jest (674). By James Sherman. Opened October 10, 1991.

*Tubes (642). Performance piece by and with Blue Man Group. Opened November 17, 1991.

Marvin's Room (214). By Scott McPherson. Opened December 5, 1991. (Closed September 6, 1992)

Sight Unseen (263). By Donald Margulies. Opened January 20, 1992. (Closed September 6, 1992)

The Substance of Fire (174). By Jon Robin Baitz. Opened February 27, 1992. (Closed July 26, 1992)

Lotto (57). By Cliff Roquemore. Opened March 15, 1992. (Changed to off-off-Broadway status May 3, 1992)

Forbidden Broadway 1992 (304). Created and written by Gerard Alessandrini. Opened April 6, 1992. (Closed December 27, 1992)

Zora Neale Hurston (60). Return engagement of the play by Laurance Holder. Opened April 29, 1992. (Closed July 5, 1992)

Ruthless! (302). Musical with book and lyrics by Joel Paley; music by Marvin Laird. Opened May 6, 1992. (Closed January 24, 1993)

Fires in the Mirror (109). Conceived, written and performed by Anna Deavere Smith. Opened May 12, 1992. (Closed August 16, 1992)

Eating Raoul (47). Musical based on the film *Eating Raoul;* book by Paul Bartel; music by Jed Feuer; lyrics by Boyd Graham. Opened May 13, 1992. (Closed June 21, 1992)

Hauptmann (22). By John Logan. Opened May 28, 1992. (Closed June 14, 1992)

PLAYS PRODUCED JUNE 1, 1992–MAY 31, 1993

Brooklyn Academy of Music. Schedule of seven productions. **Richard III** (14). Revival of the play by William Shakespeare. Opened June 9, 1992. (Closed June 21, 1992) **Les Atrides.** Repertory of four revivals in the French language: **Iphigenia in Aulis** (3) by Euripides, translated by Jean and Mayotte Bollack; **Agamemnon** (3) by Aeschylus, translated by Ariane Mnouchkine; **The Libation Bearers** (3) by Aeschylus, translated by Ariane Mnouchkine; **The Eumenides** (3) by Aeschylus, translated by Helene Cixous; presented in the Théâtre du Sol production. Opened October 1, 1992. (Closed October 11, 1992) **Peer Gynt** (5). Revival of the play by Henrik Ibsen in the Royal Dramatic Theater of Sweden production, Lars Lofgren director, in the Swedish language with simultaneous English translation; Swedish translation by Lars Forssell. Opened May 11, 1993. (Closed May 15, 1993) **Madame de Sade** (3). Revival of the play by Yukio Mishima in the Royal Dramatic Theater of Sweden production, Lars Lofgren director, in the Swedish language with simultaneous English translation; Swedish translation by Gunilla Lindberg-Wada and Per Erik Wahlund. Opened May 20, 1993. (Closed May 22, 1993) Produced by Brooklyn Academy of Music, Harvey Lichtenstein president and executive producer, *Richard III, Peer Gynt* and *Madame de Sade* at the BAM Opera House, *Les Atrides* at the Park Slope Armory.

RICHARD III

The House of York:
Edward IV . . . . Bruce Purchase
Duke of Clarence . . . . Malcolm Sinclair
Gloucester, later Richard
III . . . . Ian McKellen
(Prince of Wales) . . . . Simon Blake,
Oliver Grig, Tom Penta, Richard Puddifoot
(Duke of York) . . . . Sebastian Brennan,
James Graves, Richard Lawrence,
Marco Williamson
Duchess of York . . . . Rosalind Knight
The House of Lancaster:
Queen Margaret . . . . . . Antonia Pemberton
Lady Anne . . . . Anastasia Hille
Ghost of Henry VI . . . . Sam Beazley
The Woodvilles:
Queen Elizabeth . . . . . . Charlotte Cornwell
Lord Rivers . . . . Alan Perrin
Marquess of Dorset . . . . Paul Bazely
Lord Grey . . . . Peter Darling
Politicians:
Hastings . . . . Richard Simpson
Buckingham . . . . Terence Rigby

Stanley . . . . Richard Bremmer
Bishop of Ely . . . . David Foxxe
Lord Mayor of London . . . . . . Sam Beazley
Followers of Richard:
Catesby . . . . David Beames
Ratcliffe . . . . Tristram Wymark
Tyrrel . . . . Tim McMullan
1st Murderer; Lovel . . . Dominic Hingorani
2d Murderer . . . . Phil McKee
Officials:
Lieutenant of the Tower;
Scrivener . . . . Keith Bartlett
Keeper in the Tower;
1st Citizen . . . . Chris Walker
(Page) . . . . Simon Blake, Oliver Grig,
Tom Penta, Richard Puddifoot
Maid; Nurse; Mistress . . . . . Olivia Williams
The Tudors:
Richmond . . . . Peter Darling
Blunt . . . . David Foxxe
Herbert . . . . Richard Simpson
Oxford . . . . Bruce Purchase

(Parentheses indicate roles in which the actors alternated)

Citizens, Messengers, Soldiers: Company.

Musicians: Martin Allen percussion, Walter Fabeck keyboards, Colin Rae trumpet, drums.

Directed by Richard Eyre; design, Bob Crowley; lighting, Jean Kalman; music, Dominic Muldowney; production stage manager, Mitchell Erickson; stage manager, John Handy; press, Boneau/Bryan-Brown, Adrian Bryan-Brown, Chris Boneau, Bob Fennell.

The last major New York revival of *Richard III* took place in the New York Shakespeare Festival Shakespeare Marathon 8/3/90 for 27 performances.

LES ATRIDES

PERFORMER	"IPHIGENIA IN AULIS"	"AGAMEMNON"	"THE LIBATION BEARERS"	"THE EUMENIDES"
Simon Abkarian	Agamemnon; Achilles	Agamemnon; Messenger	Orestes; Nurse	Orestes
Miriam Azencot				Erinys
Duccio Bellugi	1st Messenger		Servant	
Juliana Carneiro da Cunha	Clytemnestra	Clytemnestra	Clytemnestra	Ghost of Clytemnestra; Athena
Daniel Domingo	Old Man			
Shahrokh Meshkin Ghalam				Apollo
Brontis Jodorowsky	Menelaus; 2d Messenger	Watchman; Aegisthus	Pylades; Aegisthus	
Nirupama Nityanandan	Iphigenia	Cassandra	Electra	Prophetess; Erinys
Catherine Schaub				Erinys

IPHIGENIA IN AULIS: Chorus Leader—Catherine Schaub; Chorists—Marc Barnaud, Duccio Bellugi, Myriam Boullay, Stephane Brodt, Sergio Canto, Nadja Djerrah, Evelyne Fagnen, Isabelle

MADAME DE SADE—Agneta Ekmanner, Anita Bjork and Margaretha Bystrom in Ingmar Bergman's Royal Dramatic Theater of Sweden production at BAM

Gazonnois, Valerie Grail, Martial Jacques, Brontis Jodorowsky, Samantha McDonald, Shahrokh Meshkin Ghalam, Christophe Rauck.

AGAMEMNON: Chorus Leaders—Simon Abkarian, Nirupama Nityanandan, Brontis Jodorowsky; Chorus Leader for the Dance—Catherine Schaub; Chorists—Marc Barnaud, Duccio Bellugi, Stephane Brodt, Sergio Canto, Laurent Clauwaert, Evelyne Fagnen, Isabelle Gazonnois, Valerie Grail, Martial Jacques, Brontis Jodorowsky, Samantha McDonald, Shahrokh Meshkin Ghalam, Christophe Rauck.

THE LIBATION BEARERS: Chorus Leader—Catherine Schaub; Chorists—Marc Barnaud, Duccio Bellugi, Myriam Boullay, Stephane Brodt, Sergio Canto, Laurent Clauwaert, Odile Delonca, Nadja Djerrah, Evelyne Fagnen, Isabelle Gazonnois, Valerie Grail, Martial Jacques, Brontis Jodorowsky, Samantha McDonald, Shahrokh Meshkin Ghalam, Christophe Rauck.

THE EUMENIDES: Chorus—Duccio Bellugi, Brontis Jodorowsky, Myriam Boullay, Stephane Brodt, Sergio Canto, Laurent Clauwaert, Daniel Domingo, Martial Jacques, Jocelyn Lagarrigue, Jean-Pierre Marry, Christophe Rauck, Nicolas Sotnikoff. Black Guards—Stephane Brodt, Nadja Djerrah, Eve Doe-Bruce, Evelyne Fagnen, Isabelle Gazonnois, Valerie Grail, Martial Jacques, Brontis Jodorowsky, Samantha McDonald, Nicolas Sotnikoff.

ALL PLAYS: Musicians—Jean-Jacques LeMêtre, Maria Serrao, Marc Barnaud.

Directed by Ariane Mnouchkine; English translations, William M. Hoffman; music, Jean-Jacques LeMêtre; scenery, Guy-Claude Francois; masks, Erhard Stiefel; costumes, Natalie Thomas, Marie-Helene Bouvet; lighting, Jean-Michel Bauer, Carlos Obregon, Cecile Allogeodt; dance direction, Simon Abkarian, Catherine Schaub, Nirupama Nityanandan; stage managers, Ly Nissay, Odile Delonca, Jean-Pierre Marry, Pedro Pinto Serra, Eve Doe-Bruce; press, Peter B. Carzasty, William Murray.

French translations (with simultaneous English translation read by Faubion Bowers) of four ancient Greek tragedies of the House of Atreus, presented in three complete ten-hour cycles of one- and two-play programs. The last major New York revivals of the plays took place as follows: *Iphigenia in Aulis* adapted as a rock musical at the Public Theater 12/16/71 for 139 performances; *Agamemnon* at the Delacorte Theater 8/2/77 for 24 performances; *The Libation Bearers (The Choephori)* and *The Eumenides (The Furies)* on the Broadway program *The House of Atreus* 12/17/68 for 17 performances.

PEER GYNT

Part I: Tales and Dreams

Ase	Bibi Andersson
Peer	Borje Ahlstedt
Aslak	Carl Magnus Dellow
Ole (Rogue)	Anders Ekborg
Finn (Rogue)	Jakob Eklund
Farmer at Haegstads	Oscar Ljung
Bridegroom	Per Mattsson
Bride's Mother	Gertie Kulle
Bride's Father	Jan Waldekranz
Synnove	Kristina Tornquist
Hilde	Gunnel Fred
Nora	Kicki Bramberg
Ingert	Anna Bjork
Solveig	Lena Endre
Solveig's Father	Tord Peterson
Solveig's Mother	Agneta Ehrensvard
Solveig's Sister Helga	Emelie Haig
Odd	Benny Haag
Egil	Thomas Hanzon
Bride Ingrid	Therese Brunnander
Nille; Herdgirl	Solveig Ternstrom
Tove; Herdgirl	Kristina Adolphson
Gerd; Herdgirl	Kicki Bramberg

Woman in Green	Gertie Kulle
Old Man at Dovre	Johan Rabaeus
Ole (His Son)	Anders Ekborg
Finn (His Son)	Jakob Eklund
Odd (His Son)	Benny Haag
Egil (His Son)	Thomas Hanzon
Synnove (His Daughter)	Kristina Tornquist
Hilde (His Daughter)	Gunnel Fred
His Wife	Kicki Bramberg
Great Grandmother	Agneta Ehrensvard
Great Grandfather Vaidur	Pierre Wilkner
Troll Child	Anna Bjork
Karl	Kristina Adolphson

Guests at the Wedding: Therese Andersson, Staffan Eek, Jesper Eriksson, Johanna Friberg, Johanna Johansson, Jukka Korpi, Pia Mucchiano, Virpi Pahkinen, Erik Winquist, Ivan Ohlin.

Bojgen: Therese Brunnander, Carl Magnus Dellow, Anders Ekborg, Jakob Eklund, Benny Haag, Thomas Hanzon, Gunnel Fred, Johanna Johansson, Jukka Korpi, Jesper Eriksson, Erik Winquist, Therese Andersson, Pia Mucchiano, Staffan Eek, Ivan Ohlin, Johanna Friberg.

Part II: Foreign Lands

Peer...................... Borje Ahlstedt
Trumpeterstrale .... Jan Waldekranz
Master Cotton .... Bjorn Granath
Monsieur Ballon .... Agneta Ehrensvard
Von Eberkopf............. Pierre Wilkner
Anitra .... Solveig Ternstrom
Asra....................... Gunnel Fred
Basra................... Kicki Bramberg
Begriffenfeldt .... Johan Rabaeus
Bearer of Mummy Apis.. Therese Brunnander
Pen .... Per Mattsson
   Other Mad People: Kristina Tornquist,
Benny Haag, Carl Magnus Dellow, Jakob Ek-
lund, Thomas Hanzon, Anders Ekborg, Jukka
Korpi, Therese Andersson, Pia Mucchiano,
Virpi Pahkinen, Erik Winquist, Ivan Ohlin.

Part III: The Homecoming

Peer..................... Borje Ahlstedt
Ship's Captain .... Tord Peterson
Strange Passenger .... Bjorn Granath

Ship's Cook .... Jakob Eklund
Aslak............... Carl Magnus Dellow
Brudgummen .... Per Mattsson
Finn....................... Gorel Crona
Ole....................... Gunnel Fred
Odd .... Kicki Bramberg
Egil .... Anna Bjork
Synnove .... Benny Haag
Hilde.................... Jakob Eklund
Nora .... Anders Ekborg
Ingert .... Thomas Hanzon
Sheriff.................... Oscar Ljung
Thoughts.................. Gertie Kulle
Songs.................. Solveig Ternstrom
Tears................. Kristina Adolphson
Ase .... Bibi Andersson
Button-Molder......... Jan-Olof Strandberg
Old Man at Dovre.......... Johan Rabaeus
Solveig...................... Lena Endre
   People at the Auction: Pia Mucchiano, Jukka
Korpi, Virpi Pahkinen, Johanna Friberg.

   Directed by Ingmar Bergman; scenery and costumes, Lennart Mork; choreography, Donya
Feuer; music, Bohuslav Martinu; lighting, Hans Akesson; sound, Jan-Eric Piper; simultaneous
translation read by Paul Luskin, Harry Carlson, Tana Ross and Eva Engman; stage manager,
Thomas Wennerberg.
   The play, in this Ingmar Bergman production, was presented in three parts. The last major New
York revival of record of *Peer Gynt* was by Classic Stage Company off Broadway 11/8/81 in two
parts for 46 performances.

MADAME DE SADE

Renee, Mme. de Sade .... Stina Ekblad
Mme. de Montreuil .... Anita Bjork
Anne .... Marie Richardson

Baroness de Simiane ... Margaretha Bystrom
Countess de Sain-Fond ... Agneta Ekmanner
Charlotte................. Helena Brodin

   Directed by Ingmar Bergman; scenery and costumes, Charles Koroly; choreography, Donya
Feuer; music, Ingrid Yoda; lighting, Sven-Eric Jacobson; sound, Jan-Eric Piper; simultaneous
translation read by Tana Ross and Eva Engman; stage manager, Stephano Mariano.
   Act I: Late summer 1977, the drawing room in the house of Madame de Montreuil. Act II:
Autumn 1778, six years later. Act III: Early spring 1790, 12 years after the second act and nine
months after the outbreak of the French revolution.
   Written in 1965 and described by its author as "de Sade seen through women's eyes." A foreign
(Japanese) play presented in this Ingmar Bergman production. The last New York revival of record
of *Madame de Sade* was by Pan Asian Repertory 4/26/88.

Red Diaper Baby (59). One-man performance by Josh Kornbluth; written by Josh Kornbluth. Produced by Michael Davis at the Actor's Playhouse. Opened June 12, 1992.
(Closed August 9, 1992)

   Directed by Joshua Mostel; scenery, Randy Benjamin; costumes, Susan Lyall; lighting, Pat
Dignan; sound, Aural Fixation; press, David Rothenberg Associates.
   The actor-author in an autobiographical comedy portrayal of a young man growing up as the son
of ardently left-wing parents on New York's Upper West Side. Previously produced off off Broad-
way by Second Stage.
   A Best Play; see pages 87, 88.

Balancing Act (56). Musical by Dan Goggin. Produced by the N.N.N. Company in association with George Graham at the Westside Theater. Opened June 15, 1992. (Closed August 2, 1992; see note)

The Main Character:	Optimistic Side . . . . Christine Toy
Ambitious Side . . . . Craig Wells	Skeptical Side . . . . J.B. Adams
Sensitive Side. . . . . Diane Fratantoni	Humorous Side . . . . Suzanne Hevner

Everybody Else (Anyone, Harriet Stottlemeier, Maisie, Mr. Revere, Jane Pickford-Bellingham, Dr. Sybil)—Nancy E. Carroll.

Musicians: Michael Rice conductor, piano; John DiPinto keyboards; Robert Falvo percussion.

Understudy: Misses Fratantoni, Toy, Hevner, Carroll—Merri Sugarman.

Directed and staged by Tony Parise and Dan Goggin; musical direction, Michael Rice; scenery, Barry Axtell; costumes, Mary Peterson; lighting, Paul Miller; sound, Craig Zaionz; orchestrations, Michael Rice, David Nyberg; production stage manager, Paul Botchis; press, The Pete Sanders Group, Robert W. Larkin.

Time: The present. Place: Hometown, U.S.A., New York and Hollywood.

An actor's efforts to succeed. Previously produced at Seven Angels Theater, Waterbury, Conn.

Note: After the end of its run, *Balancing Act* was presented on Sunday evenings beginning 8/9/92 at the Douglas Fairbanks Theater where the author's long-run musical *Nunsense* was playing.

ACT I

"Life Is a Balancing Act". . . . . Company
"Next Stop: New York City". . . . . Main Character
"Home Sweet Home". . . . . Main Character
"Play Away the Blues". . . . . Maisie
"My Bio Is a Blank". . . . . Maisie, Main Character
"A Tough Town" . . . . Main Character
"I Left You There". . . . . Sensitive Side
"A Tough Town" (Reprise) . . . . Main Character
"A Twist of Fate". . . . . Main Character
"A Casting Call". . . . . Mr. Revere, Main Character
"The Fifth From the Right" . . . . Humorous Side
"You Heard It Here First". . . . . Skeptical Side
"A Long, Long War". . . . . Optimistic Side
"The Woman of the Century". . . . . Jane, Main Character

ACT II

"Welcome, Bienvenue". . . . . Maisie
"Where Is the Rainbow" . . . . Ambitious Side
"I Am Yours". . . . . Main Character
"That Kid's Gonna Make It" . . . . Harriet
"Chew Chewy Chow". . . . . Jane, Main Character
"Hollywood 'n' Vinyl" . . . . Optimistic, Sensitive, Humorous Sides
"California Suite". . . . . Main Character, Mr. Revere
"I Am Yours" (Reprise) . . . . Main Character
"I Knew the Music". . . . . Main Character
"Next Stop: New York City" (Reprise) . . . . Main Character
"Life Is a Balancing Act" (Reprise). . . . . Company

Ethel Merman's Broadway (64). One-woman musical performance by Rita McKenzie. Produced by Eric Krebs and David Buntzman in association with Go Gi Go Productions at the John Houseman Theater. Opened June 17, 1992. (Closed August 8, 1992)

Directed by Christopher Powich; musical direction, Robert Bendorff; costumes, Gail Cooper-Hecht; lighting, Peter L. Smith; press, David Rothenberg, Terence Womble.

Ms. McKenzie as Ethel Merman in a tribute to the late Broadway star, in concert form.

Playwrights Horizons. 1991–92 schedule concluded with **Flaubert's Latest** (33). By Peter Parnell. Produced by Playwrights Horizons, Don Scardino artistic director, Paul S. Daniels executive director, at Playwrights Horizons. Opened June 21, 1992. (Closed July 19, 1992)

Colin .... Mitchell Anderson	Kuchuk Hanem .... Leila Fazel
Felix .... Mark Nelson	Gustave............... John Bedford Lloyd
Howard................ Sam Stoneburner	Louise .... Jean DeBaer
Ursula.............. Mary Louise Wilson	Jace .... Gil Bellows

Directed by David Saint; scenery, James Noone; costumes, Jane Greenwood; lighting, Kenneth Posner; original music and sound, John Gromada; dances choreographed by Paul Lester; fights, Rick Sordelet; production stage manager, William Joseph Barnes; press, Philip Rinaldi.

Flaubert returns to life to visit an American artist trying to finish Flaubert's unfinished novel.

*The Night Larry Kramer Kissed Me (309). One-man performance by David Drake; written by David Drake. Produced by Sean Strub in association with Tom Viola at the Perry Street Theater. Opened June 22, 1992. (Suspended performances January 10, 1993) Reopened February 3, 1993.

Directed by Chuck Brown; scenery, James Morgan; lighting, Tim Hunter; sound, Raymond Schilke; original music, Steven Sandberg; production stage manager, Lars Umlaut; press, Boneau/Bryan-Brown, Susanne Tighe.

David Drake, author of and performer in his solo show, *The Night Larry Kramer Kissed Me*

Sequence of Vignettes: The Birthday Triptych (Somewhere; Yeah, New York; The Night Larry Kramer Kissed Me); Owed to the Village People—Part I; Why I Go to the Gym; "12" Single;" Owed to the Village People—Part II; A Thousand Points of Light; . . . and "The Way We Were." The play was performed without an intermission.

Series of monologues depicting the childhood and New York City life of a homosexual male. Eric Paeper replaced David Drake 3/17/93.

Manhattan Theater Club. 1991–92 season concluded with **The Innocents' Crusade** (14). By Keith Reddin. Produced by Manhattan Theater Club, Lynne Meadow artistic director, Barry Grove managing director, at City Center Stage 2. Opened June 23, 1992. (Closed July 5, 1992)

Bill.....................	Stephen Mailer	Mame.....................	Debra Monk
Ms. Connell; Waitress; Ms. Cabot;		Tommy; Mr. Clancy; Mr. Coover; Evan;	
Wendy; Helen	Harriet Harris	Teller; Stephen.........	Tim Blake Nelson
Karl....................	James Rebhorn	Laura	Welker White

Directed by Mark Brokaw; scenery, Bill Clarke; costumes, Ellen McCartney; lighting, Michael R. Moody; sound, Janet Kalas; production stage manager, James FitzSimmons; press, Helene Davis, Deborah Warren.

On a trip to check out colleges with his parents, a young man embarks upon a quest for an ideal.

New York Shakespeare Festival Shakespeare Marathon. Schedule of two revivals of plays by William Shakespeare. **As You Like It** (18). Opened July 2, 1992; see note. (Closed July 26, 1992) **The Comedy of Errors** (22). Opened August 6, 1992; see note. (Closed August 30, 1992) Produced by New York Shakespeare Festival, Joseph Papp founder, JoAnne Akalaitis artistic director, Jason Steven Cohen producing director, Rosemarie Tichler artistic director, with the cooperation of the City of New York, David N. Dinkins mayor, Luis R. Cancel commissioner of cultural affairs, Betsy Gotbaum commissioner of parks & recreation, at the Delacorte Theater in Central Park.

AS YOU LIKE IT

Duke Senior	George Morfogen	Sir Oliver Mar-Text........	Boris McGiver
Duke Frederick	Larry Bryggman	Corin.....................	Brad Sullivan
Amiens	Jere Shea	Silvius	Rob Campbell
Jaques	Richard Libertini	William; Lord to	
Le Beau................	Gregory Wallace	Duke Senior..........	Michael Stuhlbarg
Charles	Mark Kenneth Smaltz	Lord to Duke Senior..........	Jim Shanklin
Oliver	Peter Jay Fernandez	Lord to Duke Frederick ...	Trellis Stepter Jr.
Jacques	Stan Cahill	Rosalind	Elizabeth McGovern
Orlando.....................	Jake Weber	Celia	Kathryn Meisle
Adam	John Scanlan	Phebe	Siobhan Fallon
Denise.....................	Viola Davis	Audrey	Kristine Nielsen
Touchstone...............	Donald Moffat		

Other Lords, Pages, Foresters, Attendants: Stan Cahill, Viola Davis, Nancy Hower, Boris McGiver, Kristine Nielsen, Jim Shanklin, Jere Shea, Mark Kenneth Smaltz, Trellis Stepter Jr., Michael Stuhlbarg, Gregory Wallace.

Understudies: Misses McGovern, Nielsen, Davis—Nancy Hower; Messrs. Weber, Smaltz, Shanklin, Stuhlbarg, Stepter—Stan Cahill; Misses Meisle, Fallon—Viola Davis; Messrs. Libertini, Moffat, Shea, Cahill—Boris McGiver; Messrs. Morfogen, Bryggman—Jim Shanklin; Messrs. Wallace, Campbell, Stuhlbarg—Trellis Stepter Jr.; Messrs. Sullivan, Scanlan, McGiver—Michael Stuhlbarg; Mr. Fernandez—Jere Shea.

Directed by Adrian Hall; music, Richard Cumming; scenery, Eugene Lee; costumes, Melina Root; lighting, Natasha Katz; dramaturge, Anne Cattaneo; production stage manager, James Bernardi; stage manager, Buzz Cohen; press, Bruce Campbell, Barbara Carroll, James L.L. Morrison.

Place: Oliver's house, the court of Duke Frederick and the Forest of Arden. The play was presented in two parts.

The last major New York revival of *As You Like It* (the 20th play to be produced in the Shakespeare Marathon) was by the Acting Company 5/22/85 for 3 performances off Broadway.

THE COMEDY OF ERRORS

Aegon . . . . Frank Raiter	Antipholus of
Duke Solinus . . . . . Helmar Augustus Cooper	Ephesus . . . . John Michael Higgins
1st Merchant; 2d Merchant. . . Joseph Palmas	Angelo. . . . . Larry Block
Antipholus of Syracuse . . . . Boyd Gaines	Nell . . . . Karla Burns
Dromio of Syracuse. . . . . Peter Jacobson	Officer . . . . Simon Billig
Dromio of Ephesus . . . . Howard Samuelsohn	Courtesan . . . . Kati Kuroda
Adriana. . . . . Marisa Tomei	Pinch. . . . . Stephen Hanan
Luciana. . . . . Kathleen McNenny	Abbess. . . . . Elizabeth Franz

Ensemble, Acrobats, Townspeople: Michael Ambrozy, Andrea Arden, Simon Billig, Robert David Carroll, Christopher Harrison, Lauren Monte, Andrew Pacho, Paul Christopher Simon, Andrea Weber.

Musicians: Regina Bellantese violin, baritone saxophone; Stephen Hanan concertina; Brian Johnson percussion; Steve Silverstein woodwinds.

Understudies: Miss McNenny—Andrea Arden; Messrs. Gaines, Higgins—Simon Billig; Messrs. Cooper, Block—Robert David Carroll; Messrs. Palmas, Hanan—Christopher Harrison; Misses Kuroda, Burns, Franz—Lauren Monte; Mr. Billig—Andrew Pacho; Messrs. Jacobson, Samuelsohn—Joseph Palmas; Miss Tomei—Andrea Weber.

Directed by Caca Rosset; original music, Mark Bennett; scenery and costumes, Jose de Anchieta Costa; lighting, Peter Kaczorowski; movement, fight and acrobatics direction, David Leong; special participation, Antigravity, Inc.; dramaturge, Jim Lewis; production stage manager, Pat Sosnow; stage manager, Liz Small.

Place: A public square in Ephesus. The play was presented in two parts.

The last major New York revival of *The Comedy of Errors* was an adaptation by The Flying Karamazov Brothers and Robert Woodruff at Lincoln Center 5/31/87 for 68 performances.

Note: Press date for *As You Like It* was 7/9/92, for *The Comedy of Errors* was 8/16/92.

Note: New York Shakespeare Festival's Shakespeare Marathon is scheduled to continue through following seasons until all of Shakespeare's plays have been presented. *A Midsummer Night's Dream, Julius Caesar* and *Romeo and Juliet* were produced in the 1987–88 season; *Much Ado About Nothing, King John, Coriolanus, Love's Labour's Lost, The Winter's Tale* and *Cymbeline* were produced in the 1988–89 season; *Twelfth Night, Titus Andronicus, Macbeth* and *Hamlet* were produced in the 1989–90 season; *The Taming of the Shrew, Richard III* and *Henry IV, Part 1* and *Part 2* were produced in the 1990–91 season, and *Othello* and *Pericles, Prince of Tyre* were produced in the 1991–92 season (see their entries in Best Plays volumes of appropriate years).

Distant Fires (54). By Kevin Heelan. Produced by the Herrick Theater Foundation in the Atlantic Theater Company production at Circle in the Square Downtown. Opened August 20, 1992. (Closed October 4, 1992)

Raymond . . . . David Wolos-Fonteno	Thomas. . . . . Ray Anthony Thomas
Angel. . . . . Todd Weeks	Beauty. . . . . Jordan Lage
Foos . . . . Giancarlo Esposito	General . . . . Jack Wallace

Understudies: Messrs. Weeks, Lage, Wallace—Todd Cattell; Messrs. Wolos-Fonteno, Esposito, Thomas—Rozwill Young.

Directed by Clark Gregg; scenery, Kevin Rigdon; costumes, Sarah Edwards; lighting, Howard Werner; executive producer, Maria Di Dia; production stage manager, James FitzSimmons; press, Peter Cromarty, David Bar Katz.

Time: The present. Place: Ocean City, Maryland. The play was presented in two parts.

Racial conflicts among construction workers on a building site. Previously presented in regional theater by the Hartford, Conn. Stage Company and off off Broadway by the Atlantic Theater Company.

1992 Young Playwrights Festival (30). Program of four one-act plays: *The P.C. Laundromat* by Aurorae Khoo, *Taking Control* by Terrance Jenkins, *Mothers Have Nine Lives* by Joanna Norland and *Mrs. Neuberger's Dead* by Robert Levy. Produced by Young Playwrights, Inc., Nancy Quinn artistic director, Sheri M. Goldhirsch managing director, in association with Playwrights Horizons at Playwrights Horizons. Opened September 15, 1992. (Closed October 11, 1992.)

The P.C. Laundromat

#1	Peter Jay Fernandez
#2	Christina Moore
#3	Erika Honda
#4	Olga Merediz

Directed by Richard Caliban; dramaturge, Morgan Jenness; stage manager, Jana Llynn.

Politics in the rhythm of washers and dryers in a laundromat.

Taking Control

Joe	Peter Jay Fernandez
Mom	Elain Graham
Nana	Novella Nelson
Nikki	Afi McClendon
Kelly	Felicia Wilson
Tarae	Bahni Turpin
Tom	Seth Gilliam

Directed by Clinton Turner Davis; dramaturge, Dennis Watlington; stage manager, Jana Llynn.

A dysfunctional family.

Mothers Have Nine Lives

Kelly	Erika Honda
Christie	Danielle Ferland
Louise; Wendy; Mia	Jennie Moreau
Gina; Katherine; Marge	Kim Yancey
Margaret; Kim; Anna	Olga Merediz

Directed by Gloria Muzio; dramaturge, Victoria Abrash; stage manager, Paul J. Smith.

Relationships between mothers and daughters.

Mrs. Neuberger's Dead

Jim	Neal Huff
Marah	Margaret Welsh
Jackie	Felicia Wilson
Aaron	Seth Gilliam

Directed by Michael Meyer; dramaturge, Morgan Jenness; stage manager, Paul J. Smith.

Young couple fighting addiction and poverty.

ALL PLAYS: Scenery, Loy Arcenas; costumes, Elsa Ward; lighting, Pat Dignan; sound, Janet Kalas; production manager, David A. Milligan; press, Alan Cohen, Pamela Johnson.

These four plays by authors 18 years old or less at the time of submission were selected from hundreds of entries in Young Playwrights, Inc.'s 11th annual playwriting contest for young people. The program was presented in two parts with the intermission following *Taking Control*.

The Roads to Home (62). By Horton Foote. Produced by Lamb's Theater Company, Carolyn Rossi Copeland producing artistic director, in association with Picture Entertainment Corporation, Lee Caplin and Mortimer Caplin producers, at the Lamb's Theater. Opened September 17, 1992. (Closed November 8, 1992)

Mabel Votaugh	Jean Stapleton	Eddie Hayhurst	William Alderson
Vonnie Hayhurst	Rochelle Oliver	Dave Dushon	Devon Abner
Annie Gayle Long	Hallie Foote	Cecil Henry	Frank Girardeau
Mr. Long	Michael Hadge	Greene Hamilton	Dan Mason
Jack Votaugh	Emmett O'Sullivan-Moore		

Directed by Horton Foote; scenery, Peter Harrison; costumes, Gweneth West; lighting, Kenneth Posner; additional costumes, D. Polly Kendrick; associate artistic director, Clark Cameron; production stage manager, Lori M. Doyle; press, Boneau/Bryan-Brown, Cabrini Lepis.

Act I, *A Nightingale*: Early April, 1924, Houston, Texas, the living room of Jack and Mabel Votaugh. Act II, *The Dearest of Friends*: Early fall, 1924, the living room of Jack and Mabel Votaugh. Act III, *Spring Dance*: Spring 1928, Austin, Tex., a garden outside an auditorium.

Three related one-acters with city-dwelling characters looking homeward nostalgically to the life and times of their youth. Previously produced at Heritage Repertory Theater, University of Virginia.

Cut the Ribbons (25). Musical revue with lyrics by Mae Richard; music by Cheryl Hardwick and Mildred Kayden; additional music by Nancy Ford. Produced by George Elmer/Phase Three Productions at the Westside Theater. Opened September 20, 1992. (Closed October 11, 1992)

Georgia Engel   Donna McKechnie
Barbara Feldon

Musicians: Sande Campbell piano, synthesizer; Ron Zito drums, percussion; Ray Kilday acoustic bass, electric bass, percussion.

Understudies: Miss Feldon—Joan Porter Hollander; Misses Engel, McKechnie—Joyce Nolen.

Directed by Sue Lawless; choreography, Sam Viverito; musical direction, Sande Campbell; scenery and lighting, Michael Hotopp; costumes, Terence O'Neill; sound, Tom Sorce; arrangements and orchestrations, Sande Campbell, Patti Wyss, Ron Zito; production stage manager, Allison Sommers; press, Peter Cromarty, David Lotz.

Relationships between mothers and daughters. In the listing below, numbers with music by Nancy

THE ROADS TO HOME—Rochelle Oliver, Hallie Foote and Jean Stapleton in a scene from Horton Foote's play

Ford are marked with an asterisk (*) and those by Cheryl Hardwick by two asterisks (**); the others are by Mildred Kayden.

MUSICAL NUMBERS, ACT I: Overture—Band; "She Loves You"—Company; "Kick Me Again"*—Donna McKechnie; "Kick Me Again" (Reprise)—Georgia Engel; "Mommy Number Four"—Barbara Feldon; "Let Her Go"*—Engel; "The Door Is Closed"*—Engel; "A Period Piece"—Company; "Let Her Go" (Reprise)—Engel; "Lookin' Good"**—Engel, McKechnie; "It's a Party"**—Engel, McKechnie; "She Loves You"—McKechnie; "Four-Two-Two"—Feldon; "Two-Two-Four"—McKechnie; "Because of Her"—Feldon, McKechnie; "Try Not to Need Her"—Feldon; "Let Her Go" (Reprise)—Engel; "Balancing"**—Company; "Mom Will Be There"—Company; "Balancing" (Reprise)—Company.

ACT II: Entr'acte—Band; "Am I Ready for This?"**—McKechnie; "Instinct"**—Feldon; "She Loves You" (Reprise)—Engel; "T'ai Chi"**—Company; "Bed"**—Feldon; "The Door Is Closed"*—McKechnie, Feldon; "Isabel"**—Feldon; "That Woman in the Mirror"**—Engel; "Where's My Picture?"—Company; "I Dare You Not To Dance"**, Take One—Feldon, Take Two—McKechnie, Take Three—Engel; "Her Career"*—Feldon; "I Just Can't Move in Her Shadow"*—McKechnie; "Cut the Ribbons"*—Feldon, McKechnie; "That Woman in the Mirror" (Reprise)—Company; "Cut the Ribbons" (Finale)—Company.

Ali (68). One-man performance by Geoffrey C. Ewing; written by Geoffrey C. Ewing and Graydon Royce. Produced by Eric Krebs Theatrical Management at the Sheridan Square Playhouse. Opened September 23, 1992. (Closed November 8, 1992)

Directed by Stephen Henderson; scenery, Sirocco D. Wilson; costumes, Ann Rubin; lighting, Robert Bessoir; sound, Tom Gould; boxing choreography, Ron Lipton; production stage manager, Patricia Flynn; press, David Rothenberg Associates.

Highlights in the life of the former world heavyweight boxing champion Cassius Clay (a.k.a. Muhammad Ali). The play was presented in two parts. Previously produced in this production off off Broadway 8/12/92.

Remembrance (142). Revival of the play by Graham Reid. Produced by David G. Richenthal and Georganne Aldrich Heller at the John Houseman Theater. Opened September 30, 1992. (Closed January 30, 1993)

Bert Andrews	Milo O'Shea	Joan Donaghy	Caroleen Feeney
Victor Andrews	John Finn	Deidre Donaghy	Terry Donnelly
Theresa Donaghy	Frances Sternhagen	Jenny Andrews	Mia Dillon

Understudies: Miss Sternhagen—Peg Small; Messrs. O'Shea, Finn—Ross Bickell; Misses Dillon, Donnelly, Feeney—Elinore O'Connell.

Directed by Terence Lamude; scenery, Bill Stabile; costumes, Barbara Forbes; lighting, John McLain; sound, Tom Gould; production stage manager, Susan Whelan; stage manager, Robin Horowitz; press, Jeffrey Richards Associates, David LeShay.

Remembrance was previously produced in New York off off Broadway in 1990 and off Broadway 4/16/91 for 40 performances by the Irish Arts Center. The play was presented in two parts.

Manhattan Theater Club. Schedule of nine programs. **Mad Forest** (70). Return engagement of the New York Theater Workshop production of the play by Caryl Churchill. Opened October 1, 1992. (Closed November 29, 1992) **Joined at the Head** (41). By Catherine Butterfield. Opened November 15, 1992. (Closed December 20, 1992) **The Last Yankee** (37). By Arthur Miller. Opened January 21, 1993. (Closed February 28, 1993) **The Years** (24). By Cindy Lou Johnson. Opened January 24, 1993. (Closed February 14, 1993) **Pretty Fire** (30). One-woman performance by Charlayne Woodard; written by Charlayne Woodard. Opened March 26, 1993. (Closed April 29, 1993) **Jenny Keeps Talking** (30). One-woman performance by Leslie Ayvazian; written by Richard Greenberg. Opened April 8, 1993. (Closed May 2, 1993) **Sondheim—Putting It Together** (59).

Musical revue with music and lyrics by Stephen Sondheim. Opened April 1, 1993. (Closed May 23, 1993) And *Playland* by Athol Fugard scheduled to open 6/8/93 and *A Perfect Ganesh* by Terrence McNally scheduled to open 6/27/93. Produced by Manhattan Theater Club, Lynne Meadow artistic director, Barry Grove managing director, at the City Center Theater, *Mad Forest, The Years, Sondheim—Putting It Together* at Stage I, *Joined at the Head, The Last Yankee, Pretty Fire, Jenny Keeps Talking* at Stage II.

MAD FOREST

Vladu Family:
Bogdan.................. Lanny Flaherty
Irina .... Randy Danson
Lucia .... Calista Flockhart
Florina..................... Mary Mara
Gabriel.............. Tim Blake Nelson
Rodica; Grandmother....... Mary Shultz
Wayne .... Christopher McCann
Grandfather; Old Aunt....... Rocco Sisto
Antonescu Family:
Mihai .... Christopher McCann
Flavia..................... Mary Shultz
Radu .... Jake Weber
Grandmother............ Randy Danson
Ianos................... Garret Dillahunt
Securitate Man; Angel; Patient; Toma;
Ghost; Waiter .... Rob Campbell

Doctor; Priest; Vampire; Someone With
Sore Throat................. Rocco Sisto
Dog................. Christopher McCann
Soldiers in Rodica's
Nightmare ... Lanny Flaherty, Rocco Sisto
Act II:
Painter .... Garret Dillahunt
Girl Student................. Mary Mara
Boy Students.. Rob Campbell, Tim Nelson
Translator .... Lanny Flaherty
Bulldozer Driver ..... Christopher McCann
Securitate Officer............. Rocco Sisto
Soldier .... Jake Weber
Student Doctor .... Calista Flockhart
Flower Seller .... Randy Danson
House Painter .... Mary Shultz
Others..................... Company

Understudies: Robin Moseley, Kimber Riddle, Michael Stuhlbarg, Tom Tammi.

Directed by Mark Wing-Davey; scenery and costumes, Marina Draghici; lighting, Christopher Akerlind; sound, Mark Bennett; fight direction, David Leong; dialect coach, Deborah Hecht; associate artistic director, Michael Bush; general manager, Victoria Bailey; production stage manager, Thom Widmann; stage manager, Cathleen Wolfe; press, Helene Davis, Deborah Warren.

Time: November 22 through December 29, 1990. Act I: Lucia's wedding. Act II: December. Act III: Florina's wedding. The play was presented in two parts with the intermission following Act II.

A foreign play previously produced at the Central School of Speech and Drama, London; the National Theater, Bucharest; the Royal Court Theater, London; and in this production off off Broadway December 4, 1991 for 54 performances and a citation as a Best Play of last season.

JOINED AT THE HEAD

Maggie Mulroney .... Ellen Parker
1st College Boy; Bill the Waiter;
Others..................... Neal Huff
2d College Boy; Crystal Salesman;
Others................... Michael Wells
1st Political Woman; Doctor;
Others.............. Sharon Washington

2d Political Woman; Nora;
Others.................. Elizabeth Perry
Engaged Man; Raymond
Terwilliger; Others ...... John C. Vennema
Engaged Woman; Coat Check Girl;
Others..................... Becca Lish
Jim Burroughs .... Kevin O'Rourke
Maggy Burroughs ..... Catherine Butterfield

Directed by Pamela Berlin; scenery, James Noone; costumes, Alvin B. Perry; lighting, Natasha Katz; sound, John Kilgore; production stage manager, Karen Moore; stage manager, Mark McMahon.

Place: In and around Boston. The play was presented in two parts.

A valiant woman's battle against cancer, viewed by a onetime close friend of the husband who can't come to grips with the invalid's suffering.

A Best Play; see page 165.

THE LAST YANKEE

Leroy Hamilton	John Heard	Patricia Hamilton	Frances Conroy
John Frick	Tom Aldredge	Karen Frick	Rose Gregorio
Patient	Charlotte Maier		

Directed by John Tillinger; scenery, John Lee Beatty; costumes, Jane Greenwood; lighting, Dennis Parichy; sound, Scott Lehrer; production stage manager, Diane DiVita; stage manager, Robert V. Thurber.

Place: A state mental hospital. The play was presented without intermission.

Wives and husbands reveal themselves and their two problematical marriages after meeting by chance in a hospital waiting room. Previously produced in an earlier version at Ensemble Studio Theater.

THE YEARS

Bartholomew	Paul McCrane	Andrew	Frank Whaley
Andrea	Nancy Hower	Eloise	Julie Hagerty
Isabella	Marcia Gay Harden	Jeffrey	William Fichtner

Understudies: Messrs. McCrane, Whaley, Fichtner—Larry Green; Miss Hower—Wendy Lawless; Misses Harden, Hagerty—Elizabeth Cuthrell.

Directed by Jack Hofsiss; scenery, Loren Sherman; costumes, Lindsay W. Davis; lighting, Peter Kaczorowski; sound, John Kilgore; fight staging, Jerry Mitchell; production stage manager, Thomas A. Kelly; stage manager, Thom Widmann.

Time: The present and over a 16-year period. The play was presented in two parts.

The whole and parts of a family examined in a series of crises.

PRETTY FIRE

Directed by Pamela Berlin; scenery, Shelley Barclay; costumes, Rita Ryack; lighting, Brian Nason; sound, Bruce Ellman; production stage manager, Allison Sommers.

Act I: *Birth, Nigger, Pretty Fire.* Act II: *Bonesy, Joy.*

Charlayne Woodard as herself in five episodes from her childhood.

JENNY KEEPS TALKING

Directed by Risa Bramon Garcia; scenery, Shelley Barclay; costumes, Rita Ryack; lighting, Brian Nason; sound, Bruce Ellman; production stage manager, Buzz Cohen.

Leslie Ayvazian as two sisters, one embittered, the other an enthusiast, and finally their grandmother. The play was presented in two parts and an epilogue. Previously produced off off Broadway at Ensemble Studio Theater in a shorter version with authorship credited to the pseudonym "Lise Erlich."

SONDHEIM—PUTTING IT TOGETHER

Julie Andrews	Michael Rupert
Stephen Collins	Rachel York
Christopher Durang	

Orchestra: Scott Frankel conductor, keyboard I; Joseph Thalken associate conductor, keyboard II; John Babich bass; Fred Landes drums, percussion.

Standbys: Miss Andrews—Jeanne Lehman; Mr. Collins—Dennis Parlato; Messrs. Durang, Rupert—Patrick Quinn; Ms. York—Juliet Lambert.

Directed by Julia McKenzie; musical staging, Bob Avian; musical direction, Scott Frankel; scenery, Robin Wagner; costumes, Theoni V. Aldredge; lighting, Tharon Musser; sound, Scott Lehrer; musical arrangements, Chris Walker; production stage manager, Franklin Keysar; stage manager, Pat Sosnow.

Couple entertaining guests in a New York penthouse is the frame for a generous collection of Sondheim numbers from his productions.

MUSICAL NUMBERS, ACT I: "Invocation and Instructions" (from *The Frogs*), "Putting It Together" (from *Sunday in the Park With George*), "Rich and Happy" and "Merrily We Roll Along" (from *Merrily We Roll Along*), "Lovely" and "Everybody Ought to Have a Maid" (from *A Funny Thing Happened on the Way to the Forum*); Sequence—"Sooner or Later" (from *Dick Tracy*), "I'm Calm" and "Impossible" (from *A Funny Thing Happened on the Way to the Forum*) and "Ah, But Underneath . . . !" (from the London *Follies*); "Hello Little Girl" (from *Into the Woods*), "My Husband the Pig"/"Every Day a Little Death" (from *A Little Night Music*), "Have I Got a Girl for You" (from *Company*), "Pretty Women" (from *Sweeney Todd*), "Now" and "Bang!" (from *A Little Night Music*), "Country House" (from the London *Follies*), "Could I Leave You?" (from *Follies*).

ACT II: "Entr'acte"/"Back in Business" (from *Dick Tracy*), "Rich and Happy" (Reprise, from *Merrily We Roll Along*), "Night Waltzes" (from *A Little Night Music*), "Gun Song" (from *Assassins*), "The Miller's Son" (from *A Little Night Music*), "Live Alone and Like It" (from *Dick Tracy*), "Sorry-Grateful" (from *Company*), "Sweet Polly Plunkett" (from *Sweeney Todd*), "I Could Drive a Person Crazy," "Marry Me a Little," "Getting Married Today" and "Being Alive" (from *Company*), "Like It Was" and "Old Friends" (from *Merrily We Roll Along*), "Putting It Together" (Reprise, from *Sunday in the Park With George*).

The Holy Terror (14). By Simon Gray. Produced by John A. McQuiggan and Donald L. Taffner in association with Diana Bliss and W. Scott & Nancy McLucas at the Promenade Theater. Opened October 8, 1992. (Closed October 18, 1992)

Mark Melon	Daniel Gerroll	Josh Melon	Noel Derecki
Edward Ewart Gladstone	Michael McGuire	Gladys Powers	Kristine Nielsen
Samantha Eggerley	Lily Knight	Kate Melon	Kristin Griffith
Michael; Jacob; Rupert;			
Graeme	Anthony Fusco		

Directed by Simon Gray; scenery, David Jenkins; costumes, David Murin; lighting, Beverly Emmons; production stage manager, George Darveris; press, Boneau/Bryan-Brown, Cabrini Lepis.

Time: Between the present and the last 15 years. Place: The Cheltenham Women's Institute and The Memory. The play was presented in two parts.

A publisher reviews events in his life in a strenuous effort to find himself and regain lost equilibrium. A foreign play previously produced in London.

New York Shakespeare Festival. Schedule of nine programs. **You Could Be Home Now** (25). One-woman performance by Ann Magnuson; written by Ann Magnuson; produced in the Women's Project & Productions production, Julia Miles artistic director, Jennifer Greenfield managing director. Opened October 11, 1992. (Closed November 1, 1992) **Texts for Nothing** (25). One-man performance by Bill Irwin; adapted by Joseph Chaikin and Steven Kent from the work by Samuel Beckett. Opened November 1, 1992. (Closed November 22, 1992) **Mo' Madness: A Festival of New Voices** (14). Multi-presentational program, George C. Wolfe curator. Opened December 1, 1992. (Closed December 13, 1992) **Woyzeck** (33). Revival of the play by Georg Buchner; translated by Henry J. Schmidt. Opened December 6, 1992. (Closed January 3, 1993) **On the Open Road** (74). By Steve Tesich. Opened February 16, 1993. (Closed March 7, 1993) **Wings** (47). Musical based on the play *Wings* by Arthur Kopit; book and lyrics by Arthur Perlman; music by Jeffrey Lunden. Opened March 9, 1993. (Closed April 18, 1993)

Also **Memory Tricks** (15) one-woman performance by Marga Gomez; written by Marga Gomez, and **Deep in a Dream of You** (16) one-man performance by David Cale; written by David Cale, original music by Roy Nathanson, presented in repertory. Opened April 4, 1993. (Closed April 25, 1993) **Marisol** (22). By Jose Rivera; produced

ON THE OPEN ROAD—Byron Jennings and Anthony
LaPaglia in a scene from the play by Steve Tesich

in association with the Hartford Stage Company, Mark Lamos artistic director, David
Hawkanson managing director. Opened May 20, 1993. (Closed June 6, 1993) Produced
by New York Shakespeare Festival, Joseph Papp founder, JoAnne Akalaitis artistic
director (George C. Wolfe producer as of 3/18/93), Jason Steven Cohen producing
director (managing director as of 3/18/93), Kevin Kline and Rosemarie Tichler artistic
associates, at the Joseph Papp Public Theater (see note).

YOU COULD BE HOME NOW

Directed by David Schweizer; original music and songs composed by Tom Judson; choreography,
Jerry Mitchell; scenery, Bill Clarke; costumes, Pilar Limosner; lighting, Heather Carson; sound, Eric
Liljestrand; "Folk Song" written by Ann Magnuson; "West Virginia's Home to Me" written by
Lyell B. Clay; sound inspirations, Tom Hawk, Galen Wade; choreography for Ballet of the Fourth
Estate, William Fleet Lively; production supervisor, Bill Barnes, press, Bruce Campbell, Barbara
Carroll, James L.L. Morrison.

Reflections on home in a series of monologues, songs, dances and character studies. The play was
presented in two parts.

TEXTS FOR NOTHING

Directed by Joseph Chaikin; scenery, Christine Jones; costumes, Mary Brecht; lighting, Beverly
Emmons; sound, Gene Ricciardi; production stage manager, Ruth Kreshka.

Adaptation of Beckett's 1955 philosophical fiction *Texts for Nothing,* ending with a brief passage from Beckett's *How It Is* (1961). Previously produced as *Texts* in experimental workshop by New York Shakespeare Festival 3/8/81 for 18 performances.

WOYZECK

Franz Woyzeck	Jesse Borrego	Carnival Showman; Karl	Richard Spore
Marie	Sheila Tousey	Christian	David E. Cantler
Captain	Zach Grenier	1st Apprentice; Carnival	
Doctor	Denis O'Hare	Worker	Robert Cicchini
Drum Major	Lou Milione	Grandmother	Ruth Maleczech
Sergeant	Michael Early	Carnival Worker	Camryn Manheim
Andres	Bruce Beatty	Girls	Pauline E. Meyer, Imani Parks
Margret	Anita Hollander	Musicians	Ashley Mac Isaac, Louis Tucci
Carnival Barker; 2d			
Apprentice	Michael Stuhlbarg		

Townspeople, Soldiers, Science Students: Robert Cicchini, Denis O'Hare, Michael Stuhlbarg, Louis Tucci, LaTonya Borsay, Lynn Hawley, Camryn Manheim.

Directed by JoAnne Akalaitis; scenery, Marina Draghici; costumes, Gabriel Berry; lighting, Mimi Jordan Sherin; sound, John Gromada; original music, Philip Glass; lyrics, Paul Schmidt; fight direction, David Leong; step dancing, Ashley MacIsaac; other movement, Jess Borrego, Juliette Carillo; film, JoAnne Akalaitis, with Jesse Borrego as Lenz; dramaturge, Bill Coco; traditional music of Cape Breton Island performed by Ashley Mac Isaac; production stage manager, Mireya Hepner; stage manager, Mark Dobrow.

The last major New York revival of *Woyzeck* was by Classic Stage Company off Broadway 3/23/81 for 30 performances. In this production the play was presented without intermission.

MO' MADNESS:
A FESTIVAL OF NEW VOICES

Festival schedule comprised the following programs:

Christopher Columbus 1992 by and with Roger Guenveur Smith; live sound design by Marc Anthony Thompson, December 1 and 5.

El Cacique Cholo in the Land of Nepantla by and with George Emilio Sanchez; director and dramaturge, Joseph Di Mattia; aria from *La Forza del Destino;* slides by *Relief Sculpture From Ancient Mexico.* December 1 and 5.

Assimilation by and with Shishir Kurup; directed and designed by Page Leong. December 2 and 4.

L.A. Real performed by Rose Portillo; conceived, written and directed by Theresa Chavez; original music, Luis Perez Ixoneztli; photo researcher, Kim Lee Kahn; scenery, Tulsa Kinney; historical consultation, Norman Klein. December 2 and 4.

Kissing and Telling: Songs About Life and the Pursuit of Love by and with Alva Rogers; Gordon Chambers vocals, Diedre Murray cello, Marvin Sewell guitar, John Sherman accordion, Wendy Ultman violin. December 3 and 6.

Memory Tricks by and with Marga Gomez; developed by Marga Gomez with David Ford; directed by David Ford. December 3 and 6.

Big Mama Nem—A Work-in-Progress by and with Phyllis Yvonne Stickney. December 4.

I Think, Therefore I Is by and with Ken Roberson; additional performance by Michelle M. Robinson; musical direction, Darius Frowner. December 6 and 13.

VivaLasVegas'ploitationclambakin' to the Beat by and with Stephanie Jones and Suzanne Y. Jones; directed by Celina Davis. With Brian Soul and the U.ltra F.unky O.rchestra. December 6 and 13.

Symbiosis choreography and scene design, Sham Mosher; original music by Adam Plack; and *Petals of the Moon* conceived and directed by Sham Mosher with Leslie Findlen; choreography and scene design, Sham Mosher; both with Sham Mosher. December 8 and 10.

Corner Store Geography—A Work-in-Progress by and with Han Ong; title slides by Chris

Komuro; photo slides by Ming Ma, Luis Alfaro and Kelly Stuart; sound recording, Guillermo Hernandez. December 8 and 10.

P.C. . . . Not Just for the Politically Correct by and with Chris Creighton-Kelly; directed by Teri Snelgrove and Dennis Maracle; additional performance by Chantell Jolly. December 9 and 11.

WOMB/man WARs by and with Judith Alexa Jackson; directed by Paul McIsaac; video technician, Steve Harris; original lighting design, Howard Thies. December 9 and 11.

The Haphazard Cabaret with Vernon Reid, comprising: *The Legendary Crowations* with the Brewery Puppet Troupe, directed by Brad Brewer; *Snapshot of Remembered Friends* with Niki Davis and Vernon Reid; *Pipe* with Garland Farwell, Eileen Kelly and Wesley Clarke; *Gringo's Paradise?* with Patricia Hoffbauer, Peter Bullock and Peter Richards, direction and concept by Patricia Hoffbauer; *Manner* with Greg Hubbard; *I'm an African American But I Was Born a Negro* with Judith Alexa Jackson; *At a Loss?—A Structured Improv* with Cynthia Oliver, original music by Jayson Finkelman; *Rhythmic Antidote* with David Pleasant; *After Virtue* with Viola Sheely and Jim Mertens; *An Improvisation* with Hank Smith; *In the Image of a Darker Truth* with Marlies Yearby and Carl Hancock Rux, text by Carl Hancock Rux, choreography and direction by Marlies Yearby, original music by Don Meissner. December 12.

Second annual festival of performance, music and dance, described by its curator George C. Wolfe as offering "a unique collective view of America from artists of radically divergent backgrounds and performance styles."

ON THE OPEN ROAD

Angel	Anthony LaPaglia	Monk	Henry Stram
Al	Byron Jennings	Jesus	Andy Taylor
Little Girl	Ilana Seagull	Boy	Sean Nelson

Directed by Robert Falls; scenery, Donald Eastman; costumes, Gabriel Berry; lighting, Kenneth Posner; sound score, John Gromada; production stage manager, Peggy Imbrie; stage manager, Andrew Neal.

Time: A time of civil war. Place: A place of civil war. The play was presented in two parts.

Mankind's future at stake in a strife-torn, unnamed country. Previously produced by the Goodman Theater, Chicago.

WINGS

Emily (Tues.–Sat. eves.)	Linda Stephens	Nurse; Mrs. Timmins	Ora Jones
Emily (mats. & Sun. eve.)	Rita Gardner	Amy	Hollis Resnik
Doctor; Mr. Brambilla	William Brown	Billy	Ross Lehman

Orchestra: Bradley Vieth conductor, keyboard I; Alex Rybeck keyboard II; William Kerr flute, clarinet; Diane Barere cello; Andrew Jones percussion.

Directed by Michael Maggio; scenery and projections, Linda Buchanan; costumes, Birgit Rattenborg Wise; lighting, Robert Christen; sound, Richard Woodbury; musical direction, Bradley Vieth; production stage manager, Deya S. Friedman.

Time: Over a period of two years. The play was performed without intermission.

Female wing-walker suffers a crippling stroke. Previously produced by the Goodman Theater, Chicago.

A Best Play; see page 194.

MEMORY TRICKS

Directed by Roberta Levitow; developed by Marga Gomez and David Ford; production design, Linda Buchanan; sound, Jeff Bova; stage manager, Liz Dreyer.

Reflections on her childhood, with portrayals of her parents, by Marga Gomez. The play was presented without intermission. Previously produced at U.C. San Diego Theater Festival and elsewhere.

DEEP IN A DREAM OF YOU

Directed by David Petrarca; production design, Linda Buchanan; sound, Rob Milburn; production stage manager, Liz Dreyer.

Twelve monologues by and with David Cale portraying people with erotic obsessions. The play was presented without intermission. Previously produced at the Goodman Theater, Chicago.

MARISOL

Angel.................... Danitra Vance	June.................... Anne O'Sullivan
Marisol................ Cordelia Gonzalez	Woman With Furs; Radio
Young Woman........... Doris Difarnecio	Announcer............. Phyllis Somerville
Man With Golf Club; Man With Ice	Guitarist .... Chris Cunningham
Cream; Lenny; Man With Scar	
Tissue.................... Skip Sudduth	

Voices, Homeless People: Doris Difarnecio, Decater James, Robert Jiminez, Anne O'Sullivan, Phyllis Somerville.

Directed by Michael Greif; scenery, Debra Booth; costumes, Angela Wendt; lighting, Kenneth Posner; sound, David Budries; violence director, David Leong; original music, Jill Jaffe; production stage manager, Lori M. Doyle; stage manager, Mark McMahon.

Time: The present, winter. Place: New York City. The play was presented in two parts.

Young career woman needs a guardian angel to get by in the violent New York of today. Previously produced in the 1992 Humana Festival of New American Plays at Actors Theater of Louisville.

Note: In the Joseph Papp Public Theater there are many auditoria. *You Could Be Home Now, On the Open Road* and *Marisol* played Martinson Hall; *Texts for Nothing, Memory Tricks* and *Deep in a Dream of You* played the Susan Stein Shiva Theater; *Woyzeck* and *Wings* played the Estelle R. Newman Theater; the programs of *Mo' Madness* played both the Susan Stein Shiva and Anspacher Theaters.

Jacques Brel Is Alive and Well and Living in Paris (131). 25th anniversary revival of the musical revue with conception, English lyrics and additional material by Eric Blau and Mort Shuman, based on Jacques Brel's lyrics and commentary; music by Jacques Brel, Francois Rauber, Gerard Jouannest and Jean Corti. Produced by Blue Curl Productions, Inc., in association with Philis Raskind, Harold L. Strauss and Stuart Zimberg at the Village Gate. Opened October 18, 1992. (Closed February 7, 1993)

Gabriel Barre	Joseph Neal
Andrea Green	Karen Saunders

Directed by Elly Stone; musical direction, Annie Lebeaux; additional movement, Gabriel Barre; scenery, Don Jensen; costumes, Mary Brecht; lighting, Graeme F. McDonnell; sound, Arnold Finkelstein; production stage manager, Phillip Price; stage manager, Arnold Finkelstein; press, M.J. Boyer.

Musicians: Annie Lebeaux conductor, pianist; Gregory M. Utzig electric guitar, mandolin; Daniel L. O'Brien acoustic bass; Eddie Caccavale percussion, marimba, chimes.

Jacques Brel Is Alive and Well, etc. opened off Broadway at the Village Gate 1/22/68 and ran for 1,847 performances, moved to Broadway 9/15/72 for 51 performances and returned to off Broadway 5/17/74 in a 125-performance revival.

MUSICAL NUMBERS, ACT I: Overture—Orchestra; "My Childhood"—Andrea Green; "Marathon"—Company; "Alone"—Joseph Neal; "Madelaine"—Company; "I Loved"—Karen Saunders; "Mathilde"—Gabriel Barre; "Bachelor's Dance"—Neal; "Timid Friede"—Green, Company; "My Death"—Saunders; "Girls and Dogs"—Neal, Green; "Jackie"—Barre; "Statue"—Neal; "The Desperate Ones"—Company; "Sons Of"—Saunders; "Port of Amsterdam"—Barre, Company.

ACT II: "The Bulls"—Barre, Company; "Old Folks"—Neal, Company; "Marieke"—Green,

Company; "Brussels"—Saunders, Company; "Fanette"—Neal; "Funeral Tango"—Barre, Company; "Middle Class"—Barre, Neal; "No Love You're Not Alone"—Green; "Next—Barre; "Carousel"—Saunders, Company; "If We Only Have Love"—Company.

The Madame MacAdam Travelling Theater (17). By Thomas Kilroy. Produced by The Irish Repertory Theater Company, Inc., Charlotte Moore and Ciaran O'Reilly artistic directors, and One World Arts Foundation, W. Scott McLucas executive director, in the Irish Repertory Theater Company production at the Actors' Playhouse. Opened October 18, 1992. (Closed November 1, 1992)

Madame MacAdam	Denise duMaurier	Jo	Rosemary Fine
Bun Bourke	Michael Judd	The Dog	Attila
1st LDF Man; Chamberlain	Dennis O'Neill	Sergeant	Michael O'Sullivan
2d LDF Man; Slipper; Simon;		Lyle Jones	W.B. Brydon
Young Maher	Brian F. O'Byrne	Sally	Ellen Adamson
Marie Therese	Fiona McCormac	Rabe	Ciaran O'Reilly

Directed by Charlotte Moore; scenery, David Raphel; costumes, David Toser; lighting, Kenneth Posner; sound, James M. Bay; production stage manager, Pamela Edlington; stage manager, Chris A. Kelly; press, Boneau/Bryan-Brown, Susanne Tighe.

Time: Fall, 1941, over a period of several days. Place: a small village in the south of Ireland. The play was presented in two parts.

English theater troupe is stuck in a small Irish town during World War II. A foreign play previously produced in Ireland.

*Circle Repertory Company. Schedule of four programs. **The Destiny of Me** (175). By Larry Kramer. Opened October 20, 1992. (Closed March 21, 1993) **Orpheus in Love** (22). Opera with words by Craig Lucas; music by Gerald Busby. Opened December 15, 1992. (Closed January 3, 1993) ***Three Hotels** (64). By Jon Robin Baitz. Opened April 6, 1993. **And Baby Makes Seven** (22). By Paula Vogel. Opened April 27, 1993. (Closed May 23, 1993) Produced by Circle Repertory Company, Tanya Berezin artistic director, Abigail Evans managing director, *The Destiny of Me* and *And Baby Makes Seven* presented by special arrangement with Lucille Lortel at the Lucille Lortel Theater, *Orpheus in Love* and *Three Hotels* at Circle Repertory.

THE DESTINY OF ME

Ned Weeks	Jonathan Hadary	Richard Weeks	David Spielberg
Nurse Hanniman	Oni Faida Lampley	Rena Weeks	Piper Laurie
Dr. Anthony Della Vida	Bruce McCarty	Benjamin Weeks	Peter Frechette
Alexander Weeks	John Cameron Mitchell		

Directed by Marshall W. Mason; scenery, John Lee Beatty; costumes, Melina Root; lighting, Dennis Parichy; original music, Peter Kater; sound, Chuck London, Stewart Werner; fight direction, Nels Hennum; production stage manager, Fred Reinglas; press, Bill Evans & Associates, Jim Randolph.

Continuing the drama of Ned Weeks, leader of the AIDS activist movement, ten years after Larry Kramer first presented this autobiographically-based material and character in the landmark drama *The Normal Heart* at the Public Theater 4/21/85 for 295 performances.

Ralph Waite replaced David Spielberg 12/1/93. Carole Shelley replaced Piper Laurie 12/8/93. A Best Play; see page 104.

ORPHEUS IN LOVE

Bass	Bradley Garvin	Bassoonist	Daniel Shelly
Bassoonist	Stephen Wisner	Mezzo Soprano	Belinda Pigeon

Soprano	Diane Ketchie	Double Bass Player	Michel Taddei
Violinist	Christina Sunnerstam	Tenor	Steven Goldstein
Violist	Scott Slapin	Pianist	Eleanor Sandresky
Cellist	Nancy Ives	Musical Director	Charles Prince

Directed by Kirsten Sanderson; musical direction, Charles Prince; scenery, Derek McLane; costumes, Walter Hicklin; lighting, Debra J. Kletter; sound effects, Stewart Werner; production stage manager, M.A. Howard; press, Bill Evans & Associates, Jim Randolph, Erin Dunn.

Place: A small community college.

The Orpheus legend superimposed on the music students and others in a college community: in the first act, Orpheus tries to sleep and dreams of his first piano, his father and a mysterious woman; in the second act, Orpheus (as a viola teacher) relives the love of his life (for Eurydice, a young student).

ACT I: Sleepsong

"Sleepsong" .... Bass, Two Bassoonists
"Little Fingers" .... Soprano
"Outdoor Quartet" .... String Players
"The Cello Lecture" .... Tenor, Cellist
"Intentional Walk" .... Bass, Soprano, Violinist, Double Bass Player
"Viola" .... Mezzo Soprano, Bass, Violist

ACT II: Orpheus in Love

"Orpheus in Love" .... Entire Company

THREE HOTELS

Kenneth Hoyle... Ron Rifkin
Barbara Hoyle .... Christine Lahti

Directed by Joe Mantello; scenery, Loy Arcenas; costumes, Jess Goldstein; lighting, Brian MacDevitt; sound, Scott Lehrer; original music, Rick Baitz; production stage manager, M.A. Howard.

Part I: The Halt & the Lame (Tangier, Morocco). Part II: Be Careful (St. Thomas, Virgin Islands). Part III: The Day of the Dead (Oaxaca, Mexico). The play was presented without intermission.

Executive of an international baby-formula company and his wife express themselves and their views on corporate responsibility in a series of monologues.

Debra Monk replaced Christine Lahti 5/11/93.

AND BABY MAKES SEVEN

Peter	Peter Frechette	Anna	Cherry Jones
Ruth	Mary Mara		

The Children: Cecil Bartholemew—Cherry Jones; Henri Dumont, Orphan McDermott—Mary Mara.

Directed by Calvin Skaggs; scenery, Derek McLane; costumes, Walter Hicklin; lighting, Peter Kaczorowski; sound, Donna Riley; incidental music, Evan Morris; production stage manager, Leslie Loeb.

Time: The present. Place: A loft apartment in New York City.

A *menage a trois* (lesbian lovers and a gay male companion) awaits the birth of a baby while playing childhood games.

*Lincoln Center Theater. Schedule of two programs. **The Sisters Rosensweig** (149). By Wendy Wasserstein. Opened October 22, 1992. (Closed February 28, 1993 and transferred to Broadway; see its entry in the Plays Produced on Broadway section of this volume) ***Playboy of the West Indies** (25). By Mustapha Matura. Opened May 9, 1993. Produced by Lincoln Center Theater, Andre Bishop and Bernard Gersten directors, at the Mitzi E. Newhouse Theater.

THREE HOTELS—Christine Lahti *(above)* and Ron Rifkin *(right)* in scenes from the Jon Robin Baitz play produced by Circle Repertory Company. These two comprise the entire cast but never are onstage in a scene together in a script composed of three monologues

THE SISTERS ROSENSWEIG

Tess Goode. . . . . Julie Dretzin	Mervyn Kant . . . . Robert Klein
Pfeni Rosensweig . . . . . . Frances McDormand	Gorgeous Teitelbaum . . . . . . Madeline Kahn
Sara Goode . . . . Jane Alexander	Tom Valiunus. . . . . Patrick Fitzgerald
Geoffrey Duncan . . . . John Vickery	Nicholas Pym . . . . Rex Robbins

Standbys: Miss Dretzin—Nile Lanning; Miss McDormand—Robin Moseley; Misses Alexander, Kahn—Lucy Martin; Mr. Vickery—Stephen Stout; Messrs. Klein, Robbins—Stan Lachow; Mr. Fitzgerald—Jonathan Friedman.

Directed by Daniel Sullivan; scenery, John Lee Beatty; costumes, Jane Greenwood; lighting, Pat Collins; sound, Guy Sherman/Aural Fixation; production stage manager, Roy Harris; stage manager, Elise-Ann Konstantin; press, Merle Debuskey, Susan Chicoine.

Time: A weekend in late August, 1991. Place: A sitting room in Queen Anne's Gate, London. The play was presented in two parts

The character and relationship of three Brooklyn-born sisters celebrating the eldest's birthday. A Best Play; see page 126.

PLAYBOY OF THE WEST INDIES

Peggy. . . . . Lorraine Toussaint	Ken . . . . Victor Love
Stanley . . . . Darryl Theirse	Mama Benin. . . . . Michele Shay
Phil . . . . Arthur French	Alice . . . . Kelly Taffe
Jimmy. . . . . Akin Babatunde	Ivy. . . . . Melissa Murray
Mikey . . . . Antonio Fargas	Mac. Terry Alexander

Citizens of Mayaro: Lou Ferguson, Elain Graham, Simi Junior, Adrian Roberts.

Musicians: Gerald Rampersad flute, Ian Japsi drums, Lloyd Boodoo bass, Larry Marsden guitar.

Understudies: Miss Toussaint—Simi Junior, Elain Graham; Messrs. Theirse, Love—Adrian Roberts; Messrs. French, Babatunde, Alexander—Lou Ferguson; Mr. Fargas—Arthur French; Miss Shay—Elain Graham; Misses Taffe, Murray—Simi Junior.

Directed by Gerald Gutierrez; scenery, John Lee Beatty; costumes, Paul Tazewell; lighting, James F. Ingalls; sound, Serge Ossorguine; original music, Andre Tanker; fight direction, David Leong; production stage manager, Michael Brunner; stage manager, Alexis Shorter.

Place: A fishing village on the east coast of Trinidad. A rum shop. Act I: 9:30 p.m. Friday. Act II: 9:30 a.m. Saturday. Act III: 5 p.m. the same day.

John Millington Synge's 1921 *Playboy of the Western World* transposed to Mayaro, Trinidad in 1950. The play was presented in three parts.

*Oleanna (249). By David Mamet. Produced by Frederick M. Zollo, Mitchell Maxwell, Alan Schuster, Peggy Hill Rosenkranz, Ron Kastner, Thomas Viertel, Steven Baruch, and Frank and Woji Gero, in association with Patricia Wolff, in the Back Bay Theater Company production, at the Orpheum Theater. Opened October 25, 1992.

John .... William H. Macy
Carol... Rebecca Pidgeon

Understudies: Mr. Macy—Jim Frangione; Miss Pidgeon—Mary McCann.

Directed by David Mamet; scenery, Michael Merritt; costumes, Harriet Voyt; lighting, Kevin Rigdon; associate producers, D'Addario/Sine Ltd., Dan Markley, Kevin McCollum; production stage manager, Carol Avery; press, Bill Evans.

Place: John's office. The play was presented in three scenes with the intermission following Scene 1.

A college professor suffers an undergraduate student's charges of sexual harrassment. Previously produced in regional theater by the Back Bay Theater Company in association with American Repertory Theater in Cambridge, Mass.

Mary McCann replaced Rebecca Pidgeon 1/26/93. Treat Williams replaced William H. Macy 3/31/93.

A Best Play; see page 150.

Spic-O-Rama (86). One-man performance by John Leguizamo; written by John Leguizamo. Produced by the Westside Theater, Marshall B. Purdy and Michael S. Bregman at the Westside Theater. Opened October 27, 1992. (Closed January 24, 1993)

Developed and directed by Peter Askin; scenery, Loy Arcenas; lighting, Natasha Katz; sound, Dan Moses Schreier; video designer, Dennis Diamond; musical supervisor, Jellybean Benitez; production stage manager, Michael Robin; press, Philip Rinaldi.

John Leguizamo portraying various members of the grievously troubled Gigante family, as seen through the eyes of a 9-year-old. The play was presented without intermission. Previously produced in regional theater by the Goodman Theater, Chicago, in association with Latino Chicago Theater Company.

A Best Play; see pages 87, 95.

FILM CREDITS

Film 1

Mr. Gabrielli	Joe Sharkey
Ivan	Hedil Noel
Puchi	Jesus Fernandez
Andre	Ricardo Bones
Quique	Carlos Fernandez
Malaria	Betsaida Aguiller

Phenomena	Julia Reyes
Eurasia	Jennifer Alicea

Film 2

Yvonne	Yelba Matamoros
Chewy	Johnny Ray
Boulevard	John Ortiz
Desert Storm Soldier	"Ninja" Peter Torres

Film 3

Females: Eileen Shea, Cathy Carlson, Justina Machado, Keli Carter, Linda Buchanan, Julieann Trowbridge, Carrie Chantler, Marcela Munoz, Theresa Tetley.

Film 4

Vanna Blanca . . . . Tammi Cubilette

Film 5

M.C. . . . . Steven Solis
Yolanda . . . . Elle Thompson
Ishmael's Tush. . . . . Giovanni Vergara
Uncle Brother . . . . Sergio Leguizamo
Aunt Oephelia . . . . Ofelia Pelaez
Offstage Voice of Gladys: Waleska Coindet

Bubbe Meises Bubbe Stories (186). One-woman musical performance by Ellen Gould; written by Ellen Gould; original songs by Holly Gewandter and Ellen Gould. Produced by Richard Frankel, Paragon Park Productions and Renee Blau at the Cherry Lane Theater. Opened October 29, 1992. (Closed March 21, 1993)

Directed by Gloria Muzio; musical direction, arrangements and pianist, Bob Goldstone; scenery, David Jenkins; costumes, Elsa Ward; lighting, Peter Kaczorowski; sound, Raymond D. Schilke; associate producer, Marc Routh; production stage manager, Stacey Fleischer; press, Boneau/Bryan-Brown, Jackie Green.

Musical play in tribute to the author's grandmothers (bubbes) who emigrated to America at the turn of the century. The play was presented without intermission.

MUSICAL NUMBERS: "Bubbe Meises Bubbe Stories," "You're Dancing Inside Me," "The Road I'm Taking," "Take More Out of Life" music and lyrics by Ellen Gould; "Fifty-Fifty" music by Joseph Romshinsky, lyrics by Louis Gilrod, English lyrics by Jacques Levy, Zalman Mlotok, Moishe Rosenfeld and Bruce Adler; "Oy, How I Hate That Fellow Nathan" music by Albert Von Tilzer, lyrics by Lew Brown; "Oy, I Like Him" (based on "Oy, I Like She") by Aaron Lebedeff and Alexander Olshanetsky, English lyrics by Jacques Levy; "It's a Bubbe Meise" music and lyrics by Holly Gewandter and Ellen Gould; "The Bridge Song" (The Bubbe Rag) music by Scott Joplin, lyrics by Holly Gewandter and Ellen Gould; "Goldstein, Swank & Gordon," "Chocolate Covered Cherries" music and lyrics by Holly Gewandter.

American Place Theater. Schedule of three programs. **Dog Logic** (15). By Thomas Strelich. Opened November 8, 1992. (Closed November 22, 1992) **The Confessions of Stepin Fetchit** (19). One-man performance by Roscoe Orman as Stepin Fetchit; written by Matt Robinson. Opened March 21, 1993. (Closed April 11, 1993) **On the Way Home** (26). One-man performance by Stephen Wade; written and collected by Stephen Wade; presented in the Merrywang, Inc. production. Opened April 24, 1993. (Closed May 23, 1993) Produced by American Place Theater, Wynn Handman director, Dara Hershman general manager, at American Place Theater.

DOG LOGIC

Hertel . . . . Darrell Larson
Dale. . . . . Joe Clancy

Kaye . . . . Karen Young
Anita. . . . . Lois Smith

Understudies: Misses Smith, Young—Joanne Pattavina; Messrs. Larson, Clancy—James McCauley.

Directed by Darrell Larson; scenery and costumes, Kert Lundell; lighting, Jan Kroeze; composers, Paul Lacques, Richard Lawrence; sound, Tristan Wilson; production stage manager, Anne Marie Paolucci; stage manager, Althea Watson; press, David Rothenberg Associates, Meg Gordean.

Pet cemetery caretaker vs. real estate interests. Previously produced at South Coast Repertory, Costa Mesa, Calif. The play was presented in two parts.

THE CONFESSIONS OF STEPIN FETCHIT

Directed by Bill Lathan; scenery, Kert Lundell; costumes, Judy Dearing; lighting, Shirley Prendergast; sound, Robert LaPierre; movement consultant, Hank Smith; production stage manager, Jacqui Casto.

Roscoe Orman as the popular black motion picture performer of the 1930s, "Stepin Fetchit" (Lincoln Perry), in the ups and downs of his prominent career. The play was presented without intermission.

ON THE WAY HOME

Directed by Milton Kramer; scenery and lighting, Milton Kramer; production stage manager, Michael Robin.

Stephen Wade with banjo and guitar accompanying his program of folklore tales. The show was presented in two parts. Previously produced in May 1989 in Washington, D.C. and on a national tour with Wade's *Banjo Dancing*.

*Playwrights Horizons. Schedule of three programs. **On the Bum, or The Next Train Through** (31). By Neal Bell. Opened November 18, 1992. (Closed December 13, 1992) **The Heliotrope Bouquet by Scott Joplin & Louis Chauvin** (25). By Eric Overmyer, based on a libretto by Eric Overmyer from an idea of Roger Trefousse. Opened February 28, 1993. (Closed March 21, 1993) ***Later Life** (9). By A.R. Gurney. Opened May 23, 1993. Produced by Playwrights Horizons, Don Scardino artistic director, Paul S. Daniels executive director, at Playwrights Horizons.

ON THE BUM, or THE NEXT TRAIN THROUGH

CAST: Eleanor Ames—Cynthia Nixon; Archie, Cop 2, Gresham, Out-of-Work Man 3, Fisherman 2, Bumfork Tramp 2—Jim Fyfe; Farker, Frank—Campbell Scott; Western Union Man, Winston—William Duell; Lila, Jessie—Joyce Reehling; Stagehand, Elmo (Cop 1), Out-of-Work Man 2, Fisherman 3, Bumfork Tramp 3, Spectacle Inspector—Bill Buell; Burley, Victor—Robert Hogan; Tramp 1, Out-of-Work Man 1, Fisherman 1, Bumfork Tramp 1, Headless Ghost, Hansford—Ross Salinger; Tramp 2, Harry—Kevin Geer; Tramp 3, Gil—James Rebhorn; Maud, Lula—Maureen Shay; Norma—J. Smith-Cameron; Oskar—John Benjamin Hickey.

Directed by Don Scardino; scenery, Allen Moyer; costumes, Sharon Lynch; lighting, Kenneth Posner; sound, John Gromada; associate artistic director, Nicholas Martin; production stage manager, Dianne Trulock; stage manager, David Hyslop; press, Philip Rinaldi.

Time: Summer of 1938. Place: New York and Bumfork, the Midwest. The play was presented in two parts.

The government and the arts: out-of-work actress goes from New York to the Midwest to work in a Federal Theater Project in the Depression era.

THE HELIOTROPE BOUQUET BY SCOTT JOPLIN & LOUIS CHAUVIN

Joplin .... Delroy Lindo	Trick John; Disappearing
Spanish Mary; Lottie; Belle ... Donna Biscoe	Sam .... Ramon Moses
Hannah.................... Tonye Patano	Turpin..................... Mike Hodge
Spice .... Amber Kain	Keeler .... Steve Harris
Joy........................ Lisa Arrindell	Chauvin .... Duane Boutté
Felicity .... Kim Yancey	Stark .... Herb Foster

Piano Player—Terry Waldo.

Directed by Joe Morton; period dances choreographed by Louis Johnson; scenery, Richard Hoover; costumes, Judy Dearing; lighting, Phillip Monat; sound, Bruce Odland; piano arrangements, Terry Waldo; production stage manager, Lloyd Davis Jr.

Time and place: A Harlem rooming house, Christmas Eve 1917, where Scott Joplin lives with his second wife, Lottie; in Dream, New Orleans, circa 1900, in a sporting house called The House of Blue Light; in the Rosebud Cafe, St. Louis, 1905; in Chicago, 1906, in an opium den called The Sportin' Life. The play was presented without intermission.

Events of Scott Joplin's life, including his friendship with the composer Louis Chauvin. Previously produced at CenterStage, Baltimore.

LATER LIFE

Ruth . . . . Maureen Anderman	Other Women . . . . Carole Shelley
Austin . . . . Charles Kimbrough	Other Men . . . . Anthony Heald

Directed by Don Scardino; scenery, Ben Edwards; costumes, Jennifer Von Mayrhauser; lighting, Brian MacDevitt; sound, Guy Sherman/Aural Fixation; production stage manager, Dianne Trulock; stage manager, John Handy.

Time: A September evening. Place: The terrace of a high-rise apartment building, overlooking Boston Harbor. The play was presented without intermission.

Comedy about unrequited love and second chances, as a man and a woman meet after not seeing each other for 30 years.

A Best Play; see page 251.

Program for Murder (17). By George W. George and Jeff Travers. Produced by Dick Feldman and Ralph Roseman in association with Frederick M. & Patricia Supper at the Variety Arts Theater. Opened November 22, 1992. (Closed December 6, 1992)

Jeremy . . . . Anthony Cummings	Frank . . . . Stephen Van Benschoten
Brenda . . . . Colleen Quinn	Alan . . . . Jon Krupp
Elizabeth . . . . Mary Kay Adams	Denny . . . . Jill Susan Margolis

Cast also includes Don Howard. Understudies: Mr. Cummings—Don Howard; Mr. Krupp—Richard Cuneo; Misses Quinn, Margolis, Adams—Ellen Lancaster; Mr. Van Benschoten—Gary Rayppy.

Directed by Allen Schoer; scenery, Edward T. Gianfrancesco; costumes, Deborah Shaw; lighting, Natasha Katz; special effects, Gregory Meeh; sound, Guy Sherman/Aural Fixation; production stage manager, Brian Meister; stage manager, Richard Cuneo; press, Jeffrey Richards Associates, David LeShay, Diane Judge, Tom D'Ambrosio.

Time: The present. Place: A Victorian house in Cambridge, Mass. The play was presented in two parts.

Thinking computer helps his beleagured master to plan a murder.

CBS Live (6). Series of episodes taken from or recreating popular TV shows; *I Love Lucy* material written by Jess Oppenheimer, Madelyn Pugh and Bob Carroll Jr.; *The Honeymooners* material written by Marvin Marx and Walter Stone; new material by Bob Bejan, Ben Garant, Michael Schwartz and S. Sydney Weiss. Produced by Polygram Diversified Theatrical Entertainment, Rascoff Zysblatt Organization executive producers, in the Controlled Entropy Entertainment, Inc. production at the Minetta Lane Theater. Opened December 1, 1992. (Closed December 6, 1992)

THE HONEYMOONERS

	"BETTER LIVING THROUGH TELEVISION"	"MAMA LOVES MAMBO"
Bob Ari	Ralph	Ralph
Jonathan Bustle	Norton	Norton
Suzanne Dawson		Mrs. Stevens
Patricia Masters	Trixie	Trixie
Marcus Neville		Carlos Sanchez
Hardy Rawls	Stage Manager	Mr. Manicotti
Sue Rihr		Mrs. Manicotti
Dana Vance	Alice	Alice

I LOVE LUCY

	"LUCY IS ENCEINTE"	"LUCY DOES A TV COMMERCIAL"
Bob Ari		Joe
Jonathan Bustle	Tony	Ross Elliott
Suzanne Dawson	Lucy	Lucy
Marcus Neville	Ricky	Ricky
Hardy Rawls	Fred	Fred
Sue Rihr	Ethel	

WORLDS COLLIDE

	"1"	"2"
Bob Ari	Ralph	Ralph
Jonathan Bustle	Norton	Norton
Suzanne Dawson	Lucy	Lucy
Patricia Masters	Trixie	
Marcus Neville	Cop	Ricky
Hardy Rawls	Butcher	Fred
Sue Rihr	Ethel	Ethel
Dana Vance		Alice

Understudies: Mr. Ari—Hardy Rawls; Misses Dawson, Rihr, Vance, Masters—Kim Cea.

Directed by Bob Bejan; scenic and mixed media imagery, Cubic B's; costumes, hair and makeup, Thomas Augustine; lighting, Peggy Eisenhauer; video montages, Ira H. Gallen; production stage manager, Allison Sommers; press, Cromarty & Company, Diane L. Blackman.

Music: Theme from *I Love Lucy* by H. Adamson and E. Daniel; theme from *The Twilight Zone* by M. Constant; "We're Having a Baby" ("My Baby and Me") by H. Adamson and Vernon Duke; "Granada" by A. Lara; "The Lady in Red" by A. Wrubell and M. Dixon; "Pisa Moreno" by TBA.

Self-described "multimediagraphic" presentation combining live action and videotape, imagining that TV waves of old shows can be received—and sometimes mixed up (*Worlds Collide 1* includes material from *The Freezer* in *I Love Lucy; Worlds Collide 2* includes material from *TV or Not TV* in *The Honeymooners*).

*Hello Muddah, Hello Fadduh (199). Musical revue with music and lyrics by Allan Sherman; conceived and written by Douglas Bernstein and Rob Krausz. Produced by Diane F. Krausz, Jennifer R. Manocherian and David A. Blumberg at Circle in the Square Downtown. Opened December 5, 1992.

Stephen Berger	Paul Kreppel
Tovah Feldshuh	Mary Testa
Jason Graae	

Directed and choreographed by Michael Leeds; musical direction and vocal arrangements, David Evans; scenery, Michael E. Downs; costumes, Susan Branch; lighting, Howard Werner; sound, Tom Morse; orchestrations, David Lawrence; production stage manager, R. Wade Jackson; press, Cromarty & Company, Peter Cromarty, David Bar Katz.

Life in a Florida retirement community as a framework for a selection of song numbers written by Allan Sherman, who died in 1973.

MUSICAL NUMBERS, ACT I: "Opening Goulash," "Sarah Jackman," "Disraeli," "Sir Greenbaum's Madrigal," "Good Advice," "I Can't Dance," "Kiss of Myer," "Hello Muddah, Hello Fadduh," "No One's Perfect," "One Hippopotami," "Phil's Medley," "Harvey and Sheila."

HELLO MUDDAH, HELLO FADDUH—Stephen Berger, Scott Robertson, Tovah Feldshuh, Jason Graae, and Leslie Klein in the new musical by Douglas Bernstein and Rob Krausz based on Allan Sherman's writings

ACT II: "Shake Hands With Your Uncle Max," "Here's to the Crabgrass," "Harvey Bloom," "Mexican Hat Dance," "Grow, Mrs. Goldfarb," "Jump Down, Spin Around," "Crazy Downtown," "Did I Ever Really Live?"*, "Like Yours,"* "Down the Drain,"* "The Ballad of Harry Lewis."
*Music by Albert Hague.
Scott Robertson replaced Paul Kreppel and Leslie Klein replaced Mary Testa 12/92.

Manhattan Moves (45). All-dancing musical revue choreographed by Michael Kessler; music by various authors (see listing below). Produced by M & M American Dance Theater, David H. Peipers and Virginia L. Dean at American Place Theater. Opened December 17, 1992. (Closed January 24, 1993)

Ms. Biz	Adrienne Armstrong	Officer Wiz	Barry Wizoreck
Con Eddie	Kevin Gaudin	Flash	Michael Kessler
Mr. Mahvuss	Andre George	Star	Melinda Jackson
Bodyworkit	El Tahra Ibrahim		

Directed by Michael Kessler; costumes, Geff Rhian; lighting, Randy Becker; sound, Ted Rothstein; musical arrangements, Jon Gordon; production stage manager, Randy Becker; stage manager, Rebecca Kreinin; press, Susan L. Schulman.
Twenty scenes with a recorded score, depicting life in Manhattan.

ACT I: New York Day—"The Street"

Manhattan Moves.. Company
   (music and lyrics written and sung by Michael Kessler)
Rhapsody in Blue Jeans .... Star, Flash, Company
   (based on a theme by George Gershwin)
Subway... Company
   (music and lyrics by John Kander and Fred Ebb, Jon Gordon, Melinda Jackson, M. Kessler)
Wall Street................... Ms. Biz, Officer Wiz, Con Eddie, Mr. Mahvuss, Bodyworkit
   (music and lyrics by Brock Walsh and Mark Goldenberg, sung by the Pointer Sisters)
Taxi................... Flash, Con Eddie, Officer Wiz, Mr. Mahvuss, Bodyworkit
   (music and lyrics by John Lennon and Paul McCartney, sung by Bobby McFerrin)
Eat .... Star, Officer Wiz, Con Eddie, Mr. Mahvuss
   (music and lyrics by Donna Summer and Michael Omartian, sung by Donna Summer)
Faux Pas de la Dee Dah... Company
   (music by Peter Tchaikowsky)
Lambatomy .... Company
   (music and lyrics by E.E. Garcia, performed by Miami Sound Machine; music by Amilcare
   Ponchielli)
Central Park...................... Flash, Mr. Mahvuss, Officer Wiz, Bodyworkit, Ms. Biz
   (music and lyrics by M. Mainieri, B. Martin and James Brown, performed by Steps Ahead and
   James Brown)
Bad News..................................... Con Eddie, Officer Wiz, Mr. Mahvuss
   (music and lyrics written and sung by Michael Kessler)
"Face the Music" .... Star, Flash
   (music and lyrics by Irving Berlin, sung by Michael Kessler)

ACT II: New York Night—"The Stage"

On Broadway.. Company
   (music and lyrics by B. Mann, C. Weil, J. Leiber and M. Stoller, sung by George Benson)
Panther... Company
   (music written and performed by Henry Mancini)
Spies .... Company
   (music by Jay Graydon, Alan Paul and David Foster, lyrics by Alan Paul, sung by The
   Manhattan Transfer)
Mermaid... Star, Flash
   (music by Mindy Jostyn, Jon Gordon and Michael Kessler, sung by Mindy Jostyn)
Ritz......................... Ms. Biz, Bodyworkit, Con Eddie, Officer Wiz, Mr. Mahvuss
   (music and lyrics by Irving Berlin, sung by Michael Kessler)
Star Spangled Breakdown........ Bodyworkit, Con Eddie, Officer Wiz, Mr. Mahvuss, Ms. Biz
   (music, "The Star Spangled Banner" by Francis Scott Key, guitars by J. Gordon)
Rainbow... Flash, Star
   (music and lyrics by Harold Arlen, sung by Joan Osborne)
Rhapsody on Broadway .... Company
   (music by Jon Gordon and Michael Kessler after themes by Mann, Weill, Leiber, Stoller and
   Gershwin)
Manhattan Moves.. Company
   (music and lyrics written and sung by Michael Kessler)

Madison Avenue (48). Cabaret musical with book by Paul Streitz; music by Gary Cherpakov and Robert Moehl; lyrics by Paul Streitz and Gary Cherpakov. Produced by Paul Streitz at the Lone Star Theater. Opened December 29, 1992 (see note). (Closed February 7, 1993)

Women on the Move........ Randi Cooper,   Bruce Singer................. Donald Fish
   Michelle McDermott, Sarah Laine Terrell   Honeydew Plushbottom ...... Nicole Sislian
Alice O'Connor .... Jordan Church   Media Rep .... Tony Rossi
J. Quinby IV............... Bill Goodman

Directed and choreographed by David C. Wright; musical direction, Joel Maisano; scenery and lighting, Chris O'Leary; costumes, Brenda Burton; sound, Frank Papitio; music and vocal arrangements, Robert Marks; production stage manager, Lisa Anne Kofod; press, Jeffrey Richards Associates, David LeShay.

Subtitled "The Subliminal Musical," a melange of housewives, secretaries, media executives, etc., stirred in a bubbling cauldron.

Note: *Madison Avenue* opened as dinner theater at the Lone Star Cafe 10/31/92 but changed to off-Broadway cabaret status as of 12/29/92.

ACT I

"Women on the Move"	Women
"A Woman at Home"	Men
"Something for Me"	Alice
"All a Matter of Strategy"	Quinby, Bruce, Plushbottom
"Thirty Seconds"	Quinby, Alice
"Client Service"	Plushbottom
"L.A. Freeway"	Media Rep
"Office Romance"	Alice, Bruce
"Typical American Consumer"	Market Researcher, Company

ACT II

"Residuals"	Krystal, Alexis
"Leonardo's Lemonade," "Lennie's Lemonade," "Leonard's Lemonade"	Bruce
"It's Not a Commercial, It's Art"	Mr. Howard
"Squeeze, Squeeze, Squeeze"	Lemons
"Thirty Seconds" (Reprise)	Quinby
"The Look"	Alice, Plushbottom
"Upper East Side Blues"	Alice
"Thirty Seconds" (Reprise)	Quinby
"Madison Avenue"	Alice, Company

*Forbidden Broadway 1993 (160). Musical revue created and written by Gerard Alessandrini. Produced by Jonathan Scharer at Theater East. Opened January 12, 1993.

<table>
<tr><td>Susanne Blakeslee</td><td>Brad Oscar</td></tr>
<tr><td>Brad Ellis</td><td>Craig Wells</td></tr>
<tr><td>Dorothy Kiara</td><td></td></tr>
</table>

Directed by Gerard Alessandrini; costumes, Erika Dyson; wigs, Teresa Vuoso; production consultant, Pete Blue; musical direction, Brad Ellis; assistant director, Phillip George; associate producer, Chip Quigley; production stage manager, Jim Griffith; press, Shirley Herz Associates, Glenna Freedman.

New edition of the revue sending up currently popular New York stage attractions. The show was presented in two parts

Note: A special holiday edition of this show entitled *Forbidden Broadway Featuring Forbidden Christmas* was presented at Theater East 12/1/92–12/27/92, following the closing of *Forbidden Broadway 1992.*

*Wrong Turn at Lungfish (113). By Garry Marshall and Lowell Ganz. Produced by James B. Freydberg, Jeffrey Ash and Kenneth D. Greenblatt at the Promenade Theater. Opened February 21, 1993.

Peter Ravenswaal	George C. Scott	Anita Merendino	Jami Gertz
Nurse	Kelli Williams	Dominic De Caesar	Tony Danza

Understudies: Mr. Scott—Stephen Pearlman; Misses Williams, Gertz—Stephanie Niznik; Mr. Danza—Victor Colicchio.

Directed by Garry Marshall; scenery, David Jenkins; costumes, Erin Quigley; lighting, Peter

Kaczorowski; sound, Tom Morse; associate producers, Jean Van Tuyle, Sandra B. Greenblatt, John Goldman; production stage manager, Wm. Hare; press, Boneau/Bryan-Brown, Chris Boneau, Cabrini Lepis.

Time: The present. Place: A hospital room somewhere in New York City. Act I, Scene 1: Noon. Scene 2: Another day, noon. Scene III: Another day, evening. Act II, Scene 1: The next day, mid-morning. Scene 2: Several hours later.

Comedy, a streetwise young woman brightens the life of an ailing and irritable college professor. Previously produced in regional theater at Steppenwolf in Chicago.

Garry Marshall replaced George C. Scott 5/4/93. Fritz Weaver replaced Garry Marshall, Michael R. Knight replaced Tony Danza, Calista Flockhart replaced Jami Gertz and Kathleen Marshall replaced Kelli Williams 5/18/93.

*Jeffrey (99). By Paul Rudnick. Produced by Thomas Viertel, Richard Frankel, Steven Baruch, Jack Viertel, Mitchell Maxwell and Alan Schuster in the WPA Theater production (Kyle Renick, artistic director) at the Minetta Lane Theater. Opened March 6, 1993.

Jeffrey . . . . John Michael Higgins
Man in Bed; Gym Rat; Skip Winkly;
  Casting Director; Waiter in Headdress;
  Man #2 with Debra; Man in Jockstrap;
  Thug #2; Dave; Angelique . . . Patrick Kerr
Man in Bed; Gym Rat; Salesman; The
  Boss; Man #1 with Debra; Man in
  Chaps; Thug #1; Young Priest;
  Sean . . . . Darryl Theirse

Man in Bed; Gym Rat; Don; Tim; Dad;
  Father Dan; Chuck Farling . . . Richard Poe
Man in Bed; Darius . . . . Bryan Batt
Man in Bed; Sterling . . . . Edward Hibbert
Man in Bed; Steve . . . . Tom Hewitt
Woman in Bed; Showgirl; Ann Marwood
  Bartle; Debra Moorhouse; Sharon; Mom;
  Mrs. Marcangelo . . . . Harriet Harris

Directed by Christopher Ashley; scenery and projections, James Youmans; costumes, David C. Woolard; lighting, Donald Holder; sound, Donna Riley; musical staging, Jerry Mitchell; executive producer, Richard Frankel Productions, Marc Routh; associate producer, Peter Breger; production stage manager, John F. Sullivan; stage manager, Robbie Young; press, Boneau/Bryan-Brown, Chris Boneau, Craig Karpel.

Time: The present. Place: New York. The play was presented in two parts.

The AIDS crisis and its tragedies viewed from the angle of black humor. Transfer of the off-off-Broadway production.

A Best Play; see page 182.

The Best of Friends (41). By Hugh Whitemore. Produced by Stonebridge Presentations, The Producer Circle Co. and Pyramid Enterprises, by arrangement with Michael Redington, at the Westside Theater. Opened March 7, 1993. (Closed April 11, 1993)

Sir Sydney Cockerell . . . . . . Michael Allinson
George Bernard Shaw . . . . Roy Dotrice

Dame Laurentia MacLachlan . Diana Douglas

Standbys: Messrs. Allinson, Dotrice—Edwin J. McDonough; Miss Douglas—Victoria Boothby.

Directed by William Partlan; scenery, Robert Klingelhoefer; costumes, Edi Giguere; lighting, Tina Charney; sound, Michael Croswell; production stage manager, Ed Fitzgerald; press, Shirley Herz Associates, Shirley Herz, Glenna Freedman.

Time: 1924 through 1962. Place: A memory of Ayot St. Lawrence, 21 Kew Gardens Road and Stanbrook Abbey.

Exchanges of ideas on various subjects among three real-life friends: a playright, a nun and a gentleman. A foreign play previously produced in London and in America at the Cricket Theater, Minneapolis and in Chester, Mass.

Aven' U Boys (48). By Frank Pugliese. Produced by Ron Kastner, William B. O'Boyle, Sonny Everett and Evangeline Morphos at the John Houseman Theater. Opened March 8, 1993. (Closed April 18, 1993)

AVEN' U BOYS—Cynthia Martells and Adrian Pasdar in a scene from the play by Frank Pugliese

Wendy	Lili Taylor	Ed	Ron Eldard
Ann	Lucinda Jenney	Charlie	Michael Imperioli
Linda	Cynthia Martells	Rocky	Adrian Pasdar

Understudy: Miss Martells—Adina Porter.

Directed by Frederick Zollo; scenery, Kert Lundell; costumes, Carol Oditz; lighting, Jan Kroeze; sound, John Kilgore; fight staging, B.H. Barry; associate producer, Randy Finch; production stage manager, Eric S. Osbun; press, Bill Evans & Associates, Jim Randolph.

Time—Act I: Then, and then, and then. Act II: Now, tonight.

The lives of three young men of Italian extraction, living in Bensonhurst, are affected by the beating of a black man.

The Second Annual Heart o' Texas Eczema Telethon (80). By Mark Dunn. Produced by Thomas Weekley and Tomarq Productions at Actors' Playhouse. Opened March 16, 1993. (Closed May 23, 1993)

Mickey Cutler	Todd Chayet	Arletta Kirby	Jennifer Tulchin
Drummer	Anthony Marchionda Jr.	Buddy Towers	Deny Staggs
Keyboardist	Kevin Jones	Tanya Towers	Elizabeth Ragsdale
Guitarist	Raymond Bally	Mime	Christopher Casoria
Gladiola Pilbeam	Sherry Locher	Jordon Isles	Wallace Wilhoit
Russ Roulez	Stephen Bauer	Ricky Duval	Adam J. Weinberg
Pristine Gibbons	Jennifer Rose	Beauty Bandit	Shannon Malone
Eve Adams	Julie Hays	Camera Person #1	Chris Northup
Sue Kwan Ling	Nancy Flom	Camera Person #2	Stephanie K. Bennett
Godfrey	Thom Fudal		

Understudies: Miss Ragsdale—Shannon Malone; Mr. Bauer—Richard DeFonzo; Messrs. Chayet, Weinberg, Wilhoit—Chris Northup; Miss Tulchin—Stephanie K. Bennett; Misses Hays, Flom, Rose—Leslie Abousamra; Mr. Northup, Miss Bennett—Jennifer Acomb.

Directed by Amy Brentano; scenery, Robert Alan Harper; costumes, Don Newcomb; lighting, Stewart Wagner; stage manager, Thom Fudal; press, Shirley Herz Associates, Miller Wright.

Time: May of this year. Place: Studio "A" at Station KHUM, Channel 27, in Humes, Texas. The play was presented without intermission.

Comedy, a small town stages a big-time telethon.

Back to Bacharach and David (69). Musical revue conceived by Steve Gunderson; music by Burt Bacharach; lyrics by Hal David. Produced by Daryl Roth, Hal Luftig, Alan D. Perry, Jim David and Kathy Najimy at Club 53. Opened March 25, 1993. (Closed May 25, 1993)

Melinda Gilb	Sue Mosher
Steve Gunderson	Lillias White

Orchestra: John Boswell conductor, pianist; Shannon Ford percussion; Brian Hamm bass.

Directed by Kathy Najimy; musical direction, vocal arrangements and orchestrations, Steve Gunderson; musical staging, Javier Velasco; scenery, Peter Rogness; costumes, David Loveless; lighting, Maura Sheridan; assistant director, Scott Alan Evans; additional piano arrangements, John Boswell Band; associate producer, 126 Second Ave. Corp.; production stage manager, Todd Gajdusek; press, Shirley Herz Associates, Miller Wright.

Collection of Bacharach & David song numbers from the 1963–1969 period, restyled for the 1990s.

MUSICAL NUMBERS: "A House Is Not a Home," "Alfie," "Always Something There to Remind Me," "Another Night," "Any Old Time of the Day," "Anyone Who Had a Heart," "Are You There With Another Girl," "Close to You," "Do You Know the Way to San Jose," "Don't Make Me Over," "I Just Have to Breathe," "I Say a Little Prayer for You," "I'll Never Fall in Love Again," "Just Don't Know What to Do With Myself," "Knowing When to Leave," "Let Me Be Lonely," "Let Me Go to Him," "Message to Michael," "My Little Red Book," "Nikki," "One Less Bell to Answer," "Promises, Promises," "Reach Out for Me," "The April Fools," "The Look of Love," "This Empty Place," "This Guy's in Love With You," "Trains and Boats and Planes," "24 Hours From Tulsa," "Walk on By," "What the World Needs Now," "Whoever You Are, I Love You," "You'll Never Get to Heaven."

Second Stage Theater. Schedule of two programs. **One Shoe Off** (22) by Tina Howe. Opened April 15, 1993. (Closed May 2, 1993) **Time on Fire** (22). One-man performance by Evan Handler; written by Evan Handler. Opened May 13, 1993. (Closed June 3, 1993) Produced by Second Stage Theater, Carole Rothman artistic director, Suzanne Schwartz Davidson producing director, *One Shoe Off* at the Anspacher Theater of the Joseph Papp Public Theater, *Time on Fire* at the McGinn/Cazale Theater.

ONE SHOE OFF

Leonard	Jeffrey DeMunn	Tate	Daniel Gerroll
Dinah	Mary Beth Hurt	Parker	Brian Kerwin
Clio	Jennifer Tilly		

Directed by Carole Rothman; scenery, Heidi Landesman; costumes, Susan Hilferty; lighting, Richard Nelson; sound, Mark Bennett; associate producer, Carol Fishman; production stage manager, Jess Lynn; stage manager, Gregg Fletcher; press, Richard Kornberg.

Time: Early November. Place: A Greek farmhouse in upstate New York. Act I, Scene 1: Early evening. Scene 2: A moment later. Scene 3: An hour later. Act II, Scene 1: Moments later. Scene 2: An hour Later. Scene 3: Late that night.

Entanglements of two couples with an extra man.

TIME ON FIRE

Directed by Marcia Jean Kurtz; set consultant, Rob Odorisio; lighting, Kenneth Posner; sound consultant, Aural Fixation; associate producer, Carol Fishman; production stage manager, Jenny Peek.

Evan Handler's autobiographical memoir of his battle against leukemia.

*Lypsinka! A Day in the Life (31). One-man musical performance by John Epperson; created by John Epperson. Produced by Sam Rudy, Michael O'Rand and Howard Danziger in association with Barbara Carrellas and Denise Cooper at the Cherry Lane Theater. Opened May 5, 1993.

With the Enrico Kuklafraninalli Puppets.

Directed and choreographed by Michael Leeds; scenery, James Schuette; costumes, Anthony Wong; lighting, Mark McCullough; sound, James M. Bay; production stage manager, Kate Broderick; press, Shirley Herz Associates, Sam Rudy.

John Epperson as "Lypsinka" in the typical day of a glamorous star who lip-synchs the voices of dozens of actresses and singers as she goes through the motions of her life; performed without intermission. Previously produced in this production off off Broadway at New York Theater Workshop 3/31/92.

*Wild Men (30). Musical with book by Peter Burns, Mark Nutter, Rob Riley and Tom Wolfe; music and lyrics by Mark Nutter. Produced by James D. Stern in association with Doug Meyer at the Westside Theater. Opened May 6, 1993.

Stuart Penn	Rob Riley	Greg Neely	Peter Burns
Donnie Lodge	David Lewman	Artie Bishop	Joe Liss
Ken Finnerty	George Wendt		

Standbys: Messrs. Lewman, Wendt, Burns, Liss—Bjorn Johnson; Mr. Riley—Mark Lotito.

Directed by Rob Riley; choreography, Jim Corti; musical direction, Lisa Yeargan; scenery, Mary Griswold; costumes, John Paoletti; lighting, Geoffrey Bushor; sound, Domenic Bucci; percussions, Judy Nielsen; production stage manager, Mary McAuliffe; press, Boneau/Bryan-Brown, Jackie Green.

Time: The present. Place: The North Woods.

Subtitled A Musical . . . Sort Of, a comedy with songs about male bonding on a weekend in the wilderness.

MUSICAL NUMBERS, ACT I: "Come Away," "What Stuart Has Planned," "True Value," "Wimmins," "Ooh, That's Hot," "We're Wild Men," "Lookit Those Stars." ACT II: "The 'Un' Song," "It's You," "My Friend, My Father," "Get Pissed," "Now I Am a Man," "Come Away" (Reprise).

CAST REPLACEMENTS AND TOURING COMPANIES

Compiled by Jeffrey A. Finn

The following is a list of the major cast replacements of record in productions which opened in previous years, but were still playing in New York during a substantial part of the 1992–93 season; or were on a first-class tour in 1992–93.

The name of each major role is listed in *italics* beneath the title of the play in the first column. In the second column directly opposite appears the name of the actor who created the role in the original New York production (whose opening date appears in *italics* at the top of the column). In shows of recent years, indented immediately beneath the original actor's name are the names of subsequent New York replacements, together with the date of replacement when available.

The third column gives information about first-class touring companies. When there is more than one roadshow company, #1, #2, etc., appear before the name of the performer who created the role in each company (and the city and date of each company's first performance appears in *italics* at the top of the column). Their subsequent replacements are also listed beneath their names, with dates when available.

BEAU JEST

	New York 10/10/91	*Los Angeles 3/6/93*
Sarah Goldman	Laura Patinkin Cindy Katz Eliza Foss 4/93	Laura Patinkin
Bob	Tom Hewitt James Michael Gregory Joe Warren Davis Sal Viviano 4/93	Joe Warren Davis

BREAKING LEGS

	New York 5/19/91	*Boston 9/29/92*
Lou Graziano	Vincent Gardenia	Vincent Gardenia Harry Guardino 1/17/93
Angie	Sue Giosa Karen Valentine 1/21/92	Karen Valentine
Terence O'Keefe	Nicolas Surovy	Gary Sandy
Mike Francisco	Philip Bosco	Joseph Mascolo
Frankie Salvucci	Larry Storch	Larry Storch

352

CATS

	New York 10/7/82	*National Tour 1992–93*
Alonzo	Hector Jaime Mercado Randy Wojcik	William Patrick Dunne
Bustopher Jones	Stephen Hanan Jeffrey Clonts	Buddy Crutchfield James Hindman
Bombalurina	Donna King Marlene Danielle	Wendy Walter Helen Frank Dana D'Amore
Carbucketty	Steven Gelfer Ray Roderick (character eliminated)	(not in tour)
Cassandra	Rene Ceballos Darlene Wilson	Laura Quinn Linda May
Coricopat	Rene Clemente Cholsu Kim	(not in tour)
Demeter	Wendy Edmead Mercedes Perez	N. Elaine Wiggins
Grizabella	Betty Buckley Liz Callaway	Mary Gutzi Natalie Toro Donna Lee Marshall
Jellylorum	Bonnie Simmons Nina Hennessy	Linda Strassler Leslie Castay
Jennyanydots	Anna McNeely Rose McGuire	Alica C. DeChant
Mistoffeles	Timothy Scott Lindsay Chambers	Christopher Gattelli John Joseph Festa
Mungojerrie	Rene Clemente Roger Kachel	Gavan Pamer Dennis Glasscock
Munkustrup	Harry Groener Dan McCoy Bryan Batt Dan McCoy	Robert Amirante
Old Deuteronomy	Ken Page Ken Prymus	Jimmy Lockett Robert DuSold Bill Lindner
Plato; Macavity	Kenneth Ard Robb Edward Morris	Taylor Wicker Jim T. Ruttman
Pouncival	Herman W. Sebek Devanand N. Janki	Joey Gyondla Joseph Favalora
Rum Tum Tugger	Terrence V. Mann BK Kennelly	David Hibbard
Rumpleteazer	Christine Langner Christine DeVito	Jennifer Cody Lori Lynch
Sillabub	Whitney Kershaw Lisa Mayer	Bethany Samuelson Joyce Chittick Holly Cruz

Skimbleshanks	Reed Jones	Carmen Yurich
	George Smyros	
Tantomile	Janet L. Hubert	(not in tour)
	Michelle Artigas	
Tumblebrutus	Robert Hoshour	Tim Hunter
	Michael Giacobbe	Marc Ellis Holland
	Marc Ellis Holland	
Victoria	Cynthia Onrubia	Tricia Mitchell
	Claudia Shell	

Note: Only this season's or the most recent cast replacements are listed above under the names of the original cast members. For previous replacements, see previous volumes of *Best Plays*.

CONVERSATIONS WITH MY FATHER

	New York 3/29/92
Eddie Goldberg	Judd Hirsch
	James Belushi
Charlie	Tony Shalhoub
	James Sutorius
Josh	Tony Gillan
	Robert Cannan
Gusta	Gordana Rashovich
Zaretsky	David Margulies
Young Joey	Jason Biggs
	Rick Faugno
Hannah Di Blindeh	Marilyn Sokol
Nick	William Biff McGuire
	Alan North

CRAZY FOR YOU

	New York 2/19/92	*Dallas 5/13/93*
Polly Baker	Jodi Benson	Karen Ziemba
Bobby Child	Harry Groener	James Brennan
Bela Zangler	Bruce Adler	Stuart Zagnit

FALSETTOS

	New York 4/29/92	*San Francisco 4/27/93*
Marvin	Michael Rupert	Gregg Edelman
	Mandy Patinkin 1/15/93	
	Gregg Edelman 6/1/93	
Whizzer	Stephen Bogardus	Peter Reardon
	Sean McDermott 4/12/93	
Trina	Barbara Walsh	Carolee Carmello
	Randy Graff 4/12/93	

Mendel	Chip Zien Jason Graae 6/4/93	Adam Heller
Jason	Jonathan Kaplan Sivan Cotel 10/15/92	Jonathan Kaplan Ramzi Khalaf
Charlotte	Heather Mac Rae	Barbara Marineau
Cordelia	Carolee Carmello Maureen Moore (9/15/92)	Jessica Molaskey

THE FANTASTICKS

New York 5/3/50

El Gallo	Jerry Orbach Christopher Innvar Paul Blankenship
Luisa	Rita Gardner Marilyn Whitehead 1/23/89
Matt	Kenneth Nelson Christopher Scott

Note: Only this season's or the most recent cast replacements are listed above under the names of the original cast members. For previous replacements, see previous volumes of *Best Plays*.

FIVE GUYS NAMED MOE

New York 4/8/92

Nomax	Jerry Dixon Weyman Thompson 12/92
Big Moe	Doug Eskew
Four-Eyed Moe	Milton Craig Nealy
No Moe	Kevin Ramsey
Eat Moe	Jeffrey D. Sams
Little Moe	Glenn Turner

FOREVER PLAID

New York 5/20/90

Sparky	Jason Graae Dale Sandish Michael Winther David Benoit Daniel Eli Friedman
Smudge	David Engel Greg Jbara John Ganun Tom Cianfichi
Jinx	Stan Chandler Paul Binotto Ryan Perry

Francis	Guy Stroman
	Drew Geraci 4/15/91
	Neil Nash
	Robert Lambert

Note: Many out-of-town stagings of *Forever Plaid* were local productions, but casts of two road companies appear in *The Best Plays of 1990–91.*

GUYS AND DOLLS

	New York 4/14/92	*Hartford 9/15/92*
Sky Masterson	Peter Gallagher	Richard Muenz
	Tom Wopat 10/12/92	
	Burke Moses 4/12/93	
Nathan Detroit	Nathan Lane	Lewis J. Stadlen
	Jonathan Hadary 5/17/93	
Sarah Brown	Josie de Guzman	Patricia Ben Peterson
Miss Adelaide	Faith Prince	Lorna Luft
Nicely-Nicely Johnson	Walter Bobbie	Kevin Ligon

JELLY'S LAST JAM

	New York 4/26/92
Jelly Roll Morton	Gregory Hines
	Brian Mitchell 5/4/93
Chimney Man	Keith David
	Ken Ard 2/9/93
	Ben Vereen 4/8/93
Anita	Tonya Pinkins
	Felicia Rashad 5/28/93
Young Jelly	Savion Glover
Jack the Bear	Stanley Wayne Mathis
Miss Mamie	Mary Bond Davis
Gran Mimi	Ann Duquesnay

LES MISERABLES

| | | *#1 Boston 12/5/87* |
| | | *#2 Los Angeles 5/21/88* |
	New York—3/12/87	*#3 Tampa 11/18/88*
Jean Valjean	Colm Wilkinson	#1 William Solo
	Gary Morris 11/30/87	Craig Schulman 4/88
	Timothy Shew 5/30/88	J. Mark McVey
	William Solo 7/3/89	Gary Morris
	Craig Schulman 1/13/90	Mark McKerracher
	J. Mark McVey 1/22/91	#2 William Solo
	Mark McKerracher 11/19/92	Jordan Bennett
	Donn Cook	Rich Hebert
		Kevin McGuire
		Richard Poole

#3 Gary Barker
   Richard Poole
   Brian Lynch
   Dave Clemmons
   Donn Cook

Javert

Terrence V. Mann
   Anthony Crivello 11/30/87
   Norman Large 1/18/88
   Anthony Crivello 3/14/88
   Norman Large 7/19/88
   Herndon Lackey 1/17/89
   Peter Samuel 1/15/90
   Robert Westenberg
   Robert DuSold
   Richard Kinsey 11/19/92
   Chuck Wagner

#1 Herndon Lackey
   Charles Pistone
   Robert DuSold
   Richard Kinsey
#2 Jeff McCarthy
   Richard Kinsey
   Tim Bowman
#3 Peter Samuel
   Paul Schoeffler
   David Jordan
   Chuck Wagner
   Michael X. Martin

Fantine

Randy Graff
   Maureen Moore 7/19/88
   Susan Dawn Carson 1/17/89
   Laurie Beechman 1/15/90
   Christy Baron
   Susan Dawn Carson 11/19/92
   Rachel York
   Donna Kane

#1 Diane Frantantoni
   Ann Crumb
   Hollis Resnik
   Kathy Taylor
   Susan Dawn Carson
   Laurie Beechman 1/89
   Susan Gilmore
   Anne Runolfsson
#2 Elinore O'Connell
   Kelly Ground
#3 Hollis Resnik
   Christy Baron
   Lisa Vroman
   Donna Keane
   Jill Geddes

Enjolras

Michael Maguire
   Joseph Kolinski
   Joe Locarro 1/15/90
   Joseph Kolinski
   Joe Mahowald
   Lawrence Anderson

#1 John Herrera
   Joe Locarro
   Pete Herber
   Christopher Yates
#2 Greg Blanchard
   Raymond Sarr
   Craig Oldfather
#3 Greg Zerkle
   Jerry Christakos
   Aloysius Gigl
   Christopher Yates
   Gary Mauer

Marius

David Bryant
   Ray Walker
   Hugh Panaro
   Matthew Porretta
   John Leone
   Eric Kunze
   Michael Lynch

#1 Hugh Panaro
   John Ruess
   Peter Gunter
#2 Reece Holland
   Peter Gantenbein
   Matthew Porretta
   John Ruess
#3 Matthew Porretta
   Gilles Chiasson
   Ron Sharpe

Cossette	Judy Kuhn Tracy Shane Jacqueline Piro Melissa Anne Davis Jennifer Lee Andrews	#1 Tamara Jenkins Melissa Errico Kimberly Behlman #2 Karen Fineman Jacqueline Piro Ellen Rockne #3 Jacqueline Piro Tamara Hayden Lisa Vroman Marian Murphy Tamara Hayden
Eponine	Frances Ruffelle Kelli James 9/15/87 Natalie Toro 7/88 Debbie Gibson 1/7/92 Michele Maika Debbie Gibson 3/29/92 Brandy Brown Lea Salonga 1/5/93 Tia Riebling	#1 Renee Veneziale Jennifer Naimo Susan Tilson #2 Michelle Nicastro Michele Maika Candese Marchese Misty Cotton #3 Michele Maika Dana Lynn Caruso Candese Marchese Angela Popello
Thenardier	Leo Burmester Ed Dixon Drew Eshelman Ed Dixon	#1 Tom Robbins Neal Ben-Ari 12/5/88 Drew Eshelman #2 Gary Beach #3 Paul Ainsley J.P. Dougherty
Mme. Thenardier	Jennifer Butt Evalyn Baron 1/15/90	#1 Victoria Clark Rosalyn Rahn #2 Kay Cole Gina Ferrall #3 Linda Kerns Diana Rogers Gina Ferrall

LOST IN YONKERS

	New York 2/21/91	*Chattanooga 10/28/91*
Grandma Kurnitz	Irene Worth Mercedes McCambridge 8/26/91 Rosemary Harris 10/14/91 Anne Jackson 6/2/92	Mercedes McCambridge Isa Thomas
Bella	Mercedes Ruehl Jane Kazmarek 8/26/91 Lucie Arnaz 6/2/92 Jane Kazmarek 12/1/92 Didi Conn 12/17/92	Brooke Adams Susan Giosa 2/23/92 Brooke Adams 5/24/92 Carolyn Swift
Louie	Kevin Spacey Bruno Kirby 8/12/91	Ned Eisenberg Bruce Kronenberg
Eddie	David Chandler Steve Vinovich 6/2/92	Michael Gaston

MAN OF LA MANCHA

	New York 4/24/92
Cervantes; Don Quixote	Raul Julia Laurence Guittard 6/30/92
Aldonza; Dulcinea	Sheena Easton Joan Diener 6/30/92
Sancho	Tony Martinez

MISS SAIGON

	New York 4/11/91	*Chicago 10/12/93*
The Engineer	Jonathan Pryce Francis Ruivivar 8/19/91 Jonathan Pryce 9/30/91 Francis Ruivivar 12/16/91 Herman Sebek	Raul Aranas
Kim	Lea Salonga Leila Florentino 3/16/92	Jennifer C. Paz Hazel Raymundo
Chris	Willy Falk Sean McDermott 12/16/91 Chris Peccaro	Jarrod Emick

OLEANNA

	New York 10/25/92	*Stamford, Conn. 4/6/93*
John	William H. Macy Treat Williams 3/31/93 Jim Frangione 7/13/93	William H. Macy
Carol	Rebecca Pidgeon Mary McCann 1/26/93	Debra Eisenstadt

THE PHANTOM OF THE OPERA

	New York 1/26/88	*#1 Los Angeles 5/31/90* *#2 Chicago 5/24/90* *#3 Seattle 12/13/92*
The Phantom	Michael Crawford Timothy Nolen 10/10/88 Cris Groenendaal 3/20/89 Steve Barton 3/19/90 Kevin Gray Mark Jacoby 2/21/91 Marcus Lovett	#1 Michael Crawford Robert Guillaume 5/1/90 Michael Crawford Davis Gaines #2 Mark Jacoby Kevin Gray Rick Hilsabeck #3 Frank D'Ambrosio
Christine Daaé	Sarah Brightman Patti Cohenour 6/7/88 Dale Kristien (alt.) 7/88 Rebecca Luker (alt.) 3/89 Rebecca Luker 6/5/89	#1 Dale Kristien Mary Darcy (alt.) #2 Karen Culliver Teri Bibb (alt.) Sarah Pfisterer (alt.)

	Katherine Buffaloe (alt.)	Teri Bibb
	Karen Culliver	
	Luann Aronson (alt.) 6/92	#3 Tracy Shane
	Mary Darcy	Lisa Vroman (alt.)
Raoul	Steve Barton	#1 Reece Holland
	Kevin Gray 9/18/80	Michael Piontek
	Davis Gaines 3/12/90	#2 Keith Buterbaugh
	Hugh Panaro	Nat Chandler 8/92
	Keith Buterbaugh	#3 Caran Sheehan

Alternates play the role of Christine Daaé Monday and Wednesday evenings.

THE SECRET GARDEN

	New York 4/25/91	*Cleveland 4/28/92*
Mary Lennox	Daisy Eagan	Melody Kay
	Kimberly Mahon	Kimberly Mahon
	Lydia Ooghe 3/12/92	Demaree Alexander
		Lydia Ooghe
Archibald Craven	Mandy Patinkin	Kevin McGuire
	Howard McGillin 8/22/91	
Lily	Rebecca Luker	Anne Runolfsson
		Jacqueline Piro
Nevile	Robert Westenberg	Douglas Sills
		Peter Samuel

SIGHT UNSEEN

	New York 1/20/92
Jonathan Waxman	Dennis Boutsikaris
	Adam Arkin 6/16/92
Patricia	Deborah Hedwall
	Margaret Colin 6/16/92
Nick	Jon De Vries
	Christopher Jones 7/10/92
Grete	Laura Linney
	Pamela Gray 6/26/92

THE WILL ROGERS FOLLIES

	New York 5/1/91	*San Francisco 8/25/92*
Will Rogers	Keith Carradine	Keith Carradine
	Mac Davis 5/18/92	
	Larry Gatlin 2/16/93	
Betty Blake	Dee Hoty	Dee Hoty
	Nancy Ringham 5/18/92	
Ziegfeld's Favorite	Cady Huffman	Leigh Zimmerman
	Susan Anton 12/9/91	
	Cady Huffman 1/27/92	
	Marla Maples 8/3/92	
	Kimberly Hester 5/4/93	
	Lisa Niemi 5/27/93	

MY FAIR LADY—Richard Chamberlain as Henry Higgins, Melissa Errico as Eliza Doolittle and Paxton Whitehead as Col. Pickering in "The Rain in Spain" number of the musical's 1993 road company

SHOWS OF OTHER YEARS
ON FIRST CLASS TOURS IN 1992–93

AND THE WORLD GOES 'ROUND

Cincinnati 9/27/92
Joel Blum
Shelley Dickinson
Marin Mazzie
John Ruess
Karen Ziemba

Note: Produced on the road under the title *The World Goes 'Round*.

ANNIE GET YOUR GUN

Baltimore 3/2/93

Annie Oakley	Cathy Rigby
Frank Butler	Brent Barrett
Charlie Davenport	Paul V. Ames
Chief Sitting Bull	Mauricio Bustamante
Dolly Tate	KT Sullivan

ASPECTS OF LOVE

Toronto 4/13/92

Rose Vibert	Linda Balgord
Alex Dillingham	Ron Bohmer
George Dillingham	Barrie Ingram
Giulietta Trapani	Kelli James Chase
Marcel Richard	David Masenheimer
Young Jenny	Maryke Hendrikse
Older Jenny	Lori Alter

CAMELOT

Detroit 9/8/92

Arthur	Robert Goulet
Guenevere	Patricia Kies
Lancelot	Steve Blanchard
Merlyn	James Valentine
Mordred	Kenneth Boys
Nimue	Vanessa Shaw

EVITA

Indianapolis 8/3/92

Eva	Valerie Perri
Che	John Herrera
Peron	David Brummel
Magaldi	Sal Mistretta
Peron's Mistress	Jennifer Rae Beck

JESUS CHRIST SUPERSTAR

Baltimore 12/12/92

Jesus of Nazareth	Ted Neeley
Mary Magdalene	Leesa Richards
Judas	Carl Anderson
Pontius Pilate	Dennis DeYoung
King Herod	Laurent Giroux
Peter	Kevin R. Wright
Caiphas	David Bedella
Simon	Steven X. Ward

JOSEPH AND THE AMAZING TECHNICOLOR DREAMCOAT

Los Angeles 2/25/93

Joseph	Michael Damien
Narrator	Kelli Rabke
Jacob/Potiphar/Guru	Clifford David
Pharoah	Robert Torti
Butler	Glenn Sneed
Baker	Bill Nolte
Mrs. Potiphar	Julie Bond

MY FAIR LADY

Ft. Meyers, Fla. 4/5/93

Henry Higgins	Richard Chamberlain
Eliza Doolittle	Melissa Errico
Freddie Eynsford-Hill	Robert Sella
Colonel Pickering	Paxton Whitehead
Alfred P. Doolittle	Julian Holloway
Mrs. Higgins	Dolores Sutton

THE SEASON
OFF OFF BROADWAY

O
O
O

OFF OFF BROADWAY

O
O
O

By Mel Gussow

THE amorphous arena of off off Broadway continued to go through changes in the 1992–93 season. Theaters closed down and others sprung up; BACA Downtown in Brooklyn returned, and there was a sense of renewal at La Mama and other valuable longstanding institutions. Some newer companies like the Signature Theater Company and Naked Angels consolidated artistic efforts and gave signs of increased durability. As always, experimentation was the key, deriving from new as well as expected sources, many of them international, taking place at the Brooklyn Academy of Music, La Mama, P.S. 122, the Kitchen, Dance Theater Workshop and other venues. The Brooklyn Academy season included *Les Atrides,* Ariane Mnouchkine's spectacular reworking of *The House of Atreus,* and ended with a two-play repertory presented by Ingmar Bergman and the Royal Dramatic Theater of Sweden. In his third visit to BAM, Bergman offered a fanciful, bucolic version of *Peer Gynt,* followed by a stunning production of Yukio Mishima's *Madame de Sade.* This portrait of the Marquis de Sade as told from the point of view of women (some real, some imagined) had two prior New York productions. Bergman's vision was revelatory. Starring an ensemble of magnificent actresses, this was the performance event of the year (and is cited as an outstanding 1992–93 OOB production).

BAM additionally certified its role as an importer of venturesome work by offering the local premiere of *Needles and Opium,* written, directed and designed by Robert Lepage, a Canadian experimentalist who was also the solo performer of his own play. Cited as an outstanding OOB production, *Needles and Opium* wove together the stories of Jean Cocteau and Miles Davis into a surrealistic jazz collage that became airborne along with its actor-author. In Lepage's hands, a monodrama was transformed into a multi-drama, and more than compensated for the director's recent bizarre, world-in-a-mudpuddle variation on *A Midsummer Night's Dream* at Britain's National Theater. The Kanze Noh Theater of Japan joined with the Metropolitan Museum of Art in presenting an historic evening of Noh in front of the Temple of Dendur, unifying several cultural traditions.

Canada's *Cirque du Soleil* paid a return visit to a tent in Battery Park City. This new-wave circus specializes in high-powered pandemonium as well as agile aerialists. Victoria Chaplin and her husband Jean Baptiste Thiérrée returned with their low-powered, vestpocket *Invisible Circus.* The couple's son James

Thiérrée, who bears a strong resemblance to his grandfather Charles Chaplin as a young man, took the spotlight with his bungee style stage flying. In the course of the year, there was an International Festival of Puppet Theater at the Joseph Papp Public Theater. Many of the foreign companies in the festival were outweighed by a troupe from Chicago, the Hystopolis Puppet Theater, which found new miniaturized life in Elmer Rice's expressionist drama, *The Adding Machine.* The Bread and Puppet Theater arrived with a new Nativity play. That Italian zany Leo Bassi came back with a one-man audience encounter session entitled *C. Colombo Inc.: Export/Import, Genoa,* which had something to do with Christopher Columbus but more to do with Bassi as a kamikaze comedian.

The Signature Theater, founded by James Houghton to produce plays by a single author for an entire season, devoted its second series to Lee Blessing, giving him four New York premieres. The work ranged from a Shakespearean spoof (the post-*Hamlet Fortinbras*) to a contemporary Gothic about child abuse (*Lake Street Extension*) to an intelligent reevaluation of headline news (*Patient A,* about Kimberly Bergalis, the young woman who contracted AIDS while being treated by her dentist). The most notable Blessing work was *Two Rooms,* a probing study of the hostage crisis and its impact on those at home. As directed by Houghton, the play is cited as an outstanding OOB production. The prolific playwright had a fifth drama for later in the year, *Down the Road,* about a serial killer collaborating on a potential best seller.

Romulus Linney, who was the subject of the first Signature season, was represented by two plays at other theaters: *Democracy and Esther,* drawn from two novels by Henry Adams, and, more evocatively, *Spain,* two counterpointed one-acts that circled a favorite Linney source, the Spanish Inquisition. A provocative double-header came from Caryl Churchill, with two of her earlier plays appearing in repertory at the New York Theater Workshop: *Owners,* her first play, about the rights and limits of ownership as applied to real estate, and *Traps,* a Mobius strip of a puzzler in which communal living is under scrutiny. *Traps* had what must have been a first for the New York stage. In the climactic moment, all six actors had to strip off their clothes and take a bath onstage, one after another in the same bathwater. The last of the six deserved special pay. The actress J. Smith-Cameron was outstanding in both Churchill plays.

Ping Chong spread his conceptual wings with *Deshima,* whose canvas reached all the way from early Dutch traders to the purchase of Van Gogh paintings by Japanese billionaires. Quarantine, on a political level, was the insistent theme in this play about the lessons of history. *Samuel's Major Problem* was this season's hermetic gift from Richard Foreman, playwright, director, designer and visionary. The problem, shared by the author, was that of man in an irrational world. John Jesurun, who mixes film and video into his media, was more communicative than usual in *Point of Debarkation,* about people fleeing to the New World from the Spanish Inquisition. Pat Oleszko, who often works on wide open stages, took a more formalized approach in *Nora's Art* (at the Kitchen), with the

Mel Gussow Citations: Outstanding OOB Productions

Above, Laura Esterman and Jeffrey Hayenga in Lee Blessing's *Two Rooms* at Signature Theater ("A probing study of the hostage crisis and its impact on those at home"); *below*, Robert Lepage in his solo show *Needles and Opium* at the Brooklyn Academy of Music ("Wove together the stories of Jean Cocteau and Miles Davis into a surrealistic jazz collage that became airborne along with its actor-author.")

performance artist-puppeteer at the center of a flotilla of airheaded balloon creatures.

More new heights of wordplay were reached by Mac Wellman in *3 Americanisms,* a Babel-like outpouring of verbiage spinning around the subject of public panic. There is no writer quite like Wellman, though his antecedents include James Joyce and Lewis Carroll. He is most contemporary in his fierce attacks on authority figures in everyday life. David Ives, another linguistic lapidarist, turned his eyes to more tangible though mysterious matters in *Long Ago and Far Away,* in the Ensemble Studio Theater's Marathon of one act plays. Other assets of this year's festival included Joyce Carol Oates's *The Rehearsal,* a Pirandello-esque confrontation between actors, and *Where's Mamie?,* a Michael John LaChiusa mini-musical about Mamie Eisenhower.

The Ridiculous Theatrical Company was in full fervor with *Brother Truckers* by Georg Osterman and *Linda,* a country western musical by Everett Quinton and Mark Bennett, a show that managed to swing from television evangelism to lesbian rights. The Pan Asian Repertory Theater challenged itself with Ernest Abuba's outspoken political musical *Cambodia Agonistes,* then slipped with an attempt to relocate *A Doll's House* in contemporary American life as *A Doll House.* With *Blue Heaven,* Karen Malpede presented an environmental reproduction of the art world of the 1960s. At one performance there was a memorable offstage event: at a ringside table, a dog fell asleep, providing an act of on-the-spot criticism.

Christopher Hampton's *Tales from Hollywood,* previously staged at Britain's National Theater and on public television, opened at La Mama. Trying to vivify Hollywood at the time of Brecht and Thomas Mann, Hampton was not abetted by an insecure production. Barbara Graham's *Camp Paradox* was a familiar summer camp coming of age yarn; the only difference was that a camper's romance was with a lesbian counsellor. In *The Arrangement,* Susan Kim unveiled a voyeur with delusions. Among the plays trying to deal with contemporary grotesqueries, one of the most impressive was *Down the Shore* by Tom Donaghy, in which dysfunctionalism defined a family. The play appeared on a double bill with *The Dad Shuttle,* a mood piece about a gay son and a reserved father. OOB had its customary share of more traditional work, including several good-old-girl comedies. Alan Ball's *Five Women Wearing the Same Dress* was marginally better than others.

In a season busy with monologues, one of the more invigorating was *Jersey Girls,* written and acted by Susan Van Allen. This was a personalized comic view of what it means to grow up in an ingrown suburban community. Deb Margolin and Rae C. Wright did something related in *The Breaks,* playing nurses revealing currents of small town life. In *My Queer Body,* Tim Miller undertook a journey of self-exposure. From Germany came Franz Xaver Kroetz's *Extended Forecast,* in which Estelle Parsons reenacted the sad solo story of a woman about to go to an old people's home.

Small companies continued to explore classics: the Jean Cocteau, the Pearl (offering a rare production of Oliver Goldsmith's *The Good Natur'd Man*) and Theater for a New Audience. That last group specializes in Shakespeare, paired with first flight directors. Barry Kyle brought over Mark Rylance from England for what turned out to be a listless *Henry V.* That was followed by a lively *Love's Labour's Lost,* directed by Michael Langham. At the CSC, now under the artistic direction of David Esbjornson, the company opened *Krapp's Last Tape* and a carnivalized *Scapin* by the team of Shelley Berc and Andrei Belgrader, with Stanley Tucci as an especially malevolent Scapin. In a change of pace, the CSC also staged Ann-Marie MacDonald's *Goodnight Desdemona (Good Morning Juliet),* a new play in a classic mode.

One fledgling company bravely undertook *On a Clear Day You Can See Forever,* the Alan Jay Lerner-Burton Lane musical, and shrunk it. One of the most zestful new musicals was *Robert Johnson: Trick the Devil,* Bill Harris's retelling of the life and legend of the celebrated blues guitarist, using Johnson's music. The show (at the New Federal Theater) reached a spirited conclusion with the title character confessing how he tricked the devil. Dan Hurlin tackles large subjects, as in *Quintland (The Musical),* an engaging docu-comedy about the Dionne Quintuplets. Hurlin played all the roles, from Quints to country doctor.

PLAYS PRODUCED
OFF OFF BROADWAY

AND ADDITIONAL PRODUCTIONS

Compiled by Camille Croce Dee

Here is a comprehensive sampling of off-off-Broadway and other experimental or peripheral 1992–93 productions in New York. There is no definitive "off-off-Broadway" area or qualification. To try to define or regiment it would be untrue to its fluid, exploratory purpose. The listing below of hundreds of works produced by more than 100 OOB groups and others is as inclusive as reliable sources will allow, however, and takes in all leading Manhattan-based, new-play producing, English-language organizations.

The more active and established producing groups are identified in **bold face type**, in alphabetical order, with artistic policies and the names of the managing directors given whenever these are a matter of record. Each group's 1992–93 schedule, with emphasis on new plays and with revivals of classics usually omitted, is listed with play titles in CAPITAL LETTERS. Often these are works-in-progress with changing scripts, casts and directors, sometimes without an engagement of record (but an opening or early performance date is included when available).

Many of these off-off-Broadway groups have long since outgrown a merely experimental status and are offering programs which are the equal in professionalism and quality (and in some cases the superior) of anything in the New York theater, with special contractual arrangements like the showcase code, letters of agreement (allowing for longer runs and higher admission prices than usual) and, closer to the edge of the commercial theater, a so-called "mini-contract." In the list below, all available data on opening dates, performance numbers and major production and acting credits (almost all of them Equity members) is included in the entries of these special-arrangement offerings.

A large selection of lesser-known groups and other shows that made appearances off off Broadway during the season appears under the "Miscellaneous" heading at the end of this listing.

American Place Theater. In addition to the regular off-Broadway season, other special projects are presented. Wynn Handman director, Dara Hershman general manager.

SISTER! SISTER! (one-woman show) (20). By and with Vinie Burrows. October 29, 1992. Costumes, Dada's Works.

American Theater of Actors. Dedicated to providing a creative atmosphere for new American playwrights, actors and directors. James Jennings artistic director.

IN THE DARK ALONG THE WAY. By David Patrick Beavers. June 3, 1992. Director, David Conroy. With John Borras, Mary Ann Emerson, Mark Scherman, Angela Simpson, Angel Stokey.

THE CHANGING WOMAN. Written and directed by James Jennings. June 3, 1992. With Anne Slattery, Greg Pekar, Stephen Wyler, James Shanley.

THE COVENANT. By Albert Lipitz Evans. June 24, 1992. Director, Michael Muzio. With Ken Braslow, Sivan Cotel, George Gerard, Eli Gurevich.

A DREADFUL HUSBAND. By Cantara Christopher. July 22, 1992. Director, Joanna Lynnsey. With Jadah Carroll, Timothy James, R. D. Thomas, Raissa Radell.

TEA WITH MRS. ADAMS. By William Heywood Kaiser. August 5, 1992. Director, Valerie Harris. With Doris St. Marie, Gerard Hanley, Allison Furman.

SHE WHO FEELS THE PAST. Written and directed by James Jennings. August 10, 1992. With Jane Culley.

THE CHAIR. By Robert William Hodge. August 12, 1992. Director, James Jennings. With Mat Sarter.

MORNING COFFEE. By Frederick Stroppel. August 19, 1992. Director, James Lorinz. With Monica Kellum, John Borras.

THE HOMEFRONT. By Gregg Feistman. August 26, 1992. Director, Mark Elliot. With Richard Villella, Jody Walker, David Justin.

DUNCE CORNER. By James Crafford. September 9, 1992. Director, Mat Sarter. With Alex Chanin, Lou Lagalante.

LOOSE by Adam Kraar, directed by John Borras; STARFISH by Marlane G. Meyer, directed by Gregory Pekar; THE SACRED DANCE OF YELLOW THUNDER by Joel Ensana, directed by Courtney Everett (one-act plays). September 23, 1992. With Alan Harris, Anna LaSpisa, James Shanley, William Hallmark, Lori Sypek, Randy Moore, Natasha, Earl Pulley, Paul Campana, Robert O'Malley, Mary Chang-Faulk.

SOMEONE. Written and directed by Tom Bruce. September 30, 1992. With Anne Correa, Eliza Miller, Larry Mitchell, Doris Reardon, Madelaine Schleyer, Anne Slattery, Christian Van Lindt.

USA TODAY. Written and directed by James Jennings. October 7, 1992. With Daniel Murray, Greg Fox, Monica Kellum, Rick Monat, Judith Boxley.

SOMEONE OUT THERE. By Frederick Stroppel. October 21, 1992. Director, David Conroy. With Marilyn Posner, Ann Day, Adam Barnett.

COULD ANGELS BE BLESSED? By Nancy Keifer. November 11, 1992. Director, Allen Lang. With Greg Fox, Perri Yeager, Connie Metroka, Anna Raviv, DeBorah Waller, Ronette Von Briel.

DIVINER. Written and directed by James Jennings. November 18, 1992. With Pat O'Neal, Christopher Jennings, Lori Sypek, Dan Murray, Kathleen Mancini.

SONG OF THE NOVA. Written and directed by James Jennings. December 2, 1992. With Gregory Pekar, Annette Laskowski, Tom Bruce.

SNAPPING. By David Gray. December 16, 1992. Director, David Conaway. With William Greene, Salli Saffioti, Philip Thron, Stuart Ward.

TRAPPISTS. By Joseph P. Ritz. January 6, 1993. Director, Mark Corum. With Bill McHugh, Mary Lynn Hetsko, Tom Bruce, Kathleen Mancini.

THE OLD FRIEND. By Gene Raskin. January 27, 1993. Director, Joanna Lynnsey. With Ed Galloway, Jadah Carroll, Andres Petruscak, Dawn Sheehan, Patti Uhrich.

THE WILL. By Dean Marc Norton. February 3, 1993. Director, James Jennings. With Adam Barnett, Madelaine Schleyer, Daniel Murray, John Koprowski, Diane Van Beuren, Ray Trail.

IF I LIE. By Sidney Sulkin. February 3, 1993. Director, Jane Culley. With Jerome Richards, Brenda Smiley.

SEMINAR. By Irving A. Leitner. February 10, 1993. Director, James Jennings. With Bill McHugh, Kevin Ewing, Louise Galanda, Damien Panczyk, Toshiro Yamamoto.

BLACK AND WHITE CITY BLUES. By Richard Vetere. February 10, 1993. Director, Allen Lang. With Tony Allen, Gretchen Clagget, Anthony DiMaria, Fernando Gomes, Anthony Lepre.

ALFRED. Written and directed by Tom Labar. February 17, 1993. With Tom Bruce.

ROSEMARIE'S COME HOME. By Jerry Kaufman. March 3, 1993. Director, James Jennings. With Ellen Bradshaw, Doris Reardon, John Borras, Anne Jennings.

'BYE, 'BYE, BLACKBIRD. By Stephen Jackson. March 17, 1993. Director, Jill Wisoff. With Mark Drew, Alyssa Reiner.

DRAWN IDENTITIES. By Sean Michael Rice. March 31, 1993. Director, Diane Van Beuren. With Joe Aycock, Angel Stokey, Charles Quinn.

GENDER IS DESTINY. By Cleo Neiman. April 7, 1993. Director, Mark Scherman. With Suzanne Bayne, Debbie Cerrito, John Knox, Frantz Hall.

MY NAME IS PABLO PICASSO. By Mary Gage. April 14, 1993. Director, James Jennings. With Mike Bernosky, Jeanne Maumus, Damien Panczyk.

MY SISTER'S KEEPER. By Debbie Pearl. April 28, 1993. Director, Constance McCord.

THE GOSSIP FROM THE STITCHING ROOM. By Alfred Dumais. May 5, 1993. Director, Leo Boylan. With Stephanie Barron, Paul Finnegan, Dawn Margolis.

AMERI-KANSA. Written and directed by James Jennings. May 26, 1993. With Joe Aycock, Suzi Chrystal, Andrew Harlan.

Atlantic Theater Company. Produces new plays or reinterpretations of classics that speak to audiences in a contemporary voice on issues reflecting today's society. Neil Pepe artistic director, Jeffrey Solis managing director.

NOTHING SACRED (33). By George F. Walker, adapted from Turgenev's *Fathers and Sons*. October 21, 1992. Director, Max Mayer; scenery, David Gallo; lighting, Donald Holder; costumes, Harry Nadal. With Larry Bryggman, Daniel De Raey, Matt McGrath, Clark Gregg, Mary McCann, Heidi Kling, Robert Bella, Damian Young, David Pittu, Steven Goldstein, Nick Phelps.

VOX POP (7). Works included THE HAPPY CAMPER by Charlie Schulman, directed by Bill Wrubel; THE GETTYSBURG SOUNDBITE by Ted Tally, directed by Todd Weeks; CEAU-CESCEAU'S DOG by Warren Leight, directed by Neil Pepe; IMAGINING AMERICA written and directed by Howard Korder; THE DEBATE by Robert Bella, directed by Daisy Mayer; A BIRD IN THE HAND by Madeleine Olnek, directed by Hilary Hinckle; A MOMENT WITH CHUCK by Michael Louden; A SPEECH FOR MICHAEL DUKAKIS by David Mamet; GLENGARRY GLEN ROSS PEROT by Jay Martel, directed by Robert Bella. October 28, 1992. Scenery, Dan Shefelman; lighting, Howard Werner. With William H. Macy, Todd Weeks, Damian Young, Kristen Johnston, Robert Bella, Jordan Lage, David Pittu, Clark Gregg, Bob Clinton, Steve Davis, Chris Jones, Craig Addams, David Valcin, Karen Kohlhaas, Robin Spielberg, Kathleen Dennehy, Michael Louden.

THE WHITE SUIT (5). Book and lyrics, Jenny Lombard; music, Neil Pepe and Marco Joachim. January 15, 1993. Director, Kate Baggott; choreography, Cyndi Lee; scenery, Dan Shefelman; lighting, Howard Werner; costumes, Jenny Lombard. With Barbara McCrane, David Phillips, Steven Goldstein, Becky Ann Baker, Trip Hamilton, Kristen Johnston, Todd Weeks, Neil Pepe.

ATLANTIC THEATER COMPANY—Clark Gregg,
Matt McGrath and Larry Bryggman in a scene from
Nothing Sacred by George F. Walker

THE DAD SHUTTLE and DOWN THE SHORE (one-act plays) (26). By Tom Donaghy.
January 25, 1993. Director, William H. Macy; scenery, James Wolk; lighting, Howard Werner;
costumes, Sarah Edwards. With Matt McGrath, Peter Maloney, Neil Pepe, Kathryn Erbe, Todd
Weeks.

Circle Repertory Projects-in-Process. Developmental programs for new plays. Tanya
Berezin artistic director, Abigail Evans managing director.

GORGEOUS MOSAIC (2). By Judith Feisher. October 26, 1992. Director, Adrienne Weiss.
With Oliver Barrero, Tai Bennett, Duane Boutte, Kay Gaynor, Chris Glenn, Samaria Graham,
Harold Perrineau, Michelle Maria Weeks.

CANNIBAL'S WALTZ (4). By Lanie Robertson. February 1, 1993. Director, Mark Ramont.
With John Dossett, Sarah Baker, Larry Bryggman, Frank Lowe, Gary Dean Ruebsamen, Kay
Walbye.

DOLORES (4). By Edward Allan Baker. February 22, 1993. Director, Ron Stetson. With
Elizabeth Charlotte Ross, Christine Farrell, Catherine Perry, Nancy Ann Chatty, Suzanne
Shepard, Ron Stetson.

Extended Readings:

SCOTLAND ROAD. By Jeffrey Hatcher. November 2, 1992. Director, Margaret Denithorne.
With Mark Blum, Leslie Lyles, Ashley Crowe, Anne Pitoniak.
TRUST ME. Written and performed by Steve Brown. January 18, 1993. Directed by Mary Beth
Easley. With Geoff Gibson, Cynthia King.
LOSING FATHER'S BODY. By Constance Congdon. April 19, 1993. Director, Ray Cochran.
With Cordelia Richards, John Hickey, Scotty Bloch, Michael Warren Powell, Peter Boyden,
Pamela Dunlap, Judith Hawking, Craig Bockhorn, Amy Hohn, Catherine Coray, Scott Cohen,
Joel Rooks, Anna Bull.

WIDESCREEN VERSION OF THE WORLD. By Han Ong. May 17, 1993. With Zar Acayan, Tina Chen, Catherine Coray, Oni Faida Lampley, Bruce Locke, Florencia Lozano, Lia Yang, Keone Young.

Classic Stage Company (CSC). Aims to produce classics with a bold, contemporary sensibility. David Esbjornson artistic director.

GOODNIGHT DESDEMONA (GOOD MORNING JULIET) (41). By Ann-Marie Mac-Donald. October 13, 1992. Director, David Esbjornson; scenery, Donald Eastman; lighting, Brian MacDevitt. With Cherry Jones, Liev Schreiber, Hope Davis, Robert Joy, Saundra McClain.

SCAPIN (53). By Molière, adapted by Shelley Berc and Andrei Belgrader. January 12, 1993. Director, Andrei Belgrader; scenery, Anita Stewart; lighting, Stephen Strawbridge; costumes, Candice Donnelly and Elizabeth Hope Clancy; music and lyrics, Rusty Magee. With Stanley Tucci, Alexander Draper, Ken Cheeseman, Sarah McCord Williams, Michael McCormick, Walker Jones, Joshua Fardon, Mary Testa, Roberta Kastelic, John August, Denis Sweeney, Jules Cohen.

KRAPP'S LAST TAPE (20). By Samuel Beckett. March 29, 1993. Director and scenic designer, David Esbjornson; lighting, Brian MacDevitt; costumes, Jessica Grace. With John Seitz.

Ensemble Studio Theater. Membership organization of playwrights, actors, directors and designers dedicated to supporting individual theater artists and developing new works for the stage. Over 250 projects each season, ranging from readings to fully-mounted productions. Curt Dempster artistic director, Mike Teele managing director.

IN THE SPIRIT (5). By Chuka Lokoli. April 6, 1993. Director, Susann Brinkley. With Chuka Lokoli, M. Cochise Anderson, Kim Basset, Irene Bedard, Elisa Cato, Steve Elm, Vickie Ramirez.

MARATHON '93 (festival of one-act plays). BED AND BREAKFAST by Richard Dresser, directed by Charles Karchmer; LONG AGO AND FAR AWAY by David Ives, directed by Christopher A. Smith; IRON TOMMY by James Ryan, directed by William Carden; JACKIE by David Rasche, directed by Peter Maloney; A FAREWELL TO MUM by Julie McKee, directed by Elinor Renfield; TUNNEL OF LOVE by Jacquelyn Reingold, directed by Ethan Silverman; RING OF MEN by Adam Oliensis, directed by Jamie Richards; FORE by Frank D. Gilroy, directed by David Margulies; SEVENTH WORD, FOURTH SYLLABLE by Susan Kim, directed by Melia Bensussen; COSMO'S IN LOVE by Bill Bozzone, directed by Shirley Kaplan; THE REHEARSAL by Joyce Carol Oates, directed by Kevin Confoy; WHERE'S MAMIE? libretto and music by Michael John LaChiusa, directed by Kirsten Sanderson. May 5–June 13, 1993.

INTAR. Mission is to identify, develop and present the talents of gifted Hispanic American theater artists and multicultural visual artists. Max Ferra artistic director, Eva Brune managing director.

ANY PLACE BUT HERE. By Caridad Svich. June 6, 1992. Director, George Ferencz; scenery, Bill Stabile; lighting, Ernie Barbarash; costumes, Sally Lesser. With Jessica Hecht, Peter McCabe, Mimi Cichanowicz Quillin, Jim Abele.

WORDS DIVINE: A MIRACLE PLAY. Translated and adapted by Lorenzo Mans from Ramon del Valle Inclan's *Divinas Palabras.* November 11, 1992. Director, Max Ferra; scenery, Rimer Cardillo; lighting, Mark McCullough; music, William Harper. With Philip Arroyo, Susan Batson, Luz Castanos, Josie Chavez, Monique Cintron, Christopher Coucill, Shelton Dane, Ron Faber, Peter McCabe, Ofelia Medina, Alec Murphy, Irma St. Paule.

NOSTALGIA TROPICAL (musical revue) (48). Conceived and directed by Max Ferra. February 21, 1993. Choreography, Victor Cuellar; scenery, Ricardo Hernandez; lighting, Jennifer

Tipton; costumes, Randy Barcelo; musical director, Meme Solis. With Hector Miguel Barrera, Merly Bordes, Aimee Cabrera, Claudina Montenegro, Gilberto C. Peralta, Orlando Rios, Marden Ramos, Victor Sterling, Ramoncito Veloz Jr. Co-produced by Light Opera of Manhattan.

Interart Theater. Committed to producing innovative work by women theater artists and to introducing New York audiences to a bold range of theater that is non-traditional in form or theme. Margot Lewitin artistic director.

Schedule included:

THE BREAKS (21). Written and performed by Deb Margolin and Rae C. Wright. April 19, 1993. Director, Cheryl Katz; scenery, Christina Weppner; lighting, Jeff Zeidman; costumes, Linda Gui.

THE GLASS WOMAN (opera in progress). Book, Sally Ordway and Nancy Rhodes; music, Sorrel Hays; lyrics, Sally Ordway and Sorrel Hays. February 25, 1993. Director, Nancy Rhodes; choreography, Michelle Jacobi; scenery, Gary Jennings; lighting, Larry Johnson; costumes, Dan Wilhelm; musical director, John Yaffe. With Michael Alhonte, Teresa Lane Hoover, Bretta Lundell, Salvatore Basile, Stephen Kalm, Claudia Mayer, Ron Edwards, Jennifer Lopez, Rebecca Mercer-White. Co-produced by Encompass Theater.

Irish Arts Center. Provides a range of contemporary Irish drama, classics and new works by Irish and Irish American playwrights. Nye Heron artistic director.

THE LAMENT FOR ARTHUR CLEARY. By Dermot Bolger. October 18, 1992. Director, Nye Heron; scenery, David Raphel; lighting, Judith M. Daitsman; costumes, Carla Gant; music; Brian O'Neill Mor and Nicholas Kean. With Ron Bottitta, Jennie Conroy, David Herlihy, Chris O'Neill, Mac Orange.

A COUPLE OF BLAGUARDS. Conceived and performed by Malachy and Frank McCourt. March 18, 1993.

La Mama (a.k.a. LaMama) Experimental Theater Club (ETC). A busy workshop for experimental theater of all kinds. Ellen Stewart founder and artistic director.

Schedule included:

KANASHIBETSU. Written and directed by Soh Kuramoto. June 18, 1992. With the Furano Group.

BABY and FOURTEEN CLOWNS AND A XYLOPHONE. By Susan Sherman. October 15, 1992. Director, John Morace; choreography, Herve Le Goff. With April Armstrong, Dennis Davis, Sheila Evans, David Huberman, Edward Porter, Helen Shumaker, Gregory St. John, Carl Sturmer.

YUNUS (folk opera). Text by Yunus Emre, translated by Talat Halman, Huseyn Kat and Erol Keskin; adaptation, music, lyrics and direction, Ellen Stewart. October 22, 1992. Scenery, David Adams, Jun Maeda, Mark Tambella; lighting, Howard Thies; costumes, Selcuk Gurisik. With Mustafa Avkiran, Du Yee Chang, Rose Davis, Abba Elethea, Kaan Erten, Nadi Guler, Jonathan Hart, Erol Keskin, Asli Ongoren, Andrea Paciotto, Ching Valdes-Aran.

BIG BUTT GIRLS, HARD-HEADED WOMEN. By Rhodessa Jones. November 5, 1992. Direction and music, Idris Ackamoor.

HIPPOLYTUS. By Euripides, translated into Kannada by Raghunandana, based on Robert Bragg's English translation. November 11, 1992. Director, Vasilios Calitisis; scenery, George Ziakas; lighting, Howard Thies; costumes, Prema Karanth; music, B. V. Karanth and Philip Kovvantis. With N. Mangala, K. R. Nandini, K. C. Raghunath.

UNDERGROUND. Conceived and directed by Theodora Skipitares. November 27, 1992. Music, Bobby Previtte.

THE BABY. Written and directed by Paola Bellu. December 5, 1992. With Tomas Aranas and The Shardana Co.

DESHIMA. Conceived and directed by Ping Chong and Michael Matthews. January 1, 1993. Scenery, Watuko Euono and Ping Chong; lighting, Thomas Hase; costumes, Carol Ann Pelletier. With Deena Burton, Barbara Chan, Ching Gonzalez, Brian Liem, Larry Malvern, Michael Matthews, Emerald Trinket Monsod, Dawn Saito, Perry Yung.

TALES FROM HOLLYWOOD. By Christopher Hampton. January 7, 1993. Director, Seth Barrish; scenery, Markas Henry; lighting, Eileen H. Dougherty; costumes, Nina Canter. With Mark Shannon, Lee Brock, Marcia DeBonis, Keely Eastley, Tom Riis Farrell, Aaron Goodwin, Shannon Jones, Michael Marcus, Denis O'Hare, Michael Warren Powell, Wendee Powell, Wendee Pratt, Paul Rice, Jeff Robbins, Natalie Ross, Stephen Singer, Judy Sullivan, John Ventimiglia.

POINT OF DEBARKATION. Written, directed and designed by John Jesurun. January 22, 1993. Choreography, Sanghi Wagner; lighting, Jeff Nash; puppets, Jane Stein; video, Richard Connors.

500 YEARS: A FAX FROM DENISE STOKLOS TO CHRISTOPHER COLUMBUS. Written, directed, choreographed and performed by Denise Stoklos. January 28, 1993. Lighting, Denise Stoklos and Annette Ter Meulen; costumes, Veronica Franca.

GHOSTS: LIVE FROM GALILEE (THE SCOTTSBORO BOYS BLUES OPERA). Libretto, Edgar Nkosi White; music, Genji Ito. February 11, 1993. Director, George Ferencz.

FAUST GASTRONOME. Text adapted and directed by Richard Schechner; music, Ralph Denzer, Michelle Kinney and Charles Gounod. February 18, 1993. Scenery, Chris Muller; lighting, Lenore Doxsee; costumes, Constance Hoffman. With Maria Vail, Jeff Rickets, Rebecca Ortese, Ulla Neuerberg, Daniel Wilkes Kelley, Leigh Brown, Shaula Chambliss, David Letwin, Laverne Summers.

EVERYDAY NEWT BURMAN (THE TRILOGY OF CYCLIC EXISTENCE) (opera). By John Moran. March 5, 1993. Director, Bob McGrath. With The Ridge Theater. Reopened May 6, 1993.

THE PRINCE OF MADNESS. Written and directed by Dario D'Ambrosi. March 25, 1993. Scenery and costumes, Carmela Spiteri; lighting, Marcello Iazetti. With Dario D'Ambrosi, Cristina Colombo, Emilio De Marchi, Remo Remotti.

LOOSENING THE SHADOW. Conceived, composed and designed by Beth Skinner, Ed Herbst and Jun Maeda. April 1, 1993. With the Thunder Bay Ensemble.

BLIND SIGHT. By Virlana Tkacz, Wanda Phipps and Watoku Ueno. April 9, 1993. Directed by Virlana Tkacz. With the Yara Arts Group.

ANGEL FROM MONTGOMERY. Book, music, lyrics and direction, Billy Boesky. May 6, 1993. Director, Richard Caliban.

EXTENDED FORECAST. By Franz Xaver Kroetz, translated by Erica Bilder and Estelle Parsons. May 28, 1993. Director, Erica Bilder; scenery and lighting, Watoku Ueno; costumes, Theodora Skipitares. With Estelle Parsons.

Lamb's Theater Company. Committed to developing and presenting new works in their most creative and delicate beginnings. Carolyn Rossi Copeland producing director.

THE ROADS TO HOME. By Horton Foote. September 11, 1992. See entry in the Plays Produced Off Broadway section of this volume.

GIFTS OF THE MAGI. Book and lyrics, Mark St. Germain, based on the O. Henry story; music and lyrics, Randy Courts. December 4, 1992. Director, Scott Harris; choreography, Janet Watson. With Kathleen Bloom, Michael Farina, Herb Foster, John Hickock, Eddie Korbich, Lou Williford.

LAMB'S THEATER COMPANY—Lily Knight and Angelina Fiordellisi in *The View From Here* by Margaret Dulaney

THE VIEW FROM HERE (44). By Margaret Dulaney. February 25, 1993. Director, Matt Williams; scenery, Michael Anania; lighting, Michael Gilliam; costumes, Elsa Ward. With Angelina Fiordellisi, Lily Knight, Tudi Roche, Adam LeFevre.

Music-Theater Group. Pioneering in the development of new music-theater. Lyn Austin producing director, Diane Wondisford general director.

COOKING THE WORLD (8). By Bob Berky; music, William Harper. October 13, 1992. Director, Paul Walker; scenery and costumes, Donna Zakowska; lighting, Paul Bartlett. With Bob Berky, Peter Francis James.

HEY, LOVE (15). Conceived and directed by Richard Maltby Jr.; music, Mary Rodgers; lyrics, Marshall Barer, Martin Charnin, John Forster, Richard Maltby Jr., Mary Rodgers, Stephen Sondheim and William Shakespeare. March 24, 1993. Musical director, Patrick S. Brady; costumes, David C. Woolard. With Karen Mason, Marcus Lovett, Mark Waldrop.

New Dramatists. An organization devoted to playwrights; member writers may use the facilities for anything from private cold readings of their material to public script-in-hand readings. Elana Greenfield director of artistic programming, Jana Jevnikar director of finance, Paul A. Slee, director of development.

Rehearsed Readings

Y YORK: NO PROPS. By and with Y York. July 8, 1992. Director, Mark Lutwak.

GREATER GOOD. By Amlin Gray. August 27, 1992. Director, Lawrence J. Jost. With Kevin Geer, Garret Dillahunt, Patrick Kerr, Peter Schmidtz, Jordan Charney, Davis Hall, Dan Ahearn, John Seitz, Mark Hammer, Ron Frazier, George McGrath.

PACIFIC OCEAN. By Roger Durling. October 1, 1992. Director, Mark Brokaw. With Jan Leslie Harding, Elzbieta Czyzewska, Leslie Nipkow, Ted Brunetti, J. Ed Araiza, Alan Brasington.

VOIR DIRE. By Joe Sutton. October 19, 1992. Director, Clinton Turner Davis. With Georgina Corbo, Conan McCarty, Ariane Brandt, Lynn Cohen, Kim Yancey, Julia Gibson.

BORDERS OF LOYALTY. By Michael Henry Brown. November 2, 1992. Director, Marion McClinton. With Matt Lamaj, Michael Potts, Betty Bynum, Erica Gimpel, Christina Moore.

HUNTERS OF THE SOUL. By Marion McClinton. November 2, 1992. Director, Seret Scott. With Novella Nelson, Willie Carpenter.

THE DAY THE BRONX DIED. By Michael Henry Brown. November 6, 1992. Director, Gordon Edelstein. With Troy Winbush, Richard Topol, Seth Gilliam, Dwayne Gurley, Cynthia Martells, Tony Donelson, Daryl Mitchell, Terry Alexander, Michael Potts, Curtis McClarin, Akile Prince, Herbert Rubens.

STUPID KIDS. By John C. Russell. November 9, 1992. Director, Michael Mayer. With Garret Dillahunt, Christina Kirk, Ben Bode.

THE BENEFITS OF DOUBT. By Joe Sutton. November 18, 1992. Director, David Chambers. With Steven Mendillo, Stephanie Mnookin, Cindy Katz, Keith Szarabajka, Mark Blum, Stephen Harrison.

CRUISING CLOSE TO CRAZY. By Laura Cunningham. November 23, 1992. Director, Jim Simpson. With Sigourney Weaver, Raynor Scheine, John Seitz, Phoebe Cates, Kevin Kline.

ANARCHY IN THE OK. Written and directed by Erik Ehn. January 16, 1993. With Alexandria Sage, David Van Tieghem, Neal Huff, Margaret Welsh, Kate Forbes, Welker White, Kevin Corrigan.

FREEFALL. By Charles Smith. February 3, 1993. Director, Jim Simpson. With Miles Watson, Jasper McGruder, Karen Kandel, Cortez Nance.

IN THE LAND OF GIANTS. By Roger Arturo Durling. February 9, 1993. Director, Travis Preston. With Chris McCann, Elzbieta Czyzewska, Tomas Milian, Roberto Jiminez, Elina Lowensohn, Clia Rivera, Sol Echeverria, S. Jason Smith.

SHOEMAN. Written and directed by Marion McClinton. March 3, 1993. With Keith Glover, Laurence Mason, Marchand Odette, Marcus Naylor, Bernard Cummings.

ENLIGHTENMENTS. Written and directed by Marion McClinton. March 3, 1993.

BENNY KOZO. Written and directed by Jim Simpson. March 31, 1993.

SACRED RHYTHMS. By Eduardo Machado; music, Paquito D'Rivera. April 2, 1993.

THIN AIR. By Lynne Alvarez. April 15, 1993. Director, David Esbjornson.

JULIE JOHNSON. By Wendy Hammond. April 26, 1993. Director, Gloria Muzio.

New Federal Theater. Dedicated to presenting new playwrights and plays dealing with the minority and Third World experience. Woodie King Jr. producer.

32 performances each

CHRISTCHILD. By J. E. Franklin. November 20, 1992. Director, Irving Vincent; scenery, Felix Cochren; lighting, Jeff Guzlik; costumes, Judy Dearing. With Patti Brown, Vincent La Mar Campbell, Lee Roy Giles, Minelva Nanton, Michele Shay, Terri Towns, Charles Malik Whitfield.

ROBERT JOHNSON: TRICK THE DEVIL. By Bill Harris. February 18, 1993. Director, Woodie King Jr.; scenery, Richard Harmon; lighting, Antoinette Tynes; costumes, Judy Dearing; music, Guy Davis. With Guy Davis, Denise Burse-Mickelbury, Grenoldo Frazier, Herman Levern Jones.

New York Shakespeare Festival Public Theater. Schedule of special projects, in addition to its regular off-Broadway productions. JoAnne Akalaitis artistic director (George C. Wolfe producer as of 3/18/93)

Schedule included:

13 MINUS ONE (staged readings and works-in-progress): D by Lynn Wachman, directed by Jessica Bauman; GARY AND THE SANDMAN by Susan Bennett, directed by Jessica Bauman; BLUES written and directed by Dor Green; FANDANGO by Donna DiNovelli, directed by Dennis Davis; THE NEURO SISTERS by Lizzie Olesker, Cora Hook and Barbara Allen; ECLIPSE IN BOTTOMVILLE written and directed by Jake-Ann Jones; STUFFED CHILDREN by Julian France, directed by James Peck; DAYBREAK—THE CHILDREN by Evangeline Johns, directed by Dennis Davis; DRIZZLE by Sung Rno, directed by Daniel Kim; LAS MENINAS by Lynn Nottage, directed by Tony Gerber; QUICK, FAST AND IN A HURRY by Dennis Moritz, directed by Mark Lord; STICKY 'N JUICY ON DA SENATE FLOOR by Honour Molloy and Donna Villella, directed by Jimbo Flynn. June 2–7, 1992.

PUPPETRY AT THE PUBLIC: THE INTERNATIONAL FESTIVAL OF PUPPET THEATER. Festival included MY CIVILIZATION and SICK BUT TRUE by Paul Zaloom, Donny Osman and Jed Weissberg, directed by Donny Osman, with Paul Zaloom; PINOKIO by M. Klima, Josef Krofta, Petr Matasek, Vladimir Zajic, directed by Josef Krofta, with Theater Drak; MANIPULATOR and UNDERDOG by and with Neville Tranter (Stuffed Puppet Theater); THE END OF THE WORLD written, directed and performed by Roman Paska. September 7–20, 1992.

Public Fringe (late night performance series)

DON'T EVER CHANGE. By and with Frank Maya. October 8, 1992.

IT'S ON THE BOARD!: DIRECTIONS FROM A SWITCHBOARD QUEEN (work-in-progress) by and with Emmett Foster; THE LATE BLOOMERS (work-in-progress) by and with Jennifer Duffy and Anne Shapiro; BOO! SEVEN CHARACTERS/NO GUARANTEES by and with Stephen Patterson. October 15, 1992.

THE DEAD CLOWN CIRCUS. November 12, 1992.

ZEL REBELS! THE STORY OF A WOMAN IN A ONE MAN SHOW. By and with Ellen Hulkower. November 19, 1992.

SHOUT & TWIST. Text and music, Johann Carlo and Michael Butler, in collaboration with Henry Stram. April 2, 1993.

UNDERGROUND GODDESS. By Abigail Gampel. April 15, 1993. Director, Anthony Koplin. With Abigail Gampel, Chris Gampel, Francis X. Dowd Jr., Judy Sanger.

THE SOLDIERS OF SOLITUDE. By and with Joey John. April 22, 1993.

NO SHAME (late night performance series) co-produced with HOME for Contemporary Theater and Art, ran throughout the 1992–1993 season.

New York Theater Workshop. Produces new theater by American and international artists and encourages risk and stimulates experimentation in theatrical form. James C. Nicola artistic director, Nancy Kassak Diekmann managing director.

PUNCH ME IN THE STOMACH (25). By Deb Filler and Alison Summers. June 2, 1992. Director, Alison Summers; scenery, George Xenos; lighting, Pat Dignan. With Alison Summers.

C. COLOMBO INC.: EXPORT/IMPORT, GENOA (14). By Leo Bassi. October 26, 1992. Director, Christopher Grabowski; scenery, costumes, and lighting, Anita Stewart. With Leo Bassi, Steve Elm, Edwin Newman.

O SOLO MIO FESTIVAL (solo performances). Schedule included: BLOWN SIDEWAYS THROUGH LIFE by and with Claudia Schear, directed by Christopher Ashley; THE LAKE LAND by and with Fanni Green; A PERFECT LIFE by and with Paul Zimet; SOMETHING

WONDERFUL by and with Tom Cayler; STATE OF THE NATION by and with Douglas McGrath; A NORMAL GUY by and with Jim Fyfe; STUFF AS DREAMS ARE MADE ON by and with Fred Curchack, adapted from William Shakespeare's *The Tempest*. December 2–20, 1992.

In Repertory:

OWNERS (14) and TRAPS (13). By Caryl Churchill. April 7, 1993. Directors, Mark Wing-Davey and Lisa Peterson; scenery, Derek McLane; lighting, Christopher Akerlind; costumes, Gabriel Berry. With John Curless, Robert Stanton, J. Smith-Cameron, Lynn Hawley, Tim Hopper, Melinda Mullins, David Alford.

The Open Eye. Goal is to gather a community of outstanding theater artists to collaborate on works for the stage for audiences of all ages and cultural backgrounds. Jean Erdman founding director, Amie Brockway artistic director.

THE ODYSSEY (11). Adapted from Homer's epic and directed by Amie Brockway; music, Elliott Sokolov. November 7, 1992. Choreography, Susan Jacobson; scenery, lighting, costumes and puppets, Adrienne J. Brockway; musical director, Richard Henson. With Ricky Genaro, John DiLeo, Jose Joaquin Garcia, Ernest Johns, Stephanie Marshall, Deborah Stein, Amy Wilson.

THE WISE MEN OF CHELM (12). By Sandra Fenichel Asher. December 12, 1992. Director, Amie Brockway; choreography, Adina Kaufman Popkin; scenery, lighting and costumes, Adrienne J. Brockway. With Stacie Chaiken, George Colangelo, Judy Dodd, Scott Facher, Larry Hirschhorn, Andrew Rogow.

FREEDOM IS MY MIDDLE NAME (12). By Lee Hunkins. January 16, 1993. Director, Ernest Johns; scenery, lighting and costumes, Adrienne J. Brockway. With Mary Cushman, John DiLeo, Bryon Easley, Keith Johnston, Sheryl Greene Leverett, Stephanie Marshall.

Pan Asian Repertory Theater. Strives to provide opportunities for Asian American artists to perform under the highest professional standards and to create and promote plays by and about Asians and Asian Americans. Tisa Chang artistic/producing director.

28 performances each

CAMBODIA AGONISTES. By Ernest Abuba. October 28, 1992. Director, Tisa Chang; scenery, Robert Klingelhoefer; lighting, Deborah Constantine; costumes, Juliet Ouyoung. With June Angela, Sam-Oeun Tes, John Baray, Richard Ebihara, Lou Ann Lucas, Virginia Wing, Ron Nakahara, Hai Wah Yung.

A DOLL HOUSE. By Henrik Ibsen, adapted and directed by John R. Briggs, based on a concept by Tisa Chang. April 28, 1993. Scenery, Robert Klingelhoefer; lighting, William Simmons; costumes, Juliet Ouyoung. With Mel Duane Gionson, Daniel Dae Kim, Karen Tsen Lee, Lou Ann Lucas, Ron Nakahara.

Playwrights Horizons New Theater Wing. Full productions of new works, in addition to the regular off-Broadway productions. Don Scardino artistic director.

14 performances each

MAN IN HIS UNDERWEAR. By Jay Tarses. December 9, 1992. Director, Kevin Dowling; scenery, Rob Odorisio; lighting, Michael Lincoln; costumes, Therese A. Bruck. With Dann Florek, Robert Joy, Dick Latessa, Debra Monk, Jennifer Van Dyck, Cordelia Richards, Cynthia Vance.

SOPHISTRY (14). By Jonathan Marc Sherman. March 17, 1993. Director, Nicholas Martin; scenery, Allen Moyer; lighting, Kenneth Posner; costumes, Michael Krass. With Linda Atkinson, Nadia Dajani, Ethan Hawke, Katherine Hiler, Scarlett Johansson, Dick Latessa, Anthony Rapp, Jonathan Marc Sherman, Steve Zahn.

Primary Stages Company. Dedicated to new American plays by new American playwrights. Casey Childs artistic director, Gina Gionfriddo general manager, Janet Reed associate director.

24 performances each

THE DOLPHIN POSITION. By Percy Granger. October 1, 1992. Director, Casey Childs; scenery, Ray Recht; lighting, Deborah Constantine; costumes, Bruce Goodrich. With Larry Pine, Charlotte d'Amboise, Richmond Hoxie, Anna Holbrook, Randell Haynes, Andrew Weems, Ilene Kristen, Justin Zaremby.

BARGAINS. By Jack Heifner. February 7, 1993. Director, Casey Childs; scenery and costumes, Bruce Goodrich; lighting, Deborah Constantine. With T. Scott Cunningham, Raynor Scheine, Sally Sockwell, Jacqueline Lucid, Celia Weston, Gregory Grove.

WASHINGTON SQUARE MOVES. By Matthew Witten. April 29, 1993. Director, Seth Gordon; scenery, Bruce Goodrich; lighting, Deborah Constantine; costumes, Amanda J. Klein. With Angela Bullock, Bert Goldstein, Dion Graham, Joe Quintero, Bert Goldstein, Dawn McClendon, Ascanio Sharpe, Jack Stehlin.

Puerto Rican Traveling Theater. Professional company presenting bilingual productions primarily of Puerto Rican and Hispanic playwrights, emphasizing subjects of relevance today. Miriam Colon Valle founder and producer.

MAMBO LOUIE AND THE DANCING MACHINE (work-in-progress) (22). By Eugene Rodriguez. August 6, 1992. Director, Alex Colon; choreography, Poli Rogers; scenery, lighting and costumes, Michael Sharp. With Jorge Castillo, Georgina Corbo, Denis Hernandez, Jose Manuel Yenke.

THE BOILER ROOM (36). By Reuben Gonzalez. January 13, 1993. Director, Alex Colon; scenery, Edward T. Gianfrancesco; lighting, Rachel Budin. With Miriam Colon, Rosalinde Milan, Joe Quintero, Ed Trucco.

THE TOOTHBRUSH (48). By Jorge Diaz, translated and directed by Alba Oms. March 3, 1993. Scenery, Miguel Lopez-Castillo; lighting, Bill Simmons. With Maria Cellario, Chris de Oni.

Quaigh Theater. Primarily a playwrights' theater, devoted to the new playwright, the established contemporary playwright and the modern (post-1920) playwright. Will Lieberson artistic director.

THE BEST OF THE DRAMATHON (20) (one-act plays): AT LIBERTY by Tennessee Williams, directed by Bill Lipscomb; THE LOCAL STIGMATIC by Heathcote Williams, directed by Will Lieberson; THE DICKS by Jules Fieler, directed by Mary Tierney; THE TIES THAT BIND by Matthew Witten, directed by Bill Lipscomb; NOW DEPARTING by Robert Mearns, directed by Will Lieberson; BREAKING IN by James T. McCartin, directed by Edward Charles Lynch. July 29, 1992. Scenery, Tobi Furukawa; lighting, Winifred Powers. With Kim Dickens, Patricia Dodd, Ned Salisbury, Robert P. King, Edward Charles Lynch, Tom Fountain, Ron Roth, Jean-Robert Cledet, Claudine Kielson, Derek LeDain, Mardina Parker, Karen Dumas.

A MAP AND A CAP (12). Written and performed by Stuart Warmflash. October 29, 1992.

YUK YUK (20). Written and directed by Will Lieberson. April 22, 1993. Scenery, Ralph Thornton; lighting, Ted Bergen; costumes, Lila Upson. With Johnny Diamond, Crystal Franklin.

Lunchtime Series. 10 performances each

GETTING OUT BEFORE YOU GET IN. By Jon DeLarmo. October 5, 1992. Director, Scott Schreiber. With Fred Marley, Erica Edson, Lucille King, Bob Aston.

PROFILES OF THE UNKNOWN. Written and directed by Robert Fields. October 19, 1992. With Stanley Kosner, Valentina Gorbunov, Tom McDonald, Olga Price.

QUAIGH THEATER—Kim Dickens and Patricia Dodd in *At Liberty*

SON OF A BEACH. By Nancy Phillips. November 2, 1992. Director, Alfred Brauer. With Tom Salsbury, Ted Vernon, David Rubin, Martin Rhodes.

ET TU, BRUTUS. By Shelly Markson. November 16, 1992. Director, Barbara Kennedy. With JoAnn Muller, James Guest, Francis Preston.

THE UNDISCOVERED. By Lorna Sirrone. November 30, 1992. Director, Janice Hannen. With Ben Ducore, Sandy Curry.

RAW SEWAGE. By Martin Randell. December 14, 1992. Director, Peter Kaufman. With Steve Nester, Paul Meredith, Edith Janes, Ann Falk.

LAST EXIT BEFORE TOLL. By Carrie Goldstein. January 11, 1993. Director, Will Lieberson. With Sara Lowell.

TOO MANY HATS. By Ralph Lesser. January 25, 1993. Director, Francine Hollander. With Jim Brady, Colette Landra.

DEADLY FLOWERS. By Jack Browning. February 8, 1993. Director, Michael Whitefield. With Gretchen Malloy, Simon Lefcort, Tillie Nash, Sandra Kelly.

THE OPERATING TABLE. By Leslie Donaldson. February 22, 1993. Director, Herschel Levine. With Mary Powell, Helen Pollock, Tony Levant, Hume Proctor.

THE RETURN OF YUK YUK. Written and directed by Will Lieberson. March 8, 1993. With Loring Powers, Tommy Shields.

BEYOND THE BEYOND. By Candice Mackelroy. March 22, 1993. Director, Robert Eagan. With Harry Hatcher, Valerie Smythe, Joyce Feldman.

THE DEADLY CHEF. By Parone March. April 19, 1993. Director, Donald Grant. With Carol Nelson, John Ford, Lisa Fernandez.

DOUBLE BILL. By Salvatore LaMatta. May 3, 1993. Director, Lester Schultz. With Roseanne Barkely, Helen Simpson, Javier Sanchez.

THE PO PO. By Tobi Furukawa. May 17, 1993. Director, Will Lieberson. With Edith Kandell, Brian Boyar, Jane Wolf.

Summer Reading Series
OUR HOUSE. By Peter Levy. July 27, 1992.
OBSESSION. By Peter Levy. August 3, 1992.
THE WILD GUY. By Rebecca Shaw and Andrew Wreggitt. August 10, 1992.

JOE DI MAGGIO MUST DIE. By Abe Polsky. August 17, 1992.
RENDEZVOUS WITH DEATH. By Paul Brandt. August 24, 1992.

The Ridiculous Theatrical Company. The late Charles Ludlam's comedic troupe devoted to productions of his original scripts and new adaptations of the classics. Everett Quinton artistic director, Steve Asher managing director.

BROTHER TRUCKERS (72). By Georg Osterman. September 17, 1992. Director, Everett Quinton; scenery, Mark Beard; lighting, Terry Alan Smith; costumes, Elizabeth Fried. With Grant Neale, Georg Osterman, Eureka, Everett Quinton, Maureen Angelos, Lisa Herbold, Stephen Pell, Noelle Kalom, Adam Weitz.

LINDA (42). Book, Everett Quinton; music, Mark Bennett; lyrics, Everett Quinton and Mark Bennett. May 2, 1993. Director, David Ganon; scenery, T. Greenfield; lighting, Richard Currie; costumes, Toni Nanette Thompson. With Chris Tanner, Grant Neale, Lisa Herbold, Bobby Reed, Everett Quinton, Brenda Cummings, Eureka.

Second Stage Theater. Committed to producing plays believed to deserve another look, as well as new works. Carole Rothman artistic director, Suzanne Schwartz Davidson producing director.

SPIKE HEELS (56). By Theresa Rebeck. June 4, 1992. Director, Michael Greif; scenery, James Youmans; lighting, Kenneth Posner; costumes, Candice Donnelly. With Tony Goldwyn, Saundra Santiago, Kevin Bacon, Julie White.

A . . . MY NAME IS STILL ALICE (97). Musical revue conceived and directed by Joan Micklin Silver and Julianne Boyd. November 22, 1992. Choreography, Hope Clarke; scenery, Andrew Jackness; lighting, David F. Segal; costumes, David C. Woolard; musical director, Ian Herman. With Roo Brown, Laura Dean, Cleo King, KT Sullivan, Nancy Ticotin.

ONE SHOE OFF. By Tina Howe. April 15, 1993. Produced at the Joseph Papp Public Theater; see its entry in the Plays Produced Off Broadway section of this volume.

TIME ON FIRE. By Evan Handler. May 13, 1993. Produced at the Joseph Papp Public Theater; see its entry in the Plays Produced Off Broadway section of this volume.

Signature Theater Company. Dedicated to the exploration of a playwright's body of work. James Houghton artistic director.

16 performances each

FORTINBRAS. By Lee Blessing. October 9, 1992. Director, Jeanne Blake; scenery, David Birn and Judy Gailen; lighting, Jeffrey S. Koger; costumes, Teresa Snider-Stein. With William Cain, Kevin Elden, Steven Guevera, Celia Howard, Albert Macklin, Archer Martin, Samantha Mathis, William Metzo, Keith Reddin, Don Reilly, Anthony Michael Ruivivar, Josh Sebers, Cynthia Vance, Kim Walsh, Timothy Wheeler.

LAKE STREET EXTENSION. By Lee Blessing. November 27, 1992. Director, Jeanne Blake; scenery, E. David Cosier; lighting, Jeffrey S. Koger; costumes, Teresa Snider-Stein. With Keith A. Brush, Joe Sharkey, Rick Telles.

TWO ROOMS. By Lee Blessing. February 12, 1993. Director, James Houghton; scenery, E. David Cosier; lighting, Jeffrey S. Koger; costumes, Teresa Snider-Stein. With A. Bernard Cummings, Laura Esterman, Jeffrey Hayenga, Madhur Jaffrey.

PATIENT A. By Lee Blessing. April 23, 1993. Director, Jeanne Blake; lighting, Jeffrey S. Koger; costumes, Teresa Snider-Stein. With Robin Morse, Jon De Vries, Richard Bekins.

Soho Rep. Dedicated to new, non-naturalistic plays. Marlene Swartz founder and executive director, Julian Webber artistic director.

CROSS DRESSING IN THE DEPRESSION (12). By Erin Cressida Wilson. November 12, 1992. Director, Marcus Stern; scenery, James Schuette; lighting, Scott Zielinski; costumes, Allison Koturbash. With Jan Leslie Harding, Mark Margolis, Erin Cressida Wilson.

YES, BUT IS IT THEATER? (festival): Schedule included WENDY IN THE WACKO WARD by and with Wendy Hammond and Patricia Scanlon; PROPHET IN LIMBO by and with Patricia Scanlon; INSTANT GIRL by and with the Wrylette Sisters; LOVE SO DEEP by and with Dancenoise. February 12–27, 1993.

DAVID'S RED-HAIRED DEATH (16). By Sherry Kramer. May 20, 1993. Director, Julian Webber; scenery, Rob Odorisio; lighting, Don Holder; costumes, Maggie Morgan. With Jan Leslie Harding, Deirdre O'Connell.

Late Night Performances

TERMINAL HIP. By Mac Wellman. May 21, 1993. Scenery, Kyle Chepulis. With Stephen Mellor.

3 AMERICANISMS. By Mac Wellman. May 22, 1993. Director, Jim Simpson; scenery, Kyle Chepulis; music, Mike Nolan. With Ron Faber, Mark Margolis, Jan Leslie Harding.

Theater for the New City. Developmental theater and new American experimental works. George Bartenieff, Crystal Field artistic directors.

Schedule included:

ANNA, THE GYPSY SWEDE. By Viveca Lindfors. June 4, 1992. Scenery and lighting, Vivien Leone; costumes, Franne Lee; music, Patricia Lee Stotter. With Viveca Lindfors, Joseph C. Davies.

CHRISTOPHER COLUMBUS! OR, BUSINESS AS USUAL (13). Book, lyrics and direction, Crystal Field; music, Chris Cherney. August 8, 1992. Scenery, Anthony Angel; costumes, Sheila Warren. With Joseph C. Davies, Crystal Field, Michael David Gordon, Mark Marcante, Mira Rivera.

BLUE HEAVEN. Written and directed by Karen Malpede. September 17, 1992. Choreography, Lee Nagrin; scenery, Leonardo Shapiro; lighting, Brian Aldous; costumes, Karen Young; music, Gretchen Langheld. With Lee Nagrin, George Bartenieff, Rosalie Triana, Lailah Hanit Bragin, Nicki Paraiso, Sheila Dabney, Christian Clifford, Joseph Kellough, Beverly Wideman.

PINEAPPLE FACE (16). By Rosalyn Drexler. November 5, 1992. Director, John Vaccaro; scenery, Noel MacFetrich and Norman Anderson; lighting, Jeff Nash; costumes, Jerry Harding. With Joe Pichette, John Vaccaro, Ruby Lynn Reyner, Emilio Cubiero, Crystal Field, Michael Brody, Tony Zanetta.

MY ANCESTORS' HOUSE. By Bina Sharif. December 3, 1992. Scenery and costumes, J. Antonio Rouco; lighting, Adam Silverman. With Glenn Athaide, Raj Shree Daryanani, Madhur Jaffrey, Sunita Mukhi, Karim Panjwani, Sol Echeverria, Tamir.

TIMES SQUARE ANGEL (15). By Charles Busch. December 3, 1992. Director, Kenneth Elliott; scenery, B. T. Whitehill; lighting, Vivien Leone; costumes, Shawn Dudley. With Theresa Aceves, Jim Borstelmann, Ralph Buckley, Guyah Clark, Kenneth Elliott, Andy Halliday, Arnie Kolodner, Jim Mahady, Cheryl Reeves, Brian Winkowski.

BREAD & PUPPET THEATER: NATIVITY 1992. Written, directed and designed by Peter Schumann. December 30, 1992. With Pedro Adorno, Emily Anderson, Mary Curtin, Michael Dennison, Pati Hernandez, Jackie O'Halloran, Michael Romanyshyn, Cathy Vigo.

THE BLUE SKY IS A CURSE: BARON BONES, written and directed by Paul Zimet; music, Ellen Maddow; BROWN DOG IS DEAD book and music, Ellen Maddow; directed by Brian Jucha; THE PLUMBER'S HELPER book and direction, Paul Zimet; music, Ellen Maddow. January 21, 1993. Scenery, Tony Carruthers; lighting, Carol Mullins; costumes, David Zinn. With William Badgett, Ellen Maddow, Terry McCarthy, Tom Nelis, Tina Shepard, Paul Zimet (The Talking Band).

GET HUR. By Ray Dobbins. February 11, 1993. Director, Bette Bourne (Bloolips); lighting, David Adams. With Bette Bourne (Bloolips), Gretel Feather, Ivan, Precious Pearl.

THE BUNDLE MAN (chamber opera) (8). Libretto, Ilsa Gilbert; music, Marshall Coid. March 11, 1993. Director, Tom O'Horgan; scenery and costumes, Perry Arthur Kroeger; lighting, Chris Dallos and Robert Williams. With Marshall Coid, Steven Goldstein, Stephen Kahn, Daryl Hanriksen.

SPAIN. Written and directed by Romulus Linney. April 1, 1993. Scenery, Mark Marcante; lighting, Jeffrey S. Koger; costumes, Teresa Snider-Stein. With Frank Anderson, Peter Ashton Wise, Fred Burrell, T. Cat Ford, Russel Lunday, Mary Beth Peil, Michael Burrell.

MASTER & MARGARITA, OR THE DEVIL COMES TO MOSCOW (16). Adapted by Jean-Claude van Itallie from Mikhail Bulgakov's work. May 13, 1993. Director, David Willinger; scenery, Mark Symczak; lighting, Tommy Barker; costumes, Tanya Serdiuk. With Eran Bohem, Lisa Nicholas, Arthur Abrams, Alison Broda, Milton Carney, Jonathan Teague Cook, Matthew Dudley, Tom Dale Keever, Gary Kimble, Rafael Mateo, Kolawole Ogundiran, Eric Rasmussen, Cesar Rodriguez.

THE HOUSEGUESTS (12). By Harry Kondoleon. May 13, 1993. Director, Tom Gladwell; scenery, Chris Fields; costumes, David Zinn. With Birgit Darby, Melissa Hurst, Tom Ledcke, Albert Macklin.

Ubu Repertory Theater. Committed to acquainting American audiences with new works by contemporary French-speaking playwrights from around the world. Francoise Kourilsky artistic director.

THE FREE ZONE (32). By Jean-Claude Grumberg, translated by Catherine Temerson. March 15, 1993. Director, Francoise Kourilsky; scenery, Watoku Ueno; lighting, Greg MacPherson; costumes, Carol Ann Pelletier. With Polly Adams, Ivan Borodin, Mildred Clinton, Ian Cohen, Dan Daily, Ronald Guttman, J. D. Hyman, Michael Ingram, Jodie Lynne McClintock, Bernie Passiltiner, Patti Perkins, Oren J. Sofer.

The Vineyard Theater. Multi-art chamber theater dedicated to the development of new plays and musicals, music-theater collaborations and innovative revivals. Douglas Aibel artistic director, Barbara Zinn Krieger executive director, Jon Nakagawa managing director.

JUNO (29). Book, Joseph Stein, based on Sean O'Casey's *Juno and the Paycock;* music and lyrics, Marc Blitzstein. October 18, 1992. Director, Lonny Price; choreography, Joey McKneely; scenery, William Barclay; lighting, Phil Monat; costumes, Gail Brassard; musical direction, Grant Sturiale. With Anita Gillette, Dick Latessa, Ivar Brogger, Anne O'Sullivan, Erin O'Brien, Malcolm Gets.

PTERODACTYLS (19). By Nicky Silver. February 24, 1993. Director, David Warren; scenery, James Youmans; lighting, Donald Holder; costumes, Teresa Snider-Stein; dinosaur design, Jim Gary. With Kelly Bishop, T. Scott Cunningham, Hope Davis, Dennis Creaghan, Kent Lanier.

THE CHOCOLATE AMBASSADOR (8). Book and lyrics, Camille Saviola and Chip Lopez; music, Charles Greenberg. April 7, 1993. Director, Andre Ernotte; choreography, Lynn Taylor; scenery, Allen Moyer; lighting, Brian Aldous; costumes, Gail Grassard. With Camille Saviola, Haigh Nayyan, Mindy Cooper, Julio Munge.

CHRISTINA ALBERTA'S FATHER (19). Book, music and lyrics, Polly Pen, based on H. G. Wells's book. May 13, 1993. Director, Andre Ernotte; choreography, Lynne Taylor-Corbett; scenery, William Barclay; lighting, Phil Monat; costumes, Gail Brassard; musical direction, Madeline Rubinstein. With Marla Schaffel, Henry Stram, Alma Cuervo, Lynette Perry, Duane Boutte, Susan Blommaert, Don Mayo, Roxie Lucas, Richard Holmes, Andy Taylor.

ALDO AND HIS MAGIC LAMP (family musical presented in addition to its regular season). Book and lyrics, Barbara Zinn Krieger and Irene Tiersten; music, James Kurtz. December 26, 1992.

The Women's Project and Productions. Nurtures, develops and produces plays written and directed by women. Julia Miles founder and artistic director.

YOU COULD BE HOME NOW (28). Written and performed by Ann Magnuson. October 11, 1992. Produced at the Joseph Papp Public Theater; see its entry in the Plays Produced Off Broadway section of this volume.

WPA Theater. Produces new American plays and neglected musicals in the realistic idiom. Kyle Renick artistic director, Edward T. Gianfrancesco resident designer, Lori Sherman managing director.

CAMP PARADOX (32). By Barbara Graham. November 4, 1992. Director, Melia Bensussen; scenery, Edward T. Gianfrancesco; lighting, Craig Evans; costumes, Mimi Maxmen. With Danielle Ferland, Christina Haag, Russell Kopland, Alix Korey, Meredith Scott Lynn, Liann Pattison, Emily Schulman.

JEFFREY (48). By Paul Rudnick. January 19, 1993. Director, Christopher Ashley; scenery, James Youmans; lighting, Donald Holder; costumes, David C. Woolard. With Peter Bartlett, Bryan Batt, Harriet Harris, Tom Hewitt, Edward Hibbert, John Michael Higgins, Patrick Kerr, Richard Poe, Darryl Theirse.

LAUREEN'S WHEREABOUTS (33). By Larry Ketron. April 7, 1993. Director, Dann Florek; scenery, Edward T. Gianfrancesco; lighting, Phil Monat; costumes, Jonathan Green. With Mark Blum, Mia Dillon, Carolyn McCormick, Kevin O'Rourke, Scott Sowers.

York Theater Company. Specializing in producing new works, as well as in reviving unusual, forgotten or avant-garde musicals. Janet Hayes Walker producing director.

NOEL AND GERTIE (27). Conceived by Sheridan Morley. December 5, 1992. Director, Brian Murray; choreography, Janet Watson; scenery, James Morgan; lighting, Mary Jo Dondlinger; costumes, Barbara Beccio; musical director, Michael Kosarin. With Jane Summerhays, Michael Zaslow.

A DISTANCE FROM CALCUTTA (22). Written and directed by P. J. Barry. January 15, 1993. Scenery, James Morgan; lighting, Mary Jo Dondlinger; costumes, Barbara Beccio. With Beth Dixon, Sally Parrish, Julie Boyd, Connor Smith, Daniel Hagen.

CARNIVAL!. Book, Michael Stewart, based on material by Helen Deutsch; music and lyrics, Bob Merrill. March 31, 1993. Direction and choreography, Pamela Hunt; scenery, James Morgan; lighting, Mary Jo Dondlinger; costumes and puppets, Michael Bottari and Ronald Case; musical director, Darren R. Cohen. With Glory Crampton, Karen Mason, Paul Schoeffler, Robert Michael Baker, Bruce Anthony Davis, Teri Furr, Susan Guinn, William Linton, Robert Lydiard, Sandra Purpuro, Rusty Reynolds.

Miscellaneous

In the additional listing of 1992–93 off-off-Broadway productions below, the names of the producing groups or theaters appear in CAPITAL LETTERS and the titles of the works in *italics.* This list consists largely of new or reconstituted works and excludes most revivals, especially of classics. It includes a few productions staged by groups which rented space from the more established organizations listed previously.

THE ACTING COMPANY. *Monday Nights at the Houseman: Mad, Bad and Dangerous to Know* compiled from Lord Byron's works by Jane McCulloch; music by Don Fraser. December 21, 1992. With Derek Jacobi, Isla Blair. *Full Gallop* (one-woman show) by Mary Louise Wilson and Mark

Hampton. January 25, 1993. Directed by Mark Hampton; with Mary Louise Wilson. *Dear Liar* by Jerome Kilty. February 15, 1993. With Julie Harris, Alvin Epstein. *A Tribute to Funny Ladies* compiled by Olympia Dukakis and Paul Walker. March 1, 1993. Directed by Paul Walker; with Olympia Dukakis. *The Lunatic, The Lover, The Poet* (one-man show) compiled from William Shakespeare's works, directed and performed by Brian Bedford. March 15, 1993.

ALICE'S FOURTH FLOOR. *The Melville Boys* by Norm Foster. August 20, 1992. Directed by Susann Brinkley; with Richard Joseph Paul, Mark Tymchyshyn, Katherine Leask, Kellie Overbey.

AMERICAN JEWISH THEATER. *A Backer's Audition* book, music and lyrics by Douglas Bernstein and Denis Markell, based on an idea by Martin Charnin, Douglas Bernstein and Denis Markell. December 7, 1992. Directed by Leonard Foglia; with Tom Riis Farrell, Gretchen Kingsley, Alice Spivak, Stan Free, Ray Wills, Charles Goff, Tom Ligon, Sheila Smith. *Born Guilty* by Ari Roth, based on Peter Sichrovsky's book. January 24, 1993. Directed by Jack Gelber; with Zach Grenier, Greg Germann, Amy Wright, Victor Slezak, Lee Wilkof, Jennie Moreau, Maggie Burke. *Another Time* by Ronald Harwood. March 31, 1993. Directed by Stanley Brechner; with Malcolm McDowell, Marian Seldes, Joan Copeland, James Waterston, Jeremy Lands, Michael Lombard.

ANTROBUS GROUP THEATER. *Crushed: Tales From the Twentynothing Generation* (one-man show) by and with Lee Rosenthal. April 8, 1993. Directed by Forrest Brakeman.

APOLLO THEATER. *The Night Before Christmas: A Musical Fantasy* book, music and lyrics by Gary D. Hines, based on Clement C. Moore's *A Visit From St. Nicholas.* December, 1992. Directed by Brian Grandison; with Sounds of Blackness.

ATLANTIC THEATER. *The Elephant's Tricycle* written and directed by Elizabeth Cashour. August 20, 1992. With Catherine Brophy, Douglas Gibson, Brennan Murphy, Lillo Way. *The Root* by Gary Richards. March 11, 1993. Directed by Matthew Penn; with Giancarlo Esposito, Joseph Siravo, Jude Ciccolella, Tony Hoty.

ALICE'S FOURTH FLOOR—Richard Joseph Paul, Kellie Overbey and Mark Tymchyshyn in a scene from *The Melville Boys* by Norm Foster

THE BALLROOM. *Lypsinka! Now It Can Be Lip-Synched* by and with John Epperson. August 18, 1992. Directed by Kevin Malony. *The Charles Busch Revue.* May 11, 1993. Directed by Kenneth Elliott; with Charles Busch, Denise Nolan.

THE BARROW GROUP. *Tales From Hollywood.* See La Mama entry. *Low Level Panic* by Clare McIntyre. May 13, 1993. Directed by Leonard Foglia; with Marcia DeBonis, Christina Denzinger, Wendee Pratt.

BROOKLYN ACADEMY OF MUSIC. *Next Wave Festival.* Works included *Frida* book and direction by Hilary Blecher; music by Robert Xavier Rodriguez; lyrics by Migdalia Cruz. October 14, 1992. With Helen Schneider, William Rhodes, Chris Fields, Karen Hale, Kristin Hurst, Andrea Kane, Stephen Kaplin, Barbara Pollitt, Alba Quezada, Michael Romanyshyn, David Toney, Byron Utley, Andrew Varela. *Power Pipes* by Spiderwoman Theater. October 21, 1992. Directed by Muriel Miguel; with Elvira Colorado, Hortensia Colorado, Lisa Mayo, Gloria Miguel, Muriel Miguel, Murielle Borst. *Einstein on the Beach* (opera) music and lyrics by Philip Glass. November 19, 1992. Directed by Robert Wilson. *Needles and Opium* (one-man show) by and with Robert Lepage. December 8, 1992.

CHICAGO CITY LIMITS. *Un-Conventional Wisdom: Campaign '92 Update* by Chicago City Limits. August, 1992. Directed by Paul Zuckerman; with Gary Adler, Carole Bugge, Wendy Chatman, Carl Kissin, Judith Searcy, Rick Simpson, John Cameron Telfer.

CLUB 53. *Back to Bacharach and David* (cabaret) music by Burt Bacharach; lyrics by Hal David. March 11, 1993. Directed by Kathy Najimy; with Melinda Gilb, Steve Gunderson, Sue Mosher, Lillias White. (Transferred to off-Broadway status 3/25/93; see its entry in the Plays Produced Off Broadway section of this volume.)

COURTYARD PLAYHOUSE. *Meet Marvin: Ruminations, Evan on Earth* and *T-Shirts* by Robert Patrick. March 26, 1993. Directed by Lawrence Lane; with David Blackman, Neil Butterfield, Erich Schmidt, Casey Wayne.

CUCHARACHA THEATER. *A Vast Wreck* written and directed by Richard Caliban; music by John Hoge. April 15, 1993.

DANCE THEATER WORKSHOP. *Quintland (The Musical)* by and with Dan Hurlin. December 15, 1992.

DEL'S DOWN UNDER. *The News in Revue* (cabaret) by Nancy Holson. July 23, 1992. Directed by Terry Long; with Monique Lareau, Jack Plotnick, Richard Rowan, Linda Strasser, Stan Taffel.

DOWNTOWN ART COMPANY. *Empty Boxes* by William Badgett. October 7, 1992. Directed by Kent Alexander; with The Talking Band.

EIGHTY EIGHT'S. *Fancy Meeting You* (cabaret) compiled from E. Y. Harburg's works and performed by Phillip Officer. August 7, 1992.

FLORENCE GOULD HALL. *L'Etranger* by Albert Camus. November 13, 1992. With Theater En Pieces.

HAROLD CLURMAN THEATER. *Anything Cole: A Cole Porter Celebration* conceived by Alfonso Annotto, Tom Klebba and Jay B. Lesiger. Directed by Tom Klebba.

INTAR THEATER. *Day Dreams: The Music and Magic of Doris Day* book by Jim Murphy; music and lyrics by David Levy and Darren Cohen. July 8, 1992. Directed by Helen Butleroff; with Patty Carver, Michelle Opperman, Mary Jane Sullivan, Michelle Blakely, Catherine DuPuis, Steve Fickinger, Billy Miller, Jeannine Moore, Danny Rutigliano, Christopher Scott. *Strangers on Earth* by Mark O'Donnell. January 13, 1993. Directed by Matthew Ames; with Jeremy Gold, Elizabeth Daly, Johanna Pfaelzer, Jesse Wolfe, Shaun Powell.

IRISH REPERTORY THEATER COMPANY. *Joyicity* by Ulick O'Connor, directed by Caroline FitzGerald, original music by Noel Eccles, one-man performance by Vincent O'Neill; and *Frankly Brendan* adapted by Chris O'Neill from the works of Frank O'Connor and Brendan Behan, one-man performance by Chris O'Neill. September 9, 1992 (in repertory). Co-produced by One World Arts Foundation. *My Oedipus Complex* (monologue) by Frank O'Connor; *Seconds Out* by Aidan Barry, Noel O'Keeffe, Josie Buckley, Noel O'Driscoll, Kieran Wiseman, Trevor O'Herlihy,

Denis Butler, William Martin. April 13, 1993. Directed by Jack Hofsiss; with Chris O'Neill, Terry Donnelly, Des Keogh, Colin Lane, Sean Michael McCarthy, Brian F. O'Byrne, Paul Ronan. Co-produced by Very Special Arts and One World Arts Foundation.

JAPAN SOCIETY. *Momi No Dan, Tsurigitsune* and *Utsubozaru* (classic Japanese comedies). September 22, 1992. With the Nomura Kyogen Theater.

JEAN COCTEAU REPERTORY. *An Old Actress in the Role of Dostoyevsky's Wife* by Edvard Radzinsky, translated by Alma H. Law. September 4, 1992. Directed by Eve Adamson; with Jere Jacob, Craig Smith. *The Idiot* by Fyodor Dostoyevsky, adapted and directed by David Fishelson; with Craig Smith, John Lenartz, Elise Stone, Adrienne Williams, Joseph Menino, Angela Vitale. *The Cenci* by Percy Bysshe Shelley. March 21, 1993. Directed by Eve Adamson; with Craig Smith, Angela Vitale, Mark Waterman.

JEWISH REPERTORY THEATER. *The Last Laugh* by Michael Hardstark. June 24, 1992. Directed by Lou Jacob; with Larry Block, Ron Faber, Adam Heller, Nick Plakias, Barbara Speigel. *God of Vengeance* by Sholem Asch, adapted by Stephen Fife. November 1, 1992. Directed by Ran Avni; with Lee Wallace, Marilyn Chris, Christine Burke, Maury Cooper. *Theda Bara and the Frontier Rabbi* book by Jeff Hochhauser; music by Bob Johnston; lyrics by Jeff Hochhauser and Bob Johnston. January 9, 1993. Directed by Lynne Taylor-Corbett; with Jeanine LaManna, Jonathan Hadley, Allen Lewis Rickman, Ellen Margulies, Robin Irwin. *The King of Carpets* by Joel Hammer. April 11, 1993. Directed by Edward M. Cohen; with Matthew Arkin, Sam Gray, Wendy Kaplan, Elaine Rinehart, David Thornton.

JOHN HOUSEMAN THEATER. *The Mystery of Anna O* by Jerome Coopersmith and Lucy Freeman. September 19, 1992. Directed by Yanna Kroyt Brandt; with C. C. Lovelace, Peter Tate, David Mazzeo, Barnard Barrow, Marilee Warner. *Talking Things Over with Chekhov* by John Ford Noonan. March 14, 1993. Directed by Maureen Heffernan; with Lou Sumrall, Roma Maffia. *Buya Africa* (one-woman show) by and with Thuli Dumakude. May 2, 1993.

JOYCE THEATER. *The Mysteries and What's So Funny?* Written and directed by David Gordon; music by Philip Glass. December 15, 1992. With Valda Setterfield, Alice Playten, Lola Pashalinski, Scott Cohen, Karen Graham, Jerry Matz, Jane Hoffman, Bill Kux, Dean Moss.

JUDITH ANDERSON THEATER. *In Plain View* (festival of one-act plays): *Disposable* by Joseph Massa; *Lucky Dog* and *Springtime* by Richard Keller; *Hopscotch* by Joseph Massa, directed by Wendy Davidson; *When They Take Me . . . In My Dreams* by Richard Holland, directed by Kathleen Bishop; *Del Muenz at the Bishoff Gallery* by Peter Morris, directed by Charles Catanese; *Who Could That Be?* by Alan Minieri, directed by Alejandra Lopez. August 7, 1992. With the Turnip Theater Festival Company. *The Yes Word* by John Tobias. September 16, 1992. Directed by Andre Ernotte; with Matthew Arkin, Stephen Lee, Cornelia Mills, Geoff Pierson, Paul Ukena Jr. *Lightin' Out* book and lyrics by Walt Stepp; music by Walt Stepp and John Tucker. December 3, 1992. Directed by Kevin Cochran; with Gordon Stanley, Robert Tate, Tony Fair, Beth Blatt. *Somewhere I Have Never Traveled* by Daniel MacIvor. March 1, 1993. Directed by Daniel Selznick; with Brad Sullivan, Raymond Haigler, Ibi Janko, Aideen O'Kelly. *Pets!* (revue) compiled and directed by Helen Butleroff. March 24, 1993.

LIGHT OPERA OF MANHATTAN. *Columbus: The Musical* book by Janet Villella; music and lyrics by Earl Wilson Jr. July 22, 1992. *Nostalgia Tropical.* See INTAR entry in main section.

LINCOLN CENTER. *Serious Fun!* Schedule included *Dr. Faustus Lights the Lights* text by Gertrude Stein, music by Hans Peter Kuhn, directed by Robert Wilson, with Thilo Mandel, Christian Ebert, Thomas Lehmann, Heiko Senst, Florian Fitz, Katrin Heller, Wiebke Kayser, Gabriele Volsch, Martin Vogel; *The Flash and Crash Days* written and directed by Gerald Thomas, with Fernanda Montenegro, Fernanda Torres; *Dog Show* by and with Eric Bogosian, directed by Jo Bonney; *49 Blues Songs for a Vampire* by Keith Antar Mason, with The Hittite Empire; *A Certain Level of Denial* by and with John Kelly; performance by David Shiner, Bill Irwin and the Red Clay Ramblers; *My Mathematics* by and with Rose English. July 7–30, 1992.

McGINN/CAZALE THEATER. *Wuthering Heights* book, music and lyrics by Paul Dick, based on Emily Bronte's novel. September 13, 1992. Directed by Jack Horner.

MANHATTAN CLASS COMPANY. *Five Women Wearing the Same Dress* by Alan Ball. February 8, 1993. Directed by Melia Bensussen; with Dina Spybey, Amelia Campbell, Ally Walker, Betsy Aidem, Allison Janney, Thomas Gibson.

MANHATTAN PUNCH LINE. Festival of One-Act Comedies: *The Fall of the House of Shlimowitz* by Michael Panes, directed by Peter Basch; *Trudy & Paul Come to the Rescue* by Michael Aschner, directed by Steve Kaplan; *The John Philip Sousa Workshop* by Stephen Gregg, directed by Cynthia Stokes; *Candy Hearts* by Theresa Rebeck, directed by Tracy Brigden; *Get a Stupid Answer* by John Holleman, directed by Margie Salvante; *Monkey Business* by David Bottrell, directed by Louis Scheeder; *The Solution* written and directed by Michael Panes; *Bus Face* by Larry Blamire, directed by Cynthia Stokes; *Sally Sees the Light* by Barbara Lindsay, directed by Barbara Klapper; *Unabridged* by Michael Dempsey, directed by Charles Karchmer. June 10–21, 1992.

METROPOLITAN MUSEUM OF ART. Kanze Noh Theater. April 22, 1993.

MICHAEL'S PUB. *Vernel Bagneris Presents Jelly Roll Morton: A Me-Morial* (one-man show) by and with Vernel Bagneris, based on Jelly Roll Morton's work. October 13, 1992.

NAT HORNE THEATER. *Property* by Otis L. Guernsey Jr. (staged reading) directed by Francine L. Trevens. June 1, 1992. With Geoffrey Dawe, Oscar Brand, James Robert Robinson, T.L. Reilly, David Middleton, Frank Biancamano, Ann Alford, Barry Phillips, Jerry Silverstein, Melissa Zullo, Bryan King. *Pie Supper* written and directed by Le Wilhelm. July 16, 1992. With Caren Alpert, Nancy McDoneil, Dustye Winniford, Kirsten Walsh.

NEW GROUP THEATER. *Make Up Your Mind* by Kurt Vonnegut. April 8, 1993. Directed by Sam Schacht; with Richard Brandon, Tom Brannum, Rod McLachlan, Miranda Sinclair.

NEW YORK GILBERT AND SULLIVAN PLAYERS. *Iolanthe.* December 26, 1992. Directed by Albert Bergeret; with Keith Jurosko, Kimilee Bryant, Stephen O'Brien, Joy Hermalyn, Nancy Evers. *H.M.S. Pinafore.* January 7, 1993. Directed by Albert Bergeret; with John Astin, Lynne Vardaman, Ray Gabbard, Richard Holmes, Joy Hermalyn, Katie Geissinger, William Swain, Philip Reilly, Alan Jacobson.

NEW YORK PUBLIC LIBRARY FOR THE PERFORMING ARTS READING ROOM READINGS. *Giants Have Us in Their Books: A Tiger in Central Park, Flowers, The Winged Man, Gas, The Crooked Cross, Tape* by Jose Rivera. October 19, 1992. Directed by Michael Greif; with Rocco Sisto, Anne O'Sullivan, Susan Knight, Rene Rivera, Karina Arroyave, Kent Faulcon, Monique Cintron, Lisa Gay Hamilton, Skip Sudduth. *Blackwater* by J. Dakota Powell. November 9, 1992. Directed by Rich Lichte; with Zoe Taleporos, W. T. Martin, Leslie Lyles, Gregory Simmons, Jeff Stafford, Danyon Davis. *Antigone in New York* by Janusz Glowacki. January 4, 1993. Directed by Michael Greif; with Joe Grifasi, John Seitz, Bob Balaban, Patricia Mauceri. *New York in Three Acts* (one-act plays): *Hopped the Curb* by Laurence Klavan, directed by Evan Yionoulis; *Waltzing De Niro* by Lynn Martin, directed by Kirsten Sanderson; *New York Actor* by John Guare, directed by Neel Keller. February 1, 1993. With Cordelia Richards, Marian Seldes, Jerry Stiller, Andre Gregory, Barry Sherman, Sharon Washington, Anne O'Sullivan, John Vickery, Stephen Pearlman. *Misha's Party* by Richard Nelson and Alexander Gelman. March 8, 1993. Directed by David Jones; with John Seitz, Maria Tucci, Gerry Bamman, Frances Conroy, Edward Herrmann, Caitlin Clarke, Judy Kuhn, Vasek Simek, Ben Bode, Elaine Stritch, Megan Dodds, John Slattery, James Murtaugh; *Alice in Bed* by Susan Sontag. April 26, 1993. Directed by Michael Kahn; with Roberta Maxwell, Lola Pashalinski, Andre Gregory, Wallace Shawn, Mary Louise Wilson, Frances Conroy, Harriet Harris, Elzbieta Czyzewska, Betty Henritze, Richard Healy. *Real Life* by Susan Yankowitz. May 10, 1993. Directed by Melia Bensussen; with Peter Simon, William Fichtner, Courtney Simon, Emily Schulman, Leslie Silva, Jim Ligon.

NUYORICAN POETS CAFE. *Life During Wartime* by Wesley Brown. June 18, 1992. Directed by Rome Neal; with Betty Vaughn, Damon Chandler, Sheryl Greene Leverett, Magaly Colimon, Carla Maria Sorey. *Meeting Lillie* by Amiri Baraka. April 8, 1993. Directed by Rome Neal; with Lawrence James, Heather Simms, Carmen Mathis, Lynn Dandridge, G. Dewey Smalls, William Williams. *Beyond the Outer Circle* (one-act plays): *The Cat* and *When Nature Calls* by Candido Tirado; *Plastic Flowers* by Carmyn Rivera. May 27, 1993. Co-produced by the Shaman Repertory Theater.

OHIO THEATER. *The American Living Room Reupholstered* (one-act plays): *Soap Opera* by Ralph Pape, directed by Elizabeth Franzen; *Dialogue With a Prostitute* written and directed by Howard

Ross Patlis. September 25, 1992. With Shannon Malone, Gerard G. Schneider, Julienne Greer, Susan Huffaker, Anthony Marshall, Howard Ross Patlis. *The Men Are Afraid of the Women* by John Kaplan. October 15, 1992. Directed by Dennis Delaney. With Kevin Agnew, Tim Barrett, Dina Dillon, Funda Duyal, Joseph McKenna, Mary McLain, Jeff Morris. *The Arrangement* by Susan Kim. March 12, 1993. Directed by Nela Wagman; with Jordan Lage, Claudia Silver, Richard Long, Seth Herzog.

ONE DREAM THEATER. *The Depression Show* by Thomas Keith and Jane Young. September 21, 1992. Directed by George Hewitt; with James Adlesic, Pamela Newkirk, William Flatley, Brian Keane. *Jersey Girls* (one-woman show) by Susan Van Allen in collaboration with David Ford. March 10, 1993. Directed by David Ford; with Susan Van Allen.

ONTOLOGICAL-HYSTERIC THEATER AT ST. MARK'S. *Samuel's Major Problem* written, directed and designed by Richard Foreman. January 7, 1993. With Thomas Jay Ryan, Jill Dreskin, Steven Rattazzi.

PEARL THEATER COMPANY. *A Moon for the Misbegotten* by Eugene O'Neill. September 20, 1992. Directed by Allan Carlsen; with Joanne Camp, Frank Lowe. *The Good Natur'd Man* by Oliver Goldsmith. January 3, 1993. Directed by Anthony Cornish; with Kurt Rhoads, Robert Hock, Bella Jarrett, Frank Lowe, Robin Leslie Brown, Jeff Woodman. *Widowers' Houses* by George Bernard Shaw. April 4, 1993. Directed by Grey Johnson; with Julie DePaul, Paul O'Brien, Sean Pratt.

PERFORMANCE SPACE 122. *The Penny Arcade Sex and Censorship Show* (revue) by Penny Arcade. July 23, 1992. With Penny Arcade, Leta Davis, Shelly Calcott, Bill Graber, Callie Ryan, Diana Moonmade, Ken Davis, Greta Watson, Taylor Mead, Bina Sharif, Ron Vawter. *My Queer Body* by and with Tim Miller. December 4, 1992.

PERFORMING GARAGE. *She Who Once Was the Helmet-Maker's Beautiful Wife* written and directed by Peter Halasz and Seth Tillett. June 11, 1992. With Cora Fisher, Peter Halasz, Agnes Santha, Seth Tillett.

PLAYGROUND THEATER. *American Lesion* (one-act plays): *Collateral Damage, Microwave Recipes* and *Hung* by Tom Gilroy. April 23, 1993. Directed by Lili Taylor, Mark Williams and Michael Imperioli; with Tom Gilroy, Fernando Gomes, Chris Rossi, Tom Kopache, John Ventimiglia, Steve Mark Friedman, Maggie Low.

PLAYHOUSE 91. *Sharon* book and lyrics by Geraldine Fitzgerald, based on John B. Keane's *Sharon's Grave;* music and direction by Franklin Micare. May 12, 1993. With Kurt T. Johns, Patrick Minogue, Deanna Wells, Ken Jennings, Michael Judd, Mark Doerr, John McDonough.

ST. MARK'S STUDIO THEATER. *Homo Alone: Lost in Colorado* (revue) by and with Planet Q. May 11, 1993.

SAMUEL BECKETT THEATER. *Bundy* by and with Dan Metelitz. June 9, 1993. Directed by Seth Gordon. *I'm Sorry . . . Was That Your World?* (one-act plays): *Big Mistake* by Theresa Rebeck, directed by Maggie da Silva; *Plumb Nuts* by Bhargavi C. Mandava, directed by Shanna Riss; *Rapid Eye Movement* by Susan Kim, directed by Jamie Richards; *Dog and Fruit* by Lisa A. Reardon, directed by Colleen McQuade and Shanna Riss; *Easy Journey to Other Planets* by Neena Beber, directed by Bonnie Mark. September 11, 1992. With Eric Lutes, Eric Nolan, Deborah Laufer, Kathryn Langwell, Jessica Hecht, Susan Bernfield, Colleen McQuade, Kevin O'Keefe. *The Black Hermit* by Ngugi Wa Thiong'o. November 6, 1992. Directed by Shela Xoregos; with Jimmy Antoine, Gordon H. Brooks, Jonathan Dewberry, Ahmat Jallo, Wasi Mekuria, Alicia Monique, Adam Otokiti, Jacqueline Pennington, Hudson Pillow, Jessie Saunders, William Francis Smith.

SCARBOROUGH PRODUCTIONS. *Under Control* by Paul Walker. October 15, 1992. Directed by Jonathan Silver; with Danna Lyons, Milton Carney, Diana Martella, Amy Pierce, Anita Pratt Morris.

STEVE McGRAW'S. *White Lies* (musical revue) sketches by Douglas Carter Beane; music and lyrics by Keith Thompson and Douglas Carter Beane. June 29, 1992. Directed by Greg Ganakas; with Nancy Johnston, Bill Kocis, Hugh Panaro, Jennifer Smith, Cheryl Stern.

SYMPHONY SPACE. *Three Shots From a Hill* (one-act plays): *The End of the Beginning, A Pound on Demand* and *Bedtime Story* by Sean O'Casey. November 4, 1992. Directed by Shivaun O'Casey; with Risteard Cooper, Patrick Fitzsymons, Pauline Flanagan, Gerard McSorley, Madeleine Potter, Shauna Rooney (The O'Casey Theater Company).

THEATER ARIELLE. *The World of Kurt Weill.* July 7, 1992. Directed by Sharron Miller; with Juliette Koka.

THEATER ROW THEATER. *Them . . . Within Us* by Todd David Ross. November 10, 1992. Directed by Allan Carlsen; with Bonnie Black, Patrick Barnes, Steven Sennett, Marceline Hugot.

TRIANGLE THEATER COMPANY. *Democracy and Esther* by Romulus Linney. October 3, 1992. Directed by Elizabeth Lewis Corley; with Priscilla Shanks, John Woodson, Mary Beth Peil, Frank Anderson, Fred Burrell, Kathleen Dennehy, Kathryn Eames, Maureen Silliman, Paul Urcioli. *Playing With Fire (After Frankenstein)* by Barbara Field. January 30, 1993. Directed by Charles R. Johnson; with Aloysius Gigl, Jennifer Petsche, Jeff Sugarman, Paul Anthony Stewart, Doug Von Nessen, Garrison Phillips.

TRIBECA LAB. *Criminals in Love* by George F. Walker. October, 1992. Directed by Lee Milinazzo; with Elizabeth Browning, Grace Campbell, Elizabeth Chapman, John McKie, Ernie Shaheen, Garland Whitt.

TRIPLEX PERFORMING ARTS CENTER. *The Ragged Child* book and lyrics by Jeremy James Taylor and Frank Whateley; music by David Nield. April 15, 1993. Directed by Jeremy James Taylor; with the National Youth Music Theater of Great Britain.

UNDER ONE ROOF. *Under Wraps: More Dangerous Ideas* (solo performance art festival). Schedule included *Christopher Columbus 1992* by and with Roger Guenveur Smith; music by Marc Anthony Thompson; *Pot Melting* by and with Danny Hoch; *Holy Cow!* by and with The Mintz & Plonka Mime Theater; *Something Wonderful* conceived and created by Clarice Marshall, Kay Cummings, Tom Cayler and Jeni Breen, performed by Tom Cayler, Kay Cummings; *What My Mother Never Told Me* by and with Lisa Lipkin. October 12–November 8, 1992. *White Cotton Sheets* book, music and lyrics by Tom Judson. January 7, 1993. Directed by Michael Sexton; with Dori Kiplock, David Pittu, Tom Judson, Stephen Pell, Francine Lobis, Chris Odo, Ellen Mittenthal, Keith Davis, Bobby Reed.

UNION SQUARE THEATER. *Tapestry, the Music of Carole King.* February 18, 1993. Directed by Jeff Martin; with Lawrence Clayton, Mary Gutzi, Pattie Darcy Jones, Vanessa Jones, Frank Mastrone, Jim Morlino. *The Invisible Circus.* May 25, 1993. With Victoria Chaplin, Jean Baptiste Thiérrée, James Spencer Thiérrée.

VIA THEATER. *The Bitter Tears of Petra von Kant* by Rainer Werner Fassbinder, translated by Denis Calandra. June 10, 1992. Directed by Brian Jucha; with Tina Shepard, Lisa Welti, Tamar Kotoske, Karla Silverman, David Kellett, Anne McKenna. *Woman in Black* and *Men in Gray* (one-act plays) written and directed by Brian Jucha. October 21, 1992. With Tamar Kotoske, Lisa Welti, David Neumann, Megan Spooner, Karla Silverman. *Via Theater Triplets* (one-act plays): *Bring Me Your Love* adapted and directed by Brian Jucha, from Charles Bukowski's story; *Southern Cross* written and directed by John Jesurun; *Behavior in Public Places* based on Erving Goffman's writings, conceived and directed by Anne Bogart and the company. April 15, 1993. With Sheryl Dold, Brian Jucha, Tamar Kotoske, Barney O'Hanlon, Tina Shepard, Megan Spooner, Lisa Welti.

VILLAGE THEATER COMPANY. *Roleplay* book by Doug Haverty; music by Adryan Russ; lyrics by Doug Haverty and Adryan Russ. July 22, 1992. Directed by Henry Fonte; with Kimberly Schultheiss, Alyson Reim, Kate Bushmann, Marj Feenan, Elizabeth Silon, Anita Lento. *The Best of Sex and Violence* by Thomas Hinton. February 24, 1993. Directed by Henry Fonte; with Christopher Bailey, Julia McLaughlin, Michael Curran, Bill Christ, Barbara Berque, Michelle Berke. *Aunt Mary* by Pam Gems. April 28, 1993. Directed by Gigi Rivkin; with Bill Christ, Michael Curran, Julia McLaughlin, David McConnell.

WAVERLY PLACE THEATER. *The Boy Who Saw True* conceived and performed by Glen Williamson. October 28, 1992.

WEILL RECITAL HALL. *The World of Ruth Draper* (one-woman show) by and with Patricia Norcia. October 18, 1992.

WESTBETH THEATER. *The Hunchback of Notre Dame* book by Anthony Scully, based on Victor Hugo's book; music by Byron Janis; lyrics by Hal Hackady. April 22, 1993. Directed by Brian Murray; with Leslie Castay, Nick Wyman, Steve Barton, Ed Dixon, Laura Kenyon, Brian Sutherland.

TRIPLEX PERFORMING ARTS CENTER—Members of the cast of Great Britain's National Youth Music Theater in their musical *The Ragged Child*

WILLIAM REDFIELD THEATER. *In This Room* (one-act plays): *The Stain* by Frank Pugliese and *Blackout* by Tom McClellan. December 8, 1992. Directed by Allen Coulter; with Elizabeth Ann Daniels, Adam Trese, Alexandra Styron, Gareth Williams.

THE WOOSTER GROUP. *The Emperor Jones* by Eugene O'Neill. January 21, 1993. Directed by Elizabeth LeCompte; with Willem Dafoe, Kate Valk.

WORKING THEATER. *I Am a Man* by OyamO. May 5, 1993. Directed by Bill Mitchelson; with Robert Arcaro, Paul Butler, A. Bernard Cummings, Guy Davis, Larry Keith, James Murtaugh, Harold Perrineau Jr., Monte Russell, Howard Samuelsohn, Mark Kenneth Smaltz, Myra Taylor.

THE SEASON
AROUND
THE UNITED STATES

O
O
O

OUTSTANDING NEW PLAYS CITED BY AMERICAN THEATER CRITICS ASSOCIATION

and

A DIRECTORY OF NEW-PLAY PRODUCTIONS

O
O
O

THE American Theater Critics Association (ATCA) is the organization of 250 leading drama critics in all media in all sections of the United States. One of this group's stated purposes is "To increase public awareness of the theater as a *national* resource" (italics ours). To this end, ATCA has cited three outstanding new plays produced this season around the country, to be represented in our coverage of The Season Around the United States by excerpts from each of their scripts demonstrating literary style and quality. And one of these—*Children of Paradise: Shooting a Dream* developed by the Theatre de la Jeune Lune Company—was designated the first-place play and received the 8th annual ATCA New Play Award of $1,000.

The process of selection of these outstanding plays is as follows: any ATCA member critic may nominate a play if it has been given a production in a professional house. It must be a finished play given a full production (not a reading or an airing as a play-in-progress). Nominated scripts were studied and discussed by an ATCA play-reading committee chaired by T.H. McCulloh of the Los Angeles *Times* and comprising Jeffrey Borak of the *Berkshire Eagle,* Richard Christiansen of the Chicago *Tribune,* Lawrence DeVine of the Detroit *Free Press,* Damien Jaques of the Milwaukee *Journal* and free-lance critic Dan Sullivan. The committee members made their choices on the basis of script rather than production, thus placing very much the same emphasis as the editors of this volume in making the New York Best Play selections. There were no eligibility requirements except that a nominee be the first full professional production of a new work outside New York City within this volume's time frame of June 1, 1992 to May 31, 1993. If the timing of nominations and openings prevents some works from being considered in any given year, they will be eligible for consideration the following year if they haven't since moved on to New York production. We offer our sincerest thanks and admiration to the ATCA members and their committee for the valuable insight into the 1992–93 theater season around the United States which their selections provide for this Best Plays record, in the form of the following excerpts from outstanding scripts illustrating their style and the nature of their content, with brief introductions provided by Dan Sullivan (*Children of Paradise: Shooting a Dream*), T.H. McCulloh (*Unfinished Stories* by Sybille Pearson) and Roger Downey (*Dark Rapture* by Eric Overmyer).

*Cited by American Theater Critics
as Outstanding New Plays
of 1992–93*

CHILDREN OF PARADISE:
SHOOTING A DREAM

A Play in Two Acts

BY STEVEN EPP, FELICITY JONES,
DOMINIQUE SERRAND AND PAUL
WALSH

BASED ON THE WORK OF MARCEL CARNE
AND JACQUES PREVERT

Cast and credits appear on page 435

CHILDREN OF PARADISE: SHOOTING A DREAM: A beautiful word, collaboration. An ugly word, too. The great 1945 French film *Children of Paradise* was a *collaboration* between director Marcel Carné and writer Jacques Prévert. But did they *collaborate* with the Nazis in order to make it? That's the question posed by *Children of Paradise: Shooting a Dream,* written and produced by the Theatre de la Jeune Lune of Minneapolis.

Written to inaugurate the company's spectacular new playing space in the city's warehouse district, the piece superbly captures the ballet of shooting a

399

movie—the camera silently rolling in to adore the star, the breakaway set, the rising tension of the repeated take. But we also track the discontinuities of life in occupied France. Like most of his fellow citizens, Carné has little use for the Nazi-supported Vichy government—and absolutely no ambition to be a Resistance hero. "I just want to make movies," he says. Therefore he must accommodate the powers-that-be. In an early scene Carné, Prévert and the young actor Jean-Louis Barrault try to find an acceptable story for Carné's next film.

PREVERT: So, what is it about—this new movie?
CARNE: I was hoping you'd know.
PREVERT: Tomatoes, then. The purest love story.
CARNE: I need something "suitable," to get past the censors.
PREVERT: There are no suitable subjects. Everything can be perverted.
BARRAULT: Do you know the story of Baptiste Deburau?
PREVERT: Who?
BARRAULT: He created the white faced Pierrot. He was like me—an inoffensive anarchist . . . consumed by a great love . . . one day on the Boulevard of Crime a man insulted his wife, and Baptiste struck him down with his cane. The man died, and Baptiste was arrested. All of Paris came to the trial. You see, no one had ever heard him speak.
PREVERT: "The mime speaks." Not much of a movie. Besides, Garbo did it years ago.
CARNE: The Boulevard of Crime—huh.
BARRAULT: Only at the Comédie Française were you allowed to talk onstage. Can you imagine . . . a monopoly on the spoken word? So, they invented a new language—and the pantomime was born.

A theater condemned to silence! One might take it as a metaphor for their stifled France. But the theme will have to be played very lightly. Discussions continue at a design meeting.

TRAUNER: How about barricades? The revolution of 1830 . . . students slaughtered in the street, blood, riots, the army marching through the mob . . .
PREVERT: No.
TRAUNER: Goose-stepping like the Nazis down the Champs Elysées.
PREVERT: That, I'm afraid, we cannot do.
TRAUNER: So we jump without a word from 1828 to 1834 as if nothing happened.
PREVERT: "In our silence, we are shouting."
KOSMA: You expect your audience to know their history.
PREVERT: We must trust our audience most of all.

Barrault will play the mime, competing with a glib matinee idol, Frederic Lemaitre, for the love of a beautiful woman of the streets, a perfect role for the most fetching actress in Paris, Arletty.

PREVERT: There is a woman—Garance . . . Arletty, of course. She is truth hidden in a well. Truth personified.

TRAUNER: Only the lighting is from the top so the johns can't see below the water line.

HERRAND: Truth, but only above the shoulders.

CASARES: Like making movies under the censorship of Vichy France.

PREVERT: Family values. It's either them or the Germans. Or both.

CARNE: She's Paris. No . . . she's France, she's occupied France, but she's free. She's beautiful, alive, always laughing.

PREVERT: She is the object of men's desires.

CASARES: Of course.

PREVERT: She sings . . . a song called "I Am What I Am."

Filming begins—and the Allied bombs start to fall. Between air raids, Carné forces himself and his actors to forget the bombs and concentrate on getting the shot.

CARNE: I would like to get a very close shot of this. You dispossess this man of the most precious sentiment he holds for you. It's instant cold.

Felicity Jones as the actress Arletty in the role of Garance with Robert Rosen as Jean-Louis Barrault in the role of Baptiste in the play *Children of Paradise: Shooting a Dream*, about the making of the great French movie *Children of Paradise*, developed by Theatre de la Jeune Lune, Minneapolis

ARLETTY: What the hell is he suppose to look like, this count?

CARNE: He looks . . . like a count.

ARLETTY: I'll pretend it's General de Gaulle.

CARNE: Think of it this way—you pick up the phone, and someone is on the line, and it didn't ring. It's your best friend. Before you can even breathe you hear: "Hi, it's me, I just died. I am on the other side." Cut. We want the shock. Would you mind starting at: "But don't ask the impossible of me."

GARANCE: "But don't ask the impossible of me. However, if you wish . . . If it would please you, tomorrow the whole of Paris shall know not only that I love you, but that I am crazy about you! Yes, crazy about you! I'll tell everybody. I'll shout it from the rooftops. But to you . . . to you alone . . ."

CARNE: Cut. Let's get closer still.

ARLETTY: If you keep moving closer, pretty soon you'll be inside me.

CARNE: But to you, to you alone, I need to be very close to feel the loneliness of your secret. I'll keep the camera rolling. We'll do these lines several times. Action.

GARANCE: "But to you . . . to you alone, my friend, I will tell you this: I have loved a man, and I love him still . . ."

CARNE: Hold. Very intimate. Again.

GARANCE: "I will tell you this: I have loved a man, and I love him still."

CARNE: Hold. Lower your eyes. Again.

GARANCE: "I have loved a man, and I love him still."

CARNE: Closer, again.

GARANCE: "I have loved a man, and I love him still."

CARNE: Repeat.

GARANCE: "I have loved a man."

CARNE: Again.

GARANCE: "I have loved a man."

CARNE: What?

GARANCE: "I have loved a man."

CARNE: I don't believe it.

GARANCE: "I have loved a man, and I love him still."

CARNE: Yes. Again.

GARANCE: "I have loved a man, and I love him still. And now I have only one thought, to go away . . . to go away."

CARNE: Cut.

ARLETTY: So . . . did you get what you want?

CARNE: I might ask the same question.

"The one thing I really love is my freedom," says Garance. It's Arletty's motto too. To ensure that freedom, she takes a Nazi lover. After the war, the actress faces a tribunal of purification. Will she play the repentant sinner? Not Arletty.

PROSECUTOR: Please state your name.

ARLETTY: Arletty, but my real name . . . my maiden name is Claire.

PROSECUTOR: Claire what?

ARLETTY: Oh, Claire de Lune.

PROSECUTOR: An actress even off the set . . . and your upbringing, I understand you are of modest origin?

ARLETTY: Modest? No. But original.

PROSECUTOR: When were you born?

ARLETTY: The same year Zola wrote *I Accuse!*.

PROSECUTOR: Madame!

ARLETTY: Mademoiselle.

PROSECUTOR: It is well documented that you maintained a relationship with a certain General Soehring of the Nazi Luftwaffe throughout the occupation.

ARLETTY: When I want to say yes, I never learned how to say no. They say there are two true men in France: General de Gaulle and Arletty. Should I be insulted?

PROSECUTOR: You willingly gave your body to an enemy of the French people. You were, might I say, intimately occupied, Mademoiselle.

ARLETTY: My heart belongs to France, but my ass belongs to the world.

Arletty escapes with a five-year prison sentence, after which she makes a stunning comeback in *A Streetcar Named Desire*. Carné retains his freedom, but was he a "collaborator?" All that can be said is that he made his choice.

JOURNALIST: Monsieur Paulvé?

PAULVE: Yes.

JOURNALIST: Your colleague Marcel Carné is accused of collaboration with the Germans for having made films during the occupation. What is your opinion?

PAULVE: You call him a collaborator, a German pawn, a traitor; Vichy called him a Jewish sympathizer, a deviant; I call him an artist, a visionary, a friend. It's all true.

Children of Paradise: Shooting a Dream *was first produced collaboratively at Theatre de la Jeune Lune, Minneapolis, November 18, 1992 under the direction of Dominique Serrand. This production was then presented at the Yale Repertory Theater, New Haven, Conn., January 15, 1993 and at the La Jolla, Calif. Playhouse in May 1993.*

UNFINISHED STORIES

A Full-Length Play in One Act

BY SYBILLE PEARSON

Cast and credits appear on page 431

UNFINISHED STORIES: As time passes and more people speak out, it begins to seem as though there is no such thing as a functional family. The three generations that make up the family in Sybille Pearson's *Unfinished Stories* find that what separates them is deeper and richer than the walls that stand between most family members. It is an intellectual compartmentalizing based in the philosophical and ideological space in which each character finds himself trapped.

Grandfather Walter (called Opa by his grandson) has never been able to rid himself of the memories of the potent philosophical thought that permeated his group of Jewish contemporaries as the Nazis came to power in the 1930s.

His son, Yves, born in Paris during Walter's flight to freedom, is an actor who has spent his career in *Man of La Mancha,* a product of America's 1950s and its golden dream. He has divorced Gaby and married a younger woman, an extension to him of that dream.

Gaby, who has continued to care for her aging father-in-law, is a 1960s radical who has never given up the fight and believes that her affection for Walter is part and parcel of that fight.

Yves and Gaby's son Daniel is a Manhattan cab driver who sees the world as a magnification of the darkness that seeps through Manhattan streets and finds solace in the lost world in which his grandfather still exists. Their stories are unshakably individual, passionate and revealing, and, in the end, unfinished, as they try to pull their separate threads together into one logical tapestry.

Yves has just returned from his honeymoon in Paris and finds himself at loggerheads with Gaby and Daniel about Walter's future and his own crumbling connection with the dramas he thinks he has left behind him.

GABY: I don't know how to do this yet. I don't know how to "lunch" with you, how to ask about your honeymoon. It's a year. You were gone this long when you were on the road. This is a divorce. You walk in like it's home. Ring the bell. I have to get to work. Enough. *(To Daniel.)* The cards aren't there. *(She exits to her room.)*

YVES: Take the day as it comes, lad. Take the day as it comes. You well, son?

DANIEL: Nothing much.

YVES: Is this early for you, or are you driving . . .

DANIEL *(cuts him off)*: It's early.

YVES *(takes watch off wrist)*: I couldn't change it back last night. Two months in Paris is hard to let go of.

DANIEL: It's 8:52.

YVES *(resets watch)*: I could have been born in Berlin. People weren't leaving Germany yet. I was born in Paris. That was *his* choice, not mine. Why? I don't know. I stopped wasting my time being upset about him telling me nothing a long time ago. You and I can't talk. *(He over-dramatizes.)* But then, never say never. One day he'll take me on his knee and say: "Son. Let me tell you my life." And Brahms's Violin Concerto will play, and who knows? With music like that, I might even be forgiven for being born in Paris. Talk about romanticism! Imagine the mileage he'll get when he finds out my child was conceived in Paris.

A pause. Yves looks at Daniel.

Karen wanted it. She wouldn't have kept it a secret for long. I should get myself ready for the jokes. Older men, younger wives . . .

DANIEL *(Yiddish accent)*: "I see it but I don't believe it."

YVES *(Yiddish accent)*: "So who are you anyway?" *(Pause.)* You upset? Shocked?

DANIEL: It wasn't something I was thinking of.

When Yves announces that he wants to take Walter to live with him and his new wife Karen, the disruption brings old antagonisms to the surface.

DANIEL *(to Yves)*: Why come here? You got your house on the East Side.

YVES: How much mileage do you think you have left playing the kid who hasn't found himself?

Gaby comes in with brush and dustpan.

DANIEL *(to Yves)*: What do you need here?

GABY *(simultaneously):* Why keep on him?

YVES: The boy who can do no wrong.

GABY: He's working days. What do you want from him?

YVES: You're working days? Why didn't you tell me?

DANIEL: Do you care?

YVES: The Jack and Jill Society. Danny and Gaby's Secret Club.

GABY: He did it without your help. With the support . . .

YVES: Without the discipline. He needed a mother . . .

DANIEL: Don't fight.

YVES: Not another best friend . . .

DANIEL: Over me.

YVES: Not someone who undermines me.

GABY: You do that.

DANIEL: I don't need protection.

GABY: You gave up all authority when Walter walked into this house.

YVES: When did you stand with me? Together with me about the boy?

GABY *(referring to Daniel):* Didn't you hear him? He just said . . .

DANIEL *(topping Gaby):* No one can breathe here without your help!

GABY: What do you do here?

DANIEL: *(refers to brush and pan in her hands):* You tell me do it. *You're* doing it.

GABY: *(drops pan and brush at his feet):* Do it.

YVES *(overlap):* Listen to your mother.

DANIEL: No one can make him a cup of coffee but you.

GABY: When the hell are you here? You're in and out when you feel like it.

YVES *(simultaneously):* Your mother takes damn good care of him. Damn good care of you.

DANIEL: I'd be dead if I didn't forget what she taught me.

GABY: What'd you learn from me?

DANIEL: The first night, the first night I ever drove. A New York City taxicab. Two in the morning. I pick up three dealers and take them to an alley in the Bronx so nobody'd think I was prejudiced.

GABY *(interjection):* That was stupid.

DANIEL *(continuing):* Your expectations are fucking mismatched with reality.

GABY: What do you know about reality?

DANIEL *(continuing):* You live in a *We Are the World* video. He lives in La Mancha. I'm out there. I'm the one out there at four in the morning, who's had a gun to his head and gotten through the night.

GABY: The world's more than streets at four in the morning. You kids don't understand . . .

DANIEL *(interrupting):* I'm not you kids.

YVES: That's enough shouting.

Joseph Wiseman *(left)* as Walter and Hal Linden as
Yves in a scene from *Unfinished Stories* by Sybille Pearson at the Mark Taper Forum

GABY *(with force):* You don't have any cop-outs.
DANIEL: Einstein wouldn't be great enough for this house.

In an attempt to bridge the gap between them after he realizes that Walter—
who refers to books by friends who committed suicide—is himself considering
suicide, Yves questions him:

YVES: This is what you will do.
WALTER: The boy told you.
YVES: He didn't.
WALTER: Good.
YVES: Gaby?
     Walter shakes his head.

WALTER *(a fact):* She has my heart. She knows that.

YVES *(points to books):* This is what you will do.

WALTER: These are important men. Do not compare me. I merely quote them. As for me . . . *(He removes syringe case from drawer and puts it on night table.)* This pain is a voice inside me. Louder each day. I do not want it to become the only thing I hear. I have morphine. It is not difficult. I am not afraid of it.

YVES: There are things you can take for this pain.

WALTER: Yes, for a short time. Then it will be small doses of morphine and then, if I am lucky, a nurse will pity me and administer one that will end my life.

YVES: You don't know this, it's fifty years since you . . .

WALTER: We have said this today.

YVES: Fifty years since you were a doctor.

WALTER: Do you ask me to bear this for you?

YVES: No.

WALTER: Then allow me some dignity.

> *A silent beat.*

YVES: I will.

WALTER: Please do not tell my Gabriella.

YVES: No.

WALTER: You said a picture of your mother.

> *After a beat, Yves removes small snapshot from his wallet and hands it to Walter.*

In Berlin. Why have you this picture?

YVES: It's before the war.

WALTER: Yes?

YVES: I like to remember her then.

WALTER: You weren't born then.

YVES: I remember her stories.

WALTER: What does she wear?

YVES: As Rosalind.

WALTER: Oh yes.

YVES: In her school play. At her high school.

WALTER *(looking at picture):* She was very attractive. At the Romanische Cafe. She sat with the poets at the poets' table. Then she painted and sat with the painters. Then with the actresses. Then with the dancers. Each table coming closer to mine. We were called the younger doctors' table. The five of us met at a worker's clinic where we gave our time. But at night we were—how do you explain? Where do you find writers, painters, critics, architects, dancers drinking coffee, drunk on wine, playing chess, reading papers, looking for women, looking for men. There was nothing here like this. No cafe like this. There was too much smoke, yes, but in the smoke was the Geist. I watched her at each table changing her life, coming closer and closer to my table. For her, "Alles war Schicksal." Everything was fate.

YVES: For you?

WALTER: Nothing was fate. *(He looks at picture.)* Beautiful. I can understand why you chose her.

YVES: Chose her?

WALTER: What child doesn't choose between his parents? Don't be naive. *(He returns the picture to Yves.)* You expect too much of me.

YVES: I don't expect anything.

Unfinished Stories *was produced at the Mark Taper Forum, Los Angeles, June 25, 1992 under the direction of Gordon Davidson.*

DARK RAPTURE

A Play in Seventeen Scenes

BY ERIC OVERMYER

Cast and credits appear on page 445 of *The Best Plays of 1991–92*

DARK RAPTURE: Eric Overmyer's *Dark Rapture* is a robust representative of an all-but-vanished species: a play which exists only to amuse, and which doesn't make one ashamed of being amused. Its plot is of Chandlerian complexity, involving a half-dozen attractively inedifying moral monsters in pursuit of a brown-paper parcel of cash, but its tone is lighter, less fraught, recalling that of Hitchcock at his most delicately ironic in films like *Notorious* and *Strangers on a Train.*

In earlier work like *Native Speech, On the Verge,* and *In Perpetuity Throughout the Universe,* Overmyer's polyvalent vocabulary and rococo syntax overwhelmed the skeleton of plot sustaining them; however attractive they were to listen to, they were, dramatically speaking, inert. The language of *Dark Rapture* is as supple and energetic as that of a first-rate screen play, throwing character into high relief even as it hurries the action forward, entertaining us with its polished surface while making us long to know what happens next. *Dark Rapture* is sophisticated fun and nothing more. When fun is this sophisticated, one realizes that nothing more's required.

For example, here is the third of its 17 scenes.

Slide: Northern California. The fire site.
Morning. Two men in suits, Vegas & Lexington, look over the charred
landscape of ash & charcoal.

LEXINGTON: X marks the spot.

VEGAS: Hard to tell.

LEXINGTON: There's the bend in the road. There's the ridge. Over there's where the big white Victorian was.

VEGAS: Sure?

LEXINGTON: Positive.

VEGAS: Kinda hard to get your bearings. In the absence of what was.

LEXINGTON: The white Victorian. Which was next to the craftsman bungalow. Which was next to the newish split-level with the leaky skylights.

VEGAS: How do you know they were leaky?

LEXINGTON: You ever heard a skylights don't leak? Can't be done. The limits of human ingenuity. We cannot keep skylights from leaking. We cannot cure the common cold. And we cannot make a good-tasting spermicidal jelly.

VEGAS: I grew up New York. You know? Always buildin' it up 'n tearin' it down. Once somethin' was gone I could never remember what it was before it wasn't. And once somethin' else went up in its place, forget about it. Walk by one day, everything's fine, like always, walk by the next day, hey, shit, it's gone, this wasn't here yesterday, what did this used to be, remember? Shit. I could never remember.

LEXINGTON: This is their house. The Gaines residence. Ray and Julia's. Where it was. Take my word for it.

VEGAS: We know where Julia is. So, where's Ray?

LEXINGTON: That's one question.

VEGAS: Think he's up here?

LEXINGTON: Possible. They're still digging 'em out. Bits and pieces.

VEGAS: Man, earthquake, flood, fire. The actuarials in this area are gettin' positively apocalyptic. What's next? Famine? I'm thinkin' about movin' somewhere safe.

LEXINGTON: Oh yeah? Somewhere safe? Where would that be?

Pause. Vegas shrugs.

VEGAS: I'll let you know.

LEXINGTON: Radio says body count's twenty-eight. So far. Another fifty-three unaccounted for. Missing.

VEGAS: Including Ray.

LEXINGTON: Including Ray. Figure most a the so-called missing are just outa town.

VEGAS: Business.

LEXINGTON: Business. Yeah. But they're all on their way back home by now. Caught the late clips on CNN, holy cow, there goes the life's savings, the whole enchilada, up in flames, browned out in their bermudas, tossed 'n turned all night, grabbed the first flight out bright and early, throwin' back the Bloody Marys and poppin' Prozac, already fillin' out claim forms, cryin' the blues over their BMWs. Couple of 'em are still stuck abroad somewhere, tryin' to get back from Paris. Prague. Constantinople. And some of 'em. Some of 'em are still blissfully unawares as to what's transpired to the old neighborhood. Yuppie scum. Fucked seven ways from Sunday and don't even know it yet. Took off for a long weekend, a little r 'n r, a little illicit extra-marital hanky panky. Bahamas. Rosarita Beach.

VEGAS: Cabo San Lucas.

LEXINGTON: Cabo San Lucas. Come home tan, laid, relaxed, got their lies and alibis all lined up like so many ducks, bang bang bang, are they in for a shock.

VEGAS: Could post-facto ruin your whole vacation. In retrospect. Cast a pall.

LEXINGTON: Doesn't do anything for my disposition. So maybe Julia is just tearin' off a piece on the side. Gets back from a little extra-marital fuckin' around, finds the house, the husband, the Mercedes up in smoke. Let's hope she didn't lose anything didn't belong to her.

VEGAS: We know Ray didn't go to Cabo.

LEXINGTON: That we know.

VEGAS: Babcock had an extended conversation with him.

Babcock appears.

LEXINGTON: Where? Here, at the house?

BABCOCK: Down there on the flat.

LEXINGTON: Fuck was he doin' down there?

BABCOCK: Who knows? Admirin' the view.

LEXINGTON: Sure it was him?

BABCOCK: Fit the description.

LEXINGTON: So you swap lies, trade recipes. Then.

BABCOCK: Then he goes back up the hill, see if the fire's gonna do his house. Guess it did, huh? He went in. He came back out. Carryin' a coupla suitcases.

LEXINGTON: Ah ha.

BABCOCK: Puts 'em down. Goes back in. Then this whole side a the hill goes up. Whoosh. Then I don't see him no more. Then I don't see nothin' no more, on account a the smoke. Then I go home. Call you guys, tell you to come up, maybe we got a problem.

LEXINGTON: So what'd you talk about? You and Ray?

BABCOCK: Natural disasters. Catastrophe theory. Chaos. Cambodia.

LEXINGTON: Cambodia.

BABCOCK: Cambodia. Jungle fires versus conflagrations in a semi-wooded urban setting.

Lexington sighs, turns to Vegas.

LEXINGTON: So Ray could be up here. Somewhere. Amongst the rubble. Last seen.

David Mong (Babcock) in a scene from *Dark Rapture*
by Eric Overmyer at the Empty Space Theater, Seattle

VEGAS: Crispy critter.

LEXINGTON: It's possible.

VEGAS: Likely, even.

LEXINGTON: Awful convenient.

VEGAS: He didn't know.

LEXINGTON: Opportunity. Window of.

VEGAS: He wasn't in on it. Assuming there's something to be in on.

LEXINGTON: You know how many people go missing every year? Never come back from that fifteen minute jaunt around the corner? Go to the market for a quart a milk and vanish into thin? Take the main chance and disappear? Walk away and don't look back?

VEGAS: I dunno. How many?

LEXINGTON: Many. I dunno. A lot. I read. A million.

VEGAS: A million a year?

LEXINGTON: Yeah. Something like that. A million. Roughly. More or less.

VEGAS: I'd say less. I mean, a million a year. Pretty soon that'd add up to nobody left to mind the fuckin' store.

LEXINGTON: Factor in babies.

VEGAS: Factor in dead people.

LEXINGTON: Okay, a lot. Less than a million. Go missing. Take off. Change their names.

BABCOCK: Guys dodgin' child support.

LEXINGTON: Not just. Not only.

VEGAS: I been tempted. Start over.

LEXINGTON: Yeah, sure. Who hasn't? A clean slate. Which takes how long you figure before it gets completely fucked up again like your old life?

VEGAS: Not long.

LEXINGTON: Not long indeed.

VEGAS: Because, like the man said, wherever you go, there you are.

LEXINGTON: Right. So we wait a few days, see if they find Ray Gaines amongst the rubble. They don't, we wait for him to fuck up his brand new last best chance.

VEGAS: Which he would be bound to do.

LEXINGTON: I feel certain of it.

VEGAS: He didn't know. He had no idea this was his main chance. The door swings open. Hallelujah. He didn't know.

LEXINGTON: Maybe he suspected. Maybe the hairs on the back a his neck stood up.

VEGAS: That happen to you?

LEXINGTON: Yeah. Happen to you?

VEGAS: Yeah. Definitely. Alla time.

LEXINGTON: Babcock. Happen to you?

BABCOCK: Never.

LEXINGTON: How come you're still alive?

BABCOCK: Just lucky, I guess.

LEXINGTON: What about the merry maybe widow?

VEGAS: Julia? Maybe.

LEXINGTON: Maybe she'll come back from Cabo.

VEGAS: If she didn't, that would be a big, big clue.

LEXINGTON: Maybe at this moment, the hairs on the back of her neck are standing up.

VEGAS: I wouldn't be surprised. What I hear, everything else was.
    They laugh.

LEXINGTON: Wonder if Ray knew about that? His wife and Danny. The stuntman.

VEGAS: Hey. Modern marriage.

LEXINGTON: Babcock. Ever been to Cabo?

BABCOCK: Baja? Sure. Tuna fishing.

LEXINGTON: Bring me back a can.
    Babcock nods, leaves.

VEGAS: Cabo. Wonder she's still there.

LEXINGTON: See how she takes the news when she gets back.

VEGAS: If she gets back.

LEXINGTON: Like you say. That would be a big, big clue.

It starts to rain.

VEGAS: Startin' to rain. Shit.

LEXINGTON: Let's get the hell outa here before the whole hillside slides into the Bay.

VEGAS: Life's little mysteries.

They go. The sound of the rain intensifies.

Dark Rapture *was produced at The Empty Space Theater, Seattle, May 1, 1992 under the direction of Kurt Beattie.*

A DIRECTORY OF NEW-PLAY PRODUCTIONS

Compiled by Sheridan Sellers

Professional 1992–93 productions of new plays by leading companies around the United States that supplied information on casts and credits at Sheridan Sellers's request, plus a few reported by other reliable sources, are listed below in alphabetical order of the locations of 61 producing organizations. Date given is opening date, included whenever a record was obtained from the producing management. All League of Resident Theaters (LORT) and other Equity groups were queried for this comprehensive Directory. Those not listed here either did not produce new or newly revised scripts in 1992–93 or had not responded by press time. Most of the productions listed—but not all—are American or world premieres. Some are new revisions, second looks or scripts produced previously but not previously reported in *Best Plays*.

Ashland, Ore.: Oregon Shakespeare Festival

(Artistic director, Henry Woronicz)

LIGHT IN THE VILLAGE. By John Clifford. March 28, 1993. Director, Kirk Boyd; scenery, Richard L. Hay; lighting, Rachel Budin; costumes, Wanda A. Walden; musical director, Todd Barton.

Actor 1: Mukherjee
& Lawyer........... Douglas Markkanen
Actor 2: Sita................... Luck Hari
Actor 3: Muntu .... Robert Lisell-Frank
Actor 4: Meena & Kali.... Demetra Pittman
Actor 5: Rhodes...... Derrick Lee Weeden
Musician............... Rustin Appleyard
One intermission.

Play Readings '93:

EMMA'S CHILD. By Kristine Thatcher. Director, Cynthia White.
HEARTSOUNDS. By Buffy Sedlachek. Director, Katherine Gosnell.
THE BEAR FACTS. By Jo Carson. Director, Cynthia White.
SIGNATURE. By Beth Henley. Director, Cynthia White.
OREGON TRAIL PLAY. By Doris Baizley. Director, Cynthia White.

Baltimore: CenterStage

(Artistic director, Irene Lewis; managing director, Peter W. Culman)

ESCAPE FROM HAPPINESS. By George F. Walker. Director, Irene Lewis; scenery, Michael Yeargan; lighting, Stephen Strawbridge; costumes, Jess Goldstein; sound, Janet Kalas.

Gail..................... Marin Hinkle
Nora .... Lois Smith
Junior .... William Youmans
Dian Black .... Annette Helde
Mike Dixon .... Jack Wallace

Tom...................... James Noah
Mary Ann............. Alexandra Gersten
Elizabeth................. Pippa Pearthree
Stevie Moore .... Liev Schreiber
Rolly Moore.................. Dan Moran
Time and Place: In the present in the worn-down kitchen of an old house in the east end of a large city. One intermission.

416

DELL'ARTE PLAYERS, BLUE LAKE, CALIF.—Joe
Dieffenbacher in the title role of *Punch* by Joan Schirle

Blue Lake, Calif.: Dell'Arte Players Company

(Artistic directors, Michael Fields, Donald Forrest, Joan Schirle)

PUNCH! By Joan Schirle. September 5, 1992.
Director, Michael Fields; scenery, Ray Gu-
tierrez; lighting, Michael Foster; costumes,
Mary Scott.

The Sweeper . . . . Linda Hayden
Punch Family:
  Pulcina . . . . Lutje Christensen
  Mama . . . . Minna Holopainen
  Grandma; Reverend Doctor
    Snortle . . . . Bob Wells
  Punchie; Reverend Doctor Fartz;
    Angel . . . . Ken Colburn
  Punch . . . . Joe Dieffenbacher
  Lent . . . . Minna Holopainen
  God . . . . Lutje Cristensen
Punch & Judy Show:
  Punch . . . . Joe Dieffenbacher
  The Doctors . . . . Themselves
  Judy; Hangman . . . . Lutje Christensen
  Baby . . . . Ken Colburn
  Cop . . . . Minna Holopainen
  Devil . . . . Ken Colburn
  Time and Place: Middle Ages in a European
village. No intermission.

THE WRECK OF THE GOOD SHIP HUM-
BOLDT. By Peter Buckley. December 19, 1992.
Director, Michael Fields; scenery, Ray Gu-

tierrez; lighting, Michael Foster; costumes,
Mary Scott; sound, Stephen Vernier.

Stanwood Ickles; Chief . . . . Rod Gerber
Mr. Paterson . . . . Bob Wells
Mr. Andersen . . . . Conny Radza
Marie Andersen; Daughter . . . Linda Fallentin
Lucille Elliot; Raven . . . . . Minna Holopainen
Rebecca . . . . Joy Fairfield
Mr. Shay . . . . Rudi Galindo
The People . . . . Bob Wells, Conny Radza
  Time and Place: On the sailing vessel Hum-
boldt at the turn of the century.

KORBEL, A HUMBOLDT SOAP OPERA.
By Michael Fields, Donald Forrest, Joan
Schirle and Jael Weisman. April 29, 1993. Di-
rector, Jael Weisman; scenery, Ray Gutierrez;
lighting, Michael Foster; costumes, Jinkie Lee
Boyce.

Organist . . . . Stephen Vernier
Soloist . . . . Leira Satlof
Reverend Cornelius . . . . Stan Mott
Mary Kimble . . . . Julie Fulkerson
Vera Carlson . . . . Jane Hill
Tommy; Ron; Liam Dugan . . Michael Fields
Rhonda . . . . Lynnie M. Horrigan
William . . . . Clay Cardozo
Lori . . . . Joan Schirle

Avery .... Arnie Warshaw
Mia; Woody; Martin Dugan. . Donald Forrest
Funeral Director .... Ralph Hall
Assistant Funeral Director . . Rochelle Jacobs
Chloe...................... Lynne Safier
Singers........ Joyce Hough, Fred Neighbor

Dorothy Dugan .... Joan Schirle
Chorus: Rudi Galindo, Patrick Gavin, Beverly Hanly, Bruce Marrs, Robin Plutchok, Martha Ricca.
Time and Place: A small rural town of Korbel in the present.

Boston: The Huntington Theater Company

(Producing director, Peter Altman; managing director, Michael Maso)

MY MOTHER SAID I NEVER SHOULD. By Charlotte Keatley. January 8, 1993. Director, Charles Towers; scenery, John Falabella; lighting, Jackie Manassee; costumes, Barbra Kravitz; sound, David Strang.

Rosie Metcalf.............. Kate Goehring
Doris Partington .... Pauline Flanagan
Margaret Bradley.......... Elizabeth Franz
Jackie Metcalfe............. Linda Emond
One intermission.

Cambridge, Mass.: American Repertory Theater

(Artistic director, Robert Brustein; managing director, Robert J. Orchard; associate artistic director, Ron Daniels)

DREAM OF THE RED SPIDER. By Ronald Ribman. February 10, 1993. Director, Ron Daniels; scenery, Ricardo Hernandez; costumes, Catherine Zuber; lighting, Frances Aronson; sound, Maribeth Back.
With Jonathan Fried, Remo Airaldi, Candy Buckley, Jack Willis, Royal Miller, Gino Montesinos; Maggie Rush, Daniel Passer, Gustave Johnson, Patti Allison, Alvin Epstein, Timothy Karcher, Jennifer London, Lisa Louise Langford, Kristen Lee Kelly, Claudia Arenas, George Drance, Karl Lampley, Alex Lorria, Michael McNeal, Richard Similio.
One intermission.

ORPHEE. Libretto and music (opera) by Philip Glass; adaptation by Philip Glass based on the film by Jean Cocteau; edited by Robert Brustein. May 19, 1993. Director, Francesca Zambello; musical direction and conductor, Martin Goldray; scenery, Robert Israel; costumes, Catherine Zuber; lighting, Pat Collins; sound, Maribeth Back; produced in association with the Brooklyn Academy of Music.
Older Poet .... James Ramlet
Princess...................... Wendy Hill
Meurteoise .... Richard Fracker
Cegeste .... Paul Kirby
(Orphée) .... Eugene Perry, Leroy Villaneuva
Policeman; Commissioner;
  Judge .... John Kuether
(Eurydice)... Elizabeth Futral, Lynn Torgove
Aglaonice .... Janice Felty
Reporter; Glazier.......... Brian Mirabile
  (Parentheses indicate roles in which the actors alternated)

Others: Linda Joy Adams, Charles Butler, Robert K. Dunn, Michael Glumicich, Rachael Lillis, Ken MacDonald, Stephen Spewock, Hester A. Tinti.
One intermission.

New Stages 93

SILENCE, CUNNING, EXILE. By Stuart Greenman. April 3, 1993. Director, Stuart Greenman; scenery, Christine Jones; costumes, Karen Eister; lighting, John Ambrosone; sound, Maribeth Back.
Suzie .... Stephanie Roth
Donald .... Royal Miller
Frank .... Jonathan Fried
Beryl .... Candy Buckley
Nicole; Emaciated
  Model................ Tresha Rodriguez
Kiki....................... Leslie Beatty
Man at Party; Isaac.......... Alvin Epstein
Transvestite; Acquaintance ...... John Payne
Boyfriend; Transient;
  Inert Man .... Richard Similio
Prostitute .... Remo Airaldi
One intermission.

THE L.A. PLAYS. By Han Ong. April 10, 1993. Director, Steven Maler; scenery, Christine Jones; costumes, Gail A. Buckley; lighting, John Ambrosone; music and sound, Don Dinicola.
With Han Ong, Jonathan Fried, Gino Montesinos, Starla Benford, Matthew Rauch, Raymond Fox, Faran Tahir, John Payne.
One intermission.

Chicago: Goodman Theater

(Artistic director, Robert Falls; producing director, Roche Schulfer)

RIVERVIEW: A MELODRAMA WITH MUSIC. By John Logan. June 22, 1992. Director, Robert Falls; musical direction, Helen Gregory; scenery, Thomas Lynch; lighting, Michael S. Philippi; costumes, Nan Cibula; sound, Richard Woodbury.

Jake	Michael O'Gorman
Dolly	Shannon Cochran
Warren	John Scherer
Nat	John Beasley
Robert	Duane Boutté
Susan	Marin Mazzie
Buddy	Frederick Charles Canada
Jem	Leelai Demoz
Uncle Moe	Robert G. Breuler
Genilli	Vito D'Ambrosio

Salt-of-the-Earth Chicagoans:

Pa	Paul Amandes
Ma	Carole Gutierrez
Maria	Jennifer Kemp
Dottie	Catherine Lee Yore
Teddy	Josh Forman
Donna	Lori Longstreth
Timmy	Louis Dickinson
Joanie	Molly Kidder
Joey	Bill Szobody
Frankie	Gary Carlson

On the Midway:

The Barker	Darren Matthias
King Popeye	Stanley White
Jimmy the Ape-Boy	Nathaniel Sanders
Linda Limber	Elyse Mirto
Gypsy	Aisha deHaas
A Guy	Seth Swoboda
Soldier	Jim Corti
Rich Man	Lee Raines
Rich Woman	Katherine Lynne Condit
Sailors	Jeffery Duke, James Zager

Warren's Dream Girls:

"Lauren Bacall"	Deidre Dolan
"Betty Grable"	Kelly Prybycien
"Rita Hayworth"	Jill Locnikar

Act I: Riverview Amusement Park, Summer of 1946. Act II: Riverview Amusement Park, Summer of 1951. One intermission.

WINGS. Book and lyrics by Arthur Perlman, music by Jeffrey Lunden. Based on the play *Wings* by Arthur Kopit. October 16, 1992. Director, Michael Maggio; musical director, Brad Vieth; scenery, Linda Buchanan; lighting, Robert Christen; costumes, Birgit Rattenborg Wise; sound, Richard Woodbury.

Emily	Linda Stephens
Doctor	William Brown
Nurse	Ora Jones
Amy	Hollis Resnik
Billy	Ross Lehman
Mr. Brambilla	William Brown
Mrs. Timmins	Ora Jones

Time: The play takes place over a period of two years.

PUDDIN 'N PETE. By Cheryl L. West. February 5, 1993. Director, Gilbert Wadadazaf McCauley; scenery, Clay Snider; lighting, Robert Shook; costumes, Yslan Hicks; sound, Richard Woodbury.

Puddin	Cheryl Lynn Bruce
Pete	Ernest Perry Jr.
Ariel	Rebecca Tennison

The Ensemble:

Rose Marie; Ms. Jordan;

Aunt	Cindy Orthal

Dehlia; Penny; Tisha;

Mama Doll	JoNell Kennedy

Tee; Skeet; Mr. Brown;

Preach	Tim Rhoze

Mr. Jansky; Boss; Sal .... John Gegenhuber

Time: The present. Place: Chicago. One intermission.

BLACK SNOW: LAUGHTER BORN OF OPPRESSION. By Keith Reddin. May 10, 1993. Director, Michael Maggio; scenery, Linda Buchanan; lighting, James F. Ingalls; sound, Rob Milburn.

Ivan Vasilievich	Jordan Charney

Rvatsky-Alyosius;

Bombardov; Bahtin	Jeffrey Hutchinson
Gavril; Shakespeare	John Mohrlein
Sergei	Bruce Norris

Likospastov; Vladychinsky;

Patrikeyev	William J. Norris

Strizh; Yegor; Molière...... Steve Pickering

Toropetzkaya;

Ludmilla	Barbara Robertson

Irinia; Mother .... Carmen Roman

Musician	Miriam Sturm

Ensemble: Seana Kofoed, Michael McAlister, Tom Mula, Ajay K. Naidu, Christopher Pieczynski, Marc Vann.

GOODMAN THEATER, CHICAGO—Lee Raines *(left foreground)* and John Beasley *(right)* in an amusement park scene from *Riverview: A Melodrama With Music* by John Logan

Chicago: Remains Theater

(Artistic director, Larry Sloan)

SNAKEBIT. By David Marshall Grant. February 7, 1993. Director, Campbell Scott; scenery, Jeff Bauer; costumes, Laura Cunningham; lighting, Kevin Snow; sound, Christian Peterson.
Jennifer . . . . Talia Balsam

Michael . . . . John Benjamin Hickey
Jonathan . . . . D.W. Moffett
Man . . . . Harry Hutchinson
One intermission.

Chicago: Steppenwolf Theater

(Artistic director, Randall Arney)

MY THING OF LOVE. By Alexandra Gersten. July 12, 1992. Director, Terry Kinney; scenery, Michael Merritt, Kurt Sharp; costumes, Erin Quigley; lighting, Kevin Rigdon; music, Rob Milburn and Michael Bodeen; sound, Rob Milburn.
Elly . . . . Laurie Metcalf
Jack . . . . Tom Irwin

Kelly . . . . Kathryn Erbe
Garn . . . . Tim Hopper
(Chris) . . . . . . Kira Spencer Hesser, Zoe Perry
(Kate) . . . . Elizabeth Armstrong, Logan Hutt
(Parentheses indicate roles in which the actors alternated)
One intermission.

GHOST IN THE MACHINE. By David Gilman. May 14, 1993. Director, Jim True; scenery, Kevin Rigdon; costumes, Allison Reeds; lighting, Christine A. Solger; sound, Eric Huffman.

Wes .... Randall Arney
Nancy .... Martha Lavey
Matt .... Rick Snyder
Kim .... Mariann Mayberry
Harper .... Del Close
Minh Schumann .... Even Chin
No intermission.

Chicago: Victory Gardens Theater

(Artistic director, Dennis Zacek; managing director, John Walker)

HOSPITALITY SUITE. By Roger Rueff. November 12, 1992. Director, John Swanbeck; scenery, William Bartelt; costumes, Claudia Boddy; lighting, Chris Phillips; sound, Galen G. Ramsey.

Phil .... Dennis Zacek
Bob .... Timothy Hendrickson
Larry .... Craig Spidle
Man .... Tom Roland
One intermission.

Cincinnati: Ensemble Theater of Cincinnati

(Artistic director, David A. White III; managing director, John W. Vissman)

DOWNWINDER DANCE. By Gary Stewart. July 10, 1992. Director, Gary Stewart; scenery, Ronald A. Shaw; costumes, Lori Schepper; lighting, Jeff Gress.

With Bo Brinkman, Andrew Prine, Sara Gilbert, Jim Nelson, Mark Mocahbee, Keith Brush, Paul Wescott.
One intermission.

CINDERELLA. By Eric Schmiedl; music by David B. Kisor. December 2, 1992. Director, David A. White III; musical direction, Matt Hisel; scenery, Ruth Sawyer; lighting, Jeff Gress; costumes, Gretchen Sears.

Whiskers .... Mark Mocahbee
Cinderella .... Julia F. White
Karma .... Shannon Rae Lutz
Cupcake .... Paula Zo
Martha .... Paul Kennedy
Hubert .... Gordon C. Greene
Wicked Chancellor .... Robert B. Rais
Mr. Who .... Richard Fleischman
Prince Charming .... Claire Slemmer
The Fairy Godmother .... Diana Rogers
Vinnie .... Matt Howell
Micette .... Sally Kenyon,
                              Greta Storace
One intermission.

LOTUS HOOKS. By Kate Dahlgren. February 3, 1993. Director, David A. White III; scenery and lighting, Ronald A. Shaw; costumes, Susan Wenman; composer, Chris Dahlgren.

Old Sylvie Janis .... Mary T. Mahler
Mary .... Jessica Sullivan
Sylvie Janis .... Claire Slemmer
Philip Janis .... Robert B. Rais
Mei Su .... Berni Weber
Thomas Fine .... Robert Allen
Ming Lui .... Sachiko Nishizawa
Ling .... Ashley Bella
   Ensemble: Tricia Allen, Jason Hays, Laura Otis, Michael Wirick.
One intermission.

FREEMEN AND LUNATICS. By Joseph McDonough. May 19, 1993. Director, Mark Mocahbee; scenery, Kevin Murphy; lighting, Jeff Gress; costumes, Susan Wenman.

Lunsford .... Drew Fracher
Abby .... Kathryne Gardette
Delta .... Nicole Callender
Harrison .... Robert B. Rais
Ramsey .... Charles Holmond
   Soldiers: Charles Holmond, Richard Fleischman, Michael Wirick.
One intermission.

ZORRO. Adapted by Drew Fracher and David Richmond. May 19, 1993. Director, Drew Fracher; composer, John Henry Kreitler; scenery, Michael J. Blankenship; lighting, Ronald A. Shaw; costumes, Gretchen H. Sears.

Diego .... Keith A. Brush
Consuela .... Shannon Rae Lutz
Capt. Ramon .... Scott New
Alcalde .... Gordon C. Greene
Fra Filepe .... Jim Nelson
Ybarrra .... Mary Scott Gudaitis
El Brujo .... Brian C. Russo
Sargent Gonzales .... William Schwarber
Senor Vega .... Gregory J. Procaccino

Dona Catalina . . . . Lee Walsh
Luisa . . . . Christine Whitley

Ensemble: Tricia Allen, Victor Dickerson, Jason Hays, Jim Neely.

Cincinnati: Playhouse in the Park

(Producing artistic director, Edward Stern)

SCOTLAND ROAD. By Jeffrey Hatcher. February 11, 1993. Director, Edward Stern; scenery, Karen TenEyck; costumes, Delmar R. Rinehart Jr.; lighting, Kirk Bookman; music, Ronald Melrose.

John . . . . Reed Birney
Malbrech. . . . . Margo Skinner
Woman . . . . Lisa Fugard
Frances Kittle. . . . . Betty Low
One intermission.

Cleveland: The Cleveland Play House

(Artistic director, Josephine Abady; managing director, Dean Gladden)

FUGUE. By Leonora Thuna. October 20, 1992. Director, Kenneth Frankel; scenery, Marjorie Bradley Kellogg; lighting, Ann G. Wrightson; costumes, Jess Goldstein; sound, Kimberley M. Long.
Mary . . . . Barbara Barrie
Zelda . . . . Susanne Marley
Dr. Danny Lucchesi . . . . . . William Atherton
Dr. Alice Oleander. . . . . Myra Taylor
Mother . . . . Augusta Dabney
Noel . . . . Kurt Deutsch
Liz Kruger . . . . Mary Layne
Tammy . . . . Chelsea Altman
Voice of Nurse . . . . Ellen Karsten
Understudy. . . . . Bryan Edward Smith
Time: The present. Place: Chicago.

JAR THE FLOOR. By Cheryl L. West. January 12, 1993. Director, Tazewell Thompson; scenery and lighting, Joseph P. Tilford; costumes, Kay Kurta; sound, Susan R. White.
MaDear . . . . Irma P. Hall
MayDee . . . . Candace Hunter
Lola. . . . . Crystal Laws Green
Vennie. . . . . Susan Payne
Raisa . . . . Josette DiCarlo
Time: The present; MaDear's 90th birthday party. Place: Park Forest, Ill. One intermission.

THE BUTCHER'S DAUGHTER. By Wendy Kesselman. March 9, 1993. Director, Leslie Swackhamer; scenery, Tony Straiges, lighting, Beverly Emmons; costumes, Paul Tazewell; sound, Jeffrey Montgomerie.
Celeste. . . . . Anney Giobbe
Executioner. . . . . Frederick Neumann
Nounou; Grandmother . . . . Jane White

Olympe (Marie Gouze) . . . . Jennifer Rohn
Pierrot. . . . . Jesse L. Martin
Executioner's Wife. . . . . Beth Dixon
Le Franc de Pompignan . . . . Ken Kliban
Philippe. . . . . Anthony Brown
Michel. . . . . Billy Radin, Kitao Sakurai
Ange . . . . Tim DeKay
Montauban Peasants; Market Women; Paris Citizens: Julie Marie Boyd, Anthony Brown, Eric Coble, Tim DeKay, Ellen Karsten, Caron Tate. Actors: Anthony Brown, Eric Coble, Tim DeKay.
Time: Before and after the Revolution of 1789. Place: France. One intermission.

HEARTBEATS. Musical with book, music and lyrics by Amanda McBroom; created by Amanda McBroom and Bill Castellino; additional music by Gerald Sternbach, Michele Brourman, Tom Snow and Craig Safan. May 4, 1993. Director and choreographer, Bill Castellino; scenery, Linda Hacker; lighting, Richard Winkler; costumes, Charlotte M. Yetman; sound, Jeffrey Montgomerie.
Annie . . . . Jan Maxwell
Steve . . . . Paul Harman
Ensemble: Michelle Blakely, Nicholas Cokas, Teri Gibson, Ric Ryder.

Work-in-Progress

GRAY'S ANATOMY. One-man performance by and with Spalding Gray. May 15, 1993. Director, Renee Shafransky. No intermission.

DiscoveRead New Play Development Series

GRACE IN AMERICA. By Antoine O'Flatharta. March 25, 1993. Directors, Josephine Abady, David F. Eliet.

ON CLEVELAND STAGES—*Left,* Lisa Seppi in the musical *The Chapel of Perpetual Desire* by Amanda Shaffer and Linda Eisenstein at Cleveland Public Theater; *right,* Jesse L. Martin and Jennifer Rohn in a scene from *The Butcher's Daughter* by Wendy Kesselman at The Cleveland Play House

A PREACHER WITH A HORSE TO RIDE. By Jo Carson. March 27, 1993. Director, Roger T. Danforth.

THE FINE THINGS IN LIFE. By Lydia Stryk. April 2, 1993. Director, Roger T. Danforth.

MAPS TO STARS' HOMES. By Jim Geoghan. April 3, 1993. Director, Scott Kanoff.

Cleveland: Cleveland Public Theater

(Artistic director, James A. Levin; producing director, Amanda Shaffer)

THE CHAPEL OF PERPETUAL DESIRE PRESENTS A LITURGICAL CIRCUS OF RELIGIOUS FERVOR AND LIVE SEX ON STAGE! Book by Amanda Shaffer, Linda Eisenstein and the CPT Ensemble; music and lyrics by Linda Eisenstein. June 12, 1992. Director, Amanda Shaffer; musical director, Karen E. Bull; scenery, Amanda Shaffer; lighting, Andrew Kaletta; costumes, Elizzabeth Gardner, Amanda Shaffer; choreography, Lisa Seppi.

With Larissa Abramiuk, Zach Berman, Laura Bishop, Allen Branstein, Lonzo Browning, Karen E. Bull, Nancy Burkinshaw, Toni Dell, Linda Eisenstein, Carol Eldridge, David Ellison, Jon Carlo Franchi, Elizzabeth Gardner, Mark Hopkins, Karry Jones, Andrew Kaletta,

Zoe Kiefer, James Levin, Linda Mason, Melissa McCall, Molly McCauley, Dave McKenzie, Berman Medley, Joe Milan, Leslie Moynihan, Sean Powers, Hazel Reid, Alec Rubin, Lisa Seppi, Amanda Shaffer, k j warren, Chris Wrabel, and Olga the Amazing Dog of Dogs.

Time and Place: A struggling contemporary Temple of Theater Art in Cleveland. One intermission.

MAP OF MY MOTHER. Written and performed by Michael Geither. August 13, 1992. Director, Rob Handel; scenery, Michael Geither; lighting, Andrew Kaletta; slides, Michael Geither, Robert Geither, Leigh Davis.

THE ANCIENTS. By James Slowiak. November 13, 1992. Conceived and directed by James Slowiak; scenery and costumes, Inda Blatch-Geib; lighting, Max Barton II; musical direction, Jennifer Lavy.

Grandparent	Larissa K. Abramiuk
Messenger	Timothy D. Askew
Father	Terence Cranendonk
Grandparent	Wesley Nicholson Jr.
Mother	J. Asha Padamadan
Grandparent	Mark R. Ross
Grandparent	Claudia Tatinge
Grandparent	Kevin Willingham

Time and Place: In the homeland of the Ancients and the desert below.

THE RECITAL OF THE BIRD. By Massoud Saidpour. November 13, 1992. Director, Massoud Saidpour; scenery and costumes, Inda Blatch-Geib; lighting, Max Barton II.

Bird	Larissa K. Abramiuk
King; Master of Workshops; Blessed Tree	Romell Ayo
Storyteller	Terence Cranendonk
Lady in Red (2)	Nicole Dollwet
Verdant One, The Executioner	Wesley Nicholson Jr.
Lady in Red (1)	Claudia Tatinge

Time and Place: In the garden of a King and the surrounding countryside.

THE LIFE OF A WORM. By k j warren. February 5, 1993. Director, Caroline Jackson-Smith; scenery, Blake Ketchum; lighting, Dennis Dugan; costumes, Hazel Reid; sound, Jordan Davis.

Malcolm	Marvin Hayes
Edge	Yusef N'Dour

Time: The present. Place: A crumbling house in Cleveland.

THE SCARLETT LETTERS. Written, designed and performed by Frank Green. March 18, 1993. One intermission.

MOTHER'S WORK. By James Slowiak. April 29, 1993. Director, James Slowiak; scenery, Douglas-Scott Goheen; lighting, Andrew Kaletta; costumes, Inda Blatch-Geib.

With Larissa K. Abramiuk, Timothy D. Askew, Lisa Black, Raymond Bobgan, Terence Cranendonk, Jairo Cuesta, J. Asha Padamadan, Holly Holsinger, Massoud Saidpour, Claudia Tatinge.

11th Festival of New Plays, January 8–24, 1993
SINS OF THE MOTHERS. By Pamela Simones. Director, Jane Armitage.
THE GAME. By Jim Kuth Sr. Director, Jan Bruml.
SEPTEMBER 11. By Guillermo Reyes. Director, Alec Rubin.
THE DOGS. By Craig Strasshofer. Director, Craig A. Webb.
THE MODERN HEART. By Kelly Easton. Director, Kelly Easton.
THE OWNER'S SHUFFLE. By Terry White. Director, Raymond Bobgan.
INTERCOURSE, OHIO. By Geralyn Horton. Director, Nancy Burkinshaw.
IN THE GIST OF TWILIGHT. By Gail Franklin Young. Director, LeRoy Lyons.
MINYA MINTZ. By Anna Baum. Director, Suzanne Strollo.
HEAVEN IN YOUR ARMS. By Toni Walker. Director, Frank Adams.
THE NANJING BANANA RACE. By Reggie Cheong-Leen. Director, Brian O'Connor.
THE UNINVITED. By Joanne Durante. Director, Victoria Karnafel.
CRITICAL MOMENTS. By Carolyn Jack. Director, Craig Rich.

Costa Mesa, Calif.: South Coast Repertory

(Producing artistic director, David Emmes; artistic director, Martin Benson)

SO MANY WORDS. By Roger Rueff. Director, Lillian Garrett-Groag; scenery, Dwight Richard Odle; lighting, Paulie Jenkins; costumes, Todd Roehrman.

SOUTH COAST REPERTORY, COSTA MESA, CALIF.—Douglas Rowe (as Ulysses S. Grant) and Jerome Butler in a scene from *Great Day in the Morning* by Thomas Babe

Pamela Avery............... Lisa Howard
Beth Barnett............... Cristina Soria
Katherine Warner ...... Chris Weatherhead
Stanley Warner............. Stephen Rowe
Waiter................. Robert L. Stewart
  Time: The present, an afternoon in late Autumn. Place: A large hotel room in Washington, D.C. One intermission.

LET'S PLAY TWO. By Anthony Clarvoe. Director, Michael Bloom; scenery, John Iacovelli; lighting, Brian Gale; costumes, Dwight Richard Odle; music and sound, Nathan Birnbaum.
Phil .... Arye Gross
Grace .... Susan Cash
  Time: 1991. Place: Minnesota. One intermission.

GREAT DAY IN THE MORNING. By Thomas Babe. Director, David Emmes; scenery, Gerard Howland; lighting, Peter Maradudin; costumes, Walter Hicklin; musical direction, original music and sound, Michael Roth.
Johnnie Goodenough........ Jerome Butler

Harry Lehr................ Michael Brian
Elizabeth.................. Gloria Biegler
Ulysses S. Grant .... Douglas Rowe
Mrs. Lucy Wharton Drexel .. Jane A. Johnston
Mrs. Caroline Astor .... Oceana Marr
Mrs. Stuyvesant Fish....... Pamela Dunlap
Charlie .... Alan Brooks
Pianist................... John Ellington
  Time: Sometime near the turn of the last century. Place: Fashionable locales along the eastern seaboard. One intermission.

NewSCRipts Readings:

SO MANY WORDS. By Roger Rueff. Director, Lillian Garrett-Groag.
THE LIGHTS. By Howard Korder. Director, David Chambers.
JACKSON BLUME. By Norman Plotkin. Director, Roberta Levitow.
MRS. ZELINSKI COMES TO CALL. By Nancy Crawford. Director, Maria Mileaf.
TO DISTRACTION. By Cecilia Fannon. Director, Steven Albrezzi.

Dallas: Addison Center Theater

(Artistic director, Kelly Cotten; executive director, David Minton)

H.I.D. (HESS IS DEAD). By Howard Brenton. July 10, 1992. Director, Kelly Cotten; scenery and lighting, Robert McVay; costumes, Diana Story; choreographer, Karen Bower Robinson.

Larry Palmer .... Dean Nolen
Charity Luber .... Ellen Locy

Nicole D'Arcy .... Lisa Lee Schmidt
Officer .... Craig Dupree
Raymond Trace .... Spencer Prokop
Istvan Luber .... Fred Churchack (video), Bruce Dubose

No intermission.

Denver: The Changing Scene

(Executive producers, Al Brooks, Maxine Munt)

Summerplay—July 9–August 23, 1992

Series I:
BUS STOP BAPTISM. By Dave Brandl. July 9, 1992. Director, Mark A. Whalin; scenery, Paul Denckla; lighting, Carol Lyn McDowell; music and sound, Chuck Rhodes.
Pearl .... Judy Phelan-Hill
George Williams .... Dean Hubbard

ROSE RED. By Christine Emmert. July 9, 1992. Director, Sallie Diamond; scenery, Paul Denckla; lighting, Carol Lyn McDowell; music and sound, Chuck Rhodes.
Rose .... Lisa Maria Mumpton

IN MEMORIAM. By Marlene Remington. August 6, 1992. Director, Elaine Hoffman; scenery, Paul Denckla; lighting, Carol Lyn McDowell; music and sound, Chuck Rhodes.
Diane Arnette .... Kami Lichtenburg
Brad Kessler .... Dan Driver
Dr. Marvin Whitby ...... William T. Casper
Miss Amanda
  Carter .... M. Catherine Rambeau
Tony Patrillo .... Michael Cross
Adam Holmes; Walter
  Chapman .... Loring Olk

CONCEPTION. By Mark Higdon. July 9, 1992. Director, Angie Lee; scenery, Paul Denckla; lighting, Carol Lyn McDowell; music and sound, Chuck Rhodes.
Jon Lucas .... Paul Denckla
Cindy Lucas .... Cindy Hoots

Series II:
HEY JOE. By Michael Storer. August 6, 1992. Director, Creston McKim; scenery, Paul Denck-

kla; lighting, Mark Priester; music and sound, Steve Stevens.
Joe .... Woody Doyle
Frank .... William H. Hunter
Announcer; Vendor .... William Victor

BELIEVING BILLY. By Jennifer Green. August 6, 1992. Director, Rochelle Obechina; scenery, Paul Denckla; lighting, Mark Priester; music and sound, Steve Stevens.
Billy Lamb .... Montgomery Christian
Mary; Doctor .... Lori Herbst
Martha; Doctor .... Janette Mattocks
Dr. Louis Fine .... Gary Stricklin
Mrs. Estelle Fine; Dona Guadalupe de
  las Pappas .... Joline Black
Angel; Doctor .... Nancy Grandfield

SPIEGAL & CALLOWAY. By Brian Quinette. August 6, 1992. Director, Trace Oakley; scenery, Paul Denckla; lighting, Mark Priester; music and sound, Steve Stevens.

RIGHT TO LIFE. By Lee Patton. August 6, 1992. Director, Henry Snow; scenery, Paul Denckla; lighting, Mark Priester; music and sound, Steve Stevens.
Todd .... Wayne Willis Waterman
Les .... Dan Driver
Soldier; Man of God; Johnny .... Eric Weber
  Place: A sauna adjacent to a lap-swimming pool within a large suburban public recreation center.

QUATREFOIL. By Brian Quinette. October 8, 1992. Director, Jennifer Thero; scenery, Tom Jones; lighting, James Connaughton; costumes, Martha Harmon Pardee; sound, Wayne Willis Waterman, Jennifer Thero.

Arthur................... Eick Sandvold
Alice .... Martha Harmon Pardee
Baxter................ Travis Shakespeare
Kate .... Marta Barnard
One intermission.

THE GIANTKILLER. By Ann Chamberlain. November 5, 1992. Director, Sara Wright; scenery, Patricia Robertson; lighting, Mark Priester; costumes, Nancy Bassett; music and sound, Jay Shaffer.
Phoebe Parkinson .... Lynn Abell
Derek Freeman .... Doug White
Hillary Freeman............ Tracey Russell
Margaret Mead .... Mary Beth Floyd
Cathy Bateson .... Joline Black
Sina Ala'ilima................ Jana Ramlet
One intermission.

DESERT TIME. By Eric Walter and Doug Goodwin. December 3, 1992. Director, Doug Goodwin; scenery, Doug Goodwin; lighting, Christy Student; sound, Wayne Waterman and Casidy McLean.
With Eric Walter, Ed Lee.

OH REVOIR, MIRABEAU! By Mark Dunn. January 14, 1993. Director, Greg Ward; sce-

nery, lighting and costumes, Tumbleweed Productions; sound, Joseph McDonald.
Grace Dobbs .... Yvonne Harrison
Dwayne Moorehouse......... Matt Bachus
Emmaline Dobbs .... Patty Mintz Figel
Cora Talbot .... Suzanne Kunze
Juanita Talbot .... Mary L. Adams
Valerie Talbot .... Jean Sorich Ward
Jedediah Dobbs .... Doug White
Prentice Culler Jr. .... Joseph McDonald
Time and Place: Not-too-distant past in the town of Mirabeau, Texas. One intermission.

THE PLAY. By Vicky Semel Hammer. March 18, 1993. Director, Henry Snow; scenery, Henry Snow; lighting, Craig Williamson; costumes, Lynn Abell; sound, Chuck Rhodes.
George Lord.................. Eric Weber
Jack................. Travis Shakespeare
Dr. Milton;
Minister .... Dennis Fisher
Tina..................... Diann Chapman
Dr. Gorman; Officer O'Brien;
Minister .... James Sullivan
Helen..................... Laura Thomas
One intermission.

Dorset, Vt.: Dorset Theater Festival

(Producing director, John Nassivera; artistic director, Jill Charles; managing director, C. Barrack Evans)

THE COUNTRY CLUB. By Douglas Carter Beane. August 13, 1992. Director, Edgar Lansbury; scenery, William John Aupperlee; lighting and sound, John Henderson; costumes, Lynda L. Salsbury.
Pooker.............. Constance Crawford
Soos..................... Cynthia Nixon
Froggy .... Shauna Hicks

Bri.................. T. Scott Christopher
Zip..................... David Lansbury
Hutch .... Jim Fyfe
Chloe Maria Donna
DeGlatalia................. Cara Buono
Place: The Cub Room of the Wyomising Country Club, not far from Reading, Pa. One intermission.

East Farmingdale, N.Y.: Arena Players Repertory Company

(Producer and director, Frederic De Feis)

SATAN IN WONDERLAND. By Ron Mark. Director, Frederic De Feis; scenery, Fred Sprauer; lighting, Al Davis; costumes, Karen Ackley.
Max Ziggerman .... Michael Fredericks
Janet Macavoy........... Jeanine Matlow
Talcott Chandler .... Edwin Young

Kasey Chandler .... Allyson Cimler
Everett Harmon............ Donald Carter
Rachel Harmon .... Sunny Taylor
John Vinetti .... John Fannon
Time: The present. Place: Changing locations. One intermission.

Fort Worth: Hip Pocket Theater

(Artistic director, Johnny Simons; producer, Diane Simons)

A SAGA OF BILLY THE KID. By Johnny Simons. June 5, 1992. Director, Johnny Simons; scenery, Lake Simons; lighting, John Leach; costumes, Diane Simons.

Sheriff Pat Garrett ... Jimmy Joe Steenbergen
Billy Bonney .... David Yeakle
Kathleen Bonney .... Peggy Bott
Jesse Evans .... Michael Joe Goggans
Salazar .... Kristi Ramos
Juanita .... Audrey Todd
Delvina .... Dena Brinkley Phillips
L.G. Murphy .... Bob Allen
John S. Tunstall .... Dick Harris
  Dirty Cowboys: Heidi Blickenstaff, Peggy Bott, Audrey Todd, Dena Brinkley Phillips, Kristi Ramos.
One intermission.

NIGHTMARE ALLEY STARRING TYRONE POWER. By Johnny Simons. September 4, 1992. Director, Johnny Simons; scenery, Mark Walker; lighting, John Leach; costumes, Diane Simons; musical director, Steve Carter.

Tyrone Power; Stan Carlisle ... Lamar Wilson
Zeena; Lilith .... Dena Brinkley Phillips
Pete; Ezra Grindle .... Dick Harris
Clem .... Mario Gonzales
Molly .... Lisa Millard
Director .... Bertolt Pfeiffer
Cameraman .... Costa Caglage

George Jessel .... Howard Robin
Geek .... Michael Joe Goggans
Addie .... Peggy Bott
Deputy .... Carl Haney
Herculo.................... Bob Allen
  Ensemble: Neanna Bodycomb, Peggy Bott, Ed Cannady, Linda Boydston Dunlap, Tricia Franks, Mary Austin Harper, Holly Nelson Leach, Kristi Ramos, Doug Vail, Melinda Wood.
One intermission.

SLEEPY HOLLOW, A HEADLESS TALE. By Johnny Simons. October 2, 1992. Director, John Murphy; scenery, Susan Marshall; lighting, John Leach; costumes, Barbara O'Donoghue.

Narrator .... Jim Hopkins
Vocalist.................. Melinda Wood
Ichabod Crane .... Perry Brown
Nicholas Pickle........ Jennifer Langenstein
Dame Van Tassel............. Peggy Bott
Katrina Van Tassel .... Kristi Ramos
Brom Bones .... Bob Allen
Hans Van Ripper; Baltus
  Van Tassel .... Dick Harris
  Ensemble: Ed Cannady, Cynthia Cranz, Kristi Price-Jenkins, Jennifer Langenstein, Doug Vail.
One intermission.

Fort Worth: Stage West

(Artistic director, Gerald Russell; associate director, James Covault)

RIPE CONDITION. By Claudia Allen. June 24, 1992. Director, Buckley Sachs; scenery, Nelson Robinson; lighting, Michael O'Brien.
Buster .... Ron Quade
Lester .... Randall D. Bonifay

Ann...................... Cheryl Norris
Time: Tornado season, 1986. Place: A rural Michigan farmhouse gone to seed. One intermission.

Hartford, Conn.: Hartford Stage

(Artistic director, Mark Lamos; managing director, David Hawkanson)

MARTIN GUERRE. Book and lyrics by Laura Harrington, music by Roger Ames. January 8, 1993. Director, Mark Lamos; scenery, Michael Yeargan; lighting, Jennifer Tipton; costumes, Jess Goldstein; sound, David Budries.
Guerre, the Father.......... Walter Charles

Pierre Guerre .... Peter Samuel
Monsieur de Rols; Coras,
  the Judge .... Don Mayo
Mireille de Rols .... Judy Kuhn
Yvette .... Joan Susswein Barber
Thomas; Yves du Tilh.......... David Eye

HARTFORD, CONN. STAGE—Patrick Cassidy and
Judy Kuhn in the musical drama *Martin Guerre* by Laura
Harrington and Roger Ames

Louise..................... Beth Fowler
Martin Guerre, Act I........ Malcolm Gets
Armand...................... John Aller
The Priest.............. Cris Groenendaal
Jean de Loze................. Luke Lynch
(Martine Guerre,
Act II) .... Patrick Cassidy, Peter Reardon
Jacques Boeri............. Walter Charles

Simon Sejas .... Deborah Bradshaw
Carbon Barrau.............. Dean Stroop
Paul Bertholet .... Craig Waletzko
(Parentheses indicate role in which the actors
alternated)
Time and Place: 16th century France in a
small village in the mountains southeast of Tou-
louse.

Hollywood, Calif.: Theater West

(Managing director, Douglas Marney)

THE ROUTINE. By David Abbott. March 6,
1993. Director, Philip Abbott; scenery, George
Landry; lighting, Marianne Schneller; costumes, Lila Mae Pace.
Chester Reese.............. David Abbott

Chip Hartfeld.............. Tom Dahlgren
Green Liquid .... Linda Pace
Konica .... Mary Van Arsdel
Place: A cabaret near Chicago and a residen-
tial hotel.

Houston: Alley Theater

(Artistic director, Gregory Boyd; executive director, Stephen J. Albert)

DANTON'S DEATH. By Georg Büchner; new English version by Robert Auletta. October 27, 1992. Director, Robert Wilson; scenery, Robert Wilson; lighting, Stephen Strawbridge, Robert Wilson; costumes, John Conklin; sound, Joe Pino; original music, Chuck Winkler.

Danton	Richard Thomas
Julie	Marissa Chibas
Herault-Sechelles	John Feltch
Adelaide	Jennifer Arisco
Rosalie	Emily York
Woman	Gage Tarrant
2d Woman	Katherine Pew
Camille	Scott Rabinowitz
Phillipeau	Jamie Callahan
Man on the Street; Warder;	
Carter	James Black
Robespierre	Lou Liberatore
Legendre	Willis Sparks
Lacroix	Jeffrey Bean
Marion	Annalee Jefferies
St. Just	Jon David Weigand
1st Gentleman	Thomas Derrah
2d Gentleman	Wade Mylius
Lucille	Melissa Bowen
Herman	Peter Webster
Thomas Paine	Gregory Boyd
Jailer; Executioner	Bettye Fitzpatrick
Fouquier	Thomas Derrah
Boy	Jeremy Montemarano

Citizens: Peter Baquet, Glenn Dickerson, Matthew Rippy.

One intermission.

Kansas City: Missouri Repertory Theater

(Executive director, James D. Costin; artistic director, George Keathley)

GREYTOP IN LOVE. By Alan Brody. June 17, 1992. Director, George Keathley; scenery and lighting, Rob Murphy; costumes, Lynda K. Myers; sound, Robert Beck.

Arnold Greytop	Forrest Compton
Carol Wilson	Cynthia Hyer
Eric Johannson	Terrell Anthony
Bella Fiedler	Dodie Brown

Time: The present. Place: Arnold Greytop's apartment in New York City. One intermission.

New Plays/Staged Readings

KNIGHT. By Nancy Axelrod. Director, Mary G. Guaraldi.

PERPETRATOR. By Tedd Smith. January 16, 1993. Director, Ron Schaeffer.

ONE-ON-ONE. By Alan Brody. January 23, 1993. Director, Mary G. Guaraldi.

HYDROPHOBIA. By Amy Freed. January 30, 1993. Director, Dale AJ Rose.

MIRROR, MIRROR. By Frank Higgins. February 6, 1993. Director, Mary G. Guaraldi.

THE IMMACULATE CONCEPTION OF MALFIE DIBBS. By B. Burgess Clark. February 13, 1993. Director, Mary G. Guaraldi.

Los Angeles: Ahmanson Theater

(Producing director, Gordon Davidson; managing director, Charles Dillingham)

MONEY & FRIENDS. By David Williamson. January 14, 1993. Director, Michael Blakemore; scenery and costumes, Hayden Griffin; lighting, Martin Aronstein; sound, Jon Gottlieb.

Margaret	Linda Thorson
Peter	Michael Gross
Conrad	John McMartin
Jaquie	Julie White
Stephen	David Selby
Penny	Lizbeth Mackay
Alex	John Gertz
Vicki	Lisa Banes
Justin	Sean O'Bryan

Time: Summer 1990. Place: The Eastern Coast of Australia near Sydney. One intermission.

Los Angeles: Colony Studio Theater

(Producing director, Barbara Beckley)

WHEN THE BOUGH BREAKS. By Robert Clyman. April 4, 1993. Director, Michael Haney; scenery, D. Silvio Volonte; lighting, Jamie McAllister; costumes, Ted C. Giammona; sound, John Fisher.

Eileen	An Dragavon
Doug	Robert O'Reilly
Susan	Melody Ryane
Beth	Bonita Friedericy
Janet	Patricia Cullen
Mary	Carissa Channing
Ivan	Greg Rusin
Hank	Gil Johnson
Orderlies	Lavinia Arriaza, Robert S. Ryan

Time and Place: A hospital in an eastern city over the course of 36 hours. One intermission.

Los Angeles: Mark Taper Forum

(Artistic director and producer, Gordon Davidson)

UNFINISHED STORIES. By Sybille Pearson. June 25, 1992. Director, Gordon Davidson; scenery, Peter Wexler; costumes, Csilla Marki; lighting, Martin Aronstein; sound, Jon Gottlieb.

Walter	Joseph Wiseman
Daniel	Christopher Collet
Gaby	Fionnula Flanagan
Yves	Hal Linden

Time: The present. Place: Upper West Side, New York City. Scene 1: Friday, 8 a.m. Scene 2: Saturday, 12 noon. Scene 3: Later that night. Scene 4: Immediately following. Scene 5: Sunday, 8 a.m. No intermission. (An ATCA selection; see introduction to this section.)

ANGELS IN AMERICA—A GAY FANTASIA ON NATIONAL THEMES. PART II: PERESTROIKA. By Tony Kushner. November 8, 1992. Director, Oskar Eustis with Tony Taccone; scenery, John Conklin; lighting, Pat Collins; costumes, Gabriel Berry; sound, Jon Gottlieb.

Hannah Pitt	Kathleen Chalfant
Belize	K. Todd Freeman
Joe Pitt	Jeffrey King
Roy Cohn	Ron Leibman
Harper Pitt	Cynthia Mace
Louis Ironson	Joe Mantello
Angel	Ellen McLaughlin
Prior Walter	Stephen Spinella
Heavenly Attendants	Eve Sigall, Pauline Lepor

Place: New York City, Salt Lake City and elsewhere. Two intermissions.

Note: This world premiere of *Perestroika* was presented together with the first part of *Angels in America (Millennium Approaches)*, which had had its world premiere in May 1991 at the Eureka Theater in San Francisco.

SCENES FROM AN EXECUTION. By Howard Barker. March 16, 1993. Director, Robert Allan Ackerman; scenery, Yael Pardess; lighting, Arden Fingerhut; costumes, Dona Granata; sound, Jon Gottlieb.

Galactia	Juliet Stevenson
Carpeta	Michael Cumpsty
Prodo	Don Amendolia
Urgentino	Frank Langella
Supporta	Olivia d'Abo
Dementia	Jodie Markell
Workman; Mustafa, the Albanian; Official; Lasagna	Tony Abatemarco
Suffici	Ben Hammer
Rivera	Natalija Nogulich
Sordo; Man in Next Cell	François Giroday
1st Sailor	Carlos Papierski
2d Sailor	Greg Naughton
Ostensibile	Richard Frank
Pastaccio; Jailer	Robert Machray
Man	Michael Forest

Workmen: Alexander Enberg, Greg Naughton, Carlos Papierski. Ensemble: Francia Di-Mase, Marcia Firesten, Roger Kern. One intermission.

ON THE ROAD: A SEARCH FOR AMERICAN CHARACTER. Conceived, written and performed by Anna Deavere Smith. May 23, 1993. Director, Emily Mann; scenery, Robert Brill; lighting, Allen Lee Hughes; costumes, Ceci; sound, Jon Gottlieb.

Taper Lab 92–93: New Work Festival

SWOONY PLANET. Written and directed by Han Ong. February 3, 1993.

THE BACCHAE. By Charles L. Mee Jr. Director, Brian Kulick. February 6, 1993.
THE INTERPRETOR OF HORROR. By Kelly Stuart. Director, Robert Egan. February 10, 1993.
SANTOS & SANTOS. By Octavio Solis. Director, Jose Luis Valenzuela. February 13, 1993.
THROUGH THE SIPAPU (OR HAROLD'S BIG FEAT). Created and performed by Wolfe Bowart. February 17, 1993. Director, Peter C. Brosius.
FRIDA/ORANGE CRUSH (COOL LIKE THAT). Written and performed by Han Ong. February 20, 1993.
A WORK IN PROGRESS. Written and performed by John Fleck. February 20, 1993.
KNIFE IN THE HEART. By Philip Kan Gotanda. February 23, 1993. Director, Oskar Eustis.
GERALD'S GOOD IDEA. By Y York. February 24, 1993. Director, Frank Dwyer.
THE DISTANCE OF YOU. By Adelaide MacKenzie. February 25, 1993. Director, Jeremy Lawrence.
STALIN'S DAUGHTER. By August Baker. February 26, 1993. Director, Oskar Eustis.
A FLAW IN THE OINTMENT. By Georges Feydeau, translated and adapted by Lillian Garrett-Groag and William Gray. February 27, 1993. Director, Dan Kern.
HAINTS, CONJURMEN AND LEAVING. By David Lee Lindsey. February 28, 1993. Director, L. Kenneth Richardson.
SAHARA. By Rosanna Staffa. March 3, 1993. Director, Peter C. Brosius.
BUYING TIME. By Michael Weller. March 6, 1993. Director, Robert Egan.
THE WAITING ROOM. By Lisa Loomer. March 10, 1993. Director, David Schweizer.
BANDIDO. By Luis Valdez. March 13, 1993. Director, Jose Luis Valenzuela.
PH*REAKS. Adapted by Doris Baizley and Victoria Ann-Lewis. March 26, 1993. Director, Victoria Ann-Lewis.

Louisville: Actors Theater of Louisville

(Producing director, Jon Jory; literary manager, Michael Dixon)

17th Annual Humana Festival of New American Plays, February 25–April 4, 1993

STANTON'S GARAGE. By Joan Ackermann. Director, Steven Albrezzi; scenery, Paul Owen; lighting, Karl E. Haas; costumes, Laura Patterson; sound, Darron L. West.

Ron . . . . Peter Zapp
Harlon . . . . Rob Kramer
Silvio . . . . Bob Burrus
Denny . . . . V Craig Heidenreich
Lee . . . . Priscilla Shanks
Frannie . . . . Jessica Jory
Mary . . . . Adale O'Brien
Aubrey . . . . Susan Barnes
    Time: The present. Place: A service station in northern Missouri. One intermission.

SHOOTING SIMONE. By Lynne Kaufman. Director, Laszlo Marton; scenery, Paul Owen; lighting, Karl E. Haas; costumes, Laura Patterson; sound, Darron L. West.

Jean-Paul Sartre . . . . Fred Major
Simone de Beauvoir . . . . Janni Brenn
Olga; Kate . . . . Kathleen Dennehy
Alphonse; Rick . . . . Brett Rickaby
Garons . . . . Christopher Murphy, Brian Worrall
    Act I: Paris, 1937. Act II: Paris, 1980. One intermission.

VARIOUS SMALL FIRES (Program of two one-act plays): WATERMELON RINDS and JENNINE'S DIARY. By Regina Taylor. Director, Novella Nelson; scenery, Paul Owen; lighting, Marcus Dilliard; costumes, Toni-Leslie James; sound, Casey L. Warren. One intermission.

Jennine's Diary

Jennine . . . . Elain Graham
Taxi Driver; Cousin Esther; Aunt Rose;
    Friend; Chorus . . . . Judy Tate
Karen; Chorus . . . . Nailah Jumoké
Terrinika; Chorus . . . . Kalimi A. Baxter
Madear; Chorus . . . . Yvette Hawkins
    Time: The past, present and future. Place: Somewhere between here and a dream called Venice.

Watermelon Rinds

Jes Semple . . . . Roger Robinson
Lottie Semple . . . . Kalimi A. Baxter
Willy Semple . . . . Donald Griffin
Liza Semple . . . . Regina Byrd Smith
Pinkie Semple . . . . Elain Graham
Papa Tommy Semple . . . . Ray Johnson
Mama Pearl Semple . . . . Yvette Hawkins
Marva Semple-Weisse . . . . Judy Tate
    Time: The present. Place: A household in an urban neighborhood.

ACTORS THEATER OF LOUISVILLE—Steven Skybell
and Tamar Kotoske in *Deadly Virtues* by Brian Jucha

THE ICE FISHING PLAY. By Kevin Kling.
Director, Michael Sommers; scenery, Paul
Owen; lighting, Karl E. Haas; costumes, Toni-
Leslie James; sound, Darron L. West.

Voice of Tim	Fred Major
Voice of Paul	Ray Fry
Ron	Kevin Kling
Shumway	Pepper Stebbins
Francis	Victor Gonzalez
Irene	Susan Barnes
Duff	Michael Kevin
Junior	William McNulty
Young Ron	Collin Sherman

Act I: The present. Act II: Three days later.
Place: A lake in northern Minnesota. One intermission.

DEADLY VIRTUES. Adapted and directed by
Brian Jucha; scenery, Paul Owen; lighting, Mar-
cus Dilliard; costumes, Laura Patterson; sound,
Darron L. West.

Created and performed by Tamar Kotoske,
Barney O'Hanlon, Steven Skybell, Regina Byrd
Smith, Andrew Weems.

KEELY AND DU. By Jane Martin. Director,
Jon Jory; scenery, Paul Owen; lighting, Marcus
Dilliard; costumes, Laura Patterson; sound,
Darron L. West.

Du	Anne Pitoniak
Walter	Bob Burrus
Keely	Julie Boyd
Cole	J. Ed Araiza
Prison Guard	Janice O'Rourke
Orderlies	Jeremy Brisiel, Jeff Sexton

Time: Now. Place: Providence, R.I.

Ten-Minute Plays

WHAT WE DO WITH IT. By Bruce Mac-
Donald. Director, Frazier W. Marsh; scenery,
Paul Owen; lighting, Karl E. Haas; costumes,
Hollis Jenkins-Evans; sound, Casey L. Warren.
John .... Ray Fry
Cheryl .... Priscilla Shanks
Time: The present. Place: An office.

TAPE. By Jose Rivera. Director, Scott Zigler;
scenery, Paul Owen; lighting, Karl E. Haas; costumes, Hollis Jenkins-Evans; sound, Casey L.
Warren.

Person .... Fred Major
Attendant .... Kalimi A. Baxter
Time: The present. Place: A dark room.

POOF! By Lynn Nottage. Director, Seret Scott;
scenery, Paul Owen; lighting, Karl E. Haas; cos-
tumes, Kevin R. McLeod; sound, Casey L.
Warren.
Loureen .... Elain Graham
Florence .... Yvette Hawkins
Time: The present. Place: Kitchen.

Lowell, Mass.: Merrimack Repertory Theater

(Artistic director, David G. Kent; general manager, Keith Stevens)

THE SURVIVOR: A CAMBODIAN ODYS-
SEY. By Jon Lipsky. March 19, 1993. Director,
David G. Kent; scenery and costumes, Gary M.
English; lighting, Kendall Smith; choreogra-
pher, Maureen Fleming; sound, Todd Shil-
hanek.
Classical Dancer .... Somaly Hay
Female Naga; Dancer; Ensemble .... Eva Lee

Male Naga; Dancer; Ensemble.... Chris Odo
Ngim; Khmer Rouge Girl .... Sophia Im
Pen Tip .... Ernest Abuba
Ngor .... Francois Chau
Huoy .... Dawn Akemi Saito
Act I: Cambodia 1975–1979. Act II: Cam-
bodia and Thailand 1979–1980 and Los Angeles
1980 to present.

Madison, N.J.: Playwrights Theater of New Jersey

(Artistic director, John Pietrowski; producing director, Josh Sommers)

DADA. By Haris Orkin. November 5, 1992.
Director, Joseph Megel; scenery, Ron Kadri;
lighting, Christopher Gorzelnik; costumes,
Tracy Christensen; sound, Joe Ramos.
David Speigel .... David Breitbarth
Karen Speigel .... Julia Glander
David's Father; David's Child .. Russell Leib
David's Mother; Teacher;
Nurse .... Suzanne Toren
David's Grandfather; Guidance
Counselor .... Michael Marcus
Doctor; James Bond;
Judge; Coach; Minister; Rabbi;
Psychologist .... T. Ryder Smith

Terry; Blonde; Playmate;
Nurse .... Emily Newman
Time: Present, past and future. Place: A hospital room and various other places. One intermission.

Staged Readings:

HOW HIS BRIDE CAME TO ABRAHAM.
By Karen Sunde. September 25, 1992. Director,
Cynthia Stokes.
EATING CHICKEN FEET. By Kitty Chen.
January 29, 1993. Director, Joseph D. Giardina.
SALLY'S PORCH. By Russell Davis. April 23,
1993. Director, John Pietrowski.

Milburn, N.J.: Paper Mill Playhouse

(Artistic director, Robert Johanson; executive producer, Angelo Del Rossi)

THE WIZARD OF OZ. By John Kane;
adapted from characters created by L. Frank
Baum and the motion picture screen play; music
by Harold Arlen; lyrics by E.Y. Harburg; background music by Herbert Stothart. Directed

and choreographed by Robert Johanson and
James Rocco; scenery, Michael Anania; cos-
tumes, Gregg Barnes; lighting and sound, David
R. Paterson; musical direction, Jeff Rizzo.
Dorothy Gale .... Kelli Rabke

Toto .... Toto
Aunt Em; Glinda .... Judith McCauley
Uncle Henry; Winkie
  General .... Michael Hayward-Jones
Hunk; Scarecrow .... Mark Chmiel
Hickory; Tin Man ...... Michael O'Gorman
Zeke; Cowardly Lion............ Evan Bell
Almira Gulch;
  Wicked Witch .... Elizabeth Franz
Professor Marvel; Wizard of Oz;
  Emerald City Guard .... Eddie Bracken
Lollipop Guild: Faye Arthurs, Juliana Louise

Biersbach, Laura Mineo. Lullabye League: Michelle Caggiano, Allegra Libonati, Rebecca Lormand. Others: Frances Barney, Patrick Boyd, Casey Colgan, Jodi Glaser, Gail Cook Howell, Michael Kuchar, Derreick McGinty, Melody Meitrott, Fleur Phillips, Gary Pratt, Joyce Pratt, Norma Pratt, Mary Ruvelo, Tim Schultheis, Christine Torre, Jamie Waggoner, John Wiltberger.

Musical numbers from the film *The Wizard of Oz*. One intermission.

Milford, N.H.: American Stage Festival

(Producing director, Matthew Parent)

THE BREAK. By Jay B. MacNamee. July 8, 1992. Director, Peter Bennett; scenery, Gary English; costumes, Amanda J. Comer; lighting, Linda O'Brien.

Linus .... Tom Celli
Eddie .... Thomas Schall
  One intermission.

Minneapolis: Theatre de la Jeune Lune

(Artistic directors, Barbra Berlovitz Desbois, Vincent Gracieux, Robert Rosen, Dominique Serrand; artistic associates, Steven Epp, Felicity Jones)

CHILDREN OF PARADISE: SHOOTING A DREAM. By Steven Epp, Felicity Jones, Dominique Serrand and Paul Walsh; based on the work of Marcel Carné and Jacques Prévert. November 18, 1992. Director, Dominique Serrand; composer, Chandler Poling; scenography, Vincent Gracieux; lighting, Frederic Desbois; costumes, Trina Mrnak.

Cast: Arletty in the Role of Garance—Felicity Jones. Jean-Louis Barrault in the Role of Baptiste Deburau—Robert Rosen. Pierre Brasseur in the Role of Frederick Lemaître—Steven Epp. Marcel Herrand in the Role of Pierre-François Lacenaire—Charles Schuminski. Robert Le Vigan in the Role of Jericho—John Clark Donahue. Maria Casares in the Role of Natalie—Sarah Corzatt. Marcel Carné—Dominique Serrand. Jacques Prévert—Vincent Gracieux. Françoise Rosay—Barbra Berlovitz Desbois.

Joseph Kosma—Eric Jensen. André Paulvé; Stage Manager of the Funambules—Brian Sostek. Alexandre Trauner; Vichy Censor; Prosecutor of the Purification—Michael Collins; Mimi—Laura Esping. Director of Photography; Priest—Joel Sass; Key Grip; Gazelle—Aimée Jacobson. Sound Engineer—Michael Harryman. François—Ben Kernan. Wardrobe Mistress—Nancy Hogetvedt. Makeup Artist; Avril—Angie Lewis. Director of the Funambules; French Militia; BBC Voice; Journalist—Terry Ward. Constable; French Militia; Mme. Hermine; Set Dresser—Cherie Anderson. (General Hans Soehring; Gaffer)—Dave Boerger, Ted Mattison. (Parentheses indicate roles in which the actors alternated.)

One intermission. (The 1993 ATCA Award winner; see introduction to this section.)

New Brunswick, N.J.: George Street Playhouse

(Producing artistic director, Gregory S. Hurst)

NEAR THE END OF THE CENTURY. By Tom Dulack. September 26, 1992. Director, Gregory S. Hurst; scenery, Deborah Jasien; lighting, Donald Holder; costumes, Barbara Forbes.

Richard Boyle .... Michael Murphy
Howie Stark .... Greg Mullavey
Trish .... Catherine Curtin
  Act I: In front of a laundromat in York Beach, Me.; 6 a.m. Act II: The following day; 6 a.m.

GEORGE STREET PLAYHOUSE, NEW BRUNS-
WICK, N.J.—Michael Murphy and Catherine Curtin in
a scene from *Near the End of the Century* by Tom Dulack

IDIOGLOSSIA. By Mark Handley. October 24, 1992. Director, Tom O'Horgan; scenery, Perry Arthur Kroeger; lighting, Paul Armstrong; costumes, Barbara Forbes.

Jake........................ Steven Keats
TC........................ Allison Janney
Claude...................... Betsy Palmer
Nell.................... Deanna Deignan
Time: The present. Place: Three rooms, Richland, Wash. One intermission.

SPINE. By Bill C. Davis. January 2, 1993. Director, Bill C. Davis; scenery, Deborah Jasien; lighting, Donald Holder; costumes, Sue Ellen Rohrer.

Claire .... Heather Gottlieb
Mike Jr. .... Justin Kirk
Lois.................... Caroline Aaron
Mike Sr.................... Mark Metcalf
Dr. Maru .... Sakina Jaffrey
Time: February, the present. Place: Northwest Connecticut.

MORNING DEW WITH TRELLIS. By Richard Browner. January 30, 1993. Director, Wendy Liscow; scenery, Atkin Pace; lighting, F. Mitchell Dana; costumes, Barbara Forbes.

Angela....................... Nancy Paul
Kay.......................... Bibi Besch
Time: The present. Place: Angela's New York apartment. One intermission.

THE FIELDS OF AMBROSIA. Book and lyrics by Joel Higgins; music by Martin Silvestri. Based on *The Traveling Executioner,* an original screen play by Garrie Bateson. March 6, 1993. Director, Gregory S. Hurst; choreographer, Lynne Taylor-Corbett; musical direction, Sariva Goetz; scenery, Deborah Jasien; lighting, Howard Werner, Donald Holder; costumes, Hillary Rosenfeld; sound, Fox and Perla, Ltd.

Pat; J.B. Tucker; Superintendent of Little Betty Troublesome Prison ...... Hal Davis
Stanley Mae .... Matthew Bennett
Caleb; Rapist .... Steve Steiner

Jonas Candide .... Joel Higgins
Eben; Roscoe .... Ted Stamp
Jimmy Crawford .... Eddie Korbich
Piquant .... Peter Samuel
Doc .... Robert Ousley
Warden Brodsky .... Nick Ullett
Willie Herzallerliebst .... Shaver Tillitt
Gretchen Herzallerliebst .. Christine Andreas
Samuel Pennybaker .... Matthew Bennett
Alice .... Elisabeth S. Rodgers
Daddy; Manager, Shoatville
  Commerce Bank .... Ron Lee Savin
Rapist .... David Mann
Local Tough-Guy Card Sharp;
  Bank Guard................... Ed Sala

Staged Readings:

MORNING DEW WITH TRELLIS. By Richard Browner. October, 1922. Director, Wendy Liscow.

STAR DUST. By Elizabeth Gould Hemmerdinger. November, 1992. Director, Wendy Liscow.

WHAT IS ART. By Bill Leavengood. December, 1992. Director, Wendy Liscow.

MADWOMAN OF ETIAN. By Suzanne Marshall. December, 1992. Director, Wendy Liscow.

SUMMER FEET HEARTS. By Lynn Martin. March, 1993. Director, Wendy Liscow.

DOUBLE SOLITAIRE. By Suzanne Marshall. March, 1993. Director, Cree Rankin.

New Haven, Conn.: Yale Repertory Theater

(Artistic director, Stan Wojewodski Jr.; managing director, Benjamin Mordecai)

SAINT JOAN OF THE STOCKYARDS. By Bertolt Brecht; translated by Paul Schmidt. February 25, 1993. Director, Liz Diamond; scenery, Adam Scher; lighting, Jennifer Tipton; costumes, Lisa Tomczeszyn; musical direction, Mark Janas; original music and sound design, Dan Moses Schreier.

With Dallas Adams, Christopher Bauer, Tom Bloom, Amy Brenneman, David Chandler, Brendan Corbalis, Jane Eden, Melody J. Garrett, Paul Giamatti, Ben Halley Jr., Rodney Scott Hudson, Sarah Knowlton, Camryn Manheim, Alessandro Nivola, Nicki Paraiso, Michael Potts, David J. Roth, Tim Salamandyk, Paul Schmidt, Peter Schmitz, Scott Sherman, Christina Sibul.

Palo Alto, Calif.: Theater Works

(Artistic director, Robert Kelley; managing director, Randy Adams)

GOD'S HANDS. Book, music and lyrics by Douglas J. Cohen. October 2, 1992. Director and choreographer, Barbara Valente; musical direction, Lita B. Libaek; scenery, Joe Ragey; lighting, Pamela Gray Bones; costumes, Loren Tripp; sound, Shari Bethel.

Rabbi Daniel Levy.......... Stephen S. Gill
Ellie Levy .... Diana Torres Koss
Rhea Levy .... Miriam Babin
Benjamin Levy .... Mark Phillips
Ruth Levy................. Rebecca Fink
  Chorus: Sandy Efseaff, Barbara Lymberis, Nick Lymberis, Michael L. Pease.

Time and Place: Various locations in the lives of Daniel and Benjamin, in California, Illinois and New York, from 1964–1981. One intermission.

Project Discovery

INTEGRITY. By Eileen Siedman. Director, Amy Gonzalez.

SAME OLD THING. By Richard Freedman. Director, Leslie Martinson.

YOU WANT THE BOSS? from MIRACLE ATTRACTIONS. Book and lyrics by Nancy Gilsenan, music by William Liberatore. Musical direction, William Liberatore.

NORA'S DAUGHTER. By Carol Lashof. Director, Kathleen Woods.

CELEBRATION/THE ROAD LEADS ON from RETURN TO EDEN: A MUSICAL ADVENTURE. Book, music and lyrics by Rich McCracken. Musical direction, William Liberatore.

SISTERSOUL II. By Ashleigh Evans. Director, Kathleen Woods.

REMEMBER from CAGLIOSTRO! By Larry Blackshere. Musical direction, William Liberatore.

REVOLUTIONARY FLORES. By Michelle Turner Cordero. Director, Amy Gonzalez.

FATHERS AT A GAME. By Trey Nichols.

PITTSBURGH PUBLIC THEATER—Shirl Bernheim
and Nan Martin in a scene from *The Old Lady's Guide to
Survival* by Mayo Simon

LETTERS FROM DIMITRI. By Jeannie Barroga. Director, David Kurtz.
UP IN ANNIE'S ROOM. By Laura Beth Slobin. Director, Jeff Bengford.

WILBUR & ME. Book and lyrics by Robert Brittan, music by Mark Barkan. Director, Christine McHugh.

Philadelphia: Walnut Street Theater

(Executive director, Bernard Havard; literary manager, Alexa Kelly)

CRIES IN THE NIGHT. By Michael Elkin. March 2, 1993. Director, Alexa Kelly; scenery and lighting, Mark R. Bloom; costumes, Jennifer Deal; sound, Ken Moreland.
Billy.................... Paul Bernardo

Ellen .... Rita Ben-Or
Eric .... Daryll Heysham
Louie..................... Hank deLuca
  Time: The present. Place: The Palermo home in Cleveland, Ohio. One intermission.

Pittsburgh: Pittsburgh Public Theater

(Managing director, Dan Fallon)

THE OLD LADY'S GUIDE TO SURVIVAL. By Mayo Simon. February 18, 1993. Director, Alan Mandell; scenery, Ray Recht; lighting, Dennis Parichy; costumes, Marianna Elliott; sound, Jim Capenos.

Netty...................... Nan Martin
Shprintzy .... Shirl Bernheim
  Place: San Diego. One intermission.

Portland, Me.: Portland Stage Company

(Artistic director, Greg Leaming; managing director, William Chance)

BORDERS OF LOYALTY. By Michael Henry Brown. March 30, 1993. Director, Marion Isaac

McClinton; scenery, Jim Noone; lighting, Kenneth Posner; costumes, Elsa Ward.

Alex.................... Rafael Clements
Mercedes............... Charlotte Gibson
Lilith..................... Gwen McGee
Becky Berenson .... Sharon Cornell
Lenny Greenhut............. Matt Lamaj
    Act I: A restaurant somewhere on Ninth Avenue in Manhattan. Act II: Becky Berenson's office. Act III: The restaurant.

4th Annual A Little Festival of the Unexpected: Staged Readings
CORNER STORE GEOGRAPHY. Written and performed by Han Ong. April 13, 1993.

SABINA. By Willy Holtzman. April 14, 1993. Director, Greg Leaming.
BLOWN SIDEWAYS THROUGH LIFE. Written and performed by Claudia Shear. April 15, 1993. Director, Christopher Ashley.
PARTIAL OBJECTS. By Sherry Kramer. April 15, 1993. Director, Victor D'Altorio.
SCOPOPHILIA. By Nicky Silver. April 16, 1993. Director, Tom Prewitt.
WHAT A CAT. By Sam Carner. April 17, 1993. Director, Lisa DiFranza.

Princeton, N.J.: McCarter Theater Center

(Artistic director, Emily Mann; managing director, Jeffrey Woodward)

MISS JULIE. By August Strindberg; adapted and directed by Emily Mann. February 9, 1993. Scenery, Tom Lynch; lighting, Pat Collins; costumes, Jennifer Von Mayrhauser.
Miss Julie .... Kim Cattrall
Jean.................. Peter Francis James
Kristin.................. Donna Murphy
    Midsummer Revelers: Scott New, Pam Ward, Kurt Coble.

Staged Readings:
THE PERFECTIONIST. By Joyce Carol Oates. Director, Loretta Greco.

GRACE IN AMERICA. By Antoine O'Flatharta. Director, Steve Stettler.
GOLDBERG VARIATIONS. By George Tabori. Director, Janice Paran.
THE SCENARIO. By Jean Anouilh. Director, Larry Sacharow.
PROOF TO THE NIGHT. By Ruth Franklin. Director, Seret Scott.
THE FINE THINGS IN LIFE. By Lydia Stryk. Director, Liz Diamond.

Providence, R.I.: Trinity Repertory Company

(Artistic director, Richard Jenkins)

NORTHEAST LOCAL. By Tom Donaghy. January 5, 1993. Director, David Petrarca; scenery, Linda Buchanan; costumes, William Lane; lighting, James F. Ingalls; music composition and sound, Rob Milburn.
Gi .... Rengin Altay
Mickey .... Ed Shea
Mair .... Jane MacIver
Jesse .... Allen Oliver
    One intermission.

THE HOPE ZONE. By Kevin Heelan. February 2, 1993. Director, Richard Jenkins; scenery and lighting, Eugene Lee; costumes, William Lane.
Countess Wilhelmina
    Leach .... Olympia Dukakis
Fern...................... Janice Duclos
Maureen .... Anne Scurria
Newton.................. Timothy Crowe
Veeche Pyle............. Robert J. Colonna
    One intermission.

Rochester, N.Y.: GeVa Theater

(Producing artistic director, Howard J. Millman; associate artistic director, Anthony Zerbe)

Reflections 92: A New Plays Festival—June 2–July 5, 1992
PEEPHOLE. By Shem Bitterman. Director, Steve Zuckerman; scenery, James Fenhagen;

lighting, Kirk Bookman; costumes, Susan E. Mickey; sound, James Wildman.
Rick........................ Josh Brolin
Doctor................ Christopher Curry

Alicia..................... Greta Lambert
Man; Patient #2; New
   Appointee .... Marcus Olson
Sheena.................... Judy Prescott
Patient #1; John #2 ...... Michael F. Park
Detective................. Tony Campisi
John #1; Deacon;
   Patient #3................ Nick Corley
   Place: Various rooms, offices, parks, cars and
by the beach in a large city.

ELLEN UNIVERSE JOINS THE BAND. By
David Rush. Director, Anthony Zerbe; scenery,
James Fenhagen; lighting, Kirk Bookman; costumes, Susan E. Mickey; sound, James Wildman.
Ellen Universe .... Bari Hochwald
Young Ellen............... Rebecca Lamb
Alan .... S. T. Lamb
Mrs. Unsworth.............. Alison Bevan
Mr. Unsworth .... Christopher Curry
Pacco..................... Josh Brolin
Peter Monarch.......... Peter Birkenhead
   The Band: Nick Corley, Marcus Olson, Michael F. Park.
   Time: About 20 years ago to the present.
Place: All over, but mostly in Chicago. One intermission.

BARBEQUE IN 29 PALMS. By Wendy MacLeod. Director, Martin L. Platt; scenery, James
Fenhagen; lighting, Kirk Bookman; costumes,
Susan E. Mickey; sound, James Wildman.
Sookie Lafever.............. Judy Prescott
Sgt. Sam Lafever .... Tony Campisi
Wanda .... Greta Lambert
Lt. Delgado .... Peter Birkenhead
   Time: Labor Day, 1989. Place: 29 Palms,
Calif., a Marine base in the middle of the
Mojave Desert. One intermission.

*Reflections 93: A New Plays Festival—May 25–
June 27, 1993*

CRIMINAL HEARTS. By Jane Martin. Director, Anthony Zerbe; scenery, Bob Thayer; lighting, Mary Louise Geiger; costumes, Susan E.
Mickey; sound, Kevin Dunayer.
Bo .... Michelle Richards
Ata .... Claire Wren
Robbie .... Kevin Donovan
Wib.................... Dennis Cockrum
   Time: The present. Place: The bedroom of an
expensive condo in Chicago. One intermission.

A PENNY FOR THE GUY. By Lanie Robertson. Director, Martin L. Platt; scenery, Bob
Thayer; lighting, Mary Louise Geiger; costumes, Susan E. Mickey; sound, Kevin
Dunayer.
Peg .... Greta Lambert
Timmy.................. Craig Shilowich
C.L............................Joel Polis
   Time: The present. Place: The kitchen of a
dingy flat in the Islington section of London.

WHAT IS ART? By William S. Leavengood.
Director, Sue Lawless; scenery, Bob Thayer;
lighting, Mary Louise Geiger; costumes, Susan
E. Mickey; sound, Kevin Dunayer.
Art..................... Peter Birkenhead
Veronique................ Greta Lambert
Fred...................... Wally Dunn
Meg....................... Claire Wren
Sid..........................Joel Polis
Biff .... Dennis Cockrum
Dot .... Jane Cronin
Dee Wraith............. Michelle Richards
Akril .... Kevin Donovan
Bhrundi...................... Ray Xifo
   Time: The present. Place: An apartment in
New York City. One intermission.

St. Louis: Repertory Theater of St. Louis

(Artistic director, Steven Woolf; managing director, Mark D. Bernstein)

SHOW AND TELL. By Anthony Clarvoe. October 22, 1992. Director, Susan Gregg; scenery
and lighting, Max De Volder; costumes, J.
Bruce Summers; original music and sound, Stephen Burns Kessler.
Corey .... Susan Ericksen
Seth........................ Jim Abele
Iris; Lucy .... Mickey Hartnett
Ann; Gail .... Kim Sebastian
Sharon; Erinn............ Brenda Denmark
Farsted .... R. Ward Duffy

   Time: The present. Place: A school building.
One intermission.

THE VOYAGE OF THE RED HAT. Adapted
by Constance Congdon. December 4, 1992. Director, Tom Martin; scenery and costumes,
Devon Painter.
   With Robert Brown, Jeff Cummings, Jodi
Jinks, Molly Olson.

RATS!! THE PIED PIPER OF HAMELIN.
Adapted by Lynne Alvarez. March 27, 1993.

REPERTORY THEATER OF ST. LOUIS—Jim Abele and Susan
Ericksen in a scene from Anthony Clarvoe's *Show and Tell*

Director, Jeffery Matthews; scenery, Nicholas
Kryah; costumes, J. Bruce Summers.

With Bob Brown, Jeff Cummings, Jodi Jinks,
Molly Olson.

San Diego: Old Globe Theater

(Artistic director, Jack O'Brien; executive producer, Craig Noel; managing director, Thomas
Hall)

BREAKING UP. By Michael Cristofer. July 8,
1992. Director, Stuart Ross; scenery, Richard
Seger; costumes, Michael Krass; lighting, Ash-
ley York Kennedy; sound, Jeff Ladman.
Steve .... Jeffrey Hayenga
Alice .... Jane Galloway
  No intermission.

LOST HIGHWAY: THE MUSIC AND LEG-
END OF HANK WILLIAMS. By Randal
Myler and Mark Harelik; music by Mark
Harelik and Dan Wheetman. August 28,
1992. Director, Randal Myler; scenery, Rich-
ard L. Hay, Bill Curley; costumes, Andrew V.
Yelusich; lighting, Peter Maradudin; sound,
Tony Tait.
Hank Williams .... Mark Harelik,
                  Michael Bryan French

Tee-Tot .... Ron Taylor
Willy .... Kevin Moore
Waitress .... Stephanie Dunnam
Hoss .... Mick Regan
Jimmy "Burrhead" .... William Mesnik
Leon "Loudmouth"........ Dan Wheetman
Mama Lilly................. Kathy Brady
Pap .... Richard McKenzie
Audrey .... Sharon Schlarth
  One intermission.

OUT OF PURGATORY. By Carol Galligan.
May 8, 1993. Director, Benny Sato Ambush;
scenery, Ralph Funicello, Jane La Motte; light-
ing, Ashley York Kennedy; costumes, Andrew
V. Yelusich; sound, Jeff Ladman.
Crista MacElroy.......... Felicity Huffman
Ari Ben David .... Bruce Nozick

Rabbi Mordechai Leventhal . . . Philip Sterling
Maria Ciccone MacElroy . . . Deborah Taylor
Time and Place: The early 1980s on Manhattan's Upper West Side. One intermission.

Staged Readings:

FELICIDAD, INC. By Toby Campion. June 15, 1992. Director, Jose Guadalupe Saucedo.

OUT OF PURGATORY. By Carol Galligan. February 1, 1993. Director, Benny Sato Ambush.

COMMON HEARTS. By Bernardo Solano. March 29, 1993. Director, Raul Moncada.

BURNING HOPE. By Douglas Michilinda. April 19, 1993. Director, Andrew Traister.

San Francisco, Calif.: American Conservatory Theater

(Artistic director, Carey Perloff; managing director, John Sullivan)

THE POPE AND THE WITCH. By Dario Fo, translated by Joan Holden. October 22, 1992. Director, Richard Seyd; scenery and lighting, Kent Dorsey; costumes, Christine Dougherty; sound, Stephen LeGrand.

Friar; Caresi . . . . Joe Bellan
Nun; Addict;
 Brazilian Nun . . . . Gloria Weinstock
Cardinal Pialli; Goon . . . . Ray Reinhardt
Sister Gabriella; Carla . . . . Maureen McVerry
Father Faggio; Goon . . . . Howard Swain
Doctor Ridolfi . . . . Dan Hiatt
Elisa . . . . Sharon Lockwood
Captain of the Swiss Guard;
 Addict; 2d Cardinal . . . . John Reynolds
Pope . . . . Geoff Hoyle
Swiss Guard; Addict . . . . . Andrew DeAngelo

Black Frairs; Cardinals . . . . . . John Martone,
                                                    Craig Mason
One intermission.

ANTIGONE. By Sophocles; translated and adapted by Timberlake Wertenbaker. February 24, 1993. Director, Carey Perloff; scenery, Kate Edmunds; costumes, Donna Zakowska; lighting, Peter Maradudin; sound, Stephen LeGrand; original music by David Lang, performed by Rova Saxophone Quartet.

Antigone . . . . Elizabeth Pena
Ismene . . . . Vilma Silva
Kreon . . . . Ken Ruta
Guard . . . . Mo-Fracaswell Hyman
Haimon . . . . Wendell Pierce
Teiresias . . . . Steven Anthony Jones
Eurydike . . . . Kay Kostopoulos

San Francisco: Magic Theater

(Artistic director, Larry Eilenberg)

THE BRIEF BUT EXEMPLARY LIFE OF THE LIVING GODDESS (AS TOLD BY HERSELF). By Neena Beber. January 13, 1993. Director, Marcus Stern; scenery, Jeff Hunt; lighting, Alex Nichols; costumes, Allison Connor; sound, J.A. Deane.

Far . . . . John Balma
Prince . . . . Michael Chinyamurindi
Hand . . . . Kathleen Cramer
Living Goddess . . . . Ellen Idelson
Starlet . . . . Lisa Porter
Time and Place: The Living Goddess resides in Katmandu, Nepal, and is considered to be the incarnation of the Hindu virgin goddess Kumari Devi.

UNQUESTIONED INTEGRITY: THE HILL/THOMAS HEARINGS. By Mame Hunt. February 17, 1993. Director, Ellen Sebas-

tian; scenery and lighting, Jeff Rowlings; costumes, Kim Porter; sound, Greg Robinson.

Senator . . . . Leo Downey
Judge Thomas . . . . Artis Fountaine
Professor Hill . . . . Margo Hall
Time and Place: The present, USA.

TROUBLE. By Steve Friedman. March 12, 1993. Director, Barbara Damashek; scenery, Marsha Ginsberg; lighting, Jim Cave; costumes, Mary Ann Flippin; sound, J. Raoul Brody.

With Joe Bellan, Susan Marie Brecht, Juanita Gricelda Estrada, Charles Shaw Robinson, Megan Blue Stermer, Jordon Lee Williams.

Time and Place: The present, USA, Bosnia-Herzegovina and Somalia.

WHY WE HAVE A BODY. By Claire Chafee. April 9, 1993. Director, Jane Wenger; scenery,

MAGIC THEATER, SAN FRANCISCO—Margo Hall as Professor Hill, Artis Fountaine as Judge Thomas and Leo Downey as a Senator in *Unquestioned Integrity: The Hill/Thomas Hearings* by Mame Hunt

Jeff Rowlings; lighting, Jim Cave; costumes, Mary Ann Flippin; sound, Bob Davis.
Mary........................ Alice Barden
Renee .... Jeri Lynn Cohen
Eleanor .... Nellie Cravens
Lili........................ Amy Resnick
  Time and Place: The present, USA, the Yucatan. One intermission.

WATCH YOUR BACK. By Gary Leon Hill. May 7, 1993. Director, David Ford; scenery, Marsha Ginsberg; lighting, Jim Cave; costumes, Mary Ann Flippin; sound, Bob Davis.
Bob Green .... Joe Bellan
Ray; Smackfreak ...... Keith Elgin Douglas

Henry .... Michael Michalske
Chuck .... Charles Shaw Robinson
Red Hen .... Cynthia Robinson-Myers
Linda........................ Regina Saisi
Sally .... Johnna Marie Schmidt
Old Man .... Malcolm A. Smith Jr.
Jack Smith; Cop.......... Dorian Spencer
  Time and Place: The present, New York City. One intermission.

Staged Reading:

GIANTS HAVE US IN THEIR BOOKS. By Jose Rivera. December 7, 1992. Director, Roberto Gutierrez Varea.

San Jose, Calif.: San Jose Repertory Theater

(Artistic director, Timothy Near; managing director, Alexandra Boisvert)

WOODY GUTHRIE'S AMERICAN SONG. Songs and writings by Woody Guthrie; conceived and adapted by Peter Glazer. October 11, 1992. Director, Peter Glazer; scenery, Philipp

Jung; lighting, Derek Duarte; costumes, Susan Snowden; sound, Stephen LeGrand.
Man....................... Roger Bearde
Woman .... Lucinda Hitchcock Cone

Young Woman............ Susan Emerson
2d Young Man............. Brian Gunter
1st Young Man .... Robert Keefe
One intermission.

THE BABY DANCE. By Jane Anderson. January 10, 1993. Director, Timothy Near; scenery and costumes, Jeffrey Struckman; lighting,

Derek Duarte; sound, Paul Preston Overton.
Wanda .... Lorri Holt
Al .... Howard Swain
Rachel..................... Kerrie Keane
Richard..................... Ed Hodson
Ron......................... Joe Vincent
Act I: A trailer park in Louisiana. Act II: A hospital maternity ward. One intermission.

Sarasota: Asolo Center for the Performing Arts

(Artistic director, Margaret Booker)

CENTERBURG TALES. Adapted by Bruce E. Rodgers. November 2, 1992. Director, Margaret Booker; scenery, David Potts; lighting, Don Holder; costumes, Barbra Kravitz; sound, Daniel Schreier.
Jenny; Ginny .... Jodi Baker
Beth; 6th Grade
    Teacher .... Wendy Barrie-Wilson
Frankie; Homer .... Michael P. Connor
Jackie; Naomi Enders .... Leslie Easterbrook
Uncle Louis; Sheriff........... John Gilbert
Ed; Barber .... Douglas Jones
Gladys; Aunt Aggie;
    Librarian .... Zoaunne LeRoy
Arnold; Chauffeur .... Brian McGovern
Grandpa Carson; Grampa
    Hercules................. Joe Ponazecki
Henry; Uncle Ulysses ..... Michael O. Smith
The Mysterious Stranger; Mr. Gabby;
    Professor Atmos P.H.Ear.. Charles Weldon
Time and Place: Suburban America, 1992 and Centerburg, Ohio, 1938.

SWEET & HOT. Music by Harold Arlen; lyrics by Harold Arlen, Truman Capote, Ira Gershwin, Ted Koehler, E.Y. Harburg, Johnny Mercer, Leo Robin, Billy Rose and Jack Yellen. Conceived and directed by Julianne Boyd; cho-

reography, Hope Clarke; musical supervision and arrangement, Danny Holgate; scenery, Ken Foy; lighting, Natasha Katz; costumes, David C. Woolard; musical direction, William Foster McDaniel; sound, Karl Richardson.
With Terry Burrell, Allen Hidalgo, Jacquey Maltby, Monica Pege, Brian Quinn, Lance Roberts.
Time: 1930s–1950s. One intermission.

LEGACIES. By Kermit Frazier. April 5, 1993. Director, Margaret Booker; scenery, G.W. Mercier; lighting, Robert Wierzel; costumes, Judy Dearing.
Diane Thompson .... Kim Brockington
Carlene Wallace.............. Fanni Green
Wanda Gentry; Young
    Carlene................. Leah Maddrie
Franklin Thompson III...... George Merritt
Franklin Thompson Jr........ Clark Morgan
Joseph Gentry .... French Napier
Bobby Thompson; Young
    Franklin................. David Rainey
Carleton Wallace ...... John Canada Terrell
Roland Battles............ Charles Weldon
Time: Fall, 1983. Place: Franklin's study and various other places, both indoors and outside. One intermission.

Seattle: A Contemporary Theater

(Artistic director, Jeff Steitzer; managing director, Susan Trapnell Moritz)

THE RED AND THE BLACK. By Jon Klein; based on the novel by Stendhal. April 29, 1993. Director, Jeff Steitzer; scenery, Neil Patel; costumes, Catherine Meacham Hunt; lighting, Brenda Barry; composer, Adam Stern; sound, Malcolm Lowe.
Count Altamira .... Stephen Yoakam
Baron; Father Chelan; Marquis
    de Croisenois.............. Anthony Lee
Lady; Mme. Derville; Mme. de
    la Mole.............. Geraldine Librandi

Julien Sorel.............. Mathew Vipond
M. de Renal; Marquis de
    la Mole............... Craig D. Huisenga
Old Sorel; Father Pirard ...... Glenn Mazen
Foqué .... Darryl Scott
Valenod................... Frank Corrado
Mme. Louise de Renal .... Kate Fuglei
Elisa; Mme. de Fervaques..... Karen Meyer
Mlle. Matilde de la Mole ... Chelsea Altman
Manservant; Porter; Others...... Bill Johns
Two intermissions.

Seattle: Group Theater

(Founding artistic director, Rubin Sierra; artistic director, Tim Bond)

DEAR MISS ELENA. By Ludmilla Razumovskaya; translated by Zoltan Smith and Roger Downey. September 16, 1992. Director, Tim Bond; dramaturge, Nancy Griffiths; scenery, Yuri P. Degtjar; costumes, Kathleen Maki; lighting, Darren McCroom; sound, Steven M. Klein.

Elena Sergeyevna	Kathryn Mesney
Volodya	Andrew De Rycke
Vitya	Alan Goldwasser
Pasha	Jose J. Gonzales
Lalya	Sol Miranda

No intermission.

Seattle: Intiman Theater Company

(Artistic director, Warner Shook; managing director, Peter Davis)

CATHERINE: CONCERNING THE FATEFUL ORIGINS OF HER GRANDEUR, WITH DIVERSE MUSICAL INTERLUDES, THREE ELEPHANTS AND NO BALLET. By Louisa Rose. June 24, 1992. Director, Elizabeth Huddle; scenery, Craig Labenz; lighting, Meg Fox; costumes, Todd Roehrman; composer and sound, Jim Ragland.

Catherine the Great	Tamu Gray
Grand Duke Paul	Timothy Jones
Denis Fonvizin	Kurt Beattie

Members of the Court:

Maria Feodorovna, playing the Young
  Catherine............... Amelia Fowler
Courtier, playing Peter III ... Mark Anders
Courtier, playing Empress
  Elizabeth................. Lois Foraker
Lanskoi, playing Catherine's
  Lovers.................. Kerry Skalsky
Courtier, playing Catherine's Mother,
  Others .... Sally Smythe
Courtier, playing the Pastor,
  Others .... Clayton Corzatte
Courtier, playing Catherine's Father,
  Others .... David Mong

Courtier, playing Babette,
  Others................... Novel Sholars
Performing Serfs in Catherine's Court:
  Angel, Others .... Peggy O'Connell
  Lead Dancer .... Igor Paramonov
  Time: Latter half of the 18th century. One
intermission.

WARRIOR. By Shirley Gee. October 7, 1992. Director, Susan Fenichell; scenery, David Zinn; costumes, Todd Roehrman; lighting, Michael Wellborn; sound, David Pascal; composer and musical direction, James Palmer; fight choreographer, Jeffrey Alm.

Hannah	Shelley Reynolds
Susan; Mrs. Sculley	Stephanie Kallos
Sculley; Ditch	John Rafter Lee
Dr. Kemp; Flagg	Joseph R. Cronin
Cumberland; Drubber	Christopher Welch
Evan Godbolt	David Mong
Cuttle	Eric Ray Anderson

Others: Carl L. Carter, Niceto Festin, Sarah Harlett, Rachel Joseph, Tom Kiehfuss, Alyce LaTourelle.
One intermission.

Silver Spring, Md.: Round House Theater

(Artistic director, Jerry Whiddon; producing associate, Tony Elliot)

THE ART OF WAITING. By Rob Shinn. March 17, 1993. Director, Tom Prewitt; scenery, Elizabeth Jenkins; lighting, Daniel Schrader and Joseph B. Musumeci Jr.; costumes, Rosemary Pardee; sound, Neil McFadden.

Mr. Showbiz	Michael Willis

Scotty Whitehead; Steve Garvey;
  Wade .... Jason Kravits

Rob	Ralph Peña

Woman at Table 4; Prosecutor;
  Therapist .... Sadiqa P. Dailey

Girls at Table 3	Toyin Fadopé, Shayla Godsey
Mommy	Betty Manuar
Don; Father	Ben Lin
Denise	Desiree Marie
Old White Guy	Michael Willis

White Children...... Joey Sorge, Kim Tuvin
Mrs. D; Miss Harrison .... Marilyn Hausfeld
Radio Raheem; Judge........... D'Monroe
Missy...................... Kim Tuvin
Danita.................... Toyin Fadopé
  Ensemble: Marilyn Hausfeld, Jason Kravits,
D'Monroe, Joey Sorge, Kim Tuvin.
  Time: Now. Place: Onstage and backstage at
Bob's Comedy Luau Hut; a Chinese restaurant
in a large American city; various other locales in
Rob's mind and/or memory.

New Voices Playreading

HEARTBEATS. By Alan Sharpe. April 5,
1993. Director, Lynnie Raybuck.
THE FLIGHT OF MRS. NEUWALD. By Er-
nest Joselovitz. April 12, 1993. Director, Nick
Olcott.
SUNDAY DINNER and BACH PLAYS THE
BLUES. By Caleen Sinette Jennings. April 19,
1993. Directors, Mary Beth Levrio and Lisa
Middleton.
MEMORIAL DAY. By Paul J. Donnelly Jr.
April 26, 1993. Director, Sue Ott Rowlands.

Skokie, Ill.: National Jewish Theater

(Artistic directors, Jeff Ginsberg and Susan Padveen; producing director, Fran Brumlik)

THE SONGS OF WAR. By Murray Schisgal.
Director, Susan Padveen; musical director, Ste-
phen Dewey; choreographer, Claire Bataille;
scenery, Richard and Jacqueline Penrod; light-
ing, Mary M. Badger; costumes, Jessica Hahn;
sound, Dabney Forest.
Calvin Saks.................. Guy Barile
Saul Sakowitz.............. Paul Amandes
Bertha Sakowitz........ Lisa Marie Schultz
Lilly Sakowitz .... Julie Greenberg
Zada .... Wantland L. Sandel Jr.
Roy Atkins................. David Nisbet
  Time: 1987. Place: A New York theater. One
intermission.

THE WIZARDS OF QUIZ. By Steve Feffer.
Director, Jeff Ginsberg; scenery, Richard and
Jacqueline Penrod; lighting, Chris Phillips; cos-
tumes, Jessica Hahn; sound, Robert Neuhaus.
Herbert Stempel.......... Edward Jemison
Charles Van Doren ...... Christopher Howe
Jack Barry .... Dev Kennedy
Daniel Enright .... Richard Wharton
Oren Harris .... David Mink
Toby Stempel................ Debra Rich
Gordon Jacobs.............. Warren Davis
  Time and Place: Various locations around
New York City, and a Congressional hearing
room in Washington, D.C. between winter,
1956 and winter, 1959. One intermission.

Tampa: Tampa Players

(Artistic and managing director, Bill Lelbach)

BEAST. By Susan Arnout Smith. January 29,
1993. Director, Bill Lelbach; scenery, Kim
Edgar Swados and Bill Lelbach; lighting, G.B.
Stephens; costumes, Loren D. Bracewell; sound,
Marc Rose.
Joe Bulling .... Steve DuMouchel
Irene Bulling........... Elizabeth Fendrick
Tommy Bulling .... Michael Schroeder

Clint Bulling......... James P. Wisniewski
Therapist............ Nancy Madeline Cole
  Beasts: Jim Joyce, Greg Pitts, Pamela Stuart,
Marybeth Young.
  Time: The present. Place: A multi-level land-
scape, the place where bad dreams grow into
nightmares.

Teaneck, N.J.: American Stage Company

(Executive producer, James M. Vaglas)

THE COVER OF LIFE. By R.T. Robinson.
November 25, 1992. Director, Richard Corley;
scenery, Christine Jones; costumes, Lindsay W.
Davis; sound, Nancy R. Mannoa; choreogra-

phy, Christopher Wells; music, Randy Courts.
Sybil .... Courtenay Collins
Addie Mae .... Cynthia Darlow
Weetsie .... Melinda Eades

NATIONAL JEWISH THEATER, SKOKIE, ILL.—Guy Barile *(center)* with ensemble members David Nisbet, Lisa Marie Schultz, Julie Greenberg and Paul Amandes in *The Songs of War* by Murray Schisgal

Tood	Alice Haining
Kate	Leslie Hendrix
Aunt Ola	Tanny McDonald
Tommy	David Schiliro

One intermission.

NIGHT SEASONS. By Horton Foote. February 26, 1993. Director, Horton Foote; scenery, Daniel Ettinger; costumes, Barbara Bell; lighting, Stuart Duke; theme and musical direction, Donald Pippin.

With George Bamford, Jo Ann Cunningham, Hallie Foote, Frank Girardeau, Michael Hadge, Howard Hensel, James Prichett, Barbara Sims.

One intermission.

Tucson: Arizona Theater Company

(Artistic director, David Ira Goldstein; managing director, Robert Aplaugh)

ONE CRAZY DAY, OR THE MARRIAGE OF FIGARO. Translated and adapted by Roger Downey. October 9, 1992. Director, David Ira Goldstein; original music and musical direction, Nicolas Reveles; scenery, Greg Lucas; lighting, Don Darnutzer; costumes, David Kay

Mickelsen; choreographer, Gema Sandoval; sound, Steven M. Klein.

Marquèz de Almaviva . . . . David Asher
Rosina . . . . Suzanne Bouchard
Figaro . . . . Al Rodrigo
Susanna . . . . Leticia Vasquez
Bartholomew T. Bankhead . . . Kurt Knudson
Marcelina . . . . Alma Martinez
Querubin . . . . Samantha Follows
Antonio . . . . Roberto Guajardo
Frasquita . . . . Kristine Goto
Pedrillo . . . . Roberto Garcia
Padre . . . . Bill Anderson
Campesina . . . . Norma Medina
Cook . . . . Gaye Lynn Scott
    Musicians: John Aldecoa, Ruben M. Moreno, Larry J. Suarez.
    Time and Place: Hacienda Aguas Frescas, in the old Southwest. One intermission.

FERTILITY RIGHTS. By Michael Michaelian. February 19, 1993. Director, David Ira Goldstein; scenery, Jeff Thomson; lighting, Tracy Odishaw; costumes, Rose Pederson; sound, Eric B. Webster.

Beth . . . . Lauren Tewes
Ernie . . . . Mark Bramhall
Leo . . . . Brain Brophy
Phil . . . . Robert Nadir
    Time: The present. Place: Beth's house in the Hollywood Hills. One intermission.

Genesis: New Play Reading Series, March 4–7, 1993

THE USUAL SUSPECTS. By Steven Dietz. Director, Matthew Wiener.
THE ROOSTER AND THE EGG. By Luis Santeiro. Director, David Vining.
PAST HISTORY. By Michael Grady. Director, Jeff Steitzer.

Washington, D.C.: Arena Stage

(Artistic director, Douglas C. Wager; executive director, Stephen Richard)

THE AFRICAN COMPANY PRESENTS *RICHARD III*. By Carlyle Brown. December 9, 1992. Director, Tazewell Thompson; scenery, Douglas Stein; lighting, Allen Lee Hughes; costumes, Paul Tazewell; sound, Susan R. White.

Stephen Price . . . . Jed Diamond
Sarah . . . . LaDonna Mabry
Ann Johnson . . . . Gail Grate
James Hewlett . . . . Leon Addison Brown
Papa Shakespeare . . . . Wendell Wright
William Henry Brown . . . Jonathan Earl Peck
Constable-Man . . . . David Marks
Members of the
    Constabulary . . . . Ed Eaton, Paul Niebanck
    One intermission.

New Voices for a New America

ANTIGONE IN NEW YORK. By Janusz Glowacki. March 5, 1993. Director, Laurence Maslon; scenery, Katherine Jennings; lighting,

Christopher V. Lewton; costumes, Marjorie Slaiman; sound, Robin Heath.

Policeman . . . . Jeffery V. Thompson
Sasha . . . . Ralph Cosham
Anita . . . . Sheila M. Tousey
Flea . . . . Richard Bauer
Paulie . . . . Tom Simpson
    Time: 6 p.m. to 6 a.m., December, 1989. Place: Tompkins Square Park, New York City. One intermission.

PlayQuest Workshop

THE AMERICA PLAY. By Suzan-Lori Parks. February 24, 1993. Director, Peter Wallace.
EAST TEXAS HOT LINKS. By Eugene Lee. March 31, 1993. Director, Clinton Turner Davis.
A SMALL WORLD. By Mustapha Matura. April 7, 1993. Director, Kyle Donnelly.

Washington, D.C.: Ford's Theater

(Producing director, Frankie Hewitt; managing director, Michael Gennaro)

CAPTAINS COURAGEOUS, THE MUSICAL. Book and lyrics by Patrick Cook; music by Frederick Freyer. September 21, 1992. Director and choreographer, Graciela Daniele; musical director, James Kowal; scenery, Christopher Barreca; lighting, Jules Fisher, Peggy Eisen-

hauer; costumes, Ann Hould-Ward; sound, Peter Fitzgerald.

Manuel . . . . John Dossett
Nate . . . . Mark Aldrich
Tom . . . . Larry Alexander
Captain . . . . Don Chastain

Simon	Frank DiPasquale	Evans	Ric Ryder
Murphy.	Michael Greenwood	Harris	Michael Shelle
Long Jack.	Walter Hudson	Ollie.	Richard Thomsen
Walters	George Kmeck	Peters	John Leslie Wolfe
Stevens	Joseph Kolinski		
Doc	Michael Mandell		
Hemans.	John Mineo		
Harvey	Kel O'Neill		

Time: Summer, 1928. Place: Various spots on the North Atlantic and in the port of Gloucester, Mass. One intermission.

Washington, D.C.: Woolly Mammoth Theater Company

(Artistic director, Howard Shalwitz; producing associate, Nancy Turner Hensley)

BILLY NOBODY. By Stanley Rutherford. October 19, 1992. Director, Howard Shalwitz; scenery, Lou Stancari; lighting, Kim Peter Kovac; costumes, Howard Vincent Kurtz; sound, Dan Schrader.

Billy.	Jason Kravits
Aurora	Paula Gruskiewicz
Lenny	Norman Aronovic
Marty	Carlos J. Gonzalez
Emily.	Bernadette Flagler
Mrs. Sagerson	Nancy Robinette
Ernie	Voice of Howard Shalwitz

One intermission.

FREE WILL AND WANTON LUST. Written and directed by Nicky Silver. January 11, 1993. Scenery, James Kronzer; lighting, David Zemmels; costumes, Rosemary Ingham; sound, Hugh Caldwell.

Claire	Kerry Waters
Tony	Christopher Lane
Amy	Audrey Wasilewski
Phillip	Jason Kravits
Vivian	Naomi Jacobson

One intermission.

THE COCKBURN RITUALS. By John Strand. April 5, 1993. Director, Jennifer Mendenhall; scenery, James Kronzer; lighting, Chris Townsend; costumes, Susan Anderson.

Female Technician One; Debbie; Student;
Social Investigator.	Holly Twyford

Female Technician Two; Dr. Dupont-Seche; Tammie; 1st
Workman.	Deborah Gottesman
Dr. Cockburn.	Buzz Mauro
Public Address; Biffie.	Delia Taylor
Nurse One	Josette Murray

Male Technician One;
Billie; Pragmatist.	Matt Howe

Male Technician Two;
Lennie; Security Guard.	Christine Lane
Dr. Yaewah	Churchill Clark
2d Workman	Dexter Hamlett
Patient.	Daniel R. Escobar

Reporters: Dexter Hamlett, Josette Murray, Matt Howe, Holly Twyford, Deborah Gottesman.

Time: January, 1985. Place: A large urban hospital. One intermission.

Waterbury, Conn.: Seven Angels Theater

(Artistic director, Semina De Laurentiis)

NUNSENSE II: THE SECOND COMING. Book, music and lyrics by Dan Goggin. November 20, 1992. Director, Dan Goggin; staging and choreography, Felton Smith; musical direction, Michael Rice; scenery, Barry Axtell; lighting, Paul Miller; sound, Snow Sound; orchestrations, Michael Rice, David Nyberg.

Sister Robert Anne	Christine Anderson
Sister Mary Amnesia . .	Semina De Laurentiis
Sister Mary Hubert	Mary Gillis
Sister Mary Regina	Kathy Robinson
Sister Mary Leo	Lyn Vaux

Musical Numbers: "Jubilate Deo," "Nunsense, the Magic Word," "Winning Is Just the Beginning," "The Prima Ballerina," "The Biggest Ain't the Best," "I've Got Pizazz," "The Country Nun," "Look Ma, I Made It," "The Padre Polka," "The Classic Queens," "A Hat and Cane Song," "Angeline," "We're the Nuns to Come To," "What Would Elvis Do?", "Yes We Can," "I Am Here to Stay," "Oh Dear, What a Catastrophe," "No One Ever Cared the Way You Do," "There's Only One Way to End Your Prayers."

One intermission.

ARIZONA THEATER COMPANY, TUCSON—Suzanne Bouchard, Leticia Vasquez and David Asher in Roger Downey's *One Crazy Day, or The Marriage of Figaro*, translated and adapted from Beaumarchais

Waterford, Conn.: Eugene O'Neill Theater Center

(Artistic director, Lloyd Richards; president, George C. White)

National Playwrights Conference, June 28–July 25, 1992

THE SPINNING TOP. By Ilya Chlakishvili. Director, Alexander Velikovsky; scenery, G.W. Mercier; lighting, Tina Charney.

Pavel	Kevin Geer
Sveta	Susan Knight
Nina	Julie Boyd

Lena .... Mia Dillon
Time: 1980s. Place: Moscow.

I HAVE OFTEN DREAMED OF ARRIVING ALONE IN A STRANGE COUNTRY. By Patricia Cobey. Director, Amy Saltz; scenery, G.W. Mercier; lighting, Tina Charney.

Kate Hennessey .... Cynthia Nixon

Maura Hennessey;
  Girl . . . . Nancy-Elizabeth Kammer
Biddy; Student . . . . Peggy Pope
Greta Sorensen; Mrs. Wallace;
  Interviewer; Mme.
  Alexandria . . . . Caroline Aaron
Girl; Student; Benjamin . . . . . Kellie Overbey
Fergus Hennessey . . . . Josh Hamilton
James Hennessey; Blind Man;
  Student . . . . Jude Ciccolella
Michael; Doctor; Student . . . . . . Joseph Urla
Martin Hennessey;
  David . . . . Justin McCarthy
Time: 1980. Place: Ireland.

HERO AT LAST. By Frederick Dillen. Director, Jay Broad; scenery, G.W. Mercier; lighting, Tina Charney.
Bruce; Chinese; Third Cook . . . . . Matt Aibel
Hero . . . . John Braden
Fedy . . . . Christopher Fields
Frenchman; Aids; Hussein; Broiler Man;
  Fat Man . . . . Clebert Ford
Molly . . . . Laurie Kennedy
Fat Tom; Bar Man; Chick . . . . Delroy Lindo
Robert; Bogart . . . . Kevin D. Mayes
Castro . . . . Victor Raider-Wexler
Andy; Third Baseman . . . . . . Michael Rogers
Woman; Beauty . . . . Lynne Thigpen
A teleplay; one intermission.

CHARLIE'S WEDDING DAY. By Patricia Goldstone. Director, William Partlan; scenery, G.W. Mercier; lighting, Tina Charney.
Ernie . . . . Paul McCrane
Helen . . . . Susan Knight
Announcer; Sir John Benjamin; Police
  Sergeant; Dean . . . . Bryan Clark
Barbara Cartland . . . . B. Buell
Nell . . . . Julie Boyd
Davey . . . . Kevin Geer
Brock . . . . William Wise
Cowboy . . . . Michael Potts
Regina . . . . Amy Wright
Frank . . . . Reed Birney
Time: The eve and morning of the wedding of Prince Charles of Wales and The Lady Diana Spencer, 29 July 1981. Place: South London tenement. One intermission.

SCOTLAND ROAD. By Jeffrey Hatcher. Director, William Partlan; scenery, G.W. Mercier; lighting, Tina Charney.
Halbrech . . . . Amy Wright
John . . . . Reed Birney
Woman . . . . Alice Haining
Frances Kittle . . . . Helen Stenborg
Time and Place: The present, a white room. One intermission.

EULOGY. By Ted Hoover. Director, Margaret Booker; scenery, G.W. Mercier; lighting, Tina Charney.
Samantha Courtney . . . . Julie Boyd
Lucy Albitz . . . . Susan Knight
Charlotte McKenney . . . . Mia Dillon
George Dobson . . . . Paul McCrane
Time and Place: New York City in the late 1980s, with two scenes taking place in a small town in Georgia. One intermission.

EMPATHY, INC. By Jerry Isaacs. Director, Oz Scott; scenery, G.W. Mercier; lighting, Tina Charney.
Guy . . . . Christopher Curry
Violet Root . . . . Peggy Pope
Joseph Root . . . . John Seitz
Owen . . . . Joseph Urla
Douglas Root . . . . Rob Neill
Time: The late 1970s in late spring. Place: Somewhere in the Midwest.

A THIMBLE OF SMOKE. By Elroyce Jones. Director, Jay Broad; scenery, G.W. Mercier; lighting, Tina Charney.
Mr. Monroe . . . . Clebert Ford
Soo Baby . . . . Lisa Gay Hamilton
Storyteller; Cakeman . . . . Delroy Lindo
Rosena Sykes . . . . Linda Maurel
Snake Doctor . . . . Michael Rogers
Baby Ta Ta . . . . Michele Shay
Miss Thelma Pearl Sykes . . . . Lynne Thigpen
Place: A Saturday in Central Mississippi. A teleplay.

STRAIGHT MAN. By Ian Kerner. Director, Jay Broad; scenery, G.W. Mercier; lighting, Tina Charney.
William Sand . . . . Michael Countryman
Jackson Sand . . . . Jay Goede
Elanor Sand . . . . Helen Stenborg
Emily . . . . Mia Dillon
One intermission.

TOUGH CALL. By Ronald Kidd. Director, William Partlan; scenery, G.W. Mercier; lighting, Tina Charney.
Leo Schult . . . . Bill Buell
Benny Lomax;
  Announcer #2 . . . . Paul McCrane
Harvey "Mook" Yablonsky . . . William Wise
Zeb McGraw . . . . Kevin Geer
Frank Barker . . . . Michael Countryman
Art Frandsen . . . . Jay Goede
Tommy Demopolis . . . . Reed Birney
Richard Rogan;
  Announcer #1 . . . . Bryan Clark
Time: Next Season. Place: Umpires' locker room of a National League ball park, over the course of a four-game series.

ARTHUR AND LEILA. By Cherylene Lee. Director, Margaret Booker; scenery, G.W. Mercier; lighting, Tina Charney.
Arthur Chin . . . . Ric Young
Leila Chin-Abernathy . . . . . . Freda Foh Shen
Time: The present. Place: Various places in Los Angeles. One intermission.

VOODOO NICKEL. By Patti Patton. Director, Oz Scott; scenery, G.W. Mercier; lighting, Tina Charney.
Audrey . . . . Lisa Gay Hamilton
Little Boy . . . . Ryan Kistner
Burly Guard . . . . John Seitz
Bud Ring . . . . Christopher Curry
Dr. Fletcher . . . . James McDaniel
One intermission.

BLACKWATER. By J. Dakota Powell. Director, Amy Saltz; scenery, G.W. Mercier; lighting, Tina Charney.
Pearl Landow . . . . Kellie Overbey
Garland Landow; Tom . . . . . . Jude Ciccolella
Jeannie Landow . . . . Leslie Lyles
Arap Ruta . . . . Count Stovall
Leslie Pike; Ebert . . . . Michael Genet
Danny Barnes; Bergner . . . . . . Josh Hamilton
Elephant . . . . Adrian Bethea
Africans: Curtis James, Ntare Mwine, Arthur Solmon.
Time: Now. Place: The landscape of a young girl's mind. One intermission.

DIFFERENT. By Susan Arnout Smith. Director, Jay Broad; scenery, G.W. Mercier; lighting, Tina Charney.
Eddie; Man; Bus Driver . . . . John Braden
Bernie . . . . Christopher Fields
Russell . . . . Clebert Ford
Heather; Jennifer; Nurse; Mary; John's
    Mother; Faye . . . . Lisa Gay Hamilton
Amanda . . . . Laurie Kennedy
Beauty Parlor Boss; Fast Food Boss;
    Coach Seger . . . . Delroy Lindo
Alec . . . . Kevin D. Mayes
Libby . . . . Linda Maurel
Bob; Man; Receptionist; Santa; Shoe
    Clerk; Announcer; Kitchen
    Boss . . . . Victor Raider-Wexler
Salesman; Technician; John;
    Carnie Man; Rick;
    Driver; Bus Boy . . . . Michael Rogers

Annie; Sally; Pregnant Woman; Woman;
    Sales Clerk; Cashier; New
    Runner . . . . Michele Shay
Chica; Joanie; Mrs. Harper; Admissions
    Lady; Hairdresser; Kate;
    Miss Woods . . . . Lynne Thigpen
Hope . . . . Zoey Zimmerman
Place: Events in and around Boulder, Colo.

National Music Theater Conference, August 9–22, 1993

AVENUE X. By John Jiler and Ray Leslee. Director, Mark Brokaw; musical director, Chapman Roberts.
Pasquale . . . . Ted Brunetti
Julia . . . . Nora Cole
Winston . . . . John-Martin Green
Barbara . . . . Colette Hawley
Milton . . . . John Lathan
Chuck . . . . John Leone
Ubazz . . . . Wilbury Pauley
Roscoe . . . . Ellis E. Williams

CHRISTINA ALBERTA'S FATHER. By Polly Pen. Director, Andre Ernotte; musical director, Kristen Blodgette.
Maj. Bone; Paul . . . . Tim Jerome
Teddy; Poet . . . . Eddie Korbich
Mr. Bone . . . . Kevin D. Mayes
Chris; Ms. Means;
    M. Solbe . . . . Lauren Mitchell
Bobby . . . . John Sloman
Christina Alberta . . . . Lannyl Stephens
Albert Edward Preemby . . . . Henry Stram
Miss Rewster; Mrs. Bone . . . . . . Mary Testa
Fay . . . . Tracy Venner

THE WILD SWANS. By Adele Ahronheim and Ben Schaechter. Director, Worth Gardner; musical director, Rob Bowman.
Matthew . . . . Danny DeVito
John . . . . Jeffrey Hutchins
Prime Minister . . . . Tim Jerome
Sir Pal . . . . Eddie Korbich
Selden . . . . Kevin D. Mayes
Lady Parsippina . . . . Lauren Mitchell
Gregory . . . . Andy Reggio
Michael . . . . Sam Brent Riegel
Prince Manley . . . . John Sloman
King Frederick . . . . Henry Stram
Forest Lady . . . . Mary Testa
Elisa . . . . Tracy Venner

Westport, Conn.: Westport Country Playhouse

(Executive producer, James B. McKenzie)

THE FOURTH WALL. By A.R. Gurney; music and lyrics by Cole Porter. August 4, 1992. Director, David Saint; scenery, Richard Ellis; costumes, David Murin; lighting, Susan Roth; music arranged and performed by Jonathan Sheffer.

Roger .... Tony Roberts
Julia........................ Kelly Bishop
Peggy.................. E. Katherine Kerr
Floyd........................ Jack Gilpin
  Musical Numbers: "I'm in Love Again," "Why Shouldn't I?", "Big Town," "After You, Who?", "Let's Be Buddies."
  One intermission.

DON'T DRESS FOR DINNER. By Marc Camoletti; adapted by Robin Hawdon. July 7, 1992. Director, Pamela Hunt; scenery, Richard Ellis; costumes, Howard Tsvi Kaplan; lighting, Susan Roth.

Bernard.................. Max Robinson
Jacqueline........... Alexandra O'Karma
Robert...................... Reno Roop
Suzette.................. Karen Valentine
Suzanne................ Caroline Lagerfelt
George .... Timothy Wheeler
  Two intermissions.

Williamstown, Mass.: Williamstown Theater Festival

(Artistic director, Peter Hunt; managing director, William Stewart)

BLACK. By Joyce Carol Oates. July 21, 1992. Director, Gordon Hunt; scenery, Tom Baker; costumes, Kimberly Schnormeier; lighting, Betsy Finston; sound, Richard Allison, Andrea Hoffman.

Jonathan Boyd.......... Anthony Edwards
Debra O'Donnell......... Felicity Huffman
Lew Claybrook .... Victor Love
  One intermission.

THE WILL AND BART SHOW. By Jim Lehrer. July 7, 1992. Director, Tina Ball; scenery, Jana Bialon; costumes, Kimberly Schnormeier; lighting, Betsy Finston; sound, Richard Allison.

Hobart R. Nielsen.............. Pat Hingle
William Samuel Michel...... Norman Lloyd

Ms. Winston............... Jessica Hendra
Male Voices .... Greg Naughton
Additional Voices............. Bill Kincaid
  One intermission.

HOTEL OUBLIETTE. By Jane Anderson. August 4, 1992. Director, Jenny Sullivan; scenery, Emily J. Beck; costumes, Kimberly Schnormeier; lighting, Betsy Finston; sound, Martin Desjardins.

Meryl .... Steven Keats
Shaw...................... Hal Holbrook
Gloria .... Marcia Hyde
Head Guard .... Phillip Wofford
  Guards: Tom Caruso, Anthony Fiorillo, Andrew Overton, David Stevens, David Walley.
  One intermission.

Worcester, Mass.: Worcester Foothills Theater Company

(Executive producer/artistic director, Marc P. Smith; associate producer, Doug Landrum)

BLOOD SUMMIT. Written and directed by Marc P. Smith. February 25, 1993. Scenery, Bill Savoy; lighting, L. Stacy Eddy; costumes, Andrew J. Poleszak; sound, Michael Versteegt.

Ben Miller.............. Thomas Ouellette
Florrie O'Connor....... Ingrid Sonnichsen
Robert E. Pierce............ Peter Bubriski
Rev. Malcolm Macpherson...... John Davin
Helmut Obermann........ Peter Husovsky

Soldier...................... Bill Savoy
Inge Obermann .... Barbara Reierson
Trudl Obermann .... Susan Zizza
Mutti Obermann .... Miriam Varon
Kyle Davenport.............. Scott Kealey
Charlie Benson................ Bill Savoy
  Time and Place: Various locations in 1958 and 1978. One intermission.

FACTS AND
FIGURES

LONG RUNS ON BROADWAY

The following shows have run 500 or more continuous performances in a single production, usually the first, not including previews or extra non-profit performances, allowing for vacation layoffs and special one-booking engagements, but not including return engagements after a show has gone on tour. In all cases, the numbers were obtained directly from the show's production offices. Where there are title similarities, the production is identified as follows: (p) straight play version, (m) musical version, (r) revival.

THROUGH MAY 31, 1993

(PLAYS MARKED WITH ASTERISK WERE STILL PLAYING JUNE 1, 1993)

Plays	Number Performances	Plays	Number Performances
A Chorus Line	6,137	Barefoot in the Park	1,530
Oh! Calcutta! (r)	5,959	Brighton Beach Memoirs	1,530
*Cats	4,447	Dreamgirls	1,522
42nd Street	3,486	Mame (m)	1,508
Grease	3,388	Same Time, Next Year	1,453
Fiddler on the Roof	3,242	Arsenic and Old Lace	1,444
Life With Father	3,224	The Sound of Music	1,443
Tobacco Road	3,182	Me and My Girl	1,420
Hello, Dolly!	2,844	How to Succeed in Business	
My Fair Lady	2,717	Without Really Trying	1,417
*Les Misérables	2,532	Hellzapoppin	1,404
Annie	2,377	The Music Man	1,375
Man of La Mancha	2,328	Funny Girl	1,348
Abie's Irish Rose	2,327	Mummenschanz	1,326
*The Phantom of the Opera	2,232	Angel Street	1,295
Oklahoma!	2,212	Lightnin'	1,291
Pippin	1,944	Promises, Promises	1,281
South Pacific	1,925	The King and I	1,246
The Magic Show	1,920	Cactus Flower	1,234
Deathtrap	1,793	Sleuth	1,222
Gemini	1,788	Torch Song Trilogy	1,222
Harvey	1,775	1776	1,217
Dancin'	1,774	Equus	1,209
La Cage aux Folles	1,761	Sugar Babies	1,208
Hair	1,750	Guys and Dolls	1,200
The Wiz	1,672	Amadeus	1,181
Born Yesterday	1,642	Cabaret	1,165
The Best Little Whorehouse in		Mister Roberts	1,157
Texas	1,639	Annie Get Your Gun	1,147
Ain't Misbehavin'	1,604	The Seven Year Itch	1,141
Mary, Mary	1,572	Butterflies Are Free	1,128
Evita	1,567	Pins and Needles	1,108
The Voice of the Turtle	1,557	Plaza Suite	1,097

Plays	Number Performances	Plays	Number Performances
They're Playing Our Song	1,082	Three Men on a Horse	835
Grand Hotel (m)	1,077	The Subject Was Roses	832
Kiss Me, Kate	1,070	Black and Blue	824
Don't Bother Me, I Can't Cope	1,065	Inherit the Wind	806
The Pajama Game	1,063	Anything Goes (r)	804
Shenandoah	1,050	No Time for Sergeants	796
The Teahouse of the August		Fiorello!	795
Moon	1,027	Where's Charley?	792
Damn Yankees	1,019	The Ladder	789
Never Too Late	1,007	Forty Carats	780
Big River	1,005	Lost in Yonkers	780
Any Wednesday	982	The Prisoner of Second Avenue	780
A Funny Thing Happened on		M. Butterfly	777
the Way to the Forum	964	Oliver!	774
The Odd Couple	964	The Pirates of Penzance (1980 r)	772
Anna Lucasta	957	Woman of the Year	770
Kiss and Tell	956	My One and Only	767
Dracula (r)	925	Sophisticated Ladies	767
Bells Are Ringing	924	Bubbling Brown Sugar	766
The Moon Is Blue	924	Into the Woods	765
Beatlemania	920	State of the Union	765
The Elephant Man	916	Starlight Express	761
Luv	901	The First Year	760
Chicago (m)	898	Broadway Bound	756
Applause	896	You Know I Can't Hear You	
Can-Can	892	When the Water's Running .	755
Carousel	890	Two for the Seesaw	750
I'm Not Rappaport	890	Joseph and the Amazing	
Hats Off to Ice	889	Technicolor Dreamcoat (r) . .	747
Fanny	888	Death of a Salesman	742
*Miss Saigon	888	For Colored Girls, etc.	742
Children of a Lesser God	887	Sons o' Fun	742
Follow the Girls	882	Candide (m, r)	740
City of Angels	878	Gentlemen Prefer Blondes	740
Camelot	873	The Man Who Came to Dinner	739
I Love My Wife	872	Nine	739
*The Will Rogers Follies	870	Call Me Mister	734
The Bat	867	West Side Story	732
My Sister Eileen	864	High Button Shoes	727
No, No, Nanette (r)	861	Finian's Rainbow	725
Song of Norway	860	Claudia	722
Chapter Two	857	The Gold Diggers	720
A Streetcar Named Desire	855	Jesus Christ Superstar	720
Barnum	854	Carnival	719
Comedy in Music	849	The Diary of Anne Frank	717
Raisin	847	I Remember Mama	714
You Can't Take It With You . .	837	Tea and Sympathy	712
La Plume de Ma Tante	835	Junior Miss	710

Plays	*Number* *Performances*	Plays	*Number* *Performances*
Last of the Red Hot Lovers ...	706	The Happy Time (p)	614
The Secret Garden	706	Separate Rooms	613
Company	705	Affairs of State	610
Seventh Heaven	704	Oh! Calcutta!	610
Gypsy (m)	702	Star and Garter	609
The Miracle Worker	700	The Mystery of Edwin Drood	608
That Championship Season	700	The Student Prince	608
Da	697	Sweet Charity	608
The King and I (r)	696	Bye Bye Birdie	607
Cat on a Hot Tin Roof	694	Irene (r)	604
Li'l Abner	693	Sunday in the Park With	
The Children's Hour	691	George	604
Purlie	688	Adonis	603
Dead End	687	Broadway	603
The Lion and the Mouse	686	Peg o' My Heart	603
White Cargo	686	Street Scene (p)	601
Dear Ruth	683	Flower Drum Song	600
East Is West	680	Kiki	600
Come Blow Your Horn	677	A Little Night Music	600
The Most Happy Fella	676	Agnes of God	599
The Doughgirls	671	Don't Drink the Water	598
The Impossible Years	670	Wish You Were Here	598
Irene	670	Sarafina!	597
Boy Meets Girl	669	A Society Circus	596
The Tap Dance Kid	669	Absurd Person Singular	592
Beyond the Fringe	667	A Day in Hollywood/A Night	
Who's Afraid of Virginia		in the Ukraine	588
Woolf?	664	The Me Nobody Knows	586
Blithe Spirit	657	The Two Mrs. Carrolls	585
A Trip to Chinatown	657	Kismet (m)	583
The Women	657	Gypsy (m, r)	582
Bloomer Girl	654	Brigadoon	581
The Fifth Season	654	Detective Story	581
Rain	648	No Strings	580
Witness for the Prosecution	645	Brother Rat	577
Call Me Madam	644	Blossom Time	576
Janie	642	Pump Boys and Dinettes	573
The Green Pastures	640	Show Boat	572
Auntie Mame (p)	639	The Show-Off	571
A Man for All Seasons	637	Sally	570
Jerome Robbins' Broadway	634	Golden Boy (m)	568
The Fourposter	632	One Touch of Venus	567
The Music Master	627	The Real Thing	566
Two Gentlemen of Verona (m)	627	Happy Birthday	564
The Tenth Man	623	Look Homeward, Angel	564
The Heidi Chronicles	621	Morning's at Seven (r)	564
Is Zat So?	618	The Glass Menagerie	561
Anniversary Waltz	615	I Do! I Do!	560

Plays	Number Performances	Plays	Number Performances
Wonderful Town.............	559	Fences	526
Rose Marie	557	The Solid Gold Cadillac.......	526
Strictly Dishonorable	557	Biloxi Blues	524
Sweeney Todd, the Demon		Irma La Douce	524
Barber of Fleet Street	557	The Boomerang..............	522
The Great White Hope	556	Follies	521
A Majority of One	556	Rosalinda...................	521
Sunrise at Campobello........	556	The Best Man	520
Toys in the Attic.............	556	Chauve-Souris..............	520
Jamaica	555	Blackbirds of 1928	518
Stop the World—I Want to Get		The Gin Game	517
Off......................	555	Sunny.....................	517
Florodora	553	Victoria Regina..............	517
Noises Off	553	Fifth of July	511
Ziegfeld Follies (1943)	553	Half a Sixpence..............	511
Dial "M" for Murder.........	552	The Vagabond King..........	511
Good News	551	The New Moon..............	509
Peter Pan (r)	551	The World of Suzie Wong.....	508
Let's Face It	547	The Rothschilds	507
Milk and Honey	543	On Your Toes (r)	505
Within the Law..............	541	Sugar	505
Pal Joey (r)	540	Shuffle Along................	504
What Makes Sammy Run?	540	Up in Central Park...........	504
The Sunshine Boys	538	Carmen Jones	503
What a Life.................	538	The Member of the Wedding ..	501
*Crazy for You..............	535	Panama Hattie	501
Crimes of the Heart	535	Personal Appearance	501
The Unsinkable Molly Brown..	532	Bird in Hand................	500
The Red Mill (r).............	531	Room Service	500
Rumors	531	Sailor, Beware!	500
A Raisin in the Sun	530	Tomorrow the World........	500
Godspell....................	527		

LONG RUNS OFF BROADWAY

Plays	Number Performances	Plays	Number Performances
*The Fantasticks.............	13,702	Little Shop of Horrors........	2,209
*Nunsense	3,097	Godspell....................	2,124
The Threepenny Opera........	2,611	Vampire Lesbians of Sodom ...	2,024
*Perfect Crime..............	2,501	Jacques Brel................	1,847
Forbidden Broadway		Vanities	1,785
1982–87	2,332	*Tony 'n' Tina's Wedding	1,705†

†Editor's note: This show fits some but not all conditions of our off-Broadway category, in which it hasn't previously been listed. We list it now for informational purposes, recognizing the unique place it has made for itself on the New York theater scene.

Plays	Number Performances	Plays	Number Performances
You're a Good Man Charlie Brown	1,597	Oh! Calcutta!	704
The Blacks	1,408	Scuba Duba	692
One Mo' Time	1,372	The Foreigner	686
*Forever Plaid	1,352	The Knack	685
Let My People Come	1,327	*Beau Jest	674
Driving Miss Daisy	1,195	The Club	674
The Hot 1 Baltimore	1,166	The Balcony	672
I'm Getting My Act Together and Taking It on the Road	1,165	Penn & Teller	666
Little Mary Sunshine	1,143	*Tubes	642
Steel Magnolias	1,126	America Hurrah	634
El Grande de Coca-Cola	1,114	Oil City Symphony	626
Tamara	1,036	Hogan's Goat	607
One Flew Over the Cuckoo's Nest (r)	1,025	Beehive	600
The Boys in the Band	1,000	The Trojan Women	600
Fool for Love	1,000	The Dining Room	583
Other People's Money	990	Krapp's Last Tape & The Zoo Story	582
Cloud 9	971	The Dumbwaiter & The Collection	578
Sister Mary Ignatius Explains It All for You & The Actor's Nightmare	947	Forbidden Broadway 1990–91	576
		Dames at Sea	575
		The Crucible (r)	571
Your Own Thing	933	The Iceman Cometh (r)	565
Curley McDimple	931	The Hostage (r)	545
Leave It to Jane (r)	928	What's a Nice Country Like You Doing in a State Like This?	543
The Mad Show	871		
Scrambled Feet	831	Forbidden Broadway 1988–89	534
The Effect of Gamma Rays on Man-in-the-Moon Marigolds	819	Frankie and Johnny in the Clair de Lune	533
A View From the Bridge (r)	780	Six Characters in Search of an Author (r)	529
The Boy Friend (r)	763	The Dirtiest Show in Town	509
True West	762	Happy Ending & Day of Absence	504
Isn't It Romantic	733		
Dime a Dozen	728	Greater Tuna	501
The Pocket Watch	725	A Shayna Maidel	501
The Connection	722	The Boys From Syracuse (r)	500
The Passion of Dracula	714		
Adaptation & Next	707		

NEW YORK DRAMA CRITICS CIRCLE AWARDS, 1935–36 to 1992–93

Listed below are the New York Drama Critics Circle Awards from 1935–36 through 1992–93 classified as follows: (1) Best American Play, (2) Best Foreign Play, (3) Best Musical, (4) Best, regardless of category (this category was established by new voting rules in 1962–63 and did not exist prior to that year).

1935–36—(1) Winterset
1936–37—(1) High Tor
1937–38—(1) Of Mice and Men, (2) Shadow and Substance
1938–39—(1) No award, (2) The White Steed
1939–40—(1) The Time of Your Life
1940–41—(1) Watch on the Rhine, (2) The Corn Is Green
1941–42—(1) No award, (2) Blithe Spirit
1942–43—(2) The Patriots
1943–44—(2) Jacobowsky and the Colonel
1944–45—(1) The Glass Menagerie
1945–46—(3) Carousel
1946–47—(1) All My Sons, (2) No Exit, (3) Brigadoon
1947–48—(1) A Streetcar Named Desire, (2) The Winslow Boy
1948–49—(1) Death of a Salesman, (2) The Madwoman of Chaillot, (3) South Pacific
1949–50—(1) The Member of the Wedding, (2) The Cocktail Party, (3) The Consul
1950–51—(1) Darkness at Noon, (2) The Lady's Not for Burning, (3) Guys and Dolls
1951–52—(1) I Am a Camera, (2) Venus Observed, (3) Pal Joey (Special citation to Don Juan in Hell)
1952–53—(1) Picnic, (2) The Love of Four Colonels, (3) Wonderful Town
1953–54—(1) Teahouse of the August Moon, (2) Ondine, (3) The Golden Apple
1954–55—(1) Cat on a Hot Tin Roof, (2) Witness for the Prosecution, (3) The Saint of Bleecker Street
1955–56—(1) The Diary of Anne Frank, (2) Tiger at the Gates, (3) My Fair Lady
1956–57—(1) Long Day's Journey Into Night, (2) The Waltz of the Toreadors, (3) The Most Happy Fella
1957–58—(1) Look Homeward, Angel, (2) Look Back in Anger, (3) The Music Man
1958–59—(1) A Raisin in the Sun, (2) The Visit, (3) La Plume de Ma Tante
1959–60—(1) Toys in the Attic, (2) Five Finger Exercise, (3) Fiorello!

1960–61—(1) All the Way Home, (2) A Taste of Honey, (3) Carnival
1961–62—(1) The Night of the Iguana, (2) A Man for All Seasons, (3) How to Succeed in Business Without Really Trying
1962–63—(4) Who's Afraid of Virginia Woolf? (Special citation to Beyond the Fringe)
1963–64—(4) Luther, (3) Hello, Dolly! (Special citation to The Trojan Women)
1964–65—(4) The Subject Was Roses, (3) Fiddler on the Roof
1965–66—(1) The Persecution and Assassination of Marat as Performed by the Inmates of the Asylum of Charenton Under the Direction of the Marquis de Sade, (3) Man of La Mancha
1966–67—(4) The Homecoming, (3) Cabaret
1967–68—(4) Rosencrantz and Guildenstern Are Dead, (3) Your Own Thing
1968–69—(4) The Great White Hope, (3) 1776
1969–70—(4) Borstal Boy, (1) The Effect of Gamma Rays on Man-in-the-Moon Marigolds, (3) Company
1970–71—(4) Home, (1) The House of Blue Leaves, (3) Follies
1971–72—(4) That Championship Season, (2) The Screens, (3) Two Gentlemen of Verona (Special citation to Sticks and Bones and Old Times)
1972–73—(4) The Changing Room, (1) The Hot 1 Baltimore, (3) A Little Night Music
1973–74—(4) The Contractor, (1) Short Eyes, (3) Candide
1974–75—(4) Equus, (1) The Taking of Miss Janie, (3) A Chorus Line
1975–76—(4) Travesties, (1) Streamers, (3) Pacific Overtures
1976–77—(4) Otherwise Engaged, (1) American Buffalo, (3) Annie
1977–78—(4) Da, (3) Ain't Misbehavin'
1978–79—(4) The Elephant Man, (3) Sweeney Todd, the Demon Barber of Fleet Street

1979–80—(4) Talley's Folly, (2) Betrayal, (3) Evita (Special citation to Peter Brook's Le Centre International de Créations Théâtrales for its repertory)

1980–81—(4) A Lesson From Aloes, (1) Crimes of the Heart (Special citations to Lena Horne: The Lady and Her Music and the New York Shakespeare Festival production of The Pirates of Penzance)

1981–82—(4) The Life & Adventures of Nicholas Nickleby, (1) A Soldier's Play

1982–83—(4) Brighton Beach Memoirs, (2) Plenty, (3) Little Shop of Horrors (Special citation to Young Playwrights Festival)

1983–84—(4) The Real Thing; (1) Glengarry Glen Ross, (3) Sunday in the Park With George (Special citation to Samuel Beckett for the body of his work)

1984–85—(4) Ma Rainey's Black Bottom

1985–86—(4) A Lie of the Mind, (2) Benefactors (Special citation to The Search for Signs of Intelligent Life in the Universe)

1986–87—(4) Fences, (2) Les Liaisons Dangereuses, (3) Les Misérables

1987–88—(4) Joe Turner's Come and Gone, (2) The Road to Mecca, (3) Into the Woods

1988–89—(4) The Heidi Chronicles, (2) Aristocrats (Special citation to Bill Irwin for Largely New York)

1989–90—(4) The Piano Lesson, (2) Privates on Parade, (3) City of Angels

1990–91—(4) Six Degrees of Separation, (2) Our Country's Good, (3) The Will Rogers Follies (Special citation to Eileen Atkins for her portrayal of Virginia Woolf in A Room of One's Own)

1991–92—(4) Dancing at Lughnasa, (1) Two Trains Running

1992–93—(4) Angels in America: Millennium Approaches, (2) Someone Who'll Watch Over Me, (3) Kiss of the Spider Woman

NEW YORK DRAMA CRITICS CIRCLE VOTING, 1992–93

The musical *Kiss of the Spider Woman* by Terrence McNally, John Kander and Fred Ebb was the only one of the three 1992–93 New York Drama Critics Award winners to be named by a simple majority, receiving eleven out of the 19 votes of the members present and voting on the first ballot for the season's best musical, as follows: *Kiss of the Spider Woman* 11 (William A. Henry III, Howard Kissel, Jack Kroll, Michael Kuchwara, Jacques le Sourd, Edith Oliver, William Raidy, David Patrick Stearns, Jerry Tallmer, Douglas Watt, Edwin Wilson), *Tommy* 4 (Clive Barnes, Greg Evans, Melanie Kirkpatrick, Jan Stuart), *Wings* 3 (Jeremy Gerard, Julius Novick, Linda Winer) and *Orpheus in Love* 1 (Michael Feingold). Of the three other members of the Circle, John Simon of *New York Magazine* was absent and Frank Rich and Mel Gussow of the *Times* are non-voters.

The other two 1992–93 Critics Award winners—*Angels in America: Millennium Approaches* by Tony Kushner (best play) and *Someone Who'll Watch Over Me* by Frank McGuinness (best foreign play)—won on second, point-weighted ballots in their categories (see summaries of the voting below), after no play received a simple majority on the first ballot. According to the Critics rules, on the second ballot they name their first, second and third choices, which are awarded 3, 2 and 1 points, respectively, for each vote. To win on this weighted ballot, a play must have a point total of three times the number of members voting (19 for best play this year; 16 for best foreign play, with three voters abstaining), divided by two, plus one. *Angels in America: Millennium Approaches* won the Critics best-play citation with 32 points, against *Someone Who'll Watch Over Me* (17), *The Sisters Rosensweig* (14), *Three Hotels* (11), *The Destiny of Me* (9), *Jeffrey* (8), *Another Time* (7), *On the Open Road* (6), *Redwood Curtain* (3), *Fires in the Mirror* (2) and 1 each for *Joined at the Head, Oleanna, Playboy of the West Indies* and *Two Rooms*.

Having chosen an American play the best of the season in any category, the Critics then voted *Someone Who'll Watch Over Me* the season's best foreign play (consistently, since it had run a clear second in the previous category) by a narrow margin of 27 points against 22 for *Les Atrides* (French-language versions of four classic Greek tragedies), 19 for *Another Time,* 13 for *Playboy of the West Indies,* 8 for *Traps,* 5 for *Needles and Opium* and 2 for *Owners.*

A previous Critics voting rule that only those plays named on a first ballot could be considered in the point voting on the second ballot was rescinded last year, so that in 1992–93 the Critics were free to name any play they chose in the second-round voting.

SECOND BALLOT FOR BEST PLAY

Critic	1st Choice (3 pts.)	2d Choice (2 pts.)	3d Choice (1 pt.)
Clive Barnes *Post*	Someone Who'll Watch Over Me	On the Open Road	Millennium Approaches
Greg Evans *Variety*	Millennium Approaches	Jeffrey	The Sisters Rosensweig
Michael Feingold *Village Voice*	Millennium Approaches	Jeffrey	Oleanna
Jeremy Gerard *Variety*	Millennium Approaches	The Destiny of Me	Jeffrey
William A. Henry III *Time*	The Destiny of Me	Three Hotels	Two Rooms
Melanie Kirkpatrick *Wall St. Journal*	Someone Who'll Watch	The Sisters Rosensweig	Redwood Curtain
Howard Kissel *Daily News*	On the Open Road	Another Time	Millennium Approaches
Jack Kroll *Newsweek*	Millennium Approaches	Jeffrey	Fires in the Mirror
Michael Kuchwara Associated Press	Millennium Approaches	Three Hotels	The Sisters Rosensweig
Jacques le Sourd Gannett Newspapers	The Sisters Rosensweig	Someone Who'll Watch	Jeffrey

| Julius Novick
Newsday | Three Hotels | The Destiny of Me | Millennium Approaches |
| Edith Oliver
New Yorker | The Sisters Rosensweig | Someone Who'll Watch | Playboy of the West Indies |
| William Raidy
Newhouse
Newspapers | Millennium Approaches | Another Time | Three Hotels |
| David Patrick Stearns
USA Today | Millennium Approaches | Joined at the Head | Three Hotels |
| Jan Stuart
Newsday | Millennium Approaches | Three Hotels | On the Open Road |
| Jerry Tallmer
Post | Another Time | The Sisters Rosensweig | Someone Who'll Watch |
| Douglas Watt
Daily News | Someone Who'll Watch | The Sisters Rosensweig | Millennium Approaches |
| Edwin Wilson
Wall St. Journal | Someone Who'll Watch | Redwood Curtain | Millennium Approaches |
| Linda Winer
Newsday | Millennium Approaches | The Destiny of Me | Fires in the Mirror |

SECOND BALLOT FOR BEST FOREIGN PLAY

Critic	*1st Choice (3 pts.)*	*2d Choice (2 pts.)*	*3d Choice (1 pt.)*
Clive Barnes	Someone Who'll Watch Over Me	Another Time	Playboy of the West Indies
Greg Evans	Les Atrides	Playboy	Someone Who'll Watch
Michael Feingold	Les Atrides	Traps	Needles and Opium
Jeremy Gerard	Les Atrides	Another Time	Someone Who'll Watch
William A. Henry III	Les Atrides	Another Time	Playboy
Melanie Kirkpatrick	Someone Who'll Watch	Another Time	Playboy
Howard Kissel	Someone Who'll Watch	Another Time	Playboy
Jack Kroll	Abstained		
Michael Kuchwara	Les Atrides	Someone Who'll Watch	Traps
Jacques le Sourd	Someone Who'll Watch	Another Time	Playboy

Julius Novick	Abstained		
Edith Oliver	Someone Who'll Watch	Playboy	Traps
William Raidy	Another Time	Someone Who'll Watch	Les Atrides
David Patrick Stearns	Les Atrides	Another Time	Needles and Opium
Jan Stuart	Needles and Opium	Owners	Traps
Jerry Tallmer	Abstained		
Douglas Watt	Someone Who'll Watch	Traps	Playboy
Edwin Wilson	Someone Who'll Watch	Another Time	Playboy
Linda Winer	Les Atrides	Playboy	Traps

CHOICES OF SOME OTHER CRITICS

Critic	Best Play	Best Musical
Alvin Klein N.Y. Times Regional	The Sisters Rosensweig	Kiss of the Spider Woman
Stewart Klein WNYW-TV	Millennium Approaches	Tommy
Richard Scholem Long Island News	Millennium Approaches	Kiss of the Spider Woman
Allan Wallach Newsday	Millennium Approaches	Kiss of the Spider Woman

PULITZER PRIZE WINNERS, 1916–17 TO 1992–93

1916–17—No award
1917–18—Why Marry?, by Jesse Lynch Williams
1918–19—No award
1919–20—Beyond the Horizon, by Eugene O'Neill
1920–21—Miss Lulu Bett, by Zona Gale
1921–22—Anna Christie, by Eugene O'Neill
1922–23—Icebound, by Owen Davis
1923–24—Hell-Bent fer Heaven, by Hatcher Hughes
1924–25—They Knew What They Wanted, by Sidney Howard
1925–26—Craig's Wife, by George Kelly
1926–27—In Abraham's Bosom, by Paul Green
1927–28—Strange Interlude, by Eugene O'Neill
1928–29—Street Scene, by Elmer Rice

1929–30—The Green Pastures, by Marc Connelly
1930–31—Alison's House, by Susan Glaspell
1931–32—Of Thee I Sing, by George S. Kaufman, Morrie Ryskind, Ira and George Gershwin
1932–33—Both Your Houses, by Maxwell Anderson
1933–34—Men in White, by Sidney Kingsley
1934–35—The Old Maid, by Zoë Akins
1935–36—Idiot's Delight, by Robert E. Sherwood
1936–37—You Can't Take It With You, by Moss Hart and George S. Kaufman
1937–38—Our Town, by Thornton Wilder
1938–39—Abe Lincoln in Illinois, by Robert E. Sherwood

1939-40—The Time of Your Life, by William Saroyan
1940-41—There Shall Be No Night, by Robert E. Sherwood
1941-42—No award
1942-43—The Skin of Our Teeth, by Thornton Wilder
1943-44—No award
1944-45—Harvey, by Mary Chase
1945-46—State of the Union, by Howard Lindsay and Russel Crouse
1946-47—No award
1947-48—A Streetcar Named Desire, by Tennessee Williams
1948-49—Death of a Salesman, by Arthur Miller
1949-50—South Pacific, by Richard Rodgers, Oscar Hammerstein II and Joshua Logan
1950-51—No award
1951-52—The Shrike, by Joseph Kramm
1952-53—Picnic, by William Inge
1953-54—The Teahouse of the August Moon, by John Patrick
1954-55—Cat on a Hot Tin Roof, by Tennessee Williams
1955-56—The Diary of Anne Frank, by Frances Goodrich and Albert Hackett
1956-57—Long Day's Journey Into Night, by Eugene O'Neill
1957-58—Look Homeward, Angel, by Ketti Frings
1958-59—J.B., by Archibald MacLeish
1959-60—Fiorello!, by Jerome Weidman, George Abbott, Sheldon Harnick and Jerry Bock
1960-61—All the Way Home, by Tad Mosel
1961-62—How to Succeed in Business Without Really Trying, by Abe Burrows, Willie Gilbert, Jack Weinstock and Frank Loesser
1962-63—No award
1963-64—No award
1964-65—The Subject Was Roses, by Frank D. Gilroy

1965-66—No award
1966-67—A Delicate Balance, by Edward Albee
1967-68—No award
1968-69—The Great White Hope, by Howard Sackler
1969-70—No Place To Be Somebody, by Charles Gordone
1970-71—The Effect of Gamma Rays on Man-in-the-Moon Marigolds, by Paul Zindel
1971-72—No award
1972-73—That Championship Season, by Jason Miller
1973-74—No award
1974-75—Seascape, by Edward Albee
1975-76—A Chorus Line, by Michael Bennett, James Kirkwood, Nicholas Dante, Marvin Hamlisch and Edward Kleban
1976-77—The Shadow Box, by Michael Cristofer
1977-78—The Gin Game, by D. L. Coburn
1978-79—Buried Child, by Sam Shepard
1979-80—Talley's Folly, by Lanford Wilson
1980-81—Crimes of the Heart, by Beth Henley
1981-82—A Soldier's Play, by Charles Fuller
1982-83—'night, Mother, by Marsha Norman
1983-84—Glengarry Glen Ross, by David Mamet
1984-85—Sunday in the Park With George, by James Lapine and Stephen Sondheim
1985-86—No award
1986-87—Fences, by August Wilson
1987-88—Driving Miss Daisy, by Alfred Uhry
1988-89—The Heidi Chronicles, by Wendy Wasserstein
1989-90—The Piano Lesson, by August Wilson
1990-91—Lost in Yonkers, by Neil Simon
1991-92—The Kentucky Cycle, by Robert Schenkkan
1992-93—Angels in America: Millennium Approaches, by Tony Kushner

THE TONY AWARDS, 1992–93

The American Theater Wing's Antoinette Perry (Tony) Awards are presented annually in recognition of distinguished artistic achievement in the Broadway theater. The League of American Theaters and Producers and the American Theater Wing present the Tony Awards, founded by the Wing in 1947. Legitimate theater productions opening in eligible Broadway theaters during the eligibility season of the current year—April 30, 1992 to May 5, 1993—were considered for Tony nominations.

Winners of the best supporting actress Tonys are pictured here: *above,* Debra Monk as Geneva in the play *Redwood Curtain; right,* Andrea Martin *(right)* as Alice Miller with Lannyl Stephens in the musical *My Favorite Year*

The Tony Awards Administration Committee appoints the Tony Awards Nominating Committee which makes the actual nominations. The 1992–93 Nominating Committee consisted of Donald Brooks, costume designer; Marge Champion, choreographer; Ted Chapin, theater executive; Betty L. Corwin, theater historian; Gretchen Cryer, composer; Jay Harnick, artistic director; Eileen Heckart, actress; Arthur Kopit, playwright; Fran Kumin, theater administrator; Suzanne Sato, arts executive; Oliver Smith, set designer; and Sister Francesca Thompson, theater educator.

The Tony Awards are voted from the list of nominees by the members of the governing boards of the five theater artists' organizations: Actors' Equity Association, the Dramatists Guild, the Society of Stage Directors and Choreographers, the United Scenic Artists and the Casting Society of America, plus the members of the designated first night theater press, the board of directors of the American Theater Wing and the membership of the League of American Theaters and Producers. Because of fluctuation within these boards, the size of the Tony electorate varies from year to year. In the 1992–93 season there were 670 qualified Tony voters.

The list of 1992–93 nominees follows, with winners in each category listed in **bold face type.**

BEST PLAY (award goes to both author and producer). *Angels in America: Millennium Approaches* by **Tony Kushner,** produced by **Jujamcyn Theaters, Mark Taper Forum/Gordon Davidson, Susan Quint Gallin, Jon B. Platt, The Baruch-Frankel-Viertel Group, Frederick Zollo, Herb Alpert;** *The Sisters Rosensweig* by Wendy Wasserstein, produced by Lincoln Center Theater, Andre Bishop, Bernard Gersten; *Someone Who'll Watch Over Me* by Frank McGuinness, produced by Noel Pearson, The Shubert Organization, Joseph Harris; *The Song of Jacob Zulu* by Tug Yourgrau, produced by Steppenwolf Theater Company, Randall Arney, Stephen Eich, Albert Poland, Susan Liederman, Bette Cerf Hill, Maurice Rosenfield.

BEST MUSICAL (award goes to the producer). *Blood Brothers* produced by Bill Kenwright; *The Goodbye Girl* produced by Office Two-One Inc., Gladys Nederlander, Stewart F. Lane, James M. Nederlander, Richard Kagan, Emanuel Azenberg; *Kiss of the Spider Woman* produced by **Livent (U.S.) Inc.;** *The Who's Tommy* produced by Pace Theatrical Group, Dodger Productions, Kardana Productions, Inc.

BEST BOOK OF A MUSICAL. *Anna Karenina* by Peter Kellogg; *Blood Brothers* by Willy Russell; *Kiss of the Spider Woman* by **Terrence McNally;** *Tommy* by Pete Townshend and Des McAnuff.

BEST ORIGINAL SCORE (music & lyrics) WRITTEN FOR THE THEATER (a tie in this category). *Anna Karenina,* music by Daniel Levine, lyrics by Peter Kellogg; *Kiss of the Spider Woman,* music by **John Kander,** lyrics by **Fred Ebb;** *The Song of Jacob Zulu,* music by Ladysmith Black Mambazo, lyrics by Tug Yourgrau and Ladysmith Black Mambazo; *Tommy,* music and lyrics by **Pete Townshend.**

BEST LEADING ACTOR IN A PLAY. K. Todd Freeman in *The Song of Jacob Zulu,* **Ron Leibman** in *Angels in America,* Liam Neeson in *Anna Christie,* Stephen Rea in *Someone Who'll Watch Over Me.*

BEST LEADING ACTRESS IN A PLAY. Jane Alexander in *The Sisters Rosensweig,* **Madeline Kahn** in *The Sisters Rosensweig,* Lynn Redgrave in *Shakespeare for My Father,* Natasha Richardson in *Anna Christie.*

BEST LEADING ACTOR IN A MUSICAL. **Brent Carver** in *Kiss of the Spider Woman,* Tim Curry in *My Favorite Year,* Con O'Neill in *Blood Brothers,* Martin Short in *The Goodbye Girl.*

BEST LEADING ACTRESS IN A MUSICAL. Ann Crumb in *Anna Karenina,* Stephanie Lawrence in *Blood Brothers,* Bernadette Peters in *The Goodbye Girl,* **Chita Rivera** in *Kiss of the Spider Woman.*

BEST FEATURED ACTOR IN A PLAY. Robert Sean Leonard in *Candida,* Joe Mantello in *Angels in America,* Zakes Mokae in *The Song of Jacob Zulu,* **Stephen Spinella** in *Angels in America.*

BEST FEATURED ACTRESS IN A PLAY. Kathleen Chalfant in *Angels in America,* Marcia Gay Harden in *Angels in America,* Anne Meara in *Anna Christie,* **Debra Monk** in *Redwood Curtain.*

BEST FEATURED ACTOR IN A MUSICAL. Michael Cerveris in *Tommy,* **Anthony Crivello** in *Kiss of the Spider Woman,* Gregg Edelman in *Anna Karenina,* Paul Kandel in *Tommy.*

BEST FEATURED ACTRESS IN A MUSICAL. Jan Graveson in *Blood Brothers,* Lainie Kazan in *My Favorite Year,* **Andrea Martin** in *My Favorite Year,* Marcia Mitzman in *Tommy.*

BEST DIRECTION OF A PLAY. David Leveaux for *Anna Christie,* Eric Simonson for *The Song of Jacob Zulu,* Daniel Sullivan for *The Sisters Rosensweig,* **George C. Wolfe** for *Angels in America.*

BEST DIRECTION OF A MUSICAL. Bill Kenwright and Bob Tomson for *Blood Brothers,* Michael Kidd for *The Goodbye Girl,* **Des McAnuff** for *Tommy,* Harold Prince for *Kiss of the Spider Woman.*

BEST SCENIC DESIGN. **John Arnone** for *Tommy,* John Lee Beatty for *Redwood Curtain,* Jerome Sirlin for *Kiss of the Spider Woman,* Robin Wagner for *Angels in America.*

BEST COSTUME DESIGN. Jane Greenwood for *The Sisters Rosensweig,* **Florence Klotz** for *Kiss of the Spider Woman,* Erin Quigley for *The Song of Jacob Zulu,* David C. Woolard for *Tommy.*

BEST LIGHTING DESIGN. Howell Binkley for *Kiss of the Spider Woman,* Jules Fisher for *Angels in America,* Dennis Parichy for *Redwood Curtain,* **Chris Parry** for *Tommy.*

BEST CHOREOGRAPHY. **Wayne Cilento** for *Tommy,* Graciela Daniele for *The Goodbye Girl,* Vincent Paterson and Rob Marshall for *Kiss of the Spider Woman,* Randy Skinner for *Ain't Broadway Grand.*

BEST REVIVAL OF A PLAY OR MUSICAL (award goes to the producer). *Anna Christie* produced by **Roundabout Theater Company, Todd Haimes;** *Saint Joan* produced by National Actors Theater, Tony Randall, Duncan C. Weldon; *The Price* produced by Roundabout Theater Company, Todd Haimes; *Wilder, Wilder, Wilder* produced by Circle in the Square Theater, Theodore Mann, George Elmer, Paul Libin, Willow Cabin Theater Company, Edward Berkeley, Adam Oliensis, Maria Radman.

SPECIAL TONY AWARDS: Richard Rodgers and Oscar Hammerstein II's musical **Oklahoma!** in recognition of the show's 50th anniversary; **La Jolla Playhouse,** San Diego, Calif.

TONY HONORS: the **International Alliance of Theatrical Stage Employees and Moving Picture Machine Operators of the United States and Canada** (usually known as I.A.T.S.E or the I.A) and **Broadway Cares/Equity Fights AIDS.**

TONY AWARD WINNERS, 1947–1993

Listed below are the Antoinette Perry (Tony) Award winners in the categories of Best Play and Best Musical from the time these awards were established until the present.

1947—No play or musical award
1948—Mister Roberts; no musical award
1949—Death of a Salesman; Kiss Me, Kate
1950—The Cocktail Party; South Pacific
1951—The Rose Tattoo; Guys and Dolls
1952—The Fourposter; The King and I
1953—The Crucible; Wonderful Town
1954—The Teahouse of the August Moon; Kismet
1955—The Desperate Hours; The Pajama Game
1956—The Diary of Anne Frank; Damn Yankees
1957—Long Day's Journey Into Night; My Fair Lady
1958—Sunrise at Campobello; The Music Man
1959—J.B.; Redhead
1960—The Miracle Worker; Fiorello! and The Sound of Music (tie)
1961—Beckett; Bye Bye Birdie
1962—A Man for All Seasons; How to Succeed in Business Without Really Trying
1963—Who's Afraid of Virginia Woolf?; A Funny Thing Happened on the Way to the Forum
1964—Luther; Hello, Dolly!
1965—The Subject Was Roses; Fiddler on the Roof
1966—The Persecution and Assassination of Marat Performed by the Inmates of the Asylum of Charenton Under the Direction of the Marquis de Sade; Man of La Mancha
1967—The Homecoming; Cabaret

1968—Rosencrantz and Guildenstern Are Dead; Hallelujah, Baby!
1969—The Great White Hope; 1776
1970—Borstal Boy; Applause
1971—Sleuth; Company
1972—Sticks and Bones; Two Gentlemen of Verona
1973—That Championship Season; A Little Night Music
1974—The River Niger; Raisin
1975—Equus; The Wiz
1976—Travesties; A Chorus Line
1977—The Shadow Box; Annie
1978—Da; Ain't Misbehavin'
1979—The Elephant Man; Sweeney Todd, the Demon Barber of Fleet Street
1980—Children of a Lesser God; Evita
1981—Amadeus; 42nd Street
1982—The Life & Adventures of Nicholas Nickleby; Nine
1983—Torch Song Trilogy; Cats
1984—The Real Thing; La Cage aux Folles
1985—Biloxi Blues; Big River
1986—I'm Not Rappaport; The Mystery of Edwin Drood
1987—Fences; Les Misérables
1988—M. Butterfly; The Phantom of the Opera
1989—The Heidi Chronicles; Jerome Robbins' Broadway
1990—The Grapes of Wrath; City of Angels
1991—Lost in Yonkers; The Will Rogers Follies
1992—Dancing at Lughnasa; Crazy for You
1993—Angels in America: Millennium Approaches; Kiss of the Spider Woman

THE OBIE AWARDS, 1992–93

The, *Village Voice* Off-Broadway (Obie) Awards are given each year for excellence in various categories of off-Broadway (and frequently off-off-Broadway) shows, with close distinctions between these two areas ignored. The 37th annual Obies for the 1992–93 season, listed below, were chosen by a panel of judges chaired by Ross Wetzsteon and comprising Michael Feingold, Alisa Solomon, Jeremy Gerard and Mary Alice.

PLAYWRITING. **Harry Kondoleon** for *The Houseguests,* **Larry Kramer** for *The Destiny of Me,* **Jose Rivera** for *Marisol,* **Paul Rudnick** for *Jeffrey.*

PERFORMANCE. **Jane Alexander** and **Robert Klein** in *The Sisters Rosensweig,* **Miriam Colon** and **Ellen Parker** for sustained excellence, **Frances Conroy** in *The Last Yankee,* **David Drake** in *The Night Larry Kramer Kissed Me,* **Giancarlo Esposito** in *Distant Fires,* **Geoffrey C. Ewing** in *Ali,* **Hallie Foote** in *The Roads to Home,* **Edward Hibbert** in *Jeffrey,* **Bill Irwin** in *Texts for Nothing,* **John Cameron Mitchell** in *The Destiny of Me,* **Linda Stephens** in *Wings.*

DIRECTION. **Christopher Ashley** for *Jeffrey,* **Michael Maggio** for *Wings,* **Frederick Zollo** for *Aven' U Boys.*

DESIGN: **Loy Arcenas** for sustained excellence of set design, **Howard Thies** for sustained excellence of lighting design.

SUSTAINED ACHIEVEMENT. **JoAnne Akalaitis.**

SPECIAL CITATIONS. *Cirque du Soleil,* **Betty Corwin, Ensemble Studio Theater** for its annual one-act play marathon, **International Festival of Puppet Theater: Puppetry at the Public,** Ariane Mnouchkine for *Les Atrides,* **Lincoln Center Serious Fun!** Festival.

VILLAGE VOICE GRANTS. **Nuyorican Poets Cafe, Pearl Theater Company.**

ADDITIONAL PRIZES AND AWARDS, 1992–93

The following is a list of major prizes and awards for achievement in the theater this season. In all cases the names and/or titles of the winners appear in **bold face type.**

1992 ELIZABETH HULL-KATE WARRINER AWARD. To the playwrights whose work dealt with controversial subjects involving the fields of political, religious or social mores of the time, selected by the Dramatists Guild Council. **Donald Margulies** for *Sight Unseen,* **Larry Kramer** for *The Destiny of Me* and **John Leguizamo** for *Spic-O-Rama.*

8th ANNUAL ATCA NEW PLAY AWARD. For an outstanding new play in cross-country theater, voted by a committee of the American Theater Critics Association. *Children of Paradise: Shooting a Dream* company-developed by Theatre de la Jeune Lune. Also cited, *Unfinished*

Stories by Sybille Pearson and *Dark Rapture* by Eric Overmyer.

12th ANNUAL WILLIAM INGE AWARD. For lifetime achievement in the American Theater. **Wendy Wasserstein.**

MARGO JONES MEDAL. For lifetime achievement in theater, in support of playwrights and playwriting. **Abbott Van Nostrand.**

15th ANNUAL KENNEDY CENTER HONORS. For distinguished achievement by individuals who have made significant contributions to American culture through the arts. **Lionel Hampton, Paul Newman** and **Joanne**

Woodward, Ginger Rogers, Mstislav Rostropovich, Paul Taylor.

9th ANNUAL GEORGE AND ELISABETH MARTON AWARD. To an American playwright, selected by a committee of Young Playwrights Inc. **Anna Deavere Smith** for *Fires in the Mirror.*

1992 JUJAMCYN THEATERS AWARD. Honoring outstanding contribution to the development of creative talent for the theater. **Yale School of Drama/Yale Repertory Theater.**

1993 ASTAIRE AWARDS. For achievement in dance in the Broadway theater. **Chita Rivera** for her performance in *Kiss of the Spider Woman,* **Wayne Cilento** for the choreography of *Tommy.*

59th ANNUAL DRAMA LEAGUE AWARDS. For distinguished performance. **Stephen Rea** in *Someone Who'll Watch Over Me,* **Chita Rivera** in *Kiss of the Spider Woman.* Special award, **Lucille Lortel.**

LONG WHARF THEATER MURPHY AWARD. Honoring an illustrious practitioner of the art of theatrical design. **Ming Cho Lee.**

1992 JOSEPH KESSELRING PRIZES. Selected under the aegis of the National Arts Club, by a committee comprising Anne Cattaneo, John Guare and John Lahr. **Marion McClinton** for *Police Boys,* **Jose Rivera** for *Marisol.*

49th ANNUAL *THEATER WORLD* AWARDS. For outstanding new talent in Broadway and off-Broadway productions during the 1992–93 season, selected by a committee comprising Clive Barnes, Douglas Watt and John Willis. **Brent Carver** in *Kiss of the Spider Woman,* **Michael Cerveris** in *Tommy,* **Marcia Gay Harden** and **Stephen Spinella** in *Angels in America,* **Stephanie Lawrence** in *Blood Brothers,* **Andrea Martin** in *My Favorite Year,* **Liam Neeson** and **Natasha Richardson** in *Anna Christie,* **Stephen Rea** in *Someone Who'll Watch Over Me,* **Martin Short** in *The Goodbye Girl,* **Dina Spybey** in *Five Women Wearing the Same Dress,* **Jennifer Tilley** in *One Shoe Off.* Special awards: **Rosetta LeNoire, John Leguizamo.**

1991–92 GEORGE JEAN NATHAN AWARD. For drama criticism, administered by Cornell University's English department. **Kevin Kelly.**

1992 MR. ABBOTT AWARD. Presented by the Stage Directors and Choreographers Foundation. **Arvin Brown.** President's award, **Al Hirschfeld.**

1993 AMERICAN THEATER WING DESIGN AWARDS. For design originating in the U.S., voted by a committee comprising Tish Dace (chair), Michael Feingold, Henry Hewes and Michael Sommers. Scenic design, **John Arnone** for *Tommy.* Lighting design, **Mimi Jordan Sherin** for *Woyzeck.* Costume design, **Elizabeth Fried** for *Brother Truckers.* Noteworthy unusual effects, **Wendall K. Harrington** for *Tommy.*

43d ANNUAL OUTER CRITICS CIRCLE AWARDS. For outstanding achievement in the 1992–93 New York theater season, voted by an organization of critics on out-of-town periodicals and media. Broadway play, *The Sisters Rosensweig.* Performance by an actor in a play, **Robert Klein** in *The Sisters Rosensweig.* Performance by an actress in a play, **Madeline Kahn** in *The Sisters Rosensweig.* Broadway musical, *Tommy.* Actor in a musical, **Martin Short** in *The Goodbye Girl.* Actress in a musical, **Tonya Pinkins** in *Jelly's Last Jam.* Off-Broadway play, *Jeffrey.* Off-Broadway musical, *Ruthless!* Revival of a play, *Anna Christie.* Revival of a musical, *Carnival.* Director of a play, **Daniel Sullivan** for *The Sisters Rosensweig.* Director of a musical, **Des McAnuff** for *Tommy.* Choreography, **Hope Clarke, Gregory Hines** and **Ted L. Levy** for *Jelly's Last Jam.* Design, *Tommy* scenery by John Arnone, costumes by David C. Woolard, lighting by Chris Parry, projections by Wendall K. Harrington. Debut of an actor, **Stephen Rea** in *Someone Who'll Watch Over Me.* Debut of an actress, **Natasha Richardson** in *Anna Christie.* John Gassner Playwriting Award, **Paul Rudnick** for *Jeffrey.*

Special achievement awards: **Julie Andrews** for "returning to her roots" in *Putting It Together.* **David Shiner** and **Bill Irwin** for writing and starring in the unique work *Fool Moon.* **Broadway Angel Records** for their *Broadway Classics* series, a distinguished preservation of original cast recordings. James H. Fleetwood Award to a promising composer, **Rusty Magee** for *Scapin.*

38th ANNUAL DRAMA DESK AWARDS for outstanding achievement, voted by an association of New York drama reporters, editors and critics. New play, *Angels in America* by Tony Kushner. New musical, *Kiss of the Spider Woman* by Terrence McNally, John Kander and Fred Ebb. Director of a play, **George C. Wolfe** for *Angels in America.* Director of a musical, **Des McAnuff** for *Tommy.* Actor in a play, **Ron Leibman** in *Angels in America.* Actor in a musical, **Brent Carver** in *Kiss of the Spider*

Woman. Actress in a play, **Jane Alexander** in *The Sisters Rosensweig.* Actress in a musical, **Chita Rivera** in *Kiss of the Spider Woman.* Featured actor in a play, **Joe Mantello** and **Stephen Spinella** (tie) in *Angels in America.* Featured actor in a musical, **Mark Michael Hutchinson** in *Blood Brothers.* Featured actress in a play, **Madeline Kahn** in *The Sisters Rosensweig.* Featured actress in a musical, **Andrea Martin** in *My Favorite Year.* Music, **John Kander** for *Kiss of the Spider Woman.* Lyrics, **Joel Paley** for *Ruthless!* Orchestration, **Steve Margoshes** for *Tommy.* Choreography, **Wayne Cilento** for *Tommy.* Revival, *Anna Christie.* Scenery, **John Arnone** and **Wendall K. Harrington** for *Tommy.* Lighting, **Chris Parry** for *Tommy.* Costumes, **Florence Klotz** for *Kiss of the Spider Woman.* Solo performance, **Anna Deavere Smith** in *Fires in the Mirror.* Sound, **Steve Canyon Kennedy** for *Tommy.* Music in a play, **Ladysmith Black Mambazo** in *The Song of Jacob Zulu.* Unique theatrical experience, *Fool Moon.*

1993 Special Awards: **Early Stages** for its tenth year of providing theater tickets to New York City school children. **International Festival of Puppet Theater: Puppetry at the Public** for presenting outstanding puppetry from around the world. **RCA Victor** for its inspired documentation of theater music, past and present.

9th ANNUAL NEW YORK DANCE AND PERFORMANCE AWARDS (BESSIES). For exceptional achievement in the field of dance and related performance in the 1991–92 New York season, presented by Dance Theater Workshop. Choreographer/creator awards, **Donald Byrd** for *The Minstrel Show,* **Ping Chong and the Fiji Company** for sustained achievement, **Frank Conversano** for his body of work, **Craig Harris** and **Sekou Sundiata** for the Fire Wall Festival, **Linda Montano** for *7 Years of Living Art,* **Bernard Djola Branner, Brian Freeman** and **Eric Gupton** for *Fierce Love: Stories From Black Gay Life,* **Marta Renzi** for *Vital Signs,* **The Rhythm Technicians and Rock Steady Crew** for body of work, **Urban Bush Women** for body of work. Performer awards, **Kim Y. Bears** for Philadanco, **Steve Mellor** in *7 Blowjobs,* **Mark Robison** for work with Ringside, **Natalie Rogers** in *Griot/New York,* **Viola Sheely** in *Praise House* and *Vanquished by Voodoo,* **Scot Willingham.** Visual design awards, **Michael Mazzola** (lighting), **Gabriel Berry** (costumes) for *The Minstrel Show* and *Place,* **Donna Dennis** (settings) for *Quintland (The Musical),* **Martin Puryear** (settings) for *Griot/New York.* Composer awards, **Leroy Jenkins** for *The Mother of Three*

Sons, **Robert Mirabal** for *Land,* **Carl Riley** for *Praise House.*

Special citations: **Chuck Davis** and **Danceafrica; Howard Moody** for establishing the Judson Church Dance Theater; **Miguel Algarin, Willie Correa, Lois Griffith, Bob Holman, Roland Legiardi-Laura** of the Nuyorican Poets Cafe.

3d ANNUAL CONNECTICUT CRITICS CIRCLE AWARDS. Outstanding playwright, **A.R. Gurney** for his body of work. Outstanding contribution to Connecticut theater, **James B. McKenzie** of Westport Country Playhouse.

11th ANNUAL ELLIOT NORTON AWARDS. For distinguished contribution to the theater in Boston. Elliot Norton Medal, **Lynn Redgrave** for *Shakespeare for My Father.* Charlotte Cushman Prize for outstanding actress, **M. Lynda Robinson.** Otis Skinner Prize for outstanding actor, **Munson Hicks.** Henry Jewett Prize for outstanding direction, **Joann Zazofsky Green.** Robert Edmond Jones Prize for outstanding stage design, **Helen Pond** and **Herbert Senn.** Creative achievement, **Terrence McNally.** Lifetime achievement, **Claire Bloom.** Citation as honorees, **Walter Pierce, Beth Soll, John Williams, Citydance** (Frank Bourman and Mel A. Tomlinson, directors).

9th ANNUAL HELEN HAYES AWARDS. In recognition of excellence in Washington, D.C. Theater, presented by the Washington Theater Awards Society. Resident shows—Play, Arena Stage production of *Hamlet.* Musical, *Assassins* by John Weidman and Stephen Sondheim. Actor in a play, **Richard Bauer** in *The School for Wives.* Actress in a play, **Franchelle Stewart Dorn** in *The Visit.* Actor in a musical, **J. Fred Shiffman** in *Falsettoland.* Actress in a musical, **Rebecca Rice** in *In Living Colors.* Supporting actor in a play, **Floyd King** in *The Lisbon Traviata.* Supporting actress in a play, **Francesca Buller** in *Hamlet.* Supporting actress in a musical, **Ella Mitchell** in *Conrack.* Director of a play, **Michael Kahn** for *Hamlet.* Director of a musical, **Eric Schaeffer** for *Assassins.* Scenery, **James Kronzer** for *The Lisbon Traviata.* Costumes, **Paul Tazewell** for *The African Company Presents Richard III.* Lighting, **Howell Binkley** for *Hamlet.* Sound, **Jens McVoy** for *The Einstein Project.* Choreography, **Dianne McIntyre** for *In Living Colors.*

Non-resident shows—Production, Royal National Theater of Great Britain's *Richard III.* Actor, **Ian McKellen** in *Richard III.* Actress, **Julie Harris** in *Lettice & Lovage.*

Charles MacArthur Award for best new play, *Those Sweet Caresses* by Lucy Tom Lehrer. Washington *Post* Award for community service to **Source Theater Company** for its Washington Theater Festival of new works. KMPG Peat Marwick Award for distinguished service to the Washington theater community, **William Beltz** of the Bureau of National Affairs. Special American Express Award, **Stephen Sondheim.**

13 ANNUAL DORA MAVOR MOORE AWARDS. For outstanding achievement in Toronto theater. New play, *Escape From Happiness* by George F. Walker. New musical, *Ontario: Yours to Recover.* Production of a drama/ comedy, *Three Sisters.* Production of a revue/musical, *Closer Than Ever.* Female lead in a drama/comedy, **Nicola Cavendish** in *Shirley Valentine.* Male lead in a drama/comedy, **Rod Beattie** in *The Wingfield Trilogy.* Performances in a revue/musical, **Richard Greenblatt** and **Norma Dell'Agnese** in *God Almighty's Second Class Saloon: A Brecht/Weill Cabaret.* Direction of a drama/comedy, **Neil Munro** for *Hamlet* and **Second City** for *Shopping off to Buffalo.* Scene design in a revue/musical, **Phillip Silver** for *Aspects of Love.* Lighting design in a revue/ musical, **Louise Guinard** for *Aspects of Love.* Sound design in a drama/comedy, **Lesley Barber** and **Shirley Eikhard** for *Escape From Happiness.*

24th ANNUAL JOSEPH JEFFERSON AWARDS. For achievement in Chicago theater during the 1991–92 season. New work or adaptation, *My Thing of Love* by **Alexandra Gersten** and *The Song of Jacob Zulu* by **Tug Yourgrau.** Production of a play, *The Good Person of Setzuan* by the Goodman Theater. Production of a musical, *Phantom* by the Candlelight Dinner Playhouse. Production of a revue, *Spunk: Three Tales by Zora Neale Hurston* by the Goodman Theater. Director of a play, **Frank Galati** for *The Good Person of Setzuan* and **Gary Griffin** for *Stand-Up Tragedy* (tie). Director of a musical, **William Pullinsi** for *Phantom.* Director of a revue, **Donald Douglass** for *Spunk.* Actress in a principal role of a play, **Cherry Jones** in *The Good Person of Setzuan* and **Laurie Metcalf** in *My Thing of Love* (tie). Actor in a principal role of a play, **Denis O'Hare** in *Hauptmann.* Actress in a principal role of a musical, **E. Faye Butler** in *Hello, Dolly!.* Actor in a principal role of a musical, **James Harms** in *La Cage aux Folles.* Actress in a revue, **JoNell Kennedy** in *Spunk.* Actor in a revue, **Ellis Foster** in *Spunk.* Actress in a supporting role of a musical, **Peggy Roeder** in *Ar-*

thur: The Musical. Actor in a supporting role of a musical, **William Brown** in *Arthur: The Musical.* Actress in a supporting role of a play, **Pamela Webster** in *Eleemosynary.* Actor in a supporting role of a play, **David Anzuelo** in *Stand-Up Tragedy* and **Si Osborne** in *The Heidi Chronicles* (tie). Choreography, **Marc Robin** for *Hello, Dolly!.* Musical direction, **Nick Venden** for *Phantom.* Original music, **Lloyd Broadnax King** for *Macbeth* and **Claudia Schmidt** for *The Good Person of Setzuan* (tie). Scene design, **Michael Merritt** for *A Summer Remembered.* Costume design, **Jack Kirkby** for *La Cage aux Folles.* Lighting design, **Robert Shook** for *Macbeth.* Sound design, **Robert Neuhaus** for *Macbeth.*

Special awards: **Stanley Freehling** and **Bruce Sagan** for life achievement; **Ladysmith Black Mambazo** for its overall role in *The Song of Jacob Zulu.*

20th ANNUAL JOSEPH JEFFERSON CITATIONS. To recognize outstanding 1992–93 achievement in professional productions of Chicago area theaters not operating under union contracts. Production and ensemble, Lookingglass Theater Company's *The Arabian Nights,* Famous Door Theater's *The Conquest of the South Pole,* Stage Left Theater's *Leander Stillwell.* Director, **Calvin MacLean** for *The Conquest of the South Pole,* **Drew Martin** for *Leander Stillwell,* **Mary Zimmerman** for *The Arabian Nights.* Actress in a principal role, **Kelly Nespor** in *Virginia,* **Lee Roy Rogers** in *Prin,* **Karen Vaccaro** in *The Rose Tattoo.* Actor in a principal role, **Jeff Atkins** in *In the Flesh,* **Tim Decker** in *The Dresser,* **Christopher Eudy** in *Buddy,* **Benjamin Werling** in *Talk Radio.* Actress in a supporting role, **Tonray Ho** in *Mother Courage and Her Children.* Actor in a supporting role, **Tim Decker** in *Prin,* **Steve Kay** in *Talk Radio.* Scene design, **Steve Pickering** and **Greg Ballman** for *In the Flesh,* **Roger Smart** for *The Dresser,* **Robert G. Smith** for *The Conquest of the South Pole.* Costume design, **Patricia L. Hart** for *Mother Courage and Her Children,* **Allison Reeds** for *The Balcony,* **Sharon Sachs** for *The Conquest of the South Pole.* Lighting design, **Jeff Pines** for *The Conquest of the South Pole* and *Shrapnel in the Heart.* Sound design, **Michael Bodeen** for *In the Flesh.* New work or adaptation, **Christopher Cartmill** for *Light in Love,* **David Connelly** for *Shrapnel in the Heart,* **Paul Edwards** for *The End of the Road,* **Mary Zimmerman** for *The Arabian Nights.* Original music, **The Arabian Nights Company** for *The Arabian Nights,* **William Underwood** for *Mother Courage and Her Children.*

Choreography, **Lanet Louer** for *Buddy*. Musical direction, **Jim O'Connell** for *Buddy*. Special Award: **Business Volunteers for the Arts/Chicago** for facilitating the much-needed contribution of business expertise to Chicago's Theater Community.

24th ANNUAL LOS ANGELES DRAMA CRITICS CIRCLE AWARDS. For distinguished achievement in Los Angeles theater during 1992. Production; *The Kentucky Cycle* at Center Theater Group/Mark Taper Forum, Gordon Davidson producer, in association with Intiman Theater Company; *Angels in America: A Gay Fantasia on National Themes* at Center Theater Group/Mark Taper Forum, Gordon Davidson producer, in association with New York Shakespeare Festival; *Melody Jones* at CAST Theater, Diana Gibson producer, with BeBe Love Productions. Lead performance: **Kandis Chappell** in *Woman in Mind*, **Charles Hallahan** in *The Kentucky Cycle*, **Ed Harris** in *Scar*, **Nan Martin** in *Odd Jobs*, **Bebe Neuwirth** in *Chicago*, **Mark Sheppard** and **Trevor Goddard** in *Cock & Bull Story*, **Morgan Weisser** in *Being at Home With Claude*. Writing: **Tony Kushner** for *Angels in America*, **Robert Schenkkan** for *The Kentucky Cycle*. Direction: **Julie Cobb** for *Twelve Angry Men*, **Oskar Eustis** and **Tony Taccone** for *Angels in America*, **Ron Link** for *Melody Jones*. Creation performance: **John Fleck** for *A Snowball's Chance in Hell*, **Charlayne Woodard** for *Pretty Fire*. Ensemble performance: **Joel Blum, Shelley Dickinson, Marin Mazzie, John Ruess** and **Karen Ziemba** in *The World Goes 'Round*. Musical direction: **Steven Applegate** for *Candide*, **John McDaniel** for *Chicago*. Choreography: **Ann Reinking** for *Chicago*, **Susan Stroman** for *The World Goes 'Round*. Costume design: **Cara Varnell, Alex Jaeger** and **Lori Martin** for *Under the Gaslight;* **Ann Bruice** for *The Philadelphia Story*. Sound design: **Scott Watson** for *Melody Jones*. Lighting design: **Ken Booth** for *Melody Jones*, **Peter Maradudin** for *The Kentucky Cycle*. Musical performance: **Djimbe West African Dancers and Drummers** in *Twelfth Night*. Scene design: **Michael Olich** for *The Kentucky Cycle*.

Margaret Harford Award for achievement by the smaller theaters: **West Coast Ensemble.** Ted Schmitt Award: **Tony Kushner** for *Angels in America*. Angstrom Lighting Award: **Peter Maradudin.** Special Awards: **Theater Row Hollywood; Shakespeare Festival/LA.**

THE THEATER HALL OF FAME

The Theater Hall of Fame was created to honor those who have made outstanding contributions to the New York theater. Members are elected annually by the nation's drama critics and editors (names of those elected in 1993 appear in **bold face type**).

GEORGE ABBOTT
MAUDE ADAMS
VIOLA ADAMS
STELLA ADLER
EDWARD ALBEE
THEONI V. ALDREDGE
IRA ALDRIDGE
WINTHROP AMES
JUDITH ANDERSON
MAXWELL ANDERSON
ROBERT ANDERSON
MARGARET ANGLIN
HAROLD ARLEN
GEORGE ARLISS
BORIS ARONSON
ADELE ASTAIRE
FRED ASTAIRE
BROOKS ATKINSON
PEARL BAILEY
GEORGE BALANCHINE
ANNE BANCROFT
TALLULAH BANKHEAD
PHILIP BARRY
ETHEL BARRYMORE
JOHN BARRYMORE
LIONEL BARRYMORE
NORA BAYES
S. N. BEHRMAN
NORMAN BEL GEDDES
DAVID BELASCO
MICHAEL BENNETT
RICHARD BENNETT
IRVING BERLIN
SARAH BERNHARDT
LEONARD BERNSTEIN
EARL BLACKWELL
KERMIT BLOOMGARDEN
JERRY BOCK
RAY BOLGER
EDWIN BOOTH
JUNIUS BRUTUS BOOTH
SHIRLEY BOOTH

ALICE BRADY
FANNIE BRICE
PETER BROOK
JOHN MASON BROWN
BILLIE BURKE
ABE BURROWS
RICHARD BURTON
MRS. PATRICK CAMPBELL
ZOE CALDWELL
EDDIE CANTOR
MORRIS CARNOVSKY
MRS. LESLIE CARTER
GOWER CHAMPION
CAROL CHANNING
RUTH CHATTERTON
PADDY CHAYEFSKY
INA CLAIRE
BOBBY CLARK
HAROLD CLURMAN
LEE J. COBB
GEORGE M. COHAN
JACK COLE
CY COLEMAN
CONSTANCE COLLIER
BETTY COMDEN
MARC CONNELLY
KATHARINE CORNELL
NOEL COWARD
JANE COWL
CHERYL CRAWFORD
HUME CRONYN
RUSSEL CROUSE
CHARLOTTE CUSHMAN
JEAN DALRYMPLE
AUGUSTIN DALY
RUBY DEE
ALFRED DE LIAGRE JR.
AGNES DEMILLE
COLLEEN DEWHURST
HOWARD DIETZ
DUDLEY DIGGES
MELVYN DOUGLAS

ALFRED DRAKE
MARIE DRESSLER
JOHN DREW
MRS. JOHN DREW
MILDRED DUNNOCK
ELEANORA DUSE
JEANNE EAGELS
FRED EBB
FLORENCE ELDRIDGE
LEHMAN ENGEL
MAURICE EVANS
JOSE FERRER
DOROTHY FIELDS
HERBERT FIELDS
LEWIS FIELDS
W. C. FIELDS
MINNIE MADDERN FISKE
CLYDE FITCH
GERALDINE FITZGERALD
HENRY FONDA
LYNN FONTANNE
EDWIN FORREST
BOB FOSSE
RUDOLF FRIML
CHARLES FROHMAN
GRACE GEORGE
GEORGE GERSHWIN
IRA GERSHWIN
JOHN GIELGUD
WILLIAM GILLETTE
CHARLES GILPIN
LILLIAN GISH
JOHN GOLDEN
MAX GORDON
RUTH GORDON
ADOLPH GREEN
PAUL GREEN
CHARLOTTE GREENWOOD
TYRONE GUTHRIE
UTA HAGEN
OSCAR HAMMERSTEIN II
WALTER HAMPDEN

OTTO HARBACH
E. Y. HARBURG
SHELDON HARNICK
EDWARD HARRIGAN
JED HARRIS
ROSEMARY HARRIS
SAM H. HARRIS
REX HARRISON
LORENZ HART
MOSS HART
TONY HART
HELEN HAYES
LELAND HAYWARD
BEN HECHT
THERESA HELBURN
LILLIAN HELLMAN
KATHARINE HEPBURN
VICTOR HERBERT
JERRY HERMAN
AL HIRSCHFELD
RAYMOND HITCHCOCK
CELESTE HOLM
HANYA HOLM
ARTHUR HOPKINS
DE WOLF HOPPER
JOHN HOUSEMAN
EUGENE HOWARD
LESLIE HOWARD
SIDNEY HOWARD
WILLIE HOWARD
BARNARD HUGHES
HENRY HULL
WALTER HUSTON
WILLIAM INGE
ELSIE JANIS
JOSEPH JEFFERSON
AL JOLSON
JAMES EARL JONES
ROBERT EDMOND JONES
JOHN KANDER
GARSON KANIN
GEORGE S. KAUFMAN
DANNY KAYE
ELIA KAZAN
GENE KELLY
GEORGE KELLY
JEROME KERN
WALTER KERR
MICHAEL KIDD
SIDNEY KINGSLEY
BERT LAHR

BURTON LANE
LAWRENCE LANGNER
LILLIE LANGTRY
ANGELA LANSBURY
CHARLES LAUGHTON
ARTHUR LAURENTS
GERTRUDE LAWRENCE
JEROME LAWRENCE
EVA LE GALLIENNE
ROBERT E. LEE
LOTTE LENYA
ALAN JAY LERNER
SAM LEVENE
ROBERT LEWIS
BEATRICE LILLIE
HOWARD LINDSAY
FRANK LOESSER
FREDERICK LOEWE
JOSHUA LOGAN
PAULINE LORD
LUCILLE LORTEL
ALFRED LUNT
CHARLES MACARTHUR
ROUBEN MAMOULIAN
RICHARD MANSFIELD
ROBERT B. MANTELL
FREDRIC MARCH
JULIA MARLOWE
MARY MARTIN
RAYMOND MASSEY
SIOBHAN MCKENNA
HELEN MENKEN
BURGESS MEREDITH
ETHEL MERMAN
DAVID MERRICK
JO MIELZINER
ARTHUR MILLER
MARILYN MILLER
HELENA MODJESKA
FERENC MOLNAR
VICTOR MOORE
ZERO MOSTEL
PAUL MUNI
THARON MUSSER
GEORGE JEAN NATHAN
MILDRED NATWICK
NAZIMOVA
JAMES M. NEDERLANDER
ELLIOT NORTON
CLIFFORD ODETS
DONALD OENSLAGER

LAURENCE OLIVIER
EUGENE O'NEILL
GERALDINE PAGE
JOSEPH PAPP
OSGOOD PERKINS
MOLLY PICON
CHRISTOPHER PLUMMER
COLE PORTER
ROBERT PRESTON
HAROLD PRINCE
JOSE QUINTERO
MICHAEL REDGRAVE
ADA REHAN
ELMER RICE
LLOYD RICHARDS
RALPH RICHARDSON
CHITA RIVERA
JASON ROBARDS
JEROME ROBBINS
PAUL ROBESON
RICHARD RODGERS
WILL ROGERS
SIGMUND ROMBERG
HAROLD ROME
LILLIAN RUSSELL
GENE SAKS
WILLIAM SAROYAN
ALAN SCHNEIDER
ARTHUR SCHWARTZ
GEORGE C. SCOTT
ROBERT E. SHERWOOD
J. J. SHUBERT
LEE SHUBERT
HERMAN SHUMLIN
NEIL SIMON
LEE SIMONSON
OTIS SKINNER
OLIVER SMITH
STEPHEN SONDHEIM
E. H. SOTHERN
KIM STANLEY
MAUREEN STAPLETON
ROBERT L. STEVENS
ELLEN STEWART
DOROTHY STICKNEY
FRED STONE
LEE STRASBERG
JULE STYNE
MARGARET SULLAVAN
JESSICA TANDY
LAURETTE TAYLOR

ELLEN TERRY

TOMMY TUNE

GWEN VERDON

ELI WALLACH

JAMES WALLACK

LESTER WALLACK

TONY WALTON

DAVID WARFIELD

ETHEL WATERS

CLIFTON WEBB

JOSEPH WEBER

MARGARET WEBSTER

KURT WEILL

ORSON WELLES

MAE WEST

ROBERT WHITEHEAD

THORNTON WILDER

BERT WILLIAMS

TENNESSEE WILLIAMS

P. G. WODEHOUSE

PEGGY WOOD

IRENE WORTH

ED WYNN

VINCENT YOUMANS

STARK YOUNG

FLORENZ ZIEGFELD

1992–93 PUBLICATION OF
RECENTLY-PRODUCED PLAYS

Angels in America—Part One: Millennium Approaches. Tony Kushner. Theater Communications Group (paperback).
Four Baboons Adoring the Sun and Other Plays. John Guare. Random House (paperback).
Kentucky Cycle, The. Robert Schenkkan. Plume/New American Library (paperback).
Lost in Yonkers. Neil Simon. Random House.
Madness of George III, The. Alan Bennett. Faber & Faber (paperback).
Marvin's Room. Scott McPherson. New American Library.
Oleanna. David Mamet. Random House (paperback).
On the Open Road. Steve Tesich. Applause (paperback).
Pope and the Witch, The. Dario Fo. Methuen.
Redwood Curtain. Lanford Wilson. Hill & Wang.
Reflected Glory. Ronald Harwood. Faber & Faber.
Ride Down Mt. Morgan, The. Arthur Miller. Penguin (paperback).
Secret Garden, The. Marsha Norman. Theater Communications Group.
Someone Who'll Watch Over Me. Frank McGuinness. Faber & Faber.
Sisters Rosensweig, The. Wendy Wasserstein. Harcourt Brace.
Small Family Business, A. Alan Ayckbourn. Faber & Faber.
Substance of Fire, The. Jon Robin Baitz. Theater Communications Group.
Two Trains Running. August Wilson. Dutton.

A SELECTED LIST OF OTHER PLAYS
PUBLISHED IN 1992–93

Best Plays of 1992 by Women Playwrights, The. Robyn Goodman and Marisa Smith, editors. Smith & Kraus (paperback).
Chekhov for the Stage. Anton Chekhov. Northwestern University Press.
Definitive Simon Gray I, The. Simon Gray. Faber & Faber.
Definitive Simon Gray, II, The. Simon Gray. Faber & Faber.
Early Plays, The. David Hare. Faber & Faber (paperback).
Fantasio and Other Plays. Alfred de Musset. Theater Communications Group.
Four Plays: De Filippo. Eduardo De Filippo. Methuen (paperback).
Gay and Lesbian Plays Today. Terry Helbing, editor. Heinemann.
Jeffrey Bernard Is Unwell and Other Plays. Keith Waterhouse. Penguin (paperback).
Le Bourgeois Gentilhomme. Molière. Absolute Classics.
New American Plays 2. David Budbill, Jo Carson, Samuel L. Kelley, Janet Noble. Heinemann.
Plays: Egmont, Iphigenia in Tauris, Torquato Tasso. Johann Wolfgang von Goethe. Continuum (paperback).
Plays From the Contemporary British Theater. Brooks McNamara, editor. New American Library (paperback).
Plays One: Aristophanes. Methuen (paperback).
Plays Two: Aristophanes. Methuen (paperback).
Plays One: Granville Barker. Methuen (paperback).
Plays One: Dario Fo. Methuen (paperback).
Plays One: Storey. David Storey. Methuen (paperback).
Plays One: Wedekind. Frank Wedekind. Methuen (paperback).
Playwriting Women: 7 Plays From the Women's Project. Julia Miles, editor. Heinemann.
Rug Merchants of Chaos, The and Other Plays. Ronald Ribman. Theater Communications Group.
States of Shock/Far North/Silent Tongue. Sam Shepard. Random House.

Stoppard: The Plays for Radio 1964–1983. Faber & Faber (paperback).
Thebans, The. Sophocles. Faber & Faber (paperback).
Three Plays—Frisch. Max Frisch. Methuen (paperback).
Three Trips to Bountiful. Horton Foote. Southern Methodist University (paperback).
Under a Mantle of Stars. Manuel Puig. Lumen Books (paperback).
Witkiewicz Reader, The. Stanislaw Ignacy Witkiewicz. Northwestern University (paperback).

NECROLOGY

MAY 1992—MAY 1993

PERFORMERS

Abbado, Joseph F. Jr. (47)—December 4, 1992
Acosta, Vince (30)—July 8, 1992
Adams, Diana (66)—January 10, 1993
Addison, Chuck (74)—February 5, 1993
Ades, Daniel (59)—May 30, 1992
Adler, Stella (91)—December 21, 1992
Aguilar, Thomas J. (41)—May 7, 1993
Ahern, Gladys (80s)—June 12, 1992
Alexander, Tom (29)—June 24, 1992
Allen, Harley (63)—April 3, 1993
Allen, Malcolm (58)—February 22, 1993
Anders, Laurie (70)—October 4, 1992
Anderson, John (69)—August 7, 1992
Anderson, Marian (96)—April 8, 1993
Andrews, Dana (83)—December 17, 1992
Arletty (94)—July 24, 1992
Arsenault, Martin—September 23, 1992
Ashby, Joan Marshall (61)—June 28, 1992
Atterbury, Malcolm (85)—August 23, 1992
Atwell, James Douglas (47)—January 21, 1993
Audley, Maxine (69)—July 23, 1992
Baker, Dorothy Helen (78)—October 15, 1992
Bakewell, Billy (85)—April 15, 1993
Banky, Vilma (93)—March 18, 1993
Battle, Edwin Louis (33)—February 23, 1993
Bechi, Gino (79)—February 2, 1993
Bee, Jimmy (59)—April 22, 1993
Bergfelt, Ula Sharon (87)—January 19, 1993
Bergman, Jerry (72)—April 12, 1993
Berini, Mario (80)—March 8, 1993
Berkeley, George (70)—February 1, 1993
Beyers, Bill (37)—May 29, 1992
Bissell, Jennifer Raine (60)—January 5, 1993
Bjorling, Rolf (64)—March 31, 1993
Bletcher, Arline (99)—July 3, 1992
Booth, Alan (46)—January 24, 1993
Booth, Shirley (94)—October 16, 1992
Bourne, Bonnie (89)—March 20, 1993
Boxer, Warren Neal (34)—May 17, 1992
Braden, Bernard (76)—February 2, 1993
Branda, Richard (57)—January 7, 1993
Briggs, Robert (39)—September 15, 1992
Britten, Enid (46)—January 22, 1993
Brocco, Peter (89)—January 3, 1993
Brooks, Beverly (63)—August 12, 1992

Brooks, Patricia (59)—January 22, 1993
Brown, Charles (38)—December 1, 1992
Brown, Eddie (74)—December 28, 1992
Brown, Georgia (58)—June 6, 1992
Brown, Lucille E. (74)—August 21, 1992
Bugler, Gertrude (95)—August 6, 1992
Burgess, Jim (39)—January 8, 1993
Burks, Stephen (36)—November 26, 1992
Burroughs, Eric (81)—November 12, 1992
Butler, Alistair (42)—September 14, 1992
Caldwell, Toy T. Jr. (45)—February 25, 1993
Cantinflas (Mario Moreno Reyes) (81)—April 20, 1993
Carey, Joyce (94)—February 28, 1993
Carnovsky, Morris (94)—September 1, 1992
Carothers, Ruth Tester (89)—March 21, 1993
Carpenter, Constance (87)—December 26, 1992
Carrol, Regina (49)—November 4, 1992
Carter, Beverly J. (51)—June 8, 1992
Casselman, Kevin M.A. (67)—February 5, 1993
Cattani, Rico (64)—November 12, 1992
Chaliapin, Feodor Jr. (87)—September 17, 1992
Claire, George (81)—April 17, 1993
Clayworth, June (early 80s)—January 1, 1993
Coles, Charles (81)—November 12, 1992
Collard, Cyril (35)—March 5, 1993
Conners, Chuck (71)—November 10, 1992
Constantine, Eddie (75)—February 25, 1993
Coolidge, Allan (43)—February 27, 1993
Corbett, Glenn (59)—January 16, 1993
Corday, Rita (68)—November 23, 1992
Cordial, Gary (39)—June 15, 1992
Cory, Ken (51)—January 15, 1993
Cronin, Laurel (58)—October 26, 1992
Danielewski, Tad Z. (71)—January 6, 1993
Davis, John H. (78)—November 3, 1992
de Groot, Katherine Hynes (88)—March 27, 1993
Delauder, Doug (38)—June 30, 1992
DeLoatch, Gary (40)—April 2, 1993
Desmond, Florence (87)—January 16, 1993
Dixon, Joan (61)—February 20, 1992
Donahue, Maugene Hughes (65)—April 1, 1993
Donn, Jorge (45)—November 30, 1992
Drake, Alfred (78)—July 25, 1992

Duffy, John Paul (42)—March 28, 1993
Duval, Jose F. (72)—February 27, 1993
Ellerbe, Harry (91)—December 3, 1992
Elliott, Denholm (70)—October 6, 1992
Ellsworth, Warren Aldrich III (42)—February 25, 1993
Evans, Geraint (70)—September 20, 1992
Ewell, Patricia B. (93)—October 25, 1992
Faye, Bobby (82)—August 12, 1992
Fennell, Willie (72)—September 8, 1992
Festa, James (36)—November 10, 1992
Fontana, Richard (40)—June 26, 1992
Ford, Constance (69)—February 26, 1993
Freeman, Tiki (69)—June 27, 1992
Frost, Terry (86)—March 1, 1993
Ganjou, Joy (80)—July 27, 1992
Garcia, Joaquin (71)—May 14, 1993
Garden, Jean Shaw (89)—July 11, 1992
Gardenia, Vincent (71)—December 9, 1992
Garrett, Joy (47)—February 11, 1993
Gavert, Paul (76)—March 11, 1992
Gentry, Minnie (77)—May 6, 1993
George, Joseph L. (65)—July 31, 1992
Gill, Ray (42)—September 27, 1992
Gish, Lillian (99)—February 27, 1993
Gordon, Sidney (72)—June 23, 1992
Grant, Michael (65)—October 15, 1992
Gregg, Martin (51)—October 11, 1992
Gregory, Dennis (40)—March 15, 1993
Greindl, Josef (80)—April 16, 1993
Haakon, Paul (80)—August 16, 1992
Hammerhead, Nicky (32)—November 20, 1992
Hancock, John (51)—October 13, 1992
Harris, Geraldine Delaney (67)—May 29, 1992
Harris, William E. (37)—June 25, 1992
Hayes, Helen (92)—March 17, 1993
Hazlett, Marlene—June 11, 1992
Hepburn, Audrey (63)—January 20, 1993
Herbert, Percy (72)—December 6, 1992
Hewitt, Paul F. (39)—October 12, 1992
Hilbert, Dora (77)—January 4, 1993
Hill, Jacqueline (63)—February 18, 1993
Hoff, Louise (69)—June 1, 1992
Holloway, Sterling (87)—November 22, 1992
Holland, John (85)—May 21, 1993
Hudnut, Bill (47)—October 24, 1992
Hunt, Frances (77)—February 6, 1993
Jacobson, Gerald E. (46)—December 26, 1992
Jarvis, Patience (56)—April 12, 1993
Jensen, Lenore Kinston (79)—May 5, 1993
Johnson, Marv (54)—May 16, 1993
Jones, Alice (87)—September 30, 1992
Jones, Allan (84)—June 27, 1992
Jones, Charlotte (76)—November 6, 1992
Jones, David C. (76)—September 14, 1992

Jones, Roderick (82)—September 16, 1992
Jonson, Kevin Joe (74)—July 12, 1992
Kane, Mardi Bayne (69)—February 27, 1993
Karas, Barry (49)—April 13, 1993
Keeler, Ruby (83)—February 28, 1993
Kelly, Jack (65)—November 7, 1992
Kendricks, Eddie (52)—October 5, 1992
Kenny, Herbert C. (78)—July 11, 1992
King, Michael (69)—June 1, 1992
Kirsten, Dorothy (82)—November 18, 1992
Krugman, Lou (78)—August 8, 1992
Lamb, Jim (29)—February 18, 1993
Landis, David (42)—August 1, 1992
Laufkotter, Karl (93)—December 14, 1992
Lee, Brandon (28)—March 31, 1993
Lee, Irving Allen (43)—September 5, 1992
Lee, Pinky (85)—April 3, 1993
LeMassena, William (76)—January 19, 1993
Leontovich, Eugenie (93)—April 2, 1993
Lessman, Hope Miller (63)—July 25, 1992
Liss, Ted (72)—March 3, 1993
Little, Cleavon (53)—October 22, 1992
Lopez-Cepero, Luis (52)—July 4, 1992
Lowenstein, Cary Scott (30)—November 29, 1992
Lynch, Frank J. (90)—September 30, 1992
Mack, Wayne (68)—April 1, 1993
Mannin, Marvelyn—September 3, 1992
Marshall, Brenda (76)—July 30, 1992
McCleod, Mercer (86)—January 20, 1993
McDonald, Michael Austin (39)—July 4, 1992
Miller, Clarence (69)—June 9, 1992
Miller, Dorothy (86)—October 15, 1992
Miller, Hope (63)—July 25, 1992
Millett, Timothy (37)—November 17, 1992
Millhollin, James (77)—May 23, 1993
Mitchell, Chuck (64)—June 22, 1992
Molinari, Antoinette (63)—October 16, 1992
Moore, Brian (59)—May 8, 1992
Moreno, Rosita (85)—April 25, 1993
Morley, Robert (84)—June 3, 1992
Morrison, Michael (33)—February 19, 1993
Munro, Nan (87)—June 16, 1992
Musselman, David (38)—September 23, 1992
Myhers, John (70)—May 27, 1992
Nabbie, Jim (72)—September 12, 1992
Naismith, Lawrence (83)—June 5, 1992
Nelson, Ruth (87)—September 12, 1992
Norman, Leslie (81)—February 18, 1993
Northern, Chauncey Scott (90)—September 22, 1992
Nureyev, Rudolf (54)—January 6, 1993
O'Brien, Mortimer J. (82)—June 18, 1992
Ochoa, Diana (80)—March 5, 1993
O'Donnell, Gene (81)—November 22, 1992
Olheim, Helen (87)—June 26, 1992
Oliver, David (30)—November 12, 1992

Olson, Howard M. (81)—June 26, 1992
O'Neal, Frederick (86)—August 25, 1992
Orloff, Thelma (76)—November 23, 1992
Outlaw, John (37)—March 8, 1993
Overton, Phyllis Hill Ferrer (72)—January 1, 1993
Ozker, Eren (44)—February 25, 1993
Palucca, Gret (91)—March 22, 1993
Parker, William (49)—March 29, 1993
Peardon, Patricia (69)—April 22, 1993
Parris, London (61)—September 7, 1992
Paxton, Marie—August 16, 1992
Peck, Ed (75)—September 12, 1992
Perkins, Anthony (60)—September 12, 1992
Peters, Lennie (59)—October 10, 1992
Phelps, Donald (61)—February 16, 1993
Philbin, Mary (59)—May 7, 1993
Porrello, Joseph (56)—June 22, 1992
Prentice, Keith (52)—September 27, 1992
Ralston, Howard—June 1, 1992
Ramos, Lou (51)—June 23, 1992
Randolph, Donald (87)—March 16, 1993
Ray, Harry Milton (45)—October 1, 1992
Reade, Charles A. (82)—August 29, 1992
Reed, Taylor (60)—March 24, 1993
Reese, Robert (66)—November 14, 1992
Reid, Kate (62)—March 27, 1993
Riley, Larry (39)—June 6, 1992
Rini, David (40)—July 20, 1992
Rio, Joan Maloney (57)—October 28, 1992
Rivera, Luis (54)—December 9, 1992
Rivers, Al (65)—February 17, 1993
Rivers, Mavis (63)—May 29, 1992
Robbins, Duke (71)—September 16, 1992
Robbins, Michael (62)—December 11, 1992
Robinson, Cardew (75)—December 27, 1992
Rowen, Glenn (59)—December 20, 1992
Rubenstein, Phil (51)—June 26, 1992
Sacha, Kenny (39)—August 1, 1992
Sachs, Scotty (39)—June 11, 1992
Sale-Wren, Virginia (92)—August 23, 1992
Sanders, Fetaque (77)—June 2, 1992
Sanderson, Joan (79)—May 24, 1992
Sanford, Mary Duncan (98)—May 9, 1993
Santos, Daniel (76)—November 27, 1992
Schwartz, Irv (75)—January 15, 1993
Schwartz, Sammy (86)—August 13, 1992
Seay, James (78)—October 10, 1992
Segal, Vivienne (95)—December 29, 1992
Seymour, Dan (78)—May 25, 1993
Shayne, Robert (92)—November 29, 1992
Sheldon, Richard (59)—February 22, 1992
Siegrist, Jeremy (20)—March 30, 1993
Siminski, Kenneth (41)—March 22, 1993
Simon, Robert F. (83)—November 29, 1992
Sinclair, Ronald (68)—Winter 1993
Singuineau, Frank—September 11, 1992

Smart, Richard (79)—November 12, 1992
Smith, Philip Justin (33)—September 17, 1992
Souez, Ina (89)—December 7, 1992
Steadman, John (83)—January 28, 1993
Steel, Pippa (44)—May 29, 1992
Strait, Ralph (56)—July 31, 1992
Sweeney, Bob (73)—June 7, 1992
Tajo, Italo (77)—March 29, 1993
Thom, Ruth Corbett (78)—December 7, 1992
Thomas, Dawn Eldridge (72)—April 1, 1993
Thorson, Marilyn McCrudden (62)—July 3, 1992
Tindall, Hilary (54)—December 5, 1992
Todd, Ann (82)—May 6, 1993
Todd, Christopher (30)—August 9, 1992
Toney, Edna Amadon (79)—April 13, 1993
Torena, Natalie Moorhead (91)—October 1992
Townsend, Patricia (67)—June 6, 1992
Trace, Christopher (59)—September 5, 1992
Turner, Teddy (75)—August 29, 1992
Valli, June (64)—March 12, 1993
Varsi, Diane (54)—November 19, 1992
Velie, Janet (96)—December 17, 1992
von Zerneck, Peter (84)—June 10, 1992
Waring, Richard (82)—January 19, 1993
Warriner, Frederic (76)—November 19, 1992
Warriss, Ben (83)—January 14, 1993
Watchetaker, George Smith (77)—May 27, 1993
Waters, Marlys Ann (64)—February 13, 1993
Webb, Tad (30)—September 9, 1992
Webber, Ron (60)—July 26, 1992
Wellington, Valerie (33)—January 2, 1993
Wells, Mary (49)—July 26, 1992
Welsh, Ronnie (52)—January 5, 1993
Whelan, Arleen (78)—April 8, 1993
Whelan, Kenneth (72)—April 4, 1993
White, Glenn (42)—May 27, 1992
White, John I. (90)—November 26, 1992
Wilbern, George E. (77)—February 17, 1993
Wilkinson, Kate (76)—February 9, 1993
Williams, Bill (77)—September 21, 1992
Williams, Franklin (45)—March 22, 1993
Williams, Tony (64)—August 14, 1992
Worden, Hank (91)—December 6, 1992
Wrightson, Earl (77)—March 7, 1993
Wulf, Richard (65)—December 17, 1992
Young, Skip (63)—March 17, 1993

PLAYWRIGHTS

Bird, David (85)—January 10, 1993
Brusati, Franco (66)—February 28, 1993
Clarke, Tom (74)—January 15, 1993

Conrad, Constance—Summer 1992
Combs, Frederick (57)—September 19, 1992
Douglas-Home, William (80)—September 28, 1992
Dunne, Philip (84)—May 2, 1992
Elverman, Bill (40)—August 13, 1992
Ephron, Henry (81)—September 6, 1992
Finsterwald, Maxine Flora (87)—April 7, 1993
Fraser, June Joyce Lewis (75)—November 28, 1992
Gow, Ronald (95)—April 27, 1993
Hailey, Oliver (60)—January 23, 1993
Hersey, John (78)—March 24, 1993
Kanin, Michael (83)—March 12, 1993
Kvares, Donald (57)—May 5, 1993
Litwak, Ezra (33)—August 31, 1992
Long, Sumner Arthur (71)—January 6, 1993
MacDougall, Roger (82)—May 27, 1993
Maddow, Ben (83)—October 9, 1992
Mankiewicz, Joseph L. (83)—February 5, 1993
McPherson, Scott (33)—November 7, 1992
Noel, Maurice (52)—July 19, 1992
Reyes, Albert Bosco (51)—October 26, 1992
Sahl, Hans (90)—April 27, 1993
Sergel, Christopher (75)—May 7, 1993
Sharkey, Jack (61)—September 28, 1992
Stevens, Dudley (57)—January 23, 1993
Swarthout, Glendon—September 23, 1992
Weiss, Karen Sue (49)—March 2, 1993

Lasser, Brian Alan (40)—November 20, 1992
Lowe, Sammy—February 18, 1993
Lunchbox, Deacon (41)—April 19, 1993
Mathias, William (57)—July 29, 1992
Miller, Roger (56)—October 25, 1992
Mondello, Toots (81)—November 15, 1992
Morse, Paul (45)—August 7, 1992
Motta, Gustavo A. Jr. (46)—February 6, 1993
Oldheim, Kevin (32)—March 11, 1993
Parish, Mitchell (92)—March 31, 1993
Pepper, Buddy (70)—February 14, 1993
Phillips, Murray (83)—January 19, 1993
Piazzolla, Astor (71)—July 6, 1992
Ross, David (58)—November 27, 1992
Rothmuller, Marko (84)—January 20, 1993
Russell, Bill (87)—August 9, 1992
Russell, Bobby (52)—November 19, 1992
Sallington, George (69)—February 15, 1993
Shapiro, Constantine (95)—May 25, 1992
Smith, Valerian (66)—November 18, 1992
Spencer, Herbert (87)—September 18, 1992
Swift, Kay (95)—January 28, 1993
Timberg, Sammy (89)—August 26, 1992
Volinkaty, John E. (49)—September 4, 1992
Walsh, Keith Keeler (40)—September 25, 1992
Wayne, Bernie (74)—April 18, 1993
Welin, Karl-Erik (58)—May 30, 1992

PRODUCERS, DIRECTORS CHOREOGRAPHERS

Adair, Tom (57)—February 1, 1993
Alum, Manuel (50)—May 10, 1993
Amon, Bob (78)—November 3, 1992
Andre, Raoul (76)—November 3, 1992
Andrews, Jerome (84)—October 26, 1992
Anthony, Joseph (80)—January 20, 1993
Banks, Danny (52)—September 27, 1992
Barclift, Edgar Nelson (76)—March 11, 1993
Bauman, Art—January 27, 1993
Bowyer, John (45)—August 10, 1992
Burstin, Joseph R. (85)—December 27, 1992
Cohen, Philip H. (80)—July 16, 1992
Cooper, Ralph (80s)—August 4, 1992
Cottle, Graham D. (51)—March 3, 1993
Darrid, William (69)—July 11, 1992
Daugherty, Herschel (82)—March 5, 1993
Eastwood, David P. (48)—June 26, 1992
Ehrlich, Henry (80)—June 12, 1992
Epstein, David S. (73)—July 7, 1992
Falco, Louis (50)—March 26, 1993
Farrell, Patric (85)—July 30, 1992
Fibich, Judith Berg (80)—August 19, 1992
Fielding, Sol Baer (83)—September 2, 1992

COMPOSERS, LYRICISTS, SONGWRITERS

Albert, Stephen J. (51)—December 27, 1992
Allen, Peter (48)—June 18, 1992
Assante, Allison (early 70s)—December 11, 1992
Barlow, Harold (77)—February 15, 1993
Batchelor, Ruth (57)—July 23, 1992
Bowles, Anthony (61)—March 15, 1993
Cage, John (79)—August 12, 1992
Cahn, Sammy (79)—January 15, 1993
Dolin, Gerald Lincoln (79)—December 31, 1992
Erkkila, Dan (51)—November 1, 1992
Franchetti, Arnold—March 11, 1993
Gaburo, Kenneth (65)—January 26, 1993
Garvarentz, George (61)—March 19, 1993
Greene, Mort (80)—December 28, 1992
Hemric, Guy Bonson (61)—January 10, 1993
Hester, Hal (63)—September 13, 1992
Jabara, Paul (44)—September 29, 1992
Johnson, David L. (47)—May 29, 1992

Foote, Lillian Vallish (69)—August 5, 1992
Foreman, John C. (67)—November 20, 1992
Foster, Skip (40)—September 5, 1992
Fournier, Bill (70)—October 28, 1992
Fournier, Robert E. (56)—March 11, 1993
Freedman, Lewis (66)—June 26, 1992
Gerberg, Gary (49)—December 29, 1992
Goodson, Mark (77)—December 19, 1992
Gordon, Michael (83)—April 29, 1993
Greer, Edward G. (73)—April 30, 1993
Hatcher, James F. Jr. (71)—March 19, 1993
Heyes, Douglas (73)—February 8, 1993
Holm, Hanya (99)—November 3, 1992
Jackson, Felix (90)—December 7, 1992
Jackson, John Henry—April 13, 1993
Jurist, Ed (76)—March 12, 1993
Keane, Joe (69)—January 4, 1993
Keegan, Terry (59)—January 29, 1993
King, Bruce (67)—January 1, 1993
King, Herman (77)—July 20, 1992
Levan, Larry (38)—November 8, 1992
Lewis, Russell L. (84)—December 9, 1992
Lynn, Jack (67)—January 20, 1993
Mattioli, Louis (38)—December 1, 1992
McMillan, Kenneth (62)—October 29, 1992
Merritt, Steve (48)—January 26, 1993
Minami, George Jr. (53)—December 28, 1992
Mitchell, Coleman (48)—November 17, 1992
Mnouchkine, Alexandre (85)—April 8, 1993
Nigro, Robert (45)—August 5, 1992
Nikolais, Alwin (82)—May 8, 1993
Nirenska, Pola (81)—July 25, 1992
Parham, Ernie (64)—January 22, 1993
Parker, Graham (61)—October 7, 1992
Parson, Lindsley Sr. (87)—October 9, 1992
Peralta, Delfor (64)—July 21, 1992
Roach, Hal (100)—November 2, 1992
Robins, Sylvia Friedlander (74)—November 7, 1992
Rosenberg, Mark (44)—November 6, 1992
Safir, Leonard (71)—December 13, 1992
Sanger, Eleanor (63)—March 7, 1993
Schaffel, Hal (78)—April 21, 1993
Schirmer, Gustave (73)—June 10, 1992
Schwab, Buddy (62)—December 1, 1992
Serpe, Ralph B. (81)—October 24, 1992
Sherman, Emilia—February 28, 1993
Sturges, John (82)—August 18, 1992
Tavares, Albert (39)—July 29, 1992
Thomas, Ted (88)—October 28, 1992
Thomashefsky, Harry (97)—January 28, 1993
Valentine, Victor (40)—October 1, 1992
Wallace, Allen (39)—December 12, 1992
Westbrook, Frank (82)—March 20, 1993
Wilder, Anne G. (63)—September 27, 1992
Wilson, Frank (37)—February 6, 1993
Wilson, Lester (51)—February 14, 1993

Wyler, Jorie (61)—October 27, 1992
Young, Howard (81)—Spring 1993

MUSICIANS

Alvarez, Alfred (72)—August 1, 1992
Babin, Vitya Vronsky (82)—June 28, 1992
Barnes, Buddy (53)—September 11, 1992
Bell, Leatha—February 18, 1993
Bond, Ronnie (51)—November 13, 1992
Burke, Louis (71)—July 6, 1992
Carisi, Johnny (70)—October 3, 1992
Carmirelli, Pina (79)—February 27, 1993
Cascella, John J. (45)—November 14, 1992
Dorsey, Thomas A. (93)—January 23, 1993
Douglas, Steve (55)—April 19, 1993
Dubman, Laura (69)—December 30, 1992
Gazzelloni, Severino (73)—November 21, 1992
Gillespie, Dizzy (75)—January 6, 1993
Harvey, Rick (43)—April 5, 1993
Hernandez, Freddy (25)—April 15, 1993
Hodes, Art (88)—March 4, 1993
Horszwoski, Mieczyslaw (100)—May 22, 1993
Jordan, Clifford (61)—March 27, 1993
King, Albert (69)—December 21, 1992
LaKind, Bobby (47)—December 24, 1992
Londin, Larrie (48)—August 24, 1992
Lorango, Thomas (33)—December 30, 1992
Madison, David (85)—July 24, 1992
Magaloff, Nikita (80)—December 26, 1993
Manchester, David—January 2, 1993
Marsh, Ozan (71)—March 15, 1993
Masselos, William (72)—October 23, 1992
McGary, Jimmy (66)—April 15, 1993
Milstein, Nathan (88)—December 21, 1992
Mitchell, Keith (65)—November 8, 1992
Montoya, Carlos (89)—March 3, 1993
Moore, Freddie (92)—November 3, 1992
Newman, Joe (70)—July 4, 1992
Norman, Fred (82)—February 19, 1993
Palmer, Singleton (80)—March 8, 1993
Peagler, Curtis (55)—December 19, 1992
Phillips, Linn III (45)—March 23, 1993
Popp, William N. (54)—August 25, 1992
Porcaro, Jeff (38)—August 5, 1992
Richley, Edward Charles (91)—January 22, 1993
Riley, Teddy (68)—November 14, 1992
Rizzi, Trefoni (69)—June 2, 1992
Roberts, Howard (62)—June 26, 1992
Ross, Rick A. (40)—January 10, 1993
Rowley, Sean (23)—November 8, 1992
Rupp, Franz (99)—May 27, 1992
Sidney, Sid—November 18, 1992

Tamburello, Tony (72)—September 29, 1992
Taylor, Alex (47)—March 12, 1993
Thomas, Theodore (84)—November 7, 1992
Wallington, George (69)—February 15, 1993
Ward, Jeff (30)—March 19, 1993
Wasowski, Andrzej (69)—May 26, 1993
Winter, Paul (78)—August 22, 1992

CONDUCTORS

Aliferis, James (78)—May 22, 1992
Bright, David (49)—November 9, 1992
Brown, H. Arthur (86)—May 27, 1992
Crosby, Bob (80)—March 9, 1993
Davison, Arthur (73)—August 23, 1992
Eckstine, Billy (78)—March 8, 1993
Grebnick, Al (73)—June 1, 1992
Groves, Charles (77)—June 20, 1992
Kirk, Andy (94)—December 11, 1992
Kojian, Varujan (57)—March 4, 1993
Oliver, Lynn (68)—July 20, 1992
Pastor, Guy (55)—October 28, 1992
Pierce, Nathaniel (66)—June 10, 1992
Routh, John (75)—January 10, 1993
Schneider, Alexander (84)—February 2, 1993
Sillet, Carl W. (88)—September 9, 1992
Smith, William (68)—March 24, 1993
Temianka, Henri (85)—November 7, 1992
Torkanowsky, Werner (66)—October 20, 1992
Wagner, Roger (78)—September 17, 1992

CRITICS

Anderson, George (60)—September 5, 1992
Barber, Charles Andrew (35)—July 4, 1992
Beaufort, John (79)—September 16, 1992
Biancolli, Louis (85)—June 13, 1992
Cohen, Stephen H. (53)—August 22, 1992
Daney, Serge (48)—June 11, 1992
Edwards, Douglas (44)—February 2, 1993
Feld, Hans (90)—July 15, 1992
Funke, Lewis B. (80)—June 26, 1992
Gertner, Richard (66)—September 14, 1992
Gilliatt, Penelope (61)—May 4, 1993
Gould, Jack (79)—May 24, 1993
Harvey, Stephen (43)—January 1, 1993
Katz, Ephraim (60)—August 2, 1992
Moore, William (59)—October 24, 1992
O'Leary, Liam (82)—December 15, 1992
Platt, David (89)—December 17, 1992
Prideaux, Tom (85)—May 8, 1993
Root, Wells (92)—March 8, 1993
Ryweck, Charles (76)—June 1, 1992

Sargent, Thornton (90)—April 22, 1993
Toita, Yasuji (77)—January 23, 1993

DESIGNERS

Buck, Gene Davis (49)—October 1, 1992
Clatworthy, William Robert (80)—March 2, 1993
Frazer, Anna Mae (90)—April 25, 1993
Gottesman, Edward H. (41)—September 28, 1992
Holamon, Ken (45)—January 9, 1993
Johnstone, Anna (79)—October 16, 1992
Juel, Gordon A. (39)—March 15, 1993
Jung, Philip C. (43)—December 10, 1992
Martin, William O. (58)—October 5, 1992
Merritt, Michael (47)—August 3, 1992
Nelson, George R. (65)—August 25, 1992
Nutter, Tommy (49)—August 17, 1992
Peak, Robert (64)—August 6, 1992
Sabatino, Anthony (48)—April 10, 1993
Savoy, Louis (89)—April 16, 1993
Snyder, Huck (39)—January 23, 1993
Stoessel, Jessica Haston (27)—July 21, 1992
Summerfield, Marvin (79)—September 13, 1992
Ter-Arutunian, Rouben (72)—October 17, 1992

OTHERS

Acuff, Roy (89)—November 23, 1992
    Country music
Allen, John E. Jr. (58)—February 25, 1993
    Founder, Freedom Theater
Andrews, Bert (63)—January 25, 1993
    Photographer
Baker, Joy (64)—April 24, 1993
    Kennedy Center
Balis, C. Wanton Jr. (86)—February 4, 1993
    Philadelphia Orchestra Assn.
Barber, Red (84)—October 22, 1992
    Sportscaster
Berg, Joseph Adam (37)—May 7, 1993
    Agent
Berliner, Dale (32)—October 31, 1992
    Press agent
Berman, Sydney (80)—February 5, 1993
    Editor
Bernstein, Jeffrey Alan (40)—July 10, 1992
    Lawyer
Bernstein, Sidney Lewis (94)—February 5, 1993
    Granada TV

Berthelson, Larry (60)—April 8, 1993
Pickwick Puppet Theater
Birmingham, Thomas (63)—March 1, 1993
Wisconsin Ballet Theater
Blasi, Rafe (55)—August 2, 1992
Editor
Blaze, Carol M. (86)—August 5, 1992
Writers Guild Theater
Brackman, Al (80)—October 9, 1992
Music publisher
Burkat, Leonard (73)—August 23, 1992
Tanglewood Music Center
Burnett, Harry (92)—May 28, 1993
Puppeteer
Caviano, Bob (42)—September 23, 1992
Agent
Charteris, Leslie (85)—April 16, 1993
Mystery writer
Christopher, Robert C. (68)—June 14, 1992
Pulitzer Prize board
Cree, George (55)—March 4, 1993
Theater manager
Crichton, Robert (68)—March 23, 1993
Novelist
Crist, William B. (81)—April 1, 1993
Public relations counselor
Devlin, Edward L. (38)—October 26, 1992
Press agent
Douds, Dave Smith (54)—June 7, 1992
Agent
Dufine, Herbert (61)—May 29, 1992
Stage manager
Frutin, Alex (89)—June 16, 1992
Scottish theater
Gaines, John (54)—November 21, 1992
Agent
Gaines, William M. (70)—June 3, 1992
Mad magazine
Giddens, Kenneth R. (84)—May 7, 1993
Voice of America
Goodman, Martin (84)—June 13, 1992
Marvel Comics
Gutman, John (90)—August 4, 1992
Metropolitan Opera
Hausman, Howard L. (77)—September 22, 1992
Agent
Henderson, Inge (72)—September 4, 1992
Alexander Technique
Homan, Melvin M. (50)—August 14, 1992
Set painter
Hopkins, Charles B. (92)—January 18, 1993
Sound engineer
Horn, John (76)—March 2, 1993
Press agent
Hughes, Herbert J. (68)—May 5, 1992
Stagehand

Imison, Richard (56)—February 9, 1993
Drama editor
Jacobs, Lou (89)—September 13, 1992
Clown
Jeffrey, Alix (63)—March 28, 1993
Photographer
Jessye, Eva (97)—February 21, 1992
Choir leader
Kaliff, Joseph (80)—November 13, 1992
Caricaturist
Knebel, Fletcher (81)—February 26, 1993
Author
Kurtzman, Harvey (68)—February 21, 1993
Mad magazine
LaBrasca, Robert (49)—September 23, 1992
LA Style
Lane, Leonard Charles (73)—September 10, 1992
Theater owner
Larsen, William W. Jr. (64)—February 11, 1993
Academy of Magical Arts
Lassner, Wynn (68)—April 6, 1993
Talent agent
Lawrence, Lawrence Shubert Jr. (76)—July 18, 1992
Shubert Organization
Levitt, Helen Slote (76)—April 3, 1993
Actors' Lab
Levine, Stanley (64)—May 1, 1992
Stage manager
Libman, Lillian (80)—August 24, 1992
Agent
Love, Stephan A. (38)—January 18, 1993
Dance instructor
Maazel, Marion S. (98)—December 12, 1992
Pittsburgh Youth Orchestra
Magerman, Les (46)—October 18, 1992
Thanos Dinner Theater
Marks, Gerson (82)—February 5, 1993
Lawyer
Maslandky, Michael (55)—March 19, 1993
Press agent
McCallum, James (48)—January 18, 1993
Musical America
McLaren, Wayne (51)—July 22, 1992
Rodeo rider
Meany, Patrick (67)—July 16, 1992
Rank Organization
Messing, Harold (57)—March 19, 1993
Lawyer
Miller, J. Howard (84)—February 15, 1993
USO, Los Angeles
Morgan, Barbara (92)—August 17, 1992
Photographer
Morgan, Edward P. (82)—January 27, 1993
Journalist

Morgan, Josephine (83)—July 3, 1992
Music school director
Morse, Carleton (91)—May 24, 1993
One Man's Family
Mosco, Teodoro (82)—June 15, 1992
Casals Music Festival
Mumford, Peter B. (48)—March 28, 1993
Stage manager
Myers, Edward (42)—February 1, 1993
Nashville Ballet
Nagler, Alois M. (85)—April 26, 1993
Theater historian
Narvid, Ethel (early 70s)—August 14, 1992
LA's Shakespeare Festival
O'Shea, Michael Sean—April 25, 1993
Press agent
Ottley, Bert (46)—October 1, 1992
Theater manger
Oxenburg, Allen Sven (64)—July 2, 1992
American Opera Society
Quinn, Nancy (46)—April 24, 1993
Young Playwrights, Inc.
Reavis, Willi (87)—August 27, 1992
Dresser
Roberson, George (55)—February 19, 1993
Stage door security
Rodgers, Dorothy (83)—August 17, 1992
Writer
Rose, Joel (77)—September 13, 1992
Press agent
Rotter, Clara (82)—September 13, 1992
NY *Times* Drama Dept.
Rudd, Hughes (71)—October 13, 1992
CBS correspondent
Salant, Richard (78)—February 16, 1993
CBS News
Sanders, Richard Brook (50)—April 7, 1993
Press agent
Schneider, Abe (87)—April 21, 1993
Columbia Pictures
Sears, David H. (44)—June 24, 1992
Dance News

Sepkowitz, Irv (55)—July 18, 1992
TV agent
Sevareid, Eric (79)—July 9, 1992
CBS News
Shawn, William (85)—December 9, 1992
The New Yorker
Shearer, Jacob (83)—August 18, 1992
Lawyer
Shuster, Joe (78)—July 30, 1992
Superman
Siff, Henrietta (96)—April 16, 1993
Theater party consultant
Sklar, Rick (62)—June 22, 1992
Disc jockey
Stabile, James A. (79)—June 28, 1992
Lawyer
Stark, Fran (72)—May 31, 1992
Fanny Brice's daughter
Stevens, Dan (50)—October 3, 1992
Agent
Stickler, Sam (37)—August 31, 1992
Production supervisor
Sudler, Louis C. (89)—August 25, 1992
Chicago Symphony Orchestra
Temmer, Stephen F. (64)—October 8, 1992
Audio technician
Waechter, Eberhard (63)—March 29, 1993
Vienna State Opera
Weatherby, William J. (62)—August 5, 1992
Author
Weaver, Jackson (72)—October 20, 1992
Voice of Smokey
White, Stephen (77)—March 27, 1993
Author
Woerner, Paul (40)—September 22, 1992
Lawyer
Wolfson, Wayne (40)—July 6, 1992
Agent
Yuter, Morris (66)—September 5, 1992
Press agent
Ziff, Charles E. (42)—July 4, 1992
Promoter

THE BEST PLAYS, 1894–1992

Listed in alphabetical order below are all those works selected as Best Plays in previous volumes of the *Best Plays* series. Opposite each title is given the volume in which the play appears, its opening date and its total number of performances. Two separate opening-date and performance-number entries signify two separate engagements off Broadway and on Broadway when the original production was transferred from one area to the other, usually in an off-to-on direction. Those plays marked with an asterisk (*) were still playing on June 1, 1993 and their number of performances was figured through May 31, 1993. Adaptors and translators are indicated by (ad) and (tr), the symbols (b), (m) and (l) stand for the author of the book, music and lyrics in the case of musicals and (c) signifies the credit for the show's conception, (i) for its inspiration.

PLAY	VOLUME	OPENED	PERFS
ABE LINCOLN IN ILLINOIS—Robert E. Sherwood	38–39.	.Oct. 15, 1938.	472
ABRAHAM LINCOLN—John Drinkwater	19–20.	.Dec. 15, 1919.	193
ACCENT ON YOUTH—Samson Raphaelson	34–35.	.Dec. 25, 1934.	229
ADAM AND EVA—Guy Bolton, George Middleton	19–20.	.Sept. 13, 1919.	312
ADAPTATION—Elaine May; and NEXT—Terrence McNally	68–69.	.Feb. 10, 1969.	707
AFFAIRS OF STATE—Louis Verneuil	50–51.	.Sept. 25, 1950.	610
AFTER THE FALL—Arthur Miller	63–64.	.Jan. 23, 1964.	208
AFTER THE RAIN—John Bowen	67–68.	.Oct. 9, 1967.	64
AGNES OF GOD—John Pielmeier	81–82.	.Mar. 30, 1982.	486
AH, WILDERNESS!—Eugene O'Neill	33–34.	.Oct. 2, 1933.	289
AIN'T SUPPOSED TO DIE A NATURAL DEATH—(b, m, l) MELVIN VAN PEEBLES	71–72.	.OCT. 7, 1971.	325
ALIEN CORN—Sidney Howard	32–33.	.Feb. 20, 1933.	98
ALISON'S HOUSE—Susan Glaspell	30–31.	.Dec. 1, 1930.	41
ALL MY SONS—Arthur Miller	46–47.	.Jan. 29, 1947.	328
ALL OVER TOWN—Murray Schisgal	74–75.	.Dec. 12, 1974.	233
ALL THE WAY HOME—Tad Mosel, based on James Agee's novel *A Death in the Family*	60–61.	.Nov. 30, 1960.	333
ALLEGRO—(b, l) Oscar Hammerstein II, (m) Richard Rodgers	47–48.	.Oct. 10, 1947.	315
AMADEUS—Peter Shaffer	80–81.	.Dec. 17, 1980.	1,181
AMBUSH—Arthur Richman	21–22.	.Oct. 10, 1921.	98
AMERICA HURRAH—Jean-Claude van Itallie	66–67.	.Nov. 6, 1966.	634
AMERICAN BUFFALO—David Mamet	76–77.	.Feb. 16, 1977.	135
AMERICAN PLAN, THE—Richard Greenberg	90–91.	.Dec. 16, 1990.	37
AMERICAN WAY, THE—George S. Kaufman, Moss Hart	38–39.	.Jan. 21, 1939.	164
AMPHITRYON 38—Jean Giraudoux, (ad) S.N. Behrman	37–38.	.Nov. 1, 1937.	153
AND A NIGHTINGALE SANG—C.P. Taylor	83–84.	.Nov. 27, 1983.	177
ANDERSONVILLE TRIAL, THE—Saul Levitt	59–60.	.Dec. 29, 1959.	179
ANDORRA—Max Frisch, (ad) George Tabori	62–63.	.Feb. 9, 1963.	9
ANGEL STREET—Patrick Hamilton	41–42.	.Dec. 5, 1941.	1,295
ANGELS FALL—Lanford Wilson	82–83.	.Oct. 17, 1982.	65
ANIMAL KINGDOM, THE—Philip Barry	31–32.	.Jan. 12, 1932.	183
ANNA CHRISTIE—Eugene O'Neill	21–22.	.Nov. 2, 1921.	177
ANNA LUCASTA—Philip Yordan	44–45.	.Aug. 30, 1944.	957
ANNE OF THE THOUSAND DAYS—Maxwell Anderson	48–49.	.Dec. 8, 1948.	286

PLAY	VOLUME	OPENED	PERFS

INDEX

Play titles appear in **bold face**. ***Bold face italic*** page numbers refer to those pages where complete cast and credit listings for New York productions may be found.